The Evolving Nature of EU External Relations Law

W. Th. Douma · C. Eckes · P. Van Elsuwege ·
E. Kassoti · A. Ott · R. A. Wessel
Editors

The Evolving Nature of EU External Relations Law

ASSER PRESS

Springer

Editors
W. Th. Douma
EU Legal—Centre for European
and International Law
The Hague, The Netherlands

C. Eckes
Amsterdam Centre for European Law
and Governance
University of Amsterdam
Amsterdam, The Netherlands

P. Van Elsuwege
Ghent European Law Institute (GELI)
Ghent University
Ghent, Belgium

E. Kassoti
T.M.C. Asser Institute
The Hague, The Netherlands

A. Ott
Faculty of Law
Maastricht University
Maastricht, The Netherlands

R. A. Wessel
Faculty of Law
Groningen University
Groningen, The Netherlands

ISBN 978-94-6265-422-8 ISBN 978-94-6265-423-5 (eBook)
https://doi.org/10.1007/978-94-6265-423-5

Published by T.M.C. ASSER PRESS, The Hague, The Netherlands www.asserpress.nl
Produced and distributed for T.M.C. ASSER PRESS by Springer-Verlag Berlin Heidelberg

This T.M.C. ASSER PRESS imprint is published by the registered company Springer-Verlag GmbH, DE part of Springer Nature
The registered company address is: Heidelberger Platz 3, 14197 Berlin, Germany

Preface: The Evolving Nature of EU External Relations Law

The European Union has more and more far-reaching competences in external relations than ever before. It is legally committed to a long list of ambitious and comprehensive foreign policy objectives. Arguably, the Union's foreign policy objectives (Article 21 TEU) are more ambitious and comprehensive than the foreign policy objectives set out in the national constitutions of the Member States. At the same time, Member States have in recent years challenged Union external actions in an unprecedented number of cases, including in order to reign in Union action and constrain Union powers.

On the one hand, in an ever more globalised world it is rational for the EU Member States to confer powers to the Union in order to have jointly a greater say of how global challenges are tackled and what role the Union and its Member States are playing internationally. On the other hand, Member States are ever more heterogeneous in their interests and views of (how to tackle) these challenges. This edited collection unearths and reflects on some of these tensions, including in the areas of the environment, migration and Brexit.

The present volume also marks the 10th anniversary of the Centre for the Law of EU External Relations (CLEER) at the T.M.C. Asser Institute. Throughout the past decade, CLEER operated as a forum for scholarly debate and as a research interface between academia and practice dealing with the legal aspects of the role of the EU in the world. It is a platform for reflection about the evolving nature of EU external relations law and that is precisely the theme of this book.

The start of CLEER coincided with significant changes to the legal framework of the EU's external action. The entry into force of the Lisbon Treaty brought the dissolution of the old pillar structure, the introduction of a single legal personality, as well as the grouping of all external action objectives—including those relating to the Common Foreign and Security Policy (CFSP)—which, together with a number of institutional innovations, aimed to increase the coherence and consistency of the EU's external activities. At the same time, questions of competence delimitation continue to keep EU external relations lawyers busy and lead to an increasing number of relevant cases being brought before the Court of Justice of the EU (CJEU). In parallel, the EU faced unprecedented political challenges. From Trump to Brexit, from the outbreak of violence at the southern and eastern borders, to economic, humanitarian and health crises, from the rise of populism to the public outcry regarding multilateral trade, all these events required a response from the EU and its Member States.

The conference "EU external relations: tackling global challenges?" organised at the T.M.C. Asser Institute from 6 to 7 December 2018 on the occasion of CLEER's 10th anniversary provided an opportunity to discuss the actions (and reactions) of the EU through external action instruments in a number of substantive areas such as migration, trade, neighbouring policies, and security and defence. It allowed to reflect on the appropriateness and effectiveness of the institutional structures underpinning the EU's external action in addressing these challenges and to suggest possible ways forward.

The present volume is the result of this exercise and aims to take stock of recent evolutions in the law and practice of the EU's external relations. In particular, it addresses the question *how the evolving legal and political framework affects the nature of EU external relations law*.

The first part of this volume tackles the EU's role as an exporter of values, rules and standards. This ambition is enshrined in Articles 3(5) and 21 TEU and constitutes the bedrock of the EU's external action. As observed by Cannizzaro, the generally formulated objectives, principles and values cut across the EU's system of competences. Hence, the question arises whether the external action objectives are only rhetorical devices or effective interpretive tools influencing the case law of the CJEU. As Cannizzaro argues, it appears that the increased focus on values and objectives since the Treaty of Lisbon does have a normative effect on the EU's external action and on the position of the CFSP in the EU legal order. Subsequent chapters critically analyse the EU's evolving practice in promoting the export of its own rules and values. The chapters by Theisinger and Douma address the limits of the EU's approach towards the promotion of sustainable development goals through Trade and Sustainable Development chapters that lack legal enforcement possibilities in recent trade agreements, whereas the chapter by Dero-Bugny and Motte-Baumvol looks into the enforcement challenges of the EU's secondary legislation with extraterritorial consequences.

The second part of this volume covers recent developments in the EU's treaty-making practice and foreign policy. Eva Kassoti focuses on the interface between EU law and international law in the case law of the CJEU. In particular, she looks at the CJEU's reliance on the international law principle of systemic integration for the interpretation of international agreements with third countries. Focusing on the Western Sahara case law, she criticises the CJEU's selective reading and instrumental use of the international rule of law and its consequences for the EU's identity as a global actor. A similar critique can be found in the contribution by Merijn Chamon, who looks at the EU's use of the mechanism of provisional application of treaties as foreseen in Article 25 of the Vienna Convention on the Law of Treaties (VCLT). In applying this mechanism within the framework of mixed agreements, the EU pragmatically operates at the international stage together with its Member States. Whereas this practice facilitates the EU's external action, it also has significant drawbacks as has been illustrated with the problematic signature and ratification process of the Comprehensive Economic and Trade Agreement (CETA) between the EU and Canada. The challenge of reconciling individual Member State interests with the ambitions of the EU as a global actor is also addressed in the chapters by Steven Blockmans and Ramses Wessel. The establishment of Permanent Structured Cooperation (PESCO) as "a microcosm" of differentiated integration is certainly one of the most significant developments in this respect. Differentiation is also increasingly visible in the broader framework of the CFSP, which not only implies the selective participation of EU Member States but also the participation of non-EU Member States. Accordingly, as concluded by Wessel, the CFSP is increasingly characterised by "a patchwork of diverging and overlapping members and non-members that—sometimes institutionalised, sometimes ad hoc—contribute to assisting the EU in achieving its objectives as a global actor."

The increasing integration with non-EU Member States is particularly visible in the EU's direct neighbourhood, as is further explained in the third part of this volume. Andrea Ott analyses the various types of international agreements and legal tools used to establish a so-called "European legal space". Adam Lazowski focuses more specifically on the EU's eastern neighbourhood and the development of relations with the associated Eastern Partnership countries (Ukraine, Moldova and Georgia). Finally, the chapters by Gatti and Larik deal with the challenge of Brexit. Since the entry into force of the Withdrawal Agreement, the UK is formally speaking a third country. In anticipation of a new legal framework for future EU-UK relations, Gatti observed that "[the UK's] legal position remains complex: as it was the least integrated member of the Union, it is now a very integrated third state". Larik further explores what is called "the Great British trade-off", i.e. the UK's regained power to negotiate its own trade agreements with third countries (also known under the narrative of "Global Britain") versus the loss of EU market power.

Finally, the last part of this volume is devoted to the substantive area of the EU's migration policies. This is certainly one of the most contentious fields of EU external relations law in the past decade. Against the background of an unfolding migration crisis, the EU's approach to migration management has become a heavily debated and politically sensitive issue in several Member States. In this context, the legal framework of the EU's role in shaping the Global Compact for Migration raises important questions. As discussed in the chapter by Pauline Melin, this inter alia includes the EU's involvement in the procedure for the negotiation of international soft law instruments and the external representation of the EU at the international stage. Apart from the challenges related to the use of soft law instruments, the EU and its Member States also increasingly transfer responsibilities to third countries. Juan Santos Vara and Laura Pascual Matellán critically analyse the implications of this practice and discuss the attribution of responsibility for breaches of human rights that might take place on the territory of third countries. Alfredo dos Santos Soares and Sophia Beck-Mannagetta focus more specifically on the EU's cooperation with Libya and question the compliance of the EU's approach with the values and principles of EU law. Narine Ghazaryan, finally, looks into the EU's policy towards combatting trafficking in human beings in its relations with the Eastern neighbourhood.

Taken together, all contributions reveal the evolving nature of EU external relations law. Whereas traditional questions of competence delimitation still largely determine the legal debate, the post-Lisbon constitutional structure requires a more holistic approach. In the light of the broadly defined objectives of the EU's external action, a neat distinction between traditional areas such as common commercial policy, development cooperation or CFSP becomes increasingly artificial. Trade agreements not only serve the economic interests of the EU but are intended to serve a broader agenda based on the export of the EU's values and norms. The CFSP is no longer a separate, intergovernmental pillar but part and parcel of the EU's constitutional structure. Differentiation, integration without membership and the creation of a "level playing field" with third countries are high on the external relations agenda, with Brexit as its most eminent example. The EU also faces new challenges and tensions. The ambition to become a global norm-setter while safeguarding its own autonomy is not always an easy exercise. The promotion of the EU's norms and values abroad may conflict with economic and security interests, as the debates in relation to the EU's trade, sustainable development and migration policies clearly illustrate. Hence, EU external relations law is in constant flux. This volume aims to shed light on the most significant developments of the past decade and provides food for thought for further research. This is precisely the ambition of CLEER for the years to come.

A 10-year anniversary is not complete without looking back at the origin of this successful endeavour. CLEER originated in Steven Blockmans' initiative in 2008 to bring a group of younger scholars together working in the field of EU external relations law. Starting off with meetings between Steven Blockmans, Wybe Th. Douma (both at the time at the T.M.C. Asser Institute), Fabian Amtenbrink (University of Rotterdam), Christophe Hillion (Leiden University), Andrea Ott (Maastricht University) and Ramses Wessel (at the time affiliated to the University of Twente), an idea developed quickly into setting up CLEER as an intra-faculty initiative with the T.M.C. Asser Institute as its base, solely devoted to the research and teaching of EU external relations law. The coordinator role at the beginning fell to Steven Blockmans but with the quick extension of tasks and his departure to the University of Amsterdam and CEPS, a number of CLEER coordinators took over the tasks to manage the manifold CLEER activities. We are very grateful to the following CLEER coordinators over the years: Tamara Takács, Aaron Matta, Luca Pantaleo, Enrico Partiti and Eva Kassoti. They have actively contributed to CLEER's success over the last ten years by managing the CLEER activities at the T.M.C. Asser Institute and elsewhere and acting together with the governing board in the management of financial applications, the editing of CLEER papers, book volumes, keeping the CLEER website up to date, editing the CLEER News Service, supervising CLEER fellowships, the organisation of workshops, training courses, CLEER summer schools and guest lectures. We are also grateful to the many trainees that helped CLEER through these years. Finally, CLEER was conceived as a hub for EU external relations law and thrives on its extensive network in and outside the Netherlands with many scholars and practitioners devoted to EU external relations law and policy. The governing board of CLEER would like to thank its advisory board and CLEER network members for their support and active engagement in the past and looks forward to a fruitful future cooperation in this dynamic and important EU policy field.

The Hague, The Netherlands — W. Th. Douma
Amsterdam, The Netherlands — C. Eckes
Ghent, Belgium — P. Van Elsuwege
The Hague, The Netherlands — E. Kassoti
Maastricht, The Netherlands — A. Ott
Groningen, The Netherlands — R. A. Wessel
June 2020

Contents

Contributors

S. Beck-Mannagetta Munich, Germany

S. Blockmans CEPS, Brussels, Belgium;
University of Amsterdam, Amsterdam, The Netherlands

E. Cannizzaro University of Rome "La Sapienza", Rome, Italy

M. Chamon Maastricht University, Maastricht, The Netherlands

D. Dero-Bugny Université de Paris, Malakoff, France

A. dos Santos Soares Universidad Pontificia Comillas, Madrid, Spain

W. Th. Douma EU Legal—Centre for European and International Law, The Hague, The Netherlands;
European Environmental Law Consultancy, The Hague, The Netherlands;
Ghent University, Ghent, Belgium;
Dutch Ministry of Social Affairs and Employment, The Hague, The Netherlands

M. Gatti University of Bologna, Bologna, Italy

N. Ghazaryan University of Nottingham, Nottingham, UK

E. Kassoti T.M.C. Asser Institute, The Hague, The Netherlands

J. Larik Leiden University, The Hague, The Netherlands

A. Łazowski University of Westminster, London, UK

P. Melin Maastricht University, Maastricht, The Netherlands

J. Motte-Baumvol Université de Paris, Malakoff, France

A. Ott Maastricht University, Maastricht, The Netherlands

L. Pascual Matellán University of Salamanca, Salamanca, Spain

J. Santos Vara University of Salamanca, Salamanca, Spain

M. Theisinger Erasmus University Rotterdam, Rotterdam, The Netherlands

R. A. Wessel University of Groningen, Groningen, The Netherlands

Part I
The EU as Exporter of Rules and Standards

Chapter 1
The Value of the EU International Values

E. Cannizzaro

Contents

Abstract This chapter focuses on the nature and effect of the values and principles enshrined in Articles 3(5) and 21 TEU, which set out the objectives and limits of the EU's external action. It begins with some introductory remarks highlighting the constitutional significance of international values aimed at giving guidance to the conduct of the EU foreign relations power. The second part explores the tendency of the CJEU to use these values and principles as a means of enlarging the functional scope of the EU competences. The problematic issues flowing from this approach, in particular the relation between general objectives of the EU's external action and particular objectives assigned to single areas, are discussed in the third part. The chapter concludes with a brief enquiry on the impact of general values and objectives on the principle of conferral.

Keywords objectives and values · external action · EU system of competences · principle of conferral · CFSP · holistic approach

E. Cannizzaro (✉)
University of Rome "La Sapienza", Rome, Italy
e-mail: enzo.cannizzaro@uniroma1.it

W. Th. Douma et al. (eds.), *The Evolving Nature of EU External Relations Law*,
https://doi.org/10.1007/978-94-6265-423-5_1

1.1 Introductory Remarks: Values, Principles, Objectives or Interests?

The Treaty on the European Union introduced provisions that were directly or indirectly borrowed from the Constitutional Treaty; a project which had never attained, as is well known, normative character. Two of them, in particular, Articles 3(5) and 21, express the international dimension of Europe's Constitutional setting. They are aimed at determining the model of relations the Union wishes to entertain with the "wider world" and to give guidance to the Union's Institutions accordingly. They set out a comprehensive and sophisticated frame of reference for the new external action of the Union, namely for the external aspects of all the policies and actions of the Union.[1]

A very superficial analysis of these provisions reveals the existence of two broad categories of directives. On the one hand, those aiming to ensure compliance with international law; namely respecting international law as it presently is. On the other hand, those that—albeit with changing tones and a varying phraseology—call upon the EU Institutions to contribute to the development of international law towards a model consistent with these fundamental values and principles of the EU.

The symbolic impact of these provisions can be hardly overstated. Articles 3(5) and 21 express the sentiment of the founding treaties towards the "wider world". Not only do they conceive international law as the indispensable tool for realizing the external dimension of the European integration, they also express a new ethical vision of international law and put the formidable power of the EU at the service of such a model: A new international Constitutionalism which takes shape through the EU's founding Treaties.[2]

Beyond their theoretical significance, however, the technical analysis of the two provisions is fraught with problematic issues. Articles 3(5) and 21 TEU do not clarify the nature and effect of the normative notions they lay down. Nor do they clarify the impact of these notions on the EU's competence system and, in particular, on the new external action of the Union. How do they relate to the principle of conferral? Do they blur the line between the diverse areas of the EU's external action? Or are they simply guidelines deprived of any normative effect?

These questions cannot be easily answered by referring to the mere terms of Articles 3(5) and 21. Quite the contrary, it is difficult to determine a coherent normative framework integrating these two provisions in the complex system of the EU's external action. The following sections will attempt to demonstrate how thorny it may be to reconcile the existence of general rules laying down objectives, principles and values, with a system of competences based on the principle of conferral. In doing so, this chapter aims to set the stage for the following chapters, most of which are—either explicitly or implicitly—based on the central notions in Articles 3(5) and 21 TEU.

---

[1] See Consolidated Version of the Treaty on the European Union, 2012, OJ C326 (TEU), Article 21(3).

[2] See Neframi 2013; Cremona 2016; Larik 2016.

1.2 Some Thoughts on the Nature and Effect of the EU International Values

The analysis starts from a terminological issue. The legal notions formulated by Articles 3(5) and 21 seem to sprout from a common root; the desire to construe an ethical framework able to give guidance to the exercise of the EU's foreign power.[3] However, the terminology used in the Treaty is highly heterogeneous. Article 3(5) talks about "values and interests"; Article 21 uses the term "objectives". Other Treaty provisions refer to the notions as "objectives and principles".[4] This uncertain terminology should warn against any attempt to draw conclusions on their definite legal nature.

The effect of these legal notions appears even more indeterminate. It is not clear whether they constitute mere guidelines for the exercise of the EU's external policies and actions or, rather, whether they have a normative effect, in general terms and, in particular, on the system of EU competence attribution.

Having identified the main controversial questions which surround the interpretation of these two provisions, one must admit that the Treaties do not provide many elements to answer them. An extensive reading is suggested by Article 21(3): "The Union shall respect the principles and pursue the objectives set out in paras 1 and 2 in the development and implementation of the different areas of the Union's external action covered by this Title and by Part Five of the Treaty on the Functioning of the European Union, and of the external aspects of its other policies". This statement is twofold. First, it suggests that the normative notions formulated under the previous paragraphs contribute *qua* principles to the standard of review for acts adopted under the EU's external action. Second, it entails that Articles 21 (1) and 21(2) provide general objectives, which add up to the specific objectives assigned to the single areas which compose the EU's external action. Article 21(3) seems thus to uphold the idea that the general objectives enshrined in Articles 21(1) and 21(2) integrate the set of objectives specifically assigned to the single policies which together form the external action, even though it remains unclear what happens in case of inconsistency between general and specific objectives.[5]

Article 3(6) strikes a different tone. It states that the objectives of the Union—which arguably include also the normative notions listed under Article 3(5), although labelled as values—must be pursued by appropriate means commensurate with the competences which are conferred upon it in the Treaties. Here the problem is the interpretation of the term "commensurate". This term implies some type of correspondence between the competences and the means to be employed to implement them; a correspondence in size, importance or quality. The most logical deduction is that Article 3(5), in conjunction with Article 3(6), does not extend the scope of the EU's competences but simply lays down general principles which must be pursued

[3]See de Witte 2008, pp. 3–15; Leino 2016, pp. 259–289.

[4]See Consolidated Version of the Treaty on the Functioning of the European Union, 2012, OJ C 326 (TFEU), Articles 2017(1), 208(1), 212(1), 214(1).

[5]Kube 2016.

through the use of the competences of the Union. These, in turn, must conform to the objectives specifically assigned to them.

A third option is provided by the specific provisions included in each single area of the EU's external action,[6] which directs these policies to be exercised in the context of or in the framework of the principles and objectives of Article 21.[7] The interpretation of notions such as "context" and "framework" appears to be particularly controversial. On the basis of a textual interpretation, reference to the context and framework entails that these principles and objectives should restrict, rather than enlarge, the scope of the policies and actions included in the EU's external action. This means that each single measure must be specifically grounded on the legal basis provided by one of these policies or action, and at the same time, respect the principles and objectives of Article 21. In other words, the principles and objectives of Article 21 cannot be invoked with a view to circumventing the objectives of the individual policy or action under which a measure is enacted.

We are therefore confronted with various interpretive options, each implying a different effect of the function of Articles 3(5) and 21: extending the scope of the policies which come within the external action, leaving it untouched, or restricting it. Behind this confusion, a major dilemma looms for the European order. Whereas an overtly restrictive interpretation can undermine the integration approach that is mirrored in the current Treaties, an expansive interpretation—providing for new and autonomous objectives for measures having external effect—may disrupt the basic foundations of the principle of conferral.

These three are not the only available interpretive options. In a more radical view, one could be tempted to accept that the establishment of an integrated external action has definitively merged together the general principles, values and objective enshrined in Articles 3(5) and 21, with the more specific objectives assigned to each single policy or action and thus instituted a holistic regime in which all these normative entities can be used interchangeably as a legal basis for measures implementing them.

In addition, all these options must be tested in the light of the legal conundrum represented by Article 40 TEU. Although this provision concerns the different issue of the choice of the legal basis for measures which, in the terminology predating the Lisbon Treaty, would have been defined as cross-pillar, it constituted a demanding test for every attempt to determine the functional scope of the various areas of the external action. The bi-lateralisation of the barrier separating the CFSP—a purely functional competence—from the TFEU policies—generally defined by reference to their substance matter—makes it equally hard for either one to expand its scope to the detriment of the scope of the other.[8]

[6] With the exception of Article 215 TFEU, concerning the restrictive measures, which, however, proceeds on the basis of a CFSP decision, subject, under Article 23 TEU, to the respect of the principles and objectives of the External Action; see TFEU, above n. 4.

[7] See, again, TFEU, above n. 4, Articles 207(1), 208(1), 212(1) and 214(1).

[8] Articles 40 also prevents a coordinated exercise of powers of actions respectively conferred upon each of these two dimensions of the European integration, either based on a combination of their

On the basis of these remarks, I will now proceed to see how Articles 3(5) and 21 have been treated in the case law of the CJEU. It is submitted that these have been treated in different ways: as a key to open up the principle of conferral, albeit in the limited field of external relations; as a mere rhetorical tool, to reinforce the persuasiveness of the decision; or, finally, as something intermediate between these two. This analysis may be useful for research projects aimed to determine the nature of effect of these quite mysterious provisions; a task, however, which largely remains outside the scope of the present chapter.

1.3 Rhetorical Device or Interpretive Effect?

Articles 3(5) and 21 have often been used in case law in their less engaging dimension, as a rhetorical tool, to confirm solutions based on different arguments or to reinforce the persuasiveness of an argument. Most commonly, by referring to these two provisions, the Court of Justice simply used them as an abbreviated way to refer to the obligation to respect international law. From the start of the process of integration, this obligation flows from Article 216(2) TFEU, under which international agreements that are binding on the EU must be complied with by the EU's Institutions. Moreover, according to settled case law, every international law rule binding on the EU is an integral part of the European legal order and constitutes a standard of review for EU domestic legislation.

Interestingly, the conception of Articles 3(5) and 21 as an abbreviated reference to the obligations imposed on the EU Institutions to comply with international law is adopted also by the referring judges. In *Western Sahara Campaign UK*,[9] for example, the referring Court submitted the following question:

> Is the Fisheries Partnership Agreement valid, having regard to the requirement under Article 3(5) TEU to contribute to the observance of any relevant principle of international law and respect for the principles of the Charter of the United Nations and the extent to which the Fisheries Agreement was concluded for the benefit of the Saharawi people, on their behalf, in accordance with their wishes, and/or in consultation with their recognised representatives?

Obviously, the validity of the Fisheries Partnership Agreement could have been more directly challenged against a standard of review composed by the rules and principles of international law that were allegedly breached, namely the principle of self-determination and the rule prohibiting to enter into agreements with a State administering non self-governing territories unless the agreement was concluded for

---

respective legal basis or on a sequence of measures, each grounded on its own legal basis. A sequential exercise of CFSP acts and of EU substantive policies acts is, notoriously, established only by Article 315 TFEU in the area of restrictive measures and, consequently, appears as a *lex specialis*, unlikely to be replicated in situations which fall outside its scope. For a more in-depth analysis of the exceptional status of Article 315, I refer to Cannizzaro 2017, pp. 531–546.

[9] Court of Justice, *Western Sahara Campaign UK,* Judgment of the Court (Grand Chamber), 27 February 2018, Case C-266/16, ECLI:EU:C:2018:118.

the benefit of the non-self-governing people, on its behalf and in accordance with its wishes. The same rationale applies to the obligation to respect the Charter of the United Nations,[10] which is arguably binding on the Union, although the Union is not among it signatories.[11]

In *Rosneft*[12] the Court used Article 21 to interpret an international agreement in light of the mandatory principles of the Charter of the United Nations. Asked to determine whether restrictive measures taken against that company were compatible with some provisions of the EU-Russia Partnership agreement, the Court observed that the conflict between the restrictive measures adopted by the EU and the EU-Russia agreement was only apparent, as that agreement contained a standard exception clause. Under this clause, each party was entitled to adopt "measures that it considers necessary for the protection of its essential security interests, particularly in time of war or serious international tension constituting a threat of war or in order to carry out obligations it has accepted for the purpose of maintaining peace and international security". Reference to this classic self-judging clause would have been sufficient to reject the claim. However, the Court went on to interpret that clause to the effect that it by no means requires the 'war' or the 'serious international tension constituting a threat of war' to take place in the territory of the invoking party.[13] In the light of this quite obvious remark, the Court felt safe to say that the contested measures had been enacted for the purpose of maintaining international peace and security and that purpose was "in accordance with the specified objective, under the first subparagraph of Articles 21(1) and 21(2)(c) TEU, of the Union's external action, with due regard to the principles and purposes of the Charter of the United Nations". In this way, the Court established a link between the two first paragraphs of Article 21 and the principles of the Charter, which were used to interpret extensively the EU-Russia agreement and, in particular, to bring within its scope a threat to international peace and security which did not concern *stricto sensu*, the relations between the two parties. Thus, reference to Articles 3(5) and 21 helped deal with complex situations where the scope of international values and principles of the EU overlapped with that of the Charter of Fundamental Rights: a rare but not impossible situation.

In Opinion 1/17,[14] concerning the consistency of the Comprehensive Economic and Trade Agreement between Canada, of the one part, and the European Union and

[10]See Hilpold 2009, pp. 141–182.

[11]Kokott and Sobotta 2012, pp. 1015–1024. This impression emerges from Court of Justice, *Kadi and Al Barakaat International Foundation v Council and Commission,* Judgment, 03 September 2008, Joined Cases C-402/05 and C-415/05, ECLI:EU:C:2008:461, paras 290–292, which, however, does not unveil the argument leading to this solution. A perspective based on the idea that the EU succeeded to the MS in the rights and duties flowing from the Charter, which fall within its competences, was set out by the GC (CFI) in Court of Justice, *Kadi v Council and Commission,* Judgment, 21 September 2005, Case T-315/01, ECLI:EU:T:2005:332, paras 193–195.

[12]Court of Justice, *Rosneft,* Judgment, 28 March 2017, Case C-72/15, ECLI:EU:C:2017:236.

[13]Ibid., para 111ff.

[14]Court of Justice, *Comprehensive Economic and Trade Agreement between Canada, of the one part, and the European Union and its Member States, of the other part (CETA),* Opinion of the Court, 30 April 2019, Opinion 1/17, ECLI:EU:C:2019:341.

its Member States, of the other part (CETA) with the EU Treaties, the Court was asked to determine whether the considerable financial risk which claimants had to bear to bring a claim to the CETA Tribunal was consistent with Article 47 of the Charter. Among the arguments which led to a positive answer, the Court recalled that the right of access to justice is inherent in the principle of free and fair trade, enshrined in Article 3(5).[15] Paradoxically, in Opinion 1/17 the Court abstained from using Articles 3(5) and 21 for what may have appeared their most logical and natural use, namely imposing a limit to the principle of autonomy of the European legal order. In this perspective, Articles 3(5), or 21 could have been used to compose the standard of review of EU acts, including acts concluding or implementing international agreements, alleged to be invalid in light of superior EU rules or principles, among which, the principle of autonomy holds a prominent place.[16]

There are elements in Opinion 1/17 which seem to demonstrate that the Court considered this line of reason, without expressly accepting it. This impression emerges from the passage where the Court, after referring to its settled case law on the compatibility with the founding Treaties of provisions of international agreements which establish judicial organs to settle disputes under that agreement, added:

> It is, moreover, precisely because of the reciprocal nature of international agreements and the need to maintain the powers of the Union in international relations that it is open to the Union … to enter into an agreement that confers on an international court or tribunal the jurisdiction to interpret that agreement without that court or tribunal being subject to the interpretations of that agreement given by the courts or tribunal of the Parties.[17]

Coherently unfolded, this line of reasoning could have led the CJEU to the conclusion that autonomy is not the (only) overarching principle governing the conduct of the EU external relations, but that it must be balanced against other Constitutional values and principles, among which those laid down by Articles 3(5) and 21 TEU, which, moreover, relate specifically to the EU's foreign affairs power.

---

[15] Ibid., para 200.

[16] This use of the general values and principles of Articles 3(5) and 21 emerges from the Opinion of AG Bot; see Court of Justice, *Comprehensive Economic and Trade Agreement between Canada, of the one part, and the European Union and its Member States, of the other part (CETA)*, Opinion of AG Bot of 29 January 2019, Opinion 1/17, ECLI:EU:C:2019:72, paras 73–78: "It is my view that examination of the compatibility of Section F of Chapter 8 of the CETA with the principle of the autonomy of EU law must be carried out taking due account of the need to preserve the European Union's capacity to contribute to achieving the principles and the objectives of its external action. … the Court should interpret the principle of the autonomy of EU law not only in such a way as to maintain the specific characteristics of EU law but also to ensure the European Union's involvement in the development of international law and of a rules-based international legal order."

[17] Opinion 1/17 (*CETA*), above n. 14, para 117.

1.4 The Impact of International Principles and Values on the System of Competences

1.4.1 The No-Effect Approach

The rhetoric use of Articles 3(5) and 21 TEU leaves unaltered the impact of these provisions on the system of the EU's competences. In this regard, the most conservative view was expressed by Sharpston AG. In her opinion pertaining to the Opinion procedure 2/15,[18] the Advocate General held, in quite clear-cut terms, that these provisions do not affect, even minimally, the system of competences. This view was expressed in response to the exclusivity claim advanced by the Commission and the Parliament. The Commission and the Parliament argued that Chapter 13 of the EU-Singapore FTA, although having as its main purpose to promote labour and environmental protection, nonetheless fell within the scope of the Common Commercial Policy by virtue of its effect of regulation of trade.

In response to these arguments, the AG followed the classic line of argumentation based on the directness and immediacy of the link between the measures of the agreements and their effect on trade. The enquiry gave negative results and the AG drew the conclusion that, on the basis of the classic criteria, Chapter 13 did not fall within the scope of the CCP.[19] To test the robustness of this analysis, the AG went on to examine whether this result could change in light of the objectives relating to sustainable development and labour protection in the EU external action, enshrined in Articles 3(5) and 21. In other words, the AG raised the issue of whether international obligations which do not pursue the objectives specifically assigned to the CCP, could nonetheless come within the exclusive purview of the EU as they pursue general objectives of external action. The answer was emphatically in the negative:

> In my opinion, Articles 3(5) and 21 TEU and Articles 9 and 11 TFEU, to which the Commission refers, are not relevant to resolving the issue of competence. The purpose of those provisions is to require the European Union to contribute to certain objectives in its policies and activities. They cannot affect the scope of the common commercial policy laid down in Article 207 TFEU.[20]

The idea that Articles 3(5) and 21 are irrelevant in the context of determining the scope of the EU's competence does not appear persuasive. Under Article 5 TEU, a competence has two components: the powers of action conferred by the Treaties and the objective which must be attained thereby. If Articles 3(5) and 32 set out the general objectives of the EU's external action, they can well provide the functional part of the single policies which compose it.

---

[18] Court of Justice, *Free Trade Agreement between the European Union and the Republic of Singapore*, Opinion of AG Sharpston, 21 December 2016, Opinion 2/15, ECLI:EU:C:2016:992.

[19] Ibid., paras 489–494.

[20] Ibid., para 495.

As said above, the text of these provisions does not help determine whether they intend to set out objectives or values, interests or principles. However, Article 207 TFEU, as well as its twin provisions concerning the other policies included in the external action, expressly use the term "objectives", thus making it clear that there are general objectives laid down by Articles 3(5) and 21, which can be attained through the means of action conferred to the EU by these provisions.

Even from a more general perspective, the sweeping assertion of the AG appears to be dismissive. Under the doctrine of competence, rules, principles and other undetermined legal notions can interfere in a variety of manners with a competence assigned to the EU. Under Article 6, for example, principles protecting fundamental rights do not extend the competence of the EU. However, this does not entail that they do not produce effect on the competence of the EU. They interfere with the issue of competence in many ways, the most obvious being that they restrict the scope of the competences of the Union. Thus, even if the notions enshrined Articles 3(5) and 21 TEU are not full-fledged objectives for the purposes of Article 5 TEU, this would not rule out the possibility that they are, nonetheless, relevant to determining the scope of the EU's competence.

1.4.2 The Holistic Approach

In Opinion 2/15 of 16 May 2017,[21] the Court of Justice did not follow the no-effect doctrine embraced by AG Sharpston and, rather, adopted a doctrine which may appear as its logical opposite. In particular, in the section concerning the consistence of the commitments on sustainable development formulated by Chapter 13 of the Agreement, the Court departed from the conclusions suggested by the Advocate General and relied on a different approach. According to the Court, Article 207 TFEU modifies the functional scope of the CCP by integrating the general objectives and principles of the EU's external action in the conduct of that policy.

> The obligation on the European Union to integrate those objectives and principles into the conduct of its common commercial policy is apparent from the second sentence of Article 207(1) TFEU read in conjunction with Article 21(3) TEU and Article 205 TFEU. Indeed, as provided in Article 21(3) TEU, the European Union is to 'pursue the objectives set out in paras 1 and 2 in the development and implementation of the different areas of the Union's external action covered by this Title and by Part Five of the [FEU Treaty] …'. Part Five of the FEU Treaty includes, inter alia, the common commercial policy.[22]

The Court went on to draw the inevitable conclusion that, although the Union has no exclusive competence to conclude an international agreement aimed to regulate the levels of social and environmental protection in the respective territories of its parties, it has the competence to regulate trade between the European Union and a

[21]Court of Justice, *Free Trade Agreement between the European Union and the Republic of Singapore*, Opinion of the Court, 16 May 2017, Opinion 2/15, ECLI:EU:C:2017:376.

[22]Ibid., paras 143–144.

third State by making this regulation conditional upon the compliance of international obligations concerning labour and environment protection.[23]

Although the Court did not unveil all the details of its reasoning, one could hardly doubt that, under that case law, Articles 3(5) and 21 are part of the system of the EU's competence. If the objectives and values set out by these provisions are incorporated in the set of objectives assigned to the common commercial policy, the most logical inference is that they can be attained by using the means of action conferred by the treaty under this policy. Since the process of incorporation is common for all the other policies of the Union, the same conclusion must be drawn for them all.

By no way does this finding exhaust all the problematic issues about the role of Articles 3(5) and 21. The first and most obvious is to determine the meaning of the term "integrate". Opinion 2/15 seems to conceive the process of integration as a sort of addition of a common set of objectives to those specifically assigned to each area of external relations. Should one then conclude that acts implementing the single areas of the external action could pursue the general objectives set out by Articles 3(5) and 21 insofar as they are not inconsistent with the specific objectives of each single policy or action? If this were the case, rather than enlarging the scope of the Union's competence, the process of integration restricts it.

This counterintuitive conclusion requires an explanation. The Court did not say that the means of action of the CCP policy can be used to attain the common objectives laid down by Articles 3(5) and 21. For example, the EU is not allowed to use the common commercial policy to attain the objective of social or environmental protection. This would have been a real extension of the functional scope of that policy. Rather, the Court held that the use of the classical instruments of the commercial policy, consistent with both the substantive and the functional scope of that policy, can be made conditional upon certain standards of social or environmental protection. In this context, the word "integration" is interpreted in the sense that Articles 3(5) and 21 TEU simply add certain objectives to the existing functional standard against which the lawfulness of a measure adopted under the CCP must be assessed.

For these reasons, the claim made in Opinion 1/15 is less revolutionary than it may appear. The Court did not restrict the CCP, as well as the other areas of the external policy, from pursuing the specific objectives assigned to it. Nor did it not uphold a one-size-fits-all effect. It simply found that the notions enshrined in Articles 3(5) and 21 extend the set of objectives assigned to each of these areas without get rid of the more specific objectives assigned to the single areas by the founding Treaties. One may be tempted to say that, in Opinion 1/15, the Court upheld a holistic effect. This approach would then require to determine the functional link between a measure and the competence to which it pertains on the basis of all the objectives: the general objectives of the external action and the more specific objectives assigned to its single areas.[24]

---

[23] Ibid., para 166.

[24] This conclusion was suggested by AG Bot in the *Mauritius*, who proclaimed his intention "to define the boundaries between the CFSP and the Union's other policies" and concluded that "(i)n so far as Article 21(2) TEU sets out the common objectives of the Union's external action, that

The relevance of Opinion 2/15, therefore, lies in the finding that the general objectives of the external action matter when determining whether a certain measure falls within the functional scope of the competence on the basis of which it was adopted. However, it did not clarify the relations between the general and the specific objectives. In particular, in case of a conflict between these two sub-set of objectives, a further clarification would be needed.

1.5 The Role of Article 40 TEU

The difficulty to determine the effect of the values and principles of Articles 3(5) and 21 increases if one adds to the picture one of the most mysterious and less explored provisions of the Treaties, namely Article 40 TEU. This provision contains in its two paragraphs, two symmetrical non-affectation clauses. The first aims to protect the procedure of the EU policies in the TFEU from CFSP measures having a substantive content. The second, conversely, aims to protect the procedure of the CFSP from politically motivated measures taken under one of the substantive TFEU policies of the EU.

This provision probably constitutes the most rigorous application of the principle of conferral and establishes a regime of separation, or even segregation, between the CFSP on the one and, the other substantive policies and action of the EU on the other. At its core, it prevents the CFSP to enter into matters entrusted to the substantive policies of the EU and, *vice versa*, these policies from intruding into the realm of the CFSP.

This model of relation between CFSP and TFEU EU policies is, under many respects, antithetical to the intent underlying the EU's external action. Whereas the latter integrates, the former segregates. More particularly, whereas the latter tends to consider the various areas of the external action of the Union as a harmonious set of legal bases for measures aimed to attain common objectives, the former tends to conceive them as monads, self-contained and devoid of any interaction, with the only exception provided for by Article 315 TFEU on restrictive measures.

The impact of Article 40 TEU on the integration of the EU's external action is far from clear. If taken at face value, this provision would, indeed, prevent any attempt to harmoniously use the various policies of the external action as a unitary tool designed to promote the common values and to attain the common objectives laid down by Articles 3(5) and 21. Yet, as seen above, this is not what emerges from the recent case law, which seems to have attenuated the strict regime of separation between the CFSP and the policies in the TFEU. The idea underlying this case law is that Articles 3(5) and 21 carve out an exception to the prohibition to pursue objectives,

provision should be read in conjunction with the more specific provisions applicable to each policy in order to determine the Union policy to which a certain objective is more specifically related"; see Court of Justice, *Parliament v Council (Mauritius)*, Opinion of AG Bot, 30 January 2014, Case C-658/11, ECLI:EU:C:2014:41, paras 87–88.

which were formerly assigned to the CFSP only, through measures taken under other EU substantive policies. However, this new judicial doctrine must still reckon with Article 40 and with its articulations described above.

Some of these issues have been considered in case C-244/17, concerning the procedure to be followed by the Council in determining the position of the EU with regard to decisions establishing the procedural rules of the cooperation council, a body set up by the Partnership and Cooperation Agreement between the EU and its MS with the Republic of Kazakhstan. It is worthwhile noticing that this agreement was concluded in mixed form and grounded, for what concerns the competence of the EU, on a combination of legal bases including the CFSP. The Council thus took the view that the position of the EU ought to be based on Article 218(9) TFEU, in conjunction with Article 31(1) TEU and, therefore, it needed to be adopted by a unanimous vote. This view was opposed by the Commission, which argued that the agreement mainly pertained to the non-CFSP areas of the external action and, therefore, the procedure had to be only determined by Article 218(9).

The AG and the Court agreed that the issue, by virtue of its instrumental character, needed to be decided on the basis of the contents and objectives of the Partnership agreement. They further agreed that the agreement contained obligations falling within the CFSP and obligations falling within the non-CFSP areas of the EU external action. Lastly, they agreed on the insufficiency of this link for the purpose of including the CFSP among the legal basis for such a decision.

This conclusion was based by the Court on the incidentality doctrine.[25] Although converging on this conclusion, the AG offered a more articulated reasoning, which also took into account Article 40 TEU. After recalling that "to comply with the spirit of Article 40 TEU, the unanimity principle of the CFSP must not be allowed to be undermined by the procedural rules of the communitised policies, nor must this unanimity principle of the CFSP be permitted to 'infect' the communitised policies", the AG turned her attention to the centre of gravity doctrine and concluded, as the Court did, that the references to the CFSP in the Partnership agreement ought to be considered as incidental vis-à-vis the provisions falling within the substantive competences of the EU. At the end of this reasoning, the AG felt the need to assess the soundness of the conclusions based on incidentality against the normative background of Article 40:

> A waiver of the reference to legal bases resulting from the area of the CFSP moreover does not lead to any weakening of the foreign and security policy component of the Partnership Agreement. This is because the aims and content of the Partnership Agreement with references to the foreign and security policy, as identified above, may not only be implemented by the conventional means of the CFSP. Rather, the commitment to democracy and the rule of law, respect for human rights, peaceful settlement of disputes and observance of international law belong to the fundamental values of the European Union, guiding it in all of its action on the international scene in accordance with the cross-cutting clause of Article 21(1)

[25] Ibid., para 46: The provisions falling within the scope of the CFSP "are not therefore of a scope enabling them to be regarded as a distinct component of that agreement. On the contrary, they are incidental to that agreement's two components constituted by the common commercial policy and development cooperation".

> TEU, that is to say not only in the context of the CFSP, but also for example in the context of the common commercial policy (Article 207 TFEU) and development cooperation (Article 208(1) and Article 209(2) TFEU).[26]

Although formulated in the specific context of the incidentality effect, this passage may have a broader scope and unveil some still hidden aspects of this troubled relation. One obvious inference is that measures taken under a TFEU competence in pursuing the objectives laid down in Articles 3(5) and 21 TEU, are perfectly consistent with Article 40, and not only incidentally.

This holding has far-reaching implications. First, it seems to entail that the Partnership agreement could, and perhaps should, have been concluded on a legal basis which excluded the CFSP. Second, and more important for our purposes, it seems to sensibly weaken the first sentence of Article 40 and to definitively pave the way for a system where the substantive policies of the Union under the TFEU can also autonomously operate to protect the values and attain the objectives of Articles 3(5) and 21 TEU. In such a system, these substantive EU policies become instrumental to the implementation of the internal values and principles of Articles 3(5) and 21, without the need of the intermediation of acts of foreign policy.

1.6 Conclusions: Beyond the Holistic Approach

Recent case law seems to establish a legal regime of EU external action dominated by the holistic approach, albeit in the restricted sense shaped in the previous section of this chapter. According to this case law, the effect of Articles 3(5) and 21 is tangible albeit limited. Far from constituting mere political or ethical directives, these provisions do have normative effect and, in particular, they enlarge the functional scope of the substantive competences of the EU's external action. The substantive policies of the EU—those expressly included in the external action and the external aspects of all the other EU policies—are now enabled to pursue the objectives laid down by these provisions. Moreover, the values, principles and objectives flowing from these provisions enter into a dynamic interrelation with the various doctrines of competences developed by the case law. The most blatant example is the incidentality doctrine, which presumably will be massively applied throughout the full spectrum of the relations between CFSP and other EU policies,[27] and may further integrate the various external policies.

It is noteworthy that this impact is not bidirectional. Articles 3(5) and 21 only extended the functional scope of the external aspects of the EU substantive competences, thus prompting a process of erosion of the monopoly of the CFSP. They do not correspondingly enlarge the substantive scope of the CFSP, which remains,

---

[26] Ibid., para 77.

[27] See Court of Justice, *Commission v Council*, Judgment of the Court, 20 May 2008, Case C-91/05, ECLI:EU:C:2008:288; see Hillion and Wessel 2009, pp. 551–86.

at least theoretically, a purely functional, de-materialised competence. Presumably, this asymmetrical upheaval of the system of compartimentalisation between TEU and TFEU competence of the EU foreign power will intensify the role of the CFSP as an instrument giving guidance to the exercise of the TFEU substantive policies.[28]

Not all the issues arising as a consequence of this abrupt change in the traditional system of the EU competences are automatically solved. In particular, the simple addition of new general objectives to the specific objectives of the substantive EU competences raises the problem to determine, in case of inconsistency, the relations among heterogeneous objectives pertaining to the same competence.

On the basis of logical considerations, a number of options are available, none of them, however, clearly superior to the others. A hierarchical order giving priority to the general objectives over those specifically assigned to the single EU's substantive policies could match the fundamental character of the general principles and values of the European legal order. The problem with this view is that it may incentivise the development of independent lines of foreign policy through the procedures pertaining to the substantive competences of the EU. One may wonder how far the relative autonomy acquired by the EU substantive policies can go in view of the recent case law without altering the institutional and normative balance reflected in the Treaties and, in particular, in Article 40 TEU.

A second option advocates the prevalence of the more specific objectives assigned to the single EU substantive policies in the TFEU. Arguably, this option is less disruptive of the classic principle of conferral, which still remains the philosophical corner stone of the process of integration. By confining the pursuance of the values and objectives of Articles 3(5) and 21 to the substantive scope of each single competence, this solution may be politically acceptable as it would maintain a role of supervision for the CFSP and avoid the development of independent lines of foreign policy through the different methods of EU decision-making.

A third, and perhaps more audacious, option is to apply the crucible approach used by international law to determine the relations between the diverse methods of interpretation of international treaties. The popularity of this approach in international law is basically due to its indeterminacy. It consists in putting together a number of methods of treaty interpretation, potentially conflicting with each other, and leaving to the interpreter the task of choosing the proper method, or a combination among some or all methods, on the basis of the contingencies of each particular case.

If applied to the objectives of the Unions' action, this option would appear to be highly innovative. The political Institutions would have great discretion to choose the objectives more appropriate for each specific measure falling within the scope of the external action. The various objectives—those generally assigned to the external action and those specifically assigned to the single policy—could be used interchangeably. However, the cost to be paid would be significantly high. The principle of conferral, and more generally the entire system of the EU's competences, would be fatally disrupted. If this system applied to the external aspects of the all the EU's policies, the magnitude of this upheaval would correspondingly increase.

[28] On that role, in the light of the pre-Lisbon institutional practice, see Cannizzaro 2007, pp. 193–234.

The quite disappointing conclusion is that the recent case law is still incapable to choose among the many ways following from the decision by the Treaty drafters to include general objectives, principles and values in the EU's external action. In turn, this inability seems to depend from the still controversial relationship between the political aspiration of the EU as a global actor, capable to use all the means at its disposal to pursue these objectives, principles, and values, and the restraints flowing from the principle of conferral. It is this untied knot which stays as an insurmountable obstacle in the way of every attempt to compose in a clear and coherent frame the diverse components of the EU foreign relations power.[29]

References

Cannizzaro E (2007) Unity and Fragmentation in the EU's Foreign relations Power. In: Barnard C (ed) The Fundamental of EU Law Revisited. Oxford University Press, Oxford, pp 193–234

Cannizzaro E (2017) The EU Antiterrorist Sanctions. In: Eeckhout P, Lopez-Escudero M (eds) The European Union's External Action in Times of Crisis. Hart Publishing, Oxford, pp 531–546

Cremona M (2016) Values in EU Foreign Policy. In: Sciso E, Baratta R, Morviducci C (eds) I valori dell'Unione europea e l'azione esterna. Giappichelli, Turin

de Witte B (2008) Too Much Constitutional Law in the European Union's Foreign Relations? In: Cremona M, de Witte B (eds) EU Foreign Relations Law—Constitutional Fundamentals. Hart Publishing, Oxford, pp 3–15

Hillion C, Wessel RA (2009) Competence distribution in EU external relations after ECOWAS: Clarification or continued fuzziness? CMLRev 46:551–86

Hilpold P (2009) EU Law and UN Law in Conflict: The Kadi Case. Max Planck Yearbook of United Nations Law 13:141–182

Kokott J, Sobotta C (2012) The Kadi Case—Constitutional Core Values and International Law—Finding the Balance? European Journal of International Law 23:1015–1024

Kube V (2016) The European Union's External Human Rights Commitment: What is the Legal Value of Article 21 TEU? EUI Department of Law Research Paper No. 2016/10

Larik J (2013) Entrenching Global Governance: The EU's Constitutional Objectives Caught Between a Sanguine World View and a Daunting Reality. In: Van Vooren B, Blockmans S, Wouters J (eds) The EU's Role in Global Governance: The Legal Dimension. Oxford University Press, Oxford, pp 7–22

Larik J E (2016) Foreign Policy Objectives in European Constitutional Law. Oxford University Press, Oxford

Leino P (2016) The Journey Towards All that is Good and Beautiful: Human Rights and Common Values as Guiding Principles of EU Foreign Relations Law. In: Cremona M, de Witte B (eds) EU Foreign Relations Law—Constitutional Fundamentals. Hart Publishing, Oxford, pp 259–289

Lonardo L (2018) Common Foreign and Security Policy and the External Action Objectives: An Analysis of Article 21 of the Treaty on the European Union. European Constitutional Law Review 14:584–608

Neframi E (2013) Les Rapports entre Objectifs et Compétences: de la Restructuration et de l'Identité de l'Union Européenne [The Relationship between Objectives and Competences: on the Restructuring and Identity of the European Union]. In: Neframi E (ed) Objectifs et compétences dans l'Union européenne [Objectives and Competences in the EU]. Bruylant, Brussels

[29] See Wessel 2020; Lonardo 2018, pp. 584–608; Larik 2013, pp. 7–22.

Wessel R A (2020) Legality in EU Common Foreign and Security Policy: The Choice of the Appropriate Legal Basis. In: Kilpatrick C, Scott J (eds) Contemporary Challenges to EU Legality: Collected Courses of the Academy of European Law. Oxford University Press (forthcoming)

E. Cannizzaro is Professor of International Law and EU Law at the University of Rome "La Sapienza" in Italy.

Chapter 2
New Approaches in the Promotion of EU Standards

M. Theisinger

Contents

Abstract This chapter addresses a potential risk of lower standards in the so-called 'new-generation' free trade agreements (FTAs) compared to earlier FTAs in closer geographical proximity to European Union (EU) borders. Economic models had anticipated a race-to-the-bottom effect of regulatory convergence, but in trade regulation practice, a tendency towards the adoption of higher regulatory standards has been found. The EU couples the adoption of higher standards with multilateral incentives for trade facilitation and sustainable development goals. Empirical research on the promotion of norms and standards in EU trade agreements, if controlled for the distance between the EU and third-country negotiation partners, shows a decline in the adoption of higher EU regulatory standards in a new generation of FTAs. This chapter identifies two central challenges in the promotion of regulatory cooperation for the EU. Firstly, regulatory cooperation is politically costlier than border measure trade liberalization. Regulatory cooperation is also not always linked to trade liberalization and may be associated with protectionist measures. Secondly, the bargaining power from the single market may not be as significant for geographically distant third-country trade negotiations. However, two new multilateral agreements could assist the EU in its attempt to promote its regulatory values and standards.

M. Theisinger (✉)
Erasmus University Rotterdam, Sanders Building (L), Area 7.21, Burgemeester Oudlaan 50, 3062 Rotterdam, The Netherlands
e-mail: theisinger@law.eur.nl

W. Th. Douma et al. (eds.), *The Evolving Nature of EU External Relations Law*,
https://doi.org/10.1007/978-94-6265-423-5_2

Keywords European neighbourhood policy · free trade agreements · new generation · geographical distance · regulatory cooperation · regulatory diffusion

2.1 Introduction

Global regulatory competition is becoming increasingly relevant[1] as global value chains (GVCs) and tradable services are of growing importance in international trade. The European Union has proven to be an influential regulator, by its market size,[2] regulatory capacities,[3] and past successes in regulatory diffusion.[4] The EU's market size makes it an important trading partner to many countries, which are anticipated to have an incentive of unilaterally adjusting their regulation to lower trade costs for their exporting companies. Additionally, the EU's regulatory capacity should facilitate the adoption of EU regulation beyond its borders. The expectation of the EU's ambitions of influencing global rules and norms in light of its standards comes from the EU's strategy papers,[5] as well as from negotiation successes in adjacent countries.[6]

For the so-called 'new generation' free trade agreements (FTAs)[7] it could be expected that standard setting is pursued in a similar way as in trade agreements under the European Neighbourhood Policy (ENP). As the binding adoption of norms and standards is lower with new-generation FTAs,[8] economic models would

[1]While the dominant consideration was to cut 'red tape', the risks of 'under-regulation' became increasingly apparent during the financial crisis of 2008. As the global economic integration continues to deepen, the regulatory capacity becomes increasingly important Baldwin et al. 2010.

[2]International Monetary Fund 2019, which estimates the Gross Domestic Product (GDP) based on Purchasing Power Parity (PPP) to be 15.79 percent with a GDP of 23.6 tn int. dollars (PPP; current prices, October 2019), compared to China 19.71 percent and the United States 14.93 percent of the global GDP.

[3]For example, in the widely cited definition of regulation as a "sustained and focused control exercised by a public agency over activities that are valued by a community." Selznick and Noll 1985, p. 363.

[4]In the context of Europeanization, Radaelli refers to "processes of (a) construction, (b) diffusion, and (c) institutionalization of formal and informal rules, procedures, policy paradigms, styles, 'ways of doing things,' and shared believes and norms…" Radaelli et al. 2003, p. 30; the process of regulatory diffusion describes the regulatory response of the adopting regulator to a neighbouring, regional or global power.

[5]European Commission 2015; European Commission 2010; European Commission 2006.

[6]Staeger et al. 2016, p. 221.

[7]New generation trade agreements denote trade agreements that go deeper than goods trade. For the EU these include Canada, Singapore, and South Korea. Here trade-related issues are of particular interest, such as rules on labour and environment.

[8]Young 2015, p. 1256.

predict a 'race-to-the-bottom effect'.[9] In practice, a more differentiated effect with regards to countries, sectors, and enforcement appears. There is a tendency towards adopting increasingly stringent minimum standards, rather than an uncoordinated race to the bottom.[10] The linkage of trade agreements with environmental, health, and labour standards can therefore be expected to increase the economic leverage and effectiveness of such norms.

The European Union's effort to promote the adoption of its key-governance features and regulatory standards have been more successful in the ENP strategy than in new-generation FTAs. Empirical legal research shows that binding commitments do not go far beyond the World Trade Organization (WTO) commitments.[11] EU FTAs also feature an apparent prevalence of non-binding provisions on regulatory cooperation compared to other FTA templates.[12] The communicated strategies of the EU show diminishingly binding language concerning disseminating regulatory preferences. If EU FTAs mention standards, there seems to be a preference for pointing to internationally adopted standards. While the EU might have placed a greater emphasis on the timely closure of negotiations exports of goods from Europe, increasing civil society pressure will make stringent and binding standards reflecting EU values a critical issue.

This chapter identifies two central challenges in the promotion of regulatory cooperation[13] for the EU. Firstly, the political cost of regulatory cooperation is higher than that of traditional trade border measures, making it more challenging to come to an agreement. Especially if there is already a highly developed pre-existing level of regulation for both negotiation partners, the initial economic cost for regulatory cooperation will be high. If there are different regulatory capacities, regulatory cooperation may be associated with protectionist intent to limit the exploitation of the comparative advantage of a negotiation partner. For instance, regulatory reform could lead to

---

[9] It refers to the regression of, e.g. regulatory standards, norms, and taxes to attract investment. Standards could be sacrificed for greater competitiveness. A historical reference of regulatory competition on attracting corporations was made with regards to taxation between countries in the United States. Grandy 1989, p. 677.

[10] See for example increasingly stringent norms in the International Labour Organization, in environmental protection such as the Paris Accord, and success in economic development in the United Nations Conference on Trade and Development.

[11] Young 2015, p. 1246.

[12] Baldwin 2014b, pp. 15–16.

[13] Regulatory cooperation refers to the pursuit of regulatory convergence. Regulatory divergence may stem from diverse sources, including regulatory asymmetries, path dependencies, regulatory preferences, and public choice outcomes. Chirico et al. 2013, pp. 13–16. The cost of regulatory convergence to the industry can lead to profitable outcomes but also sunk costs, societal costs if preferred policy interests are not met. Approaches to regulatory cooperation with the aim of regulatory convergence vary, as outlined by Bul et al. and may include forms of informal and formal dialogue, private standards, which can be extended to an intergovernmental basis, mutual recognition agreements, regulatory convergence in FTAs, and regulatory partnerships. Bul et al. 2015. Regulatory cooperation is included in Canada–European Union Comprehensive Economic and Trade Agreement (CETA) and the EU-South Korea FTA. The extent to which regulatory cooperation can contribute to regulate convergence is limited as parties only commit to regulatory cooperation as long as it does not limit domestic regulatory measures.

a diminished welfare effect of the desired trade liberalization by increasing the cost of labour with regulatory reforms in countries with a high proportion of 'low-skill labour' countries.

Secondly, the bargaining power from the EU single market may diminish with geographical distance. In analogy to the economic concept of the 'gravity equation',[14] the coercive power of market size diminishes with geographical distance and lowers concessions for the adoption of regulatory standards. Instead, the bargaining power needs to differentiate between prospects of international economic integration and access to trade in goods and services in the EU single market.

In this context, two new multilateral approaches could supplement the regulatory EU-FTA approach to promote its regulatory values and standards. The aim is to advance the understanding of the role regulatory cooperation may play in FTAs versus regulatory cooperation efforts that are linked with Aid for Trade (AfT) programs and Trade Facilitation (TF) efforts as pursued by the EU.[15] The assumption is that the EU may effectively promote standards with trade relations but outside its FTA structures.

2.2 Economic Motivation for Regulatory Convergence for the EU

Liberal trade is a part of the founding principles of European integration. The EU continues to be a strong supporter of multilateral trade liberalization, and additionally, it promotes liberal trade through bilateral FTAs. The EU's trade policy could be seen as very progressive when considering the regulatory cooperation it has achieved so far within the EU and also as part of its ENP as well as the African, Caribbean, and Pacific (ACP) countries with a historical connection to the EU. The EU estimates that trade has a significant impact on consumer welfare,[16] income, and employment.[17] The Global Europe Strategy of 2006 contribute to the understanding that the EU has not wavered in its commitment to liberal trade and regulatory cooperation on market integration.

EU deep trade agreements that include regulatory cooperation intend to obtain the benefits of trade liberalization while mitigating the risks of globalization. The Global Europe Strategy of 2006 and following EU publications on trade policy increasingly emphasize the importance of trade liberalization and the spread of good

---

[14]Schwellnus 2007, p. 21.

[15](1) The Sustainable Development Goals (SDGs), adopted in the UN Resolution A/RES/70/1, present an opportunity for the EU to point to agreed-upon international policy objectives on the multilateral level. The SDGs also identified trade regimes as an essential tool for the implementation of its norms and standards, see SDG 17.10 and the Addis Ababa Action Agenda. (2) The Trade Facilitation Agreement (TFA), annexed to the Marrakesh Agreement, could provide a tool to promote the economic integration of third-country negotiation partners into EU global supply chains and increase their willingness to make binding concessions on regulatory cooperation.

[16]Berlingieri et al. 2018, p. 1882.

[17]Rueda-Cantuche and Sousa 2016, p. 1.

regulatory practices. The formulation of the EU trade strategy reveals increasing importance of regulatory convergence: From 2002, when the EU aimed for exporting standards or compatibility with its standards;[18] to 2006 when it aimed to 'convergence whenever possible';[19] to a more open notion of addressing 'complex regulatory issues' in 2013.[20] The intent of regulatory convergence is visible, but the change of extent and strategy is changing over time.[21] The change of strategy is a reflection of the importance of regulatory convergence and patterns of economic and political influence. The following can be divided into the risks of regulatory divergence and the gains from regulatory convergence.

2.2.1 *The Risks of Regulatory Divergence*

Trade patterns and the content of trade have evolved, and deep trade agreements respond to resulting new challenges. For regulators, the 'servicification' of production and distribution patterns along the lines of value chains is a significant change in trade patterns. In this context, automated technologies also pose a challenge. For example, can the social and environmental aspects of production processes be exempt from FTAs? Which legal responsibility applies to platforms like uber, amazon, booking.com? Provisions aiming at regulatory cooperation in deep trade and investment agreements have much more in common with other areas in international law on regulatory cooperation than with traditional trade liberalization. Technological advances, adjustments to industrial organization, and changes in the global relative strengths of economies led to some critical changes in trade barriers that necessitate adjustments to trade governance. They appear to be similar to disruptive effects of former adjustments from "old trade," but pose new challenges. Through this structural change, shocks and frictions may ripple through economies globally and present a challenge to regulators. These developments may warrant another look at the effectiveness of EU efforts to mitigate risks and benefits from the welfare-enhancing effects of those new forms of trade liberalization.

As Richard Baldwin states, "twenty-first century regionalism is not primarily about preferential market access as was the case for twentieth century regionalism; it is about disciplines that underpin the trade-investment-service nexus."[22] His statement shows the profound effects of production and distribution on the political economy of FTAs. The twenty-first century version of trade flows implies greater importance of services trade and investment, as production processes, as well as distribution, are geographically dispersed. The trade-investment-service nexus also impacts taxation and the regulatory scope of governments. For this reason, some

[18] European Commission 2002, p. 4.

[19] European Commission 2006, p. 9.

[20] European Commission 2013, p. 5.

[21] Young 2015, p. 1255.

[22] Baldwin 2011, p. 3.

new FTAs also include provisions on new issues such as Foreign Direct Investment (FDI), e-commerce, and sustainable development issues.[23] Unlike regionalism, which already addresses tariffs and quotas on 'essentially all trade', regulatory cooperation is expected to address behind-the-border barriers to trade. Rather than agreeing to cut back on intervention to trade, for instance, by cutting tariffs, the aim of FTA regulation on non-tariff measures (NTMs) is to avoid disguised protectionism and additionally avoid unintentional barriers from regulatory divergence.

New generation FTAs are anticipated to go much further than trade liberalization by including regulatory cooperation to avoid unintended regulatory divergence. In general, the aim is to achieve the first-best scenario of trade liberalization, but additionally, supplement it with coordinating the regulatory processes between partners. This goes beyond disguised protectionism and focuses on the plethora of unintentional regulatory divergences. As a result, trade liberalization is being complemented by market integration, mirroring the changes in industrial organization. Based on this assumption, regulatory cooperation has the aim of market integration. Trade regulation goes beyond the assurance of non-discrimination and achieving market access. Regulatory cooperation pursues a different function of trade regulation—market integration. "Effective WTO disciplines exist on discriminatory regulatory measures, but not yet on the redundant, divergent, and unclear yet non-discriminatory rules and conformity assessments procedures that increasingly hinder trade."[24]

2.2.2 The Gains from Regulatory Convergence

Regulatory divergence is estimated to have a substantial impact on international trade and investment flows. Despite trade liberalization, the multitude of sources of diverging regulations may lead to much higher cost structures in international business operations than in domestic business operations. Diverging regulations lead to duplication costs of compliance and testing requirements, resulting in even costlier delays of market entry. This has been largely documented with case studies.[25]

The extent of the effect of divergence becomes apparent when considering the share of international corporations in international trade. The volume of foreign subsidiaries selling products abroad is estimated to be much more substantial than traditional trade flows, demonstrating the importance of regulatory impact. The share of traditional trade is only a small proportion of international trade that is taking place in transnationally operating corporations.[26] Consequently, a large proportion of trade

[23] See for example the EU-Singapore FTA Article 1.2, which aims to liberalize trade and investment, Chapter 14 on Electronic Commerce in the Comprehensive and Progressive Agreement for Trans-Pacific Partnership (CPTPP), and Trade and Sustainable Development Chapter in EU FTAs.

[24] Bollyky 2015, p. 10.

[25] Lampe 2016, p. 66.

[26] Transnational corporations are estimated to account for significant shares of exports and imports of the largest economies, e.g. 20 percent of exports and 28 percent of imports in the United States in

from internationally operating firms is directly exposed to regulatory divergence in its production processes.

Accordingly, regulatory convergence would be expected to lead to significant welfare gains from addressing such differences. Estimates on the expected effect of the Transatlantic Trade and Investment Partnership (TTIP) and Canada–European Union Comprehensive Economic and Trade Agreement (CETA) are relatively large for the overall effect of trade agreements, but they would be expected to be much more substantial given the importance of regulatory divergence.[27]

There is a positive correlation between investment in GVCs from headquarter economies and the formation of FTAs.[28] The terms-of-trade theory of classic trade theories is reversed. Instead of disguised protectionism through regulatory divergence, economies would benefit from regulatory cooperation.

In traditional goods trade, the assumption is that governments typically want to increase trade flows but improve their terms of trade.[29] Bearing in mind, even though tariffs and NTMs are treated as substitute policy measures, removing regulatory barriers does not entail a loss of government revenue. However, it may add the cost of changing regulations.

Terms-of-trade describes only a situation in which the countries attempt to use NTMs with protectionist intent. It does not describe other causes of regulatory divergence. As in the case of the "trade-investment-services nexus",[30] improving terms-of-trade may mean seeking greater regulatory convergence. Costs of protectionist trade policy will be endogenous to domestic firms taking advantage of vertical integration.[31] Companies will benefit from regulatory convergence when they produce goods for re-export. Their manufacturing processes are fragmented in order to benefit from the comparative advantage of, for instance, low wage labour supply in the country of their investment. Terms of trade become reverted in the case of investment in GVCs.

In the tradition of GATT Article XXIV, FTAs aim at the removal of barriers to trade, which is estimated to lead to welfare enhancement from the market liberalization effect. However, depending on the level of overall barriers to trade, trade diversion effects from countries outside liberalization has to be anticipated. The same should be anticipated as well for regulatory cooperation. The removal of regulatory barriers in FTAs follows a similar logic as regional trade agreements for the effects of trade creation and trade diversion from trade liberalization.[32] The challenge is that

2010, 31 percent of European exports and 24 percent of European imports in 2009, and 50 percent of Chinese exports and 48 percent of Chinese imports in 2012; see United Nations Conference on Trade and Development 2013 pp. 135–136.

[27]Francois et al. 2015, p. 20.

[28]Blanchard 2007, p. 40.

[29]The terms-of-trade theory describes a situation of passive diffusion, in which countries are trying to improve their terms-of-trade without taking into account the trade policy reaction of the other economies. Cave and Jones 1973, p. 250.

[30]Baldwin 2014a, p. 261.

[31]Blanchard 2007, p. 7.

[32]Trade creation and trade diversion effects of FTAs refer to the effect the removal of barriers to trade has on the subset of countries and third countries. An implicit baseline points to the exploitation

FTAs are, by nature, exclusionary. In contrast, regulatory cooperation would benefit from including the most significant number of countries that have the regulatory capacity to participate in regulatory integration. In regulatory practice, regulatory cooperation within the WTO is far less likely than in FTAs. A most-favored-nation (MFN) clause in FTAs may ensure that subsequent liberalization is extended to already established FTAs.

In summary, the importance of behind-the-border issues is well known, but the evolution of regulatory convergence in FTAs that include 'regulatory coherence' or 'regulatory cooperation' chapters is relatively new. New regulatory cooperation mechanisms established in FTAs set precedents for future negotiations. They shape the way future regulatory culture will be formulated, their scope and institutionalization. Regulatory diffusion and more active regulatory cooperation should be a strength of the EU. The expectation is that the EU would be leading in regulatory cooperation, to the point of pursuing outright diffusion of its regulation. There are three arguments why it would be expected that the EU pursues an active stance in regulatory cooperation: trade liberalization is considered a founding principle of the EU; it is relevant to maintain the effectiveness of global trade liberalization; as a new development in trade law, regulatory convergence provisions set precedence on future regulatory coherence efforts in FTAs.

2.3 Regulatory Convergence in New EU FTAs Lagging Behind Expectations

As the nature of trade changed, and NTMs moved to the centre of FTAs, it would be expected that the EU continues in the same line of regulatory diffusion. The expectation would be that this is an area in which the EU has large capacities and experience and could continue with the same success. However, the EU seems to be struggling with promoting its stance on regulatory cooperation after it had already been established as a 'global regulator'.[33] While the EU excelled in an area closely related to the biggest challenge in international trade, it does not appear to be pursuing the same hard strategy it had applied previously.

New generation EU FTAs have a broad scope but often remain softer, compared to US FTAs that have a narrow scope but focus on enforceability. The inherent hazard of adjusting regulation in 'new-generation' FTAs is that the cooperation described in them might not go as deep and may not be as beneficial. Old provisions include issues such as customs, industrial goods, and export taxes. Customs cooperation,

---

of comparative advantages prior to the FTA of all countries. It then takes into account distortions from divergences in tariffs between FTA partners and countries that are not included in the FTA. Post-FTA creation, trade diversion would argue a diversion of the most efficient rest of world exports contract, and the less efficient FTA partner exports expand. In a Vinerian tradition, exporters that receive trade preferences gain from FTAs and those exporters who do not receive them lose from the FTAs. This leads to ambiguous welfare effects for FTA partners. See Viner 1950.

[33] Young 2015, p. 1235.

social matters, and competition policy stand out in the new FTAs. The EU approach, compared to that of the United States (US), seems to be slightly hesitant with enforceable provisions, yet it employs soft provisions across a much larger scale. For EU FTAs, Baldwin found a broad scope of regulatory areas mentioned in trade agreements, but only with few of them as legally enforceable language within the FTAs. Those enforceable were mostly provisions covered by the WTO, but likely not to the same extent. As opposed to the US-FTAs, he found less legally enforceable language in EU FTAs in areas but with a broader scope, including areas such as 'social matters', 'data protection', and 'competition policy'.[34]

Advocates of services agreements under the WTO also pursue services agreements under FTAs.[35] Compared to other countries, the EU seemed hesitant to liberalize further subsectors that go beyond the sectors they have already committed to under the General Agreement on Trade in Services (GATS). Instead, they go more in-depth and explicitly codify the commitments they made under the GATS.[36,37]

There seems to be a shift from regulatory diffusion to regulatory convergence in the EU approach. The EU has taken a strong stance on regulatory cooperation before it became subject in new generation FTAs. It engaged in regulatory cooperation to the point of diffusion of its regulations. Leaving aside the EU integration project, it pursued regulatory diffusion not only in its ENP but also in FTAs with former colonial ties.[38] It is the EU's regulatory convergence in new FTAs compared to the old ENP agreements that is puzzling. Has the EU changed its regulatory approach with third countries?

There is a substantial body of research that sees the 'EU-as-a-global-regulator[39] The EU is deemed a strongly coherent and efficient regulator, which is why its regulatory influence has been anticipated to be extended beyond its borders. The EU's influence as a regulator has been evaluated by its outcome, achievement of regulatory aim, and secondary impacts. Its effectiveness is deemed to be in its pragmatism, without the pursuit of dogmatic means in formulating regulation.[40]

---

[34]Baldwin based on the number of times provisions are mentioned in the WTO database in the text-as-data analysis. For this he distinguished between mentions of a provision and legally enforceable language.

Baldwin 2014b, pp. 15–16 Enforceable language here does not imply dispute settlement procedures.

[35]The EU initially followed the GATS approach of positive listings, but then adjusted it to a combined approach of positive and negative listings. This converges treatment between services under mode three and specific Bilateral Investment Treaty (BITs) provisions. Combined approaches between positive and negative listing try to limit divergences between services and goods treatment. Roy 2007, p. 63.

[36]Roy et al. 2007, p. 63.

[37]Sauvé et al. 2009, p. 137.

[38]The resulting Economic Partnership Agreements (EPA) include the EU-Pacific, EU-Cariforum, EU-Eastern and Southern Africa (ESA) sub-region, EU-Central Africa EPA, EU-Southern African Development Community (SADC) EPA, EU-Ghana EPA and the EU-Côte d'Ivoire EPA.

[39]The regulatory power is mostly based on its market power. See: Sapir 2007; Birchfield 2015; Drezner 2008, p. 36; Damro 2012, p. 682.

[40]Dee 2013, p. 158.

As found above, the necessity for regulatory diffusion is closely related to technological advancements and ideational change. Regulatory diffusion implies that the "regulatory order that was shaped in some leading countries and sectors is then diffused to the rest of the world."[41] This definition paints the discourse of regulatory cooperation in a specific way.

The EU's strategy to pursue the spread of key-governance features and regulatory standards has been far deeper in the ENP than the new-generation FTAs. The EU laid out its strategy for ensuring adjacent countries to the East and South of the EU's borders would share "fundamental values and objectives"[42] to have "close and cooperative relations."[43] This is in order to achieve deep economic and political integration. It would be expected that the market integration to adapt to structural changes in the 'trade-investment-services nexus' would attempt to achieve the same. By contrast, empirical legal research indicates that the regulatory influence of the EU under the ENP exceeds its regulatory influence in its new global FTAs.[44] Previously, especially "Ukraine, Moldova, and Georgia [...] adopted significant parts of the EU acquis,"[45] a fact that EU negotiators see as a unique relationship more related to European integration.

The ENP is, however, not the only indicator of the EU's regulatory influence. In the context of multilateral trade negotiations, the EU is seen as a regulatory power because it is one of the largest *demandeurs* for multilateral and bilateral negotiations. Regulatory cooperation with the aim of market integration is seen to be underpinned by its coercive powers and it is, therefore, expected to be one of the EU's strengths in the perception of normative influence beyond its geographical scope. However, this perception may be distorted due, mostly for two reasons:

- Sectoral distortion: Putting an emphasis on instances of the EU's strong regulatory influence in one sector has extended expectations beyond its scope, which may lead to an overstatement of its factual regulatory influence beyond borders.
- Geographical scope distortion: If controlled for the distance between the EU and third-country negotiation partners, empirical research on the promotion of norms and standards in EU trade agreements shows a decline in the binding adoption of EU regulatory standards in the new generation FTAs.

2.3.1 Patterns Relying on Political Influence and Economic Strength

There are two elements of the EU regulatory diffusion identified, one of regulatory diffusion, and the other of an active pursuit of regulatory cooperation. They differ

[41] Levi-Faur 2005, p. 24.

[42] European Commission 2004, p. 5.

[43] European Commission 2004, p. 6.

[44] Young 2015, p. 1234.

[45] Malmström 2015, p. 3.

in the type of interaction and outcome of regulation. One specific understanding of EU regulatory diffusion is based on the attempt of non-EU regulators to facilitate private sector access to the EU market by pegging their regulatory standards to the EU standards. Countries that conduct a large proportion of their trade relations with the EU could lower costs structures for their exporters by adjusting their regulations in line with the EU's regulation. Unilateral adoption by third countries can be the active pursuit of cooperation between the EU and the adopting country or passive influence on third-country regulatory processes. This concept is often discussed as a positive externality of FTAs in third countries. It is also a concept closely associated with power disparity and coercion.[46] In this, lobbying would be expected to have a significant impact. Firms may lobby their governments to increase regulatory standards in order to facilitate private sector market access to the EU market.

Regulatory divergence is a common problem that internationally operating firms face, and it is known to hinder trade. Sources of regulatory divergence may be hidden to economic actors. If legal divergences cause disruptions to efficient market outcomes, it would be expected that economic actors that suffer detrimental effects from such diversions lobby their government for greater convergence and more efficient market outcomes. However, often the sources are ambiguous, in the sense that the wording is the same, but conceptually their legal effect diverges. The application of regulatory ideas is essential.

Regulatory diversity is associated with the transaction and legal risks costs for economic actors. They distort possible trade flows, and they are the central distortion that is contributing to the border effect.[47] The European Commission views regulatory diversity as a source of transaction and legal risk cost for firstly, entry into a foreign market, and secondly, for the extent of risk of violating foreign market rules or costs of compliance.[48]

In regulatory diffusion with the active pursuit by the EU, factors of coercion include market power, regulatory capacity, and stringent enforcement mechanisms. Measuring market power in trade flows could be indicative of an EU influence as a global regulator.

The EU regulatory convergence can be expressed inversely, depending on the degree of difficulty in adjusting to EU rules in other countries. The above spectrum of regulatory cooperation (Fig. 2.1) depicts a third-country point of view, with variables of difficulty and impact. On the right would be regulatory diffusion. Towards the left, it depicts adjustments to EU regulatory standards in diminishing degrees. The success of regulatory diffusion can then be equated to regulatory impact. Measures include the goal as well as the level of stringency. The diffusion approach seems less likely to occur in new generation EU FTAs. References to standardizing bodies are a way of policy coordination. This has the advantage of greater comparability, but they do not necessarily lead to regulatory convergence of existing regulations.

[46] Bradford 2013, p. 40.

[47] Anderson and Wincoop 2004, p. 691.

[48] Ilzkovitz et al. 2007, pp. 77–78.

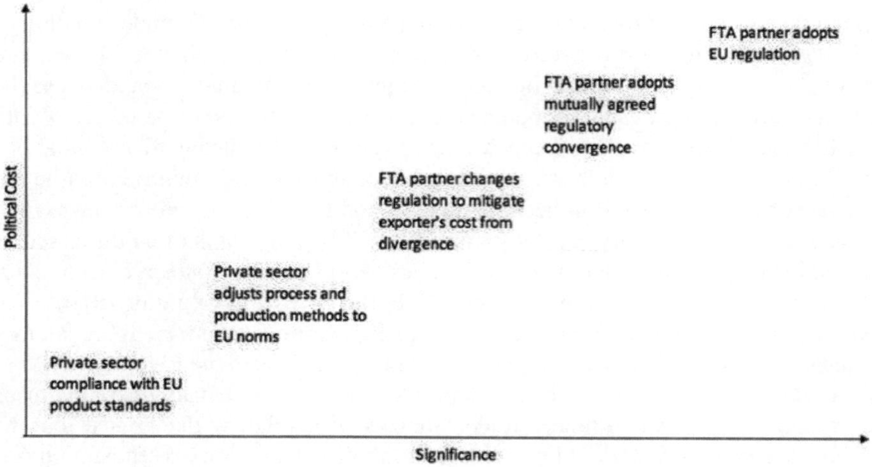

Fig. 2.1 FTA partner's political cost of regulatory convergence with EU regulations (Adapted from Young 2015, p. 1238)

Regulatory cooperation partners would not only incur costs but also benefit from cooperation with the EU. Learning effects from a cooperation with the EU would entail increasing the overall regulatory capacities of cooperation partners. In general, the learning effect from regulatory cooperation necessitates cooperation with partners with proportionally larger regulatory capacities. Cooperation with the EU would be beneficial for other countries if their regulatory capacities were very restricted.

However, there are more cooperative efforts towards regulatory convergence, including 'harmonization', 'equivalence', and 'mutual recognition' approaches. Equal to regulatory diffusion, market size and coercion seem to play an important role. Some differences are noted in the outcome. Equivalence involves a more significant measure of trust between negotiation parties on policy objectives, regulatory capacities for regulation, as well as sound implementation and enforcement. Mutual recognition requires more active and, if possible cooperative approaches, while harmonization necessitates more significant regulatory adjustments domestically.[49]

Cooperation on regulation would lower costs arising from regulatory requirements and, as a result, improve conditions for international trade and investment. At present, chapters pertaining to 'behind-the-border' regulatory choices are considered necessary, but it is still a nascent field in FTAs and clarity on the exact approach, even the consistent use of notations on regulatory convergence, is still lacking.[50]

---

[49] Mavroidis 2016, p. 7.

[50] While the notion of regulatory convergence in the broader sense is widely used and understood concept in FTAs, it is still currently evolving. See: OECD 2013, pp. 19–70. The OECD defined 11 modes of regulatory cooperation, varying in institutionalization and substantive scope - one of them is regulatory convergence under FTAs. Their applied scale reaches from exchanges of Information to discuss on an ad-hoc basis to supranational institutions with clear mandates. The OECD typology also includes FTAs with regulatory provisions. Regulatory convergence is relatively new in FTAs.

Certain EU and non-EU trade agreements in particular stand out in the discussion on regulatory convergence provisions within FTAs. A clear definition does not become apparent when comparing different FTAs. The definition, design, and scope of regulatory convergence provisions of FTAs may inform such provisions in future trade negotiations. A definition of regulatory convergence may help to indicate its institutionalization and scope in FTAs. It indicates whether it will be on a codification of sectoral issues rather than on broader good governance approaches. The extent of institutionalized approaches could range from ad hoc committee meetings to requirements of impact assessments, and active regulatory cooperation in the regulatory process.[51]

Lack of regulatory convergence in the public sector is met by the increasing development of industry standards and private label initiatives leading to even more fragmented markets and less efficient outcomes. This entails another set of inefficient outcomes to the detriment of smaller market participants.

2.3.2 *Diminishing Influence with Increasing Distance*

The differentiation depending on geographical proximity can also be reasoned with international trade flows. The different outcomes of regulatory convergence between new-generation FTAs, ENP, and ACP could be explained with the 'gravity equation', i.e. trade flows are a function which is proportional to their multiplied gross national income and inversely proportional to the distance between them. Trade flows are expected to be higher the greater their combined GDP but they diminish with the distance between trading partners or other barriers.[52] This model was introduced 50 years ago[53] and is one of the commonly used ways of estimating trade flows. It

---

The OECD also noted an international trend of "a shift away from complete harmonization" in regulation to more significant efforts of "more flexible cooperation" instead.

[51]Polanco Lazo and Sauvé 2018, p. 575. Chapter 21 of the CETA on 'regulatory cooperation' does not contain a clear definition of the term; Regulatory convergence provisions for example in the Trans-Pacific Partnership Agreement (TPP) and the Chile–Colombia– Mexico–Peru Pacific Alliance Protocol (PAAP) have included a definition of 'good regulatory practices' (Chapter 25 of TPP) and 'good international regulatory practices' in Annex 4 of the PAAP. Additionally, the private sector also has its understanding of regulatory cooperation. For example, the U.S. Chamber of Commerce published its definition of Regulatory Coherence and Cooperation for TTIP. It makes a point of regulatory practices within the country and between countries, adding another stakeholder in regulatory processes: Regulatory coherence: Regulatory practices in the domestic regulatory process; Regulatory cooperation: Regulatory practices between U.S. and EU.

[52]Deardorff and Frankel 1998, p. 9; he discusses a "standard gravity equation",

$$T_{i,j} = A\frac{Y_i Y_j}{D_{i,j}}$$

in which the total value of exports and imports T between countries i and j are determined by both their national GDPs Yi and Yj, and the distance between them, with A as a constant.

[53]See Tinbergen 1962.

was confirmed, for instance, in a meta-study that resulted in very stable results for the distance coefficient.[54]

The measure of distance can also include variables of transportation costs, regulatory divergence in the border effect,[55] and cultural divergence. The impact of the EU single market on the EU's regulatory influence can be affected by geographical and cultural distance for the adoption of EU regulation by FTA partners. The outcomes of regulatory convergence may be linked with the types of sources of regulatory divergence. They can be complex and may include different legal cultures, local preferences for specific public preferences, market failure from information asymmetries, and effects of path dependency.[56] Defining the source of the regulatory divergence is essential to determine the optimal approach for regulatory convergence.

2.3.2.1 Divergent Preferences on Policy Objectives

Every culture has its own sets of preferences and priorities. For instance, NTMs are often 'legitimate public policy goals' that aim at correcting market failures. Countries may have different optimal outcomes, e.g. regarding social policies, consumer protection, provision of public services, competitiveness, and the provision of subsidies.[57] As a result, preferred outcomes may differ and are not exclusively linked to economic interest.

2.3.2.2 Divergent Preferences Based on Development Status

Regulatory divergences may also be due to differing developmental status.[58] These would be based primarily on diverging economic preferences and additionally based on discrepancies in regulatory capacities. Protectionist intent would not be included here because, as noted above, the terms-of-trade argument in development would not be relevant in the trade-investment-services nexus.[59]

---

[54] Disdier and Head 2008, p. 37.

[55] The border effect is a strong and persistent effect of country borders on international trade even after the complete removal of trade barriers with protectionist intent and technological barriers. It can be especially narrowed down to two sources of impediments to trade: firstly, non-tariff measures from domestic regulatory and policy traditions, and secondly, barriers from linguistic, cultural, and business network effects.

[56] Chirico et al. 2013, pp. 13–16.

[57] As a principle, the Marrakesh Agreement Establishing the World Trade Organization, opened for signature 15 April 1994, 1867 U.N.T.S. 187, 33 I.L.M. 1153 (entered into force 01 January 1995), recognizes legitimate public policies as long as they are applied in a non-discriminatory way.

[58] Hoekman 2015, pp. 2–4.

[59] Baldwin 2014b.

2.3.2.3 Inefficiencies from Inertia

Path dependency[60] is one example of a network effect applied to the legal context. Regulatory convergence implies the costs of adapting regulatory cultures, inducing a shock to the path, like a critical juncture. This can entail a beneficial learning effect for countries with disparities in regulatory capacities. It becomes increasingly hard to achieve any level of convergence between regulatory systems when societies become set on a persistent path. Path dependency implies that it is not the most efficient outcome for their preferences. It seems that the costs of adaptation prevent more efficient outcomes. Legal path dependency can lead to public opposition to the proposal of convergence.[61]

2.3.2.4 Information Asymmetry

Regulatory divergence as market failure can also be due to information asymmetries and could be improved with transparency measures.[62] Divergence of legal concepts would be just one example in which different legal cultures have evolved different implications for the same term. These are often hidden and would only appear through cooperation between regulators or private sector lobbying.

2.4 Trade-Offs Between Types of Convergence Efforts

As a result of the challenges to promote its preferred regulations, regulatory convergence pursues economic benefits that run the risk of gradually reducing regulatory standards. The ‘race-to-the-bottom’ models debate the effect of competition over mobile factors as a result of jurisdictional competition, in which countries are not cooperating. A race to the bottom has been initially associated with the imposition of taxes for government spending and the preferred regulatory level. It expects efficiency outcomes at the expense of the optimal level of the ‘provision of a public good’. This implies that each country undercuts the other country in lowering taxes so that states will not be able to provide a more optimal level of public goods. The idea that globalization increases the competition between different countries to attract investment, employment opportunities and collect taxes leads to one-sided regulatory outcomes that are supportive mostly of investor interests. On the other hand, linking trade liberalization concessions with conditions of high regulatory standards can have a

[60] Path-dependency emphasizes the effects of intentional or arbitrary historical decisions. Resulting increasing returns and sunk costs have a tendency to lead to inertia.

[61] Bull et al. 2015, p. 1.

[62] Coremans et al. 2017, p. 227.

detrimental impact on developing countries.[63] The argument against linking regulatory standards with trade is that it is a way of undermining the comparative advantage of some countries relying on cheap labour and low environmental protection.[64]

The socio-economic models had predicted a low-end regulatory convergence effect of regulatory standards in accordance with the race-to-the-bottom effect. However, empirical evidence found the unilateral harmonization of regulatory standards with an improvement of regulatory practices when studying successful cases.[65] The importance of the regulatory influence has become relevant again recently with negotiation for FTAs. These arguments are often applied in a developed-developing country setting.[66]

There is empirical evidence that the race to the bottom can be observed in taxation, but the opposite has been observed in regulation. The empirical evidence of a regulatory power might still have been overstated, but the cooperation setting in which the regulatory cooperation is pursued matters for the qualitative outcome. As shown below, there is the impression that cooperation linked to an incentive is more likely to lead in turn to higher regulatory standards because there is compensation for the regulatory cost the adapting party has to incur.[67]

The political cost of regulatory convergence may give insights into the likes of the pursuit of regulatory convergence. Whereas in the WTO and the new generation FTAs, only the measures that come at a low political and regulatory cost for adapting regulations are more likely to lead to increasing regulatory standards, the ENP and the AfT for the implementation of the sustainable development goals (SDGs) would link substantive support, market access, or large-scale financial assistance and regulatory cooperation. Table 2.1 exemplifies this link with the regulatory outcomes.

2.4.1 Overcoming Divergent Regulatory Influence Through AfT and SDGs

Regulatory convergence may not be possible with some countries that have very divergent regulatory cultures, distributional systems, and understanding of best regulatory policy outcomes. As became apparent in the Singapore Issues and multilateral trade negotiations during the Doha Development Agenda (DDA), countries may have

---

[63] Vogel 1997, p. 556.

[64] Chan and Ross 2003, p. 1011.

[65] Holzinger and Sommerer 2011, p. 315.

[66] Häberli 2012, p. 287.

[67] In a scenario of race-to-the-bottom effect through deregulation the expectation is that the pursuit of increased competitiveness will lead to externalities of environmental degradation, less sustainable development and lower labour standards will occur. Singling out issues by sector over an increased period of time will more likely see an increase in regulatory standards, even if some outliers will be lower. Holzinger and Sommerer 2011, p. 315.

Table 2.1 Race to the bottom (RB) and race to the top (RT) by source of regulatory divergence

Sources of Regulatory Divergence	Regulatory Convergence by Forum: WTO	new gen. PTAs	ENP	SDGs/AfT
Policy Objectives	X	RB or RT	RT	RT
Different Preferences, development status	RB or RT	RB or RT	RT	RT
Overcoming Path Dependency	X	RB or RT	RT	RT
Information Asymmetry	RT	RT	RT	X

very different interests in regulations,[68] especially, if the sources of regulatory divergence are linked to asymmetries in development, the SDGs may have a significant impact in overcoming divergences. However, the use of SDGs with implementation mechanisms of AfT and TF may be a way of overcoming the negative correlation of the distance effect of EU influence.

Converging policy goals may be an additional approach to regulatory convergence on trade-related issues. The EU may extend its influence on regulatory convergence via other means than FTAs, such as SDGs and funding through AfT and TF programs. The EU's direct influence over other countries may diminish with geographical distance. However, its sphere of influence in its attempt to promote its regulatory

[68] Of the Singapore Issues, the EU was mainly promoting the regulation of investment, competition, and government procurement practices, but only the Trade Facilitation Agreement (TFA) was concluded. Conversely, the flexibility mechanisms in the AfT linked to conditionality may be motivated by the prospect of enhancing key country-centred goals linked to foreign policy, such as improving linkages with humanitarian, political, economic, and even military objectives. Economic efficiency, a good investment climate, and improving infrastructure are among the considerations, along with securing poverty targets, reducing the risk of the terrorist threat, and ideological indoctrination.

standards can be extended by linking SDGs to trade. They present an opportunity for the EU to point to agreed international policy objectives on the multilateral level. This is possible because the SDGs recognize trade as an important means to implement its targets.[69] The Addis Ababa Action Agenda (AAAA) provides a framework for financing the implementation of SDGs, in which trade and investment are seen as essential tools for implementing trade-related targets. Since efforts in negotiation are, to a large extent, focused on regulatory convergence, AfT and TF are expected to lead to regulatory convergence while increasing regulatory standards motivating the donating party.

The SDGs see multilateral trade as an essential tool for the implementation of its norms and standards.[70] Therefore, the SDGs could lower the costs to trade policymakers to include regulatory cooperation in trade negotiations and decrease civil society opposition. Additionally, financing through TF and AfT could provide a tool to promote the economic integration of third-country negotiation partners into EU global supply chains and increase their willingness to make binding concessions on regulatory cooperation.

The link between the SDGs and trade is especially useful due to the increased importance of investment flows and services exchange. Contrarily, traditional trade liberalization is understood to lead to overall benefits for the economy, with only the possibility of a trickling down effect throughout the economy. However, this does not necessarily lead to the good governance targets, improved consumer benefits, and economic integration.[71] The benefit of linking SDGs and trade is primarily by connecting trade liberalization with trade-related regulatory goals in regulatory cooperation.

Finally, conditionality to funding can motivate meeting targets. Via means of the imposition of conditionality on AfT and technical assistance on TF, ex ante (for example, preconditions to avoid misappropriation of funds) or ex post (for example, performance requirements and evaluation measures) assessments can ensure satisfactory outcomes.[72] Frequently used analytical tools are the Integrated Economic Analysis (IEA) developed by the Swedish International Development Cooperation Agency (Sida) and Sustainability Impact Assessments (SIA).

2.5 Conclusion

Applying regulatory cooperation as regulatory diffusion at a similar level as under the ENP has not been observed in new generation FTAs. It seems to be confirmed that geographic distance, following the gravity model, also gives a strong correlation between distance and regulatory convergence.

[69] United Nations 2015, pp. 37–42.

[70] Ibid., pp. 4–5.

[71] Cattaneo 2015, p. 18.

[72] Arruñada and Manzanares 2016, p. 217.

Some evidence points to continued regulatory convergence in international standard setting bodies and through SDGs, AfT, and TF, rather than through FTAs through mutually agreed binding standards in FTAs. Unlike the ENP, there are fewer binding obligations for the adoption of EU acquis by negotiation partners in new-generation FTAs, but rather the basis and intent for future convergence. This approach may increase the risk of a race-to-the-bottom effect, especially with large regulatory divergences and greater geographical distance.

The EU seems to pursue two approaches to counter this effect. The EU seems to pursue a mix of regulatory practices in its global policy approaches to achieve satisfactory results in regulatory convergence. Firstly, by way of referring to international standards and internationally set goals, it seems to pursue pegging regulatory convergence to international standard-setting bodies. Afterwards, it can then attempt to influence the level of regulation in standard-setting bodies. Secondly, especially in North–South regulatory convergence, the EU seems to have some potential to ensure regulatory convergence by linking SDG and trade. It increases the regulatory capacities and reduces the protectionist pressure due to the linked funds and learning effects.

Despite the greater difficulty of achieving targeted regulatory convergence in FTAs beyond the ENP and ACP-country trading partners, greater economic integration and servicification of trade make regulatory convergence a priority in trade regulation. It is to mitigate shocks, to avoid a race-to-the-bottom in regulatory standards, and to achieve desired economic outcomes from market integration.

References

Anderson J, Van Wincoop E (2004) Trade Costs. Journal of Economic literature 42:691–751

Arruñada B, Manzanares C (2016) The Tradeoff Between Ex Ante and Ex Post Transaction Costs: Evidence from Legal Opinions. Berkeley Business Law Journal 13:217–255

Baldwin R (2011) 21st Century Regionalism: Filling the Gap between 21st Century Trade and 20th Century Trade Rules. World Trade Organization (WTO) Economic Research and Statistics Division, Staff Working Paper ERSD-2011-08

Baldwin R (2014a) WTO 2.0: Governance of 21st Century Trade. The Review of International Organizations 9:261–283

Baldwin R (2014b) Multilateralising 21st Century Regionalism. OECD Conference Centre, Paris

Baldwin R, Cave M, Lodge M (2010) The Future of Regulation. In: The Oxford Handbook of Regulation https://www.oxfordhandbooks.com/view/https://doi.org/10.1093/oxfordhb/9780199560219.001.0001/oxfordhb-9780199560219-e-25 Accessed 13 February 2020

Berlingieri G, Breinlich H, Dhingra S (2018) The impact of trade agreements on consumer welfare—evidence from the EU common external trade policy. Journal of the European Economic Association 16:1881–1928

Birchfield V (2015) Coercion with Kid Gloves? The European Union's Role in Shaping a Global Regulatory Framework for Aviation Emissions. Journal of European Public Policy 22:1276–1294

Blanchard E (2007) Foreign Direct Investment, Endogenous Tariffs, and Preferential Trade Agreements. The B.E. Journal of Economic Analysis & Policy 7:1–52

Bollyky T (2015) A Role for the World Trade Organization on Regulatory Coherence. https://e15initiative.org/publications/a-role-for-the-world-trade-organization-on-regulatory-coherence/ Accessed 13 February 2020

Bradford A (2013) The Brussels Effect. https://scholarlycommons.law.northwestern.edu/nulr/vol107/iss1/1 Accessed 13 February 2020

Bull R, Mahboubi N, Stewart R, Wiener J (2015) New Approaches to International Regulatory Cooperation: The Challenge of TTIP, TPP, and Mega-regional Trade Agreements. Law and Contemporary Problems 78:1–31

Cattaneo O (2015) Promoting Greater Regulatory Coherence and Cooperation through Aid for Trade: What Could Be Done? What Role for the Private Sector and the WTO? https://e15initiative.org/wp-content/uploads/2015/09/E15-Regulatory-Coherence-Cattaneo-Final.pdf Accessed 13 February 2020

Cave R, Jones R (1973) World Trade and Payments: An Introduction. Little, Brown and Company, Boston

Chan A, Ross R (2003) Racing to the Bottom: International Trade without a Social Clause. Third World Quarterly 24:1011–1028

Chirico F, Larouche P (2013) Convergence and Divergence, in Law and Economics and Comparative Law. In: Larouche P, Cserne P (eds) National Legal Systems and Globalization. TMC Asser Press, The Hague, pp 9–33

Coremans E, Kerremans B (2017) Agents as Information Asymmetry Managers in EU Trade Policy-Making. In: Delreux T, Adriaensen J (eds) The Principal Agent Model and the European Union. Palgrave Studies in European Union Politics. Palgrave Macmillan, Cham, pp 227–253

Damro C (2012) Market Power Europe. Journal of European Public Policy 19:682–699

Deardorff A (1998) Determinants of Bilateral Trade: Does Gravity Work in a Neoclassical World? In: Frankel J (ed) The Regionalization of the World Economy. University of Chicago Press, Chicago, pp 7–32

Dee M (2013) Challenging Expectations: A Study of European Union Performance in Multilateral Negotiations https://pdfs.semanticscholar.org/297f/a15b299bc9028386bf766a625c4f5e496b86.pdf Accessed 11 February 2020

Disdier A, Head K (2008) The Puzzling Persistence of the Distance Effect on Bilateral Trade. The Review of Economics and statistics 90:38–48

Drezner D (2008) All Politics Is Global: Explaining International Regulatory Regimes. Princeton University Press, Princeton

European Commission (2002) A Policy Framework for the Facilitation of Trade in the Fields of Standardization and Conformity Assessment: A Toolbox of Instruments. https://docs.wto.org/dol2fe/Pages/FE_Search/FE_S_S009-DP.aspx?language=E&CatalogueIdList=29360&CurrentCatalogueIdIndex=0&FullTextHash=1&HasEnglishRecord=True&HasFrenchRecord=True&HasSpanishRecord=True Accessed 11 February 2020

European Commission (2004) European Neighbourhood Policy. Strategy Paper. COM 373 final. https://ec.europa.eu/neighbourhood-enlargement/sites/near/files/2004_communication_from_the_commission_-_european_neighbourhood_policy_-_strategy_paper.pdf Accessed 11 February 2020

European Commission (2006) Global Europe: Competing in the World: A Contribution to the EU's Growth and Jobs Strategy. COM(2006) 567 final.https://eur-lex.europa.eu/LexUriServ/LexUriServ.do?uri=COM:2006:0567:FIN:en:PDF Accessed 11 February 2020

European Commission (2010) Europe 2020: A Strategy for a Smart, Sustainable and Inclusive Growth. COM (2010) 2020 final. https://eur-lex.europa.eu/LexUriServ/LexUriServ.do?uri=COM:2010:2020:FIN:EN:PDF Accessed 11 February 2020

European Commission (2013) Trade: A Key Source of Growth and Jobs for the EU. https://eu2013.ie/media/eupresidency/content/documents/130207-Commission-Contribution-on-Trade-to-EC.pdf Accessed 11 February 2020

European Commission (2015) Trade for All: Towards a More Responsible Trade and Investment Policy. COM(2015) 497 final. https://ec.europa.eu/transparency/regdoc/rep/1/2015/EN/1-2015-497-EN-F1-1.PDF Accessed 11 February 2020
Francois J et al (2015) Reducing Transatlantic Barriers to Trade and Investment: An Economic Assessment. Centre for Economic Policy Research, Working Paper No. 1503, London
Grandy C (1989) New Jersey Corporate Chartermongering. The Journal of Economic History 49:677–692
Häberli C, Jansen M, Monteiro J (2012) Regional Trade Agreements and Domestic Labour Market Regulation. In: Lippoldt D (ed) Policy Priorities for International Trade and Jobs. OECD, pp 287–326
Hoekman B (2015) Trade Agreements and International Regulatory Cooperation in a Supply Chain World. https://hdl.handle.net/1814/34207 Accessed 13 February 2020
Holzinger K, Sommerer T (2011) "Race to the Bottom" or "Race to Brussels"? Environmental Competition in Europe. Journal of Common Market Studies 49:315–339
Ilzkovitz F, Dierx A, Kovacs V, Sousa N (2007) Steps Towards a Deeper Economic Integration: The Internal Market in the 21st Century, a Contribution to the Single Market Review (No. 271). https://ec.europa.eu/economy_finance/index_en.htm Accessed 13 February 2020
International Monetary Fund (2019) World Economic Outlook. https://IMF.org/external/datamapper/datasets Accessed 11 February 2020
Levi-Faur D (2005) The Global Diffusion of Regulatory Capitalism. EBOR DOI:10.1177/0002716204272371
Malmström C (2015) Trade in the 21st Century: The Challenge of Regulatory Convergence https://trade.ec.europa.eu/doclib/press/index.cfm?id=1281&title=Speech-Trade-in-the-21st-century-The-challenge-of-regulatory-convergence Accessed 13 February 2020
Mavroidis P (2016) Regulatory Cooperation: Lessons from the WTO and the World Trade Regime. https://e15initiative.org/publications/regulatory-cooperation-lessons-wto-world-trade-regime Accessed 5 July 2020
OECD (2013) International Regulatory Co-Operation: Addressing Global Challenges. OECD Publishing, Paris
Polanco Lazo R, Sauvé P (2018) The Treatment of Regulatory Convergence in Preferential Trade Agreements. World Trade Review 17:575–607
Radaelli C (2003) The Europeanization of Public Policy. In: Featherstone K, Radaelli C (eds) The Europeanization of Public Policy. Oxford University Press, New York, pp 27–56
Roy M, Marchetti J, Lim H (2007) Services Liberalization in the New Generation of Preferential Trade Agreements (PTAs): How Much Further than the GATS? World Trade Review 6:155–192
Rueda-Cantuche J, Sousa N (2016) EU Exports to the World: Overview of Effects on Employment and Income. Directorate General for Trade, European Commission, Brussels
Sapir A (2007) Fragmented Power: Europe and the Global Economy. Université Libre de Bruxelles, Brussels No. 2013/8068
Sauvé P, Ward N (2009) Services and Investment in the EC–CARIFORUM Economic Partnership Agreement: Innovation in Rule-Design and Implications for Africa, In: Faber G, Orbie J (eds) Beyond Market Access for Economic Development: EU–Africa Relations in Transition. Routledge, London, pp 137–173
Schwellnus C (2007) The Effect of Domestic Regulations on Services Trade Revisited. CEPII Working Paper, Paris
Selznick P (1985) Focusing Organisational Research on Regulation. In: Noll R (ed) Regulatory Policy and the Social Sciences. University of California Press, Berkeley, pp 363–368
Staeger U (2016) Turning a problem into a solution? The potential of interregionalism between the European Union and the Eurasian Economic Union. In: Gstöhl S, Schunz S (eds) Theorizing the European Neighbourhood Policy. Taylor & Francis, New York, pp 206–225
Tinbergen J (1962) An Analysis of World Trade Flows, Shaping the World Economy. Twentieth Century Fund, New York

United Nations (2015) The Addis Ababa Action Agenda of the Third International Conference on Financing for Development (AAAA) https://www.un.org/esa/ffd/wp-content/uploads/2015/08/AAAA_Outcome.pdf Accessed 13 February 2020

United Nations Conference on Trade and Development (2013) World Investment Report 2013: Global Value Chains—Investment and Trade for Development https://www.un-ilibrary.org/international-trade-and-finance/world-investment-report-2013_a3836fcc-en Accessed 12 February 2020

Viner J (1950) Carnegie Endowment for International Peace Division of International Law: The Customs Union Issue. Oxford University Press, New York

Vogel D (1997) Trading up and Governing across: Transnational Governance and Environmental Protection. Journal of European Public Policy 4:556–571

Von Lampe M (2016) Trade Costs in Regulatory Co-Operation: Findings from Case Studies. OECD Working Party of the Trade Committee TAD/TC/WP(2016)17/FINAL

Young A (2015) The European Union as a Global Regulator? Context and Comparison. Journal of European Public Policy 22:1233–1252

M. Theisinger is a Ph.D. researcher in EUTIP, a Marie Curie International Training Network (Horizon 2020), at the Erasmus University Rotterdam, Erasmus School of Law, Jean Monnet Chair of Economic Analysis of European Law in Rotterdam.

Chapter 3
Shaping EU External Relations Beyond Treaty-Making: The Scope of Extraterritorial EU Legislation and Its Enforcement Challenges

D. Dero-Bugny and J. Motte-Baumvol

Contents

Abstract The relationship between the European Union (EU) and its partners is essentially based on a network of bilateral, regional or multilateral treaties, broadly interpreted by the Court of Justice and analysed by legal doctrine. In recent years, however, there has been a proliferation of European secondary law that contains provisions regulating people, goods or services located outside the EU territory. Its existence raises a set of challenges that have not been examined by legal literature. The first challenge concerns the personal and material scope of the extraterritorial EU secondary law. This study reveals, in particular, the role that the European Union can play on the international scene on account of its unilateral normative activity. The second challenge concerns the implementation of extraterritorial EU secondary law. The extraterritorial nature of EU legislation should require specific implementation acts and procedures taking into consideration the difficulties arising from their extraterritorial nature. This study suggests, however, that their specific nature was not entirely taken into account by EU legislation.

D. Dero-Bugny (✉) · J. Motte-Baumvol
Université de Paris,
10 avenue Pierre Larousse, 92100 Malakoff, France
e-mail: delphine.dero-bugny@parisdescartes.fr

J. Motte-Baumvol
e-mail: julia.motte-baumvol@parisdescartes.fr

W. Th. Douma et al. (eds.), *The Evolving Nature of EU External Relations Law*,
https://doi.org/10.1007/978-94-6265-423-5_3

Keywords EU External relations · Normative action · EU secondary law · Extraterritoriality · Enforcement · Effectiveness · Competent authorities · Private actors · Commission

3.1 Introduction

Relations between the European Union and its partners are essentially founded upon bilateral, regional, and multilateral treaties concluded in conformity with the rules of international law governing the law of treaties. These treaties, and the effects that they produce, have been the subject of numerous studies.[1] The purpose of this contribution to the field is not to take an interest in the Union's conventional practice, but to address the European Union capacity to exercise an international influence, notably towards third countries, via its unilateral normative function.

To what extent can the European Union—by adopting unilateral acts such as directives, regulations, or decisions, all of which have, in principle, no purpose other than to be applied within the European Union's territory—exercise an influence on third countries' territory? This question is not simply theoretical because over the past few years we have witnessed the adoption of EU secondary legislation which will have as its purpose or effect to regulate people, goods, or services that are not located within the EU territory. For instance, Regulation 2016/79 of 27 April 2016 on the protection of personal data,[2] allows for non-European operators to be compelled to respect European regulations in terms of data protection. Similarly, Regulation 2017/821 of 17 May 2017 established supply chain due diligence obligations for Union importers of tin, tantalum and tungsten, their ores, and gold originating from conflict-affected and high-risk areas.[3]

Since the compatibility of EU extraterritorial legislation with the EU legal system has been thoroughly acknowledged,[4] this paper examines the scope of this legislation. Extraterritorial effects are scarcely addressed in European Union law, outside of

[1] Kuijper et al. 2015; Wouters et al. 2015.

[2] Regulation (EU) 2016/679 of the European Parliament and of the Council of 27 April 2016 on the protection of natural persons with regard to the processing of personal data and on the free movement of such data, and repealing Directive 95/46/EC, OJ L119, 4 May 2016 (General Data Protection Regulation), pp. 1–88.

[3] Regulation (EU) 2017/821 of the European Parliament and of the Council of 17 May 2017 laying down supply chain due diligence obligations for Union importers of tin, tantalum and tungsten, their ores, and gold originating from conflict-affected and high-risk areas, OJ L130, 19 May 2017, pp. 1–20.

[4] See, for instance, Court of Justice, *United Kingdom v Parliament and Council*, Opinion of Advocate General Jääskinen, 20 November 2014, Case C-507/13, ECLI:EU:C:2014:2394, paras 36–41 and Court of Justice, *Ahlström Osakeyhtiö a.o. v Commission*, Opinion of Advocate General Darmon, 25 May 1988, Joined Cases C-89/85, C-104/85, C-114/85, C-116/85, C-117/85 and C-125/85 to C-129/85, paras 27–30.

competition law or human rights law.[5] This effect will be understood here in a broad sense as the possibility for the European Union's unilateral acts to produce effects beyond its territory by addressing legal situations that take place in third countries, in order to regulate access to the European market, to guarantee the coherence of the European Union's actions or to promote its values and interests and contribute to the protection of its citizens (Article 3(5) TEU).[6]

The existence of European Union acts endowed with extraterritorial scope poses a certain number of challenges. These are, in the end, related more to the effectiveness of these acts than to the capacity of the European Union to adopt them, this question being to a large extent settled by the position taken by the Permanent Court of International Justice in the *Lotus* matter.[7] Indeed, within the framework of these acts, the European legislator has been compelled to develop specific implementation mechanisms to reach situations that are not found within the EU territory. Certain acts put systems for recognizing legislative equivalencies into place, entailing, at times, the adoption of a decision by the Commission. Others develop a particularly original approach by inciting an auto-regulatory activity on the part of European or non-European enterprises. These acts allow for a contemporary analysis of due diligence in that they are addressed not only to States but also to enterprises in their relations with third countries. The effects of these mechanisms remain, nonetheless, very difficult to identify, because they escape from the principle of territoriality of the law, very much present in European Union law. Their implementation nonetheless reveals the upholding of a certain territoriality because it rests essentially on the member States.

An analysis of the development of European acts with extraterritorial scope appears to be necessary before questioning the difficulties stemming from their implementation.

3.2 The Development of EU Extraterritorial Legislation

For a number of years, European regulations with extraterritorial scope have grown more diverse. An analysis of the effects of these regulations is important. It reveals, in particular, the role that the European Union can play on the international scene on account of its unilateral normative activity.

[5]Eeckman 1965, p. 499; Stoufflet 1971, p. 487; Bischoff and Kovar 1975, p. 675; Jacquet 1985, p. 327, Bazex 1987, p. 51; Groux 1987, p. 5; Milanovic 2011; Scott 2013, p. 87; Bartels 2014, pp. 1071–1091; Cannizzaro 2014, pp. 1093–1099; Martucci 2018.

[6]Stern 1986, p. 7; Bartels 2014, pp. 1071–1091.

[7]Permanent Court of International Justice, *S.S. "Lotus", France v Turkey*, Judgment, 7 September 1927, PCIJ Series A no. 10, ICGJ 248.

3.2.1 Diversification of European Acts with Extraterritorial Scope

Acts of the European Union with extraterritorial scope have known a real evolution within the past years. This is visible in both the form and the content of these acts.

3.2.1.1 Evolution of the Legal Form of Acts with Extraterritorial Scope

The adoption by European Union institutions of unilateral acts containing dispositions with extraterritorial scope is not new. As such, since the beginning of the 1980s, directives containing dispositions that either took into consideration situations existing within a third country's territory in order to draw conclusions from them within European territory, or imposed obligations on entities situated in third countries so that their merchandise or services might gain access to the European market were adopted.

Thus, the 7th Council Directive of 13 June 1983 based on Article 54(3)(g) of the Treaty on consolidated accounts[8] allows member States to exempt enterprises falling under their national law from the obligation to establish consolidated accounts as long as they constitute an affiliate of a parent company in a third country that has, that parent company itself, put into place consolidated accounts in conformity with the requirements of the directive. Article 3 of Council Directive of 6 December 1984 on the supervision and control within the European Community on the trans frontier shipment of hazardous waste imposes on the holder of the waste in a third country a notification obligation, containing a certain number of requirements, to the competent authority of the member State into which such holder has the intention of transferring the waste.[9]

The 2000s led to an increase in these types of act, which is especially visible beginning in the 2010s. The European Union's new acts with extraterritorial scope can be distinguished from those adopted in the 1980s by their legal form. Whereas during the 80s these acts were principally adopted in the form of directives, today they essentially take the form of regulations. This change in form is not insignificant. Regulations, as opposed to directives which need to be transposed into the national law of member States to take effect, are directly applicable within the member States and impose obligations by themselves on their intended targets, notably on the enterprises they address. They leave, moreover, less flexibility to the member States and avoid the existence of divergences amongst member States' legislation. This evolution in form is notable in the area of protecting personal data where the directive of 24 October 1995 on the protection of individuals with regard to the processing

[8] Seventh Council Directive 83/349/EEC of 13 June 1983 based on the Article 54(3) (g) of the Treaty on consolidated accounts, OJ L193, pp. 0001–0017.

[9] Council Directive 84/631/EEC of 6 December 1984 on the supervision and control within the European Community of the trans frontier shipment of hazardous waste, OJ L326, 13 December 1984, pp. 31–41.

of personal data and on the free movement of such data,[10] which already contained provisions with extraterritorial scope, was replaced by the regulation of 27 April 2016 on the protection of natural persons with regard to the processing of personal data and on the free movement of such data.[11]

3.2.1.2 Evolution of the Content of Acts with Extraterritorial Scope

The acts of the European Union with extraterritorial scope adopted these past years have also evolved in terms of their content and are characterized today by their diversity. This diversity is reflected most notably through the varying strength of the extraterritorial effect. Certain acts, not very numerous, can be considered extraterritorial by their purpose to the extent that they have for an objective regulating access to the internal market for merchandise, services, or workers originating from third countries. Such is the case with the regulation of 17 May 2017,[12] cited in the introduction, setting forth supply chain due diligence obligations for Union importers of tin, tantalum and tungsten, their ores, and gold originating in conflict-affected and high-risk areas. Other acts, of which the number is much higher, do not have as a specific objective ruling over a legal situation located in one or several third countries, but bring within their field of application entities that are not installed within the European Union's territory. One could cite here, by way of illustration, the regulation of 20 November 2013 on ship recycling,[13] which imposes norms on dismantling installations for merchant ships flying the flag of a member State "wherever they may be in the world".[14]

Within these different acts a distinction can be drawn between those which directly impose obligations on economic actors whose activities are conducted from third countries and those which impose obligations on actors existing within the European Union regarding relationships that they maintain with parties or circumstances in third countries.

The first hypothesis is a classic. The Union's acts in question will thus obligate operators existing in third countries to comply with the rules imposed by a regulation or in a European directive if they want to gain access to the European market. Thus, within the framework of regulation 2016/679 on the protection of personal data, the obligations set forth are also imposed on data processing managers or sub-contractors processing data who are not established within the Union when they process personal data concerning individuals who are found within the Union.

---

[10]Directive 95/46/EC of the European Parliament and of the Council of 24 October 1995 on the protection of individuals with regard to the processing of personal data and on the free movement of such data, OJ L281, 23 November 1995, p. 31.

[11]General Data Protection Regulation, above n. 2, pp. 1–88.

[12]Regulation (EU) 2017/821, above n. 3, pp. 1–20.

[13]Regulation (EU) No 1257/2013 of the European Parliament and of the Council of 20 November 2013 on ship recycling and amending Regulation (EC) n° 1013/2006 and Directive 2009/16/EC, OJ L330, 10 December 2013, pp. 1–20.

[14]Ibid, introduction, pt 22.

The second hypothesis is more innovative. For the moment, it essentially concerns acts which have for their purpose the regulation of the conditions with which specific merchandise linked to natural resources and to the protection of the environment, originating either exclusively from a third country, or third countries, or European States, can gain access the Union's internal market. The particularity of these acts is that generally they do not impose conditions directly on operators established in the third countries that produce and commercialize these products. But they put obligations on the European operators who place these products on the European market for the first time. These obligations must be complied with under penalty of sanctions. The extraterritorial effect produced is indirect here because the obligations are placed on European operators but will have repercussions on the products originating from third countries which, in order to be commercialized within the European Union, will have to comply with the norms of the producing State and international norms. The regulation of 20 October 2010[15] thus provides for an entire series of obligations imposed upon operators who place timber and its derivative products on the internal market for the first time whether the wood is of European origin or comes from a third country (obligation to not place wood that was harvested illegally on the market, obligations of traceability, setting up a system of due diligence ...). The regulation of 17 May 2017 setting out supply chain due diligence obligations for Union importers of tin, tantalum, and tungsten, their ores, and gold originating from conflict-affected and high-risk areas, bears, for its part, exclusively on products originating from third countries and imposes obligations on the European importers of ores or metals who place these specific products on the European market for the first time.

The appearance of this new form of acts with extraterritorial scope leads us to consider the effects produced by these acts both within the European Union and outside its borders.

3.2.2 Effects Stemming from the Extraterritorial Scope of European Union Acts

The effects linked to the extraterritorial scope of European Union acts should be considered through three angles: the European angle, which leads to studying the effects of this regulation within the European Union; the extra-European angle, which implies an analysis of the effects in third countries; and the international angle, which means questioning the international role of the European Union as revealed by the development of these types of acts.

[15] Regulation (EU) No 995/2010 of the European Parliament and of the Council of 20 October 2010 laying down the obligations of operators who place timber and timber products on the market, OJ L295, 12 November 2010, pp. 23–34.

3.2.2.1 Effects Within the European Union

Considering the effects within the European Union, it is worth noting that the purpose of European acts with extraterritorial scope is often the protection of the European market and the coherence of the Union's activities, most notably in making sure that goods, services, or workers originating from third countries cannot enter or exercise their functions within the European Union's territory unless they comply with European regulations. As an example, directive 2008/106/CE of 19 November 2008 concerning the minimum level of training for seafarers,[16]—which puts in place common standards for the training of seafarers working on ships flying the flag of European Union member States—institutes mechanisms to permit the assurance that residents of third countries who exercise these functions cannot do so unless they respect the rules provided for by the directive.

The protection and promotion of European values is also frequently invoked to justify the adoption of acts with extraterritorial scope. The regulation of 17 May 2017, cited above, which sets forth obligations linked to a duty of diligence with regard to European Union importers of or originating from conflict zones, can also be analysed as an instrument for promoting the European Union's values. Putting into place a responsible supply of minerals is, in effect, a means to support, in these zones, efforts in favour of the development of the rule of law which, according to Article 2 of the TUE, constitutes one of the values upon which the European Union is founded.

3.2.2.2 Effects in Third Countries

Considering the effects on third countries next, these effects act upon both States as well as private actors existing within those States (principally business enterprises).

As far as effects on States are concerned, European Union acts with extraterritorial scope can encourage third countries to develop their legislation in order to permit their enterprises, their goods, or their workers to gain access to the European Union market. In this sense, Directive 2008/101/CE of 19 November 2008 integrating aviation activities into the scheme for greenhouse gas emission allowance trading within the Community explicitly target,[17] in its introductory recitals, the encouragement of third countries to adopt equivalent measures.[18] Numerous acts endowed with extraterritorial dispositions set up equivalency systems (which sometimes presupposes the European Commission's adoption of a decision recognizing this equivalency) which are destined, once that equivalency is established, to permit the third country to gain

[16]Directive 2008/106/EC of the European Parliament and of the Council of 19 November 2008 on the minimum level of training of seafarers, OJ L323, 3 December 2008, pp. 33–61.

[17]Directive 2008/101/EC of the European Parliament and of the Council of 19 November 2008 amending Directive 2003/87/EC so as to include aviation activities in the scheme for greenhouse gas emission allowance trading within the Community, OJ L8, 13 January 2009, pp. 3–21.

[18]Ibid, Introduction, pt 17.

access to the market.[19] Within the framework of these acts, the adoption of legislation equivalent to that of the Union is thus a condition for gaining access to the internal market. As such, numerous third countries have developed their legislation to permit their enterprises to gain access to the European market. An example can be given with regard to the United States and the field of protecting personal data. Directive 95/46/EC on the protection of individuals with regard to the processing of personal data and on the free movement of such data, which was recently replaced by regulation (EU) 2016/679, already provided that member States were bound to ensure that transfers of personal data to a third country would only take place if the country in question could assure an adequate level of protection. Within the framework of this directive, the Commission was authorized to assess what constitutes an adequate level of protection in a third country. The United States had to reform their legislation in order to be recognised as having a level of protection that is adequate for the Commission. This was not recognised until the year 2000,[20] when the American Department of Commerce published an array of principles for the protection of personal data,[21] better known through the name "Safe Harbor", to which American enterprises must voluntarily adhere in order to receive personal data originating from the European Union. The Commission's decision was nonetheless invalidated by the Court of Justice in the Schrems judgment[22] which called into question the Commission's assessment when it came to the adequate level of protection of American regulations.

Acts endowed with extraterritorial scope do not only have an effect on States, they can also have consequences on the behaviour of private actors in third countries. Through its extraterritorial standard-setting, the European Union can, most notably, exercise an influence on the operating methods of enterprises existing within the territory of third countries, either by virtue of the link that these enterprises have with a European enterprise, or by virtue of these enterprises' desire to gain access to the European market. This form of influence, especially in the case of the first hypothesis, is not new,[23] and can be explained by the development of multinational enterprises which are composed of a number of entities established in a number of States (European and non-European). The European Union, in imposing obligations on companies established within its territory, can thus seek to influence the behaviour of enterprises established within the territory of third countries who constitute either

---

[19] Directive 2008/101/EC, above n. 17; Regulation (EU) No 648/2012 of the European Parliament and of the Council of 4 July 2012 on OTC derivatives, central counterparties and trade repositories, OJ L201, 27 July 2012, pp. 1–59; Directive 2008/106/EC, above n. 16, pp. 33–61.

[20] Commission Decision of 26 July 2000 pursuant to Directive 95/46/EC of the European Parliament and of the Council on the adequacy of the protection provided by the safe harbour privacy principles and related frequently asked questions issued by the US Department of Commerce, OJ L215, 25 August 2000, pp. 7–47.

[21] These principles are published in the Commission's decision.

[22] Court of Justice, *Maximillian Schrems v Data Protection Commissioner,* Judgement, 6 October 2015, Case C-362/14, EU:C:2015:650.

[23] For example: Seventh Council Directive 83/349/EEC, above n. 8, pp. 1–17.

affiliates of a European enterprise or, on the contrary, the parent company, the European enterprises being analysed thus as subsidiaries of this parent. Such is the case for Directive 2013/36 concerning access to the activity of credit institutions and the prudential supervision of credit institutions and investment firms.[24] In Article 92, this Directive expands the remuneration policies adopted within the framework of the European Union to affiliates established in third countries. It thus subjects foreign companies of a group belonging to European Union financial establishments to the regulatory framework of the European Union.

3.2.2.3 International Effects

Finally, with regard to the international effects of Union acts with extraterritorial scope, it is worth highlighting the importance of the international dimension of these acts. This dimension allows one to distinguish, most notably, the extraterritorial action of the Union from that exercised by the United States. Unlike that of the United States, the principal objective of the Union's extraterritorial action is not to impose a model on third countries, but is rather motivated by the willingness to contribute to the respect for and the development of international norms, all while preserving the European market.[25] The majority of acts containing dispositions with extraterritorial scope adopted within the last ten years have close links with international standards. The objective of these acts, thus, is either to contribute to the proper application of international standards, or to facilitate their entry into force, or to promote their utilisation.

- Certain of them thus pick back up the international standards provided for in international conventions and contribute in this way to the proper application of these standards by both member States (in giving a European footing to international standards) and by third countries who find themselves obligated to respect them in order to gain access to the European market). Directive 2008/106/EC concerning the minimal level of training of seafarers thus takes up again the training norms already decreed on the international level within the framework of the International Maritime Organisation's Convention on Standards of Training, Certification, and Watchkeeping for Seafarers. It constitutes a means of forcing European and non-European States to respect their international engagements, third countries finding themselves obligated to respect those engagements if they want their workers to gain access to the European market.
- Other acts with extraterritorial scope will have for an objective facilitating the ratification of treaties. Such is the case with regulation No. 1257/2013 of 20 November

[24]Directive 2013/36/EU of the European Parliament and of the Council of 26 June 2013 on access to the activity of credit institutions and the prudential supervision of credit institutions and investment firms, amending Directive 2002/87/EC and repealing Directives 2006/48/EC and 2006/49/EC, OJ L176, 27 June 2013, pp. 338–436.

[25]Scott 2013, p. 87.

2013 regarding ship recycling. It clearly has for its purpose facilitating early ratification, both by the Union's member States as well as by third countries, of the Hong Kong Convention, which was adopted on 15 May 2009 under the auspices of the International Maritime Organisation, by applying proportionate controls to ships and installations for the recycling of ships, based on that Convention.
- Acts endowed with extraterritorial scope can also have for an objective complementing the European Union treaty practice and/or promoting it. Regulation 995/2010 of 20 October 2010 establishing the obligations of operators who place timber and its derivative products on the market that has for its objective complementing and strengthening the voluntary partnership agreements concluded with timber-producing countries.[26]

The development and the diversification of acts endowed with extraterritorial scope necessarily leads to examining the conditions of their implementation which presupposes affecting situations existing outside of the territory of the European Union.

3.3 The Territorial Implementation of EU Extraterritorial Legislation

The extraterritorial nature of EU legislation should require specific implementation acts and procedures taking into consideration the difficulties arising from their extraterritorial nature. This study suggests, however, that their specific nature was not entirely taken into account by EU legislation. On the contrary, the implementation acts and procedures follow the general regime, assigning a fundamental role to Member State authorities who implement EU legislation inside each Member State's territory.

This territorial implementation is unfit for the purposes of such legislation and may prevent it from attaining its goals. The Commission and private actors were granted a residual role in this implementation, notably through normative mechanisms that are also supervised by Member States' competent authorities, confirming the fundamental role granted to the latter.

3.3.1 The Fundamental Role Granted to Member State Authorities

Despite their diversity, Member States' authorities were granted the main role regarding the implementation of EU extraterritorial legislation. This territorial

[26]See, for example, Regulation (EU) No 995/2010, above n. 15, pt 4; to date, this regulation has not had much effect and lacks enforcement of the due diligence system in the member States.

implementation has adverse consequences that may impede the fulfilment of the Regulations' objective.

3.3.1.1 Implementation by Member States' Competent Authorities

EU extraterritorial legislation is essentially implemented by the Member States' competent authorities. However, EU legislation does not provide for the creation of a new State authority, it rather provides for the *designation* of a competent authority—an already existing one—who will be responsible for applying EU legislation.[27] Certain EU legislation provides specific requirements concerning these authorities. The Directive on the minimum level of training of seafarers foresees, for instance, that all ships, while in the port of a Member State, will be subject to port State control by officers duly authorized by that Member State.[28] EU legislation can also require that the competent authorities have a certain level of expertise concerning the object of the Regulation to be implemented.[29]

The distinguishing aspect of these authorities is their direct relationship with Member States and their territories. Members not only designate them, but they also provide technical and financial resources to them for the effective performance of their tasks and the exercise of their powers.[30] In order to implement EU legislation, these authorities carry out "checks" within the Member's territory in order to ensure that economic operators comply with their obligations as set forth in EU legislation. These checks can apply to the activity of Union importers of minerals or metals when they want to import into the EU market,[31] to the activity of natural or legal persons who place timber or timber products in the market,[32] the activity of ship owners regarding the recycling procedures of ships flying the flag of a Member State or to ships flying the flag of a third country calling at a port or anchorage of a Member State,[33] the possession of certificates by seafarers when serving on ships flying the

[27] See for instance, Regulation (EU) 2017/821, above n. 3, Article 10(1); Directive 2003/87/EC of the European Parliament and of the Council of 13 October 2003 establishing a scheme for greenhouse gas emission allowance trading within the Community and amending Council Directive 96/61/EC, OJ L275, 25 October 2013, Articles 3(q) and 18; Regulation (EU) No 995/2010, above n. 15, Article 7(1) and Regulation (EU) No 1257/2013, above n. 13, Article 3(11); there are some exceptions in this system: according to the Regulation on ship recycling, "The competent authority, responsible for ship recycling facilities, may be a governmental authority or authorities designated by a Member State or a third country authority" (Regulation (EU) No 1257/2013, above n. 13, Article 3(11).

[28] Directive 2008/106/EC, above n. 16, Article 22(1).

[29] For instance, according to the supply chain due diligence Regulation, Member State competent authorities must have expertise as regards to raw materials, industrial processes and auditing (Regulation (EU) 2017/821, above n. 3, Article 2(n).

[30] General Data Protection Regulation, above n. 2, Article 52(4).

[31] Regulation (EU) 2017/821, above n. 3, Article 11(1).

[32] Regulation (EU) No 995/2010, above n. 15, Article 10(1).

[33] Regulation (EU) No 1257/2013, above n. 13, Articles 8, 13, 21 and 22.

flag of a Member State, or an operator's greenhouse gas emissions reports and permits in the EU system.[34]

Regarding the substance of their missions, authorities' checks encompass two main aspects, which are mainly conducted within the Member State's territory. First, they establish an examination of the system set forth in the EU legislation, which includes notably risk assessment and risk mitigation procedures and an inspection of documentation and records that demonstrate the proper functioning of the procedures and certification requirements. In order to fulfil their missions, the competent authorities are granted investigative, corrective, authorisation, and advisory powers.[35] Second, following these checks, if infringements are detected, the competent authorities may impose remedial actions based on national law, such as administrative fines[36] or they may take immediate actions such as seizing products or prohibiting their marketing[37] or detaining them in, or excluding them from, the State's ports.[38]

EU extraterritorial legislation has granted a significant role to Member States' competent authorities when implementing EU legislation. Their mission and powers are essentially territorial and directly linked to domestic law and procedures. The main question is whether this territorial application is indeed fit for the extraterritorial scope of EU legislation.

3.3.1.2 Difficulties Arising from State Implementation

State implementation of EU legislation creates difficulties that go against the very purpose of EU legislation. The Preamble of the Regulation on ship recycling clearly states that its purpose is "… also to reduce disparities between operators in the Union, in OECD countries and in relevant third countries …".[39] Yet territorial implementation increases disparities, since it promotes the development of domestic legislation and domestic monitoring procedures which are, per se, distinct from each other. One consequence of the development of divergent domestic legislation within the EU territory is the phenomenon of law shopping. States may develop their laws in order

[34]Ibid, Articles 7(1) and 2. See also Directive 2003/87/EC, above n. 27, Articles 4, 5, 6, 14 and 15; Directive 2008/106/EC, above n. 16, Article 3(1).

[35]General Data Protection Regulation, above n. 2, preamble, 51 and Articles 51(1), 51(2) and Article 58. According to Article 57 of this Regulation, each supervisory authority shall on its territory, among others, "(a) monitor and enforce the application of this Regulation". Concerning ship recycling, an inventory certificate is issued by the administration, that also operates an initial or renewal survey of the inventory (Regulation (EU) No 1257/2013, above n. 13, Article 8(7)). At the same time, port State control authorities may carry out inspections to check that either an inventory certificate or a ready for recycling certificate is kept on board (Article 11(1)).

[36]General Data Protection Regulation, above n. 2, Article 83(1).

[37]Regulation (EU) No 995/2010, above n. 15, Articles 10(5)(a) and 10(5)(b).

[38]Regulation (EU) No 1257/2013, above n. 13; Regulation (EU) 2017/821, above n. 3, Articles 11(3) and 16(3).

[39]Regulation (EU) No 1257/2013, above n. 13, preamble, 7.

to be "the most attractive and the most competitive" for foreign companies, levelling the implementation of EU legislation downwards.[40]

EU legislation has provided a safety net to prevent the negative impact of its territorial implementation. The safety net is essentially related to the principle of cooperation. First, competent authorities are asked to provide mutual assistance, "in particular for carrying out investigation or for monitoring the implementation of a measure concerning a controller or a processor established in another Member State".[41] Authorities shall also "put in place measures for effective cooperation with one another" that cover "information requests and supervisory measures such as requests to carry out prior authorisations and consultations, inspections and investigations".[42] Against this background, the General Data Protection Regulation provides for an original consistency mechanism that establishes a new body—the Board—that has the power, notably, to monitor and ensure the correct application of the Regulation, to issue guidelines, recommendations and best practices for the application of different substantive obligations provided for in the Regulation, to carry out the accreditation of certification bodies, and to issue opinions on draft decisions of supervisory authorities.[43]

This safety net can also assign a specific role to the Commission. Regulation (EU) 2017/821 provides that:

> In order to ensure clarity of tasks and consistency of action among Member State competent authorities, the Commission shall prepare non-binding guidelines in the form of a handbook detailing the steps to be followed by Member State competent authorities carrying out the *ex post* checks referred to in paragraph 1. Those guidelines shall include, as appropriate, templates of documents facilitating the implementation of this Regulation.[44]

If these different provisions attempt to mitigate the consequences of the law shopping phenomenon, they do not address the heart of the problem, which is the development of divergent domestic laws and procedures relating to the implementation of EU extraterritorial legislation. To this end, the Commission and the private sector could contribute to this endeavour, but in practice, they were granted a residual role in the implementation under Member State supervision.

---

[40] On this matter, see Assemblée nationale (15ème législ.), Rapport fait au nom de la commission des lois constitutionnelles, de législation, du suffrage universel, du Règlement et d'administration générale sur le projet de loi adopté par l'Assemblée nationale après engagement de la procédure accélérée relatif à la protection des données personnelles par S. Joissains [Report made on behalf of the Committee on Constitutional Laws, Legislation, Universal Suffrage, Regulations and General Administration on the bill adopted by the National Assembly after the initiation of the accelerated procedure on the protection of personal data by S. Joissains], n° 350, Session ordinaire 2017–2018, 14 March 2018, p. 15. See also Rodriguez 2004, pp. 330–356; Ehlermann 1995, pp. 220–227.

[41] General Data Protection Regulation, above n. 2, Article 60(2). Similarly, see Regulation (EU) 2017/821, above n. 3; Regulation (EU) No 995/2010, above n. 15, Article 12.

[42] General Data Protection Regulation, above n. 2, Article 61(1).

[43] Ibid, Articles 70(1)(a) to (y).

[44] Regulation (EU) 2017/821, above n. 3, Article 11(5).

3.3.2 The Marginal Role of the Commission and Private Actors

Both the Commission and private actors were granted a marginal role regarding the coherent implementation of EU extraterritorial legislation. The marginal character relates to two of its principal aspects. First, the Commission and private actors have residual missions concerning the implementation of EU legislation. Second, these residual missions may be reviewed by a competent member authority.

3.3.2.1 A Residual Mission Regarding the Implementation of EU Legislation

The Commission and private actors have been granted residual powers concerning the implementation of EU extraterritorial legislation. On the one hand, the Commission was granted specific powers to adopt decisions to recognise equivalency. If the recognition of equivalency is legally distinct from a mutual recognition system, it nonetheless contains certain aspects of it, since both help "intermingling domestic laws in order to constitute the global".[45]

Against this background, provisions in EU extraterritorial legislation generally require that the Commission assess whether the rules applied in certain non-EU Member States or developed by economic operators are compatible with EU legislation. For instance, according to Regulation (EU) 2017/821, the Commission is to adopt delegated acts to set out a methodology and criteria to determine that a supply chain due diligence scheme enables the importer to comply with the Regulation, and, if the result is positive, recognises the scheme and adopts implementing acts granting that scheme a recognition of equivalency with the requirements of the Regulation.[46] Similarly, concerning the minimum level of training for seafarers, when they do not possess the certificates required by the Directive, they "may be allowed to serve on ships flying the flag of a Member State, provided that a decision on the recognition of their appropriate certificate has been adopted".[47] If the certification was issued by a third country, the Member State "shall submit a request for recognition of that third country to the Commission".[48] On this matter, the Commission is assisted by the European Maritime Safety Agency, and together with "any Member State

---

[45] Nicolaidis and Shaffer 2005, p. 266.

[46] Regulation (EU) 2017/821, above n. 3, Articles 8(2) and 8(3). According to Article 8(3) of the same Regulation, "The implementing acts referred to in the first subparagraph of this paragraph shall be adopted in accordance with the advisory procedure referred to in Article 15(2)". The Commission periodically verifies that recognized supply chain due diligence schemes continue to fulfil the criteria that led to a recognition of equivalence decision adopted by it (Article 8(4)). An interesting feature of this power to recognise the equivalence of a due diligence scheme is its connection with third parties. For instance, the OECD Secretariat shall "as appropriate", be consulted prior to the adoption of the Commission's implementing acts (Article 8(3)).

[47] Directive 2008/106/EC, above n. 16, Article 19(1).

[48] Ibid, Article 19(2).

involved", is to collect the information and "carry out an assessment of the training and certification systems in the third country for which the request for recognition was submitted".[49]

The Commission may also adopt guidelines with the purpose of harmonizing the implementation of EU extraterritorial legislation. The Regulation concerning supply chain due diligence obligations for minerals provides, for instance, that "[i]n order to create clarity and certainty for and consistency among the practices of economic operators, in particular SMEs, the Commission, in consultation with the European External Action Service of the OECD, shall prepare non-binding guidelines in the form of a handbook for economic operators, explaining how best to apply the criteria for the identification of conflict-affected and high-risk areas".[50] Concerning the General Data Protection Regulation, the Commission is to adopt delegated acts for the purpose of specifying the requirements to be taken into account for data protection certification mechanisms and may adopt implementing acts "laying down technical standards for certification mechanisms and data protection seals and marks, and mechanisms to promote and recognise those certification mechanisms, seals and marks".[51] The Commission thus operates solely for the harmonisation of the implementation of EU legislation.

From the normative point of view, economic actors may also contribute to the implementation of EU legislation. For instance, associations and/or other bodies representing categories of controllers or processors may prepare codes of conduct, or amend such codes, for the purpose of specifying the application of the General Data Protection Regulation,[52] "taking into account the specific features of the various processing sectors and the specific needs of micro, small and medium-sized enterprises".[53] More precisely, in the context of the General Data Protection Regulation, codes of conduct may contribute to the fair and transparent application of the regulation,[54] the collection and the pseudonymisation of personal data, and the exercise of the rights of data subjects, among others.[55] Similarly, the General Data Protection Regulation provides for the development of certification procedures issued by certification bodies or by the competent authority.[56] Certification bodies are responsible for

---

[49]Ibid.

[50]Regulation (EU) 2017/821, above n. 3, Article 14(1). According to para 2 of the same Article, "The Commission shall call upon external expertise that will provide an indicative, non-exhaustive, regularly updated list of conflict-affected and high-risk areas. That list shall be based on the external experts' analysis of the handbook referred to in para 1 and existing information from, inter alia, academics and supply chain due diligence schemes. Union importers sourcing from areas which are not mentioned on that list shall also maintain their responsibility to comply with the due diligence obligations under this Regulation".

[51]General Data Protection Regulation, above n. 2, Articles 43(8) and 43(9); see also Directive 2003/87/EC, above n. 27, Article 14(1); Regulation (EU) No 1257/2013, above n. 13, Article 15(4).

[52]General Data Protection Regulation, above n. 2, Article 40(2).

[53]Ibid, Article 39.

[54]Ibid, Article 40(2)(a).

[55]Ibid, Artcles 40(2)(c), 40(2)(d) and 40(2)(f).

[56]Ibid, Article 42(5).

establishing data protection certification mechanisms and data protection seals and marks "for the purpose of demonstrating compliance with this Regulation" in terms of the processing operations of controllers and processors, and grants certification or the withdrawal of such certification.[57]

EU extraterritorial legislation may also provide for the creation of private bodies that can contribute to the legislation's implementation. For instance, "Data protection officers" are designated by the controller and the processor on the basis of professional qualities and may be "a staff member of the controller or processor, or fulfil the tasks on a basis of a service contract".[58] Their main task is to inform and advise the controller or processor and the employees who carry out the processing of their obligations, and to monitor compliance with "the Regulation, with other Union or Member State data protection provisions and with the policies of the controller or processor in relation to the protection of personal data, including the assignment of responsibilities, awareness-raising and training of staff involved in the processing operations, and the related audits", and to "provide advice where requested as regards the data protection impact assessment and monitor its performance".[59]

These different missions are residual in their substance, since the main tasks concerning the monitoring of EU extraterritorial legislation are still left to the national competent authorities. The residual character of the Commission's and private actors' roles is exacerbated by the review operated by the competent authority.

3.3.2.2 The Competent Authority's Power to Review the Missions of the Commission and Private Actors

The Commission and the private sector were granted a residual role in the implementation of EU regulations. Nevertheless, their role is supervised by the competent national authorities.

Concerning the Commission's power to adopt decisions of recognition of equivalency, the review issue was raised before the European Court of Justice in the *Max Schrems v. Data Protection Commissioner* case.[60] The complaint against Facebook was brought to the Irish Data Protection Commissioner by an Austrian privacy advocate. In that complaint, Mr. Schrems challenged Facebook's transfer of his data to the United States, Facebook being incorporated in Ireland. The case led the ECJ to invalidate the Safe Harbor arrangement which governed data transfers between the EU and the United States. That arrangement was based on a decision adopted by the European Commission declaring that the United States provided for adequate safeguards for data protection.[61]

According to the Court,

---

[57] Ibid, Articles 42(1), 42(4), 42(5).

[58] General Data Protection Regulation, above n. 2, Articles 37(1), 37(5) and 37(6).

[59] Ibid, Article 77(1).

[60] *Maximillian Schrems v Data Protection Commissioner,* above n. 22.

[61] Commission Decision of 26 July 2000, above n. 20, pp. 7–47.

> ... Article 28 of Directive 95:46 applies, by its very nature, to any processing of personal data. Thus, even if the Commission has adopted a decision pursuant to Article 25 (6) of that Directive, the national supervisory authorities, when hearing a claim lodged by a person concerning the data protection of his rights and freedoms in regards to the processing of personal data relating to him, must be able to examine, with complete independence, whether the transfer of that data complies with the requirements laid down by the directive. If that were not so, persons whose personal data has been or could be transferred to the third country concerned would be denied the right, guaranteed by Article 8 (1) and (3) of the Charter, to lodge with the national supervisory authorities a claim for the purpose of protecting their fundamental rights.[62]

Thus, the Commission's decision may be reviewed by national supervisory authorities. A person whose personal data has been transferred to a third country may contend before a national authority that, notwithstanding the Commission's decision, the law and practices of a particular third country do not ensure an adequate level of protection, even if the Court alone has jurisdiction to declare that an EU act is invalid.[63]

Regarding the General Data Protection Regulation, all draft codes of conduct—adopted by the private sector—must be submitted to the supervisory authority who is to approve that draft code if it finds that the code complies with the regulation.[64] The monitoring of these codes of conduct may be carried out not only by the competent supervisory authority, but also by "a body which has an appropriate level of expertise in relation to the subject-matter of the code and is accredited for that purpose by the competent supervisory authority". This body completes the tasks and powers of the competent supervisory authority, and shall "take appropriate action in cases of infringement of the code by a controller or processor, including suspension or exclusion of the controller or processor concerned from the code. It shall inform the competent supervisory authority of such actions and the reasons for taking them".[65]

Similarly, the General Data Protection Regulation provides that certification bodies are accredited by the supervisory authority and/or the national accreditation body.[66] In any case, according to the Regulation, the accreditation of certification bodies is based on criteria approved by the supervisory authority or by the Board.[67] The competent supervisory authority may also revoke an accreditation of a certification body.[68] Supervisory authorities may also carry out a review of certifications issued pursuant to Article 42(7) of the Regulation.[69] The Commission, on the other

[62] *Maximillian Schrems v Data Protection Commissioner,* above n. 22.

[63] Ibid, para 60.

[64] General Data Protection Regulation, above n. 2, Articles 40(5) and 55; codes of conduct related to processing activities in several Member states are, once approved, submitted to the Commission, who may decide that the codes of conduct "have general validity within the Union" in accordance with the examination procedure set out in Article 93(2) of the Regulation (Article 40(9)).

[65] Ibid, Article 41(4).

[66] Ibid, Article 43(1).

[67] Ibid, Article 43(3).

[68] Ibid, Article 43(7).

[69] Ibid, Article 58(1)(c).

hand, shall "adopt delegated acts in accordance with Article 92 for the purpose of specifying the requirements to be taken into account for the data protection certification mechanisms" and "may adopt implementing acts laying down technical standards for certification mechanisms and data protection seals and marks, and mechanisms to promote and recognise those certification mechanisms, seals and marks".[70]

Regulation (EU) 995/2010 provides that a monitoring organisation, whose role is to evaluate and verify the proper application of the due diligence system set out in the Regulation, and to take "appropriate action in the event of failure by an operator to properly use its due diligence system, including notification of competent authorities in the event of significant or repeated failure by the operators",[71] is verified by the competent authority. The latter determines that if the monitoring organisation no longer fulfils its functions or no longer complies with the requirements laid down in the Regulation, it is to inform the Commission without delay, who may withdraw recognition of a monitoring organisation.[72]

Competent authorities review a part of the Commission's and the private sector's missions. This review constitutes an obstacle to the coherent implementation of EU legislation, since it opens a new window for law shopping by economic operators. This phenomenon could be counterbalanced by the principle of mutual recognition which presupposes upstream coordination between EU Member States. The Directive 2008/106/EC on the minimum level of training of seafarers sets an interesting example on this matter, particularly because the purpose of that legislation is to "define a minimum level of training for seafarers in the Community".[73] On the one hand, the current version of the Directive stipulates that a Member State that recognises a certificate under the procedure laid down in the Directive shall endorse that certificate to attest to its recognition.[74] On the other hand, the proposal for a Directive amending the current Directive promotes the "mutual recognition of seafarers' certificates issued by Member States".[75] The Article, which only covers certificates issued by EU Member States, promotes the full harmonisation of Certificates of Proficiency and Documentary evidence issued by another Member State. Mutual recognition of professional certification is particularly straightforward within the EU legal system. It is possible, nevertheless, to question whether mutual recognition could be adaptable to due diligence schemes or to data protection certification.

---

[70]Ibid, Article 43(8) and 43(9).

[71]Regulation (EU) No 995/2010, above n. 15, Articles 8(1)(a), 8(1)(b) and 8(1)(c).

[72]Ibid, Article 8(6).

[73]Directive 2008/106/EC, above n. 16, pp. 33–6, Preamble, 7.

[74]Ibid, Article 4(6).

[75]Proposal for a Directive of the European Parliament and of the Council, amending Directive 2008/106/EC on the minimum level of training of seafarers and repealing Directive 2005/45/EC, 2018/0162 (COD), para 4.

3.4 Conclusion

Alongside its classical treaty-making approach, the European Union's external relations action is currently being followed by the adoption of acts—mainly regulations—with extraterritorial scope. These regulations innovate specially in their indirect extraterritorial effect: they do not impose conditions directly on operators established in the third countries that produce and commercialize EU products, but they put obligations on the European operators who place these products on the European market for the first time. Their purpose is to contribute to the respect for and the development of international norms, since they either contribute to the proper application of international standards, or they facilitate their entry into force, or to promote their utilisation. The main challenge faced by these EU acts concern their effectiveness mechanism. Member States' competent authorities were granted a significant role when implementing EU extraterritorial legislation. However, since their mission and powers are essentially territorial and directly linked to domestic law and procedures, they increase disparities and promote the law shopping phenomenon. The Commission and the private sector are not able to support a homogeneous enforcement of EU extraterritorial since they were granted a residual role in the implementation of EU extraterritorial regulation and their action and because their action is supervised by the competent national authorities.

References

Bartels L (2014) The EU's Human Rights Obligations in Relation to Policies with Extraterritorial Effect. EJIL 25: 1071–1091

Bazex M (1987) L'affirmation de compétence extraterritoriale des Communautés européennes [The affirmation of the European Communities Extraterritorial competence]. In: Stern B (ed) L'application extraterritoriale du droit économique [The extraterritorial application of economic law]. Cahiers du CEDIN, Montchrestien, Paris, pp 51–66

Bischoff J-M, Kovar R (1975) L'application du droit communautaire de la concurrence aux entreprises établies à l'extérieur de la Communauté [The application of Community competition law to undertakings established outside the Community]. JDI 102:675–684

Canizzaro E (2014) The EU's Human Rights Obligations in Relation to Policies with Extraterritorial Effects: A Reply to Lorand Bartels. EJIL 25:1093–1099

Eeckman P (1965) L'application de l'article 85 du Traité de Rome aux ententes étrangères à la CEE mais causant des restrictions à la concurrence à l'intérieur du marché commun [The application of Article 85 of the Treaty of Rome to cartels outside the EEC but causing restrictions on competition within the common market]. RCDIP 54:499–528

Ehlermann C D (1995) Compétition entre systèmes réglementaires [Competition between regulatory systems]. RMCUE 387:220–227

Groux J (1987) Territorialité et droit communautaire [Territoriality and Community law]. RTDE 23:5–33

Jacquet J-M (1985) La norme juridique extraterritoriale dans le commerce international [The extraterritorial legal norm in international trade]. JDI 112:327–405

Kuijper P J, Wouters J, Hoffmeister F, De Baere G, Ramopoulos T (2015) The law of EU external relations: Cases, materials, and commentary on the EU as an international legal actor. Oxford University Press, Oxford

Martucci F (2018) L'extraterritorialité en droit de la concurrence [Extraterritoriality in competition law]. Cahiers de Droit de l'Entreprise 4:29

Milanovic M (2011) Extraterritorial Application of Human Rights Treaties. Oxford University Press, Oxford

Nicolaidis K, Shaffer G (2005) Transnational Mutual Recognition Regimes: Governance Without Global Government. Law and Contemporary Problems 68:263–317

Rodriguez K (2004) L'attractivité, nouvelle perspective du droit national des sociétés [Attractiveness, a new perspective on national company law]. Bull Joly Sociétés 2:330–356

Scott J (2013) Extraterritoriality and Territorial Extension in EU Law. American Journal of Comparative Law 62:87–126

Stern B (1986) Quelques observations sur les règles internationales relatives à l'application extraterritoriale du droit [Some observations on international rules relating to the extraterritorial application of the law]. AFDI 32:7–52

Stoufflet J (1971) La compétence extraterritoriale du droit de la concurrence de la CEE [Extraterritorial jurisdiction of EEC competition law]. JDI 98:487–493

Wouters J, Marx A, Geraets D, Natens B (2015) Global Governance Through Trade—EU Policies and Approaches. Edward Elgar Publishing, Cheltenham

Delphine Dero-Bugny is Professor at Faculté de droit, d'économie et de gestion, Université de Paris.

Julia Motte-Baumvol (Ph.D.) is Maître de conférences en droit public at Faculté de droit, d'économie et de gestion, Université de Paris.

Chapter 4
CETA: Gold Standard or Greenwashing?

W. Th. Douma

Contents

Abstract The EU Treaties demand that EU trade policy must contribute to the sustainable development of the EU and its trading partners. It is investigated whether CETA is in conformity with this requirement and thus can form a gold standard for future trade agreements. The investor-state dispute settlement (ISDS) part of CETA, the Trade and Sustainable Development (TSD) chapters and the statements attached to the agreement are concentrated on. These aspects are investigated against the background of the manner in which EU trade agreements are negotiated, the role of the Trade Sustainability Impact Assessment (TSIA) system and public participation aspects. Under CETA's Investment Court System (ICS, a form of ISDS), the national judiciary is bypassed, and states can be ordered to pay compensation for adopting non-discriminatory measures aimed at the protection of legitimate public welfare objectives, such as health, safety and the environment. This can cause a regulatory chill and hinder the 'right to regulate' in practice at a time where the adoption of

W. Th. Douma (✉)
EU Legal—Centre for European and International Law, Van Loostraat 32, 2582 XD The Hague, The Netherlands
e-mail: W.T.Douma@EULegal.nl

European Environmental Law Consultancy, The Hague, The Netherlands

Ghent University, Ghent, Belgium

Dutch Ministry of Social Affairs and Employment, The Hague, The Netherlands

W. Th. Douma et al. (eds.), *The Evolving Nature of EU External Relations Law*,
https://doi.org/10.1007/978-94-6265-423-5_4

climate changes measures already poses formidable challenges. Neither the TSD chapters nor the statements take away these concerns, notably because the chapters lack an enforcement mechanism with sanctions and because the statements lack clear explanations that could be of legal value. The manner in which the precautionary principle is dealt with in the TSD chapters and the statements is used as a case in point. CETA forms no gold standard, it is concluded, and should definitely not be mirrored in other EU FTAs like the EU-Mercosur agreement.

Keywords EU trade agreements · ISDS · ICS · Sustainability · Labour · Environment · Enforceability · Precaution

4.1 Introduction

The year is 2016. The European Union is entirely in favour of CETA. Well, not entirely…. One small region of indomitable Walloons still holds out against the trade agreement. And life is not easy for the CETA proponents in the rest of the European Union. Fast forward to March 2020. CETA is provisionally applied, minus the controversial provisions regarding Investment-State Dispute Settlement (ISDS). So far, thirteen of the 27 EU Member States have ratified the agreement.[1] The Netherlands is not yet among these states. In Dutch parliament, a narrow majority of the Second Chamber voted in favour of the ratification. The Dutch senate (the First Chamber), where the government coalition lacks a majority, might still oppose. Whether all remaining Member States will ratify is also still uncertain.[2] As a direct result of Wallonia's resistance, the Belgian State indicated that it would only ratify after further adjustments to the Investor-State Dispute Settlement (ISDS) system that CETA encompasses under the name Investment Court System (ICS). A second condition was a favourable opinion from the Court of Justice of the European Union (CJEU) on the compatible of ICS with European law. That opinion was delivered on 30 April 2017 and found that the ICS part of CETA is indeed compatible with primary EU law.[3] Still, Belgium is among the Member States that did not ratify CETA by the end of March 2020. While Opinion 1/17 attracted scholarly attention that mostly focused on the issue of autonomy, this chapter investigates CETA's sustainable development aspects. More specifically, ICS is scrutinised where its potential effects on public policy measures, for instance on climate change, are concerned. Furthermore, the non-enforceability of the sustainable development chapters will be focused on. Both aspects play a role in the debates in the Dutch and Walloon parliaments regarding CETA.

[1] http://consilium.europa.eu/en/documents-publications/treaties-agreements/agreement/?id=2016017&DocLanguage=en. Accessed 1 April 2020.

[2] Italy also indicated that it was unwilling to ratify CETA because Canada's commitments under the agreement do not provide sufficient coverage of Italian products in terms of Designation of Origin or Geographical Indication protections. See Landini 2018 Italy won't ratify EU free-trade deal with Canada: farm minister www.reuters.com/article/us-italy-minister-canada-trade/italy-wont-ratify-eu-free-trade-deal-with-canada-farm-minister-idUSKBN1JA0TR. Accessed 20 May 2020.

[3] Court of Justice, *Comprehensive Economic and Trade Agreement between Canada, of the one part, and the European Union and its Member States, of the other part (CETA),* Opinion of the Court of 30 April 2019, Opinion 1/17, ECLI:EU:C:2019:341.

Initially, the Commission wanted to avoid involving national parliaments. It favoured presenting CETA as an 'EU only' agreement.[4] In that case, it would only need to be ratified by the Union. Instead, it was presented as an optional mixed agreement. Former EU Trade Commissioner Malmström put it as follows: "From a strictly legal standpoint, the Commission considers this agreement to fall within exclusive EU competence. However, the political situation in the Council is clear, and we understand the need for proposing it as a 'mixed' agreement, in order to allow for a speedy signature."[5] The CJEU begged to differ. It ruled that the inclusion of ICS in EU trade agreements meant that the Union was not entitled to conclude such an agreement without its member states.[6] Put differently, the suggested optional mixity turned out to be mandatory—from an actual strictly legal standpoint.

With mixed agreements especially, the chances are that one or more countries decide or are forced not to ratify. Could the part of CETA that is being provisionally applied remain in force in such a case, as some have suggested?[7] While this question is intriguing,[8] it is less relevant for future EU trade agreements. They do not include an ISDS/ICS part anymore. Instead, a separate investment agreement encompassing ISDS/ICS is now proposed to trading partners. These mixed investment agreements need to be concluded by both the EU and its Member States. The remaining issues dealt with in the trade agreements fall under the EU's exclusive competence. These agreements only need to be ratified by the Union. Mixity is thus not becoming more common, in other words.

A pertinent question that remains is whether EU trade agreements are able to ensure that increased trade will also lead to stimulating sustainable development, in spite of ICS and non-binding sustainable development chapters. That is of the utmost relevance from the point of view of the fight against climate change, but also where the

[4] Schöllmann 2016.

[5] https://europa.eu/rapid/press-release_IP-16-2371_en.htm. Accessed 5 April 2020.

[6] Court of Justice, *Free Trade Agreement between the European Union and the Republic of Singapore*, Opinion of the Court, 16 May 2017, Opinion 2/15, ECLI:EU:C:2017:376, paras 285-293. The German Constitutional Court (Bundesverfassungsgericht, BVerfG) had also ruled that ICS concerned a shared power and forbade Germany from agreeing to the provisional application of this part of CETA (BVerfG cases 2 *BvR 1368/16, 2 BvE 3/16, 2 BvR 1823/16, 2 BvR 1482/16* and 2 *BvR 1444/16*, 13 October 2016).

[7] Hosuk Lee-Makiyama, director of trade think-tank ECIPE, argued that the EU could continue to apply all parts of the agreement aside from investment dispute settlement. See Sisto A and Jones G 2018 Italy says it won't ratify EU-Canada trade deal; Canada plays down threat. www.reuters.com/article/us-italy-canada-trade/italy-says-it-wont-ratify-eu-canada-trade-deal-canada-plays-down-threat-idUSKBN1K318Q. Accessed 20 May 2020. A partner at Tereposky & Derose LLP (International Trade and Investment Lawyers) stated that the elements of the CETA that are being applied provisionally will remain in force regardless of the decisions taken by individual EU member states concerning ratification. Hohnstein 2018 Italy's decision on CETA ratification—what does it really mean? https://www.lexology.com/library/detail.aspx?g=cd0a9158-ba06-4451-9922-1dd31bfda6c6. Accessed 15 December 2020.

[8] See Van der Loo and Wessel 2017, pp. 735–770 on this question. Further, according to Suse and Wouters 2018, an argument can be made that where a Member State permanently and definitively fails to ratify a mixed agreement, the EU is under an obligation, as a matter of EU law to terminate the provisional application of that agreement.

protection of workers and the environment in general are concerned. These issues also form self-imposed obligations, notably under article 11 TFEU ("Environmental protection requirements must be integrated into the definition and implementation of the Union's policies and activities, in particular with a view to promoting sustainable development."), article 3(5) TEU ("In its relations with the wider world, the Union ... shall contribute to the sustainable development of the Earth") and article 21(2)(f) TEU (external action is to contribute to ensuring sustainable development).[9] Where the EU trade relationship with developing countries is concerned, the Union is to define and pursue common policies and actions in order to "foster the sustainable economic, social and environmental development of developing countries" (article 21(2)(d) TEU).

CETA is an agreement in a series of new generation trade agreements that the European Union has concluded with a range of third countries since 2008.[10] Negotiations with a number of other countries are still ongoing.[11] The parties to CETA

[9]See for a more detailed account Douma 2017, pp. 193–212.

[10]The first treaty was EU-CARIFORUM; see Council Decision of 15 July 2008 on the signature and provisional application of the Economic Partnership Agreement between the CARIFORUM States, of the one part, and the European Community and its Member States, of the other part, OJ L289, 30 October 2008; followed by the treaties with Korea (Council Decision of 16 September 2010 on the signing, on behalf of the European Union, and provisional application of the Free Trade Agreement between the European Union and its Member States, of the one part, and the Republic of Korea, of the other part, OJ L127, 14 May 2011), Colombia, Peru, Ecuador (Council Decision of 31 May 2012 on the signing, on behalf of the Union, and provisional application of the Trade Agreement between the European Union and its Member States, of the one part, and Colombia and Peru, of the other part, OJ L354, 21 December 2012 and Council Decision (EU) 2016/2369 of 11 November 2016 on the signing, on behalf of the Union, and provisional application of the Protocol of Accession to the Trade Agreement between the European Union and its Member States, of the one part, and Colombia and Peru, of the other part, to take account of the accession of Ecuador, OJ L356, 24 December 2016); Central America, which encompasses Costa Rica, El Salvador, Guatemala, Honduras, Nicaragua and Panama Central America (encompassing Costa Rica, El Salvador, Guatemala, Honduras, Nicaragua and Panama) Council Decision of 25 June 2012 on the signing, on behalf of the European Union, of the Agreement establishing an Association between the European Union and its Member States, on the one hand, and Central America on the other, and the provisional application of Part IV thereof concerning trade matters, OJ L346, 15 December 2012; and Moldova, Association Agreement between the European Union and the European Atomic Energy Community and their Member States, of the one part, and the Republic of Moldova, of the other part, opened for signature 27 June 2014, OJ L260/4 (entered into force 1 July 2016). The EU-Japan Economic Partnership Agreement came into force on 1 February 2019. Discussions on a separate Investment Protection Agreement (IPA) were fruitful regarding substantive aspects, yet procedural aspects regarding ICS were not accepted by Japan. For the time being, no further discussions are foreseen; see https://trade.ec.europa.eu/doclib/docs/2006/december/tradoc_118238.pdf. Accessed 29 February 2020. The EU-Singapore Agreement entered into force on 21 November 2019, while the IPA awaits ratification by all EU Member States before it can enter into force. The CJEU issued Opinion 2/15 *(Singapore FTA)*, above n. 6, on this agreement, making it clear that it falls within the Union's exclusive competence except for the provisions dealing notably with investment protection and ISD that fall within the competences shared with the Member States. The parts dedicated to the environment, labour and sustainable development formed a part of the Union's exclusive competences.

express their "commitment to promote sustainable development and the development of international trade in such a way as to contribute to sustainable development in its economic, social and environmental dimensions".[12] The agreement contains chapters on trade and sustainable development (Chapter 22), trade and labour (Chapter 23) and on trade and environment (Chapter 24) that should ensure the protection of the environment and human health in the EU and in Canada. These Trade and Sustainability (TSD) chapters lack an enforcement mechanism with sanctions. The parties can merely ask for non-binding advice in cases of violation of these norms.

The question as to the sustainability aspects is pertinent because CETA has been presented as a 'gold standard' for future trade agreements.[13] That would imply that a similar agreement could be concluded with countries with less well-developed rule of law systems and larger sustainability challenges. Indeed, the EU aims at concluding a new EU-Mercosur agreement that in many respects resembles CETA. Mercosur is the regional economic organization formed by Argentina, Brazil, Paraguay and Uruguay.[14] With its 264 million inhabitants and a GDP of around 4.6 trillion US dollars in 2019, it belongs to the five largest internal markets in the world. At the same time, it is clear that in a country like Brazil, currently the balance between economic, social and environmental dimensions of sustainable development is lacking.[15] The proposed chapters on sustainable development, environment and labour in the EU-Mercosur agreement largely mirror the ones in CETA and thus lack an effective enforcement mechanism. Hence, the question is whether such provisions would actually work in a relationship with countries like Brazil, or whether further improvements are called for.

Attention to sustainability issues in trade treaties is not an entirely new phenomenon. For example, the preamble to the 1994 World Trade Organization Agreement also highlights the objectives of sustainable development and environmental protection,[16] but by their very nature such provisions only have a limited

---

[11]FTA negotiations are currently taking place with Australia, Chile, India, Indonesia, Mexico (political agreement was reached, New Zealand and the USA (on the elimination of tariffs for industrial goods and on conformity assessment); political agreement was reached, see https://trade.ec.europa.eu/doclib/press/index.cfm?id=1830. Accessed 7 July 2020.

[12]Preamble, 9th point CETA.

[13]Malmström and Freeland 2016.

[14]Venezuela's membership has been suspended since 1 December 2016 due to the political situation in the country.

[15]According to Brazil's National Institute for Space Research (INPE), since president Bolsonaro was elected in October 2018, deforestation increased by 30%, partially by dismantling the institutions responsible for the protection of the environment. See Londoño and Casado 2019 Amazon deforestation in Brazil rose sharply on Bolsonaro's watch. http://nytimes.com/2019/11/18/world/americas/brazil-amazon-deforestation.html. Accessed 20 May 2020.

[16]It stipulates that the Parties to the WTO Agreement recognise that their relations in the field of trade and economic endeavour should be conducted "with a view to raising standards of living, ensuring full employment and a large and steadily growing volume of real income and effective demand, and expanding the production of and trade in goods and services, while allowing for the optimal use of the world's resources in accordance with the objective of sustainable development, seeking both to

impact.[17] Compared to the WTO, the new generation of EU trade agreements certainly are more progressive. Perhaps surprisingly, in some respects US Trade agreements contain stricter environmental and labour provisions than CETA that—contrary to CETA—are actually enforceable.[18] The 2019 US—Canada—Mexico Agreement (USMCA) that will replace NAFTA forms a recent case in point here. When that agreement was presented to US Congress in 2018, the Democrats insisted on more stringent labour and environment rules in terms of the rules themselves and the monitoring and enforcement mechanisms in place. This resulted in further negotiations in 2019 and a Protocol of Amendment.[19] The revised USMCA was heralded as "the gold standard by which all future trade agreements will be judged" by US Trade Representative Robert Lighthizer.[20]

The new generation of EU trade agreements include comprehensive chapters that should benefit environmental protection and sustainable development of the European Union and of its trading partners, but are less ambitious than the USMCA. The EU agreements' ultimate objective has been described as fostering "real and lasting change on the ground, through the effective application of enhanced social and environment standards, to the direct benefit of the citizens of [the EU's] FTA partners",[21] yet the extent to which such chapters actually have such a positive influence in practice is unclear. What is clear is that the sustainability provisions are excluded from regular dispute settlement mechanisms (see articles 23.11(1) and 24.16(1) CETA) and thus lack an effective enforcement mechanism.

Furthermore, the latest EU trade treaties can also bring about restrictions in practice on the possibilities for environmental policy. This is particularly the case if, through the ISDS/ICS mechanism, foreign investors are given the opportunity to claim sky-high compensation from the EU or from an EU Member State if environmental measures reduce the value of their investments.[22] ISDS—the 'most toxic

protect and preserve the environment and to enhance the means for doing so in a manner consistent with their respective needs and concerns at different levels of economic development".

[17]The provision did play a role in the US—Shrimp dispute. See WTO Appellate Body, *United States—Import Prohibition of Certain Shrimp and Shrimp Products*, Report, 12 October 1998, DSR 1998:VII, 2755, WT/DS58/AB/R, paras 129 and 153. See also Schurmans 2015, pp. 28–34.

[18]For example, the Dominican Republic-Central America-United States Free Trade Agreement, opened for signature 05 August 2004, 19 USC 4001(entered into force 01 March 2006) (CAFTA-DR).

[19]Investment Treaty News 2020 Trump signs USMCA, bringing NAFTA's replacement closer to entry into force https://cf.iisd.net/itn/2020/03/10/trump-signs-usmca-bringing-naftas-replacement-closer-to-entry-into-force/. Accessed 20 May 2020.

[20]Office of the United States Trade Representative 2020 Ambassador Lighthizer statement on Canada's approval of the USMCA https://ustr.gov/about-us/policy-offices/press-office/press-releases/2020/march/ambassador-lighthizer-statement-canadas-approval-usmca. Accessed 20 May 2020.

[21]EC Trade 2018.

[22]In contravention of (in particular) Comprehensive Economic and Trade Agreement between Canada, of the one part, and the European Union and its Member States, of the other part, opened for signature 30 October 2016, OJ L 11/23 (entered into force (provisionally) 21 September 2017) (CETA), article 8(9).

acronym in Europe'[23]—was one of the reasons for fierce debates and many critical publications.[24] In the run-up to CETA, there was also a wide focus on previous trade conflicts with Canada concerning GMOs, asbestos, seal products and hormone meat.[25] Canadian tar sands oil[26] and lower animal welfare requirements[27] were also critically discussed.

These issues make it worthwhile to examine CETA and some aspects of the future EU-Mercosur agreement. Instead of calling CETA a gold standard, its sustainability provisions have also been described as a form of 'greenwashing' and symbolic legislation to create the appearance that the agreement contributes to the protection of workers and the environment.[28] And if CETA is a gold standard, why were some 40 declarations and statements added by the Council, the European Commission and numerous EU Member States (discussed in Sect. 4.2.4 below) How come that CETA's impact assessment concluded that there was no need for ISDS, yet CETA was proposed with ISDS? Can CETA-like provisions promote sustainability in future trade agreements with (groups) of countries that have much lower levels of protection, where enforcement leaves a great deal to be desired and corruption is rampant? Can they even prevent serious negative developments, like steep increases in deforestation?

To answer these questions, this chapter first discusses the unconventional manner in which CETA came about in Sect. 4.2. By describing the legal and factual context surrounding the adoption of CETA it becomes possible to find answers, and to find out whether CETA can ensure that increased trade under its regime will also

---

[23]EU Trade Commissioner Cecilia Malmström, Speech at the Center for Strategic and International Studies Stateman's Forum, Washington, 4 May 2015. See Palmer 2015 'Malmström to unveil investment dispute plan for TTIP' http://politico.eu/article/eu-malmstrom-unveils-ttip-investment-dispute-settlement-plan/. Accessed 20 May 2020.

[24]For instance, Koeth 2016; Corporate Europe Observatory 2016.

[25]In all these cases, Canada accused the EU and its Member States of introducing trade barriers that were incompatible with WTO law.

[26]Canada produces a lot of oil from tar sands, which causes 23% more greenhouse gas emissions than regular oil and poses a risk to local biodiversity. The European Parliament reiterated its concern to this issue, noting under point 13 that CETA should not affect the EU's right to legislate in the fuel quality directive, see European Parliament resolution of 8 June 2011 on EU-Canada trade relations (P7TA(2011)0267). These concerns disappeared in the end, as shows from the 2014 support in parliament to stop labelling oil from tar sands as dirty. See also Guibert 2017 EU opens door to Canada's dirty oil, www.euractiv.com/section/ceta/news/eu-opens-door-to-canadas-dirty-oil/. Accessed 20 May 2020. Berke 2017 'No country would find 173 billion barrels of oil in the ground and just leave them': Justin Trudeau gets a standing ovation at an energy conference in Texas https://markets.businessinsider.com/commodities/news/trudeau-gets-a-standing-ovation-at-energy-industry-conference-oil-gas-2017-3-1001825435. Accessed 20 May 2020; EurActiv and Reuters 2014 Activist MEPs put tar sands 'dirty label' back on the agenda www.euractiv.com/section/energy/news/activist-meps-put-tar-sands-dirty-label-back-on-the-agenda/. Accessed 20 May 2020. And Trew 2014 Another big winner from CETA: the tar sands https://canadians.org/analysis/another-big-winner-ceta-tar-sands. Accessed 20 May 2020.

[27]Kikou 2016, p. 54.

[28]Marx et al. 2017a, pp. 78–88 wonder whether the inclusion of social sustainability requirements is primarily intended to favour interest groups, rather than to actually have any significant impact.

benefit sustainable development. It will be discussed that CETA negotiations took place against the backdrop of the Transatlantic Trade and Investment Partnership (TTIP) talks with the United States. Both negotiations encompassed an investor-state dispute settlement (ISDS) system (Sect. 4.2.1). The functioning of the system of Trade Sustainability Impact Assessments is also commented upon (Sect. 4.2.2). In Sect. 4.2.3, the bumpy road from provisional application of CETA minus ICS to ratification by the EU and the individual EU member states is looked into. As a final part of Sect. 4.2, the unilateral declarations attached to CETA and the Joint Interpretation Instrument are discussed (Sect. 4.2.4). Section 4.3.1 examines several substantive aspects of the CETA sustainability chapters. One particular aspect that is zoomed in on is the question of whether the precautionary principle is sufficiently enshrined (Sect. 4.3.2). Section 4.3.3 discusses the lack of a proper enforcement mechanism for the chapters on sustainable development, labour and environment. Throughout Sect. 4.3, suggestions for improvement, notably by looking at the USMCA example, are touched upon. Section 4.4 contains some final remarks and conclusions.

4.2 The Emergence of CETA

4.2.1 TTIP, ISDS and CETA

The negotiation of CETA took place at a turbulent moment in time. This was mostly due to the fact that at the same time the EU wanted to conclude TTIP with the US.[29] Negotiations with Canada began in May 2009, with the USA in early 2013. Initially, there was little or no attention for the CETA negotiations. Only when aspects of TTIP became known attention for and the protest against CETA—which in many ways resembles TTIP—grew. Many feared that the ISDS mechanism contained in these two agreements would undermine environmental and other public interests.[30]

Since the Treaty of Lisbon came into force, the EU has become competent in the field of investor protection. Previously, this was a competence of the EU Member States. They concluded numerous Bilateral Investment Treaties (BITs) in order to protect investors. Such treaties were initially concluded with former colonies. The BITs, which have been in place since 1959, contain rules requiring the parties not to discriminate against foreign investors and to compensate them in case of expropriation or in case of measures reducing the value of investments if these can be equated to expropriation. The withdrawal of an environmental permit or the adoption of stricter environmental legislation are examples of measures for which compensation would need to be paid, even if they do not discriminate and are for the public good.

[29] The Transatlantic Trade and Investment Partnership (TTIP) negotiations were launched in 2013 and ended without conclusion at the end of 2016. Instead, the conclusion of a limited agreement that would notably encompass mutual acceptance of conformity assessment is being discussed.

[30] For a more detailed account of that topic, see Douma 2021.

In the case of disputes, the investor had to ask a national court in the host country to rule on the matter, or their home country could be requested to take up the case. From the late 1960s onwards, an Investor-State Dispute Settlement (ISDS) system was gradually added to the BITs. The annual number of ISDS cases grew steadily and by 2018 had reached over seventy cases per year.[31]

ISDS gives investors the right to claim damages from the host country in which they invested if their rights were violated under a BIT. Decisions in these ISDS cases are taken by private arbitrators. The advantage is that one does not depend on national judges in less developed legal systems with challenges in the areas of independence, corruption, etc. However, ISDS comes with a multitude of disadvantages. Because the possibility of appeal is lacking, decisions are not always consistent. They are often not made public. The claims frequently concern environmental protection measures, for example the refusal to grant a permit for an oil pipeline, gold mine or shale gas drilling, the prohibition of harmful additives in petrol or the granting of a permit with strict environmental conditions. Under the North American Free Trade Agreement (NAFTA) between the US, Canada and Mexico, there are numerous examples of these kinds of disputes. In one such case, the NAFTA tribunal found that Canada was to compensate the US mining company Bilcon because it was unfairly treated, according to two of the three arbiters.[32] As a result of these and other ISDS decisions limiting its regulatory space, Canada opted out of the ISDS provisions under NAFTA's successor, the United States Mexico Canada Agreement (USMCA).[33]

ISDS can indeed stand in the way of public policy decisions, like energy transition measures under the Paris Climate Agreement.[34] Compensation can be much higher than under national or EU law and encompass many millions or even billions. Vattenfall's pending case against Germany over the decision to phase out nuclear power following the Fukushima disaster forms a €4.7 billion compensation claim,[35] and the Canadian company Gabriel Resources demands US$ 4.4 billion over a conflict regarding a Romanian gold mine.[36] Such compensation claims may result in countries waiving decisions to promote the public interest. This is referred to as the 'regulatory chill' or 'regulatory freeze' effect. New Zealand's decision not to pass legislation on

---

[31] https://investmentpolicy.unctad.org/investment-dispute-settlement. Accessed 20 March 2020.

[32] PCA, *Bilcon of Delaware* et al. *v. Government of Canada*, Award on Damages, 10 January 2019, Case No. 2009-04.

[33] See Ahuja 2019; Baltzan B 2020 NAFTA's Replacement Gives Labor Some Shelter From Globalization's Storms. https://foreignpolicy.com/2020/01/16/usmca-mexico-canada-trump-workers-democrats-naftas-replacement-gives-labor-some-shelter-from-globalizations-storms/. Accessed 20 May 2020. Also see Sect. 4.2.2.

[34] Compare the German company Uniper that is contemplating bringing a claim of reportedly € 850 million against the Dutch law phasing out the generation of coal-fired power plants after 2030. See Niemelä et al. 2020. At the start of April 2020, it became clear that owners of coal-fired power plants in the Netherlands are negotiating compensation for the phase out (NOS 2020 Kabinet neemt toch nu klimaatmaatregelen; productie kolencentrales omlaag [Government adopts climate measures after all; decrease in production of coal fires power plants] nos.nl/artikel/2329160-kabinet-neemt-toch-nu-klimaatmaatregelen-productie-kolencentrales-omlaag.html Accessed 20 May 2020).

[35] ICSID, *Vattenfall v Germany II*, Case No. ARB/12/12.

[36] ICSID, *Gabriel Resources Ltd. and Gabriel Resources (Jersey) v. Romania*, Case No. ARB/15/31.

plain cigarette packaging (without brand logos) constitutes an example of this effect. The country awaited the outcome of the ISDS case brought by Philip Morris Asia against a similar Australian law.[37] The disadvantages of ISDS brought a number of countries, including South Africa, India and Indonesia (and Canada in its relation with the USA and Mexico as mentioned above), to reject ISDS and sometimes even to cancel trade agreements that contained ISDS mechanisms.

The European Commission organised a public consultation on ISDS over a period of 3.5 months in 2014.[38] It centred on the question whether a proposed new approach towards ISDS would be able to achieve a proper balance between protecting investors on the one hand and ensuring the right and ability of governments to enact rules in the public interest on the other hand. Excluding ISDS from EU trade agreements altogether was not raised as an option. Nevertheless, a significant proportion of the 150,000 responses expressed themselves in favour of doing exactly that.

A Commission report summarised the results of the consultation. The broad-based rejection of ISDS was brushed aside as it "addresses a broader issue than the one that was the subject of this consultation". Instead, it was proposed that "this wider question should be answered, in light of the ongoing EU efforts to reform substantially the investment protection and ISDS system and an assessment of such efforts."[39] In addition, the Commission argued that EU Member States had unanimously entrusted the negotiations on ISDS to it, provided that the final result is in line with the EU's interests.[40] The decision whether or not to include ISDS should therefore only be taken in the final phase of the negotiations, the Commission claimed. In this way, the

[37]Phillip Morris's claim was brought under the 1993 Hong Kong-Australia investment agreement. The claim was launched in 2012 at the Permanent Court of Arbitration (PCA), after an unsuccessful attempt to have the measure overturned by the Australian high court. On 17 December 2015, the PCA dismissed the claim as it constituted an abuse of rights. See PCA, *Philipp Morris Asia Limited v Commonwealth of Australia*, Award on Jurisdiction and Admissibility, 17 December 2015, Case No. 2012-12. Shortly before the claim was issued, the US company had moved ownership of its Australian operations to Hong Kong for the principal, or even sole, purpose of taking advantage of the ISDS provisions in the agreement. The final award regarding costs ordered Philip Morris to pay half of Australia's legal costs, while not disclosing the amount. The full amount turned out to be almost $A24 million (around US$ 16 million). Hence Australia might feel like it won when in reality it lost some $12 million (or US$ 8 million) in legal fees plus €333,059.91 in arbitrator's fees. See PCA, *Philipp Morris Asia Limited v Commonwealth of Australia*, Final Award Regarding Costs, 8 March 2017, Case No. 2012-12. See also Hepburn J 2019 Final costs details are released in Philip Morris v. Australia following request by IAReporter. www.iareporter.com/articles/final-costs-details-are-released-in-philip-morris-v-australia-following-request-by-iareporter/. Accessed 20 May 2020. Together with a WTO case on the same issue and the high court case, Australia's legal costs were about $39 million (Hutchens and Knaus 2018) Revealed: $39 m cost of defending Australia's tobacco plain packaging laws. www.theguardian.com/business/2018/jul/02/revealed-39m-cost-of-defending-australias-tobacco-plain-packaging-laws. Accessed 20 May 2020.

[38]European Commission 2015; In March 2020, this document was not available in the Eurlex databases, but could be accessed at https://ec.europa.eu/transparency/regdoc/rep/10102/2015/EN/10102-2015-3-EN-F1-1.Pdf. Note that since the public consultation was held between 27 March and 13 July 2014, it took over half a year to prepare the report.

[39]Ibid., p. 3.

[40]The same argument had already been used in response to critical questions from the European Parliament, as set out below in Sect. 4.2.2.

call to opt out of ISDS was rejected, citing the previously granted mandate[41] and the reform plans for ISDS. Fobbing off those rejecting ISDS in such a manner appears disingenuous, especially when noting that once negotiations are over, critics tend to be told that it is impossible to change anything at that moment in time.

Shortly after the public consultation had confirmed the broad objections to ISDS, CETA was presented in September 2014. To the dismay of many, it included an 'old-style' ISDS system, as if the consultation did not matter one iota. In the ensuing legal scrubbing phase, which is only intended to rid the text of small irregularities and not to bring about substantial changes,[42] a revised ISDS mechanism was worked out behind the scenes. This was presented under the title Investment Court System (ICS). Contrary to the 'old-style' ISDS system, ICS includes a permanent tribunal, the possibility of appeal (which should contribute to the consistency of decisions), mandatory disclosure of decisions and better safeguards on the independence of arbitrators.[43]

Another feature of CETA worth mentioning is the stipulation that non-discriminatory measures taken by a party with regard to legitimate objectives of public well-being such as health, safety or the environment do not constitute indirect expropriations. This removes some of the concern about the impact of ISDS on environmental protection. Unfortunately, this exception does not apply in the case where "the consequences of a measure or a series of measures are so serious that they are clearly excessive in relation to its purpose".[44] In such cases, compensation may nevertheless be awarded by the ICS arbitrators in connection with environmental measures or other decisions for the benefit of the public.

The revised version of CETA was published on 29 February 2016.[45] On 5 July 2016, the Commission proposed to the Council to sign the agreement. After lengthy debates regarding the opposition from the side of the Walloons against CETA (who insisted on renegotiating aspects of the agreement)[46] the Council did so on 30 October 2016.[47] Instead of substantial changes, a Joint Interpretation Instrument was adopted and a series of other declarations were made on the part of the EU institutions and

[41]The original negotiating mandate from 2009 was amended in 2011. The latter adjustment prompted the Commission to provide a state-of-the-art investor-state dispute settlement mechanism in the agreement. According to Council Press Release 920/15, these decisions were not made public until 15 December 2015. https://www.consilium.europa.eu/en/press/press-releases/2015/12/15/eu-canada-trade-negotiating-mandate-made-public/. Accessed 7 July 2020.

[42]Legal scrubbing is the final process in which legal specialists comb through an agreement word by word, basically to make sure there are no typos or out-and-out errors.

[43]See Edward et al. 2017.

[44]CETA, above n. 22, annex 8-a, article 3.

[45]See European Commission Press release IP/16/399 (2016b) CETA:EU and Canada agree on new approach on investment in trade agreement. https://europa.eu/rapid/press-release_IP-16-399_en.htm. Accessed 7 July 2020.

[46]De la Baume 2018 Walloon parliament rejects CETA deal www.politico.eu/article/walloon-parliament-rejects-ceta-deal/. Accessed 20 May 2020.

[47]Council Decision (EU) 2017/37 of 28 October 2016 on the signing on behalf of the European Union of the Broad Economic and Trade Agreement (CETA) between Canada, of the one part, and the European Union and its Member States, of the other part, OJ L11, 14 January 2017, p. 1; see

some member states.[48] On 15 February 2017, the European Parliament (EP) agreed with CETA, despite the fact that the agreement did not meet the requirements flagged in a number of its own resolutions.[49] Although parliament does not formally have an amendment right, it has a veto right over trade agreements.[50] As a result, the EP can, through resolutions etc., try to ensure that these agreements meet certain conditions. CETA is applied provisionally since 21 September 2017 (except for those elements for which the EU is not exclusively competent, notably the ICS part). As already mentioned, the ratification process is still proceeding and will be discussed in more detail in Sect. 4.2.4.

4.2.2 Participation and Advice During the Negotiations (TSIA)

The EU is obliged to integrate environmental protection into EU trade policy in order to ensure that sustainable development is stimulated.[51] To achieve this, the EU Trade Sustainability Impact Assessment (TSIA) system has been developed. It was introduced in 1999 at the time of preparations for the multilateral trade negotiations in Seattle.[52] Since then, 27 assessments have been completed.[53] The basic rules for the system are laid down in a handbook with European Commission guidelines, a form of soft law in which the Commission explains how the system should function.[54] Unfortunately, not abiding by the rules set out in this handbook carries no consequences.

---

also https://www.consilium.europa.eu/en/meetings/international-summit/2016/10/30/. Accessed 7 July 2020.

[48]See Sect. 4.2.4.

[49]For example, European Parliament's Res P8_TA-PROV called for the enforceability of application and compliance with environmental and labour law provisions through regular dispute resolution mechanisms, including the positive experience with this in the US trade agreements. See European Parliament resolution of 8 July 2015 containing the European Parliament's recommendations to the European Commission on the negotiations for the Transatlantic Trade and Investment Partnership (TTIP) [2014/2228(INI)]; This aspect is returned to in Sect. 4.3.3. An overview of the many aspects of CETA that did not live up to Parliament's demands can be found in de Ville 2016.

[50]The EP vetoed the Anti-Counterfeiting Trade Agreement (ACTA) in 2012, for instance.

[51]Consolidated Version of the Treaty on the Functioning of the European Union, 2012, OJ C 326 (TFEU), article 11: "The environmental protection requirements should be integrated into the definition and implementation of the Union's policies and actions, in particular with a view to promoting sustainable development".

[52]The fierce protests of 'anti-globalists' around the WTO summit became known as the 'battle of Seattle' and led to planned decisions being pushed to a new summit in Doha (Qatar), a place with significantly fewer opportunities for protests.

[53]For an up-to-date overview, see https://ec.europa.eu/trade/policy/policy-making/analysis/policy-evaluation/sustainability-impact-assessments/index_en.htm#study-3. Accessed 7 July 2020.

[54]European Commission 2017a.

Under the TSIA system, an independent adviser provides the European Commission with an in-depth analysis of the potential economic, social, human rights, and environmental impacts of ongoing trade negotiations. The adviser issues recommendations on how adverse effects can be prevented and positive consequences can be encouraged. Before making such recommendations, consultations with stakeholders in both the EU and in the partner country are organised. Once the recommendations have been published, the Commission must respond to them in the form of a so-called 'position paper' in which it is set out which recommendations are adopted, which ones rejected and for which reasons. The recommendations and the position paper are to guide EU negotiators in their work and should therefore be available well before the end of the negotiations.

In the case of CETA, the TSIA was ready in June 2011, which was well in time. In line with the handbook, it assessed the potential impacts of CETA's economic, social and environmental impacts in Canada and the EU. Furthermore, the possible effects of CETA on the US, Mexico and other countries and regions, including a number of developing countries and European overseas countries were mapped. A number of consultations had preceded it.[55] On ISDS, the assessment noted that "the conflicting costs and benefits of such a mechanism make it doubtful that its inclusion in CETA would create a net/overall (economic, social and environmental) sustainability benefit for the EU and/or Canada. There is no solid evidence to suggest that ISDS will maximise economic benefits in CETA beyond simply serving as one form of an enforcement mechanism, just as state-state dispute settlement is also an enforcement mechanism. And the policy space reductions caused by ISDS allowances in CETA, while less significant than foreseen by some parties, would be enough to cast doubt on its contribution to net sustainability benefits. As such, the study's assessment suggests that a well-crafted state-state dispute settlement mechanism might be a more appropriate enforcement mechanism in CETA than ISDS."[56] In spite of the stress put by the Commission on better regulation (which includes basing measures on solid arguments), and in violation of the TSIA Handbook, the recommendation to leave ISDS out of CETA was ignored. Instead, as already explained, CETA was presented with an ISDS mechanism.

Several MEPs asked the Commission why the ISDS recommendation was not followed. They were told, among other things, that it did not constitute the Commission's opinion, and that the EP and the Council had agreed to ISDS in CETA.[57] The Commission also pointed out that in some cases European companies had not been

[55] Inter alia meetings with civil society (in Brussels and Ottawa with a wide range of interest groups and trade unions), a stakeholder workshop (in Ottawa with trade associations, labour organisations, trade unions and environmental organisations) and a website with a discussion forum.

[56] Development Solutions 2011.

[57] Answer given by Mr. De Gucht on behalf of the Commission on 5 February 2013. https://www.europarl.europa.eu/sides/getAllAnswers.do?reference=E-2012-011275&language=EN. Accessed 7 July 2020; see also https://eur-lex.europa.eu/legal-content/EN/TXT/?uri=OJ:C:2013:321E:TOC. Accessed 7 July 2020. Also compare the comments above in Sect. 4.2.1 on the ISDS consultation.

given access to the Canadian courts. Exactly how many times this had happened and when was not made clear.[58]

Remarkably, the Commission's response to the TSIA in the form of a position paper did not appear until 4 April 2017, almost six years after the release of the TSIA.[59] This late response is contrary to the Commission's own guidelines.[60] By that moment in time, negotiations were long over and the Council and the EP had already agreed to CETA. Thus, the meagre explanations as to why the recommendation to exclude ISDS from CETA was rejected were too little, too late. Remarkably enough, the Commission notes that where the comparison made to NAFTA is concerned, the TSIA itself indicated that there is "no available evidence which convincingly suggests that the ISDS mechanism in NAFTA has created significant policy space reductions." Merely two years later, Canada eliminated US-Canada ISDS in NAFTA's successor USMCA, notably because the country took particular offense to the outcome of the *Bilcon* v *Canada* dispute.[61] The reason for Canada's resentment was the tribunal's seemingly arbitrary decision in favour of a U.S. mining company which significantly reduced Canada's policy space to regulate in environmental matters.[62] The Canadian Minister of Foreign Affairs put it as follows: "ISDS elevates the rights of corporations over those of sovereign governments. In removing it, we have strengthened our government's right to regulate in the public interest, to protect public health and the environment, for example."[63]

Unfortunately, this CETA experience with the EU impact assessment system does not constitute an isolated phenomenon. The impact assessments and the Commission's responses to them are often not available in time to influence the negotiations and the content of the trade agreements, in violation of the Handbook rules.[64] In practice, the manner in which the duty to integrate environmental and sustainability interests in EU trade agreements leaves much to be desired. Codifying the impact assessment rules in binding legislation could form a step forward. After all, binding European rules on environmental impact assessment have been around since 1985.[65]

---

[58] Answer by Mr. De Gucht on behalf of the Commission on 29 January 2013. https://eur-lex.europa.eu/legal-content/EN/TXT/?uri=OJ:C:2013:321E:TOC. Accessed 7 July 2020.

[59] EC Trade 2017a.

[60] European Commission 2016a. This was the first version of the handbook.

[61] *Bilcon of Delaware* et al. *v. Government of Canada,* above n. 32.

[62] Aldin 2019; Doelle 2019; Quinn 2018; Canadian opposition to Nafta's Chapter 11 gives Trudeau leeway, http://bloomberg.com/news/articles/2018-04-17/canadian-opposition-to-nafta-s-chapter-11-gives-trudeau-leeway. Accessed 20 May 2020.

[63] Prime Minister Trudeau and Minister Freeland speaking notes for the United States-Mexico-Canada Agreement press conference (2018). https://pm.gc.ca/en/news/speeches/2018/10/01/prime-minister-trudeau-and-minister-freeland-speaking-notes-united-states. Accessed 7 July 2020.

[64] At the time of completion of this contribution (April 2020), work on the TSIA on the EU-Mercosur Treaty still has not finished (in February 2020 an interim report was published), while negotiations are already nearing completion. While negotiations with Mexico were completed in April 2018, only an inception report had been presented at that moment in time (LSE Enterprise 2017). At the presentation of the report complaints were raised regarding these violations of the TSIA handbook; see European Commission 2017b.

[65] For a more detailed discussion of the EU's TSIA system, see Douma 2017, pp. 193–212.

4.2.3 From Provisional Application to Ratification

On 16 May 2017, the CJEU confirmed in Opinion 2/15 on the EU-Singapore Free Trade Agreement that the EU does not have exclusive jurisdiction where ISDS is concerned.[66] This was in line with the German Constitutional Court's ruling of 16 October 2016 in which it was decided that the ICS part of CETA could not provisionally enter into force for the same reason.[67] Opinion 2/15 concerns only the question of competence and not the question of whether an ISDS system is compatible with European law. This question was answered in Opinion 1/17 at the request of Belgium, as will be returned to below.

As of 21 September 2017, CETA is provisionally applied, with the exception of parts which are not part of the exclusive powers of the EU, such as the ICS part. The provisional application encompasses the chapters on sustainability and the environment to be discussed in the next section. Moreover, the Council stated that "[i]f the ratification of CETA fails permanently and definitively because of a ruling of a constitutional court, or following the completion of other constitutional processes and formal notification by the government of the concerned state, provisional application must be and will be terminated. The necessary steps will be taken in accordance with EU procedures."[68]

Latvia was the first Member State to ratify, followed by the Czech Republic, Denmark, Malta, Croatia, Estonia, Spain, Portugal, Lithuania, Sweden, Finland, Austria and Slovakia, bringing the total to thirteen.[69] The Netherlands had indicated that it would wait until the CJEU issues Opinion 1/17.[70] By that moment in time, the Dutch referendum law was repealed, avoiding cumbersome situations like the one the Dutch had to face where the ratification of the EU-Ukraine Association Agreement was concerned.[71] As explained above, at the time of rounding up this

[66]See n. 6 above.

[67]BVerfG Cases *2 BvR 1368/16, 2 BvE 3/16, 2 BvR 1823/16, 2 BvR 1482/16 and 2 BvR 1444/16*, above n. 6 As explained above, ICS is a form of ISDS.

[68]Statement no. 20 from the Council. See https://data.consilium.europa.eu/doc/document/ST-13463-2016-REV-1/en/pdf. Accessed 7 July 2020.

[69]www.consilium.europa.eu/en/documents-publications/treaties-agreements/agreement/?id=2016017. Accessed 20 May 2020.

[70]Letter of Dutch Minister Kaag of Foreign Trade and Development Cooperation to the House of Representatives of 26 April 2018, www.rijksoverheid.nl/binaries/rijksoverheid/documenten/kamerstukken/2018/04/26/kamerbrief-over-investeringsakkoorden-met-andere-eu-lidstaten/kamerbrief-over-investeringsakkoorden-met-andere-eu-lidstaten.pdf. Accessed 7 July 2020.

[71]On 6 April 2016, a majority of 61% of the participants in a referendum voted against the law on the approval of the EU-Ukraine Association agreement. Merely 32% of the voters turned up to cast their votes. As the referendum was not binding, the Dutch government was able to vote in favour of the agreement after adding a declaration in which it was underlined *inter alia* that the agreement would not automatically lead to Ukraine's EU membership. See Lambie and Koole 2016 Reconstructie Oekraïne-referendum: Hoe de nee-stem een ja wordt [Reconstruction Ukraine-referendum; How a no-vote becomes a yes] https://www.rtlnieuws.nl/nederland/politiek/artikel/346556/reconstructie-oekraine-referendum-hoe-de-nee-stem-een-ja-wordt. Accessed 7 July 2020; Aalberts 2016 Wat deed Rutte met de uitslag van het Oekraïne-referendum [What did Rutte do with

contribution the Dutch senate still needs to cast its vote on CETA ratification, which poses a challenge for the government that does not have a majority there.

Ratification by Belgium is also not a foregone conclusion. At Wallonia's insistence, the country indicated that it does not intend to ratify if the part on ICS is not modified further.[72] Slovenia has also expressed objections to the ICS system and expressed the expectation that the relevant CETA provisions will be adapted to introduce improvements already before a multilateral investment tribunal is established.[73] So there is pressure from different sides to amend the ICS even further. In addition, the Italian Minister of Agriculture indicated that CETA does not provide sufficient protection for Italian food specialties, and that therefore Italy would not be able to ratify CETA.[74]

Belgium asked the CJEU on 13 October 2017 to verify through a binding Opinion 1/17 whether the ICS provisions of CETA[75] are compatible with the European Treaties, including fundamental rights.[76] Some claimed that from the Achmea judgment, in which the CJEU found that ISDS is incompatible with European law in investment treaties between EU Member States,[77] it may inferred that an ISDS mechanism such as ICS is also contrary to EU law.[78] It was also submitted that Member States should at least wait to ratify that Convention until the CJEU has issued its CETA Opinion 1/17.[79]

---

the result of the Ukraine-referendum] https://www.ftm.nl/artikelen/wat-deed-rutte-met-uitslag-oekraine-referendum. Accessed 7 July 2020.

[72]Council of the European Union 2016, Statement No. 37.

[73]Council of the European Union 2016, Statement No. 23.

[74]Rios 2018 Italy threatens to block CETA ratification www.euractiv.com/section/ceta/news/italy-threatens-to-block-ceta-ratification/. Accessed 20 May 2020.

[75]More specifically Chapter 8 ("Investments") and Section F ("Investor-State Investment Dispute Resolution"). See CETA, above n. 22.

[76]Opinion 1/17: Request for an opinion submitted by the Kingdom of Belgium pursuant to Article 218(11) TFEU, OJ C 369, 30 October 2017. In concrete terms, Belgium asked the Court on ICS' compatibility with the exclusive jurisdiction of the EU Court to give a definitive interpretation of EU law; the general principle of equality and the requirement for the useful functioning of EU law; the right to access the courts and the right to an independent and impartial justice system. On the latter point, Belgium seeks advice on the conditions relating to remuneration, appointments and release of the judges, the Guidelines of the International Bar Association on conflicts of interest in international arbitration and the introduction of a code of conduct, and external professional activities relating to the judges' investment disputes. See further https://diplomatie.belgium.be/sites/default/files/downloads/ceta_summary.pdf. Accessed 20 May 2020.

[77]Court of Justice, *Slowakische Republik (Slovak Republic) v Achmea,* Judgment, 6 March 2018, Case C-284/16, ECLI:EU:C:2018:158 *(Achmea).* The Luxembourg judges did not follow the conclusion of Advocate General Wathelet of 19 September 2017 (ECLI:EU:C:2017:699) in this case. As a result of this ruling, Achmea is unlikely to be entitled to compensation of more than €22 million from Slovakia awarded by ISDS arbitrators.

[78]Schepel 2018. See also Ankersmit and Hughes 2018.

[79]Eckes 2018 Teken het handelsverdrag tussen EU en Canada nu nog niet [Don't sign the EU-Canada trade treaty yet] http://volkskrant.nl/columns-opinie/teken-het-handelsverdrag-tussen-eu-en-canada-nu-nog-niet~bc5b971a/. Accessed 7 July 2020; Krajewski 2018.

As indicated above, ICS includes a number of improvements compared to the old ISDS. Although these improvements are a clear step in the right direction, the dispute resolution system continues to allow investors to let their dispute be decided by arbiters rather than by national judges and the CJEU. The fact that the CJEU is being side-lined may even be contrary to European law, according to several experts.[80] This point was addressed in Opinion 1/17, where the CJEU found ICS not to be contrary to EU law.

4.2.4 *Joint Interpretative Instrument and Unilateral Statements and Declarations*

4.2.4.1 Joint Interpretative Instrument

CETA adopted a Joint Interpretative Instrument, which initially had the more common designation 'interpretive statement'.[81] The reason for the name change remains unclear. A perceived reason might have been that the article 31(2)(b) Vienna Convention on the Law of Treaties (VCLT)—to which the parties refer—uses the term 'instrument',[82] yet the name is less relevant than the content of the document. And the latter aspect is where the real challenges lies.

If we examine some aspects relating to sustainability of the content, it shows first of all that the parties recognise the significance of the right to regulation in the public interest, among other things, and confirm that CETA will not affect standards and regulations relating to food safety, product safety, consumer protection, health, environmental or labour protection.[83] Fine as that sounds, it does not shield the parties against other CETA provisions that restrict the introduction or application of environmental standards.

With regard to trade and sustainable development, it is explained that CETA reconfirms the parties' longstanding commitment to sustainable development and is "designed to foster the contribution of trade to this objective. Accordingly, CETA

---

[80] See for instance Ankersmit 2016, pp. 46–63; Kokott and Sobotta 2016, p. 1; Krajewski and Hoffmann 2016; Govaere 2016. Legal Service of the European Parliament 2016, arriving at a different conclusion on the compatibility with the Treaties of investment dispute settlement provisions in EU trade agreements.

[81] Joint Interpretative Instrument on the Comprehensive Economic and Trade Agreement (CETA) between Canada and the European Union and its Member States, OJ L11/3, 14 January 2017.

[82] Vienna Convention on the Law of Treaties, opened for signature 23 May 1969, 1155 UNTS 331 (entered into force 27 January 1980) (VCLT), article 31, which provides among other things, that a treaty shall be interpreted in good faith in accordance with the ordinary meaning to be given to the terms of the treaty in their context and in the light of its object and purpose, and that this context shall comprise, in addition to the text: ... any instrument which was made by one or more parties in connexion with the conclusion of the treaty and accepted by the other parties as an instrument related to the treaty.

[83] Joint Interpretative Instrument on CETA, above n. 81, point 1(d).

includes comprehensive and binding commitments for the protection of workers' rights and the environment."[84] Comprehensive and binding as these commitments may be, in practice they might have little or no effect. The assurance that the parties "attach the highest priority to ensuring CETA delivers tangible outcomes in these areas, thereby maximising the benefits the agreement will bring for workers and for the environment"[85] does not alter this.

According to the Joint Interpretative Instrument, stakeholders, including employers, unions, labour and business organisations and environmental groups, have a key role to play in supporting the effective implementation of CETA. The Parties are committed to seeking regularly the advice of stakeholders to assess the implementation of CETA. They support their active involvement, including through the establishment of a CETA Civil Society Forum.[86] While this initiative can be welcomed, the manner in which the opinion of civil society was brushed aside on key aspects of CETA while the treaty was being negotiated might have dampened interest for such a forum.

As was briefly indicated above, CETA's Chapters 22 (Trade and Sustainable Development), 23 (Trade and Labour) and 24 (Trade and Environment) are excluded from the regular dispute resolution mechanisms, and the flawed mechanism foreseen in these chapters does not provide for imposing sanctions in case of a violation of the norms. Instead, only a non-binding recommendation can be made by an expert panel.[87] In the Joint Interpretative Instrument, the Parties undertake to initiate an early review of these provisions, "including with a view to the effective enforceability of CETA provisions on trade and labour and trade and the environment".[88] The need for an evaluation of the flawed dispute settlement mechanism in Chapters 22–24 of CETA is actually unnecessary. Similar mechanisms can already be found in existing EU treaties, and evaluations have already noted that their effectiveness needs to be improved. This issue is returned to in Sect. 4.3.3.

The preamble of the Joint Interpretative Instrument states that it provides, in the sense of article 31 VC, 'clear and unambiguous statement' of what Canada, the EU and its Member States agreed in a number of CETA provisions.[89] But just how clear and unambiguous are these explanations actually? The Council Legal Service confirmed that the Joint Interpretative Instrument, by virtue of Article 31(2)(b) VC, "constitutes a document of reference that will have to be made use of if any issue arises in the implementation of CETA regarding the interpretation of its terms". The service adds that "[t]o this effect, it has legal force and a binding character".[90] In the

[84] Ibid., point 7.

[85] Ibid.

[86] Ibid., point 10.

[87] CETA, above n. 22, article 24.25.

[88] Ibid. Note that the French, Portuguese, Spanish and Swedish versions more accurately talk about effective applicability rather than about enforceability, given the absence of sanction that could force a party violating the sustainability provisions to change its behaviour.

[89] Joint Interpretative Instrument on CETA, above n. 81, preamble, sub. (e).

[90] Council of the European Union 2016, Statement No. 38.

Netherlands is was also stressed that, pursuant to Article 31 VC and international customary law, parties are obliged to take into account the content of the Instrument when interpreting and applying CETA.[91]

Despite all these assurances, the Joint Interpretative Instrument can hardly be called an instrument in the sense of the VC. The authoritative International Law Commission (ILC) describes interpretive statements as statements by states or international organisations specifying or clarifying the meaning of provisions in a treaty.[92] They serve to clarify the existing obligations in the text of the Treaty,[93] and may constitute an authentic interpretation of the relevant Treaty if it is approved by both Parties.[94]

Interpretative statements are common practice in EU trade agreements, and are regularly included to clarify human rights provisions.[95] However, they usually relate to specific articles of the text of the agreement, and, for example, provide real clarification of the definitions of certain concepts.[96] Because the formulations used in the Joint Interpretative Instrument are so vague and general, no specific provisions of CETA are clarified. The Instrument therefore contains little or no meaningful evidence to support the interpretation of CETA provisions by a judge or arbitrator.[97]

The reference to the precautionary principle forms a case in point. It reads: "The European Union and its Member States and Canada reaffirm the commitments with respect to precaution that they have undertaken in international agreements."[98] It is unlikely that such an extremely short provision will have any significant added value. Firstly, the reference is only made to the precautionary principle in international law, while most concerns relate to the specific way in which the precautionary principle has been shaped under European law. Secondly, an interpretative instrument cannot alter the content of an agreement. CETA includes, for example, the Sanitary and Phytosanitary (SPS) rules successfully invoked by Canada and other countries against precautionary food safety measures and the measures aimed at avoiding the spread of plant diseases from the EU, Japan, Korea and Australia.[99] The Interpretative Instrument will not be able make a difference here, as a judge/arbiter will not be able to go against the letter of the CETA/SPS provisions. This topic will be returned to below in Sect. 4.3.2.

[91] Tweede Kamer, Brief van de Minister voor Buitenlandse Handel en Ontwikkelingssamenwerking [Letter from the Minister of Foreign Trade and Development Cooperation] 31985 No. 54, 25 September 2017, 44.

[92] ILC 2011, para 1.2.

[93] UN 2012, para 3.6.1.

[94] ILC 2011, para 1.6.3.

[95] Joint Interpretative Instrument on CETA, above n. 81, preamble, sub (d).

[96] See, for example, Free trade Agreement between the European Union and its Member States, of the one part, and the Republic of Korea, of the other part, opened for signature 6 October 2010, OJ L127 (entered into force 13 December 2015), articles 45 and 46, regarding the common interpretative declaration.

[97] Compare Shyrbman 2016; Griller et al. 2017; and Lester 2016.

[98] Joint Interpretative Instrument on CETA, above n. 81, preamble, sub. (d).

[99] See for further details Douma 2019.

All in all, the legal value of the Joint Interpretation Instrument on CETA is quite limited. The document neither clarifies the provisions of CETA, nor does it have an affirmative role because of the vague wording chosen. It is therefore unlikely that the Joint Interpretation Instrument will be of added value in dispute resolution procedures.

4.2.4.2 Unilateral Statements and Declarations

The Joint Interpretative Instrument discussed in the previous section could have been of legal value because it was agreed to by all parties to the agreement. Besides that joint statement, numerous unilateral statements and declarations were made. By their very nature, such documents have a more limited legal value. For a start, as the International Law Commission sets out in this respect, it is "a well-established rule of international law that obligations cannot be imposed by a State upon another State without its consent".[100] In the context of the law of treaties, this principle has been codified in article 34 VC. It adds that "[n]o obligation may result for other States from the unilateral declaration of a State. However, the other State or States concerned may incur obligations in relation to such a unilateral declaration to the extent that they clearly accepted such a declaration".[101] This implies that the other State has to unequivocally accept the obligations resulting from that declaration, the ILC added. In that light, the 38 unilateral statements and declarations appear to be much ado amounting to nothing, or at least nothing much. Nevertheless, it is worth our while to look at a couple of the statements dealing with sustainability issues. It can be added that by not objecting to the unilateral declarations, they might be relied upon as legal norms.[102]

One of the concerns existing with regard to CETA is that the European market would have to be opened up to beef from cows raised with the help of growth hormones. That kind of meat is banned in the EU to protect consumers, as a precaution.[103] In one of the unilateral declarations, the European Commission underlines that CETA will not affect that ban.[104] While it might be hard for Canadian farmers

---

[100] ILC 2006.

[101] Ibid.

[102] Compare UK Attorney's General Office 2019, who on the one hand submits that "[a] unilateral declaration by one party to a bilateral agreement constitutes an authentic interpretation of the treaty if it is accepted by the other party" while adding that he understands that the EU has agreed it will not object to the Unilateral Declaration, and that this confirms that the UK can rely on the declaration.

[103] Directive 96/22/EC concerning the prohibition on the use in stockfarming of certain substances having a hormonal or thyrostatic action and of ß-agonists, OJ L125, 23 May 1996, pp. 3–9, as amended by Directive 2003/74/EC, OJ L262, 14 October 2003, pp. 17–21, and Directive 2008/97, OJ L318, 28 November 2008, pp. 9–11.

[104] Council of the European Union 2016, Declaration No. 26.

to get rid of the ban under CETA, it would have been better if this particular point—around since two decades—had been covered in CETA itself or in the Joint Interpretative Instrument, instead of in a unilateral declaration. Similar concerns can be raised regarding the assurance that CETA does not involve any changes in the field of genetically modified organisms (GMOs).[105]

With regard to the precautionary principle in general, the Commission confirms that CETA preserves the ability of the EU and its Member States to apply their fundamental principles governing regulatory activities. For the EU, those principles include those established in the EU Treaties and include, in particular, the precautionary principle as mentioned in Article 191 and reflected in Articles 168(1), 169(1) and (2) TFEU. Consequently the Commission confirms that nothing in CETA prevents the application of the precautionary principle in the EU as set out in the TFEU.[106] In Sect. 4.3.2 it will be demonstrated that in spite of these assurances, this unilateral declaration does not prevent CETA from imposing restrictions regarding the application of the precautionary principle by the Union, both from a legal point of view and in practice.

In another statement, the Commission indicated that it would continue to evaluate the dispute settlement mechanism (ICS) without delay, and to ensure independence, impartiality and the highest degree of competence where judges are concerned. The ethical requirements for judges will be worked out in detail in the form of an "obligatory and binding code of conduct".[107] The latter point seems to incorporate a contradictio in terminis, since codes of conducts usually are not binding. At any rate, while it is to be welcomed that ICS overcomes some of the weaknesses that characterised the old style ISDS system, the principle objection to a parallel law system that in practice is used mainly by large multinationals in order to fight public policy measures remains.

4.3 The CETA Chapters on the Environment and on Sustainable Development

4.3.1 Sustainable Development, Labour and Environment in CETA

EU trade policy should be promoting sustainable development, also on the territory of our trading partners.[108] To this end, CETA encompasses three chapters: one on Trade

---

[105] Ibid., Declaration 30.

[106] Ibid., Declaration 7.

[107] Ibid., Statement 36.

[108] As explained in the introduction this forms a constitutional obligation enshrined notably in TFEU, above n. 51, articles 3(5) and 11. See also Consolidated Version of the Treaty on the European Union, 2012, OJ C326 (TEU), article 21.

and Sustainable Development (Chapter 22), one on Trade and Labour (Chapter 23) and one on Trade and Environment (Chapter 24), also known as the TSD chapters. Do the provisions of these chapters ensure that sustainable development, which encompasses economic development that meets the needs of the present without endangering the needs of future generations,[109] is indeed promoted on the ground? That question will first be discussed from the point of view of the substantive provisions in these chapters in this section. After that, a particular contentious point, the possibility to adopt precautionary measures, will be zoomed in on (Sect. 4.3.2). The last section (Sect. 4.3.3) will discuss the lack of enforceability of CETA's TSD chapters. A few times, the contrast with US trade agreements will be highlighted as some of their labour and environmental provisions are enforceable and contain alternatives that are worth analysing.

4.3.1.1 Sustainable Development (Chapter 22)

Chapter 22 of CETA on trade and sustainable development comprises only five articles. Three of them are substantive, the last two are institutional in nature. The three substantive provisions are formulated in a rather precatory manner: although they are binding because they are included in CETA, they do not actually create concrete legal obligations. That the "parties recognise that economic and social development and environmental protection are closely linked and mutually reinforcing components of sustainable development", and that they reaffirm their commitment "to promote the development of international trade in a way that contributes to the objective of sustainable development, for the well-being of current and future generations"[110] are, for example, provisions that belong in the preamble to a treaty rather than in a substantive chapter. Similar thoughts come to mind when reading that the Parties "aim to promote sustainable development",[111] "promote dialogue and cooperation in the environmental field"[112] and encourage the development of voluntary best practices of corporate social responsibility, such as those in the OECD guidelines for multinational companies.[113]

Promising to promote sustainable development is easily said. The challenge is in defining what this means in practice, defining instruments, setting measurable goals and timeframes to achieve these, and evaluating progress. The Trade and Sustainability chapter in CETA fails to do all that. What about the chapters dealing with the labour and environment components? Are these more to the point?

---

[109] The definition that was introduced by the World Commission on Environment and Development 1987.

[110] CETA, above n. 22, article 22(1) lid 1.

[111] Ibid., article 22.1(3)(a).

[112] Ibid., article 22.1(3)(b).

[113] Ibid., article 22.3(2)(b).

4.3.1.2 Labour and Environment (Chapters 23 and 24)

Chapter 23 deals with Trade and Labour. In many respects, it is similar to Chapter 24 on Trade and Environment. The chapters comprise 11 and 16 provisions, respectively. The Parties, among other things, confirm their international obligations and promise to implement environmental treaties effectively.[114] Furthermore, each Party seeks to ensure that legislation and policies provide high levels of protection and promote them, and strives to continually improve its laws, regulations and policies as well as their underlying levels of protection of workers and the environment.[115] They recognise that it is "not appropriate to weaken or reduce the levels of protection" provided for by their labour laws and environmental legislation in order to "encourage trade or investment".[116] Such behaviour is thus labelled 'inappropriate', but apparently not so inappropriate that it is actually prohibited under CETA.

Furthermore, the parties promise not to encourage trade and investment by not effectively enforcing their environmental and labour legislation 'continuously and repeatedly'.[117] Again, CETA does not prohibit non-enforcement of environmental legislation per se: it is only contrary to the agreement if this is done to encourage trade and investment. This raises the burden of proof rather high. Even in situations where a party clearly lowers its protection standards or repeatedly fails to enforce them, it will be difficult or impossible to prove that this happened with the aim of promoting trade, as the USA-Guatemala case discussed below in Sect. 4.3.3 demonstrates.

Access to remedies and procedural safeguards under the obligation of respect for levels of protection is defined as a duty of care. Each Party shall ensure that its enforcement authorities take due account of alleged violations of labour and environmental law.[118] Furthermore, each Party shall ensure that appropriate remedies in the event of infringements of its labour and environmental law are open to persons with a legally recognised interest in a particular matter or who claim that there is an infringement of a right under its internal law, administrative or judicial proceedings with a view to effective action against infringements of its labour and environmental law.[119]

Then there is the obligation to ensure that labour and environmental procedures must be fair and equitable (plus transparent, but remarkably only for environmental procedures) and not unnecessarily complicated or prohibitively costly. If appropriate, injunction relief should also be provided.[120]

The provisions on information and awareness of the general public are again formulated in a precatory manner. Parties should encourage public debates as regards the development and definition of policies that may lead to the adoption of labour and

[114] Ibid., article 24.4 lid 2.
[115] Ibid., articles 23.2 and 24.3.
[116] Ibid., articles 23.4(1) and 24.5(1).
[117] Ibid., articles 23.4(3) and 24.5(3).
[118] Ibid., articles 23.5(1)(a) and 24.6(1)(a).
[119] Ibid., articles 23.5(1)(b) and 24.6(1)(b).
[120] Ibid., articles 23.5(2) and 24.6(2).

environmental and standards. Interestingly enough, while the labour chapter lacks a duty to actually take the views expressed by the public into account, according to the environment chapter each Party "shall be open to receive and shall give due consideration to submissions from the public on matters related to this Chapter, including communications on implementation concerns." Furthermore, parties shall encourage public debate with and among non-state actors and promote public awareness about labour and environmental standards, as well as enforcement and compliance procedures.[121]

As was already noted, the environment chapter has more provisions than the one on labour. One provision that is specific for the former chapter underlines that the parties are "resolved to make efforts to facilitate and promote" trade and investment in environmental goods and services.[122] Being resolved to make efforts forms yet another example of the wavering wording in which CETA provisions relating to protection of the environment are cast. The environmental chapter also includes two specific provisions on forestry and fisheries, which confirm, among other things, that parties are in favour of sustainable management of these natural resources.[123] The precatory wording of these provisions will hardly suffice to deter a further increase in deforestation on the territory of the EU trading partners. The same holds true for the final substantive provision of Chapter 24, in which parties promise to cooperate on a range of trade-related environmental issues such as climate change.[124]

4.3.1.3 Concluding Remarks on the Substantive Parts of CETA's Sustainability Chapters

Most of the provisions in the TSD chapters do not entail clear obligations. The mainly contain best effort obligations. While the norms formally speaking are binding, substantively they resemble soft law because they lack actual bite. Where norms are a bit more precise, for instance where the lowering or non-enforcement of standards is concerned, the burden of proof makes it hard or impossible to conclude norms were violated. This particular hurdle could be overcome by altering the burden of proof where conditions like "to encourage trade and investment" are concerned.

The latter solution was embraced in the USMC. For purposes of dispute settlement, violations of labour and environmental provisions are assumed to be in a manner affecting trade unless the other party demonstrates otherwise.[125] The burden of proof is thus reversed so that the responding Party is tasked with demonstrating that the

[121] Ibid., articles 23.6 and 24.7.

[122] Ibid., article 24.9. Environmental goods and services are designed to protect the environment, such as windmills and processes to save energy. Within the WTO, for years there have been attempts to agree on reducing tariffs and non-tariff barriers to these goods and services.

[123] Ibid., arts, 24.10 and 24.11, respectively.

[124] Ibid., article 24.12.

[125] The USMCA sets out that a panel "shall presume that a failure is in a manner affecting trade or investment between the Parties, unless the responding Party demonstrates otherwise".

labour or environmental violations are not related to trade or investment. Since the USMCA forms an agreement between the USA, Mexico and Canada surely it would be feasible to agree on such an amendment in CETA.

Furthermore, in order to ensure that sustainability provisions stand a chance of actually achieving positive changes on the ground, as the EU claims to be striving for, the USMCA improvements definitely need to be embraced in future EU trade agreements with Mercosur and other countries. After all, with more progressive features in US trade agreements, claiming that CETA forms a gold standard becomes less convincing.

4.3.2 CETA and the Precautionary Principle

The word precaution does not appear in CETA. The Parties do stress they "shall take into account relevant scientific and technical information and related international standards, guidelines, or recommendations" when preparing and implementing measures aimed at environmental protection that may affect trade or investment between the Parties. The same provision adds that "where there are threats of serious or irreversible damage, the lack of full scientific certainty shall not be used as a reason for postponing cost-effective measures to prevent environmental degradation".[126] A similar provision is included in Chapter 23 on Trade and Labour.[127]

The CETA provisions stimulating precautionary environmental and labour related measures were supplemented by the comments mentioned above in the Joint Interpretation Instrument and in a unilateral statement from the EU. Is this sufficient to ensure that the EU and its Member States can implement the precautionary principle laid down in the EU constitutional legal order in the form of a treaty provision (article 191 para 2 TFEU), numerous directives and regulations and the case law of the CJEU? According to a comprehensive report prepared by four authors (including myself) in 2016, that is not the case.[128] In this contribution, I will briefly refer to some conclusions of that report, and some of the reactions to it from EU Trade Commissioner Malmström.[129]

A first concern is that the precautionary provisions in CETA apply only to the protection of the environment and workers. In the EU, the precautionary principle was codified in the part dealing with the protection of the environment, but through the jurisprudence of the CJEU now has a much wider scope and also covers issues such as the protection of human health, food safety, the protection of life and health of animals and so forth.[130] While the two CETA provisions open the door slightly

[126] CETA, above n. 22, article 24.8.

[127] Ibid., article 23.3(3).

[128] Stoll et al. 2016, For further arguments, see Foodwatch and the Council of Canadians 2020.

[129] See Douma 2016 for a comprehensive discussion of the arguments that EU Trade Commissioner Malmström and Dutch Minister Ploumen put forward.

[130] Stoll 2019; Douma 2003.

for precautionary measures, they only apply to environmental and labour measures respectively. Even when one might assume that they would apply—for instance where the protection of bees against certain pesticides is concerned—in practice other, more specific CETA chapters (in casu the SPS Chapter 5) can apply. Those more specific chapters do not carve out room for precautionary measures, or only to a much more limited degree than under EU law.

Furthermore, the parties to CETA affirm their rights and obligations under the WTO's SPS Agreement. Under the rules of the latter agreement, numerous disputes in which scientific uncertainties played a role have been adjudicated since 1995. In fact, Canada already instituted several proceedings against the EU in disputes such as the ones on Beef hormones[131] and on GMOs.[132] Both cases were decided in Canada's favour. In fact, not only the Union was told its precautionary measures violated WTO law, but each and every time that WTO members (including Australia, Japan and Korea) tried to justify their precautionary measures they were unsuccessful.[133] On the one hand, they were told that they could not adopt precautionary measures because sufficient scientific evidence to complete a risk analysis and adopt regular protection measures was available.[134] Under such circumstances, it is impossible to invoke a provision that allows for measures in situations where there is insufficient scientific evidence to carry out an 'objective' risk analysis (article 5.7 SPS Agreement). On the other hand, regular protection measures were rejected due to the absence of sufficient scientific evidence.[135] In other words, the WTO judiciary has rejected precautionary measures because of the absence of a lack of evidence, while regular protection measures were rejected because of a lack of evidence. This explanation of WTO law makes it extremely difficult—and for the time being even impossible—for WTO members to adopt precautionary measures. If this case law is compared to that of the CJEU, it is noticeable that the latter leaves much more policy space to the

---

[131] The European precautionary ban on beef hormones was approved by the Court in Case C-331/88, while the WTO dispute resolution body found the same ban contrary to WTO law in EC—Hormones (United States). See, respectively, Court of Justice, *The Queen v Minister of Agriculture, Fisheries and Food and Secretary of State for Health, ex parte: Fedesa and others,* Judgment, 13 November 1990, Case C-331/88, ECLI:EU:C:1990:391; WTO Appellate Body, *European Communities—Hormones (United States),* Report, 13 February 1998. WT/DS26/AB/R, WT/DS48/AB/R.

[132] WTO Panel Body, *European Communities—Biotech (Canada),* Report, 29 September 2009, WT/DS291/R; WT/DS292/R; WT/DS293/R. See also Arcuri 2017, pp. 35–58 finding that CETA offers ample margin to apply the agreement in a way respectful of stringent regulatory standards and of the precautionary principle, while warning that it remains to be seen whether this path will be followed in practice.

[133] Douma 2019, pp. 163–200.

[134] This happened in the following disputes: WTO Appellate Body, *Japan—Agricultural products II,* Report, 22 February 1999, WT/DS76/AB/R; WTO Appellate Body, *Japan—Measures Affecting the Importation of Apples,* Report, 23 June 2005, WT/DS245/AB/R; WTO Appellate Body, *Korea—Import Bans, and Testing and Certification Requirements for Radionuclides,* Report, 26 April 2019, WT/DS495/AB/R.

[135] E.g. *Japan—Agricultural products II,* Ibid.

EU legislature in cases where they have to take decisions in situations of scientific uncertainty.[136]

What is more, the WTO dispute settlement body rejects the absence of scientific *certainty* as a reason for taking precautionary measures, because article 5.7 SPS Agreement only refers to insufficient scientific *evidence*.[137] This explanation is far more restrictive than the one given to the precautionary principle in the EU. In the EU, the focus is on potential risks that cannot be determined with sufficient certainty by a scientific evaluation. This may be due to a lack of evidence, but also a lack of suitable scientific models.[138] By allowing only the lack of scientific evidence as a reason for precautionary measures, under WTO law—and hence under CETA—an entire category of cases is thus excluded. The WTO's dispute settlement body's stance is also contrary to the Rio Declaration, in which the principle is defined as follows: 'Where serious or irreversible damage is imminent, the lack of complete scientific *certainty* should not be used as an argument for delaying cost-effective measures to prevent environmental degradation.' All in all, instead of merely referring to the SPS Agreement in CETA, the Commission should have made clear that the agreement does not preclude the possibilities of the EU to continue applying the precautionary principle in the manner in which the CJEU holds this appropriate. In this way, CETA would have offered far more leeway to adopt precautionary measures than is the case now. The assertion by EU Trade Commissioner Malmström that in the negotiations on EU trade agreements, the precautionary principle as laid down in various EU Treaty as well as in EU directives and regulations is always fully respected, does not alter this conclusion.[139]

A report to the French Prime Minister on the precautionary principle[140] confirms that the EU could have done more to strengthen the European version of the precautionary principle. The authors rightly point out that the SPS agreement, and now CETA as well, places very high demands on the level of scientific evidence to be provided by the party that wishes to take precautions. CETA therefore raises questions about the future of the precautionary policy that includes various public policy areas in Europe, the authors warn.

---

[136]Dutch Minister Ploumen's assertion (letter dated 17 August 2016, copy in the possession of author) that article 24.8 of CETA allows for precautionary measures fails to address the wider scope of the principle in the EU. She also argued that the CJEU's rulings on precautionary measures will keep their validity under CETA. However, the fact that the CJEU allows for EU precautionary measures does not mean that international dispute settling bodies will do the same. In fact, such situations have already arisen where it concerns the EU's beef hormones ban.

[137]*Japan—Measures Affecting the Importation of Apples*, above n. 134. Japan had argued that there was no certainty as to how diseases spread (they did) and therefore claimed to be entitled to take the certain uncertainty (but this was not allowed).

[138]European Commission 2000, pp. 14–15.

[139]EU Commissioner Malmström, letter of 16 November 2016, copy in the possession of author. She referred to articles 168(1), 169(1) and (2) and 191 TFEU that deal with the protection of public health, consumers and the environment respectively. It can be noted that EU directives and regulations are not mentioned in unilateral declaration nr 7 (see Sect. 4.2.4.2 above).

[140]Commission Indépendante 2017.

The same report also contains an interesting *gaffe*. CETA talks about adopting "*cost-effective* measures to prevent environmental degradation", while according to the French authors the 1992 Rio Declaration would only involve adopting "*effective* measures to prevent environmental degradation". That is true if one only takes notice of the French version, as apparently happened. However, the English version of the Rio Declaration shows that it does refers to "*cost-effective* measures to prevent environmental degradation", as do the Russian and Spanish language versions.[141] The difference between CETA and the Rio Declaration is thus based on a mistake in the French translation of the latter document.

In France, the precautionary principle forms a constitutional standard, which has been formulated as an obligation to act.[142] French parliamentarians asked the Constitutional Council (*Conseil Constitutionnel*) whether joining CETA was contrary to that standard.[143] They claimed that CETA infringed the precautionary principle because it is not mentioned, because even in the case of impending serious or irreversible damage no obligations are imposed on the parties, and because the precautionary principle would be affected by several CETA provisions. The Constitutional Council disagreed, but with all due respect not all the reasons that it put forward are equally convincing. First of all, the Council indicated that Chapter 22 of CETA frequently refers to the importance of sustainable development. How this prevents the precautionary principle from being violated remains unclear, however. More to the point, the Council noted that the absence of a specific reference to the precautionary principle does not in itself constitute a violation of the French constitutional standard. Furthermore, Article 24.8(2) of CETA recognises that where there is a threat of serious or irreparable harm, the absence of complete scientific certainty should not be used as a reason for delaying cost-effective measures to prevent environmental degradation. While the Council is right to point at the possibility of taking precautionary measures that CETA refers to here, it fails to address the lack of an obligation to do so as contained in the French constitutional rule and the other objections set out above.

The Constitutional Council also refers to the obligation of the Joint Committee under CETA[144] to comply with the precautionary principle as required by European

[141] The Russian and Spanish versions encompass "принятия *экономически эффективных* мер по предупреждению ухудшения состояния окружающей среды"[taking cost-effective measures to prevent environmental degradation] and "la adopción de medidas *eficaces en función de los costos* para impedir la degradación del medio ambiente" [the adoption of cost-effective measures to prevent environmental degradation] respectively.

[142] Article 5 Environment Charter (Charte de l'Environnement de 2004, NOR:JUSX0300069L, 02 March 2005) states: "When the occurrence of any damage, albeit unpredictable in the current state of scientific knowledge, may seriously and irreversibly harm the environment, public authorities shall, with due respect for the principle of precaution and the areas within their jurisdiction, ensure the implementation of procedures for risk assessment and the adoption of temporary measures commensurate with the risk involved in order to preclude the occurrence of such damage".

[143] Conseil Constitutionnel [Constitutional Council of France], *Comprehensive Economic and Trade Agreement between Canada, on the one hand, and the European Union and its Member States, on the other,* Decision No. 2017-749 DC of 31 July 2017.

[144] Established under CETA, above n. 22, article 26.1.

law, and in particular Article 191 TFEU. However, this obligation can only apply to the EU representatives of this Committee and not to the Canadians. Finally, the Council referred to Article 9 of the Joint Interpretation Instrument annexed to CETA, in which the Parties promise to promote a high level of environmental protection[145] and the right of Canada, the EU and its Member States to set their own environmental priorities, set their own levels of environmental protection and adopt or amend their legislation and policies accordingly, taking into account their international obligations. The latter arguments again fail to convince. The Joint Interpretation Instrument was also endorsed by Canada, and thus formally forms a binding means of interpretation within the meaning of article 31 VC. However, it fails to mention a right to take precautionary measures. Hence, this provision cannot guarantee such a right to take precautions, for instance in cases regarding technical barriers to trade.[146] Nevertheless, the Council concludes that the provisions mentioned together ensure sufficient respect for the French precautionary principle, and that the provisions in various CETA chapters are not contrary to the precautionary principle.

In practice, Canada has already urged the EU to lower some of its standards in order to facilitate export of agricultural products.[147]

4.3.3 Enforceability of Environmental Provisions

The CJEU underlined that a breach of the provisions concerning protection of workers and the environment set out in TSD chapters of EU trade agreements authorises the other party—in accordance with the rule of customary international law codified in Article 60(1) VC—to terminate or suspend the liberalisation, provided for in the other provisions of the envisaged agreement, of that trade.[148] The Union does not seem to have considered this line of action as an option. In fact, so far it has refused to even consider introducing sanctions regarding violations of TSD norms in its trade agreements itself, even though the US has included such provisions in its trade agreements.

Under Chapters 23 and 24 of CETA, the Parties may only invoke the rules and procedures provided for in these chapters. CETA's general dispute resolution procedures do not apply.[149] Both chapters contain the possibility of consultations in the case of differences of opinion.[150] If the dispute is not resolved, a Panel of Experts

---

[145] Ibid, article 9(a), which states: "CETA commits the European Union and its Member States and Canada to establish and promote high levels of environmental protection, and to seek to continually improve their legislation and policies in this area as well as the underlying levels of protection".

[146] Ibid., article 4.2(1), incorporating and making part of the agreement article 2 TBT.

[147] See Douma 2020.

[148] Opinion 2/15 *(Singapore FTA)*, above n. 6, para 161.

[149] CETA, above n. 22, articles 23.11(1) and 24.16(1).

[150] Ibid, articles 23.9 and 24. 14.

may be asked to draw up recommendations.[151] Although article 23.11(3) CETA suggests otherwise by underlining that "the obligations included under this Chapter are binding and enforceable through the procedures for the resolution of disputes provided in Article 23.10", the dispute resolution on labour and environmental issues lacks a 'stick' in the form of sanctions. It is also in stark contrast to the possibility for investors that can bring their claims against states or the EU through ICS. Why standards protecting investors should be enforceable, contrary to standards protecting the environment, remains difficult to grasp.

The idea that the norms of Chapters 23 and 24 should become legally enforceable through binding dispute resolution has many proponents.[152] Others point out that "effective enforceability"[153] includes all mechanisms that encourage compliance with provisions, and call for improvements to the existing system without the introduction of legally binding dispute resolution.[154]

In 2010, as regards labour and environment standards in EU trade agreements, the European Parliament had insisted on recourse to a dispute settlement mechanism on an equal footing with the other parts of the agreement, with provision for fines to improve the situation in the sectors concerned, or at least a temporary suspension of certain trade benefits provided for under the agreement, in the event of an aggravated breach of these standards should be introduced.[155]

While the text of CETA had been adopted without a dispute settlement mechanism like the one the EP had called for in the TSD chapters, the EU and Canada did agree to an early review of the existing mechanisms in these chapters, including with a view to the "effective enforceability" of CETA's TDS provisions.[156] The results of an investigation into a sanctions mechanism for labour and environmental standards could be taken into account in this review, it was explained in the Dutch parliament.[157] That investigation was carried out by the University of Leuven[158] and sets out several options, including traditional intra-state dispute resolution. Various US trade agreements include such an option.

Such dispute resolution systems do not warrant improved implementation of labour and environmental provisions in practice. The 2017 arbitral decision in a dispute between the United States of America and Guatemala under The Dominican

[151] Ibid, articles 23.10 and 24.15.

[152] See for example Gruni 2017; De Ville 2016.

[153] The term used in point 10(a) of the Joint Interpretative Instrument on CETA, above n. 81; see Sect. 4.2.4.1 above.

[154] Alexovicová and Prévost 2018.

[155] European Parliament resolution of 25 November 2010 on human rights and social and environmental standards in international trade agreements (2009/2219(INI)), point 22(c); European Parliament resolution of 5 July 2016 on implementation of the 2010 recommendations of Parliament on social and environmental standards, human rights and corporate responsibility (2015/2038(INI)), points 21 (c) and (d).

[156] Joint Interpretative Instrument on CETA, above n. 81, point 10(a).

[157] Tweede Kamer, Brief van de Staatssecretaris van Economische Zaken [Letter from the State Secretary for Economic Affairs],11 October 2016, 31985 No. 44.

[158] Marx 2017b.

Republic-Central America (CAFTA-DR) Free Trade Agreement demonstrates that the burden of proof was too high.[159] CAFTA-DR contains a provision encompassing that "[a] Party shall not fail to effectively enforce its labour laws, through a sustained or recurring course of action or inaction, in a manner affecting trade between the Parties".[160] The Panel concluded that Guatemala had failed to effectively enforce applicable labour laws regarding 74 workers in eight workplaces. At the same time, the Panel found that in a number of cases "the United States has not proven that the failures to effectively enforce labour laws … were in a manner affecting trade"[161] while in other cases the country had failed "to effectively enforce court orders which "conferred some competitive advantage upon it".[162] In a number of cases, the United States could not provide sufficient evidence that the failure to maintain employment standards had an impact on trade.[163] The Panel therefore concluded that "[w]hen Guatemala's law enforcement failures are looked at collectively, they show (on an *arguendo* basis) a sustained or recurring course of action or inaction, but not conduct in a manner affecting trade."[164] The US action was therefore rejected. It can be noted that the Panel set the bar very high. Other Panels could conclude that the systematic failure to maintain social or environmental standards has an impact on trade in principle. The wording of standards in treaties could also be tailored to this aspect of enforceability, as the example of the USMCA discussed above demonstrates.

At the end of 2017 and the beginning of 2018, two 'non-papers' from the European Commission on the environmental and sustainability aspects of EU Trade Agreements were published. The first 'non-paper' explains that the Union wants to ensure that obligations included in bilateral trade and investment treaties are met in areas such as trade, labour standards, climate and environmental protection. A model with sanctions is discussed at some length.[165] A short while later, the second non-paper rejects that option. Ignoring the absence of consensus on introducing an ISDS mechanism in CETA, the Commission notes that the "absence of consensus on a sanctions-based model makes it impossible to move to such an approach." Other reasons are uncertainty about the manner in which a breach of social or environmental standards can be translated into economic compensation, and the wider scope of EU trade agreements compared to the scope of trade agreements that do include sanctions.[166] Referring to the Commission's own 2017 evaluation, the non-paper indicates that the trade and sustainable development (TSD) chapters of EU trade agreements "have,

---

[159] Dominican Republic—Central America—United States Free Trade Agreement, Arbitral Panel Established pursuant to Chapter XX, *Guatemala—Issues Relating to the Obligations Under Article 16.2.1(a) of the CAFTA-DR*, Final Report, 14 June 2017.

[160] CAFTA-DR, above n. 18, article 16.2.1(a).

[161] *Guatemala—Issues Relating to the Obligations Under Article 16.2.1(a) of the CAFTA-DR*, above n. 159, points 465 and 496.

[162] Ibid., point 491.

[163] Ibid, point 496.

[164] Ibid, point 505.

[165] EC Trade 2017b.

[166] Ibid, p. 3.

in broad terms, worked well".[167] In reality, the Commissions own implementation report found that in general, the agreements "seek to provide a useful framework for addressing issues that may arise regarding the interaction between trade, social and environmental objectives. But the work on TSD has yet to realise its full potential. Further efforts will have to be made to further improve labour and environmental policies".[168] The non-paper did reflect the latter part of the report when admitting that there is a clear consensus that the implementation of three TSD chapters must be stepped up and improved.[169]

One of the reasons for opposing sanctions (the 'stick' method) as a means of enforcement of the TSD norms in EU trade agreements has been their alleged limited effectiveness. The USA-Guatemala case has been cited in this respect. Some comments need to be made regarding that position. First of all, as demonstrated above, the Panel in that dispute opted for a restrictive interpretation of the applicable norms which led the USA to introduce improvements in the form of a reversal of the burden of proof in the USMCA. These improvements will definitely raise the chances of successful enforcement actions under that agreement. Secondly, the 'stick' is not going to replace the 'carrot'. Sanctions only come into play once the persuasive instruments remain ineffective to solve a dispute. Thirdly, relying solely on the persuasion method also proved ineffective in encouraging a trading partner to better protect social rights.[170] Independent sources concluded that in general, the current operation of TSD chapters suffer from a series of important limitations and failings with in a variety of different contexts. The dispute resolution process is viewed as insufficient: it "lacks a credible enforcement mechanism so as to induce compliance with obligation contained in the TSD chapters".[171]

In any case, the implementation of the TSD chapters in EU trade treaties can and should be improved.[172] Some of these improvements could be made without any adjustments to the existing agreements. Giving more systematic follow-up to such input from local organisations could already bring about an improvement. More openness could also be made to developments under the trade agreements. The meeting reports currently being published of the discussions on labour and environmental issues are not useful for lack of details; they should be expanded and include the different positions taken by the Parties on specific issues, rather than the mere mentioning of the fact that an issue was discussed. Furthermore, in cases where a trading partner is acting contrary to the TSD chapters, the EU could use the existing possibilities to make a formal complaint about it. Other improvements could require

---

[167]EC Trade 2018.

[168]EC Trade 2017a, point 6.4 at p. 28.

[169]EC Trade 2018, p. 2.

[170]As Gruni 2017 demonstrates regarding the rights of workers in Korea under the EU-Korea Free Trade Agreement, above n. 96, which came into force (provisionally) on 1 July 2011.

[171]Barbu et al. 2017; Marx 2016; Ebert 2016.

[172]This is also argued in The Netherlands at International Organisations 2020. Also see Brunsden and Mallet 2020 France and Netherlands call for tougher EU trade conditions. Bloc urged to enforce environmental and labour standards through tariffs www.ft.com/content/e14f082c-42e1-4bd8-ad68-54714b995dff. Accessed 20 May 2020.

adjustment of agreements, which would necessitate the approval of trading partners. In doing so, the option to enforce the TSD provisions through sanctions should not be ignored and excluded from the discussions, but be further explored.

4.4 Concluding Remarks

Representatives of various countries around the globe with which the EU is negotiating trade agreements have asked if they could expect restrictions ensuing from proposed TSD chapters. The manner in which the provisions in these chapters are worded at the moment means that they need not worry too much. Their wording is precatory, expressing mostly wishes that rather belong in preambles. Where provisions are a bit more concrete, conditions raise hurdles so high that complaints hardly stand a chance to be successful.

The European Commission remains firm in its rejection of sanctions in TSD chapters, and excludes them from the regular intra-state dispute resolution. For the time being, the Commission only wants to encourage trading partners to take greater care of the environment and sustainability through persuasion (the 'carrot' method). It was argued that in order to increase the effectiveness of these chapters and their effect on the ground, the introduction of sanctions would form an improvement, also because the effectiveness of the EU's persuasion method leaves a lot to be desired. Other improvements could include more systematic following up on suggestions from local organisations and the publication of meeting reports that make clear what the positions of the parties are regarding points discussed.

The way in which EU trade treaties are prepared, and in particular the role played by Trade Sustainability Impact Assessment (TSIA) system needs urgent improvement. The assessment on CETA recommended, among other things, that ISDS should not be included. According to its own rules, the Commission should have responded to this recommendation in time for the EU negotiators to take this response into account. However, the response was only issued well after the negotiations had already been concluded. The TSIA rules were also ignored during the negotiations with Mexico and Mercosur. It is not acceptable for the Commission to ignore its own guidelines in these. TSIAs are intended to provide room for participation and to steer the negotiations and should therefore be available well before the end of the negotiations. The European Commission should comment on these independent recommendations and should explain in more detail why certain recommendations are rejected. Furthermore, consultations under TSIA processes should be announced not only on the websites of the contracted consultants, but also on those of the European Commission. Finally, the TSIA system should be based on legislation rather than mere guidelines. Such improvements can contribute to preventing the unintended consequences of trade treaties and ensure a positive sustainability impact of new agreements.

The way in which general consultations are set up should also be improved. The consultations on ISDS and those on improvements in the effectiveness of the sustainability chapters (as described in the non-papers of the Commission services) leave a lot to be desired. These processes are not conducive to the confidence in the EU, they are not sufficiently democratic and in stark contrast with the assurances about increased transparency on EU trade agreements.

Considering the track record of Canadian investors under ISDS provisions in trade agreements with other countries, it is likely that sooner rather than later they will rely on CETA's investment chapter and seek compensation from individual EU Member States or from the European Union. The suggestion that it is unlikely in the case of the Netherlands, based on the fact that the country was never accused of violating a trade agreement with ISDS constitutes pulling the wool over the eyes of Dutch parliament, as past results are no guarantee for the future, given the amount of investments that Canadians invest in the EU[173] and considering the fact that Canadian investors occupy the sixth spot in the global ranking of initiating ISDS claims.[174] Furthermore, it should not be forgotten that ICS does not form an improvement where the situation in all but eight (mostly Eastern European) member states is concerned. Only eight countries[175] currently have BITs with Canada encompassing old-style ISDS at the moment. For the remaining 19 EU member states, introducing ICS means providing Canadian investors with a new forum to introduce claims against states and allowing them to bypass national courts.[176]

For the non-ICS parts of CETA and future treaties, it is important to note that these can be concluded exclusively by the EU. Consequently, it will be particularly important to engage the EP, which can ultimately veto such agreements it does not agree with their content. In order to improve the effectiveness of environmental provisions in EU trade treaties, institutional and other changes need to be made. These changes could primarily focus on complementing and clarifying existing key rules and making better use of existing possibilities. In addition, it would be a good thing if a stick was also put behind the door in the form of access to a regular dispute resolution mechanism. The obligations contributing to environmental protection should ultimately be enforceable for those cases where persuasion does not work.

With regard to the precautionary principle, EU trade agreement should enable the EU to continue to apply this in the way it is customary in the EU. It definitely does not suffice to refer only to WTO rules or environmental treaties, as this restricts the possibility to adopt precautionary measures by the EU and its Member States.

[173] According to the Canadian ambassador to the Netherlands during the expert meeting in the Dutch Senate on 19 May 2020, Canadians invested 25 billion Euro in The Netherlands in 2018. http://youtube.com/watch?v=TvCqFhO98. Accessed 20 May 2020.

[174] See http://tweedekamer.nl/kamerstukken/plenaire_verslagen/detail/b85c005d-1215-4151-89f9-4ec67b88a658. Accessed 8 July 2020; and UNCTAD 2019.

[175] Croatia, the Czech Republic, Latvia, Malta, Poland, Romania and the Slovak Republic. See CETA, above n. 22, Annex 30-A.

[176] In theory investors could bring their claims to national courts, but this forms "merely a possibility in the discretion of the claimant investor" as the latter can decide "to submit the dispute to arbitration, without that Member State being able to oppose this". Opinion 2/15 *(Singapore FTA)*, above n. 6, paras 290–292.

Finally, the EU introduced the obligation to integrate environmental protection considerations in EU trade policy in 1986. The TSIA instrument that was introduced to operationalise this integration principle was launched in 1999. Trade agreements with sustainability chapters have been around since 2008. A decade later, it was clear that improvements are called for. The debates on CETA and TTIP mean that attention has increased for EU trade agreements. At present, the actual effect on the ground of the EU's persuasive approach to TSD chapters leaves much to be desired. As long as that is the case, the EU runs the risk of being accused of greenwashing rather than achieving a gold standard. Both CETA and the upcoming EU-Mercosur agreement form an optimal opportunity to go for gold in the form of firm, enforceable TSD norms.

References

Ahuja N (2019) USMCA: An Analysis of the Proposed ISDS Mechanism http://arbitrationblog.kluwerarbitration.com/2019/11/26/usmca-an-analysis-of-the-proposed-isds-mechanism/ Accessed 20 May 2020

Aldin E (2019) A Solution Due South: Canada, Mexico, and Investor-State Arbitration in the U.S.M.C.A. Michigan Journal of International Law Online. http://www.mjilonline.org/a-solution-due-south-canada-mexico-and-investor-state-arbitration-in-the-u-s-m-c-a/ Accessed 20 May 2020

Alexovicová I, Prévost M D (2018) Afdwingbaarheid van bepalingen inzake duurzame ontwikkeling in EU-handelsovereenkomsten [Enforceability of provisions on sustainable development in EU Trade Agreements]. SEW 66:3:82–96

Ankersmit L (2016) The compatibility of investment arbitration in EU trade agreements with the EU judicial system. Journal for European Environmental & Planning Law 13:46–63

Ankersmit L, Hughes L (2018) Implications of Achmea: how the Achmea judgment impacts investment agreements with non-EU countries. https://www.ciel.org/wp-content/uploads/2018/04/Implications-of-Achmea.pdf Accessed 20 May 2020

Barbu M et al. (2017) Response to the Non-paper of the European Commission on Trade and Sustainable Development (TSD) chapters in EU Free Trade Agreements (FTAs) https://www.qmul.ac.uk/geog/media/geography/docs/research/working-beyond-the-border/A-Response-to-the-Nonpaper-26.09.17.pdf Accessed 20 May 2020

Commission Indépendante (2017), L'impact de l'Accord Économique et Commercial Global entre l'Union européenne et le Canada (AECG/CETA) sur l'environnement, le climat et la santé [The impact of Comprehensive Economic and Trade Agreement (CETA) on the environment, climate and health] https://www.gouvernement.fr/sites/default/files/document/document/2017/09/rapport_de_la_commission_devaluation_du_ceta_-_08.09.2017.pdf Accessed 20 May 2020

Corporate Europe Observatory (2016) Statement against Investor Protection in TTIP, CETA and other trade deals https://corporateeurope.org/sites/default/files/attachments/s2b_statement_isds_ics_engl.pdf Accessed 20 May 2020

Council of the European Union (2016) CETA—Statements to the Council Minutes. https://data.consilium.europa.eu/doc/document/ST-13463-2016-REV-1/en/pdf Accessed 7 July 2020

De Ville F (2016) In pursuit of a consistent European Parliament position on two transatlantic trade agreements. Analysis of the conformity of CETA with the European Parliament's 8 July 2015 Resolution on TTIP. http://www.s2bnetwork.org/wp-content/uploads/2015/09/De-Ville-2016-CETA-report-bonne-version.pdf Accessed 20 May 2020

Development Solutions (2011) A Trade SIA relating to the negotiation of a Comprehensive Economic and Trade Agreement (CETA) between the EU and Canada. https://trade.ec.europa.eu/doclib/docs/2011/september/tradoc_148201.pdf Accessed 7 July 2020

Doelle M (2019) The Bilcon NAFTA arbitration: the damages ruling. https://blogs.dal.ca/melaw/2019/03/01/the-bilcon-nafta-arbitration-the-damages-ruling/

Douma W Th (2003) The precautionary principle. Its application in international, European and Dutch law. Dissertation, Groningen

Douma W Th (2016) Sustainability and precautionary aspects of CETA dissected. ELNI Review 12:2:58–63

Douma W Th (2017) The promotion of sustainable development through EU trade instruments. European Business Law Review 28:2:193–212

Douma W Th (2019) The limits to precaution in international trade law: from WTO law to EU trade agreements. In: Squintani L, Darpö J, Lavrysen L, Stoll PT (eds) Managing facts and feelings in environmental governance. Elgar, pp 163–200

Douma W Th (2020) CETA's disbalans tussen handel en duurzaamheid [CETA's disbalance between trade and sustainability]. https://www.milieurecht.nl/bestanden/ceta-handel-duurzaamheid-douma-position-paper.pdf Accessed 20 May 2020

Douma W Th (2021) Investor-state dispute settlement in EU trade agreements in the light of EU policy and law. In: Andenas M, Pantaleo L, Happold M, Contartese C (eds) EU External Action in International Economic Law. T.M.C. Asser Press, The Hague

Ebert F (2016) Labour Provisions in EU Trade Agreements. International Labour Review 155:407–433

EC Trade (2017a) Position paper on the trade sustainability impact assessment of a Comprehensive Economic & Trade Agreement between the EU and Canada https://trade.ec.europa.eu/doclib/docs/2017/april/tradoc_155471.pdf Accessed 20 May 2020

EC Trade (2017b) Trade and Sustainable Development (TSD) Chapters in EU Free Trade Agreements (FTAs). https://trade.ec.europa.eu/doclib/docs/2017/july/tradoc_155686.pdf Accessed 20 May 2020

EC Trade (2018) Feedback and way forward on improving the implementation and enforcement of Trade and Sustainability chapters in EU Free Trade Agreements. https://trade.ec.europa.eu/doclib/docs/2018/february/tradoc_156618.pdf Accessed 20 May 2020

Eckes C (2018) Teken het handelsverdrag tussen EU en Canada nu nog niet [Don't sign the EU-Canada treaty yet]. www.volkskrant.nl/columns-opinie/teken-het-handelsverdrag-tussen-eu-en-canada-nu-nog-niet~bc5b971a/ Accessed 9 December 2020

Edward R et al. (2017) From arbitration to the investment court system (ICS): The evolution of CETA rules. European Parliamentary Research Service, www.europarl.europa.eu/RegData/etudes/IDAN/2017/607251/EPRS_IDA(2017)607251_EN.pdf Accessed 20 May 2020

European Commission (2000) Communication on the precautionary principle, COM(2000)1

European Commission (2015) Report: Online public consultation on investment protection and investor-to-state dispute settlement (ISDS) in the Transatlantic Trade and Investment Partnership Agreement (TTIP). https://ec.europa.eu/transparency/regdoc/rep/10102/2015/EN/10102-2015-3-EN-F1-1.Pdf Accessed 20 May 2020

European Commission (2016a) Handbook for Trade Sustainability Impact Assessment (1st edn)

European Commission (2016b) Handbook for Trade Sustainability Impact Assessment (2nd edn). https://trade.ec.europa.eu/doclib/docs/2016/april/tradoc_154464.PDF Accessed 20 May 2020

European Commission (2017a) Report on the implementation of free trade agreements 1 January 2016—31 December 2016, COM(2017)654 final. https://ec.europa.eu/transparency/regdoc/rep/1/2017/EN/COM-2017-654-F1-EN-MAIN-PART-1.PDF Accessed 20 May 2020

European Commission (2017b) Meeting on EU-Mexico Sustainability Impact Assessment—Draft Inception Report. https://trade.ec.europa.eu/doclib/docs/2018/january/tradoc_156555.pdf Accessed 7 July 2020

Foodwatch and the Council of Canadians (2020) The potential dangers of CETA committees on Europe. https://www.foodwatch.org/fileadmin/-NL/Potential_dangers_of_ceta_committees_on_Europe.pdf Accessed 20 May 2020
Govaere I (2016) TTIP and Dispute Settlement: Potential Consequences for the Autonomous EU Legal Order. Collège d'Europe Research Paper in Law 01/2016
Griller S, Obwexer W, Vranes E (2017) Mega-Regional Trade Agreements. New orientations for EU external relations? Oxford University Press, Oxford
Gruni G (2017) Labor standards in the EU-South Korea Free Trade Agreement, Pushing labor standards into global trade law? European Journal of International and Comparative Law 5:100–121
Hepburn J (2019) Final costs details are released in Philip Morris v. Australia following request by IAReporter. https://www.iareporter.com/articles/final-costs-details-are-released-in-philip-morris-v-australia-following-request-by-iareporter/ Accessed 20 May 2020
Hohnstein D (2018) Italy's decision on CETA ratification–what does it really mean? https://www.lexology.com/library/detail.aspx?g=cd0a9158-ba06-4451-9922-1dd31bfda6c6 Accessed 15 December 2020
Hutchens G, Knaus C (2018) Revealed: $39m cost of defending Australia's tobacco plain packaging laws. https://www.theguardian.com/business/2018/jul/02/revealed-39m-cost-of-defending-australias-tobacco-plain-packaging-laws Accessed 20 May 2020
ILC (2006) Guiding Principles applicable to unilateral declarations of States capable of creating legal obligations, with commentaries thereto. https://legal.un.org/ilc/texts/instruments/english/commentaries/9_9_2006.pdf Accessed 20 May 2020
ILC (2011) Guide to Practice on Reservations to Treaties, UN Doc. A/66/10, pp 56–76
Kikou O (2016) Animal welfare for farm animals. In: Mertins-Kirkwood H et al. (eds) Making sense of CETA, 2nd edn. PowerShift, Berlin/Ottawa
Koeth W (2016) Can the Investment Court System (ICS) save TTIP and CETA? https://www.eipa.eu/wp-content/uploads/2017/11/20161019072755_Workingpaper2016_W_01.pdf Accessed 20 May 2020
Kokott J, Sobotta C (2016) Investment Arbitration and the EU law. Cambridge Yearbook of European Legal Studies 1
Krajewski M (2018) Die Auswirkungen des Achmea-Urteils des EuGH auf die EU Investitionspolitik [The consequences of the CJEU's Achmea judgment for EU investment policy]. https://power-shift.de/wp-content/uploads/2018/03/PowerShift_BriefingPaper_Krajewski-Folgen-AchmeaUrteil-EU-Investitionspolitik-3-2018.pdf Accessed 20 May 2020
Krajewski M, Hoffmann R T (2016) The European Commission's Proposal for Investment Protection in TTIP. https://www.fes-europe.eu/fileadmin/public/editorfiles/events/Juni_2016/FES_2017plus_Krajewski_ENGL.pdf Accessed 20 May 2020
Legal Service of the European Parliament (2016) Legal opinion on compatibility with the Treaties of investment dispute settlement provisions in EU trade agreements
Lester S (2016) Interpreting the CETA Joint Interpretative Instrument. https://ielp.worldtradelaw.net/2016/11/the-ceta-joint-interpretative-instrument.html Accessed 20 May 2020
Londoño E, Casado L (2019) Amazon deforestation in Brazil rose sharply on Bolsonaro's watch. https://www.nytimes.com/2019/11/18/world/americas/brazil-amazon-deforestation.html Accessed 20 May 2020
LSE Enterprise (2017) Sustainability Impact Assessment (SIA) in support of the negotiations for the modernization of the trade pillar of the Global Agreement with Mexico: Inception report. https://trade.ec.europa.eu/doclib/docs/2017/december/tradoc_156422.pdf Accessed 7 July 2020
Malmström C, Freeland C (2016) Joint statement Canada-EU Comprehensive Economic and Trade Agreement (CETA). https://trade.ec.europa.eu/doclib/docs/2016/february/tradoc_154330.pdf Accessed 7 July 2020
Marx A et al. (2016) The protection of labour rights in trade agreements: the case of the EU-Colombia Agreement'. Journal of World Trade 50:4:587–610

Marx A et al. (2017a) Strengthening labour rights provisions in bilateral trade agreements: making the case for voluntary sustainability standards. Global Policy 8:3:78–88

Marx A et al. (2017b) Dispute settlement in the trade and sustainable development chapters of EU trade agreements. https://ghum.kuleuven.be/ggs/publications/books/final-report-9-february-def.pdf Accessed 20 May 2020

Niemelä P et al. (2020) Risky business: Uniper's potential investor-state dispute against the Dutch coal ban. EJIL: Talk! https://www.ejiltalk.org/risky-business-unipers-potential-investor-state-dispute-against-the-dutch-coal-ban/ Accessed 20 May 2020

Quinn G (2018) Canadian opposition to Nafta's Chapter 11 gives Trudeau leeway. https://www.bloomberg.com/news/articles/2018-04-17/canadian-opposition-to-nafta-s-chapter-11-gives-trudeau-leeway Accessed 20 May 2020

Rios B (2018) Italy threatens to block CETA ratification. https://www.euractiv.com/section/ceta/news/italy-threatens-to-block-ceta-ratification/ Accessed 20 May 2020

Schepel H (2018) From conflicts-rules to field preemption: Achmea and the relationship between EU law and international investment law and arbitration. European Law Blog. https://europeanlawblog.eu/2018/03/23/from-conflicts-rules-to-field-preemption-achmea-and-the-relationship-between-eu-law-and-international-investment-law-and-arbitration/ Accessed 20 May 2020

Schöllmann W (2016) Is CETA a mixed agreement? European Parliamentary Research Service. https://www.europarl.europa.eu/RegData/etudes/ATAG/2016/586597/EPRS_ATA(2016)586597_EN.pdf Accessed 20 May 2020

Schurmans M (2015) Sustainable development is emerging as a core tenet of WTO case law. To what extent has it helped enshrine this as a legal concept? European Energy and Environmental Law Review 24:2:28–34

Shyrbman S (2016) CETA: The Effect of an Interpretative Declaration by Canada and EU Commission. http://www.meco.lu/wp-content/uploads/2016/10/02_Juristesch-Analyse-Etude.pdf Accessed 20 May 2020

Sisto A, Jones G (2018) Italy says it won't ratify EU-Canada trade deal; Canada plays down threat. http://www.reuters.com/article/us-italy-canada-trade/italy-says-it-wont-ratify-eu-canada-trade-deal-canada-plays-down-threat-idUSKBN1K318Q Accessed 20 May 2020

Stoll PT (2019) Of fear and prudence: precaution through better regulation and innovation. In: Squintani L et al (eds) Managing facts and feelings in environmental governance. Elgar, Cheltenham, pp 137–162

Stoll PT et al. (2016) CETA, TTIP and the European precautionary principle. A study on the regulations on sanitation and phytosanitary measures, technical barriers to trade and regulatory cooperation in the CETA agreement and the EU proposals for TTIP.www.foodwatch.org/uploads/media/2016-06-21-_Studie_Vorsorgeprinzip_TTIP_CETA_01.pdf Accessed 20 May 2020

Suse A, Wouters J (2018) The provisional application of the EU's mixed trade and investment agreements. https://ghum.kuleuven.be/ggs/publications/working_papers/2018/201suse Accessed 20 May 2020

The Netherlands at International Organisations (2020) Non-paper from the Netherlands and France on trade, social economic effects and sustainable development https://www.permanentrepresentations.nl/documents/publications/2020/05/08/non-paper-from-nl-and-fr-on-trade-social-economic-effects-and-sustainable-development Accessed 20 May 2020

UK Attorney General's Office (2019) Legal opinion on the Joint Instrument and Unilateral Declaration concerning the Withdrawal Agreement. https://assets.publishing.service.gov.uk/government/uploads/system/uploads/attachment_data/file/785188/190312_-_Legal_Opinion_on_Joint_Instrument_and_Unilateral_Declaration_co..___2_.pdf Accessed 8 July 2020

UN (2012) Treaty Handbook, Revised edition. https://treaties.un.org/doc/source/publications/THB/English.pdf Accessed 7 July 2020

UNCTAD (2019) Fact sheet on Investor-State Dispute Settlement Cases in 2018 https://unctad.org/en/PublicationsLibrary/diaepcbinf2019d4_en.pdf Accessed 20 May 2020

Van Der Loo G, Wessel R (2017) The non-ratification of mixed agreements: Legal consequences and solutions. CMLRev 54:3:735–770

World Commission on Environment and Development (1987) Our Common Future: Report, Annex to UNGA Doc. No. A/42/427

W.Th. Douma is an Independent legal expert at European Environmental Law consultancy and EU Legal—Centre for European and International Law, voluntary researcher at Ghent University and Senior Legal Adviser at Dutch Ministry of Social Affairs and Employment.

Part II
The EU, Treaty-Making, and Foreign Policy

Chapter 5
The CJEU and the Potential and Limitations of Systemic Integration

E. Kassoti

Contents

Abstract This chapter enquires into the CJEU's increasing reliance on the international law principle of systemic integration in the context of interpreting international agreements concluded with third parties. The main argument advanced here is that, despite the principle's potential as a tool for achieving the harmonious co-existence between EU and international law, the CJEU's application of the principle in practice is problematic. The chapter argues that as long as the Court is unwilling to use international law rules as these are understood and applied in international judicial practice, systemic integration cannot be convincingly conceived as a mechanism for promoting the international rule of law within the EU legal order.

Keywords Interpretation · CJEU · systemic integration · Article 31(3)(c) VCLT · international rule of law · interpretative methods

E. Kassoti (✉)
T.M.C. Asser Institute, The Hague, The Netherlands
e-mail: E.Kassoti@asser.nl

W. Th. Douma et al. (eds.), *The Evolving Nature of EU External Relations Law*,
https://doi.org/10.1007/978-94-6265-423-5_5

5.1 Introduction

This chapter enquires into the CJEU's increasing reliance on the international law principle of systemic integration in the context of interpreting international agreements concluded with third parties. The main argument advanced here is that, despite the principle's potential as a tool for achieving the harmonious co-existence between EU and international law, the CJEU's application of the principle in practice is problematic. More specifically, the chapter identifies a worrisome trend in the Court's case-law. In many cases, where the Court used international law as an interpretative tool, it did so in a way that few international lawyers would recognise. Particularly in its more recent case-law on Western Sahara, the Court has shown its readiness to rely on international law principles without actually taking into account how these principles are understood and applied by international courts and tribunals. The rest of this introductory section will briefly sketch out the *problematique* surrounding the topic in order to provide the necessary background to the discussion that will unfold in the following sections and it will also provide the structure of the chapter.

The concept of autonomy is central to the history of international organizations and it may also serve as a cognitive tool in order to comprehend the ambivalent relationship between global institutions and the international rule of law. The recognition of the importance of the autonomy of international organizations in securing the rule of law at the international level has been a recurrent feature in international legal scholarship over the past century.[1] In fact, for a long time the prevailing view among many international lawyers was that whatever the degree of independence an organization gained vis-à-vis its member States was necessarily good for the functioning of the organization and, thus, also good for the advancement of the international rule of law[2]—since organizations with a large degree of autonomy may be more likely to achieve their foundational objectives without being hindered by the political interests of States.[3] As Schermers and Blokker put it: "[T]he lack of a central, supranational authority at the global level and the resulting horizontal nature of international law have been compensated for by the creation and functioning of international organizations. International organizations have therefore remedied, to some extent, what has been called the *carence institutionelle* of the international legal order."[4] However, as the number and normative influence of international organisations grew, the benefits of autonomy have begun to be perceived in more cautious terms—with autonomy seen as potentially threatening the international rule of law. Concerns have been raised about the fact that increasingly autonomous institutions are causing both a (normative and institutional) fragmentation of the unity of the

---

[1]Collins and White 2011, p. 1 at p. 2.

[2]Regarding the rule of law as a concept that applies both to national and international law, see Nollkaemper 2012, p. 3. Kanetake 2016, p. 11 at pp. 18–22. See also Crawford 2003.

[3]Collins 2011, p. 22 at pp. 22–24. Klabbers 2015, p. 29.

[4]Schermers and Blokker 2011, p. 6.

international legal order[5] and there is a growing awareness that the policy choices and agendas of institutions may be threatening values most associated with the rule of law.[6]

The European Union is an institutional order where the 'tug of war' between autonomy and the international rule of law manifests itself in a most dramatic manner. From the Union's early days, the concept of 'internal autonomy', namely the idea that the EU is not only a new legal order, but also one that is distinct from its Member States has been instrumental in forming its identity.[7] More recently, the focus on internal autonomy has given way to the protection of the external dimension of autonomy.[8] The idea that EU law could be undermined not only by conflicting national legislation, but also by international law has emerged and gained traction in the case-law of the CJEU.[9] According to the Court, the EU is a self-referential order with its own (internal) claim to validity.[10] Being a (self-proclaimed) autonomous legal order does not imply that EU law does not interact with international law at all; rather, it means that the rules governing this interaction are governed by the internal (Union) rules.[11] Autonomy does not merely form part of the CJEU's constitutional rhetoric but it has also strongly influenced the way in which the Court gauges the interplay between

[5]In its normative aspect, fragmentation can be seen as the offshoot of the erosion of general international law through the "splitting up of the law into highly specialised "boxes" that claim relative autonomy from each other and from the general law". This erosion carries the risk of the emergence of conflicting norms for the solution of the same legal issue (normative fragmentation). International Law Commission (ILC) (2006) paras 8–13. In its institutional aspect, the term is used to describe the ramifications of the recent proliferation of international courts and tribunals. The mushrooming of new international courts and tribunals coupled with the lack of any structural co-operation—let alone hierarchy—among the different judicial *fora* carry the risk of divergent (but "equally authoritative") interpretations of international law (substantive fragmentation). ILC 2006, ibid. See also Webb 2013, p. 6.

[6]Court of Justice, *NV Algemene Transport-en Expeditie Onderneming van Gend and Loos v Netherlands Inland Revenue Administration,* Judgment, 05 February 1963, Case 26/62, ECLI:EU:C:19631, p. 12. Collins and White 2011, p. 2. See also Alvarez 2016, pp. 30–47.

[7]Court of Justice, *Costa v ENEL,* Judgment, 16 July 1964, Case 6/64 ECLI:EU:C:1964:66, p. 593. Weiler and Haltern 1996, p. 411.

[8]On the 'internal' and 'external' dimension of the concept of autonomy (or autonomy as 'political independence' or 'institutional independence', see D'Aspremont 2011, p. 63; Brölmann 2007, pp. 29–33.

[9]For case-law and analysis, see van Rossem 2013, p. 13; Contartese 2017.

[10]See Tsagourias 2011, p. 339, at p. 340. "By appropriating the instruments of its creation, the Union liberated itself from external—international contingencies and also moved the source of its validation from the international legal order to the Union … As a result, the chain of validity in the Union begins and ends with the treaties which are autochthonous Union Instruments." See also Odermatt 2018, p. 291, at pp. 297–308.

[11]As A.G. Maduro famously put it in *Kadi,* the autonomy of the Union legal order: "does not mean, however, that the Community's municipal legal order and the international legal order pass by each other like ships in the night …" but "[t]he relationship between international law and the Community legal order is governed by the Community legal order itself, under the conditions set by the constitutional principles of the Community." See Court of Justice, *Kadi and Al Barakaat International Foundation v Council and Commission*, Opinion of AG Maduro, 16 January 2008, Joined Cases C-402/05 and C-415/05, ECLI:EU:C:2008:11 *(Kadi 2008),* paras 22 and 24.

EU and international law.[12] In the literature, it has been noted that in its more recent case-law the Court has taken a distinctly more cautious approach to international law—by way of contrast to its earlier openness thereto.[13] In this context, it has been further highlighted that autonomy—either expressly or implicitly—underpins this increasingly restrictive approach towards international law—as evidenced by the Court's reasoning.[14] As De Búrca notes: "The CJEU has undeniably become more concerned with the internal constitutional unity of the EU and the external autonomy of its legal order from the international legal order."[15] On the other hand, respect for international law, and thus by extension for the international rule of law, has become a core constitutional norm of the EU[16]—something acknowledged by the CJEU itself.[17] This reveals an intrinsic tension lying at the heart of the EU's identity as an international actor: while the Union claims that its relations with the 'outside world' are governed by EU law principles, its external mandate requires that these relations be conducted within the legal environment of international law.[18]

How does the Court navigate between autonomy and the international rule of law? While there is a cottage industry of legal commentary concerning the relationship between international and EU law,[19] the main focus of the debate (until recently at least) has been on questions of validity, direct effect and supremacy.[20] In other words, these concepts are the standard tools used to decide on the role of international norms within the EU[21]—and thus, by extension the standard framework within which the tension between the EU's autonomy and the need to maintain the international rule of law is explored.

---

[12]Odermatt 2018, p. 291, at pp. 297–308. De Witte 2010, p. 150.

[13]Eckes 2012, p. 353, at p. 368. Ziegler 2011, p. 681. De Búrca 2015, p. 1002.

[14]Apart from *Kadi* (Judgment, 3 September 2008, ECLI:EU:C:2008:461), there is a series of other cases where the Court has limited the invocability and enforceability of international law norms. Some textbooks examples include Court of Justice, *The Queen, on the application of International Association of Tanker Owners and Others v Secretary of State for Transport,* Judgment, 03 June 2008, Case C-308/06, ECLI:EU:C:2008:312 *(Intertanko)*; Court of Justice, *Air Transport Association of America and others v Secretary of State for Energy and Climate Change,* Judgment, 21 December 2011, Case C-366/10, ECLI: EU:C:20011:864 *(ATAA)*. For more case-law and analysis, see Ziegler 2011, pp. 683–684. De Búrca 2015, p. 1002, van Rossem 2013, p. 13. Odermatt 2018, p. 305.

[15]De Búrca 2015, p. 1003. According to Klabbers: "[T]he EU has a much less friendly disposition towards international law than is commonly assumed." Klabbers 2012, p. 111, at p. 112.

[16]Consolidated Version of the Treaty on the European Union, 2012, OJ C326 (TEU), Articles 3(5), 21(1).

[17]*ATAA*, above n. 14, para 101. Court of Justice, *Commission and Others v. Kadi,* Judgment, 18 July 2013, Joined Cases C-584/10 P, C-593/10 P and C-595/10 P, ECLI:EU:C:2013:518 *(Kadi 2013)*, para 103.

[18]Cremona 2018, p. 3, at p. 26.

[19]See for example Klabbers 2011, p. 95; Wouters et al. 2014, p. 249.

[20]Wessel 2012, p. 7, at pp. 18–22.

[21]Ibid., pp. 18–19.

So far, other ways of maintaining an equilibrium between autonomy and the international rule of law, such as through interpretation, remain largely under-researched.[22] A subtler way in which the CJEU has given effect to international law is through the application of the Vienna rules on treaty interpretation.[23] While the claim of autonomy means that the Court has generally refrained from applying the Vienna rules to the founding instruments of the Union,[24] the CJEU, as it will be seen below, has made extensive use of Article 31 VCLT[25] in interpreting agreements before it. Of particular importance here is the Court's recourse to Article 31(3)(c) VCLT which incorporates the principle of systemic integration, namely the process whereby international obligations are interpreted by reference to their normative environment.[26] The principle is grounded on the premise that, despite the fragmented and decentralised nature of international law-making, all new rules are made against the backdrop of existing rules of international law.[27] In this sense, the principle of systemic integration presupposes the formal unity of the international legal system.[28] While the principle does not point towards a particular interpretative outcome (as it will be discussed in more detail below), it does mandate the interpreter to engage with other relevant rules of international law—thereby minimizing the possibility of interpretation in clinical isolation from the *corpus juris* of international law.[29]

In the context of the discussion regarding the tension between the autonomy of the Union legal order and the need to maintain the international rule of law, it would be interesting to examine how the CJEU has applied the principle of systemic integration in the interpretation of agreements concluded between the EU and third parties. Does the Court's use of Article 31(3)(c) VCLT qualify the more restrictive turn noted in the literature towards international law and to what extent can it inform the debate about the EU's autonomy?

In this light, this contribution seeks to explore the potential and (possible) limitations of the principle of systemic integration as a technique for striking a balance between the EU's autonomy and the need to respect the international rule of law. The chapter begins by mapping out the operation and limitations of Article 31(3)(c) VCLT as a means of interpretation (Sect. 5.2). Against this backdrop, the chapter zooms in on the relevant CJEU jurisprudence in order to examine whether the Court's practice of interpreting EU law in the light of international law is actually conducive to the maintenance of the international rule of law (Sect. 5.3). The chapter argues that, in this line of case-law, the Court has proffered its own version of international law in the context of interpretation on the basis of Article 31(3)(c) VCLT, and that,

---

[22] A notable exception is Ziegler 2011.

[23] Odermatt 2015, pp. 130–134.

[24] Gardiner 2015, p. 136.

[25] Vienna Convention on the Law of Treaties, opened for signature 23 May 1969, 1155 UNTS 331 (entered into force 27 January 1980) (VCLT).

[26] ILC 2006, para 413.

[27] MacNair 1961, p. 466.

[28] D'Aspremont 2012, p. 141, at p. 148.

[29] Ziegler 2011, p. 690.

by doing so, it has, in its practice, reintroduced the element of autonomy through the backdoor. As long as the Court is unwilling to use international law rules as these are understood and applied in international judicial practice, systemic integration cannot be convincingly conceived as a mechanism for promoting the international rule of law within the EU legal order.

The chapter concludes by canvassing some general remarks on the repercussions of the Court's approach as this was described above (Sect. 5.4). The international rule of law has never been a mere political project for the EU but has been central to its identity. By displaying a cavalier attitude towards international law, the CJEU runs the risk of undermining the international rule of law as well as the very identity of the EU as a global actor.

5.2 The Principle of Systemic Integration (Article 31(3)(C) VCLT): Potential and Limitations

Although it would be beyond the scope of this chapter to provide a detailed account of Article 31(3)(c) VCLT, a few general points regarding its content, operation as well as its limitations need to be made from the outset in order to provide the necessary background to the discussion that will unfold in the following sections.[30] The provision states that 'any relevant rules of international law applicable in the relations between the parties' will be taken into account in the context of interpretation. The principle (whose customary law status is widely acknowledged)[31] recognises that international law constitutes a legal system in which a treaty co-exists with (rather than being clinically isolated from) other rules and norms.[32] In this sense, Article 31(3)(c) VCLT allows the interpreter to take into account the interpretive relevance of extraneous sources and thus, to consider—in their quest for attributing meaning to treaty terms—the broader normative environment.[33] In this respect, the ICJ has stressed that: "an instrument has to be interpreted and applied within the framework of the entire legal system prevailing at the time of the interpretation."[34]

At first sight, the provision lays down specific criteria triggering its application; Article 31(3)(c) VCLT refers to "relevant" "rules of international law" which must

[30]For an overview of the principle of systemic integration, see generally Merkouris 2015; Gardiner 2015, pp. 289–334. Klabbers 2007, p. 141. Villiger 2009, pp. 432–434. McLachlan 2005, p. 279.

[31]ICJ, *Guinea-Bissau v Senegal,* Arbitral Award, 31 July 1989, ICJ Rep 1991, p. 53, at para 48. ICJ, *Certain Questions of Mutual Assistance in Criminal Matters (Djibouti v France)*, Judgment (Merits), 4 June 2008, [2008] ICJ Rep 2008, p. 177, at para 112.

[32]Wouters et al. 2019, p. 103. D'Aspremont 2012, p. 148.

[33]ICJ, *Case concerning Oil Platforms (Iran v U.S.A)*, Separate Opinion of Judge Kooijmans to the Judgment (Merits), 6 November 2003, [2003] ICJ Rep 2003, p. 246, at para 23. Tzevelekos 2010, at p. 631. Orakhelashvili 2008, pp. 366–367.

[34]ICJ, *Legal Consequences for States of the Continued Presence of South Africa in Namibia (South West Africa) notwithstanding Security Council Resolution 276 (1970)*, Advisory Opinion, 21 June 1971, [1971] ICJ Rep 1971, p. 16 *(Namibia Advisory Opinion),* para 53.

be "applicable in the relations between the parties". However, the application of these criteria in practice has not been entirely consistent or uncontroversial.[35] For present purposes, it suffices to note here that 'relevant' rules of international law are those which may provide interpretative guidance in establishing the meaning of a treaty provision.[36] In other words, and at a minimum, an extraneous rule is considered relevant when it relates to the same subject matter as the treaty term under interpretation.[37] When it comes to customary international law rules, in practice, international judicial bodies typically have recourse thereto either when a treaty term is unclear or open-textured and reference to such a rule will aid in determining the meaning of the term;[38] or, when a treaty term has a recognized meaning in customary law to which the parties can thus be safely assumed to have intended to refer.[39]

Apart from constituting the background against which a treaty's provisions are to be interpreted, Article 31(3)(c) VCLT also gives rise to two concrete interpretative presumptions which are reflected in practice;[40] first that, in entering into treaty obligations, the parties did not intend to act inconsistently with customary rules or previous treaty obligations (negative presumption);[41] and secondly, that the parties intended to resort to general principles of international law for all issues that the treaty does not regulate expressly or in a different manner (positive presumption).[42]

Turning to the normative weight to be ascribed to extraneous rules in the context of treaty interpretation, Article 31(3)(c) VCLT requires the interpreter simply to "take into account" such rules—thereby suggesting a weak form of interaction.[43] In other words, the provision serves as an interpretation tool to assist in the clarification of the meaning of one term by reference to another and does not require the interpreter

---

[35]D'Aspremont 2012, p. 151. Orellana Zabalza 2012, pp. 269–274.

[36]Gardiner 2015, p. 305. Orakhelashvili 2003, p. 537.

[37]ICJ, *Maritime Delimitation in the Indian Ocean (Somalia v Kenya)*, Judgment (Preliminary Objections), 2 February 2017, [2017] ICJ Rep 2017, p. 3, at para 89; ICJ, *Case concerning Oil Platforms*, Separate Opinion of Judge Higgins, above n. 33, p. 225, at para 46; WTO Appellate Body, *United States—Definitive Antidumping and Countervailing Duties on Certain Products from China*, Report, 11 March 2011, DSR 2011:V, 2869, WT/DS379/AB/R, para 308. WTO Appellate Body, *European Communities and Certain Member States—Measures Affecting Trade in Large Civil Aircraft*, Report, 18 May 2011, DSR 2011:II, 685, WT/DS316/AB/R, para 846. Dörr 2012, p. 559, at p. 610.

[38]*Case concerning Oil Platforms*, above n. 33, p. 161, paras 40–41. WTO Appellate Body, *United States—Import Prohibition of Certain Shrimp and Shrimp Products*, Report, 12 October 1998, DSR 1998:VII, 2755, WT/DS58/AB/R, para 158. Iran—United States Claims Tribunal, *Amoco International Finance Corporation v Iran*, Award No. 310-56-3, 14 July 1987, 15, IRAN—US CTR 189, para 112. Iran—United States Claims Tribunal, *Nasser Esphahanian v Bank Tejarat*, Award No. 31-157-2, 29 March 1983, 2 IRAN—US CTR 157, pp. 160–161. ILC 2006, para 467. McLachlan 2005, p. 312.

[39]NAFTA Arbitral Tribunal, *Pope and Talbot Inc. v Canada*, 31 May 2002, 31 ILM 1347, para 46. ILC Report 2006 on Fragmentation, ibid. McLachlan 2005, ibid.

[40]Jennings and Watts 1992, p. 1275. ILC 2006, ibid., para 465. McLachlan 2005, ibid., p. 311.

[41]ICJ, *Right of Passage over Indian Territory (Portugal v India)*, Judgment (Merits), 26 November 1957, [1957] ICJ Rep 1957, p. 125, at p. 142.

[42]*Georges Pinson* Case, Award, 13 April 1928, 5 RIAA 327 (1952), para 50(4).

[43]Ziegler 2011, p. 690.

to give effect substantively to the extraneous rule.[44] As Orakhelashvili notes: "The purpose of interpreting by reference to "relevant rules" is, normally, not to defer the provisions being interpreted to the scope and effect of those "relevant rules", but to clarify the content of the former by referring to the latter."[45]

The ILC's report on fragmentation posits that the provision plays a more fundamental role in treaty interpretation. According to the Commission, Article 31(3)(c) VCLT goes further than merely restating "the applicability of general international law in the operation of treaties" giving rise to a duty of "integration into the process of legal reasoning … of a sense of coherence and meaningfulness".[46] The elevation of Article 31(3)(c) VCLT to a stand-alone interpretative principle requiring the interpreter to read a treaty by reference to relevant rules of international law *with the particular objective* of integrating different rights and obligations into a coherent whole remains questionable.[47] It suffices to note here that such a far-reaching reading of Article 31(3)(c) VCLT, namely as a principle which points to a *particular interpretative result* (that of achieving coherence and meaningfulness), is not readily reconcilable with the language and purpose of Article 31 VCLT—which conceptually relates to *interpretative methods and means.*[48] In this respect, it has been noted that: "From the perspective of the law of interpretation, reference to relevant rules of international law will in some cases produce the result of integration while in some cases it will not … Although the integration of extraneous rules into a treaty can be an interpretative outcome in some cases, it is certainly not a principle, still less a principle that applies across the board."[49]

Against this background, the section continues by highlighting certain caveats relating to the application of Article 31(3)(c) VCLT. First, it should be borne in mind that the principle of systemic integration is not a stand-alone principle enjoying priority over the other means of interpretation enshrined in Article 31; it is merely one of the several means to ascertain the common intention of the parties to a treaty

[44] Ibid. Orakhelashvili 2008, p. 366. Tzevelekos 2010, p. 635. See also *Certain Questions of Mutual Assistance in Criminal Matters,* above n. 31, paras 113–114: "The provisions of the 1977 Treaty of Friendship and Co-Operation are 'relevant rules' within the meaning of Article 31, para (3)(c), of the Vienna Convention … The Court thus accepts that the Treaty of Friendship and Co-operation of 1977 does have a certain bearing on the interpretation and application of the Convention on Mutual Assistance in Criminal Matters of 1986. *But this is as far as the relationship between the two instruments can be explained in legal terms.*" (Emphasis added). WTO Appellate Body, *European Communities—Measures Affecting the approval and Marketing of Biotech Products*, Report, WT/DS291/R, WT/DS292/R, WT/DS293/R, 29 September 2006, 285, para 7.69: "It is true that the obligation is to "take account" of such rules and thus no particular outcome is prescribed." *European Communities and Certain Member States—Measures Affecting Trade in Large Civil Aircraft,* above n. 37, para 841. *Amoco International Finance Corporation v Iran*, above n. 38, para 112.

[45] Orakhelashvili 2003, p. 537.

[46] ILC 2006, paras 415, 419.

[47] Rachovitsa 2017, p. 557. Tzevelekos 2010, pp. 631–636. Orakhelashvili 2008, p. 367.

[48] Orakhelashvili 2008, ibid.

[49] Ibid.

reflected in the Article.[50] Interpretation, under the Vienna Convention, is envisaged as a 'holistic process'[51] where the interpretative outcome results from the combined application of *all* elements contained in Article 31 VCLT.[52] Secondly, in using Article 31(3)(c) VCLT as part of the interpretative process, the interpreter should take great care not to conflate interpretation by reference to relevant rules of international law with application of those rules directly to the facts of the case.[53] Although closely intertwined, these two normative processes are distinct.[54] Interpretation is the process of determining "the meaning of a text", whereas application is "the process of determining the consequences which, according to the text, should follow in a given situation".[55] Thus, interpretation, at least in the relatively strict sense referred to in the VCLT, is "a matter of definition",[56] namely a matter of giving meaning to the terms of a treaty.[57] In international judicial practice, interpretation precedes the application of a treaty text.[58] As Schwarzenberger put it: "any application of a treaty, including its execution, presupposes ... a preceding conscious or subconscious interpretation of the treaty."[59] The distinction between the normative processes of interpretation and application demonstrates the inherent limitations of Article 31(3)(c) VCLT. It is one thing to seek interpretative guidance from the general principles of international law in order to clarify the meaning of a treaty term, and quite another to apply these principles independently of interpretation.[60] As Gardiner notes:

> Located in its immediate context of treaty interpretation, article 31(3)(c) implicitly invites the interpreter to draw a distinction between using rules of international law as part of the apparatus of treaty interpretation and applying the rules of international law directly to the

---

[50] *United States—Definitive Antidumping and Countervailing Duties on Certain Products from China*, above n. 37, para 312.

[51] Abi-Saab 2006, p. 453, at p. 459.

[52] ILC, Draft Articles on the Law of Treaties with commentaries, Yearbook of the International Law Commission, 1966, vol. II, p. 219, para 8. ICSID, *Aguas del Tunari v Bolivia*, Award, 21 October 2005, Case No ARB/02/03, para 91. WTO Appellate Body, *European Communities—Customs Classification of Frozen Boneless Chicken Cuts*, Report, 27 September 2005, WT/DS286/AB/R, WT/DS269/AB/R, DSR:XIX, 9157, para 177. Torres Bernárdez 1998, p. 721, at p. 726.

[53] Separate Opinion of Judge Higgins in *Case concerning Oil Platforms*, above n. 37, para 49. Separate Opinion of Judge Kooijmans in *Case concerning Oil Platforms*, above n. 33, paras 42–43.

[54] Separate Opinion of Judge Higgins, ibid. See also generally Gourgourinis 2011.

[55] Harvard Law School 1935, pp. 938–939. See also PCIJ, *Case concerning the Factory at Chorzow (Germany v Poland)*, Dissenting Opinion of Judge Ehrlich to the Decision on Jurisdiction, 26 July 1927, [1927] 26 PCIJ Rep 1927, Series A-No 9, p. 35, at p. 39. Haraszti 1973, p. 18.

[56] ICJ, *Fisheries Jurisdiction Case (Spain v Canada)*, Judgment (Jurisdiction), 4 December 1998, [1998] ICJ Rep 1998, p. 432, para 68.

[57] Pauwelyn 2003, p. 245.

[58] ICJ, *Applicability of the Obligation to Arbitrate under Section 21 of the United Nations Headquarter Agreement of 26 June 1947*, Separate Opinion of Judge Shahabuddeen, Advisory Opinion, 26 April 1988, [1988] ICJ Rep 1988, p. 57, p. 59.

[59] Schwarzenberger 1969, p. 212.

[60] *European Communities—Customs Classification of Frozen Boneless Chicken Cuts*, above n. 52, para 177. Gourgourinis 2011, p. 51.

> facts in the context of which the treaty is being considered. The former is within the scope of the Vienna rules, the latter not.[61]

Finally, turning to the negative presumption that Article 31(3)(c) VCLT gives rise to (namely that in entering treaty obligations the parties did not intend to act inconsistently with general international law), it needs to be stressed that this is merely a *presumption*, namely the starting point in attributing meaning to relevant treaty terms and thus, the normative weight attached thereto needs not be exaggerated. As Jenks writes: "the presumption against conflict is not, however, of an overriding character. It is one of the elements to be taken into account in determining the meaning of a treaty provision, but will not avail against clear language or clear evidence of intention."[62] By according undue weight to Article 31(3)(c) VCLT and to the presumption of compliance with international law the interpreter runs the risk of replacing the enquiry into the common intention of the parties with an enquiry into what the parties *should have intended* according to general international law. As Thirlway acutely observes: "There must be a danger … of confusing what, on the basis of available evidence, may be found to have been the actual intention of the parties concerned, and what is judged, with the benefit of hindsight, to be what *ought* to have been their intention."[63]

Against this backdrop the next section explores how the CJEU has used Article 31(3)(c) VCLT in its case-law.

5.3 The Relevant Jurisprudence of the CJEU: From Indifference to (an Ambivalent) Engagement?

The CJEU's acceptance of the applicability of the principle of systemic integration in the context of interpretation of agreements concluded between the EU and third parties has been rather slow and incremental. As it will be shown below, the Court in its earlier case-law either refrained from engaging with Article 31(3)(c) VCLT altogether (*Anastasiou*[64]) or it did so without expressly referring thereto (*Brita*[65]). It was only in the context of the Western Sahara litigation (*Front Polisario,*[66] *Western*

[61] Gardiner 2015, p. 320.

[62] Jenks 1953, p. 403.

[63] Thirlway 1989, pp. 136–137. (Emphasis added).

[64] Court of Justice, *The Queen v Minister of Agriculture, Fisheries and Food, ex parte Anastasiou,* Judgment, 05 July 1994, Case C-432/92, ECLI:EU:C:1994:277 *(Anastasiou).*

[65] Court of Justice, *Firma Brita GmbH v Hauptzollamt Hamburg-Hafen,* Judgment, 25 February 2010, Case C-386/08, ECLI:EU:C: 2010:91 *(Brita).*

[66] Court of Justice, *Council of the European Union v Front populaire pour la libération de la saguia-el-hamra et du rio de oro,* Judgment, 21 December 2016, Case C-104/16 P ECLI:EU:C:2016:973 *(Front Polisario 2016).*

Sahara Campaign UK[67]) that the Court fully embraced the principle of systemic integration and expressly acknowledged the interpretative relevance of general international law. While at first blush this may seem as a positive development marking a retreat from its previous restrictive approach towards international law, in reality, the picture is much more complex. As it will be discussed in detail below, the Court has, in the context of the Western Sahara litigation, applied the principle of systemic integration in ways that few international lawyers would recognise. By doing so, the Court has in essence re-introduced the element of autonomy through the backdoor. While seemingly relying on relevant rules of international law, the Court has, upon closer inspection, misused international law rules in order to avoid pronouncing on the legal consequences of the EU's approach towards Western Sahara.

5.3.1 *The* Anastasiou *Judgment*

The first case which involved an (at least indirect) invocation of Article 31(3)(c) VCLT was *Anastasiou.* The case arose from an action brought by a number of Greek Cypriot producers before the UK High Court of Justice for judicial review of the practice of UK authorities of accepting origin certificates (pursuant to the 1977 Protocol regarding products originating from Cyprus)[68] and phytosanitary certificates (pursuant to Directive 77/93/EEC on protective measures against the introduction into the Community of organisms harmful to plants or plant products)[69] issued by the authorities of the self-proclaimed Turkish Republic of Northern Cyprus ('TRNC').[70] The Court stated that the non-recognition of the TRNC either by the EU, or by its Member States precluded the possibility of mutual reliance and co-operation between the entity's authorities and those of the Member States according to the 1977 Protocol.[71] On this basis, it was held that "the acceptance of movement certificates not issued by the Republic of Cyprus would constitute … a denial of the very object and purpose of the system established by the 1977 Protocol."[72]

During the proceedings the Commission put forward an argument that could be viewed as an invocation of a relevant rule of law applicable in the relations between

[67] Court of Justice, *Western Sahara Campaign UK v Commissioners for Her Majesty's Revenue and Customs, Secretary of State for Environment, Food and Rural Affairs*, Judgment, 27 February 2018, Case C-266/16, ECLI:EU:C:2018:118 (*Western Sahara Campaign UK).*

[68] Council Regulation 290/77 of 20 December 1977 on the conclusion of the Additional Protocol to the Agreement establishing an Association between the European Economic Community and the Republic of Cyprus, OJ L339/1, 28 December 1977.

[69] Council Directive 77/93/EEC of 21 December 1976 on protective measures against the introduction into the Community of organisms harmful to plants or plant products, OJ L26/20.

[70] Talmon 2001, pp. 734–737.

[71] *Anastasiou*, above n. 64, paras 39–40.

[72] Ibid., para 41.

the parties. More particularly, the Commission invoked the so-called 'Namibia exception'—enunciated by the ICJ in its *Namibia* Advisory Opinion.[73] According to the ICJ, despite the existence of an unlawful situation which should not enjoy recognition at the international level, minor administrative acts undertaken by the non-recognised regime, such as "the registration of births, deaths and marriages" and acts of benefit to the local population remain valid[74] as they are "untainted by the illegality of the administration".[75] On this basis, the Commission claimed that the non-recognition of the TRNC should not be to the detriment of the local population and that this rule should have a bearing upon the interpretation of the EC—Cyprus Association Agreement and the relevant protocols.[76] However, both the Advocate General[77] and the Court[78] rejected this proposition. Significantly, for present purposes, neither the Advocate General, nor the Court went on to establish whether the 'Namibia exception' constitutes an extraneous rule that may have some interpretative relevance in the case at hand. On the contrary, the argument was dismissed solely on the grounds that the special situation of Namibia was not comparable to that of Cyprus and "[c]onsequently, no interpretation can be based on an analogy between them."[79] The fact that the Court viewed this as an argument by analogy rather than as an invocation of the interpretive relevance of Article 31(3)(c) VCLT evidences that, at that stage at least, the Court was disinclined to view general international law as the background against which a treaty's provisions are to be interpreted.

In fact, in *Anastasiou*, the Court's reasoning was not based on international law at all. On the contrary, the Court framed its analysis in terms of the need to maintain the uniform application of Community rules in its trade relations.[80] The ECJ underscored that a strict interpretation of the 1977 Protocol was required "in order to ensure uniform application of the [EU-Cyprus] Association Agreement in all the Member States".[81] According to Koutrakos, this approach shows that the Court sought to ensure the uniformity and effectiveness of EU law "whilst intervening as little as possible in an issue which is highly charged in in political terms".[82]

---

[73] *Namibia Advisory Opinion,* above n. 34, p. 16.

[74] Ibid., para 125.

[75] Crawford 2006, p. 167.

[76] *Anastasiou,* above n. 64, para 33.

[77] Court of Justice, *The Queen v Minister of Agriculture, Fisheries and Food, ex parte Anastasiou,* Opinion of Advocate General Gulmann, 20 April 1994, Case C-432/92, ECLI:EU:C:1994:159, paras 57–59.

[78] *Anastasiou,* above n. 64, para 49.

[79] Ibid.

[80] Emiliou 1995, p. 209.

[81] *Anastasiou,* above n. 64, para 54.

[82] Koutrakos 2003, at p. 492. Skoutaris 2011, p. 130.

5.3.2 *The* Brita *Judgment*

In *Brita*, the Court relied (albeit not expressly) on Article 31(3)(c) VCLT in order to make use of the principle of *pacta tertiis*,[83] according to which treaties do not create obligations or confer rights upon third States without their consent—a principle of customary international law[84] codified in Article 34 VCLT. In *Brita*, the ECJ was confronted with the question of the territorial scope of the EU-Israel Association Agreement.[85] The case concerned the import to Germany of goods from an Israeli company located in the West Bank.[86] The German authorities withdrew the benefit of preferential treatment on the ground that it could not be conclusively established that the imported goods fell within the scope of the EU-Israel Association Agreement.[87] Brita, the company that imports the products in question, brought the issue before the German courts, which then submitted a preliminary question to the ECJ.[88]

The Court employed the *pacta tertiis* principle in order to interpret Article 83 of the EU—Israel Association which established the territorial scope of the agreement. It ruled that the EU-PLO Association Agreement[89] implicitly restricted the territorial scope of the EU-Israel Association Agreement.[90] According to the Court, construing the territorial clause of the EU-Israel Agreement:

> as meaning that Israeli customs authorities enjoy competence in respect of products originating from the West Bank would be tantamount to imposing on the Palestinian customs authorities an obligation to refrain from exercising the competence conferred upon them by virtue of the … provisions of the EC-PLO Protocol. Such an interpretation, the effect of which would be to create an obligation for a third party without its consent, would thus be contrary to the principle of general international law, '*pacta tertiis nec nocent nec prosunt*'.[91]

Nevertheless, the Court's first foray into interpretation by reference to relevant rules of international law was not unproblematic. Here, the Court in essence opposed to Israel an agreement to which it is not a party (EU-PLO Association Agreement)—to the extent that it is this agreement that needed to be taken into account in order to reasonably interpret Article 83 of the EU—Israel Association Agreement in the

---

[83]Wouters et al. 2019, p. 103.

[84]See with reference to practice Proells 2012, p. 655, at p. 657.

[85]Euro-Mediterranean Agreement establishing an association between the European Communities and their Member States, of the one part, and the State of Israel, of the other part, opened for signature 20 November 1995, OJ L147/3 (entered into force 01 June 2000) (EU-Israel AA).

[86]*Brita*, above n. 65, para 30.

[87]Ibid., para 33.

[88]Ibid., paras 35–36.

[89]Euro-Mediterranean Interim Association Agreement on trade and cooperation between the European Community, of the one part, and the Palestine Liberation Organization (PLO) for the benefit of the Palestinian Authority of the West Bank and the Gaza Strip, of the other part, opened for signature 24 February 1997, OJ L187/3 (entered into force 01 July 1997) (EU-PLO AA).

[90]*Brita*, above n. 65, paras 50–53.

[91]Ibid., para 52.

light of the *pacta tertiis* principle.[92] In other words, by means of the principle of systemic integration, the Court introduced into the context of interpretation of the territorial scope of EU—Israel Association Agreement rules not applicable between the parties, (i.e. the territorial scope of the EU—PLO Association Agreement). The Court's use of Article 31(3)(c) VCLT in this case has been criticised in the literature.[93] As Cannizzaro notes:

> In spite of its persuasive force, this approach can hardly have a legal basis in the international principles of treaty interpretation, which limit the relevance of other rules to those applicable between the parties. One fails to see how the agreement between the EC and the Palestinian authority can be taken into account in the interpretation of another unrelated agreement between the EC and Israel.[94]

Secondly, (and this is a point which will be explored in more detail below),[95] the ECJ did not examine the applicability of the *pacta tertiis* vis-a-vis non-State entities (PLO) before bringing it into the equation. More particularly, the Court here merely assumed that the principle to the effect that a treaty does not create obligations for *third States* is equally applicable to *third parties* in general (PLO). Thus, the Court extended the application of Article 34 VCLT (which clearly refers to third States and not to third parties in general) to non-State actors—without, however, actually furnishing proof thereof. Under customary international law, however, it is highly questionable that the principle applies to third parties other than States.[96] In this light, more by way of evidence was needed in favour of the proposition that the rule in question also extends to entities that are not subjects of international law.

Finally, it is not readily apparent to an international lawyer why the *pacta tertiis* rule would be the most 'relevant' rule in the context of interpreting the concept of "territory of the State of Israel".[97] In this context, one would have expected the Court to utilise international law in order to answer questions of borders, sovereignty—and thus to directly confront the issue of occupation of Palestinian territory.[98] Despite an express invitation by the Advocate General to analyse the legal status of Israel's presence in the West Bank for the purpose of establishing the territorial scope of the Association Agreement,[99] the Court decided the matter solely with reference to the "politically-detached" principle of *pacta tertiis*.[100] In this light, it is difficult to escape the conclusion that, by not relying more heavily on international law, the

---

[92] Kuijper 2010, p. 249.

[93] Kuijper 2010, ibid., Aust et al. 2014, p. 103; Cannizzaro 2011, p. 425, p. 432.

[94] Ibid., Cannizzaro 2011.

[95] See below p. 19.

[96] Proells 2012, pp. 661–663. See also Milanovic 2011, p. 39.

[97] Harpaz and Rubinson 2010, p. 562.

[98] Ibid.

[99] Court of Justice, *Firma Brita GmbH v Hauptzollamt Hamburg-Hafen*, Opinion of Advocate General Bot, 29 October 2009, Case C-386/08, ECLI:EU:C:2009:674, paras 109–112.

[100] Harpaz and Rubinson 2010, p. 566.

Court sought to achieve conformity with EU law while avoiding being drawn into contentious political issues.[101]

5.3.3 The **Front Polisario** *Judgment*

Against this backdrop, the remainder of this section zooms in on the Western Sahara litigation before the CJEU—a line of case-law that is of particular significance since the Court made extensive use of Article 31(3)(c) VCLT in order to interpret the territorial scope of the relevant EU-Morocco agreements. A few general remarks regarding the Morocco—Western Sahara dispute need to be made at this juncture. Western Sahara is a non-self-governing territory that has been under Moroccan occupation since Morocco invaded it in 1975.[102] Despite an ICJ Advisory Opinion[103] and numerous UN Security Council and General Assembly resolutions[104] affirming the Sahrawi peoples' right to self-determination, a political solution regarding the future of Western Sahara has not yet been reached and the territory remains under Moroccan control.

In *Front Polisario*, the ECJ was faced with the question of interpretation of the territorial scope of the 1996 EU-Morocco Association Agreement[105] as well as of the 2010 EU-Morocco Agreement on agricultural, processed agricultural and fisheries products ('Liberalization Agreement').[106] The Grand Chamber overturned the

[101] Ibid.

[102] The UN General Assembly has twice characterized the presence of Morocco in Western Sahara as 'occupation'; see UNGA 1979, para 5. UNGA 1980, para 3. See also African Union 2015, para 21. High Court of South Africa—Eastern Cape Local Division Port Elizabeth, *Saharawi Arab Democratic Republic and Another v Owner and Charterers of the MV 'Cherry Blossom' and Others*, Judgment, 15 June 2017, [2017] ZAECPEH 31, para 38. Court of Justice, *Western Sahara Campaign UK v Commissioners for Her Majesty's Revenue and Customs Secretary of State for Environment, Food and Rural Affairs*, Opinion of AG Wathelet, 10 January 2018, Case C-266/16, ECLI:EU:C:2018:1, para 246.

[103] ICJ, *Western Sahara,* Advisory Opinion, 16 October 1975, [1975] ICJ Rep 1975, p. 12, para 162.

[104] See UNGA 1979, para 1; UNGA 1980, para 1. See also UNSC 2011, para 6. UNSC 2016, para 9.

[105] Euro-Mediterranean Agreement establishing an association between the European Communities and their Member States, of the one part, and the Kingdom of Morocco, of the other part, opened for signature 26 February 1996, OJ L70/2 (entered into force 01 March 2000) (Hereinafter referred to as the 'Association Agreement').

[106] Agreement in the form of an Exchange of Letters between the European Community and the Kingdom of Morocco concerning reciprocal liberalisation measures on agricultural products, processed agricultural products, fish and fishery products, the replacement of Protocols 1, 2 and 3 of and their Annexes and amendments to the Euro-Mediterranean Agreement establishing an association between the European Communities and their Member States, of the one part, and the Kingdom of Morocco, of the other part, opened for signature 13 December 2010, OJ L241 (entered into force 01 September 2013) (Hereinafter referred to as the 'Liberalisation Agreement').

General Court's judgment[107] rendered a year earlier. The Grand Chamber decided that Front Polisario, the main Sahrawi liberation movement, did not have legal standing to bring an action for annulment against the Council decision[108] adopting the Liberalization Agreement since, in its view, neither the Liberalization Agreement nor the Association Agreement (on which the former is based) legally extend to the territory of Western Sahara.[109] The ECJ ruled that the General Court erred in interpreting the territorial scope of the Liberalization Agreement as extending to Western Sahara to the extent that it failed to take into account Article 31(3)(c) VCLT.[110] The Court pointed out three relevant rules of applicable international law that the General Court failed to take into account: the right to self-determination; Article 29 VCLT relating to the territorial scope of international agreements; and the principle of the relative effect of treaties (the principle of *pacta tertiis*).[111]

According to the Court, the right to self-determination is an *erga omnes* right and one of the essential principles of international law, as evidenced by the relevant case-law of the ICJ,[112] applicable to all non-self-governing territories and to all peoples who have not yet achieved independence.[113] As a non-self-governing-territory whose peoples have an internationally recognized right to self-determination, Western Sahara has a legal status separate and distinct from that of Morocco and this legal status precludes the legal application of Article 94 of the Association Agreement to the territory.[114]

Next, the Court turned to the 'territorial scope' rule enshrined in Article 29 VCLT.[115] In the Court's view, the wording of the article implies that an international agreement is applicable only within the geographical space within which a State exercises its *full* sovereign powers and does not extend to other territories under its jurisdiction or international responsibility—unless the treaty expressly provides for such an extension.[116] This reading of Article 29 VCLT precluded Western Sahara,

---

[107] General Court, *Front Polisario v. Council of the European Union,* Judgment, 10 December 2015, Case T-512/12, ECLI:EU:T:2015:293 *(Front Polisario 2015).* For an analysis, see Kassoti 2017a.

[108] Council Decision of 8 March 2012 on the conclusion of an Agreement in the form of an Exchange of Letters between the European Union and the Kingdom of Morocco concerning reciprocal liberalisation measures on agricultural products, processed agricultural products, fish and fishery products, the replacement of Protocols 1, 2 and 3 and their Annexes and amendments to the Euro-Mediterranean Agreement establishing an association between the European Communities and their Member States, of the one part, and the Kingdom of Morocco, of the other part, OJ L241/2, 08 March 2012.

[109] *Front Polisario 2016*, above n. 66, paras 92, 123, 132, 133.

[110] *Front Polisario 2016,* above n. 66, para 86.

[111] Ibid., para 87.

[112] Ibid., para 88. The ECJ cited the ICJ's Advisory Opinion on *Western Sahara* and the *East Timor* case. *Western Sahara,* above n. 103, paras 54–56; ICJ, *Case concerning East Timor (Portugal v Australia),* Judgment (Jurisdiction), 30 June 1995, [1995] ICJ Rep 1995, p. 90, para 29.

[113] Ibid., para 88.

[114] Ibid., paras 89–92.

[115] Ibid., paras 94–99.

[116] Ibid., paras 94–96.

as a non-self-governing territory, from being regarded as falling under Article 94 of the Association Agreement.[117]

In its analysis of the relevant rules of international law applicable between EU and Morocco, the Court finally relied on the principle of the relative effect of treaties (*pacta tertiis* principle) enshrined in Article 34 VCLT.[118] It was asserted that Western Sahara's status as a non-self-governing territory means that it constitutes a third party (*tertius*) in relation to the EU and Morocco.[119] Thus, the Association Agreement could not, in the Court's view, be interpreted as being applicable to the territory of Western Sahara to the extent that its people had not expressly consented thereto.[120]

Finally, the Court also disagreed with the General Court's assessment of the role of 'subsequent practice' in interpreting the Liberalization Agreement pursuant to Article 31(3)(b) VCLT.[121] The ECJ held that the General Court failed to establish the requisite elements of Article 31(3)(b) VCLT. In the Court's opinion, the instances of de facto application of the Association and Liberalization Agreements to Western Sahara did not warrant the conclusion that the EU and Morocco had actually *agreed* to extend the application of those treaties to the territory in question.[122] In the light of the finding that the Liberalization Agreement is not legally applicable to the territory of Western Sahara, the ECJ held that Front Polisario did not have legal standing to bring an action of annulment against the Council Decision approving the Liberalization Agreement and accordingly, it dismissed its action as inadmissible.[123]

The judgment has been criticised in the literature mainly because of the ECJ's selective and artificial reliance on international law.[124] More particularly, as Odermatt observes, the judgment is an example of the Court "instrumentalizing" international law.[125] Though purportedly relying on international law, upon closer scrutiny, the Court's reasoning and findings are far from convincing from the vantage point of the international legal order since the ECJ applied principles of international law without taking into consideration how these principles are actually understood in international law and in international judicial practice.

The Court's excessive reliance on Article 31(3)(c) VCLT and the fact that it paid little or no attention to other elements contained therein go against the 'holistic

[117] Ibid., para 97.

[118] Ibid., paras 100–107.

[119] Ibid., paras 104–106.

[120] Ibid., paras 106–107.

[121] Ibid., paras 117–125. According to the text of Article 31(3)(b) VCLT, account must be taken, together with the context, of "any subsequent practice in the application of the treaty which establishes the agreement of the parties regarding its interpretation".

[122] Ibid., paras 121–122.

[123] Ibid., paras 131–134.

[124] Kassoti 2017b, p. 41. Odermatt 2017, pp. 737–738. Van der Loo 2019, p. 1, 17. Hilpold 2017, p. 908.

[125] Odermatt 2017, p. 737.

approach' to interpretation envisaged by the ILC and actually employed in international judicial practice.[126] Rather than starting with the treaty terms and applying the whole process of the Vienna Convention systematically, the ECJ "turned treaty interpretation on its head" and relied almost exclusively on Article 31(3)(c) VCLT. This, however,[127] does not comport with the Vienna rules.

Furthermore, it is questionable to what extent the rules invoked and relied upon by the Court constitute in reality "relevant rules of international law applicable in the relations between the parties" within the meaning of Article 31(3)(c) VCLT. As seen above, in order for a rule to be considered 'relevant' within the meaning of Article 31(3)(c) VCLT, it needs to relate to same subject matter as the treaty term under interpretation. In *Front Polisario*, it is questionable that the rules invoked relate to the same subject matter as the territorial clause of the agreements. The Court's reliance on the principle of self-determination of the peoples of Western Sahara, as a non-self-governing territory, for the purpose of interpreting the territorial scope of the EU-Morocco Association Agreement is particularly problematic. The Court found that the right of peoples to self-determination is a right *erga omnes* and as such it is applicable to the relations between the EU and Morocco.[128] It then relied on the Friendly Relations Declaration,[129] according to which a non-self-governing territory has "under the [UN] Charter, a status separate and distinct from the State administering it", in order to conclude that the Association Agreement cannot be interpreted in such a way as to include Western Sahara within its territorial scope.[130] The Court here drew conclusions regarding the territorial status of Western Sahara vis-à-vis Morocco without inquiring into the exact legal consequences that might flow from a non-self-governing-territory possessing "separate and distinct status".[131] The Friendly Relation's Declaration reference to the "separate and distinct" status of non-self-governing territories is generally understood to mean that these territories enjoy a measure of international legal personality, but not necessarily a measure of territorial sovereignty[132]—as the ECJ seems to imply here. Indeed, there is evidence to suggest that, in the context of non-self-governing territories, sovereignty and territorial title remain with the administering State.[133]

Moreover, it is difficult to see how the extract from the Friendly Relations Declaration is relevant for the purpose of interpreting what constitutes the "territory of the Kingdom of Morocco"; the extract clearly refers to, and defines, the legal status of non-self-governing territories vis-à-vis their *administering* States. However, Morocco does not administer Western Sahara under Article 73 of the UN Charter

---

[126] See above notes 51 and 52.

[127] Kassoti 2017b, p. 31. Odermatt 2017, p. 735.

[128] *Front Polisario 2016*, above n. 66, paras 88–89.

[129] UNGA 1970.

[130] *Front Polisario 2016*, above n. 66, para 92.

[131] Kassoti 2017b, pp. 32–34. Odermatt 2017, p. 735.

[132] Crawford 2006, pp. 618–619. Schwed 1982, p. 452.

[133] Crawford 2006, pp. 613–615. Gowlland-Debbas 1990, p. 157.

but militarily occupies it, something that renders the rule 'not relevant' in the present context.

Similarly, the proposition that Article 29 VCLT supports the finding of legal inapplicability of the agreements at hand to the territory of Western Sahara is open to doubt.[134] Here the Court relied on Article 29 VCLT in order to argue that whenever an international agreement is intended to produce extraterritorial effect, the wording of its 'territorial scope' clause is formulated in such a way as to expressly provide for this effect.[135] Short of a provision expressly allowing the extraterritorial application of the Association Agreement to Western Sahara, it was concluded that its scope could not be understood as including that territory.[136] The Court's argument to the effect that Article 29 VCLT creates a presumption against extraterritoriality does not comport with the drafting history of the Article. The ILC, in its 1966 commentary, made it abundantly clear that the matter of extraterritorial application of treaties was too complicated and it decided to leave it aside.[137] Furthermore, as Odermatt stresses, according to the ILC, Article 29 VCLT was designed to apply in cases where a treaty does not define its territorial application—something that is not the case in relation to the agreement at hand.[138] In this light, the Court's conclusion that Article 29 VCLT corroborates the view that the territorial scope of the Association Agreement does not extend to Western Sahara seems unsubstantiated.

As was the case with *Brita* (Sect. 5.3.2), the ECJ's interpretation and application of the principle of *pacta tertiis* has also been criticised in the literature to the extent that the applicability of this principle to international legal persons other than States remains unclear.[139] The principle's conceptual roots in the notions of State sovereignty and sovereign equality arguably preclude its application to non-State actors.[140] In the light of the State-centric nature of the principle, the Court's unqualified assertion that it applies to relations between States and non-State actors falls short of convincing.

The overwhelming majority of commentators have found the Court's reluctance to engage extensively with the parties' 'subsequent practice in the application of the treaty' under Article 31(3)(b) VCLT for the purpose of interpreting the territorial scope of the Association and Liberalization Agreement particularly problematic.[141] The importance attached to the subsequent practice of the parties to a treaty in its

---

134 Kassoti 2017b, pp. 34–35. Odermatt 2017, p. 736.

135 *Front Polisario 2016*, above n. 66, paras 94–96.

136 *Front Polisario 2016*, above n. 66, paras 95–97.

137 ILC Draft Articles on the Law of Treaties with commentaries, above n. 52, pp. 213–214, para 5.

138 Odermatt 2017, p. 736. ILC Draft Articles on the Law of Treaties with commentaries, above n. 52, p. 213, para 2.

139 Ryngaert (2017). Hilpold 2017, p. 917. Kassoti 2017b, pp. 35–37. Odermatt 2017, p. 736. Van der Loo 2019, p. 17.

140 ILC Draft Articles on the Law of Treaties with commentaries, above n. 52, p. 226, para 1.

141 Cannizzaro 2018, at p. 578. Hilpold 2017, p. 917. Kassoti 2017b, pp. 37–40. Odermatt 2017, p. 737. Van der Loo 2019, p. 16.

interpretation constitutes one of the most distinctive features of the Vienna rules.[142] International courts and tribunals routinely have recourse to the subsequent practice of the parties in order to establish the 'ordinary meaning' of a treaty term in accordance with Article 31(1) VCLT, or it can enter the reasoning at a later stage, in order to confirm the result reached from the initial textual interpretation.[143] The ECJ has also recognised the relevance of the "settled practice of the parties to the Agreement" for the purpose of treaty interpretation[144] and it has even argued that "the subsequent practice followed in the application of a treaty may override the clear terms of that treaty if that practice reflects the parties' agreement."[145]

However, the Court in *Front Polisario* completely ignored a discernible pattern of acts and pronouncements that strongly points to the conclusion that, in their subsequent practice in the application of the treaties at hand, EU and Morocco treated Western Sahara as falling within the territorial scope of the agreements at hand.[146] The negative presumption that Article 31(3)(c) VCLT gives rise to (namely the presumption that in entering treaty obligations the parties did not intend to act inconsistently with general international law) discussed above[147] played a crucial role in the Court's dismissal of the subsequent conduct by the EU and Morocco as an interpretative element relevant to the case at bar. According to the Court, had the EU intended the agreements to apply to the Western Sahara, that "would necessarily have entailed conceding that the European Union intended to implement those agreements in a manner incompatible with the principles of self-determination and of the relative effect of treaties, even though the European Union repeatedly reiterated the need to comply with those principles."[148] The Court's over-reliance on the presumption of compliance with international law to the exclusion of clear evidence of intention on the basis of the parties' subsequent practice goes far beyond what is allowed under Article 31(3)(c) VCLT and casts doubt on the Court's interpretative outcome. The Court's tortured logic according to which "there could not be what must not be"[149] has been also vociferously criticised in the literature.[150] At the very minimum, one would have expected the Court to explain why the EU's and Morocco's subsequent practice in the application of the treaties was not relevant for the purpose of treaty

[142] ILC Draft Articles on the Law of Treaties with commentaries, above n. 52, p. 221, para 15.

[143] See for example ICJ, *Case concerning Kasikili/Seduku Island (Botswana/Namibia)*, Judgment (Merits), 13 December 1999, [1999] ICJ Rep 1999, p. 1045, para 50. WTO Appellate Body, *Japan-Taxes on Alcoholic Beverages*, Report, 04 October 1996, WT/DS8/AB/R, WT/DS10/AB/R, WT/DS11/AB/R, DSR 1996:I, pp. 12–13.

[144] Court of Justice, *Leonce Cayrol v Giovanni Rivoira and Figli*, Judgment, 30 November 1977, Case C-52/77, ECLI:EU:C:1977:196, para 18. *Anastasiou,* above n. 64, paras 43, 50.

[145] Court of Justice, *Europäische Schule München v Silvana Oberto and Barbara O'Leary,* Judgment, 11 March 2015, Case C-464/13, ECLI:EU:C:2015:163, para 61.

[146] *Front Polisario 2016,* above n. 66, paras 117–118. *Front Polisario 2015*, above n. 107, paras 78–80.

[147] See above pp. 7–9.

[148] *Front Polisario 2016*, above n. 66, para 123.

[149] Hilpold 2017, p. 916.

[150] Cannizzaro 2018, p. 12. Van der Loo 2019, p. 16. Odermatt 2017, p. 737.

interpretation.[151] Overall, the ECJ's artificial and selective reliance on international law in the *Front Polisario* case leaves much to be desired from an international legal perspective.

5.3.4 *The* Western Sahara Campaign UK *Judgment*

The judgment followed a request for a preliminary ruling by the High Court of England and Wales in a case brought by Western Sahara Campaign UK, a voluntary organisation whose aim is to support the right of the people of Western Sahara to self-determination.[152] In the context of the national proceedings the applicant challenged the validity of the EU-Morocco Association Agreement, the Fisheries Partnership Agreement ('FPA'),[153] the 2013 Fisheries Protocol[154] as well as the relevant EU implementing legislation insofar as these instruments are applicable to the territory of Western Sahara and to the waters adjacent thereto.[155] According to the applicant, the inclusion of that territory and of those waters within the territorial scope of the relevant EU-Morocco agreements violates Article 3(5) TEU, under which the Union is required to respect international law.[156] More particularly, the applicant claimed that such inclusion is incompatible with the right to self-determination, the duty of non-recognition, the duty of non-assistance as well as the principle of permanent sovereignty over natural resources.[157]

In this case, the Court closely followed its previous approach in *Front Polisario* and concluded that neither the FPA nor the 2013 Fisheries Protocol extend to the territory and waters off the coast of Western Sahara.[158] In order to reach this conclusion the ECJ relied almost exclusively on Article 31(3)(c) VCLT—thereby replicating the weaknesses of the *Front Polisario* judgment. As seen above, one of the most striking aspects of the *Front Polisario* judgment—and one that has attracted a fair amount of criticism in the literature—was the Court's over-reliance on the presumption of the (EU's) compliance with international law. The same argument to the effect that 'there could not be what must not be' permeates the *Western Sahara Campaign UK* judgment. The Court had recourse to this argument twice; both in interpreting what

---

[151] Kassoti 2017b, p. 29.

[152] *Western Sahara Campaign UK*, above n. 67, paras 30–31.

[153] Fisheries Partnership Agreement between the European Community and the Kingdom of Morocco, opened for signature 26 July 2006, OJ L141/4 (entered into force 28 February 2007).

[154] Protocol between the European Union and the Kingdom of Morocco setting out the fishing opportunities and the financial contribution provided for in the Fisheries Partnership Agreement between the European Union and the Kingdom of Morocco [2013] OJ L328/2.

[155] *Western Sahara Campaign UK*, above n. 67, para 32.

[156] Ibid.

[157] Ibid., Opinion of AG Wathelet, above n. 102, para 26.

[158] Ibid., paras 64, 73.

constitutes the concept of 'territory' of Morocco[159] and in interpreting what constitutes 'waters falling within the sovereignty' of Morocco.[160] According to the judgment, if the EU-Morocco fisheries agreements extended to the territory of Western Sahara and the waters adjacent thereto, "this would be contrary to certain rules of international law … which the European Union must observe."[161]

This line of reasoning is deeply problematic on a number of grounds. The extreme version of the argument advanced by the Court holds that the EU could never be found in breach of international law simply because this would run counter to its express commitment to upholding international law and irrespective of the actual evidence on the ground. In this sense, in the context of judicial review of the compatibility of the EU's international agreements with international law, all conflicts between what the EU *should do* according to international law and what it actually *does* in the application of an agreement could simply be 'interpreted away'.

More fundamentally, this line of reasoning raises questions in relation to the weight and role that the presumption of compliance with international law may have in the process of treaty interpretation. As seen earlier, this is merely a *presumption* and thus, the normative weight attached thereto needs not be exaggerated. Here, the Court treated the EU's professed commitment to international law not merely as the starting point in the quest for ascertaining the meaning of the relevant treaty terms, but as an overriding principle of treaty interpretation—something that does not comport with the interpretative process under Article 31 VCLT.

Furthermore, the argument according to which 'there could not be what must not be' seems to conflate interpretation with application. As discussed above, although closely intertwined, these two normative processes are (and should remain) distinct.[162] Here, the Court set out to interpret the terms 'territory' of Morocco and 'waters falling within the sovereignty' of Morocco, but it did so *by directly applying* the principle of self-determination and the principle of relative effect of treaties to the facts of the case.[163] Having concluded that the application of those principles would lead to a finding of breach by the EU of its international law obligations, the Court reverted back to the process of interpretation and informed the meaning of the relevant treaty terms on the basis of the juridical consequences resulting from the application of the relevant rules.[164] Thus, in essence, the Court here reversed the sequence of the interpretation-application processes in order to reach a conclusion that would not entail the breach by the EU of any of its international law obligations. By doing so, the Court blurred the distinction between clarifying the meaning of a treaty provision by reference to relevant rules of international law and applying those

[159] Ibid., para 63.
[160] Ibid., para 71.
[161] Ibid., paras 63, 71.
[162] See above p. 9.
[163] Ibid., paras 63, 71–73.
[164] Ibid.

rules directly to the facts in the context of which a treaty is being considered—the latter being impermissible under the Vienna rules.[165]

Furthermore, as in *Front Polisario*, the Court in *Western Sahara Campaign UK* relied almost exclusively on the normative context of the dispute under Article 31(3)(c) VCLT in order to define the territorial scope of the agreement. More particularly, the Court relied exclusively on Articles 55 and 56 United Nations Convention on the Law of the Sea (UNCLOS)[166] in order to interpret the territorial clause of the FPA[167] and did not engage at all with the other means of interpretation listed in Article 31 VCLT. The Court's excessive reliance on Article 31(3)(c) VCLT and the fact that it did not take into account the other means of interpretation contained in the Article go against the letter and spirit of the Vienna rules.

As discussed above, the overwhelming majority of commentators have found the Court's reluctance to engage extensively with the parties' "subsequent practice in the application of the treaty" under Article 31(3)(b) VCLT in the context of the *Front Polisario* case particularly problematic.[168] The same reluctance to engage with the parties' subsequent practice for the purpose of interpreting the territorial scope of the FPA and the 2013 Protocol permeates the Court's judgment in *Western Sahara Campaign UK*. At the same time, as also highlighted in the Advocate General's Opinion,[169] there is abundant evidence that the subsequent practice of the parties in the application of the FPA and the 2013 Protocol reveals their common understanding that the waters adjacent to Western Sahara are included in the territorial scope of the agreements.[170] Here, as in *Front Polisario*, the Court failed to explain why this practice has no bearing in the context of interpretation of the territorial clauses of the EU-Morocco agreements.

Overall, the ECJ in *Western Sahara Campaign UK* followed the same judicial strategy as in *Front Polisario*, namely one of 'instrumentalization' of international law. In both cases, the Court made extensive use of Article 31(3)(c) VCLT and of the normative context of the dispute and it pointedly ignored the factual application of these agreements to the territory and waters adjacent to Western Sahara. Furthermore, in both cases, the Court stretched the limits of the principle of systemic integration to a breaking point, in a rather overt attempt to achieve conformity with international law without having to pronounce on the legal repercussions of the EU's policy and practice towards Western Sahara.[171]

---

[165] Gardiner 2015, p. 320.

[166] United Nations Convention on the Law of the Sea, opened for signature 10 December 1982, 1833 UNTS 397 (entered into force 16 November 1994).

[167] *Western Sahara Campaign UK*, above n. 67, paras 66–69.

[168] Cannizzaro 2018, p. 578. Kassoti 2017b, pp. 37–40. Odermatt 2017, p. 717. Hilpold 2017, p. 917.

[169] *Western Sahara Campaign UK* (Opinion of A.G. Wathelet), above n. 102, paras 60–75.

[170] Kassoti 2019, pp. 225–229.

[171] Odermatt 2017, pp. 737–738. Kassoti 2019, p. 235.

5.4 Conclusions

The chapter has shown that the CJEU's embrace of Article 31(3)(c) VCLT in its later case-law concerning Western Sahara is not as innocuous as it may seem at first sight. Far from signalling the Court's willingness to engage more extensively with international law, the principle of systemic integration was used in this line of case-law as a heuristic device in order to shield the Union from the obligations incumbent upon it under international law. From the broader perspective of autonomy, the Court's line of argumentation in the Western Sahara case-law makes sense if one recalls the type of agreements that were brought before the Court. Here, the Court was faced with questions of validity of association and free trade agreements, namely agreements that "radiate EU law outwards", in the sense of agreements that are substantively based on EU law and aim to export it to third States.[172] Overall, the Court has been quite well-disposed towards this class of agreements since they reinforce its autonomy as a global actor that can shape law and policy beyond its borders.[173] To the extent that the agreements in question do not threaten but reinforce the distinctiveness of the EU legal order, the Court is unwilling to employ rules originating outside the legal order to challenge them.

This line of case-law confirms the observations made in the literature regarding the increasingly restrictive approach that the Court has adopted towards international law in its later case-law. More particularly, this approach vindicates the view that the practice of the CJEU evidences that the Union is not interested in being international-law friendly, but rather "in guarding its own identity. If and when possible it will happily do so in harmony with international law, but if and when it is impossible to do so harmoniously, international law will have to take the backseat."[174] However, the 'instrumentalization' of international law in this line of case-law has significant repercussions both for the international rule of law and for the very identity of the EU as a global actor. As Klabbers explains: "the Rule of Law has never been a mere particularist political project for the EU, but has been central to its own identity."[175] Displaying a cavalier attitude towards international law endangers the loss of legal certainty (itself a core element of the international rule of law)[176] and undermines the very identity of the EU as a global actor with a particular fidelity to international law.

---

[172] Klabbers 2018, p. 1208, p. 1217.

[173] Ibid., pp. 1216–1220.

[174] Klabbers 2011, p. 97.

[175] Klabbers 2018, p. 1233.

[176] Peters 2017, p. 679.

References

Abi-Saab G (2006) The Appellate Body and Treaty Interpretation. In: Sacerdoti G, Yanovich Bohanes J, Yanovich A (eds) The WTO at Ten—The Contribution of the Dispute Settlement System. Cambridge University Press, Cambridge

African Union (2015) Legal Opinion on the legality in the context of international law, including the relevant United Nations resolutions and organization of African Unity/African Union decisions, of actions allegedly taken by the Moroccan authorities or any other State, group of States, foreign companies or any other entity in the exploration and/or exploitation of renewable and non-renewable natural resources or any other economic activity in Western Sahara, Annex to the letter dated 9 October 2015 from the Permanent representative of Zimbabwe to the United Nations addressed to the President of the Security Council, UN Doc. S/2015/786

Alvarez JE (2016) International Organizations and the Rule of Law: Challenges Ahead. https://papers.ssrn.com/sol3/papers.cfm?abstract_id=2793924. Accessed 2 December 2019

Aust H, Rodijes A, Staubach P (2014) Unity or Uniformity? Domestic Courts and Treaty Interpretation. LJIL 27:75–112

Brölmann C (2007) The Institutional Veil in Public International Law: International Organisations and the Law of Treaties. Hart Publishing, Oxford

Cannizzaro E (2011) A Higher Law for Treaties? In: Cannizzaro E (ed) The Law of Treaties beyond the Vienna Convention. Oxford University Press, Oxford

Cannizzaro E (2018) In Defence of *Front Polisario*: The ECJ as a Global *Jus Cogens* Maker. CMLRev 55:569–587

Collins R (2011) Modernist-Positivism and the Problem of Institutional Autonomy in International Law. In: Collins R, White ND (eds) International Organizations and the Idea of Autonomy: Institutional Independence in the International Legal Order. Routledge, London

Collins R, White ND (2011) International Organizations and the Idea of Autonomy: Introduction and Overview. In: Collins R, White ND (eds), International Organizations and the Idea of Autonomy: Institutional Independence in the International Legal Order. Routledge, London

Contartese C (2017) The Autonomy of the EU Legal Order in the ECJ's External Relations Case Law: From the "Essential" to the "Specific Characteristics" of the Union and Back Again, CMLRev 54:1627–1672

Crawford J (2003) International Law and the Rule of Law. Adel L Rev 24:3

Crawford J (2006) The Creation of States in International Law, 2nd ed. Clarendon Press, Oxford

Cremona M (2018) Structural Principles and their Role in EU External Relations Law. In: Cremona M (ed) Structural Principles of EU External Relations. Hart Publishing, Oxford

D'Aspremont J (2011) The Multifaceted Concept of the Autonomy of International Organizations and International Legal Discourse. In: Collins R, White ND (eds) International Organizations and the Idea of Autonomy: Institutional Independence in the International Legal Order. Routledge, London

D'Aspremont J (2012) The Systemic Integration of International Law by Domestic Courts: Domestic Judges as Architects of the Consistency of the International Legal Order. In: Fauchald OK, Nollkaemper A (eds) The Practice of International and National Courts and the (De-) Fragmentation of International Law. Hart Publishing, Oxford

De Búrca G (2015) Internalization of International Law by the CJEU and the US Supreme Court. Int'l J Const L 13:987–1007

De Witte B (2010) European Union Law: How Autonomous is Its Legal Order? Zeitschrift für öffentliches Recht 65:141–155

Dörr O (2012) Article 31: General Rule of Interpretation. In: Dörr O, Schmalenbach K (eds) Vienna Convention on the Law of Treaties: A Commentary, 2nd ed. Springer, Berlin

Eckes C (2012) International Law as Law of the EU: The Role of the European Court of Justice. In: Cannizzaro E, Palchetti P, Wessel R (eds) International Law as Law of the European Union. Martinus Nijhoff, Leiden

Emiliou N (1995) Cypriot Import Certificates; some hot potatoes. E L Rev 20:202–210

Gardiner R (2015) Treaty Interpretation, 2nd ed. Oxford University Press, Oxford
Gourgourinis A (2011) The Distinction between Interpretation and Application of Norms in International Adjudication. JIDS 2:31–57
Gowlland-Debbas V (1990) Collective Responses to Illegal Acts in International Law: United Nations Action in the Case of Southern Rhodesia. Martinus Nijhoff, Dordrecht
Haraszti G (1973) Some Fundamental Problems in the Law of Treaties. Akadémiai Kiadó, Budapest
Harpaz G, Rubinson E (2010) The Interface between Trade, Law and Politics and the Erosion of Normative Power Europe: Comment on Brita. EL Rev 35:551–570
Harvard Law School (1935) Draft Convention on the Law of Treaties: Article 19. Interpretation. AJIL Suppl 29:937
Hilpold P (2017) "Self-Determination at the European Courts: The *Front Polisario* Case" or "The Unintended Awakening of a Giant". European Papers 2:907–921
International Law Commission (ILC) (2006) 'Fragmentation of International Law: Difficulties Arising from the Diversification and Expansion of International Law—Report of the Study Group of the International Law Commission', UN Doc. A/4/682 (finalised by Martti Koskenniemi). http://legal.un.org/ilc/documentation/english/a_cn4_l682.pdf. Accessed 2 December 2019
Jenks W (1953) The Conflict of Law-Making Treaties. BYIL 30:401–453
Jennings R, Watts A (1992) Oppenheim's International Law, 9th edn, Vol. I. Longman, London
Kanetake M (2016) The Interfaces Between the National and the International Rule of Law: A Framework Paper. In: Nollkaemper A, Kanetake M (eds) The Rule of Law at the National and International Levels. Hart Publishing, Oxford
Kassoti E (2017a) The Front Polisario v Council Case: The General Court, *Völkerrechtsfreundlichkeit and the External Aspect of European Integration.* http://europeanpapers.eu/en/system/files/pdf_version/EP_EF_2017_I_010_Eva_Kassoti_3.pdf. Accessed 3 December 2019
Kassoti E (2017b) The Council v Front Polisario Case: The Court of Justice's Selective Reliance on Treaty Interpretation. European Papers 2:23–42
Kassoti E (2019) The ECJ and the Art of Treaty Interpretation: *Western Sahara Campaign UK*. CMLRev 56:209–236
Klabbers J (2007) Reluctant Grundnormen: Articles 31(3)(c) and 42 of the Vienna Convention on the Law of Treaties and the Fragmentation of International Law. In: Craven M, Fitzmaurice M, Vogiatzi M (eds) Time, History and International Law. Martinus Nijhoff, Leiden
Klabbers J (2011) Völkerrechtsfreundlichkeit? International Law and the EU Legal Order. In: Koutrakos P (ed) European Foreign Policy. Edward Elgar Publishing, Cheltenham
Klabbers J (2012) The Validity of EU Norms Conflicting with International Obligations. In: Cannizzaro E, Palchetti P, Wessel R (eds) International Law as Law of the European Union. Martinus Nijhoff, Leiden
Klabbers J (2015) The EJIL Foreword: The Transformation of International Organizations Law. EJIL 26(9):9–82
Klabbers J (2018) The Reception of International Law in the EU Legal Order. In: Schütze R, Tridimas T (eds) Oxford Principles of European Union Law: Volume I: The European Union Legal Order. Oxford University Press, Oxford
Koutrakos P (2003) Legal Issues of EC-Cyprus Trade Relations. ICLQ 52:489–498
Kuijper PJ (2010) Case C-386/08, Brita GmbH v Hauptzollamt Hamburg-Hafen Judgment of the European Court of Justice of 25 February 2010. Legal Issues of Economic Integration 37:241–251
MacNair A (1961) The Law of Treaties. Oxford University Press, Oxford
McLachlan C (2005) The Principle of Systemic Integration and Article 31(3)(c) of the Vienna Convention. ICLQ 54:279–319
Merkouris P (2015) Article 31(3)(c) VCLT and the Principle of Systemic Integration: Normative Shadows in Plato's Cave. Martinus Nijhoff, Leiden
Milanovic M (2011) Is the Rome Statute Binding on Individuals? (And Why We Should Care). JICJ 9:25–52
Nollkaemper A (2012) National Courts and the International Rule of Law. Oxford University Press, Oxford

Odermatt J (2015) The Use of International Treaty Law by the Court of Justice of the European Union. Cambridge Yearbook of International Legal Studies 17:121–144
Odermatt J (2017) Council of the European Union v. Front populaire pour la libération de la saguia-el-hamra et du rio de oro (Front Polisario). AJIL 111:731–738
Odermatt J (2018) The Principle of Autonomy: An Adolescent Disease of EU External Relations Law? In: Cremona M (ed) Structural Principles of EU External Relations. Hart Publishing, Oxford
Orakhelashvili A (2003) Restrictive Interpretation of Human Rights Treaties in the Recent Jurisprudence of the European Court of Human Rights. EJIL 14:529–568
Orakhelashvili A (2008) The Interpretation of Acts and Rules in Public International Law. Oxford University Press, Oxford
Orellana Zabalza G (2012) The Principle of Systemic Integration: Towards a Coherent International Legal Order. Lit Verlag, Berlin
Pauwelyn J (2003) Conflict of Norms in Public International Law: How WTO Law Relates to Other Rules of International Law. Cambridge University Press, Cambridge
Peters A (2017) The Refinement of International Law: From Fragmentation to Regime Interaction and Politicization. Int'l J Const L 15:671–704
Proells A (2012) Article 34: General rule regarding third States. In: Dörr O, Schmalenbach K (eds) Vienna Convention on the Law of Treaties: A Commentary, 2nd edn. Springer, Berlin
Rachovitsa A (2017) The Principle of Systemic Integration in Human Rights Law. ICLQ 66:557–588
Ryngaert C (2017) The Polisario Front Judgment of the EU Court of Justice: A Reset of EU-Morocco Trade Relations in the Offing http://blog.renforce.eu/index.php/nl/2017/01/15/the-polisario-front-judgment-of-the-eu-court-of-justice-a-reset-of-eu-morocco-trade-relations-in-the-offing. Accessed 3 December 2019
Schermers HG, Blokker N (2011) International Institutional Law: Unity within Diversity. Martinus Nijhoff, Leiden
Schwarzenberger G (1969) Myths and Realities of Treaty Interpretation: Articles 27–29 of the Vienna Draft Convention on the Law of Treaties. Current Legal Problems 22:205–227
Schwed A (1982) Territorial Claims as a Limitation to the Right to Self-Determination in the Context of the Falkland Islands Dispute. Fordham Int'l L J 6:443–471
Skoutaris N (2011) The Cyprus Issue: The Four Freedoms in a Member State under Siege. Hart Publishing, Oxford
Talmon S (2001) The Cyprus Question before the European Court of Justice. EJIL 12:727–750
Thirlway H (1989) The Law and Procedure of the International Court of Justice 1969–1989, Part One. BYIL 60:1–157
Torres Bernárdez S (1998) Interpretation of Treaties by the International Court of Justice following the Adoption of the 1969 Vienna Convention on the Law of Treaties. In: Hafner G et al. (eds) Liber Amicorum Ignaz Seidl-Hohenveldern in honour of his 80th Birthday. Kluwer Law International, The Hague
Tsagourias N (2011) Conceptualising the Autonomy of the European Union. In: Collins R and White ND (eds) International Organizations and the Idea of Autonomy: Institutional Independence in the International Legal Order. Routledge, London
Tzevelekos V (2010) The Use of Article 31(3)(c) of the VCLT in the Case Law of the ECtHR: An Effective Anti-Fragmentation Tool or a Selective Loophole for the Reinforcement of Human Rights Teleology. Mich. J Int'l L 31:621–690
UNGA (1970) Resolution 25/2625, Declaration on Principles of International Law concerning Friendly Relations and Co-operation among States in accordance with the Charter of the United Nations, UN Doc. A/RES/25/2625
UNGA (1979) Resolution 34/37 of 21 November 1979, UN Doc. A/RES/34/37
UNGA (1980) Resolution 35/19 of 11 November 1980, UN Doc. A/RES/35/19
UNSC (2011) Resolution 1979/2011 of 27 April 2011, UN Doc. S/RES/1979
UNSC (2016) Resolution 2285/2016 of 29 April 2016, UN Doc. S/RES/2285

Van der Loo G (2019) Law and Practice of the EU's Trade Agreements with Disputed Territories. In: Garben S, Govaere I (eds) Interfaces between EU and International Law. Hart Publishing, Oxford (forthcoming)
van Rossem JW (2013) The Autonomy of EU Law: More is Less? In: Wessel RA, Blockmans S (eds) Between Autonomy and Dependence: The EU Legal Order under the Influence of International Organisations. T.M.C. Asser Press/Springer, The Hague
Villiger M (2009) Commentary on the 1969 Vienna Convention on the Law of Treaties. Martinus Nijhoff, Leiden
Webb P (2013) International Judicial Integration and Fragmentation. Oxford University Press, Oxford
Weiler JHH, Haltern UR (1996) The Autonomy of the Community Legal Order: Through the Looking Glass. Harv. Int'l L J 37:411–448
Wessel R (2012) Reconsidering the Relationship between International and EU Law: Towards a Content-Based Approach? In: Cannizzaro E, Palchetti P, Wessel R (eds) International Law as Law of the European Union. Martinus Nijhoff, Leiden
Wouters J, Odermatt J, Ramopoulos T (2014) Worlds Apart? Comparing the Approaches of the European Court of Justice and the EU Legislature to International Law. In: Cremona M, Thies A (eds) The European Court of Justice and External Relations Law. Hart Publishing, Oxford
Wouters J, Ryngaert C, Ruys T, De Baere G (2019) International Law: A European Perspective. Hart Publishing, Oxford
Ziegler K (2011) Beyond Pluralism and Autonomy: Systemic Harmonization as a Paradigm for the Interaction of EU Law and International Law. YEL 35:667–711

E. Kassoti is Senior Researcher in European and International Law and the Academic coordinator of CLEER at the T.M.C. Asser Institute.

Chapter 6
Provisional Application's Novel Rationale: Facilitating Mixity in the EU's Treaty Practice

M. Chamon

Contents

Abstract This chapter argues that the EU has created a new use for the mechanism of provisional application of treaties foreseen in Article 25 VCLT. Differently from established rationales for relying on provisional application, the EU as a federal polity uses it to allow effective external action of the federal level without pushing out the Member States from the international plane (as would be the case in a typical federal polity). In EU terms, the PIL mechanism of provisional application facilitates the internal EU decision for mixed agreements. While useful and rather elegant, reliance on this mechanism also raises a host of further legal questions, both under PIL and EU law. The present chapter focuses on the latter and looks into how the Council of the EU defines the scope of provisional application; how these decisions should in theory be informative of the delimitation of competences within the EU but in practice are not; and how provisional application can be terminated on the EU side.

Keywords mixed agreements · provisional application · article 25 VCLT · EU exclusive competences · national exclusive competences

M. Chamon (✉)
Maastricht University, Maastricht, The Netherlands

W. Th. Douma et al. (eds.), *The Evolving Nature of EU External Relations Law*,
https://doi.org/10.1007/978-94-6265-423-5_6

6.1 Introduction

The European Union (EU) is a prolific actor on the international plane with an ever-expanding list of multilateral and bilateral agreements.[1] In its treaty practice it regularly relies on the technique of provisionally applying agreements before their entry into force, a by now also common practice in general state practice in international law.[2] Although the EU relies on the device of provisional application for all sorts of agreements, it is an especially characterizing feature of the EU's so called bilateral mixed agreements. These are agreements concluded by both the EU and its 27 individual Member States as one meta-EU party with a third country (or group of third countries). The present chapter argues that the EU, through its practice of mixed agreements, relies on an entirely novel rationale, hitherto unknown in international law, in its recourse to the technique of provisional application. As will be shown, it facilitates the external action of a federal polity like the EU without requiring its constituent Member States to retreat from the international arena.

This chapter will first explore the general issue of provisional application foreseen in Article 25 of the Vienna Convention on the Law of Treaties (VCLT) and the traditional rationales underpinning the technique. Next the EU's practice in concluding mixed agreements, i.e. agreements to which both the EU and its Member States are parties together with one or more third countries or international organisations, will be briefly commented and explained in light of the EU's constitutional order of competences.

Having laid down this groundwork, the contribution will subsequently focus on the EU's practice of provisionally applying bilateral mixed agreements signed or concluded after the entry into force of the Lisbon Treaty, showing a new rationale for provisional application.[3] This practice will be looked at in light of the work by the International Law Commission (ILC) and the draft Guidelines on provisional application which it is developing.[4] Despite the Lisbon Treaty already having entered into force more than ten years ago, the EU legal framework governing this area is still developing through the jurisprudence of the Court of Justice. As a result, throughout the discussion, reference will also be made to the impact of recent case law on the conduct of EU external relations.

Finally, three key legal issues in relation to the provisional application of bilateral mixed agreements will be explored. First the different practices in partial provisional application by the EU will be scrutinized. Second it will be tested whether the Council's decisions on provisional application can help us in determining the

---

[1] Odermatt 2017, p. 504.

[2] Arsanjani and Reisman note that "*the urgent need for provisional application of more contemporary treaties soon expanded to other matters [than peace treaties]*," Dalton adds that "*[i]n recent years, the incidence of provisional application between States has continued to increase.*" See Arsanjani and Reisman 2011, p. 88; Dalton 2012, p. 221.

[3] The post-Lisbon agreements covered are listed in n. 29.

[4] For a more internal EU-perspective on provisional application, see Flaesch-Mougin and Bosse-Platière 2014, pp. 293–323.

precise division of competences between the EU and its Member States (as in theory it ought to). As will be shown, this is particularly problematic for the EU's partners which are effectively burdened with the EU's own problematic internal division of competence. Lastly, the issue of the termination of provisional application will be explored in light of recent developments in relation to the Comprehensive Economic and Trade Agreement (CETA) between the EU, its Member States and Canada.

6.2 Provisional Application of International Agreements

In international state practice, the provisional application of international agreements is (by now) common practice,[5] even if the topic is hardly discussed in scholarly contributions.[6] A desire to ensure that the VCLT would reflect actual practice indeed explains why a clause on provisional application was ultimately included in the final text.[7] The parties agreed on Article 25 VCLT following intense debates on i.a. the legal status of provisionally applied agreements and the relationship with national constitutional law.[8] Article 25 of the VCLT reads:

1. *A treaty or a part of a treaty is applied provisionally pending its entry into force if*
   (a) *the treaty itself so provides; or*
   (b) *the negotiating States have in some other manner so agreed.*
2. *Unless the treaty otherwise provides or the negotiating States have otherwise agreed, the provisional application of a treaty or a part of a treaty with respect to a State shall be terminated if that State notifies the other States between which the treaty is being applied provisionally of its intention not to become a party to the treaty.*

The lack of legal precision for which Article 25 VCLT has been criticized[9] must then be understood as part of the tradeoff between the sensed need to acknowledge the existing practice of provisional application and the lack of a more broad consensus on the detailed rules that ought to govern provisional application. This lack of a broader consensus may have been the result of limited practice but also has implications for the question on the status of Article 25 VCLT as part of customary international

[5]Lefeber 2011, para 1.

[6]Hafner also observes this, see Hafner 2014, p. 146.

[7]For legibility reasons, reference will be made to the 1969 VCLT rather than the 1986 VCLT even if the EU's practice as an international organization is discussed. This since Article 25 1986 VCLT simply mirrors Article 25 1969 VCLT. Vienna Convention on the Law of Treaties, opened for signature 23 May 1969, 1155 UNTS 331 (entered into force 27 January 1980) (VCLT).

[8]Mathy 2006, p. 1050.

[9]Geslin 2005, p. 111; Rogoff and Gauditz 1987, p. 41.

law.[10] Although this falls outside the scope of this chapter, it may be noted that, so far, the clarification and interpretation of this provision have for a large part been left to arbitration tribunals.[11] While arbitration awards are only binding inter partes and their precedential value depends on the quality of the reasoning and the reception thereof in the legal community, there are clear legitimacy concerns in promoting the development of international law by such tribunals.[12] While not critical of this development, ILC Member Giorgio Gaja indeed referred to these arbitration decisions when discussing the outstanding issues related to provisional application[13] which led the ILC to appoint a Special Rapporteur, Juan Manuel Gómez-Robledo, to map and analyse state practice on provisional application in order to draft a Guide to Provisional Application of Treaties.[14]

6.2.1 The Reasons for Resorting to Provisional Application

Although Lefeber notes that identifying the reasons why parties decide on provisional application "*involves a degree of speculation*",[15] there seem to be two generally accepted ones. It is thus relied upon in treaty practice (i) to address urgent issues, e.g. peace treaties, crisis management, and (ii) to ensure continuity, e.g. when an agreement establishing an international organization is reviewed and replaced by a new agreement.[16] In addition to these two universally accepted reasons, Michie has identified a further four based on state practice, adding (iii) the (interim) application

---

[10] Mathy notes that it was possible to regard Article 25(1) VCLT as crystallizing established practice, while Article 25(2) VCLT clearly did not codify customary international law and was an instance of the progressive development of international law. See Mathy 2006, p. 1049. Dalton, citing Villiger, notes that subsequent developments in state practice have meant that Article 25(2) VCLT now also reflects custom. See Dalton 2012, p. 232.

[11] Notably the elaborate provisional application clause of the Energy Charter Treaty has been interpreted, together with Article 25 VCLT by arbitration tribunals. See for instance the decisions in the *Yukos* and *Kardassopoulos* cases to the effect that Article 26 VCLT (*pacta sunt servanda*), rather than Article 18 VCLT applies to provisionally applied agreements, see PCA, *Yukos*, Interim Award on Jurisdiction and Admissibility, 30 November 2009, Case No. AA 228, paras 319–320; ICSID, *Kardassopoulos*, Decision on Jurisdiction, 6 July 2007, Case No. ARB/05/18, paras 205 et. seq. In *Petrobart* an arbitration tribunal had to decide whether the ECT was still provisionally applied by the UK on behalf of Gibraltar, even if the UK had excluded Gibraltar from in its instrument of (final) ratification. See Arbitration Institute of the Stockholm Chamber of Commerce, *Petrobart*, Arbitral Award, 29 March 2005, Arbitration No. 126/2003, pp. 62–63. The Swedish Court of Appeal upheld the award on this point. See the unofficial English translation published in (2007) 4 Transnational Dispute Management 5, p. 8.

[12] See von Bogdandy and Venzke 2012, pp. 18–19.

[13] See ILC 2011, Annex C, para 5.

[14] For the most recent draft, see ILC 2018.

[15] Lefeber 2011, para 2.

[16] ILC 2013b, pp. 11–15. Mathy 2006, pp. 1050–1052; Arsanjani and Reisman 2011, pp. 87–90.

of non-urgent treaties where future ratification is guaranteed,[17] (iv) legal consistency, (v) facilitating the setting up of new international organisations and (vi) the circumvention of obstacles to entry into force.[18]

Turning to the EU's treaty practice, the EU (then European (Economic) Community)[19] initially indeed resorted to the technique of provisional application for the reasons generally identified in international state practice. One of the first agreements that was provisionally applied by the EU was the Fifth International Tin Agreement.[20] As Michie notes, a classic example of resort to provisional application in order to ensure legal continuity is that of the commodity agreements.[21] Further, ever since the EU acquired the (exclusive) competence to conclude fisheries agreements, it has consistently relied on the option to provisionally apply such agreements. The 1979 agreement with Senegal for instance was provisionally applied before entry into force and this for reasons of urgency, given the approaching fishing season.[22] Any subsequent agreements, renewing both parties' commitments, are then typically provisionally applied to ensure continuity.[23] More recently however, a third reason why the EU resorts to the device of provisional application may be identified in that it allows the EU to circumvent the delay caused by the lengthy ratification procedures for its so called 'mixed' agreements (see below).[24] It is this specific function of the technique of provisional application in the EU's treaty practice that will be further analysed in this chapter.

---

[17]This was also specifically noted by the Expert Consultant, Mr. Waldcock, during the Vienna Conference. See ILC 2013b, p. 13.

[18]Michie 2009, pp. 23–47. Lefeber 2011, para 2, who identified the adoption of confidence building measures as another function which Michie includes in the sixth category. In his first report on the provisional application of treaties, Special Rapporteur Juan Manuel Gómez-Robledo essentially comes to the same conclusion but proposes a slightly different typology. See ILC 2013a, pp. 6–9.

[19]In the remainder of this chapter, EU will be used to refer to both the EU (pre- and post-Lisbon) and the EEC and EC (pre-Lisbon).

[20]See Council Decision 76/626 of 21 June 1976 on the provisional application of the Fifth International Tin Agreement, OJ L222/1, 14 August 1976.

[21]See Michie 2009, p. 33. See also Arsanjani and Reisman 2011, pp. 89–90.

[22]See Council Decision 79/569 of 12 June 1979 concerning the conclusion of the Agreement in the form of an exchange of letters on the provisional application of the Agreement between the Government of the Republic of Senegal and the European Economic Community on fishing off the coast of Senegal and of the Protocol and the exchanges of letters relating thereto, OJ L154/25, 21 June 1979.

[23]See e.g. Council Decision 81/1055 of 21 December 1981 on the conclusion of an Agreement in the form of an exchange of letters providing for provisional application of the Agreement between the Government of the Republic of Senegal and the European Economic Community amending the Agreement on fishing off the coast of Senegal, and of the Protocol thereto, OJ L379/64, 31 December 1981.

[24]Hoffmeister 2010, p. 257.

6.2.2 Alternatives to Provisional Application

Before elaborating on the notion of a 'mixed agreement' and before setting out the precise legal context in which this type of agreement is concluded by the EU, it may already be noted that while provisional application is by now part and parcel of the EU's practice in mixity, this was not always so. Originally, the bilateral mixed agreements which the EU and its Member States concluded with third countries were typically complemented by bilateral 'interim agreements'. The interim agreements contained all those provisions of the mixed agreement for which the EU had exclusive competence and which therefore could be concluded by the EU on its own, without the formal involvement of the Member States as individual subjects of international law being required or even permitted. As a consequence, the interim agreements could enter into force speedily following ratification by the EU and the third state concerned. Once the mixed agreement (containing but not limited to all the provisions of the interim agreement) was ratified by all parties (thus including the EU Member States), it would subsume the interim agreement. Of course, since the interim agreement contained only the provisions coming under EU exclusive competence, and given the perennial disagreements within the EU (typically between the Commission on the one side and the Member States and the Council on the other side) on the precise scope of the EU's exclusive competence, the typical interim agreement only contained provisions for which the EU's exclusive competence was beyond any doubt. In practice this meant that only the trade component of the mixed agreement was replicated in the interim agreement.[25]

This situation was remedied by the Amsterdam Treaty which amended then Article 300 EC to include a clause allowing a decision on the signature of an agreement to "*be accompanied by a decision on provisional application before entry into force*". At the time Dashwood rightly foretold that this new provision would "*make it no longer necessary to enter into freestanding interim agreements*".[26] Indeed, today, the technique of the interim agreement is not relied upon anymore.[27] However, while from a material point of view the techniques of the interim agreement and provisional application are identical, this is very much different from a procedural point of view.

For EU purposes, provisional application is decided upon by the Council upon a proposal by the Commission. In contrast, since an interim agreement still is a fully-fledged agreement, it is subject to the proper ratification procedure as now

[25] Some years before the practice of concluding interim agreements was effectively discontinued, the EU also concluded an interim agreement containing provisions on public procurement and competition next to the traditional trade component. See Council Decision 98/504 of 29 June 1998 concerning the conclusion of the Interim Agreement on trade and trade-related matters between the European Community, of the one part, and the United Mexican States, of the other part, OJ L226/24, 29 June 1998.

[26] Dashwood 1999, p. 206.

[27] The last examples pre-date the entry into force of the Lisbon Treaty and are the interim agreements concluded with a number of Western Balkan states, reproducing some of the trade related provisions of the Stabilisation and Association Agreements (SAAs) concluded with these countries. On the SAAs, see Maresceau 2006, p. 365 et seq.

defined in Article 218 TFEU. Whereas pre-Lisbon trade agreements (which the interim agreements essentially were) did not require the consent of the European Parliament, such consent is now prescribed by Article 218(6)(a)(v) TFEU. As a result, the internal procedural differences for deciding on an interim agreement or on provisional application have accrued. Provisional application of the trade provisions of an agreement do not require the Parliament's consent,[28] while the approval of an interim agreement containing the very same trade provisions would.

In addition, from an international law perspective there are also significant differences. Since an interim agreement is a proper international agreement, it is essentially governed by the relevant rules on issues such as reservations, entry into force, suspension and termination as codified in Articles 19–24 and 54 and 56–62 of the VCLT. In contrast the same issues relating to the provisional application of an agreement are not elaborately spelled out by Article 25 VCLT, if at all, hence the current work of the ILC.

While post-Lisbon the practice of concluding interim agreements has perished, that of provisionally applying signed agreements prior to their entry into force has seen significant developments. Of the 270 or so international agreements signed by the EU post-Lisbon, some 117 contain a provisional application clause. Of those agreements figuring such a clause, around 38 are mixed (out of the 61 mixed agreements).[29] Focusing on the bilateral mixed agreements, the current practice also goes

---

[28] A gentleman's agreement has nonetheless been worked out between the Parliament and the Commission that foresees the Parliament giving (or withholding) its consent before the decision on provisional application is taken. See Suse and Wouters 2018, pp. 9–11; Passos 2016, pp. 122–123. Three important caveats may be noted however: (i) while it is the Commission that proposes the provisional application (together with the proposal for signature) of an agreement, the decision itself is taken only by the Council; (ii) the practice only relates to trade agreements and association agreements (which always contain an important trade component), not to other agreements; (iii) while the Commission committed itself to follow this new practice it also reserved to itself a possibility to derogate in those cases where the file at issue is particularly urgent or technical.

[29] The figures are based on a search on the EU Treaties Database on 11 December 2019 (http://ec.europa.eu/world/agreements/default.home.do). The mixed agreements (and the concomitant Council decisions on signature and provisional application) that figure in the present contribution are the Air Transport Agreement with Canada, OJ L207/30, 6 August 2010; the Air Transport Agreement with the US, Iceland, Norway and the Ancillary Agreement with Iceland and Norway, OJ L 283/1, 29 October 2011; the Aviation Area Agreement with Georgia, OJ L321/1, 31 May 2013; the Euro-Mediterranean Aviation Agreement with Jordan, OJ L 334/1, 6 December 2012; the Common Aviation Area Agreement with Moldova, OJ L292/1, 20 October 2012; the Euro-Mediterranean Aviation Agreement with Israel, OJ L 208/1, 2 August 2013 (as regards air transport); the Stepping Stone Agreement with Côte d'Ivoire, OJ L 59/1, 3 March 2009; the Interim Agreements on Economic Partnership Agreements (EPA) with the SADC and ESA States, [2009] OJ L111/1 & [2009] OJ L 319/1, 6 May 2010; the EPA with the Eastern and Southern African States OJ L 111/1, 24 April 2012; the EPA with the SADC States OJ L 250/3, 16 September 2016; the Stepping Stone EPA with Ghana, OJ L 287/1, 21 September 2016 (as regards trade and development agreements); the Partnership and Cooperation Agreement (PCA) with Iraq OJ L204/20, 31 July 2012; the Framework Agreement with Korea OJ L20/2, 23 January 2013; the Enhanced PCA with Kazakhstan OJ L29/1, 4 February 2016; the Partnership Agreement on Relations and Cooperation with New Zealand, OJ L321/3, 29 November 2016; the Strategic Partnership Agreement with Canada, see OJ L329/43, 3 December 2016; the Political Dialogue and Cooperation Agreement with Cuba OJ L337I/1, 13

beyond only provisionally applying some trade related and institutional provisions (see Sect. 6.4).

6.3 On EU Mixed Bilateral Agreements and Their Provisional Application

Mixed agreements are international agreements concluded by both the EU and (some or all of) the EU Member States, on the one hand, and one (or more) subject(s) of international law, on the other hand.[30] They are a necessity whenever an agreement contains provisions that touch both on EU exclusive competence and Member States' retained competences. Alternatively, if the international agreement does not cover areas coming under exclusive Member State competence, it could be concluded as an EU-only agreement. For this to happen, the Council of the EU would have to decide to exercise the EU's competences to the fullest, thereby pre-empting the Member States.[31] However, in so far as the international agreement covers areas coming under shared competence, an option always remains to allow the Member States to be formal parties to the agreement, thus resulting in a facultatively mixed agreement.

Indeed, in practice, the Member States in Council typically limit the EU's exercise of competence in the external sphere to the areas coming under its exclusive competence when horizontal, rather than sector specific, agreements are concluded. For the other areas, the Council will typically decide that the EU elects not to exercise its shared competences, leaving the necessary legal space for the Member States to be involved.

The reasons why the EU Member States insist on the EU refraining from exercising its shared competences when concluding international agreements have been amply discussed elsewhere and do not require an extensive discussion here.[32] Suffice to note that the choice for a mixed agreement means that Member States will be *formal* parties to the agreement, one of the most visible acts of their retained sovereignty, and this

December 2016; the Cooperation Agreement on Partnership and Development with Afghanistan OJ L 67/1, 24 October 2017; the Framework Agreement with Australia OJ L237/5, 15 September 2017; the Strategic Partnership Agreement with Japan OJ L 216/1, 10 July 2018 (as regards horizontal cooperation agreements); the EU-Korea Free Trade Agreement (FTA) OJ L127/1, 14 May 2011; the EU-Central America AA OJ L 346/1, 15 December 2012; the Trade Agreement with Colombia and Peru OJ L 354/1, 21 December 2012; the EU-Ukraine AA OJ L161/3, 29 May 2014; the EU-Moldova AA L260/1, 30 August 2014; the EU-Georgia AA L261/1, 30 August 2014; the Comprehensive Economic and Trade Agreement with Canada (CETA) OJ L 11/1, 14 January 2017; the EU-Armenia AA OJ L23/1, 26 January 2018 (trade or association agreements); the Cooperation Agreement on Satellite Navigation with Norway OJ L53/11, 29 October 2010; the Agreement on Galileo with the USA OJ L348/1, 31 December 2011; the European Satellite Navigation Programmes Cooperation Agreement with Switzerland OJ L15/1, 20 January 2014 (other sectoral agreements).

[30] Kadelbach 2014, p. 227.

[31] See Consolidated Version of the Treaty on the Functioning of the European Union, 2012, OJ C 326 (TFEU), Article 2(2).

[32] See notably one of the first contributions on the topic, Ehlermann 1983, pp. 3–21.

choice thereby ensures that the Member States retain an identity on the international plane. It also allows the Member States to contain the EU's reach and possible pre-emptive effects of the EU concluding an agreement which might otherwise reduce the possible scope for Member State action through a reverse *ERTA* effect.[33] In terms of competences, mixity is convenient because it allows the precise division of competences between the EU and the Member States to be held in abeyance.[34] By concluding the agreement as one meta-party, all the matters under the agreement are by definition covered in terms of competences.[35] In terms of decision-making power, the choice for a mixed (rather than an EU-only) agreement typically does not strengthen a Member State's hand. While a mixed agreement evidently gives every Member State a veto right, the Member States will most often already have a veto right in the Council of the EU. This will be the case at least for the politically significant agreements, since these will normally come under one of the exceptions of Articles 218(8) TFEU and 207(4) TFEU which provide that the Council must conclude an agreement by unanimity rather than by qualified majority vote.

In short, mixity remains very attractive to the Member States despite all the practical and legal problems raised by concluding a facultative EU-only agreement as a facultative mixed agreement. Out of those problems,[36] perhaps the most pressing practical issue resulting from concluding an international agreement as a mixed agreement is that in an EU of 27 Member States, at least 28 different ratification procedures have to be completed on the EU side before the agreement can enter into force. This is where the technique of provisional application enters the stage as it is relied upon by the EU precisely to offset the negative effects of the considerable delays between the signing of a mixed agreement and its formal entry into force.[37] Where provisional application has become a common technique, it still remains an exception for most agreements concluded by states.[38] For the EU's mixed bilateral agreements however, it has become the rule. Considering the different functions of provisional application identified above, the provisional application of mixed agreements would then *prima facie* seem to come under that of 'the circumvention of obstacles to entry into force.' However, the examples cited in this regard by Michie relate purely to *political* impediments in bilateral relations.[39] These are of a different nature than the *legal* impediments to the entry into force of a mixed agreement.[40] Indeed, the provisional application of EU bilateral mixed agreements is always *originally* envisaged and is an almost automatic corollary to the decision on the mixed

[33] See the discussion at n. 81.

[34] Van der Loo & Wessel 2017, p. 738.

[35] See Consolidated Version of the Treaty on the European Union, 2012, OJ C326 (TEU), Article 5(2).

[36] See Rosas 2020, pp. 9–12.

[37] Michie 2009, pp. 3–4.

[38] Kempen and Schiffbauer 2017, p. 99.

[39] Ibid., 35–36.

[40] This was also noted as such by Special Rapporteur Juan Manuel Gómez, see ILC 2013a, above n. 18, p. 9.

nature of the agreement. In fact, it is only when the internal constitutional law of the partner third country does not allow provisional application that the agreement will not contain a clause on provisional application.[41]

The present chapter therefore argues that the EU has created a new and specific function for the legal device of provisional application: in a composite federal system whereby treaty-making powers are shared between the federal and the state level, provisional application facilitates the decision to turn a facultative EU-only agreement into a facultative mixed agreement, by formally concluding an agreement in mixed form but (partially and temporarily) applying it as if it were an EU-only one. The device of provisional application allows the Member States in Council to reconcile two conflicting objectives: on the one hand the Member States do not want to wait several years before seeing the effective application of the commitments entered into by virtue of an international agreement. On the other hand, the Member States want to remain being involved as formal parties to major agreements, something which becomes impossible if those agreements are concluded by the EU on its own. Provisional application then creates a way out of this dilemma and facilitates the decision in favour of 'mixity'. It thereby also allows the EU and its Member States (as a meta-party) to remain an attractive partner to the outside world even when agreements are concluded as mixed agreements.[42]

Assuming this practice by the EU is legally sound,[43] an inherent limit to the decision on provisional application, which is taken by the Council pursuant to Article 218(5) TFEU, is that it can only relate to those provisions of the agreement for which the EU (i) has been conferred a competence and (ii) for which it also exercises a competence (cf. the EU may have a competence without exercising it). Yet, if the exact scope of the provisional application is spelled out methodically in the EU's decision on provisional application this would again make the technique less attractive and would go against part of the raison d'être of having mixed agreements in the first place (cf. *supra*), since it would require the EU and the Member States to articulate the division of competences between the EU and the Member

[41]See for instance the Framework Agreement on Comprehensive Partnership and Cooperation between the European Union and its Member States, of the one part, and the Socialist Republic of Vietnam OJ L 137/1, 3 December 2016.

[42]Of course, the device of provisional application is no miracle cure either. As the CETA saga shows, mixity still has the potential of significantly undermining the EU's attractiveness as an international partner. The Commission was of the opinion that CETA should be an EU-only agreement but for political reasons agreed to have it signed and concluded as a mixed agreement. Just before the planned signature of CETA however, the government of one of the Belgian regions blocked the procedure (which it could because of CETA's mixed nature), a compromise being reached only at the eleventh hour, allowing for CETA's signature and provisional application.

[43]I.a. Kempen and Schiffbauer claim that the EU's practice is illegal. This, based on the premise that a provisionally applied agreement is a separate but accessory agreement to the main agreement, and that therefore the parties to both agreements ought to be the same (which they are not in current EU practice). If they are not the same Kempen and Schiffbauer argue that the provisionally applied agreement is not 'accessory' anymore and requires its own negotiating and ratification process (which it does not in current EU practice). See Kempen and Schiffbauer 2017, pp. 116–117. Similarly, see Bäumler 2016, p. 626.

States with precision. As will be illustrated below however, the EU Council's decisions on provisional application are drafted in rather ambiguous terms, allowing the provisional application of (parts) of an agreement without definitively settling the question whether the EU has exercised competence for these parts, thus adding to the attractiveness (for EU Member States) of the technique of provisional application.[44]

6.4 The Practice of Provisionally Applying Mixed Agreements Post-Lisbon

The very first application of this new (or EU-specific) function of the device of provisional application related to the 1995 Interregional Framework Cooperation Agreement (IFCA) between the EU and its Member States with the Mercosur and its Party States. The provisional application only extended to some of the trade related clauses[45] of the IFCA and the institutional provisions facilitating the implementation of the agreement.[46] Materially then the scope of provisional application was the same as the typical scope of the interim agreements concluded by the EU (cf *supra*).[47]

Since the IFCA itself did not foresee in its provisional application, the provisional application was put into effect through a separate exchange of letters.[48] In addition, given that the EU Treaties at the time did not explicitly allow recourse to provisional application, the Council's decision on the provisional application did not identify a specific legal basis in the Treaties.[49]

---

[44] Subject to this caveat, it is therefore doubtful to claim that "*it is not guaranteed that the mixed agreement will be subject to provisional application in all of the member states in regard to those aspects of the mixed agreement that do not fall within the Union's competence*" as does Paz Andrés Sáenz de Santa María, since the duty to provisionally apply the agreement also in the Member States is purely an EU-obligation similarly to the duty to apply agreements *formally concluded* by the EU pursuant to Article 216(2) TFEU. See Paz Andrés Sáenz de Santa María 2019, p. 731.

[45] Notably the provision on cooperation in relation to intellectual property (and for the agreement with Chile, cf. infra) also the provision on public procurement) was not provisionally applied.

[46] An identical procedural approach was taken for the provisional application of the framework cooperation agreement with Chile OJ L 209/2, 19 August 1996.

[47] As Neframi rightly notes, given that it is the Council of the EU deciding on either provisional application or an interim agreement, such a decision cannot (in principle) cover the agreement's provisions coming under Member State competence. See Neframi 2007, p. 297 at n. 509.

[48] See Interregional Framework Cooperation Agreement between the European Community and its Member States, of the one part, and the Southern Common Market and its Party States, of the other part - Joint Declaration on political dialogue between the European Union and Mercosur OJ L69, 19 March 1996.

[49] See Council Decision 96/205/EC of 20 November 1995 concerning the provisional application of certain provisions of the Interregional Framework Cooperation Agreement between the European Community and its Member States, of the one part, and the Southern Common Market and its Party States, of the other part OJ L69, 19 March 1996; Council Decision 96/504/EC of 18 July 1996 on the Exchange of Letters between the European Community and Chile concerning the provisional application of certain provisions of the Framework Cooperation Agreement leading ultimately to the establishment of a political and economic association between the European Community and

Considering the changes introduced by the Amsterdam Treaty (cf. *supra*), it is by now established practice for the Commission to include a clause on provisional application in the agreement's general provision on its entry into force and for the Council to decide on the provisional application in the same decision as the one authorizing the signature of the agreement. The old practice of provisionally applying agreements through separate exchange of letters has thus been discontinued. In the mixed agreements which the EU concludes, provisional application commences when both parties have exchanged notifications informing that the necessary internal procedure for provisional application have been completed. The agreements thereby typically prescribe provisional application in a mandatory manner although some agreements merely allow for provisional application.[50] The EU's rather consistent practice is therefore a more refined version of the second type of source of provisional application identified by Special Rapporteur Gomez-Robledo,[51] i.e. the obligation to provisionally apply the agreement arises out of the signature of the parties but the commencement depends on a further reciprocal unilateral decision.

Despite the very high degree of consistency in the EU's approach to provisional application, some differentiation in the Council's approach may still be noted: its decisions identifying precisely which provisions of the (to be signed) agreement will be provisionally applied vary greatly and the extent to which the identified provisions will be provisionally applied will also be qualified (Sect. 6.4.1). In theory this practice should shed light on the difficult internal division of competences within the EU (Sect. 6.4.2). Lastly, this chapter will also look at the question who at the EU side may terminate the provisional application of mixed agreements (Sect. 6.4.3).

6.4.1 Defining the Scope and Qualifying the Extent of Provisional Application

In terms of defining the scope of provisional application, two basic approaches are typically followed by the Council in its decisions on signature and provisional application.[52] Pursuant to a positive approach the Council identifies those provisions that

its Member States, of the one part, and the Republic of Chile, of the other part OJ L 209, 19 August 1996 (agreement with Chile).

[50] An example of the latter exception may be found in the PA with New Zealand.

[51] See ILC 2014, pp. 7–9.

[52] For an exception where it did, see e.g. Article 117 of the PCA with Iraq. An even more remarkable variant of this approach may be found in relation to the Korea Framework Agreement, above n. 29, where the entire agreement is provisionally applied. See Council Decision 2013/40 of the European Parliament and of the Council of 12 August 2013 on attacks against information systems and replacing Council Framework Decision 2005/222/JHA OJ L218, 14 August 2013. Since this is a mixed agreement, it is of course legally impossible for the Council to decide on the full provisional application in absence of a delegation by the Member States. Kleimann and Kübek seem to refute this by noting past institutional practice whereby the (Member States in) Council agree(d) to a provisional application which *prima facie* extended to provisions coming under national exclusive

will be provisionally applied, while a negative approach will list the provisions that will not be provisionally applied.

Of course, in practice, different variations on these basic approaches exist. Sometimes the Council opts for a combination of the positive and negative approach.[53] In a number of other cases, such as that of the Framework Agreement with Korea,[54] a remarkable variant is followed whereby the *entire* agreement is provisionally applied.[55] From a legal perspective this is problematic, since by definition a mixed agreement implies that at least some commitments of the agreement are entered into (on behalf of the EU-meta-party) by the Member States. In so far as the Member States have not given a mandate to the EU Council to decide on the provisional application for those commitments, the Council would act *ultra vires* when deciding on the provisional application of the entire agreement.[56]

For this reason, a practice was developed among the Member States in Council whereby the single decision on the signature and provisional application was not just taken by the Council but by 'the Council and the Representatives of the Governments

competence. See Kleimann and Kübek 2018, pp. 27–28. However, "*[i]n accordance with settled case-law, a mere practice on the part of the Council cannot derogate from the rules of the Treaty and cannot therefore create a precedent that is binding on the EU institutions.*" See Court of Justice, *Commission v. Council*, Judgment, 25 October 2017, Case C-687/15, ECLI:EU:C:2017:803, para 42. As a result and a fortiori, institutional practice, even if settled, cannot in any event override the principle of conferral laid down in Article 5 TEU. Other cases (apart from the Korea Framework Agreement) where the Commission proposed the full provisional application without recourse to a hybrid act are the Euro-Med Aviation Agreement with Israel (see COM (2012) 688 final), the FTA with Korea (see COM (2010) 136 final), the Satellite Agreement with Norway (see COM (2009) 453 final), the Stepping Stone EPA with Ghana (see COM (2008) 440 final), the CETA with Canada (see COM (2016) 470 final), etc. The alternative option to decide on the full provisional application of a mixed agreement through a single decision jointly taken by the EU and the Member States has been ruled unconstitutional by the Court of Justice in the *Hybrid Acts* case. See Court of Justice, *Commission v. Council*, Judgment, 28 April 2015, Case C-28/12, ECLI:EU:C:2015 282. Following this judgment, the Council changed its practice but according to some it still does not comply with the spirit of *Hybrid Acts*. See e.g. Castillo de la Torre 2020, pp. 231–234.

[53] See i.a. the Council Decisions on the SPA with Japan, the EU-Armenia AA, the EU-Georgia AA, above n. 29.

[54] See above n. 29.

[55] As noted, this would seem legally contradictory unless the Commission proposes a hybrid act (allowing the simultaneous action of the Council of the EU and its separate Member States in a single decision). Other cases (apart from the Korea Framework Agreement) where the Commission proposed the full provisional application without recourse to a hybrid act are the Euro-Med Aviation Agreement with Israel (see COM (2012) 688 final), the FTA with Korea (see COM (2010) 136 final), the Satellite Agreement with Norway (see COM (2009) 453 final), the Stepping Stone EPA with Ghana (see COM (2008) 440 final), the CETA with Canada (see COM (2016) 470 final), etc.

[56] Kleimann and Kübek seem to refute this by noting past institutional practice whereby the (Member States in) Council agree(d) to a provisional application which *prima facie* extended to provisions coming under national exclusive competence. See Kleimann and Kübek 2018, pp. 27–28. However, "*[i]n accordance with settled case-law, a mere practice on the part of the Council cannot derogate from the rules of the Treaty and cannot therefore create a precedent that is binding on the EU institutions.*" See *Commission v. Council*, above n. 52, para 42. As a result and a fortiori, institutional

of the Member States'.[57] Such a 'hybrid' act allowed for the full and simultaneous provisional application of mixed agreements. However, it is equally clear that such 'hybrid' acts, intermingle the supranational decision-making procedure prescribed by Article 218 TFEU with the intergovernmental decision-making typical of ordinary public international law. Even when it had proposed such hybrid decisions in the past itself,[58] the Commission eventually took the Council to Court over this practice. In the 2015 *Hybrid acts* case, the Court of Justice found such intermingling to undermine both the autonomy of EU law and the principle of institutional balance and thus held the practice to be unlawful under EU law.[59] While hybrid acts cannot be adopted anymore,[60] the practice of the Council deciding on the full provisional application of a mixed agreement is still not destined to die out. For instance, the above noted Framework Agreement with Korea was fully provisionally applied by the Council acting alone, without any reservation.[61] Another example may be found with the Cooperation Agreement with Norway on Satellite Navigation which itself provides in the (full) provisional application, limited by the (unnecessary but equally unhelpful) qualifier that it relates only to the elements falling within the competence of the EU.[62]

This of course puts the third country concerned in a very peculiar position. In addition, the EU also applies a differentiated approach in relation to how the scope of provisional applications is determined, depending on the precise partner involved. For instance, a very elaborate clause can be found in the CETA, the Korea FTA and the EUSFTA (in its draft version before Opinion 2/15) where the parties agreed to provisionally apply the agreement but equally providing that "In the event that certain provisions of [the] Agreement cannot be provisionally applied, the Party which cannot undertake such provisional application shall notify the other Party of the provisions which cannot be provisionally applied." Subsequently if the other Party "does not object to provisional application within ten days of the notification that certain provisions cannot be provisionally applied, the provisions of [the] Agreement which have not been notified shall be [provisionally applied]."[63] In contrast, the SPA

---

practice, even if settled, cannot in any event override the principle of conferral laid down in TEU, above n. 35, Article 5.

[57] See e.g. for the Air Transport Agreement with Canada, above n. 29; Euro-Mediterranean Aviation Agreement with Jordan, above n. 29. For the latter (like the one with Georgia), the Commission had proposed a hybrid act itself, see COM (2010) 303 final. This is also true for its proposal to sign and provisionally apply the Galileo agreement with the US, see SEC(2004) 640 final/2.

[58] See above n. 57.

[59] See *Commission v. Council*, above n. 52. On whether the principle of institutional balance played a role in this case, see Hillion 2018, pp. 144–145.

[60] While the Court did not prohibit these acts completely, the only possible scope left for them would seem to be when both the supranational and intergovernmental decision-making procedure are identical. See Chamon 2018, p. 163.

[61] See Council Decision 2013/40, above n. 52.

[62] Norway Satellite Agreement, above n. 29, Article 12(4) of the Agreement. Similarly, see the Interim Agreements on EPAs with the SADC and ESA States and the Stepping Stone EPA with Ghana (above n. 29).

[63] See Article 17.12(4) of the original EUSFTA (on file with the author); EU-Korea FTA, above n. 29, Article 15.10.5; see also CETA, above n. 29, Article 30.7(3)(a).

with Canada provides that the EU will decide on which parts of the agreement it will provisionally apply and subsequently foresees a decision by Canada through which it needs to agree to the scope as set out by the EU before provisional application can commence.[64] Such measure of formal equality (albeit completely tailored to fit the EU's needs) between contracting parties seems absent in the PACD with Afghanistan and the Association Agreements with Ukraine, Georgia and Moldova which provide that both Parties "agree to provisionally apply [the] Agreement in part, *as specified by the Union*".[65] For the latter partners, an agreement with the EU was apparently deemed so important that they accept this inequality. However, given the flexibility of Article 25 VCLT, as reflected on this point in the ILC's draft Guideline 4,[66] this practice would still appear to be in conformity with international law.

As the just mentioned Cooperation Agreement with Norway on Satellite Navigation shows, in practice both the negative and positive approach to determining the provisional application of a mixed agreement are almost always complemented with a further qualification of the extent of provisional application.[67] In the aviation agreements, the clauses on entry into force contain a general reservation to the effect that the agreement will be provisionally applied in so far as possible under domestic law.[68] For the EU meta-party this reference captures the limitations flowing from EU's lack of full competences. Still other agreements are explicit on this, referring to provisional application in so far as the provisions come under EU competences.[69] I.a. in those cases, the Council subsequently decides that the EU will not simply provisionally apply a number of provisions but only so "to the extent that they cover matters falling within the Union's competence" which may include "matters falling within the Union's competence to define and implement a common foreign and security policy [CFSP]". Sometimes it is added that the provisional application "does not prejudge the allocation of competences between the Union and its Member States". When this limit on the extent of provisional application is also foreseen in the agreement itself, such as in the case of the Cooperation Agreement with Norway on

---

[64] See Canada SPA, above n. 29, Article 30(2).

[65] See Afghanistan PCAD, above n. 29, art 59(2); See EU-Ukraine AA, above n. 29, Article 486(3); EU-Georgia AA, above n. 29, Article 431(3); EU-Moldova AA, above n. 29, Article 464(3) (emphasis added).

[66] See above n. 14.

[67] See e.g. Norway Satellite Agreement, above n. 29, Article 12(4). Similarly, see the Interim Agreements on EPAs with the SADC and ESA States and the Stepping Stone EPA with Ghana (above n. 29).

[68] See Aviation Agreement with Israel, above n. 29, Article 30(1); Aviation Agreement with Moldova, above n. 29, Article 29(2); Ancillary Agreement, above n. 29, Article 8; Accession Agreement to the US Air Transport Agreement, above n. 29, Article 5; Air Transport Agreement with Canada, above n. 29, Article 23(2); Aviation Agreement with Jordan, above n. 29, Article 29(2); Aviation Area Agreement with Georgia, above n. 29, Article 29(2).

[69] See EPA with the SADC States, above n. 29, Article 113(3); Interim EPA with the SADC States, above n. 29, Article 105(4); Norway Satellite Agreement, above n. 29, Article 12(4); EPA with the Eastern and Southern African States, above n. 29, Article 62(4); European Satellite Navigation Programmes Cooperation Agreement with Switzerland, above n. 29, Article 27(2).

Satellite Navigation,[70] the EU's contracting party has also accepted this. However, when the Council only adds this qualifier at a later stage when it adopts its decision on provisional application,[71] the situation is much less clear (cf. *infra*).

From an internal EU perspective, these qualifiers are superfluous and redundant: if the Council decides on provisional application, the latter can by definition only relate to provisions for which the EU is competent in the first place[72] as a Council decision on provisional application cannot in any way alter the Treaty-defined allocation of competences. This also holds true for any references to the CFSP. Since the Council's decision on provisional application will cite a CFSP legal basis it is evident that the provisional application also extends to the CFSP provisions.

However, also on this point a recent decision of the Court might frustrate future mixed action. In the 2018 *Kazakhstan* case,[73] the Court of Justice effectively ruled that horizontal cooperation agreements concluded by the EU (encompassing different topics ranging from trade to CFSP) may not be based on a CFSP legal basis if the agreement's provisions related to CFSP are ancillary in quantitative and qualitative terms. The Court in *Kazakhstan* applied its well-established centre of gravity test, albeit, and this for the first time, in relation to the choice between a TEU and TFEU legal basis (rather than between two or more TFEU legal bases). This sits uneasily with Article 47 TEU which essentially provides that both the TEU and TFEU will not encroach upon each other. This legal question aside, the future decisions authorizing the signature and conclusion of this type of horizontal cooperation agreements can therefore only be based on TFEU legal bases. Council decisions providing that the provisional application on the part of the EU also covers matters coming under CFSP would then become very relevant. Whether this approach will indeed be taken is far from clear, since *Kazakhstan* could also result in the Member States insisting that future agreements' provisions on CFSP matters will not be entered into by the EU but by the Member States individually.[74]

---

[70]Norway Satellite Agreement, above n. 29, Article 12(4), that provides, i.a.: "*Norway and the European Union, as regards elements falling within its competence, agree to apply provisionally this Agreement*" (emphasis added).

[71]See e.g. recital 9 of the preamble to Council Decision 2011/265 on the signing and provisional application of the FTA with Korea, OJ L127/1, 14 May 2011.

[72]As noted above, this could only be different if the Member States mandate the Council to decide on the provisional application on their behalf. However, as a general rule for any delegation, a mandate cannot be presumed but must be granted explicitly. See, analogously, Court of Justice, *Tralli v. ECB*, Judgment, 26 May 2005, Case C-301/02 P, ECLI:EU:C:2005:306, para 43.

[73]See Court of Justice, *Commission v. Council (Kazakhstan Agreement)*, Judgment, 4 September 2018, Case C-244/17, ECLI:EU:C:2018:662.

[74]See e.g. Van Elsuwege and Van der Loo who noted that "the addition of a CFSP legal basis seemed to be a potential instrument to avoid the conclusion of mixed agreements." Van Elsuwege and Van der Loo 2019, p. 1350. Currently, a new case is pending before the Court where the Commission also challenges the legality of the Council's new approach, whereby the Council adopts two separate decisions, thereby splitting the CFSP apart from the rest of the agreement. See Case C-180/20, *Commission v. Council*, pending.

Other clarifications on the scope of the decision on provisional application are legally significant but equally legally doubtful. For instance, the Association Agreement with Central America itself provides that the parties *may* provisionally apply Part IV of the agreement. Here provisional application itself is clearly optional but there does not seem to be a choice on its scope (i.e. either the whole part IV is applied provisionally or there is no provisional application at all). Still, in its decision, the Council confirmed the provisional application of Part IV with the exclusion of Article 272 on the criminal enforcement of IP infringements. The aspect of criminal enforcement is typically something which the Member States perceive as coming under exclusive national competences, but this also means that the EU has unilaterally altered the extent of provisional application. In its decision on the signature and provisional application of the Strategic Partnership Agreement with Japan the Council for the very first time explicitly clarified that the EU will provisionally apply a number of provisions "to the extent that they cover matters for which the Union has already exercised its competence internally".[75] This type of clarification will probably figure more prominently also as an indirect consequence of the Court's jurisprudence, notably the 2017 *COTIF* case.[76]

Prior to that case, a significant number of EU Member States had consistently defended the view, both in the Council and before the Court, that the only type of competences which the EU has in external relations are exclusive competences. Hence, if in absence of an explicit competence in the Treaties it could not be shown that the EU had a priori exclusive competence (now codified in Article 3(1) TFEU) or that the EU had an exclusive competence by virtue of the *ERTA* doctrine (now codified in Article 3(2) TFEU),[77] the EU did not have any external competence at all. From this perspective, restricting the provisional application to the "matters falling within the Union's competence" is the same as restricting it to the "matters falling within the Union's exclusive competence". While this view was hardly, if at all, defended in legal doctrine (and was also contradicted by the Council's practice),[78] it took until the end of 2017 for the Court in the *COTIF* case to unequivocally confirm that the EU might also enjoy and exercise a *shared* external competence.

When the Council subsequently had to decide on the provisional application of the agreement with Japan, a number of Member States insisted that the EU should not exercise a shared competence and that instead it should only exercise its exclusive competences. Despite Article 47 of the agreement not referring back to the internal law of the parties when listing the parts of the agreement that would be provisionally applied, the Council in its decision added that part of the agreement's provisions would be provisionally applied "*to the extent that they cover matters for*

[75] The first time the Council included such a provision was in its decision on the Strategic Partnership Agreement with Canada, above n. 29.

[76] See Court of Justice, *Germany v. Council*, Judgment, 5 December 2017, Case C-600/14, ECLI:EU:C:2017:935.

[77] On the latter codification, see Chamon 2018a, pp. 1101–1142.

[78] For instance, readmission agreements have been concluded as EU-only agreements, although they clearly come under shared competence.

which the Union has already exercised its competence internally".[79] This hints at an *ERTA* effect[80] but also redefines the extent of the agreement's provisional application compared to what had been agreed with Japan. It should be noted that for the Member States this is not just an issue of principle but also one with potentially significant practical ramifications. After all, one of the (few) legal reasons why Member States might want to insist on facultative mixity is to pre-empt a so called 'reverse' *ERTA* effect. Indeed, while the traditional *ERTA* effect is well-established and accepted, it only covers situations in which the EU acquires an *exclusive external* competence as a result of having exercised a *shared internal* competence. One of the so far unsolved legal questions resulting from the *ERTA* doctrine is whether the EU exercising a shared external (rather than internal) competence could also trigger an *ERTA* effect. This would be a 'reverse' *ERTA* effect.[81] Of course, under the view that a shared external competence does not exist in the first place, the possibility of a reverse *ERTA* effect could be categorically ruled out. But with the Court's clarification in *COTIF* also comes the need to rule out any possible finding (by the Court) of a reverse *ERTA* by limiting the EU's exercise of competence.

6.4.2 The Provisional Application as a Proxy for the Precise Delimitation of Competences Between the EU and Its Member States

As already noted above, one of the key features of mixed bilateral agreements which makes them attractive to both the Member States and the EU, is that they allow the exact delimitation of competences between both of them to be held in abeyance. While the multilateral agreements which are open to regional economic integration

[79] See Council Decision (EU) 2018/1197 of 26 June 2018 on the signing, on behalf of the European Union, and provisional application of the Strategic Partnership Agreement between the European Union and its Member States, of the one part, and Japan, of the other part, OJ L216, 24 August 2018, Article 4(b).

[80] The word *hint* is important here, since for the *ERTA* test to be met under Article 3(2) TFEU, as interpreted by the Court, there needs to be a risk that common rules are affected or that their scope is altered. The simple fact that there are common rules in place (i.e. that that Union has already exercised its competence internally) is not sufficient. For this distinction see also the pre-Lisbon *Mox Plant* case, Court of Justice, *Commission of the European Communities v Ireland*, Judgment of 30 May 2006, Case C-459/03, ECLI:EU:C:2006:345 (Mox Plant); paras 105–106.

[81] Dony notes that there are elements for and against such an effect in the Court's case law and that the original draft Constitutional Treaty of 2003 explicitly referred to *internal* common rules being affected, whereas the final and current Article 3(2) TFEU only generally refers to common rules being affected. See Dony 2018, pp. 163–164. See also Klamert 2014, p. 186; Cremona 2014, p. 70; Groux 1978, p. 24; Dashwood and Heliskoski 2000, p. 14; Heliskoski 2019, p. 310.

organisations (REIOs) typically require REIOs to provide a declaration of competence,[82] such declarations are never foreseen in the EU's bilateral (mixed) agreements. Instead, the other party accepts that the Member States and the EU as a meta-party cover all of the commitments laid down in the agreement.

Van der Loo and Wessel note that in principle the veil over the division of competences may be pierced by the decision on provisional application, if there is one,[83] since it should give indications on that division.[84] However, they also note that the resulting picture is far from clear or perfect. This already follows from the discussion in the previous section. To illustrate, when the Council decision on the provisional application of the Comprehensive and Enhanced Partnership Agreement with Armenia foresees in the provisional application of Titles I and V of the agreement, one cannot simply infer that the EU is competent for those Titles since the decision equally restricts this to 'the extent that those Titles cover matters falling within the Union's competence.' As a result, in effect no clear conclusions on the precise delimitation of competences can be drawn from a decision on provisional application. In contrast, these decisions do allow a veil to be pierced in so far as they sometimes reveal disagreements between the Commission and the Council. After all, pursuant to Article 218(5) TFEU a Council decision authorizing the signature and provisional application of a negotiated agreement is always based on a Commission proposal (1).[85] These decisions may also help to identify those (remaining) areas that come under exclusive Member State competence (2).

6.4.2.1 Inter-institutional Disagreements on the Scope of EU Competences

Sometimes the Council simply endorses the scope of provisional application as proposed by the Commission. This may also happen when the Commission proposes the provisional application of the full agreement, which is questionable for a mixed agreement (cf. *supra*). The Council will then typically add a qualification that the provisional application only extends to the 'elements falling within the competence of the EU.'[86] However the Council may also opt for a more restricted scope than that proposed by the Commission by proceeding to a precise indication of the agreement's

---

[82]On this practice, see Delgado Casteleiro 2012, pp. 491–509.

[83]As noted, not all bilateral mixed agreements are provisionally applied. This is typically the case when the constitutional rules of the third country with which an agreement is signed do not allow for provisional application. See for instance the Framework Agreement on Comprehensive Partnership and Cooperation with Vietnam, above n. 41.

[84]Van der Loo and Wessel 2017, p. 754.

[85]To be precise, the proposal is made by the actor that has negotiated the agreement. Only for CFSP agreements will this be the High Representative rather than the Commission. A joint proposal by the Commission and the High Representative is also possible, albeit that also on this issue the Court's decision in *Kazakhstan* will have an impact, see above n. 73.

[86]In relation to the Stepping Stone EPA with Ghana, compare the proposal in COM (2008) 440 final with Council Decision 2016/1850, [2016] OJ L287/1.

provisions. The Council will do so through the negative[87] or positive[88] approach or a combination of both (cf. *supra*).[89]

Considering most Member States' pre-*COTIF* (cf. *supra*) understanding of the scope of EU external competences, one would expect the Council to follow a rather consistent approach in that only those provisions coming under a priori or supervening exclusive competences (cf. *supra*) would be provisionally applied. However, the decision on the scope of provisional application seems inspired as much by reasons of political expediency as for legal reasons. A first very clear area in this regard are the provisions coming under the CFSP which are routinely provisionally applied, yet clearly do not fall under the EU's exclusive competences.[90]

The provisions which the Council in the past has excluded from provisional application, sometimes in disagreement with the Commission, are varied in terms of their nature and content: WMD clauses;[91] clauses setting norms on administrative and judicial proceedings;[92] clauses on consular protection;[93] clauses on protection of intellectual property;[94] clauses on criminal enforcement;[95] clauses on cooperation with the International Criminal Court;[96] clauses on money laundering;[97] clauses on

---

[87] See i.a. Council Decision 2012/735 on the trade agreement with Columbia and Peru, OJ L354, 21 December 2012.

[88] See i.a. the Council Decisions on the Framework Agreement with Australia (Council Decision 2017/1546, OJ L 237, 15 September 2017) and on the Cooperation Agreement on Partnership and Development with Afghanistan (Council Decision 2017/434) above n. 29.

[89] See i.a. Council Decision 2017/38 on the CETA with Canada, above n. 29.

[90] According to Bribosia (at least under the original Constitutional Treaty) CFSP is a special kind of shared competence, see Bribosia 2005, p. 63.

[91] See the horizontal agreements with Australia, Afghanistan, Japan and Iraq, the AAs with Ukraine and Armenia and the Trade Agreement with Colombia and Peru, above n. 29.

[92] See CETA, above n. 29, Articles 27.3 and 27.4; EU-Ukraine AA, above n. 29, Articles 285 and 286; Trade Agreement with Colombia and Peru, above n. 29, Articles 291 and 292. The decisions for CETA and the Ukraine DCFTA explicitly provide that provisional application is only excluded in relation to national procedures.

[93] See Cuba PDCA, above n. 29, Article 35; EU-Armenia AA, Article 21.

[94] See Trade Agreement with Colombia and Peru, above n. 29, Article 202.

[95] See CETA, above n. 29, Article 20.12; EU-Ukraine AA, above n. 29, Article 158; EU-Central America AA, Article 272.

[96] See the horizontal agreements with Australia, Afghanistan, Iraq and Japan and the AAs with Ukraine and Armenia, above n. 29.

[97] See Cuba PDCA, above n. 29, Article 29; EU-Armenia DCFTA, above n. 29, Article 18; Japan SPA, above n. 29, Article 34; Iraq PCA, above n. 29, Article 107.

maritime transport;[98] taxation;[99] border security;[100] non-agricultural appellations of origin;[101] clauses on cultural cooperation;[102] forestry;[103] portfolio investment.[104]

These clauses should fall in either of two categories: a first group concerns matters which the Member States in Council (rightly or wrongly) believe to come under exclusive Member State competence (see also *infra*). Yet, two very similar provisions may sometimes be provisionally applied for one agreement and be excluded from provisional application for another agreement (on this, cf. *infra*). A second group of clauses comes under EU shared or supporting competences but are not provisionally applied because of reasons of political expediency. The broad horizontal partnership and cooperation agreements which the EU has concluded with Australia, Afghanistan, Canada, Cuba, Korea, New-Zealand, Iraq, Japan, etc., are a case in point. These horizontal agreements have been concluded with very diverse countries, but all follow a similar structure and content, although, evidently, the detailed provisions and exact commitments vary.

Of these horizontal agreements only the one with Korea was provisionally applied in full (cf. *supra*). For the others, a significant number (sometimes most) of the provisions are excluded from provisional application, even if these provisions *prima facie* come under EU (shared) competence and even if they do not impose clear obligations. One example here are the provisions on money laundering, which are typically excluded from provisional except in the case of the Korea Framework Agreement. Legally speaking the clauses on money laundering could be included in the provisional application but for political reasons (on the side of the EU or the third country) these commitments are only taken up with the formal entry into force.

The typical WMD clause which figures in every horizontal agreement is another example of a clause which, from a legal point of view, could perfectly be included in the provisional application (given the EU's competence in CFSP). This makes it all the more remarkable that is rather consistently excluded, the exceptions being the PDCA with Cuba and the FA with Korea.

Even more pointed cases are the provisions on taxation, portfolio investment and cultural cooperation. These are areas which, at least in the mind of the Member States, come close to exclusive national competence. In fact, one of the oft cited reasons for explaining the mixed nature of the Korea Free Trade Agreement was its protocol on cultural cooperation.[105] Yet, the provision on cultural cooperation in the

---

[98] See Cuba PDCA, above n. 29, Article 55.

[99] Ibid., Article 58; see also EU-Armenia AA, above n. 29, Chapter 2 of Title IV; Japan SPA, above n. 29, Article 19.

[100] See Cuba PDCA, above n. 29, Article 71.

[101] Ibid., Article 73.

[102] See EU-Korea FTA, above n. 29.

[103] See EU-Armenia, above n. 29, Article 46(e).

[104] Ibid., Article 205; see also CETA, above n. 29, Chapter 8.

[105] Given the limited substantive commitments made in relation to cultural cooperation, it is challengeable however whether the protocol indeed triggered a legal need for mixity. See Chamon 2018, p. 152.

Strategic Partnership Agreement with Japan is provisionally applied.[106] Conversely, and as Kleimann and Kübek note, the provisions on portfolio investment of the Korea FTA were provisionally applied.[107] In relation to taxation, the relevant provisions in CETA, the SADC Interim EPA and the PCA with Iraq are provisionally applied. As a result, and in relation to the Iraq PCA, the EU can be deemed to have exercised a competence when agreeing that both its Member States and Iraq remain free to fiscally discriminate on the basis of a taxpayer's place of residence.[108] Of course, the Council's decision contains the proviso that provisional application is limited to matters coming under the EU's competence but if the provision on taxation would be deemed not to be covered, it would mean that MFN treatment granted under the PCA's trade chapter would effectively extend to tax matters which arguably could not have been the intention of the Council.

6.4.2.2 The Theoretic Existence of Exclusive National Competences and Possible Work-Arounds

Some provisions are typically excluded from provisional application suggesting that these come under exclusive national competence. Perhaps the best example is the criminal enforcement of intellectual property law, although again this was included in the provisional application of the Korea FTA. Yet in relation to the Association Agreement with Central America where the Commission also proposed the full provisional application, the Council excluded the single clause of the agreement which dealt with criminal enforcement. From a legal perspective, such clauses indeed seem to fall outside EU competence if they cannot be brought under Article 83(2) TFEU or if they cannot be qualified as ancillary to the substantive commitments the enforcement of which they facilitate. That provision only allows for the adoption of minimum rules on criminal offences and sanctions in so far as necessary to ensure the effective implementation of harmonized EU rules.

The mixed agreements' provisions setting out certain guarantees for administrative and judicial proceedings which the Council typically excludes from provisional application (cf. *supra*) could also be said to come under exclusive national competence. At least for judicial proceedings this finds some support in the Court's Singapore Opinion where it ruled that the agreement's Investor State Dispute Settlement (ISDS) provisions did not come within the EU's exclusive competence given their impact on national jurisdictions.[109] Crucially however, the Court did not arrive at

[106] Admittedly, the commitments vis-à-vis Korea were indeed more far-reaching than those laid down in Article 41 of the Japan agreement but it is still remarkable that provisional application was agreed to in this sensitive area.

[107] Kleimann and Kübek 2018, p. 27.

[108] See Iraq PCA, above n. 29, Article 26(3).

[109] Court of Justice, *Free Trade Agreement between the European Union and the Republic of Singapore*, Opinion of the Court, 16 May 2017, Opinion 2/15, ECLI:EU:C:2017:376, paras 292–293.

this conclusion by finding that this area comes under exclusive national competence but only because the provisions on ISDS could not be qualified as ancillary.[110]

This indeed raises one critical issue: although the existence of exclusive national competence is generally presumed, it is far from straightforward to actually identify an area or subject that is completely out of reach of EU law. As Lenaerts noted in 1990 "[t]here simply is no nucleus of sovereignty that the Member States can invoke, as such, against the [EU]."[111] This is because the ECJ follows a similar approach whenever reserved national competences (i.e. matter explicitly excluded from EU competence in the Treaties) or retained national competences (i.e. matters for which competence is not explicitly conferred on the EU in the Treaties) clash with EU law requirements imposed on the Member States.[112] Indeed, as Dashwood has also noted, the scope of EU law is even more vast than the competences of the EU.[113] Is it then sufficient for ancillary provisions to come within the scope of EU law or is EU competence required?

Further, even if a core of exclusive national competence can be identified, a long-lingering legal question has come to forefront rather recently: if an agreement concluded by the EU contains provisions coming under exclusive national competence, can such an agreement still be an EU-only (rather than compulsory mixed) agreement? Or can the Council include provisions of the agreement coming under exclusive national competence within the scope of the agreement's provisional application. Kleimann and Kübek note that the Council could rely on Article 352 TFEU to do so,[114] but this would imply that the matter at issue is not a genuinely exclusive national competence to begin with. A second option may be envisaged in so far as those provisions are purely ancillary. The application of the absorption doctrine is indeed well established in the case law of the Court of Justice but only so when a choice has to be made between two (or more) different legal bases in the TFEU, and following the *Kazakhstan* case also in relation to legal bases in the TEU and TFEU. In contrast, the Court has not been explicit on whether the absorption doctrine can also be applied in vertical (rather than horizontal) configurations. While some see scope for such an application of the doctrine,[115] Advocate General Kokott has dismissed the possibility, noting that it would violate the principle of conferred powers.[116]

If one were to accept a vertical application of the absorption doctrine, it would undermine the legal case for excluding provisions in international agreements coming under exclusive national competence from provisional application by the EU (or conclusion by the EU for that matter). In this regard, three different types of ancillary provisions may be identified: those that constitute commitments only for the other

[110]See Chamon 2019, pp. 44–45.

[111]Lenaerts 1990, p. 220.

[112]De Witte 2017, pp. 59–73.

[113]See Dashwood 1996, p. 114.

[114]See Kleimann and Kübek 2018, p. 28.

[115]See Chamon 2019, pp. 44–45; see also Prete 2020.

[116]Court of Justice, *Commission v. Council*, Opinion of AG Kokott, 31 May 2018, Joined Cases C-626/15 and C-659/16, ECLI:EU:C:2018:362 (MPA Antarticque), para 82.

party,[117] those that are a necessary adjunct to ensure the effectiveness of the main provisions[118] and substantive provisions that are only limited in scope.[119] The provisions on safeguards in administrative and judicial proceedings, criminal enforcement, etc., which the Council typically leaves to the Member States would then come under the second category and would not legally *require* Member State involvement. Similarly, provisions on political dialogue, WMD, etc., while symbolically important, only prescribe limited (if any) clear obligations which means they could come under the third type of ancillary provisions. Of course, these hypotheses are contested (cf. *supra*) and remain to be tested by the Court of Justice. In addition, even if the Court would confirm that the absorption doctrine may be applied vertically, it would only mean that in a number of scenarios compulsory mixity would morph into facultative mixity, i.e. the Member States' involvement would not be legally required anymore but it would still be permissible and possible if the (Member States in the) Council insist(s) on leaving a legal space for the Member States.

In summary, while the decision on the provisional application of a mixed agreement in principle ought to be informative of the division of competences between the EU and the Member States (the EU not being able to apply provisions for which the Member States are competent), in practice this is not the case. The scope of provisional application should therefore not be equated with the scope of EU competences. This is so firstly because the Council's decision on provisional application is not guided purely by legal considerations, i.e. provisions for which the EU is undoubtedly competent might still be excluded from provisional application for political reasons. Secondly, provisions that are provisionally applied cannot *a fortiori* be considered to come under EU competence in light of the Council's rather consistent practice to subject its decision to a sweeping reservation, limiting the provisional application of specifically identified provisions 'to the extent that they come under EU competence' or 'to the extent that the EU cover matters for which the EU has acted internally'.

6.4.3 Terminating the Provisional Application of a Bilateral Mixed Agreement: The Case of CETA

A final issue that has surfaced more recently raises the question as to what happens to a (partially) provisionally applied mixed agreement when one of the EU's Member

[117] Court of Justice, *Competence of the Community to conclude international agreements concerning services and the protection of intellectual property*, Opinion of the Court, 15 November 1994, Opinion 1/94, ECLI:EU:C:1994:384, para 68.

[118] Court of Justice, *Commission v. Council*, Judgment, 22 October 2013, Case C-137/12, ECLI:EU:C:2013:675, para 70.

[119] Court of Justice, *Portugal v. Council*, Judgment of the Court, 3 December 1996, Case C-268/94, ECLI:EU:C:1996:461, paras 75–76.

States subsequently refuses to ratify the agreement.[120] Regarding the termination of provisional application, Article 25(2) VCLT first refers back to the (or an) agreement between the parties themselves, adding a second option allowing the unilateral termination of provisional application by a party if it has ultimately decided not to be a party to the agreement. This is also reflected in draft Guideline 8 of the ILC[121] which foresees that apart from the situation in which a state or international organisation does not intend to become a party to the agreement, the termination of provisional application may be provided for in the agreement itself or if it is otherwise agreed. This leaves the question *when* termination is required and *who* may terminate provisional application.

The provisions in the EU's mixed bilateral agreement do not always contain specific rules on a possible termination of the provisional application of the agreement[122] (and this for instance unlike the elaborate provision in Article 45(3) of the Energy Charter Treaty).[123] The question therefore arises whether under Article 25(2) VCLT and draft Guideline 8, the provisional application *must* be terminated when one Member State of the EU decides not to ratify the mixed agreement, a question which is never foreseen in either the EU's mixed agreements or the Council's decision on provisional application.[124] A related question is whether Article 25(2) VCLT and draft Guideline 8, as a reflection of customary international law,[125] *exhaustively* regulate the scenarios in which provisional application may be terminated.[126]

---

[120] Another question is whether an individual EU Member State can terminate the provisional application (decided upon by the Council of the EU) of a mixed agreement. Although it should evidently be answered in the negative, the question is still raised because of the blatantly erroneous finding of the German Constitutional Court (in interim proceedings on the validity of CETA), arrogating this power to the German government. See BVerfG, *Judgment of the Second Senate*, 13 October 2016, 2 BvR 1368/16, ECLI:DE:BVerfG:2016:rs20161013.2bvr136816, para 72. For a more elaborate challenge of the German Constitutional Court's assertion, see Suse and Wouters 2018, pp. 20–22; Kleimann and Kübek 2018, pp. 29–30.

[121] See above n. 14.

[122] For those that do, see i.a. EU-Ukraine AA, above n. 29, Article 486(7); EPCA with Kazakhstan, above n. 29, Article 281(10); EU-Korea FTA, above n. 29, Article 15.10(5)(c); CETA, above n. 29, Article 30.7(3)(c).

[123] For a discussion see Dalton 2012, p. 241 et seq.

[124] Only because of the obstacles putting into doubt the signature of the CETA did the Council include a clear statement on the fate of provisional application when ratification remains forthcoming, see also infra n. 126.

[125] See above n. 10.

[126] Although that question will not be further addressed here, Bartels seems to assume it does, all the while noting that Article 25(2) VCLT cannot be considered customary international law if it precludes parties from terminating provisional application as a means to put pressure on other contracting parties to ensure the proper ratification of the agreement. See Bartels 2012, p. 118.

This has become relevant following the uncertain ratification procedure of the CETA with Canada.[127] Poland has for instance objected to the envisaged composition of the dispute settlement body.[128] The former Italian populist government had also threatened to refuse ratification because CETA would insufficiently safeguard Italian appellations of origin,[129] and the Cypriot parliament has even rejected the agreement because of its insufficient protection of Cypriot Halloumi. Even after the Court's positive Opinion 1/17, a government party in a pro-trade Member State such as the Netherlands is making objections to the investment rules in CETA.[130] In this regard, Van der Loo and Wessel note that "*as long as not all the parties have ratified the agreement, the provisional application can continue indefinitely, [since t]he clauses on provisional application in mixed agreements or the respective Council decisions do not impose a "deadline" on the provisional application.*"[131] According to both authors, the situation would be different when a Member State gives *formal* notification of its intent not to ratify the agreement. Since the agreements' provisions on entry into force and the Council's decisions on provisional application typically foresee in the provisional application *pending* the agreement's entry into force. Van der Loo and Wessel, relying also on a formal Council position adopted at the occasion of the signature of CETA,[132] argue that provisional application would have to be terminated given that the formal entry into force would be definitively forthcoming.[133] Suse and Wouters acknowledge that this may be so under EU law but argue that under international law this is not the case. This since the decision on provisional application by the Council can only relate to those provisions for which the EU is competent, meaning that "*the Member States do not qualify as 'States between which the treaty is being applied provisionally' […] in the sense of Article 25(2) VCLT*".[134] While correct on its terms, the reasoning of Suse and Wouters loses force when ones takes into account that the 1969 VCLT only relates to the treaties between states and in no way envisages the possibility of mixed agreements.

[127] This is not to say that CETA is the first case in which the entry into force (or provisional application) of a mixed agreement is put into doubt because of objections raised by individual Member States subsequent to the signature of the mixed agreement. In this regard Rosas notes the so-called Grappa incident of 1999–2000, see Rosas 2010, p. 368. Van der Loo and Wessel also draw attention to the Dutch referendum rejecting the Association Agreement with Ukraine, see Van der Loo and Wessel 2017, p. 735 et seq.

[128] See Shotter J and Brunsden J (2017) Poland threatens to block part of EU-Canada trade deal. https://www.ft.com/content/9c83f060-9321-11e7-a9e6-11d2f0ebb7f0. Accessed 13 May 2020.

[129] Sisto A and Jones G (2018) Italy says it won't ratify EU-Canada trade deal; Canada plays down threat https://www.reuters.com/article/us-italy-canada-trade/italy-says-it-wont-ratify-eu-canada-trade-deal-canada-plays-down-threat-idUSKBN1K318Q Accessed 8 July 2020.

[130] See Alonso S (2019) Is er nog een toekomst voor het CETA-verdrag? [Is there still a future for CETA?]. https://www.nrc.nl/nieuws/2019/10/15/is-er-nog-een-toekomst-voor-het-ceta-verdrag-a3976870. Accessed 8 July 2020.

[131] Van der Loo and Wessel 2017, p. 759.

[132] See the statement of the Council (no 20) regarding the termination of provisional application of CETA, OJ L11/15, 14 January 2017.

[133] See Van der Loo and Wessel 2017, p. 760.

[134] Suse and Wouters 2018, p. 18.

The EU's mixed bilateral agreements themselves typically contain a provision identifying the parties to the agreement, providing that "*the Parties mean, on the one hand, the European Union or its Member States or the European Union and its Member States within their respective areas of competence as derived from the Treaty on European Union and the Treaty on the Functioning of the European Union (hereinafter referred to as the 'EU Party')*".[135] In the terms of a (bilateral) mixed agreement itself, there is always one third country on the one part and the Member States and the EU on the other part (constituting a meta-party). The 'States' to which Article 25(2) VCLT refers must then in the context of a mixed agreement be interpreted as the third country on the one hand and the EU meta-party on the other hand. Since a mixed agreement can only enter into force once it is ratified by all constituent parts of the EU-party, a definite refusal by just one of these constituent parts would be sufficient to meet the requirement for termination under Article 25(2) VCLT.[136] The key issue then is when the impediment to ratification can be deemed to be permanent and definitive.[137] As Suse and Wouters correctly point out, only rarely would this threshold be met in practice.[138] An initial averse ruling by a national constitutional court or a failure to ratify by a national parliament, such as in the case of Cyprus, in itself would not be sufficient in this regard. Instead, one could argue that under the EU principle of sincere cooperation, which requires Member States to "facilitate the achievement of the Union's tasks",[139] they would first have to seek and exhaust possible solutions to overcome any legal and political obstacles to ratification. In addition, under the very same principle, combined with the principle of conferral, the legal and political obstacles raised at national level could in the first place also only relate to matters for which the Member States are competent.[140]

In light of this, the possible Polish, Dutch, Cypriot and Italian objections to CETA are also markedly different. While the Court of Justice in Opinion 2/15 has confirmed that the EU's exclusive competence did not extend to the investor state dispute settlement mechanism,[141] it has equally confirmed in the case on the Lisbon Agreement on Appellations of Origin and Geographical Indications that the EU's exclusive

---

[135] See e.g. EU-Korea FTA, above n. 29, Article 1.2.

[136] While the requirements of Article 25(2) VCLT would be met, it is unclear whether Article 25(2) VCLT would also require the termination of the provisional application. While it would appear to make little sense in provisionally applying an agreement for which it is positively assured that it will never enter into force, an obligation to terminate provisional application does not follow from the text of Article 25(2) VCLT itself.

[137] A 'permanent and definite' failure to ratify the agreement is the threshold identified in the Council statement above at n. 131.

[138] Suse and Wouters 2018, p. 20.

[139] See TEU, above n. 35, Article 4(3).

[140] On this see Opinion 2/15 *(Singapore FTA)*, above n. 109, Opinion of AG Sharpston, 21 December 2016, ECLI:EU:C:2016:992, para 568. See also Van der Loo and Wessel 2017, p. 745.

[141] Opinion 2/15 *(Singapore FTA)*, above n. 109, paras 290–293.

competence in Common Commercial Policy extends to both agricultural and non-agricultural appellations of origin.[142] While the Polish and Dutch objections would relate to issues coming under shared competence (or perhaps even exclusive national competence), Italy and Cyprus would be acting ultra vires since only the Council of the EU is competent to decide on commitments under the CCP.

Finally, this brings us to the second issue, which is that of the actor that may terminate provisional application. As noted by Paz Andrés Sáenz De Santa María, a number of Member States have claimed the competence to terminate the provisional application of the CETA agreement.[143] It is also the position defended by the German government before the German Constitutional Court and endorsed by the latter[144] but it stands in contrast with the Council's view that the provisional application would be terminated "*in accordance with EU procedures*".[145] That arguably is indeed the better view since the decision on provisional application is also taken by the Council and in accordance with EU procedures. EU Member States claiming this competence results in a serious risk of a second Grappa-incident. As Rosas explains, when the provisional application of the association agreement with South Africa was about to commence (on the first of January 2000), Italy made certain last minute demands and threatened that it would not ratify the agreement, meaning that the agreement could not be provisionally applied either (pursuant to Article 25 VCLT). A solution was ultimately negotiated but the Commission also took the position that EU Member States had no independent say anymore in so far as the Council had decided on provisional application.[146] For the EU's partners, this internal EU issue of course results in a great deal of legal uncertainty.

As a result, it would have been welcome if the draft Guideline 8 of the ILC or the commentary thereto had been more explicit thereon. Draft Guideline 8 could have for instance referred back to the internal law of the parties, given that such a reference has also been included in draft Guideline 11 or be more explicit on the identity of the terminating state or international organization by clarifying that the termination may be notified *only* by the State or international organization that decided on the commencement of provisional application in line with draft Guideline 5.

[142] Court of Justice, *Commission v. Council*, Judgment, 25 October 2017, Case C-389/15, ECLI:EU:C:2017:798.

[143] Paz Andrés Sáenz de Santa María 2019, p. 733. Poland, Germany and Austria (but not Belgium) have noted they would do so "in accordance with EU procedures" but this of course is impossible. If EU procedures are followed it can only be the Council that terminates provisional application, not the individual Member States. See Statements to be entered in Council Meetings No. 21, 22 and 37, OJ L11/15, 14 January 2017.

[144] The Court observed that Germany's statement provided that this would be done "in accordance with EU procedures" but then noted that "*it is not apparent that this reference would restrict the right deriving from Article 30.7(3) letter c CETA to unilaterally terminate the provisional application of the Agreement.*" See BVerfG, *Order of the Second Senate,* 7 December 2016 - 2 BvR 1444/16, ECLI:DE:BVerfG:2016:rs20161207.2bvr144416, para 30. See also *Judgment of the Second Senate,* above n. 120, para 72.

[145] See the statement of the Council (No 20) regarding the termination of provisional application of CETA, above n. 143.

[146] Rosas 2010, pp. 368–369.

6.5 Conclusion

Reliance on the device of provisional application is by now part and parcel of the EU's treaty making practice. In addition, it has become a quasi-automatic corollary to the Council of the EU's decisions to sign mixed bilateral agreements. The EU as an international law actor has thereby devised a new function for the instrument of provisional application. Provisional application allows federal polities such as the EU, where both levels of government are constitutionally competent to act (independently) on the international plane, to pursue effective external action, minimizing the cumbersome effects of the polity's complex internal division of competences.

Conversely, the technique of provisional application has allowed the EU Member States, as constituent parts of the EU federal polity, to remain visible actors on the international plane, since provisional application also minimizes the cumbersome legal and practical consequences of concluding a facultative EU-only agreement as a facultative mixed agreement. Without a possible recourse to provisional application, the instrument of a mixed agreement would be far less attractive to the EU Member States and more agreements would be concluded by the EU alone.

While aiming for greater consistency in the EU's external action, the Treaty of Lisbon has not done away with the practice of concluding facultative bilateral mixed agreements. The EU's practice in provisionally applying agreements remains a rich and vibrant area of study. A number of conclusions may then be drawn from the Council's practice of provisionally applying mixed agreements. First, since the provisional application (as decided upon by the Council) can in principle only relate to those provisions of the agreement for which the EU has competence, the scope or extent of provisional application should inform us of the extent of the (exercise of) EU's competences. However if the decision on provisional application would be preconditioned on a precise distinction between EU and Member State competences, the instrument of the mixed agreement itself would lose much of its attractiveness since it precisely allows the EU and the Member States to keep the exact delimitation of competences in abeyance. This also translates in the Council's decision-making practice whereby the scope of provisional application is conditioned on both self-evident and unhelpful qualifiers limiting the provisional application to 'matters falling within the EU's competence.

Recent post-Lisbon jurisprudence of the Court of Justice will impact on the Council's practice, since recourse to hybrid acts seems now excluded (*Hybrid acts*), as well as recourse to a dual TEU/TFEU legal bases for horizontal cooperation agreements (*Kazakhstan*). In addition, with the Court's confirmation in *COTIF* that the EU can act externally even when it merely has a shared competence, fears on the part of the Member States of a reverse *ERTA*-effect will be resuscitated. This may then result in Member States attempting to pre-empt this effect through an even more cumbersome definition of the scope of the provisional application of mixed agreements. The recent decision on the provisional application of the SPA with Japan seems a case in point.

It is interesting to note that so far, the EU's partners accept the peculiar burden of the EU imposing its burdensome internal competence-disagreements, as part of the price to pay to establish a legal relationship with the EU. This is even clearer for those partners that go as far as accepting that EU unilaterally determines the precise scope of provisional application.

Lastly, the disadvantages that come with concluding facultative mixed agreements have recently been highlighted again by the problematic signature and ratification processes of the CETA with Canada. Just like the Council in its decision can in principle only decide on the provisional application of provisions coming under EU competence, only the Council, and therefore not the individual Member States, can terminate the provisional application. Whether international law requires the Council to do so when just one EU Member State refuses to ratify a mixed agreement may be an open question but the Council in any event may be required to do so under EU law. However, before such a point of no return is reached (and the termination of provisional application is required), EU Member States would have to explore appropriate legal and political solutions overcoming any obstacle (at national level) to ratification. In addition, in accordance with the principles of conferral and loyal cooperation, Member States could not refuse the ratification of a mixed agreement if their objections relate to issues coming under EU exclusive competence.

References

Arsanjani M, Reisman M (2011) Provisional Application of Treaties in International Law: The Energy Charter Treaty Awards. In: Cannizaro E (ed) The Law of Treaties beyond the Vienna Convention. Oxford, Oxford University Press, pp 86–104

Bartels L (2012) Withdrawing Provisional Application of Treaties: Has the EU Made a Mistake? CJICL 1:112–118

Bäumler J (2016) Vom Vertragstext zum Inkrafttreten: Das Vertragsschlussverfahren im Mehrebenensystem am Beispiel CETA [From the text of the Treaty to its entry into force: The contract conclusion procedure in the multi-level system using the example of CETA]. Europarecht 51:607–630

Bribosia H (2005) La répartition des compétences entre l'Union et ses Etats members [The Division of Competences between the EU and MS]. In: Dony M, Bribosia E (eds) Commentaire de la Constitution de l'Union européenne. Editions de l'Université de Bruxelles, Brussels, pp 47–83

Castillo de la Torre F (2020) On 'Facultative' Mixity: Some Views from the North of the Rue de la Loi. In: Chamon M, Govaere I (eds) EU External Relations Post-Lisbon: The Law and Practice of Facultative Mixity. Martinus Nijhoff Brill, Leiden, pp 229–250

Chamon M (2018) Constitutional Limits to the Political Choice for Mixity. In: Neframi E, Gatti M (eds) Constitutional Issues of EU External Relations Law. Nomos, Baden-Baden, pp 137–166

Chamon M (2018) Implied exclusive powers in the ECJ's post-Lisbon jurisprudence: The continued development of the ERTA doctrine. CMLRev 55:1101–1142

Chamon M (2019) Mixity in the EU's post-Lisbon free trade agreements. In: Bosse-Platière I, Rapoport C (eds) The conclusion and the implementation of EU free trade agreements: constitutional challenges. Edward Elgar, Cheltenham, pp 39–57

Cremona M (2014) EU External Relations: Unity and Conferral of Powers. In: Azoulai L (ed) The Question of Competence in the European Union. Oxford University Press, Oxford, pp 65–85

Dalton R (2012) Provisional Application of Treaties. In: Hollis D (ed) The Oxford Guide to Treaties. Oxford University Press, Oxford, pp 220–247
Dashwood A (1996) The limits of European Community powers. EL Rev 21:113–128
Dashwood A (1999) External Relations Provisions of the Amsterdam Treaty. In: O'Keeffe D, Twomey P (eds) Legal Issues of the Amsterdam Treaty. Hart, Oxford, pp 202–224
Dashwood A, Heliskoski J (2000) The Classic Authorities Revisited. In: Dashwood A, Hillion H (eds) The General Law of EC External Relations. Sweet & Maxwell, London, pp 3–19
De Witte B (2017) Exclusive Member State Competences – Is There Such a Thing? In: Garben S, Govaere I (eds) The Division of Competences between the EU and the Member States. Hart, Oxford, pp 59–73
Delgado Casteleiro A (2012) EU Declarations of Competence to Multilateral Agreements: A Useful Reference Base. EFAR 17:491–509
Dony M (2018) Retour sur les compétences externes implicites de l'Union [Review of the Union's Implied External Competences]. Cahiers de droit européen 54:109–176
Ehlermann C-D (1983) Mixed Agreements: A List of Problems. In: O'Keeffe D, Schermers H (eds) Mixed Agreements. Kluwer, Deventer, pp 3–21
Flaesch-Mougin C, Bosse-Platière I (2014) L'application provisoire des accords de l'Union européenne [Provisional application of EU Agreements]. In: Govaere et al. (eds) The European Union in the World – Essays in Honour of Marc Maresceau. Martinus Nijhoff, Leiden, pp 293–323
Geslin A (2005) La mise en application provisoire des traités [Provisional application of treaties]. Editions A. Pedone, Paris
Groux J (1978) Le parallelisme des compétences internes et externes de la Communauté européenne [The parallelism of the internal and external competences of the European Community]. Cahiers de droit européen 14:3–32
Hafner G (2014) Die vorläufige Anwendung internationaler Verträge [The provisional application of international treaties]. In: Benedek W et. al. (eds) Bestand und Wandels des Völkerrechts. Peter Lang, Vienna, pp 145–156
Heliskoski J (2019) The Exercise of Non-Exclusive Competence of the EU and the Conclusion of International Agreements. In: Lenaerts K et al. (eds) An Ever-Changing Union? Perspectives on the Future of EU Law in Honour of Allan Rosas. Hart Publishing, Oxford, pp 293–310
Hillion C (2018) Conferral, Cooperation and Balance in the Institutional Framework of EU External Action. In: Cremona M (ed) Structural Principles in EU External Relations Law. Hart Publishing, Oxford, pp 117–174
Hoffmeister F (2010) Curse or Blessing? Mixed Agreements in the Recent Practice of the European Union and its Member States. In: Hillion C, Koutrakos P (eds) Mixed agreements revisited: The EU and its member states in the world. Hart, Oxford, pp 249–268
ILC (2011) Report of the ILC of its Sixty-third session: Guide to Practice on Reservations to Treaties, UN Doc. A/66/10
ILC (2013a) Secretariat of the International Law Commission, Memorandum on Provisional Application of Treaties, UN Doc. A/CN.4/658
ILC (2013b) First Report on the Provisional Application of Treaties, UN Doc. A/CN.4/664
ILC (2014) Second report on the provisional application of treaties, UN Doc. A/CN.4/675
ILC (2018) Guide to the Provisional Application of Treaties, Texts and titles of the draft guidelines adopted by the Drafting Committee on first reading, UN Doc. A/CN.4/L.910
Kadelbach S (2014) Handlungsformen und Steuerungsressourcen in den EU-Außenbeziehungen. In: Hatje A, Müller-Graf P-C (eds) Europäische Außenbeziehungen. Nomos, Baden-Baden, pp 207–271
Kempen B, Schiffbauer B (2017) Die vorläufige Anwendung völkerrechtlicher Verträge im internationalen Mehrebenensystem. ZaöRV 77:95–124
Klamert M (2014) The Principle of Loyalty in EU Law. Oxford University Press, Oxford
Kleimann D, Kübek G (2018) The Signing, Provisional Application, and Conclusion of Trade and Investment Agreements in the EU: The Case of CETA and Opinion 2/15. LIEI 45:13-45

Lefeber R (2011) Treaties, Provisional Application. Max Planck Encyclopedia of Public International Law

Lenaerts K (1990) Constitutionalism and the Many Faces of Federalism. American Journal of Comparative Law 38:205–263

Maresceau M (2006) Bilateral Agreements concluded by the European Community. Martinus Nijhoff, The Hague

Mathy D (2006) Article 25. In: Corten O, Klein P (eds) Les Conventions de Vienne sur le Droit des Traités - Commentaire Article par Article. Bruylant, Brussels, pp 1047–1073

Michie A (2009) The provisional application of treaties with special reference to arms control, disarmament and non-proliferation instruments (unpublished PhD Thesis). University of South Africa, Pretoria

Neframi E (2007) Les accords mixtes de la Communauté européenne: aspects communautaires et internationaux. Bruylant, Brussels

Odermatt J (2017) The development of customary international law by international organizations, International and Comparative Law Quarterly 66:491–511

Passos R (2016) The External Powers of the European Parliament. In: Eeckhout P, Lopez-Escudero M (eds) The European Union's External Action in Times of Crisis. Hart, Oxford, pp 85–128

Paz Andrés Sáenz de Santa María M (2019) The European Union and the Law of Treaties: A Fruitful Relationship. EJIL 30:721–751

Prete L (2020) Some offstage reflections on the constitutional limits to the choice of mixity after EUSFTA, COTIF I, MPA Antarctic and COTIF II. ELRev. 45:113–127

Rogoff M, Gauditz B (1987) The Provisional Application of International Agreements. Maine Law Review 39:29–82

Rosas A (2010) The Future of Mixity. In: Hillion C, Koutrakos P (eds) Mixed agreements revisited: the EU and its member states in the world. Hart, Oxford, pp 367–374

Rosas A (2020) Mixity Past, Present and Future: Some Observations. In: Chamon M, Govaere I (eds) EU External Relations Post-Lisbon: The Law and Practice of Facultative Mixity. Martinus Nijhoff Brill, Leiden, pp 8–19

Suse A, Wouters J (2018) The Provisional Application of the EU's Mixed Trade and Investment Agreements, Working Paper No. 201

Van der Loo G, Wessel R (2017) The Non-Ratification of Mixed Agreements: Legal Consequences and Solutions. Common Market Law Review 54:735–770

Van Elsuwege P, Van der Loo G (2019) Legal basis litigation in relation to international agreements: Commission v. Council (Enhanced Partnership and Cooperation Agreement with Kazakhstan). CMLRev. 56:1333–1353

von Bogdandy A, Venzke I (2012) In Whose Name? An Investigation of International Courts' Public Authority and Its Democratic Justification, EJIL 23:7–41

M. Chamon is Assistant Professor of EU Law at Maastricht University in The Netherlands. An earlier version of this chapter, which focuses on the EU's contribution to the development of public international law through the mechanism of provisional application, has been accepted for publication in the European Journal of International Law. The present chapter studies the mechanism of provisional application from an EU law perspective.

Chapter 7
PESCO's Microcosm of Differentiated Integration

S. Blockmans

Contents

Abstract Differentiation, or what some have called the 'negative starting point' of integration, has always been the norm in EU defence policy. Political leaders in the European Council are nevertheless mindful of the need to protect their citizens against security threats from within and outside the EU's borders. For this reason, a package of defensive measures has been developed with remarkable speed since 2016. Permanent Structured Cooperation (PESCO) is the most prominent innovation in this field. Somewhat surprisingly, PESCO has produced the most inclusive expression of enhanced cooperation, even if it is the most flexible of the differentiated integration mechanisms provided by the Treaties. This is largely the result of a German push for inclusivity, which prevailed over a French desire for a higher level of ambition. Driven by the European Defence Fund (EDF), PESCO has been touted as the formula to generate 'positive differentiation', or greater convergence in Europe's defence sector. With varied clusters of member states lining up behind different types of projects, this chapter looks at the deeper forms of differentiated integration that are maturing below the Treaty level in EU defence. Is PESCO developing in the way that Germany envisaged or France wanted?

Keywords European Union · CSDP · differentiated integration · European Defence Union · PESCO · defence industries

S. Blockmans (✉)
CEPS, Brussels, Belgium
e-mail: steven.blockmans@ceps.eu

University of Amsterdam, Amsterdam, The Netherlands

W. Th. Douma et al. (eds.), *The Evolving Nature of EU External Relations Law*,
https://doi.org/10.1007/978-94-6265-423-5_7

7.1 Multi-layered Differentiation

Differentiated integration in the EU has been the subject of academic theory for decades. Seen through a legal-institutional lens, the most notable examples of differentiated integration are either 'opt-outs'[1] by a few member states from designated policy areas laid down in primary EU law, or the advance of a majority of them, in areas such as: the passport-free travel area of Schengen, the common currency eurozone and, more recently, Permanent Structured Cooperation (PESCO) in the area of defence. Special protocols either condition these forms of enhanced cooperation or address individual member states' concerns by granting derogations from treaty obligations. The scope and content of those advances or derogations vary widely. In fact, primary-level cases constitute the most far-reaching forms of differentiated integration,[2] in domains characterised by their proximity to the central functions of state: migration, money and security. Member states have been able to secure opt-outs from primary law as they have strong bargaining power in intergovernmental negotiations: EU treaty revision generally requires unanimous agreement and national ratification. That makes member state governments and parliaments veto players. Status quo countries[3] can be convinced to waive their veto by accepting opt-outs from policies they find too integrationist. If they cannot be convinced, the other member states need to conclude a treaty outside the EU treaty framework.[4]

Permanent Structured Cooperation in Defence falls within the remit of the Common Security and Defence Policy (CSDP), which itself is an integral part of the Common Foreign and Security Policy (CFSP). Whereas the operationalisation of CSDP is subject to the rules of and differentiated integration in CFSP,[5] Article 46 TEU on PESCO is a *lex specialis* that foresees a 'structured' form of cooperation (see Sect. 7.2). Moreover, the membership of PESCO need not overlap with those in enhanced, let alone temporary, forms of differentiation under either the CFSP or the CSDP.[6]

One level down from EU primary law, differentiated integration can be secured through the adoption of secondary legislation. Following a case-by-case logic and specific procedures laid down in the treaties, secondary-level differentiation can be defined as a provision, often of a more technical nature, that formally exempts at least one member state from applying a legal rule otherwise valid for all EU member

[1] These can be either complete opt-outs from policy fields or the right to opt-out on a case-by-case basis. Opting in from opt-out areas is also possible, when contractually agreed.

[2] De Neve 2007, p. 505.

[3] Those countries that would rather not agree to attribute competences to the EU in designated fields.

[4] See Schimmelfennig 2018, p. 1158.

[5] Blockmans 2013, p. 53.

[6] Ibid. The differences in support for CSDP missions were already visible with the adoption by the Council of the CFSP decision to launch *EULEX Kosovo*, which benefitted from the constructive abstention by Cyprus, and the operationalisation thereof, which also excludes Spain but includes fellow non-recognisers Romania and Slovakia.

states.[7] Legally binding acts such as EU regulations and decisions may exempt individual member states from applying them or individual provisions contained therein, or introduce special rules applied to an *avant garde* of a minimum of nine member states to establish enhanced cooperation in a non-exclusive competence area with the aim of furthering the objectives of the Union, protecting its interests and reinforcing its integration process (cf. Article 20(1) TEU and Articles 326–335 TFEU). Mimicking this philosophy, Article 46 TEU provides a unique legal basis for the adoption of Council decisions that lay down governance rules for states participating in PESCO,[8] which—in turn—may leave the possibility for further downstream differentiation (see Sect. 7.4). Yet, fluctuating empirical realities in the realm of PESCO have so far not supported sophisticated theories of multi-layered differentiation.

Cooperation between clusters of member states in PESCO is best understood as 'negative differentiation': "a status quo that poses severe obstacles to integration—rather than a formula that allows for diverse experiences and approaches to facilitate integration ('positive integration')".[9] Differences between large and small countries, nuclear/non-nuclear states, expeditionary and territorial armed forces, allies and neutrals, professional and conscript armies, big and small spenders, naval and land army states, and those with or without a defence industrial base have long prevented them from moving beyond the 'negative starting point' of differentiated integration.

And yet, in response to geopolitical shifts around the world, an increasingly volatile neighbourhood and the spectre of Brexit, great strides have been made to create a defence architecture for the European Union. A permanent headquarters for military operations has been set up, located within the European External Action Service (EEAS) in Brussels; the 22 member states that are also NATO allies pledged to increase defence spending to 2% of their GDP and to earmark 20% of that sum for investment in defence capabilities; a Coordinated Annual Review on Defence (CARD) mechanism now monitors the implementation of commitments on defence spending and capability development of member states; PESCO was formally launched in December 2017; and a multi-billion European Defence Fund (EDF) has been proposed to stimulate the development of military capabilities. Given the ulterior aim of creating a single market and operationalising European capabilities to serve common strategic interests, can we observe any greater convergence between defence sectors that so far have been siloed?

While it is too early to draw any definitive conclusions in this regard, especially since it takes years, if not decades, to develop and procure the most ambitious of platforms, one can discern the potential and the limitations of positive differentiation in the area of defence. With the launch of two waves of 17 projects in both 2017 and 2018 and a third wave of 13 projects in November 2019, early dynamics of secondary-level differentiation in the field of EU defence integration have been

---

[7] See Duttle et al. 2007, p. 410.

[8] Cf. Council Decision (CFSP) 2018/909 of 25 June 2018 establishing a common set of governance rules for PESCO projects, OJ L161/37, 26 June 2018.

[9] See Howorth 2019, p. 261.

observed. Following a brief look at the origins of primary-level differentiation in EU defence integration (Sect. 7.2), this chapter offers elements for an emerging narrative of 'positive differentiation' in participating states' modular approach to PESCO project cooperation (Sect. 7.3). It then drills down within the projects to examine whether tertiary-level flexible arrangements in the governance of these projects are being applied (Sect. 7.4).

7.2 Participation in PESCO

Article 42(6) TEU allows for the creation of a permanent structured cooperation between willing member states "whose military capabilities fulfil higher criteria and which have made more binding commitments to one another in this area with a view to the most demanding missions". This provision encapsulates the *raison d'être* of PESCO: participating states commit to spend more, and more intelligently, on defence training, equipment and capabilities so that they are better able to conduct operations at the higher end of the military spectrum. On top of the entry criteria for PESCO laid down in Article 1 of Protocol No. 10, i.e. proceeding more intensively to develop defence capacities and having the capacity to supply troops and kit, Article 2 adds the following baseline commitments for continued participation in the structured framework:

(a) cooperating with a view to achieving higher levels of investment expenditure on defence equipment in the light of, inter alia, international (especially NATO) responsibilities;
(b) aligning the defence apparatus by identifying military needs, pooling and specialising capabilities, and encouraging cooperation in training and logistics;
(c) taking concrete measures to mobilise forces;
(d) reducing capability shortfalls and gaps; and
(e) participating in major joint or European equipment programmes in the framework of the European Defence Agency (EDA).

Despite early attempts by Belgium, Hungary and Poland in a 2010 non-paper of their trio presidency to outline thoughts on how cooperation might be made inclusive and effective,[10] and a written request by Italy and Spain to HR/VP Ashton in May 2011 to put PESCO on the agenda of the Foreign Affairs Council, it took until June 2016 for a High Representative to suggest in the EU Global Strategy that "[e]nhanced cooperation between Member States should be explored, and might lead to a more structured form of cooperation, making full use of the Lisbon Treaty's potential". The December 2016 European Council responded by tasking the HR and member states to present "elements and options for an inclusive Permanent Structured Cooperation based on a modular approach and outlining possible projects".

---

[10] See Biscop and Coelmont 2011, p. 149.

Unlike the Common Security and Defence Policy (CSDP) writ large, which suffers from an opt-out by Denmark, EU defence integration in a narrower sense takes the unique form of enhanced cooperation between 25 member states (Denmark, Malta[11] and the UK[12] chose to stand aside). Compared to other cases of enhanced cooperation that are built around one piece of legislation,[13] PESCO establishes differentiated integration in an entire policy field;[14] a microcosm in which secondary level differentiation is taking shape.

Counterintuitively, PESCO has so far produced the most inclusive expression of enhanced cooperation.[15] This is largely the result of a German push for inclusivity, which prevailed over a French desire for a higher level of ambition. But rather than presenting this as a binary choice to the other member states, Berlin and Paris agreed to compromise by applying a "modular approach"[16] to enhanced cooperation in the field of defence.[17] Paradoxically, this modular approach also serves as a permanent vehicle for opt-outs and exemptions in the area of defence. For PESCO to succeed, the key challenge, therefore, is "to develop a modus operandi [which is] flexible [enough] to manage diversity [and] solid [enough] to generate tangible collective gains".[18]

---

[11] Malta invoked a constitutional commitment to neutrality and non-alignment but kept the door open for future participation depending on the course of implementation of PESCO. See Lazarou and Friede 2018, p. 6.

[12] Ibid: "The UK welcomed the launch of PESCO and 'its ambition to develop military capabilities that address the shortfalls in EU and NATO contexts', as stated by the British Minister of State for Europe, Alan Duncan, in his answer to the House of Commons."

[13] So far, the general instrument of enhanced cooperation has been triggered only four times. See Council Regulation (EU) 2017/1939 of 12 October 2017 implementing enhanced cooperation on the establishment of the European Public Prosecutor's Office ("the EPPO") OJ L283/1, 31 October 2017; Council Decision of 12 July 2010 authorising enhanced cooperation in the areas of the law applicable to divorce and legal separation, OJ L189/12, 22 July 2017; Council Decision of 10 March 2011 authorising enhanced cooperation in the area of the creation of unitary patent protection, OJ L76/53, 22 March 2011; and Proposal for a Council Directive implementing enhanced cooperation in the area of financial transaction tax, COM(2013)71 final (currently at a standstill). In all these cases, legislative proposals failed to obtain unanimous support for EU-wide implementation, with individual countries blocking the adoption of secondary legislation and sub-groups of member states forging ahead by way of enhanced cooperation.

[14] Council Decision (CFSP) 2017/2315 of 11 December 2017 establishing permanent structured cooperation (PESCO) and determining the list of participating Member States, OJ L331/57, 14 December 2017.

[15] Prior to PESCO, the most inclusive of enhanced cooperative frameworks was the establishment of the EPPO by 16 member states, joined later by 4 more. See Wolfstädter and Kreilinger 2017.

[16] European Council Conclusions, EUCO 34/16, 15 December 2016, para 11.

[17] See Blockmans 2018, p. 1785.

[18] See Fiott et al. 2017, p. 53.

7.3 Explaining Positive Integration in European Defence[19]

Cooperation (or non-cooperation) naturally stems from factors that unite (or divide) certain member states. For PESCO, these factors are primarily structural and economic in nature.[20] Firstly, it is intuitive to examine the factors that bring certain member states together within PESCO through an industrial lens. By comparing the share of the average value of PESCO participating states' arms export licences from 2012 to 2017, the average share of PESCO state-owned or transnational corporations in the SIPRI Top 100 of total arms sales worldwide from 2012 to 2017, the average defence expenditures per member state from 2012 to 2017 and the amount of active military personnel in 2019, one can observe that four PESCO participating states are the defence frontrunners: France, Italy, Germany and Spain, with Poland, Greece and Belgium in a second tier. In 9 of the 47 PESCO projects, all four of these member states are present and three of them are all members in an additional five projects.[21]

Smaller projects in which three or all of the big four are present are those which, according to the data currently available, might reward the national defence technological and industrial base (NDTIBs) of the big four. Examples of these include the natural heirs of off-the-shelf Organisation for Joint Armament Cooperation (OCCAR) projects such as ESSOR (Leonardo), European Attack Helicopters TIGER Mark III (Airbus) and the MALE RPAS Eurodrone project (Airbus, Leonardo, Dassault Aviation and Aero Vodochody). This could indicate that the financial incentives, in the form of a 10% co-financing bonus offered by the future EDF may, at times, be the sole reason for projects born outside of the PESCO framework to join. This could hold true as well for projects in which any of the big four are collaborating on a bilateral or trilateral basis with smaller member states such as the EU Beyond Line of Sight Land Battlefield Missile Systems (to be based on the Airbus, BAE, Leonardo conglomerate MBDA's MMP land combat missile system) or the Armoured Infantry Fighting Vehicle/Amphibious Assault Vehicle/Light Armoured Vehicle project (all of these are state-of-the-art Iveco products). In these cases, increased cooperation could be explained by certain member states' willingness to tap into the expertise and resources made available by the largest multinational corporations in the defence industry.

The trend of looking toward each member state's National Defence Technological and Industrial Base (NDTIB) is confirmed by the companies involved in some of the trial-run projects under the Preparatory Action for Defence Research, a EDF trial experiment under the current multi-annual financial framework: OCEAN2020

---

[19]This section draws on the empirical research presented in Blockmans and Macchiarini Crosson 2019.

[20]Other factors could be considered, such as the strength of ties as expounded upon by ECFR's Coalition Explorer. However, this data primarily relies on perceptions.

[21]Of note, there are only three projects in which none of the big four is present. These are: Maritime (semi-) Autonomous Systems for Mine Countermeasures (Belgium, Greece, Latvia, the Netherlands, Poland, Portugal, Romania), the Joint EU Intelligence School (Greece, Cyprus), and One Deployable Special Operations Force (SOF) Tactical Command and Control (C2) Command Post (CP) for Small Joint Operations (SJO)—(SOCC) for SJO (Greece, Cyprus).

Table 7.1 Multi-sectoral and operational defence cooperation in Europe

Cooperation format	Member states
Lancaster House Treaties	France and non-PESCO UK
Élysée/Aachen Treaties	France and Germany
Nordic Defence Cooperation (NORDEFCO)	Sweden, Finland and non-PESCO Denmark, along with non-EU Norway and Iceland
Visegrád 4	Poland, Hungary, the Czech Republic and Slovakia
Benelux Defence Cooperation (2012 Declaration to further defence cooperation)	Belgium, the Netherlands and Luxembourg
Baltic Defence Cooperation	Estonia, Latvia and Lithuania
Central European Defence Cooperation	Hungary, the Czech Republic, Slovakia, Austria, Croatia and Slovenia (with Poland as an observer)

Treaty between the United Kingdom of Great Britain and Northern Ireland and the French Republic for Defence and Security Co-operation, opened for signature 2 November 2010, No. 36(2011) (entered into force 1 July 2011), Articles 1–2; Franco-German Treaty of Aachen, opened for signature January 2019, Article 4; Nordic Defence Cooperation 2009; Visegrad Group EU 2014, point 1; Central European Defence Cooperation, "light institutionalisation" agreed to in May 2015 in Brno, Slovenia, mentioned in Mueller 2016, p. 30; Ministry of National Defence of the Republic of Lithuania 2019, point 4; the constituent document of the Central European Defence Cooperation could not be retrieved. Academic papers are sceptical of its utility. See Lang and Schwarzer 2011
Source Blockmans and Crosson 2019

and the Generic Open Soldier Systems Reference Architecture (GOSSRA) projects involve industrial partners such as Leonardo, MBDA, Fincantieri, Saab, Rheinmetall and PGZ, i.e. all corporations in the SIPRI Top 100 of total arms sales worldwide.[22] On the other hand, the projects in which all of the big four are present and have the output goal of stimulating coordination, harmonising standards, and jointly defining operational frameworks (instead of industrial production), tend to be larger. Examples of these are the Military Mobility, the Network of Logistic Hubs in Europe and Support to Operations, the European Military Command and Co-basing projects.[23]

Another way of explaining cooperation between participating states (also outside of the big four) is to examine previous frameworks for bilateral, trilateral, and minilateral defence cooperation in Europe. Distinctions should be made between operational and capabilities-oriented cooperation, and among different forms of operational cooperation, i.e. those that are multi-sectoral and those that are limited to one sector only. In doing so, forms of cooperation as spin-offs of NATO, such as the Joint Expeditionary Force, created at the 2014 NATO Wales Summit, or the broader concept of EU pooling and sharing, are left out. Table 7.1 presents an overview of the first type of cooperation, i.e. multi-sectoral and involving operational elements.

[22]These findings are based on original empirical research presented in Blockmans and Macchiarini Crosson 2019.

[23]Ibid.

These forms of cooperation concern both operations and acquisition of capabilities. The 2010 Lancaster House Treaties for Defence and Security Co-operation, the 2019 Franco-German Treaty of Aachen marking 56 years from the Élysée Treaty, the NORDEFCO Memorandum of Understanding, the Long Term Vision of the Visegrád Countries on Deepening their Defence Cooperation, and the 2012 Benelux Declaration on Defence Cooperation formally structure cooperation between the parties to those agreements. Baltic Defence Cooperation is not formally structured in one document yet is still multi-sectoral in nature. Other forms of bilateral, trilateral, and minilateral defence cooperation do exist, however. Examples include BeNeSam Naval Cooperation between Belgium and the Netherlands, Polish-German Submarine Cooperation, and Dutch-German Battalion and Air Force Cooperation, all operational in nature but limited in scope. Finally, on the acquisition side of things, France, Italy, Spain, Belgium, Germany, and the non-PESCO United Kingdom are all full members of OCCAR. This organisation has the objective of facilitating joint production and procurement programmes for defence equipment. The Netherlands, Poland, Lithuania, Sweden, Finland and (for now) EU accession country Turkey are observers and participate in a limited number of these projects.

These pre-existing forms of bilateral, trilateral, and minilateral cooperation in Europe only explain PESCO cooperation to a certain extent. Benelux cooperation and Baltic cooperation remain strong in PESCO, whereas Franco-German, Nordic and Visegrád cooperation is surprisingly low. In the Franco-German case this could be due to their different views on how PESCO should be run, reflective of increasing tensions between the two sides of the Rhine since the beginning of Emmanuel Macron's presidency. Finland and Sweden, the only PESCO participating states in NORDEFCO, have different preferences vis-a-vis partners, with Finland preferring to cooperate with the German-Dutch-Polish axis and Sweden choosing France and Spain as its preferred partners. This could be seen through a European Intervention Initiative (EI2) lens.[24] Sweden, not a member of this France-led initiative to develop a common strategic culture in Europe, may want to keep strong ties to its French counterparts, whereas Finland, a member of EI2, would prefer to strengthen its relationship with the more reluctant Germany,[25] followed in this case by Poland and the Netherlands, with which it shares staunch support for a leading role for NATO in providing for Europe's collective security. As for the Visegrád countries, Poland prefers to partner with the Dutch, the Czech Republic with Germany, and Hungary and Slovakia with Italy. This raises the question of whether these seemingly unexpected partnerships

[24] See Zandee and Kruijver 2019.

[25] German participation in the EI2 could be seen as a way to control the French initiative and prevent it from superseding PESCO as the main experiment in European-wide defence cooperation. Indeed, the potential for duplication, in particular with PESCO's German-led EUFOR Crisis Response Operation Core (EUFOR CROC) project, is real. While stressing the "need to further develop the emergence of a shared strategic culture through the European Intervention Initiative" in their Meseberg Declaration of 19 June 2018, Macron and Chancellor Merkel agreed to link EI2 "as closely as possible with PESCO". For that to happen though, the associate status of the respective non-members is essential. See https://www.elysee.fr/emmanuel-macron/2018/06/19/meseberg-declaration-renewing-europes-promises-of-security-and-prosperity.en. Accessed 8 July 2020.

are born out of natural synergies in member states' strategic cultures (cf. EI2) and/or particularly strong integrated value chains.[26]

One key underlying element of PESCO's 20 binding commitments is the pursuit of alignment in strategic cultures at the EU level. As others have noted, EU member states can be largely categorised into three clusters based on their level of ambition in international security policy, the scope of action for the executive branch in military-security decision-making, their foreign policy orientation and their willingness to use military force (linked to threat perceptions).[27] The clusters that emerge from their analysis, displayed in Table 7.2, prove to be interesting input for the discussion on PESCO groupings.

Two main conclusions can be drawn from this attempt to cluster EU member states' strategic cultures. First, strategic culture alignment plays a role in determining the extent of participation of certain member states in PESCO. In fact, those states with a strategic culture aimed at protecting and projecting their state power generally participate in more projects, thanks to the larger margin for manoeuvre of the executive branch of government and a generally high willingness to use military force. This is true for France, the Netherlands, Greece and Poland. Furthermore, those member states that use their security policy to gain visibility and credibility on the international stage have more heterogeneous participation rates in PESCO. In the final cluster, for those states that use their security policy as an international bargaining tool, there is some variation. A schism emerges in this cluster between Atlanticist, pro-NATO and generally Central and Eastern European member states that are less involved in PESCO, and Europeanist, Western European member states with higher participation, which could be explained by their 'functional foreign policy orientation' (see Table 7.2).

Moreover, strategic culture alignment can explain cooperation among certain member states within PESCO. First, while there is greater variation in participation among those states that use their security policy as a tool for international bargaining, the states within this cluster tend to cooperate more among themselves than the states in other clusters do. This could indicate that such a strategic culture is correlated with an institutional tendency towards cooperation. A case in point is Croatia's strong preference to partner with like-minded strategic partners within PESCO. Furthermore, some bilateral cooperation within PESCO might be explained by the alignment of strategic cultures. This could be said for Portuguese cooperation with both Austria and Finland.

Other variables could also partially explain why states participating in PESCO prefer each other as partners. Chief among these is geography. Countries like the Czech Republic, Croatia, Bulgaria, and Estonia have stronger partnerships with one or more bordering countries or countries in the immediate vicinity. The Baltics and Balkan countries, in particular, show a high level of cohesion among themselves.

---

[26]According to Pannier and Schmitt 2014, and "contrary to the arguments of many discussions, think-tank reports and political actors, there is no evidence that institutionalised cooperation leads to policy convergence as far as defence is concerned."

[27]See Biehl et al. 2013.

Table 7.2 Strategic cultures within PESCO-involved EU member states

	Security policy as a manifestation of statehood	Security policy as international bargaining	Protecting and projecting state power
The level of ambition in international security policy	Relatively high (often 'punching above its weight' in order to gain international visibility and credibility)	Low to medium (activities are expected to lead to indirect effects, i.e. a seat at the table)	High
The scope of action for the executive in decision-making	Strong legislative rights	Strong legislative rights	High flexibility for the executive (Presidential or majoritarian parliamentary system) or strong informal ties between the executive and legislative branches
Foreign policy orientation	Tendency toward the EU	Functional: NATO for collective defence, otherwise EU preference	Strong advocates for either EU or NATO
The willingness to use military force	Low	High for defence purposes, lower for crisis management	High
Countries	Austria, Cyprus, Finland, Hungary, Ireland, Luxembourg, Portugal	Belgium, Bulgaria, the Czech Republic, Estonia, Germany, Italy, Latvia, Lithuania, Romania, Slovakia, Slovenia, Spain (and potential third country participant Norway)	France, Greece, the Netherlands, Poland, Sweden (and potential third country participant UK)

Source Blockmans and Crosson 2019

Geography plays another role in the scope of cooperation. For example, all the states participating in maritime capabilities projects are seafaring. This is unsurprising from both a practical and industrial standpoint, yet one could suppose that certain components or competences are not necessarily strictly maritime, i.e. the Hungarian river minesweeping fleet for the Danube. Secondly, linguistic and cultural proximity could explain strong Belgian-French, Belgian-Dutch and, above all, Greek-Cypriot cooperation within PESCO. Finally, it seems that in a few cases, a strong pro-NATO stance (and consequently a more open position vis-a-vis third country participation) brings EU member states together in PESCO. Strong Polish-Dutch-Finnish-Baltic cooperation could be framed by the NATO narrative.[28]

Having established some of the most important push-pull factors that energise this secondary-level field of PESCO, it remains to be seen whether further differentiation might emerge within the projects.

7.4 Governance within PESCO Projects

Tertiary-level differentiation refers to the individual project arrangements, as loosely set out in Article 7(1) of Council Decision (CFSP) 2018/909 of 25 June 2018 establishing a common set of governance rules for PESCO projects. The most prominent modes of deep differentiated integration in EU defence could hypothetically take place in the form of a change to decision-making procedures.

In spite of the low threshold for launching PESCO (by qualified majority vote, or QMV), decisions and recommendations taken within the framework are adopted by unanimity, constituted by the votes of the representatives of all participating member states (Article 46(6) TEU). However, Article 4(4) of the governance rules on PESCO allows "project members [to] agree among themselves by unanimity that certain decisions, such as those relating to administrative matters, will be taken according to different voting rules", such as QMV. The likelihood that states participating in individual PESCO projects would adapt the governance rules for individual PESCO projects in order to take decisions by QMV is not great, however. As a result, decision-making by unanimity will prolong consensus politics. Poland may well replace the UK as the member state that most frequently slams on the brakes. In the face of Russian aggression, the country relies on the hard security guarantees provided by the US. Warsaw has long resisted the idea of EU defence integration for fear of undermining NATO's resolve to come to the rescue in the hour of need. Political market forces unleashed by the prospect of Brexit and the Trump presidency have ultimately led the Polish government to sign up to PESCO.[29]

If not through a change in decision-making, then tertiary differentiation in the PESCO ecosystem could manifest itself through implementation of Article 7(1) of the governance rules on PESCO:

---

[28] This is supported by the 'food-for-thought' paper encouraging an inclusive vision for third country participation put out by the Benelux countries and supported by Lithuania, Estonia, Latvia, Poland, Slovakia, the Czech Republic, Bulgaria, Portugal, Sweden and Finland. See Blockmans 2017, p. 223.

[29] In a joint letter of 13 November 2017 addressed to the HR, the Ministers of Foreign Affairs and National Defence of Poland set out three conditions for Poland's participation in PESCO: primacy of NATO's defence planning process; competitive, innovative and balanced development of the European defence industry in order to suit the needs of all the member states involved; and a "360-degree approach" to security threats with particular attention paid to the eastern flank. See Consilium Europa 2017.

> The arrangements that the project members may agree among themselves, where appropriate in writing, within each PESCO project […] include [… the] invitation to the Commission to be involved, as appropriate, in the proceedings of the project.

To date, this has not materialised. Considering, however, that EDF funding will be allocated by the Commission and that certain elements of PESCO have implications for the single market, the argument could be made for Commission participation in project proceedings to be mandatory. This could increase the potential for upward convergence between projects.

7.5 Conclusion

The political momentum generated by PESCO has been characterised by high-level officials as a game-changer in EU defence integration.[30] This is largely attributed to the involvement of the European Commission, brandishing a new Directorate General for Defence Industry and Space, in offering funding for both research in innovative defence products and technologies, and the development and procurement of key capabilities. Clusters of participating states can now bid for the type of defence projects (training, equipment and capabilities) that they and the PESCO Secretariat believe to be of most value added.

Having spurred 47 projects in its first two years, PESCO presents a microcosm of differentiated integration. Below the primary law commitments to which 25 member states have signed up, membership and observer status in the projects is in flux in at least three ways. First, overall numbers of states participating in designated projects has dropped as a result of the quick succession of more ambitious projects in the first two years since the launch of PESCO. A potential downscaling of project management from the political to the technical level may well be the consequence of that. Secondly, the differences in participation extend to the project clusters as well as to country-pairings within projects belonging to different clusters. And thirdly, the possibility of third country participation is still under discussion and may, if agreed, lead to a rise in the participation of certain projects.

Empirical research shows that, two years on, four states are PESCO frontrunners: France, Italy, Germany and Spain, with Poland, Greece, the Netherlands and Belgium in a second tier. In nine projects, all four of these member states are present and three of them are all members in an additional five projects. There are only three projects in which none of the big four are present.

The various collaborative clusters are defined by factors that unite and divide participants. These factors are primarily structural and economic in nature. Among the major factors that explain why member states gravitate towards each other, industrial cooperation and integrated supply chains play an important role. Clustering is also the result of member states' foreign policy orientation, their level of ambition

[30] See, e.g., several of the contributions in European Defence Agency 2018.

in international security policy, willingness to use military force and scope of action for the executive branch in military-security decision-making. These factors have led to various extra-EU cooperative frameworks in the area of defence, from the 2010 Lancaster House Treaties between France and the UK to the 2019 Franco-German treaty signed at Aachen but could be gold-plated in the PESCO framework.

With subsequent waves of PESCO projects becoming more ambitious, costly and exclusive, an early trend of re-ordering can be observed. Two different scenarios may emerge if France continues to power ahead with its PESCO commitments while Germany and Italy lose appetite and stretch their military and administrative resources. On the one hand, if political enthusiasm remains, the future of EU defence could be defined along French-industry lines. On the other hand, if political momentum is lost due to growing indifference by participating state governments toward PESCO, it could be that the Commission's newly created DG Defence Industry and Space (even under the current French Commissioner Thierry Breton) takes the lead on defence matters at a more technical level.

With the focus in coming years shifting away from the launch of new initiatives to implementation of what has been put in place, one may well expect projects to merge or disappear altogether, depending on the level of member state commitment and synergies developed with other projects. Such 'positive differentiation' is not a foregone conclusion, however. Further industrial and operational convergence may lead to new siloes around 'European champions', thus hampering a proper functioning of the envisaged single market of defence. Based on the principle of an open and fair market, it will be up to the HRVP and the European Commission to ensure that EU defence integration remains high on the political agenda and that (vested) industry interests do not undermine the ulterior objective of European strategic autonomy.

References

Biehl H, Giegerich B, Jonas A (2013) Strategic Cultures in Europe. Springer, Wiesbaden

Biscop B, Coelmont J (2011) CSDP and the Ghent framework: The Indirect Approach to Permanent Structured Cooperation. EFAR 16:149–167

Blockmans S (2013) Differentiation in CFSP. Studia Diplomatica LXVI:53–67

Blockmans S (2017) The Benelux Approach to EU Integration and External Action. Global Affairs 3:223–235

Blockmans S (2018) The EU's Modular Approach to Defence Integration: An Inclusive, Ambitious and Legally Binding PESCO? CMLRev 55:1785–1826

Blockmans S, Macchiarini Crosson D (2019) Differentiated Integration Within PESCO: Clusters and Convergence in EU Defence. https://www.ceps.eu/wp-content/uploads/2019/12/RR2019_04_Differentiated-integration-within-PESCO.pdf. Accessed 24 May 2020

Consilium Europa (2017) Notification on Permanent Structured Cooperation (PESCO) to the Council and to the High Representative of the Union for Foreign Affairs and Security Policy. https://www.consilium.europa.eu/media/31511/171113-pesco-notification.pdf. Accessed 8 July 2020

De Neve J (2007) The European Onion? How Differentiated Integration is Reshaping the EU. JEI 29:503–521

Duttle T et al. (2007) Opting Out from European Union Legislation: The Differentiation of Secondary Law. JEPP 24:406–428

European Defence Agency (2018) Quantum Leap: How PESCO Could Shape European Defence. https://www.eda.europa.eu/docs/default-source/eda-magazine/edm-issue-15_web. Accessed 24 May 2020

Fiott D, Missiroli A, Tardy T (2017) Permanent Structured Cooperation: What's in a Name? ISSUE Chaillot Paper No 142:5–66

Howorth J (2019) Differentiation in Security and Defence Policy. CEP 17:261–277

Lang K-O, Schwarzer D (2011) Consolidating the Weimar Triangle. https://www.files.ethz.ch/isn/134241/2011C30_lng_swd_ks.pdf. Accessed 24 May 2020

Lazarou E, Friede A (2018) Permanent Structured Cooperation (PESCO): Beyond Establishment. https://www.europarl.europa.eu/thinktank/en/document.html?reference=EPRS_BRI(2018)614739. Accessed 8 July 2020

Ministry of National Defence of the Republic of Lithuania (2019) Baltic Defence Ministers agreed on mutual positions on aspects of the NATO deterrence and defence measures at the meeting in Tartu. https://kam.lt/en/news_1098/current_issues/baltic_defence_ministers_agreed_on_mutual_positions_on_aspects_of_the_nato_deterrence_and_defence_measures_at_the_meeting_in_tartu.html. Accessed 24 May 2020

Mueller P (2016) Europeanization and regional cooperation initiatives: Austria's participation in the Salzburg Forum and in Central European Defence Cooperation. OZP 45:23–34

Nordic Defence Cooperation (2009) Memorandum of Understanding. https://www.nordefco.org/Files/nordefco-mou.pdf. Accessed 24 May 2020

Pannier A, Schmitt O (2014) Institutionalised Cooperation and Policy Convergence in European Defence: Lessons from the Relations Between France, Germany and the UK. European Security 23:270–289

Schimmelfennig F (2018) Brexit: Differentiated Disintegration in the European Union. JEPP 25:1154–1173

Visegrad Group EU (2014) Long Term Vision of the Visegrad Countries on Deepening their Defence Cooperation: Political declaration. http://www.visegradgroup.eu/about/cooperation/defence. Accessed 24 May 2020

Wolfstädter L, Kreilinger V (2017) European Integration via Flexibility Tools: The Cases of EPPO and PESCO. https://institutdelors.eu/wp-content/uploads/2018/01/europeanintegrationviaflexibilitytools-kreilingerwolfstdter-nov17.pdf. Accessed 24 May 2020

Zandee D, Kruijver K (2019) The European Intervention Initiative: Developing a Shared Strategic Culture for European Defence https://www.clingendael.org/sites/default/files/2019-09/The_European_Intervention_2019.pdf. Accessed 24 May 2020

S. Blockmans is Director of the Brussels-based think tank CEPS and Professor of EU External Relations Law and Governance at the University of Amsterdam.

Chapter 8
The Participation of Members and Non-members in EU Foreign, Security and Defence Policy

R. A. Wessel

Contents

Abstract The idea of a common policy is, firstly, that it includes *all* Member States, and, secondly that it should include EU *members only*. The present contribution aims to assess how the Union has attempted to overcome the tension between the ambition to create a common foreign policy as a clear *Union* policy, and the need to pragmatically accept the fact that not all Member States are always onboard (and that third states sometimes are). The notion of 'EU membership' is thus approached from two different angles: 1. to what extent does EU membership entail the demand that all Member States agree to and implement CFSP decisions; and 2. to what extent is it legally possible for third states to participate in CFSP?

Keywords Common Foreign and Security Policy · CFSP · differentiated integration · EU membership · participation of third states · Brexit

R. A. Wessel (✉)
University of Groningen, Groningen, The Netherlands
e-mail: R.A.Wessel@rug.nl

W. Th. Douma et al. (eds.), *The Evolving Nature of EU External Relations Law*,
https://doi.org/10.1007/978-94-6265-423-5_8

8.1 Introduction: Between a Common and a Differentiated Policy

Post-Brexit and in the framework of the Conference on the Future of Europe,[1] debates on more, or less, European integration as well as on possibilities for differentiation between EU Member States as to their participation in certain policy fields have re-emerged.[2] Some of these debates echo the well-known discussions in the 1990s on differentiated integration, flexibility, multi-speed Europe, concentric circles and possibilities for a *geometrie variable*.[3]

The focus of current contribution is on one particular policy field only: the EU's Common Foreign and Security Policy (CFSP)—including the Common Security and Defence Policy (CSDP). From the outset, the Union has been struggling with the ambition to create and uphold a *common* policy and the often diverging views of the Member States.[4] The—at least initial—requirement of unanimity for each and every (implementing) decision was necessary to convince certain Member States that Union foreign policies would never conflict—let alone set aside—national foreign policies. The creation of CFSP was a compromise born out of the development of the European Political Cooperation in the 1970s and 80s and the wish to create something of a 'European Political Union' alongside the Economic and Monetary Union.[5] The idea was to unite Member States on foreign policy issues to allow the Union to act as a cohesive force in external relations.

Given the—perceived—more intergovernmental nature of CFSP, a variation in participation in this policy area is often seen as easier to realise than in certain parts of the internal market; as was exemplified by the wish of the UK government to stay closely connected to CFSP in contrast to other policy areas.[6] While CFSP indeed started out as 'the odd one out', over the more than 25 years of its existence we have slowly witnessed a 'normalisation' of this policy area.[7] Analyses of this normalisation highlighted the consolidation of EU foreign policy—as well its constitutionalisation as part of the Union's legal order—by subsequent treaty modifications (*inter alia* integrating the Union's external objectives[8]) as well as institutional adaptations (such as the introduction of the European External Action Service (EEAS) and the

[1] See https://ec.europa.eu/commission/presscorner/detail/en/ip_20_89. Accessed 8 July 2020; see also Communication from the Commission to the European Parliament and the Council, COM(2020) 27 final, 22 January 2020.

[2] See for instance Fabbrini 2019.

[3] See for instance De Witte et al. 2001. See also more recently Blockmans 2014b; De Witte et al. 2017; Della Cananea 2019.

[4] See Wessel 2007.

[5] See on the origins and early days of CFSP: Wessel 1999.

[6] See Wessel 2019.

[7] See (also for many references to earlier studies): Wessel 2018b; Editorial Comments 2018, Sánchez-Taberno 2017.

[8] Consolidated Version of the Treaty on the European Union, 2012, OJ C326 (TEU) Article 21(3); see below. See also Lonardo 2018. As argued by Larik 2013, pp. 10–11 "The Lisbon Treaty has both expanded and streamlined the Union's global objectives. [W]e can see that the EU Treaties codify

combination of the High Representative for CFSP and the Commission for external relations[9]). These changes have largely made an end to the (partly perceived[10]) distinction between CFSP and other external Union policy areas.

This, however, has not changed the fact that is remains difficult to reach consensus among the Member States on EU external action, despite the ambition that CFSP covers "*all* areas of foreign policy and *all* questions relating to the Union's security, including the progressive framing of a common defence policy that might lead to a common defence" (Article 24(1) TEU).[11] The idea of a common policy is, firstly, that it includes *all* Member States. The notion of normalisation, secondly, strengthened the idea that—because of the links between CFSP and other EU external policies such as trade and development—it should include EU *members only*. As to the first element, practice revealed the many difficulties of establishing a common foreign policy by the Union without having recourse to the usual machinery of the ordinary legislative procedure and the familiar role of the Institutions.[12]

While it has been observed that "Flexibility has been inherent in the very design of the legal set of rules which governs CFSP/CSDP",[13] the present contribution aims to assess how the Union has attempted to overcome the tension between the ambition to create a common foreign policy as a clear *Union* policy, and the need to pragmatically accept the fact that not all Member States are always onboard (and that third states sometimes are). The focus on CFSP as a Union policy implies that we leave out initiatives that are developed outside the Union's framework, such as the 'European Intervention Initiative' that was initiated by French President Emmanuel Macron in 2017.[14] The notion of 'EU membership' will thus be approached from two different angles: 1. to what extent does EU membership entail the demand that all Member States agree to and implement CFSP decisions; and 2. to what extent is it legally possible for third states to participate in CFSP?

---

a range of global objectives both in terms of substance but also specifically harnessing law […] Together, these elements coincide with the idea of the Union as a 'transformative power', changing not only fundamentally the relations among its members but also of the world around it."

[9]On the EEAS, see for instance Gatti 2017; and De Baere and Wessel 2015. On the High Representative, see Helwig 2015.

[10]Cardwell 2015 pointed to the difficulty to change the "tradition of otherness" in analyses of CFSP, which made it difficult to fully value the (post-Lisbon) changes. See also Wessel 2021a.

[11]Emphasis added.

[12]Cf. Blockmans 2014a, p. 46: "More often than not, a common commitment to a shared strategic vision, treaty-based values and norms, is an insufficient basis for policy consensus on what are still perceived as different foreign policy interests and threat perceptions by individual member states."

[13]Koutrakos 2017.

[14]The European Intervention Initiative (EI2) is a joint military project between 14 European countries outside of the existing structures. See for instance Zandee and Kruijver 2019.

8.2 Treaty Rules on Differentiated Integration and Voting in CFSP

8.2.1 Voting and Its Consequences

It is well known that CFSP is formed on the basis of "specific rules and procedures" (Article 24(1) TEU). This is characterised in particular by the exclusion of the use of 'legislative acts'[15] (Article 23(1) TEU); and thereby the use of the legislative procedure which is the regular decision-making procedure for most other Union policies, and by unanimity rather than qualified majority voting (QMV) as the default voting rule.[16] This does not imply that all Member States necessarily agree with all CFSP decisions. Article 31(1) TEU allows Member States to abstain from Council decision-making. On the basis of the second subparagraph "any member of the Council may qualify its abstention by making a formal declaration". The consequence of an abstention is that the member in question shall not be obliged to apply the decision, but shall accept that the decision commits the Union". In a spirit of mutual solidarity, [that] Member State shall refrain from any action likely to conflict with or impede Union action based on that decision, and the other Member States shall respect its position". The latter requirement is a logical implication of the general duty of loyal cooperation in CFSP: it "shall refrain from any action which is contrary to the interests of the Union or likely to impair its effectiveness as a cohesive force in international relations" (Article 24(3) TEU).

While an abstention obviously does not change the concept of membership, it is interesting to see that it does create different membership duties. For instance, it allows the abstaining Member States not to participate in the operational management of a CSDP mission (which is conducted within the Committee of Contributors), while at the same time it remains involved in the political and strategic decision-making in the Political and Security Committee.[17] The overall idea of constructive abstention is that the decision remains a Union decision, based on a Union competence,[18] but that variations occur in the way in which Member States engage in the implementation of that decision. In the words of Blockmans: "the mechanism of constructive abstention aims at reconciling the position held by the majority of member states with the reservations and concerns of some."[19] Obviously, there are limits to the number of abstentions and as in the end the idea of a 'common' policy needs to be preserved. Article 31(1) second subparagraph TEU provides that if constructive abstentions

[15]Note that this does not imply that CFSP acts are not binding on Member States; see Wessel 2015.

[16]TEU, above n. 8, Article 24(1): "Unanimity continues to form the basis for CFSP decisions, "except where the Treaties provide otherwise".

[17]Cf. also Törő 2005, p. 63.

[18]TEU, above n. 8, Article 24(1): "The *Union's* competence in matters of common foreign and security policy shall cover all areas of foreign policy and all questions relating to the Union's security, including the progressive framing of a common defence policy that might lead to a common defence." (emphasis added).

[19]Blockmans 2014a, p. 49. See also Törő 2005.

"represent at least one third of the member states comprising at least one third of the population of the Union, [then] the decision shall not be adopted." This may form a reason why constructive abstentions are a rare phenomenon.[20]

At the same time it is important to note that QMV is possible even in relation to CFSP decision-making in various situations,[21] and that Article 31(3) TEU enables the European Council to extend the cases of QMV by unanimously adopting a decision stipulating that the Council shall act by qualified majority in other cases, with the exception of decisions having military or defence implications (Article 31(4) TEU). Indeed, the latter is the clear treaty exception to the use of QMV. In addition, Member States may block a shift towards QMV and pull the so-called 'emergency brake'. Article 31(2) TEU provides that

> If a member of the Council declares that, for vital and stated reasons of national policy, it intends to oppose the adoption of a decision to be taken by qualified majority, a vote shall not be taken. The High Representative will, in close consultation with the Member State involved, search for a solution acceptable to it. If he does not succeed, the Council may, acting by a qualified majority, request that the matter be referred to the European Council for a decision by unanimity.

The fact that the use of QMV is ruled out in CSDP underlines that—at all stages of the decision-making process—all Member States need to be onboard (see also Article 42(4) TEU). In that respect, it is striking that QMV is allowed for the establishment of closer military cooperation between (groups of) Member States, resulting in the so-called permanent structured co-operation (PESCO).[22] Article 46 TEU provides:

> 1. Those Member States which wish to participate in the permanent structured cooperation referred to in Article 42(6), which fulfil the criteria and have made the commitments on military capabilities set out in the Protocol on permanent structured cooperation shall notify their intention to the Council and to the High Representative of the Union for Foreign Affairs and Security Policy.

---

[20] In fact, so far, constructive abstention has been used only once, by a Member State. See the abstention by Cyprus in 2008 when the Council adopted the Decision establishing the EULEX Kosovo mission; Council Joint Action 2008/124/CFSP of 4 February 2008 on the European Union Rule of Law Mission in Kosovo, EULEX Kosovo, OJ L42/92, 16 February 2008; Final Communication from the Commission to the European Council, the European Parliament and the Council: A stronger global actor: a more efficient decision-making for EU Common Foreign and Security Policy, COM(2018) 647, 12 September 2018.

[21] In that respect it is interesting to point to the fact that apart from the previously existing possibilities for QMV under CFSP which mainly related to implementation acts, it is now possible for the Council to adopt measures on this basis following a proposal submitted by the High Representative (TEU, above at n. 8, Article 31(2)). Such proposals should, however, follow a specific request by the European Council, in which, of course, Member States can foreclose the use of QMV. In addition, QMV may be used for setting up, financing and administering a start-up fund to ensure rapid access to appropriations in the Union budget for urgent financing of CFSP initiatives (TEU, Article 41(3)). This start-up fund may be used for crisis management initiatives as well, which would potentially speed up the financing process of operations. In addition, QMV may be extended to new areas on the basis of a decision by the European Council (TEU, above n. 8, Article 31(3))

[22] See also Blockmans 2018.

> 2. Within three months following the notification referred to in paragraph 1 the Council shall adopt a decision establishing permanent structured cooperation and determining the list of participating Member States. The Council shall act by a qualified majority after consulting the High Representative.

The absence of the unanimity requirement returns in paras 3 and 4 in relation to the decision to allow states to join PESCO at a later stage, or to suspend a participating state. Unilateral withdrawal from PESCO can simply take place on the basis of a notification by the Member State (para 5).

It is also worth noting that the requirement for unanimity does not prevent smaller groups of Member States to go ahead in case there are simply no objections from others. As noted by Törő: "Although unanimity is prescribed, it is important to note that full consensus is not required. In other words, the Council cannot take decisions on any organisational or operational (military or civilian missions) aspect of the common security and defence policy unless and until all formal and open disagreement has been overcome by mutually acceptable compromise, even in the absence of full consensus."[23] This implies that those members of the Union with no intention of participating in a proposed CSDP mission have the opportunity to allow a smaller group to establish the mission nevertheless.

More in general, the unanimity requirement in CFSP is currently under debate. In his State of the Union speech of 2017, President Juncker suggested "looking at which foreign policy decisions could be moved from unanimity to qualified majority voting",[24] and in 2018 the Commission drafted a proposal towards more effective decision-making in CFSP.[25] The Commission argued the following:

> In the future [...] certain Common Foreign and Security Policy decisions should be taken by qualified majority. The use of qualified majority would make the Union a stronger, more effective and more credible international actor, as it would make it easier for the Union:
>
> - To act on the global scene on the basis of robust and consistent positions;
> - To react with speed and efficiency to pressing foreign policy challenges, both where a new position needs to be established and in the implementation of an agreed strategy;
> - To strengthen the resilience of the EU by shielding Member States from targeted pressure by third countries that try to divide the EU.

Taken together, this would help the Union to pull its weight acting in concert as more than the sum of its parts. Experience from other policy areas where qualified majority is the rule shows that qualified majority fosters common solutions.[26]

---

[23] Törő 2005, p. 67.

[24] http://europa.eu/rapid/press-release_SPEECH-17-3165_en.htm; 13 September 2017.

[25] Communication from the Commission to the European council, the European parliament and the Council, A stronger global actor: a more efficient decision-making for EU Common Foreign and Security Policy, Brussels, 12.9.2018 COM(2018) 647 final (https://ec.europa.eu/commission/sites/beta-political/files/soteu2018-efficient-decision-making-cfsp-communication-647_en.pdf).

[26] Ibid., p. 3.

Obviously, other Union policy areas have shown us that an increase in QMV possibilities does not necessarily affect the unity among members and the process of European integration. At the same time, it may be good to keep the specific nature of CFSP in mind, as also reflected in the fact that Article 40 TEU still exist, despite its limited value these days.[27] As earlier held by one observer more than twenty years ago: "[A] majority decision on a foreign policy matter is totally different in character from a majority decision on an EC legal act: adopted against the will of some Member States it would lose much or even most of its international credibility and could be easily subverted by signals from the opposing Member States through its national diplomatic channels."[28] While there is still a lot of truth in this statement, CFSP—as we have seen—is much more part of the Union's legal order than it was twenty years ago.

8.2.2 *Forms of Differentiated Integration in CFSP and CSDP*

8.2.2.1 Principles of EU External Action

The 'common' nature of the EU's foreign and security policy has not prevented Member States to develop initiatives in which not all of them participate. Given the different (geo-)political interests of the Member States this should not come as a surprise.[29] The present section aims to list the main possibilities to break the 'unity of membership'. It should be kept in mind, however, that both in their internal EU cooperation as in dealing with third states, Member States remain bound by the principles underlying all EU external action (including the principles of sincere cooperation and consistency. Indeed, as argued elsewhere,[30] the presumption is that all structural as well as more substantive principles apply to the CFSP and, moreover, that it would not be easy to rebut this presumption. This conclusion can be drawn on the basis of the Treaty provisions themselves, which are usually phrased in quite general terms, and are not excluding specific policy areas. This holds true for all key EU principles, including the principles of cooperation, the principles of conferral, subsidiarity and proportionality, more substantive principles, as well as some general principles of international law referred to in the Treaties.

One might even argue that structural principles are particularly important in the area of CFSP—where Member States, as at least perceived, play a larger role—to live up to the requirement of "consistency, effectiveness and continuity of its policies

[27] Wessel 2021a.

[28] Monar 1997.

[29] Cf. Koutrakos 2017: "As foreign policy and security and defence lie at the core of national sovereignty, their conduct is in greater need of being attuned to the different interests which Member States have in the area of high politics. This is all the more so in the light of the wide range of diverse Member States – small and large, north and south, new and old, rich and poor."

[30] Wessel 2021b.

and actions".[31] On top of this, all of this seems to be confirmed by Article 24(2) TEU, which provides that the Union shall conduct, define and implement a common foreign and security policy "[w]ithin the framework of the principles and objectives of its external action". The reference to 'external action' cannot be read as restricting the list of principles to that particular dimension of the Union's policies. In fact, Article 21(1) TEU clearly links the principles as applied in the internal context to external action: "The Union's action on the international scene shall be guided by *the principles* which have inspired its own creation, development and enlargement, and which it seeks to advance in the wider world [...]".[32]

This notion is further strengthened by the requirement of consistency, which is not termed a principle in the treaties,[33] but nevertheless guides the EU's external action more generally and functions as a principle to work towards the attainment of the objectives.[34] Both in Article 3(5) and in Article 21 TEU on the external objectives of the Union specific references to CFSP are absent. Indeed, the Lisbon Treaty consolidated the Union's external relations objectives and CFSP is just one of the means to attain these objectives. The requirement of consistency in Article 21(3) TEU is meant to prevent a fragmentation of the Union's external action.[35] Specifically through the case-law of the Court of Justice the obligation of loyalty has become directly connected to the objective of "ensur[ing] the coherence and consistency of the action and its [the Union's] international representation".[36]

[31] TEU, above n. 8, Article 13(1), as well as other provisions, including Article 21(3). Cf. also Azoulai 2018, p. 33: "Structural principles are seen as forms of rationalisation of a highly valuable but essential unstable project. To make EU law subject to structural principles is to make it and the EU more resilient".

[32] Emphasis added. As these principles, the Article mentions: "democracy, the rule of law, the universality and indivisibility of human rights and fundamental freedoms, respect for human dignity, the principles of equality and solidarity, and respect for the principles of the United Nations Charter and international law.

[33] Nevertheless, Article 22 TEU refers to "the principles and objectives set out in Article 21".

[34] See also Estrada Cañamares 2018, p. 256: "Because of its location under Article 7 TFEU, coherence can be considered a 'Principle' of 'General Application' to the Union." Cf. Larik 2014, p. 962, who argues that the EU objectives "provide a sense of purpose as to the exercise of powers through the structures of the constitutionalised legal order".

[35] It provides that: "[...] The Union shall ensure consistency between the different areas of its external action and between these and its other policies. The Council and the Commission, assisted by the High Representative of the Union for Foreign Affairs and Security Policy, shall ensure that consistency and shall cooperate to that effect." Cf. also Consolidated Version of the Treaty on the Functioning of the European Union, 2012, OJ C 326 (TFEU), Article 7: "The Union shall ensure consistency between its policies and activities, taking all of its objectives into account and in accordance with the principle of conferral of powers." The TEU contains four other provisions which pertain to coherence in its material and institutional dimensions. All in their own way, these provisions strengthen the relationship (or in fact, the integration) between CFSP and other external relations policies. See more extensively Wessel and Larik 2020; as well as Hillion 2012.

[36] Court of Justice, *Commission* v *Luxembourg*, Judgment of the Court (First Chamber), 2 June 2005, C-266/03, para 60; Court of Justice, *Commission* v *Germany*, Judgment of the Court, 5 November 2002, C-476/98, para 66. See further on the role of the Court in CFSP: Hillion and Wessel 2018.

It is essential to keep this in mind when assessing the different forms of differentiated integration in CFSP.

8.2.2.2 Enhanced Cooperation in CFSP

A first form of closer cooperation is termed 'Enhanced cooperation' and is introduced in Article 20 TEU. It can be used in CFSP, including CSDP and allows smaller groups of Member States to move ahead in certain policy or security fields.[37] Article 331(2) TFEU provides:

> Any Member State which wishes to participate in enhanced cooperation in progress in the framework of the common foreign and security policy shall notify its intention to the Council, the High Representative of the Union for Foreign Affairs and Security Policy and the Commission.
>
> The Council shall confirm the participation of the Member State concerned, after consulting the High Representative of the Union for Foreign Affairs and Security Policy and after noting, where necessary, that the conditions of participation have been fulfilled. The Council, on a proposal from the High Representative, may also adopt any transitional measures necessary with regard to the application of the acts already adopted within the framework of enhanced cooperation. However, if the Council considers that the conditions of participation have not been fulfilled, it shall indicate the arrangements to be adopted to fulfil those conditions and shall set a deadline for re-examining the request for participation.
>
> For the purposes of this paragraph, the Council shall act unanimously and in accordance with Article 330.

Articles 326-328 TFEU provide that enhanced cooperation shall comply with the Treaties and Union law, that is shall not undermine the internal market or economic, social and territorial cohesion and that it shall not constitute a barrier to or discrimination in trade between Member States, nor shall it distort competition between them. In addition, enhanced cooperation shall respect the competences, rights and obligations of those Member States which do not participate in it.

Despite this possibility, that was introduced by the Lisbon Treaty, enhanced cooperation in CFSP was a clear compromise and a number of criteria were introduced that are not easy to meet: a minimum number of nine participants, the requirement of unanimity in the Council for authorising any kind of enhanced cooperation in CFSP, and the requirement of the consent of the European Parliament.[38] Furthermore, the treaty has made clear that "The decision authorising enhanced cooperation shall be adopted by the Council as a last resort, when it has established that the objectives of such cooperation cannot be attained within a reasonable period by the Union as a whole" (Article 20(2) TEU). Any decision on differentiated integration can therefore not be taken lightly and, so far, practice shows that Member States have not been able to agree on establishing any kind of enhanced cooperation in CFSP.

[37] Cf. Cremona 2009.

[38] See also Piris 2010.

8.2.2.3 Other Forms of Closer Cooperation

While formally institutionalised enhanced cooperation may be difficult to realise, practice has revealed the creation of coalitions of Member States working closer together. Blockmans distinguishes between three different types of coalitions, that may partly overlap:[39]

- permanent (e.g. Benelux) and ad hoc (e.g. the UK and France pushing the EU on lifting the ban on arming opposition forces in Syria);
- institutionalised (e.g. Visegrad Group) and loosely organised (e.g. the EU Core Group on Somalia, created early 2004, consisted primarily of the UK, Italy, Sweden and the European Commission, and was endorsed by the Council);
- regional (e.g. Baltic Council of Ministers), inter-regional (e.g. the partnership framework of the Baltic and Benelux countries and that of Nordic, Baltic and Visegrad countries), and thematic (e.g. mediation or reconciliation efforts). While there is always the risk that the 'Common' in CFSP is affected, it has been argued that these initiatives may actually be helpful in strengthening CFSP, e.g. through the taking of new initiatives or a smoother implementation.[40]

Differentiation in Member State participation also occurs in a CSDP context, and is far from new.[41] The most far-reaching form is the opt-out granted to Denmark in relation to defence matters. This opt-out basically allows an EU Member State non-participation in a common policy. Article 5 of Protocol 22 reads as follows:

> With regard to measures adopted by the Council pursuant to Article 26(1), Article 42 and Articles 43 to 46 of the Treaty on European Union, Denmark does not participate in the elaboration and the implementation of decisions and actions of the Union which have defence implications. Therefore Denmark shall not participate in their adoption. Denmark will not prevent the other Member States from further developing their cooperation in this area. Denmark shall not be obliged to contribute to the financing of operational expenditure arising from such measures, nor to make military capabilities available to the Union.

While this is an express opt-out for one Member State, the Treaty also seems to allow all Member States to take a step back in case their EU obligations would get in the way of, in particular, NATO commitments. Article 42(2) TEU provides:

> The policy of the Union in accordance with this Section shall not prejudice the specific character of the security and defence policy of certain Member States and shall respect the obligations of certain Member States, which see their common defence realized in the North Atlantic Treaty Organisation (NATO), under the North Atlantic Treaty and be compatible with the common security and defence policy established within that framework.

This provision seems to apply to NATO members only (and hence not to Austria, Finland, Sweden, Ireland, Malta and Cyprus). Yet, the first part ("the specific character of the security and defence policy of certain Member States") seems more

[39] Blockmans 2014a, p. 53.

[40] Keukeleire 2006.

[41] Missiroli 2000.

general and has been interpreted as to accommodate the security and defence considerations prevailing in different Member States.[42]

The most obvious example of ad hoc opt-outs and opt-ins is provided by the fact that in most EU military missions not every Member State is involved. But 'less close cooperation' may also be the result of what has been termed "flexibility in execution", which implies that not all Member States are forced to implement CSDP decisions in the same manner.[43] The reason for this is believed to be found in "historical reservations when it came to defence-related issues from Denmark (with its opt-out on all defence-related provisions of the TEU), as well as the political or constitutional concerns of the neutral or non-aligned EU member states (Austria, Finland, Ireland and Sweden)".[44]

The Treaty, in fact, expressly foresees the possibility of differentiation in security and defence policy. Article 42(5) TEU allows for the Council to "entrust the execution of a task, within the Union framework, to a group of Member States in order to protect the Union's values and serve its interests". While membership differentiation in this area has thus been built into the Treaty, an overall responsibility for the Council remains. Article 44 TEU stresses that Member States participating in the task "shall keep the Council regularly informed of its progress on their own initiative or at the request of another Member State. Those States shall inform the Council immediately should the completion of the task entail major consequences or require amendment of the objective, scope and conditions determined for the task […]".

In a more institutionalised sense, closer cooperation in CSDP can take the form of the so-called permanent structured cooperation (PESCO).[45] It is interesting to note that the Treaty does not merely allow for this form of differentiated integration, but actually seems to *encourage* states to engage in it, Article 42(6) TEU provides:

> Those Member States whose military capabilities fulfil higher criteria and which have made more binding commitments to one another in this area with a view to the most demanding missions *shall establish* permanent structured cooperation within the Union framework.[46]

The details of PESCO are spelled-out in Protocol No. 10 that is annexed to the Treaties.[47]"(a) proceed more intensively to develop its defence capacities …; and

---

[42]Koutrakos 2017. Cf. also Declaration No. 13, indicating that the CFSP provisions: "do not affect the responsibilities of the Member States, as they currently exist, for the formulation and conduct of their foreign policy nor of their national representation in third countries and international organisations. […]". And, Declaration No. 14, that these provisions "will not affect the existing legal basis, responsibilities, and powers of each Member State in relation to the formulation and conduct of its foreign policy, its national diplomatic service, relations with third countries and participation in international organisations, including a Member State's membership of the Security Council of the United Nations".

[43]Törő 2005, p. 63.

[44]Duke 2003.

[45]See Blockmans 2018.

[46]Emphasis added. See also Törő 2005, p. 70.

[47]Article 1 of Protocol No. 10 thus spells out that any Member State wishing to participate in PESCO should:

(b) have the capacity to supply … targeted combat units for the missions planned, structured at a tactical level as a battle group, with support elements, including transport and logistics, capable of carrying out the tasks referred to in Article 43 (TEU), within a period of five to 30 days, in particular in response to requests from the (UN), and which can be sustained for an initial period of 30 days and be extended up to at least 120 days". Despite the fact that the possibility was already formally included through the Lisbon Treaty, and despite earlier cooperation in the form of for instance 'Battlegroups',[48] PESCO was only vitalised in its current form in December 2017.[49] All Member States are onboard, except for Denmark (because of its CSDP opt-out), and Malta (for constitutional reasons related to neutrality). Differentiation largely occurs through the ways in which the different Member States participate in the (now) 47 'PESCO projects' that were defined by the Council.[50] The projects in the areas of capability development and in the operational dimension range from the establishment of a European Medical Command, an EU Training Mission Competence Centre, Cyber Rapid Response Teams, Mutual Assistance in Cyber Security, Military Disaster Relief or an upgrade of Maritime Surveillance to the creation of an European Military Space Surveillance Awareness Network, a joint EU Intelligence School, specialised Helicopter Training as well as co-basing, which would allow the joint use of national and overseas bases.[51]

PESCO consists of "legally binding commitments" aimed to prepare the Union to be ready to perform all crisis management tasks listed in Article 43 TEU. As Blockmans argued, PESCO faces at least three key challenges: "raising the level of ambition while ensuring inclusivity; maintaining credibility in case Member States do not comply with their commitments; and ensuring coherence with the many other building blocks in Europe's defence architecture".[52]

Finally, practice has revealed the possibility of closer cooperation between EU members, but *outside* the EU framework. EUROCORPS, the Franco-German Brigade, with units from Spain, Belgium and Luxembourg as national contributions is the most prominent example. In addition, we have witnessed other institutionalised groups of EU members, such as the EUROMARFOR (naval forces bringing together France, Italy, Spain, Portugal), the European Air Group (Germany, Belgium, Spain, France, Italy, the UK) and the German-Netherlands First Corps (Germany, the Netherlands, the UK). Looser cooperation frameworks (lacking a joint HQ) also exist, as exemplified by the Spanish-Italian Amphibious Force.[53]

---

[48] Van Eekelen and Kurpas 2008.

[49] Council Decision (CFSP) 2017/2315 of 11 Dec. 2017 establishing permanent structured cooperation (PESCO) and determining the list of participating Member States, OJ 2017, L 331/57.

[50] Council Decision (CFSP) 2018/1797 of 19 November 2018 amending and updating Decision (CFSP) 2018/340 establishing the list of projects to be developed under PESCO, OJ L 294/18, 21 December 2018.

[51] See also the PESCO Factsheet; https://eeas.europa.eu/sites/eeas/files/pesco_factsheet_november_2018_en_0.pdf.

[52] Blockmans 2018, p. 1811.

[53] See more extensively Törő 2005.

One could safely say that the above overview reveals that differentiation in member participation has been part and parcel of the EU's security and defence policy. At the same time—as we see with the development of PESCO in particular—the initiatives are perceived as contributing to a stronger Union and not to fragmentation.[54] As observed by Törő, "The repeated examples of Common Security and Defence Policy missions by variable combinations of states from inside and outside the Union illustrate a consolidated pattern of practice. Acting in coalition by some or many of the member states representing the entire EU continues to define the prevailing mode of execution of CSDP missions."[55]

8.3 Beyond EU Membership: Possibilities for Third State Participation in CFSP

The possibilities for non-EU members to participate in CFSP have gained more attention now that the United Kingdom has indicated that, post-Brexit, it would be interested in continuing cooperating on foreign policy.[56] In fact, in the UK's view, in this area EU membership should be replaced by a new security partnership, "that is deeper than any other third country partnership and that reflects our shared interests, values, and the importance of a strong and prosperous Europe".[57] Despite these clear intentions of the UK, participation of third states in foreign, security and defence matters raises a number of questions under both EU and international law.

After all, the Treaties have established a cooperation between the Union and its Member States on foreign and security policy; no reference is made to any participation of third states in this policy area. On the contrary perhaps, as the treaty provisions underline the need for consistency in many provisions (see above), imposing a binding obligation of coherence in EU external relations on the Union. CFSP is clearly connected to many other external policies of the Union, including sanctions, migration, trade, development, and environmental and energy policy.

---

[54] Cf. "We have activated a Permanent Structured Cooperation on Defence – ambitious and inclusive. Member States have committed to join forces on a regular basis, to do things together, spend together, invest together, buy together, act together. The possibilities of the Permanent Structured Cooperation are immense." Federica Mogherini, High Representative/ Vice-President (December 2017).

[55] Törő 2005, p. 67.

[56] See already the remarks made by Prime Minister Cameron after the referendum; Tannock 2016: The EU's negotiating guidelines for Brexit note that, "The EU stands ready to establish partnerships in areas unrelated to trade, in particular the fight against terrorism and international crime, as well as security, defence and foreign policy."; European Council, 'Conclusions: Negotiating Guidelines for Brexit' EUCO XT 20004/17, 7. See also the position paper in HM Government 2017.

[57] Ibid. See also the speech by PM Theresa May on 17 February 2018: "Europe's security is our security. And that is why I have said – and I say again today – that the United Kingdom is unconditionally committed to maintaining it. The challenge for all of us today is finding the way to work together, through a deep and special partnership between the UK and the EU, to retain the co-operation that we have built and go further in meeting the evolving threats we face together."; https://www.gov.uk/government/speeches/pm-speech-at-munich-security-conference-17-february-2018.

It will not be easy to uphold these rules and principles when participating third states are not equally bound by them. In that respect it should also be underlined once more that CFSP is a *Union* competence (e.g. Articles 24(1), 25 TEU; Article 2(4) TFEU). In fact, throughout Title V TEU (on CFSP) it is made clear that *the Union* is in charge, loyally *supported* by the Member States (Article 23(3) TEU). Furthermore, international agreements in the area of CFSP are 'exclusively' concluded by the Union as so-called 'EU only' agreements; there are no mixed agreements in CFSP.[58] This is not to say that third state participation in EU mixed agreements would be easy as these agreements are concluded between 'the European Union and its *Member States*' and other states.[59] Moreover, it has increasingly become difficult to isolate CFSP issues in international agreements from other EU policy areas and the Court established that it not necessary to include a CFSP basis merely because there are CFSP elements in a certain agreement.[60]

8.3.1 Legal Institutional Possibilities and Obstacles

To start with the obvious: the term 'common' in Common Foreign, Security, and Defence Policy refers to the Union and its *Member States*. Article 26(2) TEU entails a general competence for the Council to "frame the common foreign and security policy and take the decisions necessary for defining and implementing it on the basis of the general guidelines and strategic lines defined by the European Council". The Council, in turn, "shall consist of a representative of each Member State at ministerial level, who may commit the government of the Member State in question and cast its vote" (Article 16(2) TEU). The CFSP provisions do not foresee the participation of non-EU states in the decision-making process. And, indeed, Article 28(2) TEU provides that the CFSP Decisions "shall commit *the Member States* in the positions they adopt and in the conduct of their activity".[61] In short, as also explained by the Comments on the Council's Rules of Procedure:

> It should be noted that it follows from the system of the Treaties, and from Article 16 TEU in particular, that the representation of the governments of the Member States of the Council is composed of nationals of the Member State concerned or, in any event, of a national of one of the Member States of the European Union. Therefore, *the presence at a Council meeting of a national of a third State as a member of the delegation of a member of the Council should be ruled out*, as it could be regarded by the other members of the Council as a factor which could affect the decision-making autonomy of the Council.[62]

---

[58] See Van der Loo and Wessel 2017.

[59] Wessel 2018a.

[60] Court of Justice, *Commission v Council (Kazakhstan PCA)*, Judgment of the Court of Justice, 04 September 2018, C-244/17, ECLI:EU:C:2018:662.

[61] Emphasis added.

[62] Comments on the Council's Rules of Procedure, 2016, p. 16; https://www.consilium.europa.eu/media/29824/qc0415692enn.pdf. Accessed 8 July 2020. Emphasis added.

This also prevents that—on the basis of Article 4 of the Council's Rules of Procedure—"a member of the Council who is prevented from attending a meeting may arrange to be represented" by a third state representative. Any attempt to provide a formal role to third states in CFSP decision-making would thus require a treaty modification. This is not to say that all forms of third state participation in CFSP and CSDP are excluded (see also below). In institutional terms, several options have been discussed in the literature. First of all, the treaties themselves are silent on the *presence* of third countries during the EU decision-making procedures. Yet, in the above interpretation offered by the Comments on the Rules of Procedure, the "presence" of third states during Council—and European Council—meetings seems excluded.[63] At the same time, the Rules seem to provide some leeway to invite representatives of third countries to attend some of the Council's work. In view of the importance of this issue for a possible UK (or other third state) presence during Council meetings, the Comments on the Council's Rules of Procedure deserve to be quoted in length (emphasis added):

> Participation in Council meetings must not be confused with the *occasional presence of representatives of third States* or of international organisations, who are sometimes invited as observers to attend certain Council meetings or meetings of Council preparatory bodies concerning a specific item.
>
> Article 6(1) CRP provides that '[…] the deliberations of the Council shall be covered by the obligation of professional secrecy, except insofar as the Council decides otherwise'. Under this article, the Council may, whenever it considers it appropriate, decide by a simple majority to open its deliberations – or to disclose their content, inter alia by forwarding documents – to certain persons (or categories of persons).
>
> *The presence of observers* must be authorised by the Council for a specific item on the agenda. In this case, the Presidency must warn the Council members of this fact in advance. In respect of this item, the Council (or the relevant preparatory body) implicitly decides, by simple majority, to set aside the professional secrecy provided for in Article 6(1). The observer must leave the room once the deliberations on this item have ended, or when requested to leave by the Presidency. The third-party observer may be invited by the Council Presidency to state his or her views or inform the Council concerning the subject at issue.
>
> From a legal point of view, *the third party does not participate in the deliberations leading to the taking of a decision by the Council*, but simply provides the Council with information which it can draw upon before taking its decision.
>
> *The same rules apply to meetings of the Council's preparatory bodies.* The Presidency is responsible for organising the proceedings so as to preserve the Council's decision-making autonomy.[64]

With regard to the European Council, the regulatory provisions are (even) stricter as its Rules of Procedure provide that "meetings in the margins of the European Council

[63]While the Rules of Procedure of both the Council and the European Council do not address this issue expressly, these Rules imply that only representatives of Member States are present.

[64]Comments, above n. 62, p. 39; emphasis added. See also the European Parliament study 'CSDP after Brexit: the way forward', Directorate-General for External Policies, Policy Department, May 2018; http://www.europarl.europa.eu/RegData/etudes/STUD/2018/603852/EXPO_STU(2018)603852_EN.pdf.

with representatives of third States [...] may be held in exceptional circumstances only, and with the prior agreement of the European Council, acting unanimously, on the initiative of the President of the European Council".[65] Here, any presence of third countries during formal meetings seems to be fully excluded and even meetings 'in the margin' of the European Council are subject to strict conditions.[66]

But, what about the lower organs? While the same rules apply to "the Council's preparatory bodies", participation of third states in the Political and Security Committee (PSC) or in Working Parties has proven to be possible in practice, albeit not in Coreper (see further below). At the same time, the question is whether presence at *informal* Council meetings (e.g. so-called 'Gymnich meetings' organised by the rotating Presidency) is also to be excluded and to what extent participation in specific CSDP bodies, such as the European Institute for Security Studies, the European Defence Agency, and the European Satellite Centre is allowed.[67]

While the above rules seem to underline that even on the basis of a special agreement an observer status of third states at Council or Coreper meetings would be in conflict with primary law rules,[68] such a status could perhaps be foreseen for in certain working parties.[69] However, the Brexit debate has revealed that EU does not seem to be in favour of any form of 'half-member' status, let alone of voting rights for non-members.[70] While High Representative Mogherini seemed ready to explore the options,[71] the idea met with some critics among other officials, even where observer status in the PSC would be concerned.[72]

[65]Rules of Procedure of the European Council, Article 4(2).

[66]However, despite the fact that for third states being present at European Council meeting might politically be important, the influence of this Institution on key foreign policy issues has been doubted. See Lonardo 2019, p. 51: "[...] while it is true that the European Council is influential in the external relations of the EU, this might be the case only on non-critical issues. Instead, it fails to express an influential position when highly divisive topics are on the table, and there is no evidence of its influence."

[67]Cf. in relation to Brexit: Article 156 WA that deals with the budgetary questions during transition: "Until 31 December 2020, the United Kingdom shall contribute to the financing of the European Defence Agency, the European Union Institute for Security Studies, and the European Union Satellite Centre, as well as to the costs of Common Security and Defence Policy operations [...]".

[68]Something for instance suggested by Whitman 2016.

[69]See also Piris 2016; Blunt 2017.

[70]See also European Commission 2018.

[71]Remarks by Mogherini on EU-UK future partnership CFSP, 2018; https://eeas.europa.eu/headquarters/headquarters-homepage/44528/remarks-hrvp-mogherini-eu-institute-security-studies-event-future-eu-foreign-security-and_en.

[72]Lis 2017.

8.3.2 *Third Country Participation in CFSP in Practice*

Despite to institutional obstacles assessed above, the participation of third states in CFSP and CSDP policies and actions has become common practice and one could even argue that it seems to contribute to the objective in Article 21 TEU that "The Union shall seek to develop relations and build partnerships with third countries, and international, regional or global organisations which share [its] principles". EU-third state cooperation on foreign affairs usually takes place on the basis of some form of agreement that functions as the base for their cooperation. Some third states—Norway and Iceland in particular—take part in various theme specific Council working groups.[73] Candidate countries show that it is even possible to be an observer in the PSC.[74] However, the EU has no experience with giving observer rights that include the right to speak and agenda making to a non-EU member/non-candidate country in high-level formations such as the PSC, Coreper or the Foreign Affairs Council. Apart from the legal obstacles discussed above, granting such rights to third states could also have political consequences. It has been observed that it could open the door to many requests from non-EU members such as Switzerland, Norway, or Turkey that currently have close relations with the Union (see further below). Moreover, it can possibly create political tensions in certain EU Member States, like Sweden, Denmark and others, where Eurosceptic political parties could be tempted to push for 'half-member' status.[75]

8.3.2.1 Templates for Third Country Participation in CFSP

In practice, third country participation in CFSP currently takes place on the basis of agreed frameworks for cooperation. The first type of cooperation is formed by the EFTA/EEA agreements.[76] While these agreements do not formally include cooperation on foreign and security policy, the EU has the habit of inviting EFTA/EEA countries to join EU statements and position on foreign policy.[77] Furthermore, the EEA Council meets twice a year with representatives of the Commission and the EEAS. Representatives of the European Council are present at those meetings as well as the representatives of the rotating Council presidency. During this EEA Council meeting, foreign policy is openly discussed while searching for consensus between the EU

[73] Rieker 2017; Hillion 2019.

[74] Lis 2017.

[75] Piris 2016. The possibility of voting rights for the UK was also excluded by the HR/VP in answering questions by reporters (Remarks by Mogherini on EU-UK future partnership CFSP, retrieved from: https://eeas.europa.eu/headquarters/headquarters-homepage/44528/remarks-hrvp-mogherini-eu-institute-security-studies-event-future-eu-foreign-security-and_en) as well as by the European Parliament in a 2018 Resolution; see European Parliament 2018.

[76] See on the EEA in relation to Brexit: Hillion 2018.

[77] See also Zarembo 2011; Isleifsson 2014.

and the EEA nations.[78] The EU-Norway relationship serves as a good example of a continuous dialogue with the EU on numerous foreign policy issues.[79] This is done through a formal format that consists of two meetings per year between the Norwegian foreign minister and the foreign ministers of the EU. Additionally, there are several meetings where officials from Norway meet together with their counterparts from Iceland and Liechtenstein in CFSP working groups. So far Norwegian officials have participated in CFSP working groups that operate in policy areas that Norway has an interest in, such as the Balkans, Russia, anti-terrorism coordination and the Middle-East peace process. In the end, Norway is invited to sign EU foreign policy statements and thus to align its position to that of the EU.[80] Norway's policy is to join EU statements whenever possible.[81] It has been observed that "Norway has thus been involved in essentially all of the core aspects of the EU CFSP".[82] Apart from Norway (and Iceland) as active CFSP participants, Switzerland is worth mentioning as well. As a non-EEA EFTA member Switzerland joins the EEA Council meetings and regularly joins EU foreign statements and participates in EU missions.[83]

Third country participation in CFSP is also possible on the basis of a Partnership and Cooperation Agreement (PCA). While some PCAs do not expressly refer to foreign policy cooperation (e.g. the one with the Philippines), the EU-Ukraine PCA did as the provisions on 'political dialogue' allowed Ukraine to join EU statements and positions as well as having high-level dialogues at ministerial level and regular meetings at senior official level.[84]

More comprehensive and in-depth cooperation is possible on the basis of an Association Agreement (AA). In the, more recent, AA between the EU and Ukraine, for example, Article 7 concerns cooperation on foreign and security policy and provides that: "The Parties shall intensify their dialogue and cooperation and promote gradual convergence in the area of foreign and security policy, including the Common Security and Defence Policy (CSDP), and shall address in particular issues of conflict prevention and crisis management, regional stability, disarmament, non-proliferation, arms control and arms export control as well as enhanced mutually-beneficial dialogue in the field of space."

Similar cooperation can be found in a number of Stabilisation and Association Agreements (SAAs).[85] Thus, in the EU-Serbia SAA Article 10 provides for "an increasing convergence of positions of the Parties on international issues, including

[78] See for instance: EEA Council meetings (46th), 2016; http://www.efta.int/sites/default/files/documents/eea/eea-news/2016-11-15-eea-council-conclusions.pdf. Accessed 8 July 2020.

[79] See Hillion 2018.

[80] Rieker 2006; Sjursen 2015.

[81] Norwegian Ministry of Foreign Affairs 2018.

[82] Hillion 2019, p. 5.

[83] Cf. EU-Switzerland relations. http://www.consilium.europa.eu/en/press/press-releases/2017/02/28/conclusions-eu-swiss-confederation/. Accessed 8 July 2020.

[84] Partnership and Cooperation Agreement between the European Communities and their Member States, and Ukraine (Section II), opened for signature 14 June 1994, OJ L 49/3 (entered into force 1 March 1998).

[85] Cf. Đukanović 2015.

CFSP issues, also through the exchange of information as appropriate, and, in particular, on those issues likely to have substantial effects on the Parties" as well as "common views on security and stability in Europe, including cooperation in the areas covered by the CFSP of the European Union".[86] In general, candidate countries—which basically are almost all countries that have signed an SAA—are invited to join Gymnich meetings and participate as observers in the PSC.

More generally, the EU has gained experience with third country participation in CFSP through its European Neighbourhood Policy (ENP). As the agreements are all tailored made, they do not all deal with foreign policy issues in the same manner. An example can be found in the EU Georgia Action Plan, which—as 'Priority area 7'—mentions the goal to "Enhance EU-Georgia cooperation on Common Foreign and Security Policy, including European Security and Defence Policy. Georgia may be invited, on a case by case basis, to align itself with EU positions on regional and international issues."[87]

Similar notions may be found in so-called Framework Agreements. Thus, Article 3 of the 2017 Agreement with Australia provided for political dialogues and cooperation in the area of foreign policy.[88] Similar provision can also be found in the Strategic Partnership Agreement with Canada, that was negotiated alongside CETA.[89]

These examples reveal the experience of the European Union with the participation of third states in foreign and security policy. In addition, ad hoc alignment with EU policies and actions remains possible,[90] including sanctions.[91]

8.3.2.2 Third Country Participation in CSDP

Finally, third country participation has proven to be possible in CSDP missions, both civilian and military. Around 45 non-EU countries have contributed troops to CSDP missions and operations (approximately 30 if one detracts third countries that have since then become member states). As calculated by Törő, "The variety of potential partners from outside the Union envelops European NATO members (Norway,

---

[86] Stabilisation and Association Agreement between the European Communities and their Member States, of the one part, and the Republic of Serbia, of the other part, 2013.

[87] 2006 EU-Georgia Action Plan; https://library.euneighbours.eu/content/eu-georgia-action-plan.

[88] Framework Agreement between the European Union and its Member States, of the one part, and Australia, of the other part, opened for signature 07 August 2017, OJ L 237 (entered into force 15 September 2017).

[89] Strategic Partnership Agreement between the European Union and its Member States, of the one part, and Canada, of the other part, OJ L 329 (entered into force 28 October 2016).

[90] It has been observed that the 'European Union Withdrawal Bill 2017-19' will copy existing EU sanctions measures into UK law and may also provide a legal basis for new sanctions regimes. See Lonardo 2019.

[91] See the Council's Guidelines on implementation and evaluation of restrictive measures (sanctions) in the framework of the EU Common Foreign and Security Policy (No. 11205/12, 15 June 2012) in which paras 56–57 aim at strengthening restrictive measure by the adoption of similar measures by third countries.

Turkey or Albania), EU candidates (Croatia, FYROM or Montenegro), other states from Europe (Switzerland) or partners from other continents (the US, Brazil, Canada and South Africa) interested in, and capable of contributions to a given joint security enterprise under the EU' banner and direction."[92] Four non-EU countries have participated in EU Battlegroups: Turkey, Norway, Ukraine and Macedonia.[93] This has included, for example, all NATO members, and all EU candidate countries. The legal basis for such cooperation has been a treaty in the form of a Framework Participation Agreement (for more structural participation in CSDP missions), or a Participation Agreement (for ad hoc participation in a mission). These agreements are concluded in the form of bilateral EU-only agreements on the basis of Articles 37 TEU and 218 TFEU.[94] Thus, for instance, the FPA with Turkey reveals the procedural rights of the participating country: "The Republic of Turkey shall have the same rights and obligations in terms of day-to-day management of the operation as European Union Member States taking part in the operation, in accordance with the legal instruments referred to in Article 2(1) of this Agreement".[95] This principle returns in all FPAs. Third countries are not involved in drafting the operations. They typically receive access to relevant documents once the participation has been accepted by the Political and Security Committee (PSC). In practice, third countries are expected and required to accept the EU's schedule and procedures, and "by nature, non-member states' participation in EU operations requires a certain degree of acceptance of EU practices, as well as a degree of subordination".[96]

The latter point underlines that full participation of non-EU members in the preparation and formation of CSDP missions through, *inter alia*, the Civilian Committee, the EU Military Committee, the Politico-Military Group, the Civilian Planning and Conduct Capability, and the EU Military Staff will be difficult to realise. Apart from legal obstacles, it is politically difficult to differentiate between different EU partners as they expect equal treatment.[97] This is not to say that the different arrangements the EU has with external partners are all alike. The example of Norway shows that country not only contributed assets and personnel to a large variety of CSDP missions and operations, but also that it has access to a regular dialogue with regards to EU foreign and security policy. Moreover, Norway's agreement allows the country to join CSDP

---

[92] Törő 2005, pp. 66–67. See also Törő 2010.

[93] See Bakker et al. 2017. This report also provides a good overview of the current and past participation of the UK in CSDP missions.

[94] See also Lonardo 2019, p, 10; Bakker et al. 2017.

[95] Agreement between the European Union and the Republic of Turkey establishing a framework for the participation of the Republic of Turkey in the European Union crisis management operations, OJ L 189 12 July 2006, annex II, Sectio 2, Article 6(5).

[96] Tardy 2014.

[97] See also the European Parliament study 'CSDP after Brexit: the way forward', *op.cit.*, at 19: "should London be granted too many privileges, many other countries would go back on the attack to call for similar rights."

missions and operations, as well as cooperation in the European Defence Agency (EDA).[98] Nevertheless, Norway struggles with similar decision-shaping problems.[99]

8.4 Conclusion: CFSP as a Common Policy Between the EU and Its Members?

The Common Foreign, Security and Defence Policy is characterised by the EU Treaties in three ways: (1) as a *common* policy of the Union, supported by its members; (2) as an *EU-only* policy on the basis of a Union competence that is also used for the conclusion of EU-only agreements with third states; and (3) as an *exclusive* EU policy that is not designed for third state participation. Perhaps paradoxically, on all accounts the practice of CFSP is different.[100] First of all, the notion of a 'common' policy is put into perspective by the many forms of differentiated cooperation among smaller groups of Member States. Secondly, Member States have an essential role in CFSP. Unlike for instance the Common Commercial Policy, the Common Foreign, Security and Defence Policy is much more built on coalitions of members. Thirdly, while third state participation in CFSP is nowhere mentioned in the Treaties, in all areas of CFSP and CSDP—ranging from political cooperation, to sanctions or military missions—non-EU members participate; either through an alignment with EU policies or on the basis of an almost equal participation in the implementation of decisions and actions.

Perhaps much more than any other EU policy, CFSP is characterised by a patchwork of diverging and overlapping members and non-members that—sometimes institutionalised, sometimes ad hoc—contribute to assisting the EU in achieving its objectives as a global actor. To some extent, primary law indeed allows for, or even encourages working in smaller groups. One reason may also have been to simply accept that this is the closest thing to a common foreign policy among 27 sovereign states, while at the same time preventing that they seek their options outside the EU framework.[101] Yet, the downside is equally obvious. With the increasing 'normalisation' of CFSP it has become part and parcel of the overall external relations regime of the Union and it becomes difficult to clearly separate foreign policy from other EU external action. This also points to another looming risk: fragmentation in CFSP may make it more difficult to live up to many of the principles that are at the basis of EU law and cooperation. In the further development of CFSP a balance will have to be sought between the advantages of working in smaller groups of both EU

[98] Cameron 2017.

[99] Koenig 2018.

[100] Cf. Koutrakos 2017: "flexibility has been inherent in the conduct of the policy as a matter of practice and quite independently from the legal mechanisms set out in the Union's primary rules."

[101] See on this argument already Wessel 2007.

and non-EU members[102] and the need to uphold the principles of consistency and loyalty that are key to any common policy.

Acknowledgments Credits are due to Richard Haringsma and Eduard Hoek for their valuable work on this topic in their master theses for the European Studies programme at the University of Twente. These theses are accessible here: https://essay.utwente.nl.

References

Azoulai L (2018) Structural Principles in EU Law: Internal and External. In: Cremona M (ed) Structural Principles in EU External Relations Law. Hart Publishing, Oxford, pp 31–45

Bakker A, Drent M, Zandee D (2017) European defence: how to engage the UK after Brexit? Clingendael Report. https://www.clingendael.org/sites/default/files/2017-07/Report_European_defence_after_Brexit.pdf Accessed 6 May 2020

Blockmans S (2014a) In: Blockmans S (ed) Differentiated Integration in the EU. From the Inside Looking Out. Centre for European Policy Studies (CEPS), Brussels, pp 46–56

Blockmans S (ed) (2014b) Differentiated Integration in the EU. From the Inside Looking Out. Centre for European Policy Studies (CEPS), Brussels. https://www.ceps.eu/ceps-publications/differentiated-integration-eu-inside-looking-out/ Accessed 28 June 2020

Blockmans S (2018) The EU's Modular Approach to Defence Integration: An inclusive, ambitious and legally binding PESCO? CMLRev 55:1785–1826

Blunt C (2017) Post-Brexit EU-UK Cooperation on Foreign and Security Policy. Discussion paper. https://www.blunt4reigate.com/sites/www.blunt4reigate.com/files/2017-04/Post-Brexit%20EU-ΩK%20cooperation%20on%20foreign%20%26%20security%20policy%20April%202017.pdf Accessed 6 May 2020

Cameron F (2017) After Brexit: Prospects for UK-EU cooperation on foreign and security policy. European Policy Centre. http://www.epc.eu/en/Publications/After-Brexit-Prospects-for-UK-EU-cooperation-on-foreign-and-security~210714 Accessed 6 May 2020

Cardwell PJ (2015) On 'ring-fencing' the Common Foreign and Security Policy in the legal order of the European Union. Northern Ireland Legal Quarterly 64: 443–463

Cremona M (2009) Enhanced cooperation and the European Foreign and Security and Defence Policy. In: Beneyto JM (ed) Unity and Flexibility in the future of the European Union: The Challenge of Enhanced Cooperation. CEU Ediciones, Madrid

De Baere G, Wessel RA (2015) EU Law and the EEAS: Of Complex Competences and Constitutional Consequences. In: Bátora J, Spence D (eds) The European External Action Service: European Diplomacy Post-Westphalia. Palgrave MacMillan, Basingstoke, pp 175–193

De Witte B, Hanf D, Vos E (eds) (2001) The Many Faces of Differentiation in EU Law. Intersentia, Antwerp

De Witte B, Ott A, Vos E (eds) (2017) Between Flexibility and Disintegration: The Trajectory of Differentiation in EU Law. Edward Elgar, Cheltenham/Northampton

Della Cananea G (2019) Differentiated Integration in Europe After Brexit: A Legal Analysis, European Papers 4:447–469

Đukanović D (2015) The Process of Institutionalization of the EU's CFSP in the Western Balkan Countries during the Ukraine Crisis. Croatian International Relations Review, 21:81–106

[102]Cf. Keukeleire 2006: "[U]nder certain conditions, the specialisation and division of labour among EU member states [big and small] can strengthen both the effectiveness and legitimacy of the foreign policy of the EU […]."

Duke S (2003) The Convention, the Draft Constitution and External Relations: Effects and Implications for the EU and its international role. EIPA Working Paper No. 2003/W/2
Editorial Comments (2018) CMLRev 55:1–10
Estrada Cañamares M (2018) Building Coherent Responses: Coherence as a Structural Principle in EU External Relations. In: Cremona M (ed) Structural Principles in EU External Relations Law. Hart Publishing, Oxford, pp 244–262
European Commission (2018) Foreign, Security and Defence Policy Slides. https://ec.europa.eu/commission/sites/beta-political/files/slides_on_foreign_security_defence_policy.pdf. Accessed 8 July 2020.
European Parliament (2018) EP resolution on the framework for EU-UK cooperation; http://www.europarl.europa.eu/sides/getDoc.do?pubRef=-%2F%2FEP%2F%2FTEXT%2BMOTION%2BB8-2018-0135%2B0%2BDOC%2BXML%2BV0%2F%2FEN&language=EN Accessed 8 July 2020
Fabbrini F (2019) The Future of the EU27. EJLS 305–333
Gatti M (2017) European External Action Service: Promoting Coherence through Autonomy and Coordination. Brill|Nijhoff, The Hague
Helwig N (2015) The High Representative of the Union: The Quest for Leadership in EU Foreign Policy. In: Bátora J, Spence D (eds) The European External Action Service: European Diplomacy Post-Westphalia. Palgrave MacMillan, Basingstoke, pp 87–104
Hillion C (2012) Cohérence et action extérieure de l'Union Européenne [Coherence and external action of the European Union], EUI Working Papers Law, No. 2012/14
Hillion C (2018) Brexit Means Br(EEA)xit: The UK Withdrawal from the EU and its Implications for the EEA. CMLRev 55:135–156
Hillion C (2019) Norway and the changing Common Foreign and Security Policy of the European Union. NUPI Report. https://www.nupi.no/en/Publications/CRIStin-Pub/Norway-and-the-changing-Common-Foreign-and-Security-Policy-of-the-European-Union Accessed 6 May 2020
Hillion C, Wessel RA (2018) The Good, the Bad and the Ugly: Three Levels of Judicial Control over the CFSP. In: Blockmans S, Koutrakos P (eds) Research Handbook in EU Common Foreign and Security Policy. Edward Elgar Publishing, Cheltenham/Northampton, pp 65–87
HM Government (2017), 'Foreign policy, defence and development: a future partnership paper'; https://www.gov.uk/government/uploads/system/uploads/attachment_data/file/643924/Foreign_policy__defence_and_development_paper.pdf Accessed 8 July 2020
Isleifsson A (2014) Brothers without Arms: Explaining Iceland's Participation in European Union CSDP Operations. https://pdfs.semanticscholar.org/45f3/523f19fc8f045f77c5dbf338f1563429d20c.pdf Accessed 6 May 2020
Keukeleire S (2006) EU Core Groups – Specialisation and division of labour in EU foreign policy. CEPS Working Document No. 252. https://www.ceps.eu/ceps-publications/eu-core-groups-specialisation-and-division-labour-eu-foreign-policy/ Accessed 28 June 2020
Koenig N (2018) Towards Norway Plus? EU-UK defence cooperation post-Brexit. Jacques Delors Institut Berlin. https://www.delorscentre.eu/en/publications/detail/publication/towards-norway-plus-eu-uk-defence-cooperation-post-brexit/ Accessed 6 May 2020
Koutrakos P (2017) Foreign Policy between opt-outs and closer cooperation. In: De Witte B et al. (eds) Between Flexibility and Disintegration: The Trajectory of Differentiation in EU Law. Edward Elgar, Cheltenham/Northampton, pp 405–424
Larik J (2013) Entrenching Global Governance: The EU's Constitutional Objectives Caught Between a Sanguine World View and a Daunting Reality. In: Van Vooren B et al. (eds) The EU's Role in Global Governance: The Legal Dimension. Oxford University Press, Oxford, pp. 7–22
Larik J (2014) From Speciality to the Constitutional Sense of Purpose: On the Changing Role of the Objectives of the European Union. ICLQ 63:936
Lis J (2017) Brexit's toll on foreign policy: Losing our reputation day after day. http://www.politics.co.uk/comment-analysis/2017/07/17/brexit-s-toll-on-foreign-policy-losing-our-reputation-day-af Accessed 6 May 2020

Lonardo L (2018) Common Foreign and Security Policy and the EU's External Action Objectives: An analysis of Article 21 of the Treaty on the European Union. European Constitutional Law Review 14:584–608

Lonardo L (2019) The Relative Influence of the European Council in EU External Action. JCER 15:36–56

Missiroli A (2000) CFSP, Defence, and Flexibility. Chaillot Paper No. 38, WEU Institute for Security Studies. https://www.iss.europa.eu/sites/default/files/EUISSFiles/cp038e.pdf Accessed 28 June 2020

Monar J (1997) The European Union's Foreign Affairs System after the Treaty of Amsterdam: A 'Strengthened Capacity for External Action'? EFAR 2:418

Norwegian Ministry of Foreign Affairs (2018). Cooperation on foreign and security policy. https://www.regjeringen.no/en/topics/european-policy/Norways-relations-with-Europe/eu_fusp/id684931/ Accessed 6 May 2020

Piris J-C (2010) The Lisbon Treaty: A Legal and Political Analysis. Cambridge University Press, Cambridge, pp 89–90

Piris J-C (2016) If the UK votes to leave: The seven alternatives to EU membership. Centre for European Reform. http://www.cer.eu/sites/default/files/pb_piris_brexit_12jan16.pdf Accessed 6 May 2020

Rieker P (2006) Norway and the ESDP: Explaining Norwegian participation in the EU's Security policy. European Security 15:281–298

Rieker P (2017) Outsidership and the European Neighbourhood Policy: The Case of Norway. Global Affairs 3:1–13

Sánchez-Taberno SR (2017) The Choice of Legal Basis and the Principle of Consistency in the Procedure for Conclusion of International Agreements in CFSP Contexts: Parliament v. Council (Pirate-Transfer Agreement with Tanzania). CMLRev 54:899–920.

Sjursen H (2015) Reinforcing executive dominance: Norway and the EU's foreign and security policy. In: Eriksen EO, Fossum JE (ed) The European Union's Non-Members: Independence under Hegemony? Routledge, pp 189–208

Tannock C (2016) Brexit: The Security Dimension. http://www.charlestannock.com/brexit-security-dimension.pdf. Accessed 8 July 2020

Tardy T (2014) CSDP: Getting third states on board. European Union Institute for Security Studies. https://www.iss.europa.eu/sites/default/files/EUISSFiles/Brief_6_CSDP_and_third_states.pdf Accessed 6 May 2020

Törő C (2005) The Latest Example of Enhanced Cooperation in the Constitutional Treaty: The Benefits of Flexibility and Differentiation in European Security and Defence Policy Decisions and their Implementation. European Law Journal 11:641–656

Törő C (2010) External State Partners in ESDP missions: Third Country Participation in EU Crisis Management. EFAR 15:325–345

Van der Loo G, Wessel RA (2017) The Non-Ratification of Mixed Agreements: Legal Consequences and Options. CMLRev 54:735–770

Van Eekelen WF, Kurpas S (2008) The Evolution of Flexible Integration in European Defence Policy: Is Permanent Structured Cooperation a Leap Forward for the Common Security and Defence Policy? CEPS Working Document No. 296. http://aei.pitt.edu/9316/2/9316.pdf Accessed 28 June 2020

Wessel RA (1999) The European Union's Foreign and Security Policy: A Legal Institutional Perspective. Kluwer Law International, The Hague

Wessel RA (2007) Differentiation in EU Foreign, Security, and Defence Policy: Between Coherence and Flexibility. In: Trybus M, White N (eds) European Security Law. Oxford University Press, Oxford, pp 247–248

Wessel RA (2015) Resisting Legal Facts: Are CFSP Norms as Soft as They Seem? EFAR 20:123–145

Wessel RA (2018a) Consequences of Brexit for International Agreements Concluded by the EU and its Member States. CMLRev 55:101–132

Wessel RA (2018b) Integration and Constitutionalisation in EU Foreign and Security Policy. In: Schütze R (ed) Governance and Globalization: International and European Perspectives. Cambridge University Press, Cambridge, pp 339–375

Wessel RA (2019) Friends with Benefits? Possibilities for the UK's Continued Participation in the EU's Foreign and Security Policy. European Papers, 4:427–45

Wessel RA (2021a) Legality in EU Common Foreign and Security Policy: The Choice of the Appropriate Legal Basis. In: Kilpatrick C, Scott J (eds) Contemporary Challenges to EU Legality (Collected Courses of the Academy of European Law). Oxford University Press, Oxford (forthcoming)

Wessel RA (2021b) General Principles in CFSP Law. In: Moreno-Lax V et al. (eds) Research Handbook on General Principles of EU Law. Edward Elgar Publishing, Cheltenham/Northampton (forthcoming)

Wessel RA, Larik J (2020) EU External Relations Law: Text, Cases and Materials. Hart Publishing, Oxford

Whitman RG (2016) The UK and EU Foreign and Security Policy: An Optional Extra. The Political Quarterly 87:254–26

Zandee D, Kruijver K (2019) The European Intervention Initiative: Developing a shared strategic culture for European defence. Clingendael Report. https://www.clingendael.org/sites/default/files/2019-09/The_European_Intervention_2019.pdf Accessed 6 May 2020

Zarembo K (2011) Ukraine in EU security: an undervalued partner. https://www.files.ethz.ch/isn/131810/Ukraine_in_EU_Security_PB_88.pdf Accessed 6 May 2020

Part III
The EU and Third European Countries

Chapter 9
The Building Blocks and Stumbling Stones of Constructing the European Legal Space

A. Ott

Contents

Abstract The integration of third European countries into the EU's framework of policies and rules is a trajectory of renewed attention in law and politics. The international agreements setting up a legal relationship between the EU and the third European country might differ in detail, but are characterized by similar legal building blocks and legal tools. This chapter explains which categories of international agreements exist and which legal tools are employed to build a European Legal Space in which the EU rules and policies are extended to third countries. The legal content and the legal tools extending EU rules and enforcing and safeguarding their application in international agreements are decisively shaped by the EU's formal, political and judicial conditions. These conditions are characterized by respecting EU's competences, safeguarding the integrity of EU law and the autonomy of the EU courts.

Keywords European Legal Space · EEA · Switzerland · Brexit · Integrity and Autonomy of EU Law

---

A. Ott (✉)
Faculty of Law, Maastricht University, Maastricht, The Netherlands
e-mail: a.ott@maastrichtuniversity.nl

W. Th. Douma et al. (eds.), *The Evolving Nature of EU External Relations Law*,
https://doi.org/10.1007/978-94-6265-423-5_9

9.1 Introduction

The extension of European Union (EU) rules and policies beyond its territory and on third countries—so creating a European Legal Space—has moved from a matter of technical importance for lawyers and politicians to the daily news. The possible post-Brexit relations between the EU and the United Kingdom (UK) are captured in the options of the Norway, Ukraine or Turkey 'models', all symbolizing existing forms of bilateral cooperation of the EU with third countries. At the same time, when these cooperation models are compared, the EU has been busy updating bilateral relations with other non-EU countries in Europe. The EU aims to modernize relations with the so-called European microstates (Andorra, San Marino and Monaco).[1] Furthermore, the EU has been negotiating a new institutional framework agreement with Switzerland to update the management of the Bilaterals, the EU-Swiss sectoral agreements.[2] Finally, the EU has developed ideas to update the EU-Turkey customs union, which are, however, currently shelved for political reasons.[3]

All of these negotiations and the political discussions surrounding the integration of third countries demonstrate that negotiations have become cumbersome and time-consuming, influenced by legal concerns and political interests on both sides. The contribution will demonstrate that the EU might offer different models of cooperation—ranging from sectoral agreements to association agreements. In essence, however, the EU applies the same legal building blocks to extend EU rules on third countries in its proximity, independently whether dealing with small states such as Andorra or big states such as the UK. This rigidity is caused by the EU's toolbox to enable the third countries successful and effective participation in internal market rules or other core policies and rules such as on the Eurozone and the Schengen rules. The content of the norms establishing a European Legal Space are decisively shaped by the European Court of Justice (ECJ)'s case law on previous international agreements. Consequently, the contribution highlights the three EU legal and political constraints that emerge when constructing a common legal space. These conditions are that the extension of EU rules complies internally with EU competences, the integrity of EU law and the level playing field is preserved, and, finally, the EU's courts autonomy remains untouched. Moreover, the contribution aims to point out the hidden stumbling blocks at the entrance into that Space, so which legal problems arise enabling third country integration.

---

[1] See for instance Council Conclusions on a Homogeneous Extended Single Market and EU Relations with non-EU Western European Countries, Brussels 16 December 2014, 16583/14; European Parliament Recommendation of 13 March 2019 to the Council, to the Commission and to the Vice-President of the Commission/High Representative of the Union for Foreign Affairs and Security Policy on the Association Agreement between the EU and Monaco, Andorra and San Marino, P8_TA(2019)0188.

[2] Draft Institutional Framework Agreement with Switzerland. https://www.fdfa.admin.ch/dam/dea/fr/documents/abkommen/Acccord-inst-Projet-de-texte_fr.pdf. Accessed 29 June 2020.

[3] European Commission 2016.

9.2 The EU as a Regional Rule-Maker: Exporting the Brussels Rules

The integration of a non-EU Member State into the EU legal set of rules can be approached from different conceptual perspectives and requires a certain form of categorization at the risk of simplifying complex realities. The EU operates as the largest and most successful regional international organization worldwide. It is equipped with a functioning customs union and internal market. It is further based on other, more variable, common aims such as common borders, currency, security, and foreign policy. The EU, despite all its shortcomings, still acts as an attractive role and rule model for other regional integration areas globally and third countries integrated into the European Legal Space regionally. This expression 'European Legal Space', coined by Christopher Harding some 19 years ago in his mapping exercise on legal regimes in Europe, denotes very well the impact of the EU's legal system beyond the EU's territory and the increasing overall convergence between legal regimes in Europe.[4] The extension of rules and regimes to its immediate neighbours forms part of the EU's ambition as a global rule-maker. Third countries align, either voluntarily or mandatory, to EU rules because these states want to join the Union in the future, trade with the Union and import their products or services to the EU's internal market. The EU aims not to govern by stealth, but by law; it is a regulatory actor or soft power compared to nation states and superpowers.[5]

The EU has a global mission and this is stated in Article 3(5) TEU: "In its relations to the wider world, the Union shall uphold and promote its values and interests and contribute to the protection of its citizens." This is twinned with Article 8 TEU. It aims to establish a "special relationship with neighbouring countries" founded on the values for the Union.[6] These provisions flag that this organization is more than a trading block extending its rules. Its dogmatic self-understanding as a supranational legal order of constitutional nature is carved out in the ECJ's early jurisdiction.[7] The EU acts as a self-contained system in international law.[8] It has been lately reconfirmed in the 2018 *Achmea* judgment and the *Wightman* case by emphasising that "EU law is characterized by the fact that it stems from an independent source of law, the Treaties, by its primacy over the laws of the Member States, and by the direct effect of a whole series of provisions which are applicable to their nationals and to the Member States themselves. Those characteristics have given rise to a

[4]Harding 2000, pp. 28–147; see also Von Bogdandy 2016, who borrows this term more recently to replace European Legal Space for European Legal Order, pp. 519–538.

[5]European Commission 2007.

[6]See generally on Article 8 TEU: Wessel and Larik 2020, p. 441.

[7]Court of Justice, *Costa* v. *Enel*, Judgment of the Court, 15 July 1964, Case 6/64, ECLI:EU:C:1964:66; see further: Czuczai 2012, pp. 452–472.

[8]International Law Commission 2006, defining a self-contained regime as a group of rules and principles concerned with a particular subject matter may form a special regime ("Self-contained regime") and be applicable as *lex specialis*. Such special regimes often have their own institutions to administer the relevant rules.

structured network of principles, rules and mutually interdependent legal relations binding the EU and its Member States reciprocally and binding its Member States to each other."[9]

The Union extends its regulatory model and its 'structured network of rules and principles' in different forms and under varying conditions but at the same time the supranational legal order is distinguished from the international agreements copying 'Brussels rules' or third countries adapting to these rules.[10] Brussels rules can be exported by unilateral EU legislation or bilateral/multilateral agreements. In the former situation, the EU adopts legislation with an extraterritorial reach[11] or third countries voluntarily copy EU legislation. Especially in the policy fields relating to the internal market and the rights of citizens and businesses, it can be recognized that the EU aims to protect its own standards by exporting them or by legislating with an extraterritorial reach.[12] The external reach of the subject matter—competition law, environmental law and fundamental rights—impacts third countries. The Union becomes a global rule-maker—though in a clustered way—and many theories have dealt with the Brussels effect, norm diffusion, and territorial expansion to describe this development.[13] Yet, the most effective and structured approach to extend Brussels rules to third countries is by the conclusion of mutually binding international agreements. And this is achieved in a more effective and sustainable way in the nearer neighbourhood by this regional organization than in the global arena.[14]

The focus of this contribution rests on countries in the Union's proximity. In its direct neighbourhood, the EU acts as an important regional rule-maker. These countries either do not wish to join the EU political and economic project for diverse reasons and instead aim to remain close, (Switzerland, Norway, Iceland and Liechtenstein, the microstates Andorra, Monaco, San Marino, Vatican City) or hold the ambition to join in the future (Ukraine) and are candidate countries (the Western Balkans states).[15] Or, finally, they are countries whose status is unclear and in transition (the UK left the Union but its future relation still needs to determined and Turkey

[9]Court of Justice, *Slowakische Republik (Slovak Republic) v Achmea,* Judgment, 6 March 2018, Case C-284/16, ECLI:EU:C:2018:158; Court of Justice, *Wightman and Others v Secretary of State for Exiting the European Union,* Judgment of the (full) Court, 10 December 2018, Case C-621/18, ECLI:EU:C:2018:999, para 45.

[10]See on this point European Court of Justice, *Draft Agreement relating to the creation of the European Economic Area,* Opinion of 14 December 1991, Opinion 1/91, ECLI:EU:C:1991:490, paras 20–21.

[11]We witness recently many examples of this option, namely the REACH Chemicals Regulation, OJ 2006 L 396/1-849; the Timber Regulation, OJ 2010 L 295 p. 23–34; Saving Seals Regulation, OJ 2009 L 286/36–39 or the Data Protection Regulation, OJ 2016 L 119/1–88.

[12]In the 2007 Commission Staff Working Paper, the Commission referred to the success stories on the multilateral level involving food safety, public health, climate change, maritime safety and financial services.

[13]Bradford 2012, p. 1; Scott 2014, p. 1343; Damro 2012, p. 682; De Hert and Czerniawski 2016, pp. 230–243; Scott 2015, pp. 92–120; Cremona and Scott 2019.

[14]Like-minded countries with similar standards and expectations such as Canada and Chile are an exception to this rule.

[15]Although Ukraine has currently no perspective of joining the Union.

is a candidate country without realistic accession prospects).[16] These countries have an economic, financial, political and strategic interest to participate in some of the EU's aims and objectives but on their own terms, respecting their sovereign rights and specific interests.[17]

The landscape of third countries' integration into the EU's legal space is variable: some cooperations establish a customs union with the EU (the European microstates[18] and Turkey[19]), or form a free trade area (as, for instance, the EU candidate countries).[20] Other concepts provide for a tailor-made access to parts of the internal market (Switzerland) or offer the internal market with an enhanced FTA (European Economic Area including Norway, Iceland and Liechtenstein),[21] or may include the possibility of partial access to the internal market in the future (Ukraine).[22] In addition, and depending on the extent of third countries' legal commitments, these countries align to the EU's *acquis* in certain policy fields (Schengen, CFSP),[23] participate

[16]Over the years, Switzerland, Iceland and Norway applied for accession. But due to referenda either the application was withdrawn (in case of Switzerland and Iceland) or an accession treaty was not ratified (in the case of Norway). See Tatham 2009, pp. 175–192; and on Iceland: Avery 2012.

[17]See also Van Elsuwege 2019, pp. 637–650.

[18]For instance, Andorra: Council Decision of 10 May 2005 on the conclusion of a Cooperation Agreement between the European Community and the Principality of Andorra; OJ L 2005 L 135/12.

[19]Decision No 1/95 of the EC-Turkey Association Council of 22 December 1995 on Implementing the Final Phase of the Customs Union, OJ 1996 L 35/1–46.

[20]Stabilisation and Association Agreement between the European Communities and their Member States, of the one part, and the Republic of Serbia, of the other part, opened for signature 29 April 2008, OJ L 278/14 (entered into force 1 September 2013).

[21]Agreement on the European Economic Area, opened for signature 2 May 1992, OJ L 1/3–522 (entered into force 1 January 1994) (EEA Agreement).

[22]Association Agreement between the European Union and its Member States, of the one part, and Ukraine, of the other part, opened for signature 21 March 2014, OJ L 161/3–2137 (entered into force 1 September 2017) (EU-Ukraine Association Agreement).

[23]Switzerland is associated to Schengen: Agreement between the European Union, the European Community and the Swiss Confederation on the Swiss Confederation's Association with the Implementation, Application and Development of the Schengen Acquis, opened for signature 25 October 2004, OJ L53 (entered into force 28 February 2008). Monaco participates in Schengen, and San Marino which is not part of Schengen but no border control between Italy and San Marino are implemented: see Communication from the Commission to the EP, the Council, ECOSOC and the Committee of the Regions, EU relations with the Principality of Andorra, the Principality of Monaco and the Republic of San Marino, COM (2012) 680 final/2, Brussels 11.1.2013, pp. 9–10. See for CFSP participation, for instance: Agreement between the European Union and the Republic of Albania on the participation of the Republic of Albania in the European Union Military Operation in the Republic of Chad and in the Central African Republic, opened for signature 13 July 2008, OJ L217/19 (entered into force 13 August 2008).

in programmes (ERASMUS, Jean Monnet and Horizon 2020),[24] Euro currency[25] and EU agencies (accession candidates and EFTA countries).[26]

This past diversity is, however, constrained increasingly by the EU's experience of which cooperation forms work or do not work. In addition, the closer a third country aligns to core EU policies such as internal market, currency or Schengen, the more closely-knit the system of effective rule-application and compliance control has to be. The EU institutions remain in the European Legal Space the rule-maker and the ECJ is interpreting EU rules and concepts extended on third countries. The decision-shaping influence of third countries in this process is minimal, as politicians and lawyers from the EFTA states have experienced with growing frustration.[27] And the ECJ decisively shapes the content and legal framework of these integration-oriented international agreements.[28] Firstly, the Court became more reluctant to provide a dynamic reading of such international agreements in line with the EU legal order. This has become visible in the case law on the Swiss bilateral on persons and the Turkish association.[29] Secondly, the ECJ has carved out its own rigid red lines securing the EU's primacy in bilateral rule-making. The judges cemented the EU's autonomy towards international law in the famous *Costa* v. *Enel*, the *EEA* and *ECHR* Opinions but also lesser known ones as the Opinion 1/76 (*European Laying-up Fund*) or the *ECAA* Opinion.[30]

---

[24] See for instance: Commission Decision approving, on behalf of the European Union, an Agreement on the Participation of Albania in "Erasmus+": the Union Programme for Education, Training, Youth and Sport, C(2014)1937/F1.

[25] This concerns the micro-states: Council Decision of 26 November 2009 on the position to be taken by the European Community regarding the renegotiations of the Monetary Agreement with the Republic of San Marino, OJ 2009 L 322/12. Monetary Agreement between the European Union and the Republic of San Marino, OJ 2012 C 2012/5.

[26] Decision no 1/2018 EU/Serbia SAA Council of 8 May 2018 on the Participation of Serbia as an Observer in the European Union Agency for Fundamental Rights' Work and the Respective Modalities thereof, within the framework of Council Regulation (EC) No 168/2007 [2018/1228], OJ 2018 L 229/9.

[27] On the EU's political institutions unwillingness to use the twin pillar system: Iceland Monitor 2018; See also Frederiksen 2010, pp. 481–499.

[28] See on this term: Maresceau 2012, pp. 315–340; see also Maresceau 2013a, p. 153.

[29] Court of Justice, *Demirkan v Bundesrepublik Deutschland*, Judgment of the Court (Grand Chamber), 24 September 2013, Case C-221/11, ECLI:EU:C:2013:583, para 44; Court of Justice, *Grimme v Deutsche Angestellten-Krankenkasse*, Judgment of the Court (Fourth Chamber), 12 November 2009, Case C-351/08, ECLI:EU:C:2009:697; Court of Justice, *Hengartner and Gasserv Landesregierung Vorarlberg*, Judgment of the Court (Third Chamber), 15 July 2010, Case C-70/09, ECLI:EU:C:2010:430; Court of Justice, *Fokus Invest AG v FIAG*, Judgment of the Court (Third Chamber), 11 February 2010, Case C-541/08, ECLI:EU:C:2010:74.

[30] Court of Justice, *Draft Agreement establishing a European Laying-up Fund for Inland Waterway Vessels*, Opinion of 26 April 1977, Opinion 1/76, ECLI:EU:C:1977:63; Opinion 1/91 *(EEA),* above n. 10; Court of Justice, *Draft agreement between the Community, on the one hand, and the countries of the European Free Trade Association, on the other, relating to the creation of the European Economic Area,* Opinion of 10 April 1992, Opinion 1/92, ECLI:EU:C:1992:189; Court of Justice, *Draft Agreement between the European Community and non-Member States on the establishment of a European Common Aviation Area*, Opinion of 18 April 2002, Opinion 1/00, ECLI:EU:C:2002:231; Court of Justice, *Commission of the European Communities v Ireland*, Judgment, 30 May 2006, Case C-459/03, ECLI:EU:C:2006:345 (Mox Plant); Court of Justice, *Kadi and Al Barakaat International*

The chapter now illustrates how the EU consolidates its position as a regional rule-maker in the European Legal Space. In addition, it will demonstrate that former UK prime minister Theresa May's reference in her Florence speech of September 2017 to the EU's creative arrangements with third countries is based on a wrong assumption.[31] These arrangements are not creative and this not because lawyers lack imagination but is caused by the 'building plan' for the European Legal Space. The varying objectives of the cooperation in form of customs union, free trade area or internal market are related to their historical and specific context. Certain constructions were set up but have proven not to be necessarily sustainable in practice or compatible with the judicial red lines set by ECJ in its subsequent case law.

The chapter now elucidates the legal building blocks the Union employs and explains the three EU legal and political constraints that emerge when constructing a common legal space. It finally will also point to the hidden stumbling blocks at the entrance into that Space.

9.3 The EU Legal Building Blocks and Legal Tools Managing a European Legal Space

9.3.1 Categories of Agreements

In the 2012 Communication on European microstates, the European Commission explains the underlying aims of third country integration. These aims are in essence the same, irrespective whether it concerns small Andorra or Great Britain:[32] Internal market access can be provided under the conditions that "mutual benefits through a level playing field"[33] and "cooperation in support of shared objectives" are safeguarded.[34] This Communication also decoded the applicable current categories of

Foundation v Council and Commission, Judgment of 3 September 2008, Joined Cases C-402/05 and C-415/05, ECLI:EU:C:2008:461; Court of Justice, *Draft Agreement on the Creation of a Unified Patent Litigation System,* Opinion of 8 March 2011, Opinion 1/09, ECLI:EU:C:2011:123; Court of Justice, *Draft Agreement on the Accession of the European Union to the European Convention for the Protection of Human Rights and Fundamental Freedoms,* Opinion of 18 December 2014, Opinion 2/13, ECLI:EU:C:2014:2454.

[31] Former Prime Minister Theresa May's Florence speech: "Instead let us be creative as well as practical in designing an ambitious economic partnership which respects the freedoms and principles of the EU, and the wishes of the British people", UK Government 2017.

[32] Communication from the Commission to the EP, the Council, ECOSOC and the Committee of the Regions, EU relations with the Principality of Andorra, the Principality of Monaco and the Republic of San Marino, COM (2012) 680 final/2, Brussels, 11 January 2013.

[33] See above n. 28.

[34] Ibid.

cooperation outside membership in the form of 1. sectoral agreements, 2. association agreements, and 3. European Economic Area (EEA) membership, possibly in parallel, with 4. membership in regional international organizations covering sectoral policies.

9.3.1.1 Sectoral Agreements

Sectoral agreements provide tailor-made access to parts of the internal market (such as in the area of persons or goods), complemented by coverage of other internal market related policies (for instance transport, competition, Schengen rules) in separate international agreements. This piecemeal approach is visible in EU-Swiss relations, characterized by a patchwork of more than 120 sectoral agreements (the so-called Bilaterals I and II) governed by 27 joint committees and a clustered, variable dispute settlement. It achieves a tailor-made and flexible access to the EU's internal market policies which has been critically depicted as 'cherry-picking' and is criticism for its byzantine structure by EU institutions. They have unanimously dismissed the Swiss experience in the last nine years for its "unmanageable complexity" and as being plagued by "legal uncertainty".[35] Consequently, the EU has promoted—without resonance, however, on the Swiss side—Swiss EEA membership or at least a comprehensive Framework Association Agreement. Since 2008, the EU has pursued to monitor the internal market related Swiss Bilaterals by way of an overarching institutional framework agreement. This framework agreement has been negotiated since 2014. The draft—finalized on the technical level—at the end of 2018, however, holds only a 50/50 percent chance to be signed and ratified.[36] To a lesser extent, we also witness a sectoral approach in the current relations with the micro-states,[37] however, negotiations aim to transfer them into framework associations, either through a general association agreement with individual protocols or individual association agreements.

---

[35] European Union External Action (2010) Council conclusions on EU relations with EFTA countries 3060th GENERAL AFFAIRS Council meeting, Brussels, 14 December 2010: "Since Switzerland is not a member of the European Economic Area, it has chosen to take a sector-based approach to its agreements in view of a possible long-term rapprochement with the EU. In full respect of the Swiss sovereignty and choices, the Council has come to the conclusion that while the present system of bilateral agreements has worked well in the past, the challenge of the coming years will be to go beyond this complex system, which is creating legal uncertainty and has become unwieldy to manage and has clearly reached its limits. In order to create a sound basis for future relations, mutually acceptable solutions to a number of horizontal issues, set out below, will need to be found."

[36] The fate of this draft is also linked to a pending Swiss referendum whether the free movement of persons between the EU and Switzerland should be abolished, see Draft Institutional Agreement with Switzerland, above n. 2.

[37] So are currently monetary, taxation, customs and cooperation agreements in place and they also align to Schengen and the CFSP. See Murray 2006, p. 185.

9.3.1.2 Association Agreements

Association agreements in the European Legal Space constitute a framework to establish a free trade area (with the exception of Turkey and the micro-states which established a customs union) with preferential access to the EU market.[38] Their flanking measures and horizontal policies provide a platform of participation in other areas of EU activity. In the past, the formation of a customs union was only agreed exceptionally, as in the case of Turkey and its association agreement. Currently, association agreements of different generations are in place with Turkey, the Western Balkans states (as so-called accession associations) and with the countries of the Eastern Partnership (Ukraine, Moldova, Armenia and Georgia). As the Association Agreement with Ukraine demonstrates, a deep and comprehensive free trade area might open the path for gradual integration into the EU internal market.[39] This promise, based on preferential market access for goods, is, however, conditional on the third countries' successful legislative approximation to EU rules.[40]

9.3.1.3 Participation in the European Economic Area (EEA)

While the EEA agreement is based on the association policy legal basis, it belongs to a category *sui generis* in terms of its structural and institutional set-up. The EEA extends the internal market to the participating EFTA states (Norway, Iceland and Liechtenstein). Next to the extension of internal market policies (including the four freedoms), the EEA aligns competition and state aid rules with EU rules, but also the following horizontal policies: consumer protection, company law, environment, social policy and statistics. The institutional framework of the EEA consists of two pillars; the EU and its institutions constitute the first pillar, whereas the EEA/EFTA bodies, form the second pillar and mirror EU institutions. Joint bodies implementing the EEA Agreement establish the link between these pillars. Both legal orders are synchronized and the EEA pillar is safeguarded by the EFTA Surveillance Authority and the EFTA court. A dynamic adoption of the relevant EU *acquis* is established[41]

[38] Some sectors provide for tariff-free access. According to the famous definition in the Demirel case an association agreement creates "special, privileged links with a non-member country which must, at least to a certain extent, take part in the Community system", see Court of Justice *Demirel v Stadt Schwäbisch Gmünd,* Judgment of 30 September 1987, Case 12/86, ECLI:EU:C:1987:400 para 9. See, for comments, amongst others, Van Elsuwege and Chamon 2019.

[39] See on this Van der Loo 2016, p. 63 where he discusses the aspects of different types of legislative approximation mechanisms.

[40] Van der Loo characterizes this as market access conditionality, above n. 28, p. 66.

[41] EEA Agreement, above n. 21, Article 102 "In order to guarantee the legal security and the homogeneity of the EEA, the EEA Joint Committee shall take a decision concerning an amendment of an Annex to this Agreement as closely as possible to the adoption by the Community of the corresponding new Community legislation with a view to permitting a simultaneous application of the latter as well as of the amendments of the Annexes to the Agreement. To this end, the Community shall, whenever adopting a legislative act on an issue which is governed by this Agreement, as soon as possible inform the other Contracting Parties in the EEA Joint Committee".

and extensive homogeneity principles guide the interpretation of EEA law by the EFTA court and the other EEA institutions.[42]

9.3.1.4 Regional Organizations Covering Sectoral Policies (Aviation, Energy, Transport)

Finally, from these three bilateral cooperation forms, the sectoral and regional organizations have to be separated. They operate in parallel to existing association agreements. The EU established with neighbouring countries (mainly the Western Balkans states and Eastern ENP countries) an Energy[43] (2005, EnCT) and Transport Community (2017, TCT).[44] Furthermore, the European Common Aviation Area (ECAA) applies the EU's aviation *acquis* to the EEA, accession candidates and European Neighbourhood Partnership (ENP) countries.[45] These regional organizations extend the EU rules in energy, aviation and transport but also in related areas such as environment, competition law and public procurement. EU market access is made conditional upon satisfactory implementation of the sectoral EU acquis.[46] Coined sector-based multilateralism, it overcomes the deficiencies of the current enlargement and ENP process which cannot offer any medium-term and realistic incentives for these third countries and aims instead for legal integration in specific policy sectors.[47]

9.3.2 The Legal Tools Integrating Third States into the European Legal Space

For all these categories or building blocks, a toolbox of norms is designed to ensure an effective and coherent application of EU rules in the European Legal Space.

[42]Lazowski 2006, p. 95.

[43]The following third countries are members: Albania, Bosnia and Herzegovina, Kosovo, the Former Yugoslav Republic of Macedonia, Georgia, Moldova, Montenegro, Serbia and Ukraine. Armenia, Norway and Turkey take part as Observers. Energy Community Treaty, opened for signature 25 October 2005, OJ L 198/16-37 (entered into force 1 July 2006).

[44]Albania, Bosnia and Herzegovina, the Former Yugoslav Republic of Macedonia, Kosovo, Montenegro, the Republic of Serbia; See Transport Community Treaty, opened for signature 09/10/2017, OJ L 278/3-53 (entered into force provisionally).

[45]Albania, Bosnia and Herzegovina, Croatia, the Former Yugoslav Republic of Macedonia, Montenegro, Serbia, Kosovo under UNSCR 1244, Norway and Iceland; see Multilateral Agreement between the European Community and its Member States, the Republic of Albania, Bosnia and Herzegovina, the Republic of Bulgaria, the Republic of Croatia, the Former Yugoslav Republic of Macedonia, the Republic of Iceland, the Republic of Montenegro, the Kingdom of Norway, Romania, the Republic of Serbia and the United Nations Interim Administration Mission in Kosovo on the establishment of a European Common Aviation Area, opened for signature 9 June 2006, OJ 2006 L 285/3-46 (entered into force 1 December 2017) (ECAA Agreement).

[46]For an overview of the Air Services agreements concluded by the EU, see: EP Study 2013, p. 48.

[47]See further: Blockmans and Van Vooren 2012, p. 577.

These legal tools can be grouped for their two-fold purposes: (1) Extending EU rules and ensuring their compliance and (2) enforcing EU rules and safeguarding their consistent interpretation and development. Concrete examples of these two forms of legal tools can be found, for instance, in the EC-Swiss agreement on air transport,[48] the Association Agreement with Ukraine,[49] the EEA agreement[50] and the Transport Community Treaty (TCT).[51]

9.3.2.1 Extending EU Rules and Ensuring Their Compliance

To achieve a homogeneous legal space, rules—phrased identically to the respective EU rules or referring to a concept or acquis established under EU law[52]—are introduced into these international agreements. They secure the extension, for instance, of the customs union, internal market or Schengen common border rules to the third countries. Furthermore, the contracting parties should aim for a homogeneous interpretation of the international agreement provisions with EU norms[53] (or rules which are identical in substance to EU law[54]). In addition, the relevant rulings of the ECJ (and even Commission decisions as in the case of the Transport Community Treaty) are to be considered. The provisions of the Transport Community Treaty are directly effective, individuals can rely on them. Overall, if other bilateral agreements are to be relied by individuals this is now clearly indicated in the more recent bilateral agreements.[55] This condition of directly effective norms differentiates these bilateral agreements from trade agreements updating WTO rules which explicitly deny direct effect in national courts.[56] This consistent interpretation is aided by non-discrimination clauses and good faith norms.[57] The evolution of the interpretation of

[48]Agreement between the European Community and the Swiss Confederation on Air Transport, opened for signature 21 June 1999, OJ L114/73-90 (entered into force 1 June 2002), (EC-Swiss Bilateral Agreement).

[49]EU-Ukraine Association Agreement, above n. 22.

[50]EEA Agreement, above n. 21.

[51]Transport Community Treaty, above n. 44.

[52]Knöpfel and Najy 2018.

[53]EEA Agreement, above n. 21, Article 6.

[54]Transport Community Treaty, above n. 44, Article 19.

[55]Ibid., Article 18(1).

[56]For instance: Article 30.6 CETA, the Comprehensive Economic and Trade Agreement (CETA) between Canada, of the one part, and the European Union and its Member States, of the other part, opened for signature 30 October 2016, OJ L 11/23 (entered into force (provisionally) 21 September 2017); see also Ghazaryan 2018, pp. 27–74; see also Court of Justice, *Comprehensive Economic and Trade Agreement between Canada, of the one part, and the European Union and its Member States, of the other part (CETA),* Opinion of AG Bot of 29 January 2019, Opinion 1/17, ECLI:EU:C:2019:72.

[57]EC-Swiss Bilateral Air Transport Agreement, above n. 48, Article 17 “The Contracting Parties shall take all appropriate measures, whether general or particular, to ensure fulfilment of the obligations arising out of this Agreement and shall refrain from any measures which would jeopardise attainment of the objectives of this Agreement”.

EU law norms and principles in the ECJ's jurisdiction cannot, though, be reflected in these international agreements. The contracting parties can only consider precedential case law decided before the signature of the agreement and "future developments of case law" are only communicated to the contracting parties.[58]

9.3.2.2 Enforcing EU Rules and Safeguarding Their Consistent Interpretation and Development

To prevent divergences in interpretation between EU rules and the rules of these organizations and agreements in the European Legal Space in the long term, several models in different generations of international agreements exist. They can be generally split up into a diplomatic resolution between the contracting parties (1) or adjudication by ECJ, EFTA court or arbitrators (2) (or a combination of two of them).[59]

Enforcement mechanisms, the governance rules on state-to-state arbitration, have become more sophisticated over the years. This development is related to, on the one hand, past experiences with ineffective diplomatic dispute resolution and on the other hand, by the evolution of ECJ's jurisdiction on dispute resolution. Not many cases have become public where disputes arose in Association Councils and Joint Committees, but these conflicts are subsequently not resolved in the diplomatic fora.[60]

In more recent international agreements, the drafters depart from the diplomatic conflict resolution and employ a quasi-judicial resolution. The great variety, especially in the procedural details, is related to the respective generation, as mentioned, but also whether and how far the agreement extends core policies of the EU to a third country (namely the internal market, customs union, Schengen rules, currency).[61] The more these agreements touch upon core policies and especially internal market policies, the more effective the dispute settlement system in these international agreements is regulated. Newer cooperation agreements include a termination clause and

---

[58] EEA Agreement, above n. 21, Article 6 "Relevant rulings of the Court of Justice given prior to the date of signature of this Agreement"; Further, Article 16 of the EC-Swiss Bilateral Agreement, above n. 48, provides that: "insofar as the application of this agreement involves concepts of Community law, account shall be taken of the relevant case-law (…) prior to the date of signature"; ECAA Agreement, above n. 45, Article 16 provides that "insofar as the provisions of this agreements and the provisions of the acts specified in Annex I are identical in substance to corresponding rules of the EC Treaty and to acts adopted pursuant to the EC Treaty (…) be interpreted in conformity with the relevant rulings and decisions".

[59] These disputes can concern the interpretation of homogenous norms or the general application and interpretation of the agreement.

[60] So is the dispute between the EU and Switzerland on the flanking measures stuck in the Joint Committee of the Swiss bilateral on persons. Regarding the restrictions to the movement of service providers (the so-called "flanking measures"), the EU requested the revision of the discriminatory and disproportionate aspects of some of those measures, such in the case of the so-called "eight-day-rule" and the compulsory deposit. See Europa Consilium 2012.

[61] See, generally, Vajda 2018, pp. 205–224.

allow for suspension measures in case of irreconcilable divergences.[62] These tools serve the purpose of strengthening the enforcement of agreement[63] and applying conditionality tools on the third country.[64] To better understand the limits set to the cooperation with third countries, the following part will set out the political and legal conditions framing the use of these building blocks.

9.4 The EU's Legal and Political Conditions for Third Country Integration

International agreements governing the European Legal Space have evolved into complicated legal designs. They navigate a thin line ensuring compliance with exported EU rules, on the one hand, and compliance with the EU and the third countries' red lines, on the other.

What are the EU conditions framing every current and future third country integration? These criteria can be broken down into complying with EU competences, EU integrity and autonomy. These three criteria shape the content of these international agreements and have been carved out—more or less—in the ECJ jurisdiction but are also mirrored in current political negotiations with third European countries. Primarily, an international agreement that the EU concludes with a third country and which extends Brussels rules on third countries cannot alter the essential characteristics of the EU. Essential characteristics or elements, according to the Court, are the existing division of competences between the EU, its institutions and Member States, and that the international agreement does not affect the special legal order with its supranational principles of EU primacy and direct effect. Finally, it requires that such an agreement does not touch upon tasks assigned to the national courts and the Court of Justice to apply and interpret EU law.[65] Consequently, a decisive

---

[62]The EEA Agreement and the ECAA Agreement state that the Parties can refer the dispute to the ECJ; see ECAA Agreement, above n. 45, Article 20(4). The internal market-related Swiss bilateral agreements also include a guillotine clause, according to which the termination of one of these agreements leads automatically to the termination of the others; See Agreement between the European Community and its Member States, of the one part, and the Swiss Confederation, of the other, on the free movement of persons, opened for signature 21 June 1999, OJ L 114 (entered into force 30 April 2002), Article 25.

[63]These structures, however, are also visible in exceptional situations such as the case of Member State integration by international law. This is the case of Denmark, which has a permanent opt-out from the area of freedom, security and justice and concluded, for instance, an international agreement with the EU on participation in Europol.

[64]The tool of conditionality has been mainly known and employed in the pre-accession context but also has a post-accession dimension and is employed throughout the EU's external relations.

[65]Court of Justice, *Comprehensive Economic and Trade Agreement between Canada, of the one part, and the European Union and its Member States, of the other part (CETA)*, Opinion of the Court of 30 April 2019, Opinion 1/17, ECLI:EU:C:2019:341, paras 111–117; Opinion 2/13 (*Accession to the ECHR*), above n. 30, para 166; Opinion 1/09 *(Patent Court)*, above n. 30, paras 76–85. See the

element in the assessment plays which role is assigned or not assigned to the ECJ in the dispute settlement involving rules of EU law origin.

In light of the complexity of the concept of the EU's autonomy in international law and its chameleonic interpretation by the ECJ, three different scenarios can be distinguished. However, only the last one is of relevance to this contribution. The first scenario relates to the EU's involvement in international dispute settlement beyond the borders of the European Legal Space. The EU participates since 1994 in the WTO dispute settlement and in an increasing number of arbitration structures established on a bilateral and multilateral level.[66] The bilateral agreements involving investor-to-state dispute settlement in trade and investment agreements have, in particular, raised issues of compatibility with the EU legal order. The Court's jurisdiction finally addresses such a situation in the 1/17 (CETA) Opinion. In this Opinion, the judges argued that the investor-state dispute settlement (ISDS) introduced in the EU-Canada free trade agreement is compatible with EU law. Decisive is according to the EU judges that the dispute resolution under CETA has no jurisdiction to interpret and apply rules of EU law other than the provisions of the CETA agreement and then this interpretation is guided only by international law. In addition, the CETA ruling argues that the agreement has no effect on the operation of the EU institutions in accordance with the EU constitutional framework, namely the rulings cannot affect the legislative autonomy of the EU concerning the level of protection of public order or public safety.[67] This dispute settlement between the EU and a third country stands outside the EU judicial system, no references for a preliminary reference are enabled and the principle of mutual trust does not find application between the EU and Canada.[68]

The second scenario of dispute settlement concerns the situation when the EU and/or its Member States participate in a specialized and autonomous dispute settlement system in the European Legal Space. The compatibility with EU law was addressed in *Achmea* case on intra-EU investment disputes, the Patent Court Opinion on European patent protection (Opinion 1/09), the EU accession to the ECHR Opinion (Opinion 2/13) and the Opinion 1/76 on the Rhine inland waterways management.[69] These cases have in common that the EU and/or its Member States delegated or outsourced specific judicial functions to an international organization and its court system in the European Legal Space, taking away this function from the ECJ and its

extensive discussion in the literature on autonomy: De Witte 2013, p. 33; De Witte 2010, pp. 141–155; Govaere 2010, p. 187; Thym 2011, p. 320–322; Odermatt 2018, pp. 291–316; Contartese 2017, pp. 1627–1671.

[66]Such arbitration is agreed, for instance, in 1994 Energy Charter Treaty and in the UN Convention on the Law of the Sea, opened for signature 10 December 1992, UNTS 397 (entered into force 16 November 1994), (UNCLOS).

[67]Opinion 1/17 *(CETA),* above n. 65, paras 120–161.

[68]Ibid., paras 106–134; Rosas 2003, p. 284.

[69]The Rhine Navigation case could also be categorized under the third category because it dealt with a mini-court of EC and Swiss judges in a legal space mainly within the EC legal space, see further on this: De Witte 2013, p. 35.

Member States courts.[70] These judicial constructions have been consistently critically assessed by the Court and condemned as a breach of the EU's autonomy.

The third and final scenario is the only one relevant for the integrating of third countries into the European Legal Space and differs from the first and especially second one. In this situation, the EU and a third country establish a joint dispute settlement system through an international agreement to manage a common legal space. This situation has been only so far assessed in the *EEA* and *ECAA* Opinions.[71] The court appears to be more benevolent as all these dispute settlement constructions and cooperation forms found the approval of the Court. However, these dispute settlement mechanisms have to comply with the three conditions which will be outlined now. This third scenario decisively differs from the second scenario as such that the EU does not participate in an autonomous dispute settlement in competition to EU jurisdiction but extends EU rules in the European Legal Space. For these rules the EU remains in the rule-maker and the third country in the role of the rule-taker. And the Court of Justice will be the final arbiter involving disputes on rules of EU law origin.

9.4.1 EU Competences—A Formal Condition

The first condition on EU competences can be addressed briefly, since the Court tends to apply a broad-brush approach when considering it. The ECJ, instead, focusses on its role in the dispute resolution of these agreements and the potential withdrawal of disputes under EU law, which is as a judicial condition covered under point 9.4.33.

The EU can participate, in principle, in such international agreements and the EU court jurisdiction can be extended to third countries when EU competences are respected.[72] Whether the EU competences are affected, is primarily a question of the intra-EU relations between EU and Member States and what the content of the international agreement regulates. Third country cooperation based on mixed agreements—so agreements concluded by EU and Member States with a third country—can form more of a stumbling block for a successful integration into the European Legal Space than EU-only agreements. In practice, the picture is not coherent; some of the currently applicable bilateral agreements are EU only agreements (the Swiss bilateral agreement on transport, EnCT, TCT, the Swiss association to Schengen, the Kosovo Association Agreement or the EU-UK withdrawal agreement), but others are mixed agreements (for instance, the ECAA, EEA, the Swiss bilateral agreement on persons, the EU-Ukraine Association Agreement and Stabilization and Association agreements).

---

[70] Rosas 2003.

[71] Opinion 1/91 *EEA*, above n. 10; Opinion 1/92 *EEA*, above n. 30; Opinion 1/00 *(ECAA)*, above n. 30.

[72] Opinion 1/09 (*Patent Court*), above n. 30, paras 74–75.

These EU mixed agreements raise primarily issues regarding the relationship between the EU and its Member States including their courts but also concerning mixed agreements' practical implementation. EU and national parliaments of EU Member States and the third country ratify these agreements.[73] This process is cumbersome and time-consuming, it could involve referenda by the third country, as happened in case of Switzerland, but also by an EU Member State (the Netherlands on the Ukrainian Association Agreement)[74] or might raise concerns by national courts or individual Member States for political and constitutional reasons.[75] In the first Court case addressing EU autonomy, Opinion 1/76, the peculiar situation of 'partial mixity' was critically assessed. This concerned the participation of some Member States and the EC at the time in a Draft agreement on a European laying-up fund on the Rhine and Moselle. The management of waterway vessels and preventing overcapacities required the participation of Switzerland. The Court criticized the "mixed organization"[76] for its "ambiguity". It argued that it was a surrender of the independence of action (autonomy) of the Union in its external relations and constituted a harmful influence on the position of the institutions and the Member States vis-à-vis one another.[77]

In contrast, EU-only agreements pose less of a risk to the EU that such diplomatic or dispute settlement bodies could determine and impact the intra-EU relations between EU and Member States.[78] The Court confirmed the conformity of an EU-only agreement in the *ECAA* Opinion. Such an agreement would not affect the allocation of powers because the Member States would not be parties to this ECAA Agreement. Decisively, the Court explained that the disputes between Member States or third countries and Union institutions on Union law applicable to air transport were not withdrawn from the EU system in line with Article 344 TFEU.[79] However, despite this warning, the final agreement was ratified as a multilateral EU and Member States mixed agreement.[80] Until now, this competence condition appears more as a formal than substantial condition. It has been submerged in the question how far the dispute settlement in these international agreements touches upon the EU courts' autonomy.

[73]Frederiksen and Franklin 2015, pp. 629–684.

[74]See for instance Wessel 2016.

[75]See the German Constitutional Court and the provisional application of the CETA agreement or the difficulty in the past of the ratification of the Europe Agreement by Italy due to the Italian-Slovenian border conflict on the Osimo Agreements: Vehar and Ilesic 2002.

[76]Opinion 1/76 (*European Laying-up Fund*), above n. 30, para 14.

[77]Ibid., paras 8, 12.

[78]Opinion 1/00 (*ECAA)* above n. 30, para 16 with reference to the opposite situation in Opinion 1/91, above n. 10, paras 31–36.

[79]Ibid., Opinion 1/00 *(ECAA),* paras 16 and 17: "will continue to be dealt exclusively by the machinery provided for by the Treaty".

[80]Eckes 2013, p. 97; see also Govaere 2010, p. 193.

9.4.2 Integrity of EU Law and Creating a Level Playing Field: A Political Condition?

The 'integrity of EU law' features prominently in the discussion on third country integration recently.[81] Often narrowed down to the integrity of the internal market and the customs union,[82] it has been—especially in the Brexit debate—more broadly interlinked with the integrity of the EU legal order and the autonomy of its decision-making.[83] This all-encompassing definition finds its origin in the Court's position that the essential character of the powers of the Union and its institutions remain unaltered.[84]

The underlying understanding behind the integrity argument is more political than legal. The EU rules come with rights and obligations for third countries but also that a dividing line between members and non-members remains. It excludes third countries from gaining equal rights in EU institutions[85] or having a free choice as to which EU integration policies they join in. It is reflected in the Brexit negotiations when references to the long-term relationships are made. The European Council stressed in this context a balance of rights and obligations, the preservation of a level playing field and the integrity and proper functioning of the Single Market.[86]

Behind this integrity condition, looms the economic and political consideration of securing a level playing field.[87] Fair and equal conditions for traders internally are present in the internal policies (internal market and competition law), for some time and frequent references to the external dimension can be traced back to 2010. In the Commission Communication on European microstates, the Commission explains that "the backbone of the EU's internal market are common rules and standards and

[81] See in this respect the European Council Negotiating Guidelines and the Draft Political Declaration setting out the Framework for the Future Relationship between the European Union and the United Kingdom, para 4, Brussels, 22 November 2018, XT 21095/18.

[82] European Council Negotiating Guidelines, Brussels 29 April 2017, Speech by Michel Barnier at the Centre for European Reform on 'The Future of the EU', European Parliament resolution of 13 December 2017 on the state of play of negotiations with the United Kingdom (2017/2964(RSP)).

[83] European Parliament resolution of 13 December 2017 on the State of Play of Negotiations with the United Kingdom (2017/2964(RSP)); European Parliament resolution of 14 March 2018 on the Framework of the Future EU-UK relationship (2018/2573(RSP)).

[84] Opinion 1/00 (*ECAA*), above n. 30, para 12.

[85] See case involving Switzerland where Switzerland could not be claim to be treated—comparable to a Member State—in regard to the bilateral agreement on transport as a privileged applicant in the Article 263 Procedure; see General Court, *Confédération Suisse v European Commission,* Judgment of the General Court (Grand Chamber), 9 September 2010, T-319/05, ECLI:EU:T:2010:367.

[86] European Council Guidelines, 15 December 2017, EUCO XT 20011/17, para 7; European Council Conclusions, EUCO XT 20022/18, "The European Council underlines that the backstop is intended as an insurance policy to prevent a hard border on the island of Ireland and ensure the integrity of the Single Market".

[87] Van Miert 1998.

a thorough policy on enforcement and governance. In principle, both the EU and the small-sized countries should benefit from the extension of the EU's internal market acquis to them as this would ensure a level playing field for both businesses and persons."[88]

Thus, if third countries, their citizens and businesses profit from EU rules and freely trade with the Union, its citizens and businesses, they should play along with the rules and including the EU's social values and environmental concerns. The Brexit and Swiss examples of throwing this level playing field off balance nourish the concerns about this level playing field. Switzerland has been able, since 2004, to differentiate between EU citizens from existing and new Member States, to keep restrictions on the job market in place and finally to invoke a safeguard clause to limit unilaterally residence permits for EU nationals in Switzerland.[89] Besides, posted EU workers have fallen since 2004 under the Swiss flanking measures to protect Swiss labour conditions, namely compliance with minimum wages and an eight-days rule applies according to which EU companies need to register with the Swiss authorities eight days in advance before providing services. This unequal treatment might be legally acceptable but difficult to justify and undermines the level playing field—especially from the perspective of EU citizens.

9.4.3 Autonomy of EU Courts: A Legal Condition?

Autonomy of EU judges and courts has become an overarching precondition for the EU legality of third country integration.[90] It has decisively shaped the juridification and standardization of bilateral compliance control and dispute settlement. However, at the same time, EU autonomy has been chameleonic and ever-evolving since its introduction by the ECJ's case law.[91] In the beginning, the focus rested on the Union competences and the functioning of the common policies (requirements of unity and solidarity, Opinion 1/76 European Laying-up fund), as already highlighted. In later case law, the role of ECJ in this international dispute settlement became the point of contestation (EEA opinions, ECAA and Patent Court Opinions, Opinion on the accession to the ECHR) and even broadened to Member States courts (Opinion on the accession to the ECHR, Achmea, CETA). EU national courts and tribunals are

[88] "In view of the need for a level playing field for all economic operators of the parties concerned and the continued development of internal market relevant acquis, the EU and the EFTA States should ensure homogeneity in the implementation of the acquis and the good functioning of the institutions" in Council Conclusions on EU relations with EFTA countries, Council meeting, Brussels, 14 December 2010, para.7.

[89] See Ott 2017.

[90] It has been even promoted in the literature into a principle, see Odermatt 2018; see also Hindelang 2019, pp. 383–400.

[91] De Witte calls it 'fuzzy', in De Witte 2018, p. 8220; Contartese employs the term 'nebulous' in Contartese 2017, p. 1628.

entrusted with the tasks of ensuring the interpretation and application of EU law and are linked with the Union in a network of principles and rules.[92]

While a lot has been written in the literature about these characteristics and what the inner core of judicial autonomy entails, it boils down in essence to two readings: (1) The Court of Justice has the interpretation monopoly over EU law and its progeny international norms and (2) EU law disputes cannot be withdrawn from the jurisdiction of the Member States courts and the ECJ. These judicial conditions can be defended: When the Union extends EU law to third countries (the EU regulatory space), then the ECJ can insist of remaining the final arbiter on EU rules. This also serves the purposes of protecting the EU competences and the level playing field discussed earlier. However, also limits to this framework need to be established as the international agreement remains international law and cannot form a simple EU law-annex.

So far, the ECJ has approved two dispute settlement systems for the European Legal Space: The one-pillar structure of the special Common Aviation Area where the ECJ gives the final verdict on the application and interpretation of the agreement[93] or the two-pillars system of the EEA, with the EFTA court ruling for the EEA EFTA members. The latter system can be, however, be better described as a one-and-half pillar. The EFTA court is independent from the ECJ but succumbs to the ECJ lead role, providing the ECJ with the last say on the interpretation of the EEA.[94] Also, this system includes the possibility, after a conflict reached the Joint Committee and the dispute has not been settled, that both Contracting parties can agree to refer to the ECJ to give an interpretation ruling.[95] The attempt, by both the former EFTA court president Carl Baudenbacher and ECJ president Koen Lenaerts, to advocate this system as the best way forward for third countries concerned about foreign judges in their long-term relations with the EU, appears to ignore the dependency of the EFTA court on the ECJ.[96]

The third, and most recent, system containing an arbitration dispute settlement between the parties in combination with the ECJ has operated so far underneath the judicial radar. It possibly points to the direction of the most feasible solution for future bilateral rules outside the EEA and integrating third countries into the European Legal Space. This Dispute Settlement was introduced in the Association Agreement with Ukraine (Article 322),[97] has inspired the UK Withdrawal Agreement

---

[92]Court of Justice, *Associacao Sindical dos Juizes Portugueses*, Judgment of the Court (Grand Chamber) of 27 February 2018, Case C-64/16, ECLI:EU:C:2018:11, para 34.

[93]ECAA Agreement, above n. 45, Article 20.

[94]Frederiksen 2010, p. 490.

[95]EEA Agreement, above n. 21, Article 111.

[96]See further Taylor 2018; Baudenbacher 2016; The Times 2017.

[97]EU-Ukraine Association Agreement, above n. 22, Article 322, in relation to Dispute settlement relating to regulatory approximation: "1. The procedures set out in this Article shall apply to disputes concerning the interpretation and application of a provision of this Agreement relating to regulatory approximation contained in Chapter 3 (Technical Barriers to Trade), Chapter 4 (Sanitary and Phytosanitary Measures), Chapter 5 (Customs and Trade Facilitation), Chapter 6 (Establishment, Trade in Services and Electronic Commerce), Chapter 8 (Public Procurement) or Chapter 10

and Draft Institutional Framework Agreement with Switzerland. Conflicts are not settled by a diplomatic body (a joint committee) but by an appointed arbitration panel under procedural conditions, review mechanisms and remedies for non-compliance.

The first-generation international agreements extending Brussels rules excluded any arbitration mechanism. The 1963 Association Agreement with Turkey include an archaic arbitration system[98] and the former 1971 Association Agreement between the EEC and Malta establishing a customs union included no reference to any form of diplomatic dispute settlement.[99] More recent international agreements include arbitrators in the dispute resolution between the parties[100] with notable exceptions of the 2002 EU-Swiss sectoral bilateral on persons and the 2008 Schengen association of Switzerland.[101] This diplomatic dispute settlement has turned out in practice to be problematic for the application of Brussels rules and policies. In the EU-Joint Committee on Free Movement of Persons Agreement, the reintroduction of Swiss quotas on eight recently joined EU Member States and the restrictions to EU movement of services providers (so-called flanking measures) were raised by the EU as discriminatory but to no avail.[102] Consequently, the EU insists in all the recent dispute settlement rules that the arbitration system moves away from a solely diplomatic dispute settlement and each side can initiate the arbitration.[103]

(Competition), or which otherwise imposes upon a Party an obligation defined by reference to a provision of EU law. 2. Where a dispute raises a question of interpretation of a provision of EU law referred to in para 1, the arbitration panel shall not decide the question, but request the Court of Justice of the European Union to give a ruling on the question. In such cases, the deadlines applying to the rulings of the arbitration panel shall be suspended until the Court of Justice of the European Union has given its ruling. The ruling of the Court of Justice of the European Union shall be binding on the arbitration panel".

[98] The Association Agreement with Turkey foresees in its Article 24(2) that "The Council of Association may settle the dispute by decision; it may also decide to submit the dispute to the Court of Justice of the European Communities or to any existing court or tribunal." This reference mechanism has never been used in practice. See Agreement Creating an Association between the European Economic Community and Turkey, opened for signature 12 September 1963, OJ L 35 (entered into force 1 December 1964) (EU-Turkey Association Agreement).

[99] Agreement establishing an Association between the EEC and Malta, opened for signature 5 December 1970, OJ 1971 L 61/3-75 (entered into force 1 April 1971).

[100] Such as the cooperation agreement with San Marino; see Agreement on Cooperation and Customs Union, opened for signature 16 April 1991, OJ L 84/43-52 (entered into force 1 April 2002); see also EC-Swiss Bilateral Air Transport Agreement, above n. 48, Article 20: "All questions concerning the validity of decisions of the institutions of the Community taken on the basis of their competences under this Agreement, shall be of the exclusive competence of the Court of Justice of the European Communities".

[101] In these agreements only the joint committee is responsible resolving disputes; see EC-Swiss Bilateral Agreement on the Free Movement of Persons, above n. 48, Article 19; see also Agreement between the European Union, the European Community and the Swiss Confederation on the Swiss Confederation's Association with the Implementation, Application and Development of the Schengen Acquis, OJ L114/6-72 (entered into force 28 January 2008), Article 10.

[102] "Due to disagreement between both delegations, the Joint Committee could not pronounce itself on this issue", see on this Europa Consilium 2012.

[103] See Monetary Agreement between the European Union and the Principality of Monaco, opened for signature 24 December 2001, OJ C310 (entered into force 13 October 2012), Article 12: "If no

And—in line with the jurisdiction on EU's courts autonomy—the arbitrators have to refer the dispute relating to the interpretation of the EU law-related provisions to the ECJ. As these recent international agreements clarify, such a reference is obligatory when a question arises on "a provision of EU law" in form that it relates to regulatory approximation, or "an obligation defined by reference to a provision of EU law" or "a rule having an EU law origin".[104]

9.5 Conclusion

Third countries in the proximity of the Union struggle to find their spot half in and half out. However, the EU is also challenged by the tailor-made integration of third countries. Third country integration is organized around legal building blocks that have been refined over the years to fit the legal and political preconditions established by the EU rule-makers and -shapers. The three EU formal, political and judicial constraints demand that the EU institutions and the competence divide between EU and Member States remains untouched, the extension of Brussels rules does not result in disadvantages for EU businesses and citizens (the level playing field) and the EU's courts exclusive jurisdiction on EU rules is secured. Especially the latter condition restricts the involvement of other forms of arbitration and courts (so foreign judges for the EU) ruling on EU rules or rules of EU law origin. Hence, the technical detailed task emerges as to how to recognize which international agreements provisions are of EU law origin and which are not. This requires, firstly, a clear-cut categorization as to how far the EU extends the core characteristics of the EU legal order (in the form of the internal market or customs union). Secondly, it requires that any agreement extending Brussels rules also needs to determine in great technical detail

amicable conclusion can be reached, the European Union—acting on a recommendation from the Commission, after consultation with the French Republic and the ECB on matters falling within its field of competence—or the Principality of Monaco may bring the matter before the Court of Justice, if the Joint Committee determines that one of the parties has not fulfilled an obligation or provision under the present Agreement. The judgment of the Court shall be binding on the Parties, which shall take the necessary measures to comply with the judgment within a period to be decided by the Court in its judgment, monetary agreement with Monaco"; See also Draft Institutional Framework Agreement with Switzerland, above n. 2, Article 10(2); Agreement on the withdrawal of the United Kingdom of Great Britain and Northern Ireland from the European Union and the European Atomic Energy Community, opened for signature 24 January 2020, OJ C 384I, entered into force 1 February 2020, Article 170.

[104] See for these dispute mechanism, ECAA Agreement, above n. 45, Articles 15, 16; EU-Ukraine Association Agreement, above n. 21, Article 322; Transport Community Treaty, above n. 44, Article 19(2) as preliminary ruling system from the regional court and Article 37 by the dispute parties, as well as annex IV; Monetary Agreement with Monaco, above n. 103, Article 12; Draft Institutional Framework Agreement with Switzerland, above n. 2, Article 10(2); UK Withdrawal Agreement, above n. 103, Article 174(1).

the circumstances under which an ECJ reference is required. This latter aspect is partially reflected in both agreements – the Swiss draft and the British version—but still might result in disputes.[105]

Finally, these integration models have to also sustain the practicability test, once they have survived the negotiation and ratification phase. While the EEA has fared better than other forms of bilateralism and sectoral multilateralism until now,[106] the EEA (as the most dynamic parallel system) also struggles to keep pace. The EU Charter of Fundamental Rights and the adoption of the EU citizenship directive without a parallel concept of citizenship in EEA law posed legal challenges.[107] Other forms of cooperation have become outdated (the Turkey association and the cooperation with the micro-states), too complex and static (Switzerland), or have not yet proven whether they will fulfil their potential to achieve sectoral legal approximation (the ECAA, Energy and Transport Communities).[108]

Acknowledgements This work is part of the research programme Westerdijk Talentimpuls with project number 014.041.097, which is partly financed by the Dutch Research Council (NWO). The author would like to thank Sonja Boelaert, John Cotter, Bruno De Witte, Pauline Melin, Christa Tobler and Peter Van Elsuwege for their valuable comments and suggestions. The usual disclaimer applies.

References

Avery G (2012) The European Economic Area Revisited. https://www.epc.eu/en/Publications/The-European-Economic-Area-rev~2450e0. Accessed 1 July 2020

Baudenbacher C (2016) After Brexit: Is the EEA an Option for the United Kingdom? https://www.kcl.ac.uk/law/tli/about/Baudenbacher-Kings-College-13-10-16.pdf. Accessed 1 July 2020

Blockmans S, Van Vooren B (2012) Revitalizing the European Neighbourhood Economic Community: The Case for Legally Binding Sectoral Multilateralism. EFARev 17:577

Bradford A (2012) The Brussels Effect. Northwestern University Law Review 107

Commission Communication on Micro-States (2012) Ensuring a Level Playing Field by Promoting Adequate Standards in Third Countries and by Acting against Abusive Use of TDI. https://trade.ec.europa.eu/doclib/docs/2010/july/tradoc_146391.pdf. Accessed 30 June 2020

Communication from the Commission to the EP, the Council, ECOSOC and the Committee of the Regions, EU relations with the Principality of Andorra, the Principality of Monaco and the Republic of San Marino, COM (2012) 680 final/2, Brussels, 11 January 2013

Contartese C (2017) The Autonomy of the EU legal order in the ECJ's external Relations Case Law: From the "Essential" to the "Specific Characteristics" of the Union and Back Again. CMLRev 54:1627–1671

[105] Ibid., UK Withdrawal Agreement, Article 174; Draft Institutional Framework Agreement with Switzerland, above n. 2, Article 10(3).

[106] On this term see Lazowski 2008, p. 1433.

[107] Haukeland Frederiksen and Franklin 2015, pp. 629–684. See on the details Maresceau 2013b, pp. 769–773; Tobler 2018, pp. 1429–1451.

[108] Energy Community Secretariat 2018; Deitz et al. 2019; European Parliament 2018; see on this for the ECAA, and the sectoral and regional communities on Energy and Transport: Lazowski and Blockmans 2014, p. 108.

Cremona M, Scott J (2019) EU Law Beyond EU Borders: The Extraterritorial Reach of EU Law. Oxford University Press, Oxford
Czuczai J (2012) The Autonomy of the EU legal order and the Law-Making Activities of International Organizations. Some Examples Regarding the Council's Most Recent Practice. YEL 31:452–472
Damro C (2012) Market Power Europe. Journal of European Public Policy 19:682
De Hert P, Czerniawski M (2016) Expanding the European Data Protection Scope Beyond Territory: Article 3 of the General Data Protection Regulation in its Wider Context. International Data Privacy Law 6:230–243
De Witte B (2010) European Union law: How autonomous is its legal order? Zeitschrift für Öffentliches Recht 65:141–155
De Witte B (2013) A Selfish Court? The European Court of Justice and the Design of International Dispute Settlement beyond the European Union. In: Cremona M, Thies A (eds) The European Court of Justice and External Relations Law. Hart Publishing, Oxford
De Witte B (2018) European International Law. In: Schütze R (ed) European Solutions. Cambridge University Press
Deitz L et al. (2007) The Energy Community of South East Europe: Challenges of, and Obstacles to Europeanisation - Association agreements between the EU and Moldova, Georgia and Ukraine. http://competitionpolicy.ac.uk/documents/107435/107587/ccp08-4.pdf. Accessed 10 October 2019
EC Europa (2007) Commission Staff Working Document. http://ec.europa.eu/citizens_agenda/docs/sec_2007_1519_en.pdf. Accessed 5 January 2019
EC Trade (2016) Study of the EU-Turkey Bilateral Preferential Trade Framework, Including the Customs Union, and an Assessment of Its Possible Enhancement. https://trade.ec.europa.eu/doclib/docs/2017/january/tradoc_155240.pdf. Accessed 1 June 2020
Eckes C (2013) The European Court of Justice and (Quasi-)Judicial Bodies of International Organisations. In: Wessel R, Blockmans S (eds) Between Autonomy and Dependence. T.M.C. Asser Press, The Hague, p. 85
Energy Community Secretariat (2018) Annual Implementation Report. https://www.energy-community.org/implementation/IR2019.html. Accessed 30 June 2020
EP Study (2013). http://www.europarl.europa.eu/RegData/etudes/note/join/2013/495849/IPOL-TRAN_NT(2013)495849_EN.pdf. Accessed 30 June 2020
Europa Consilium (2012) The EU-Switzerland Joint Committee on Free Movement of Persons Agreement meets in Brussels. https://www.consilium.europa.eu/uedocs/cms_data/docs/pressdata/EN/foraff/131319.pdf. Accessed 30 June 2020
European Commission (2016). https://trade.ec.europa.eu/doclib/docs/2017/january/tradoc_155240.pdf. Accessed 1 June 2020
European Parliament (2018) European Implementation Assessment. https://www.europarl.europa.eu/RegData/etudes/STUD/2018/615668/EPRS_STU(2018)615668_EN.pdf. Accessed 30 June 2020
European Parliament resolution of 13 December 2017 on the state of play of negotiations with the United Kingdom (2017/2964(RSP))
European Parliament resolution of 14 March 2018 on the framework of the future EU-UK relationship (2018/2573(RSP))
European Union External Action (2010) Council conclusions on EU relations with EFTA countries 3060th GENERAL AFFAIRS Council meeting, Brussels, 14 December 2010
Frederiksen H (2010) One Market, Two Courts: Legal Pluralism vs. Homogeneity in the European Economic Area. Nordic Journal of International Law 79:481–499
Frederiksen H, Franklin C (2015) Of Pragmatism and Principles: The EEA Agreement 20 Years On. CMLRev 2015, 52:629–684.
Ghazaryan N (2018) Who Are the 'Gatekeepers'?: In Continuation of the Debate on the Direct Applicability and the Direct Effect of EU International Agreements. YEL 37: 27–74

Govaere I (2010) Beware of the Trojan Horse: Dispute Settlement in (Mixed) Agreements and the Autonomy of the EU Legal Order. In: Koutrakos P, Hillion C (eds) Mixed Agreements Revisited: The EU and its Member States in the World. Hart Publishing, Oxford, p. 187

Harding C (2000) The Identity of European Law: Mapping Out the European Legal Space. ELJ 6:28–147

Hindelang S (2019) Conceptualisation and Application of the Principle of Autonomy of EU Law – The CJEU's Judgement in Achmea Put in Perspective. ELRev 44383–400

Iceland Monitor (2018) Brussels Reluctant to Use the EEA Two Pillar System. https://icelandmonitor.mbl.is/news/politics_and_society/2018/04/14/brussels_reluctant_to_use_the_eea_two_pillar_system/. Accessed 29 June 2020

International Law Commission (2006) Fragmentation of International Law: Difficulties Arising from the Diversification and Expansion of International Law, A/CN.4/L.682

Knöpfel L, Najy C (2018) Breaking the Deadlock, A proposal for a Genuine Arbitration Mechanism to Solve Disputes between Switzerland and European Union. https://www.foraus.ch/publications/breaking-the-deadlock-a-proposal-for-a-genuine-arbitration-mechanism/. Accessed 1 July 2020

Lazowski A (2006) EEA Countries. In: Blockmans S, Lazowski A (eds) The European Union and its Neighbours: A Legal Appraisal of the EU's Policies of Stabilisation, Partnership and Integration. T.M.C. Asser Press, The Hague

Lazowski A (2008) Enhanced Multilateralism and Enhanced Bilateralism: Integration without Membership in the European Union. CMLRev 45:1433

Lazowski A, Blockmans S (2014) Between Dream and Reality. In: Van Elsuwege P, Petrov R (eds) Legislative approximation of EU law in the Eastern Neighbourhood of the European Union. Routledge, p. 108

Maresceau M (2012) Turkey: A Candidate State Destined to Join the Union. In: Shuibhne N, Gormley L (eds) From Single market to Economic Union—Essays in Memory of John A. Usher. Oxford University Press, Oxford, pp. 315–340

Maresceau M (2013a) Les Accords d'Intégration dans les Relations de Proximité de l'Union Européenne [Integration Agreements in EU Neighbourhood Relations]. In: Blumann C (ed) Les frontieres de l'Union Européenne [The Frontiers of the EU]. Bruylant, Brussels, p. 151

Maresceau M (2013b) On the External Dimension of Directive 2004/38/EC. In: Govaere I, Hanf D (eds) Scrutinizing Internal and External Dimensions of European Law - Liber Amicorum Paul Demaret. Peter Lang Publisher, pp. 769–773

Murray F (2006) Micro-States (Andorra, Monaco, San Marino and the Vatican City). In: Blockmans S, Lazowski A (eds) The European Union and its Neighbours. T.M.C. Asser Press, The Hague, p. 185

Odermatt J (2018) The Principle of Autonomy: An Adolescent Disease of EU External Relations Law? In: Cremona M (ed) Structural Principles in EU External Relations Law. Hart Publishing, Oxford, pp. 291–316

Ott A (2017) Free Movement Rights in an Enlarged European Union. In: De Witte B et al (eds) Between Flexibility and Disintegration. Edward Elgar Publishing, Cheltenham/Northampton

Rosas A (2003) International Dispute Settlement: EU Practices and Procedures. GYIL 46:284

Scott J (2014) The New Extraterritoriality. CMLRev 51:1343

Scott J (2015) The Geographical Scope of the EU's Climate Responsibilities. Cambridge Yearbook of European Legal Studies 17:92–120

Tatham A (2009) Enlargement of the European Union. Kluwer Law International, Alphen aan den Rijn

Taylor R (2018) Britzerland: The Problem of Dispute Resolution Post-Brexit. http://blogs.lse.ac.uk/brexit/2018/10/29/britzerland-the-problem-of-dispute-resolution-post-brexit/. Accessed 1 July 2020

The Times (2017) European Court of Justice President offers a Solution to Brexit Conundrum. https://www.thetimes.co.uk/article/european-court-of-justice-president-koen-lenaerts-offers-european-free-trade-association-as-solution-to-brexit-conundrum-dnwf83zxw. Accessed 30 June 2020

Thym D (2011) Foreign Affairs. In: Von Bogdandy A, Bast J (eds) Principles of European Constitutional Law, 2nd edn. Hart Publishing/Beck Publishers, Oxford, pp. 320–322

Tobler C (2018) Free Movement of Persons in the EU v. in the EEA: Of Effect-related Homogeneity and a Reversed Polydor Principle. European Papers, 3:429–1451

UK Government (2017) PM's Florence Speech: A New Era of Cooperation and Partnership between the UK and the EU. https://www.gov.uk/government/speeches/pms-florence-speech-a-new-era-of-cooperation-and-partnership-between-the-uk-and-the-eu. Accessed 29 June 2020

Vajda C (2018) The EU and Beyond: Dispute Resolution in International Economic Agreements. EJIL 29:205–224

Van der Loo G (2016) The EU-Ukraine Association Agreement and Deep and Comprehensive Free Trade Area: A New Legal Instrument for EU Integration without Membership? Brill Nijhoff

Van Elsuwege P (2019) Exporting the Internal Market beyond the EU's borders: Between Political Ambition and Legal Reality. In: Amtenbrink F, Davies G, Kochenov D, Lindeboom J (eds) European Integration, Essays in Honour of Laurence W Gormley. Cambridge University Press, pp. 637–650

Van Elsuwege P, Chamon M (2019) The Meaning of 'Association' under EU law - A Study on the Law and Practice of EU Association Agreements. https://www.europarl.europa.eu/thinktank/nl/document.html?reference=IPOL_STU%282019%29608861. Accessed 30 June 2020

Van Miert K (1998) What does a level playing field mean in the global economy? http://ec.europa.eu/competition/speeches/text/sp1998_031_en.html. Accessed 2 November 2018

Vehar P, Ilesic P (2002) Slovenia. In: Ott A, Inglis K (eds) Handbook on European Enlargement. T.M.C. Asser Press, The Hague

Von Bogdandy A (2016) European Law Beyond 'Ever closer Union' Repositioning the Concept, its Thrust and ECJ's Comparative Methodology. ELJ 22:519–538

Wessel R (2016) The EU Solution to Deal with the Dutch Referendum Result on the EU-Ukraine Association Agreement. http://www.europeanpapers.eu/en/europeanforum/eu-solution-deal-dutch-referendum-result-on-the-eu-ukraine-association-agreement. Accessed 30 June 2020

Wessel R, Larik J (2020) EU External relations, 2nd edn. Hart Publishing, Oxford

Prof. A. Ott is professor of EU external relations law at the Law Faculty of Maastricht University in The Netherlands. The contribution is based on her inaugural lecture held on 18 January 2019.

Chapter 10
Where Do We Go from Here? EU Relations with the Eastern Partnership *Avant Garde*

A. Łazowski

Contents

Abstract This chapter looks at the relations between the European Union and the Eastern Partnership *avant garde*, that is Ukraine, Georgia, Moldova. In the course of the last ten years these three countries negotiated and signed very ambitious Association Agreements, which promise enhanced bilateral relations but without an explicit offer of EU membership on the horizon. At the same time, the signals coming from Kyiv, Tbilisi and (occasionally) Chișinău indicate that the choice of a pro-EU trajectory is there to stay. With this in mind the analysis looks at the heart of the Association Agreements, that is, law approximation and, in broader terms, the way in which the association is developing. The author argues that the EU is reaching a point when, as in any close relationship, it will have to make its future intentions clear. Towards the end of the chapter a few suggestions as to the next steps forward are made. The easiest, and the most do-able option is to regularly update the lists of the EU *acquis* pencilled in for approximation. Furthermore, the relations could be upgraded by a reformed institutional framework, potentially modelled on the draft EU-Swiss Institutional Agreement and the EU-UK Withdrawal Agreement. The parties may also wish to explore additional areas of co-operation, going beyond the current parameters of the Association Agreements. The EU also needs to be prepared that at some point in the future applications for membership may arrive.

A. Łazowski (✉)
University of Westminster, London, UK
e-mail: a.lazowski@westminster.ac.uk

W. Th. Douma et al. (eds.), *The Evolving Nature of EU External Relations Law*,
https://doi.org/10.1007/978-94-6265-423-5_10

Keywords European Neighbourhood Policy · Eastern Partnership · Association Agreements · Association Agendas · law approximation · conditionality · rule of law · EU *acquis*

10.1 Introduction

Over recent years the European Union has concluded a number of very ambitious and comprehensive free trade agreements with countries around the world.[1] This includes a set of Association Agreements aiming at the creation of Deep and Comprehensive Free Trade Areas (DCFTAs) with three Eastern Partnership (EaP) countries: Ukraine,[2] Georgia[3] and Moldova.[4] In 2020 all three Agreements came fully into force and, despite a not very favourable political and economic environment, they are being gradually implemented by the respective associated countries.[5] Sectoral integration is also pursued *qua* the Energy Community[6] and, in the case of Moldova and Georgia, by respective Civil Aviation Agreements.[7] However, quite inevitably, questions are being asked as to the next steps in the *rapprochement* of the three associated countries with the European Union. There is no denying that in many EU capitals there is no political climate even to mention the prospect of a membership offer to be sent to Kyiv, Tbilisi or Chișinău.[8] At the same time, there is general consensus on

[1] Melo Araujo 2016.

[2] Association Agreement between the European Union and the European Atomic Energy Community and its Member States, of the one part, and Ukraine, of the other part, opened for signature 21 March 2014, OJ L 161/3–2137 (entered into force 1 September 2017) (EU-Ukraine AA). See further Emerson and Movchan 2018; Van Der Loo 2016.

[3] Association Agreement between the European Union and the European Atomic Energy Community and their Member States, of the one part, and Georgia, of the other part, opened for signature 27 June 2014, OJ L 261/4 (entered into force 1 July 2016) (EU-Georgia AA). See further Emerson and Kovziridze 2018.

[4] Association Agreement between the European Union and the European Atomic Energy Community and their Member States, of the one part, and the Republic of Moldova, of the other part, opened for signature 27 June 2014, OJ L 260/4 (entered into force 1 July 2016), (EU-Moldova AA). See further Emerson and Cenuşa 2018.

[5] See, *inter alia*, European Commission, Association Implementation Report on Ukraine, SWD (2019) 433 final; European Commission, Association Implementation Report on Georgia, SWD (2020) 30 final; European Commission, Association Implementation Report on Moldova, SWD (2019) 325 final.

[6] See Buschle and Talus 2015; Buschle 2016; Buschle and Karova 2019; Blockmans and Van Vooren 2012.

[7] Common Aviation Area Agreement between the European Union and its Member States and the Republic of Moldova, opened for signature 26 June 2012, OJ L 292/3 (entered into force (provisionally) 26 June 2012); Common Aviation Area Agreement between the European Union and its Member States, of the one part, and Georgia, of the other part, opened for signature 2 December 2010, OJ L 321/3 (entered into force 18 June 2019).

[8] See Łazowski 2021a.

the European credentials of the EaP *avant garde*[9] and the pro-EU trajectory Ukraine, Georgia and Moldova opted for when signing the Association Agreements.[10] Hence, the challenge is how to take their association with the EU to the next levels. One ought to remember that standing still is not part of the European integration DNA; it needs goalposts. The EU is certainly getting closer to the point where the major next steps will have to be determined as the three associated countries are starting to make their voices heard more loudly. Alas, the most recent policy paper on the future of Eastern Partnership, published by the European Commission and the High Representative, offers disappointingly little and, together with preceding consultations, it is likely to come down in history as a wasted opportunity for a proper overhaul of the policy in question.[11] Thus, the time is right to ask a fundamental question: *quo vadis*?

The aim of this chapter is to provide some food for thought. The starting point is a stock-taking exercise aimed at identification of the experience gained thus far and at pinpointing the challenges that lie ahead. While the centre of gravity is on the legal matters, excursions into the worlds of politics and international relations are inevitable (Sect. 10.2). The section that follows focuses on the implementation of the political conditionality employed *vis-à-vis* the EaP countries *qua* jointly developed European Agendas. As elaborated in Sect. 10.3 of the present chapter, they are a rather tricky affair with the EU's legitimacy to pursue the rule of law desiderata seriously undermined by the cases of constitutional vandalism courtesy of the Polish and Hungarian authorities. The last part of the chapter offers ideas on how the Association Agreements could be upgraded to offer the next steps in the *rapprochement* with Ukraine, Georgia and Moldova (Sect. 10.4).

10.2 Association Agreements: Ambitious and Demanding

10.2.1 The Big Picture

As well documented in the academic literature, the Association Agreements with Ukraine, Georgia and Moldova made history even before they entered into force.[12] In simple terms, the pro-EU orientation of respective EaP countries has not been

---

[9]See diplomatically-framed allusions to the European perspective in preambles to all three Association Agreements.

[10]The only exception is Moldova, which has been in permanent political turmoil, with pro-Russia and pro-EU parties swinging in regular intervals to the left and to the right. See further Nizhnikau 2019.

[11]European Commission and High Representative of the Union for Foreign Affairs and Security Policy, Joint Communication to the European Parliament, the European Council, the Council, the European Economic and Social Committee and the Committee of the Regions. Eastern Partnership policy beyond 2020. Reinforcing Resilience-an Eastern Partnership that delivers for all, JOIN (2020) 7 final. For a commentary, see Emerson et al. 2020. An inventory of previous ENP/EaP policy papers is available in Gstöhl 2016a, p. 7.

[12]See Van der Loo 2016, pp. 100–164.

welcomed with open arms by the political elites in the Kremlin. *Au contraire*, Russia has engaged in numerous activities broadly aimed at blocking the *rapprochement* on the Euro-Atlantic trajectory that some of the former Soviet Union countries opted for. This policy bore fruit in relation to Armenia, which—at the last minute—decided to do a reverse ferret and join the Eurasian Union instead.[13] The same tactic pursued by Russia proved to be futile in the cases of Georgia, Moldova and Ukraine, even though in the case of the latter it led to the *Maidan* revolution, the ousting of the pro-Russian administration in Kyiv and prompting the Russian invasion of Donbas and Crimea. Consequentially, all three EaP countries have entered the association with the European Union with quite a number of commonalities, past and present. Not only for decades were they forcefully part of the Soviet Union but they have also had—in the past decades—their territories sliced by the very much not welcome Russian, or Russian-sponsored, forces.[14] One needs to bear in mind that such factors not only have political consequences, but they also make a long-lasting impact on the economies and the political climate, which—in turn—may affect the implementation of the Association Agreements. On top of this, the infamous referendum on the Ukrainian Association Agreement, held in the Netherlands, had a great potential to serve as the straw that broke the camel's back. After all, it only delayed the ratification of the Agreement in question, but—at the same—it put the EU's credibility at risk when, in the wake of Russia's illegal activities, a unified stance was most desired.[15] Thanks to political and legal acrobatics, the Agreement was eventually ratified by the EU and all its Member States, yet the entire ordeal sent a worrying signal and left a rather bitter aftertaste among the political elites in the EU's pro-European eastern vicinity.

10.2.2 Implementation of the Association Agreements

Association Agreements with Ukraine, Georgia and Moldova are frequently referred to as 'very ambitious and comprehensive agreements'.[16] They envisage the creation of DCFTAs and a widespread *rapprochement* in many areas. Approximation of legislation of the associated countries with the EU *acquis* constitutes the backbone of this process. In this respect, the methodology employed by the drafters resembles the foundations of the European Economic Area (EEA), with lengthy lists of EU

---

[13] See Emerson and Kostanyan 2013; Vilpišauskas 2016. It is notable that Armenia eventually signed a pruned agreement with the EU. See Comprehensive and Enhanced Partnership Agreement between the European Union and the European Atomic Energy Community and their Member States, of the one part, and the Republic of Armenia, of the other part, opened for signature 20 November 2017, OJ L 23/4 (entered into force (provisionally) 20 November 2017).

[14] For a comparative analysis of frozen conflicts in this region and troubles in the Western Balkans, see Brsakoska Bazerkoska 2016.

[15] This was amplified by the shenanigans associated with ratification of the CETA. See further Wessel and Van der Loo 2017.

[16] Van der Loo 2019, p. 115.

secondary legislation destined for the approximation exercise.[17] It should be noted, however, that the EU *acquis* does not have to be approximated lock, stock and barrel; the system designed by the Association Agreements is much more nuanced.[18] The lists of relevant EU legislation, as well as deadlines for compliance, were negotiated either before the entry into force of the Agreements or, in several sectors, at later stages.[19] This stands in stark contrast to the Stabilisation and Association Agreements concluded with potentially future members of the EU from the Western Balkans.[20] In the latter case, no such exhaustive lists are available. Only vague and general law approximation clauses are expected to suffice.[21] One may genuinely argue for hours over the advantages or drawbacks of either methodology. The incontestable fact is, though, that the model opted for the new generation of association agreements with the EaP *avant garde* makes the basic parameters clear, and by the same token, it gives more clarity and enhances transparency. It allows for relatively easy identification of obligations resting on the shoulders of the Kyiv, Tbilisi or Chișinău authorities and, in general terms, it facilitates verification of the levels of implementation of the respective Association Agreements. At the same time, it leaves the associated countries rather exposed and may potentially undermine their EU membership aspirations. To put it differently, delays in meeting the deadlines for approximation laid

[17] Agreement on the European Economic Area, opened for signature 2 May 1992, OJ L 1/3–522 (entered into force 1 January 1994). See further Arnesen et al. 2018; Baudenbacher 2015.

[18] The Association Agreements contain a plethora of law approximation clauses. See, for instance, EU-Georgia AA, above n. 3, Article 47 (approximation with technical regulations), Article 55 (gradual with sanitary and phytosanitary, animal welfare and other legislative measures), Article 75 (approximation with customs acquis), Article 103 (gradual approximation with services legislation), Article 113 (approximation with acquis on electronic communication), Article 122 (approximation in the area of financial services), Article 126 (approximation with transport legislation), Articles 141(2), 145–146 (approximation with EU public procurement legislation), Articles 417–419 (dynamic approximation).

[19] This applies to SPS, where the lists of *acquis* pencilled in for approximation have been developed in tailor-made action plans.

[20] Stabilisation and Association Agreement between the European Communities and their Member States, of the one part, and the Former Yugoslav Republic of Macedonia, of the other part, opened for signature 9 April 2001, OJ L 84/1 (entered into force 1 April 2004); Stabilisation and Association Agreement between the European Communities and their Member States, of the one part, and the Republic of Albania, of the other part, opened for signature 12 June 2006, OJ L 107/116 (entered into force 1 April 2009); Stabilisation and Association Agreement between the European Communities and their Member States, of the one part, and the Republic of Montenegro, of the other part, opened for signature 15 October 2007, OJ L 108/3 (entered into force 1 May 2010); Stabilisation and Association Agreement between the European Communities and their Member States, of the one part, and the Republic of Serbia, of the other part, opened for signature 29 April 2008, OJ L 278/14 (entered into force 1 September 2013); Stabilisation and Association Agreement between the European Communities and their Member States, of the one part, and Bosnia and Herzegovina, of the other part, opened for signature 16 June 2008, OJ L 164/2 (entered into force 1 June 2015); Stabilisation and Association Agreement between the European Union and the European Atomic Energy Community, of the one part, and Kosovo*, of the other part, opened for signature 27 October 2015, OJ L 71/3 (entered into force 1 April 2016). See further on this family of association agreements Phinnemore 2003.

[21] Łazowski and Blockmans 2014.

down in the Association Agreements may undermine the credibility of—for now hypothetical—EU accession bids and, at the same time, they may give the European Commission ammunition to deliver negative opinions on potential applications for EU membership.[22]

When compared to the vague approximation clauses known from other association agreements, the listing methodology brings an additional challenge: keeping the lists up to date. The EU legal order, just like national legal systems, is prone to constant development. Both legislative and non-legislative acts are regularly subject to minor revisions, codification exercises or even major overhauls. In the past decade, EU law has also been subjected to a comprehensive decluttering exercise, resulting in the repeal of redundant legislation.[23] Hence, when the Association Agreements with the EaP *avant garde* were being negotiated, it was clear that a *modus operandi* for regular updates of annexes would have to be developed. Accordingly, the Agreements provide for a number of procedures, either tailor-made for the DCFTA parts[24] or of a horizontal nature, applicable to all other non-DCFTA parts of the Agreements.[25] The system, although sometimes referred to as dynamic approximation is, however, dynamic in name only. Procedurally, it sits oceans apart from the dynamism of the European Economic Area, where annexes to the EEA Agreement are updated almost on a monthly basis.[26] In the case of Association Agreements with EaP countries, the existing *modi operandi* for updates are not utilised frequently. The end result is that the Agreements in question are now considerably outdated with plentiful references to the EU *acquis* that is either no longer applicable in the European Union or will soon lose force.[27] This has considerable implications, which are elaborated in turn.

Firstly, it creates uncertainty as to the best options to proceed, which inevitably is a challenge for the Ukrainian, Georgian and Moldovan authorities. A fundamental question is whether to follow old EU legislation, as listed in the Association Agreements, or—in the alternative—opt for newly adopted EU *acquis*. To ease the pain, it would be tempting to develop a standard uniform approach. Alas, such a *modus operandi* would be counterproductive and potentially detrimental. To put it differently, it would be rather unwise to approximate by default only with old EU legislation or automatically follow the newly adopted *acquis*. A one-size-fits-all approach should not be on the menu, as in some cases the legislation appearing on the lists in the Agreements may prove to be more beneficial (or less detrimental) for the

[22] As the first step of the EU accession process the European Commission presents so called *avis*—an opinion on candidates' compliance with the EU entry criteria. As the cases of Turkey and Albania prove, it is not a *fait accompli*. See Commission of the European Communities. Commission opinion on Turkey's request for accession to the Community, SEC (89) 2290 final; Commission Opinion on Albania's application for membership of the European Union, SEC (2010) 1335.

[23] See further Refit EU 2018.

[24] See, for instance, EU-Georgia AA, above n. 3, Article 274(1), EU-Moldova AA, above n. 4, Article 410(1).

[25] EU-Ukraine AA, above n. 2, Article 463(3): EU-Georgia AA, above n. 3, Article 418; EU-Moldova AA, above n. 4, Article 449.

[26] Wernø Holter 2017.

[27] Van der Loo and Akhvlediani 2020.

associated country than recent EU legal acts. It may perfectly well be the other way around. Directive 90/314 on package holidays may serve as a very good example to demonstrate the dilemmas of the associated countries.[28] While it is listed in all three Agreements, it is no longer in force in the European Union as it has been replaced by Directive 2015/2302.[29] The new legal regime is not a mere facelift of the previous legislation but rather a completely new framework, taking the consumer protection standards to new levels. Hence, addressing the conundrum 'new or old' is a major policy choice. On the one hand, enhancing consumer rights is traditionally a crowd pleaser. On the other hand, imposing even more requirements on the business community at the time of economic woes exacerbated by the Covid-19 pandemic may not be the preferred choice.

One needs to remember that the one-size-fits-all approach to new/old EU legislation is also not advisable for other reasons. For instance, not all changes to EU law carry the same weight. New legal acts codifying or recasting the existing *acquis* usually provide little substantive change to the legal framework. Many a time the *raison d'être* behind their adoption is more improving the clarity of the legislation than setting new legal standards. With this in mind such legislation seems to be perfectly fit for dynamic approximation, even on a voluntary basis without a formal revision of the Association Agreements. Obviously, major overhauls of EU secondary legislation are a different kettle of fish. Each and every legal act should be put by the associated countries under a microscope to determine the best way forward.

Another vital aspect of law approximation, although frequently forgotten, is the role of case-law of the Court of Justice of the European Union (CJEU). The position of the Court and importance of its jurisprudence for the everyday application of EU law is well-rehearsed and documented in the academic literature.[30] However, its impact on the shaping of the legislation of third countries and its role in the practice of national courts is of lesser interest among the academic community.[31] For the purposes of the present contribution a few points merit attention. To begin with, with very few exceptions, the associated countries are not under an obligation to take into account the jurisprudence of the CJEU.[32] Hence, if they do so, that would be largely on a voluntary basis. As compilations of relevant judgments prove, this is of particular importance in such areas as employment, equality, VAT or consumer protection, where the jurisprudence of the Court at Kirchberg is particularly prolific.[33] With this

---

[28] Council Directive 90/314/EEC of 13 June 1990 on package travel, package holidays and package tours [1990] OJ L 158/59.

[29] Directive (EU) 2015/2302 of the European Parliament and of the Council of 25 November 2015 on package travel and linked travel arrangements, amending Regulation (EC) No 2006/2004 and Directive 2011/83/EU of the European Parliament and of the Council and repealing Council Directive 90/314/EEC [2015] OJ L 326/1.

[30] See, *inter alia*, Saurugger and Terpan 2016; Sindbjerg and Martinsen 2015; Rosas et al. 2013.

[31] See, however, Rodin and Perišin 2015; Łazowski 2020; Petrov and Kalinichenko 2011.

[32] See EU-Ukraine AA, above n. 2, Articles 153, 264; EU-Georgia AA, above n. 3, Article 146; EU-Moldova AA, above n. 4, Articles 273, 340.

[33] See, *inter alia*, a manual on the jurisprudence of the Court of Justice relevant for the Ukrainian authorities: Association4U 2018.

in mind it is hard to imagine that law approximation would be limited merely to copy-pasting listed EU regulations or EU directives into Ukrainian, Georgian and Moldovan laws. Yet, at the same time, while such a desideratum is plausible for legal purists, it fails to take into account the reality on the ground. One needs to be aware of the pressures faced by the law drafters in the associated countries and the simple fact that frequently they operate in an environment which is not fertile ground for such a generous approach to law approximation. With ever-pressing deadlines for the domestication of EU laws, an opportunity to venture into the case law of the Court to make sure that the approximation effort is properly done is simply an intellectual luxury that only a few can afford.

Above all, law approximation is a tedious and fairly bureaucratic endeavour. A matter often overlooked in the academic literature is the technical side of this exercise. Be it as it may, the properly organised implementation of law approximation obligations laid down in the Association Agreements requires proper institutional set-ups, with clear-cut procedures and allocation of roles between different actors as well as robust planning combined with comprehensive monitoring.[34] Furthermore, a good degree of cooperation between the executive and the legislature is a *conditio sine qua non*. From the political perspective, law approximation and partisan politics are not bedfellows by any stretch of the imagination. Alas, not always are these requirements met by the associated countries in question. This is further exacerbated by the economic and political price tag that implementation of the Association Agreements may come with.[35] Many of the required law approximation efforts may bring positive results only in the long-term perspective. At the same time, the authorities regularly face a difficult challenge of persuading the business community to invest into endeavours with no clear mercantile benefits on the horizon. This is exacerbated by the lack of a clearly spelled out EU membership perspective, which traditionally serves the power of persuasion. A *cliché* as it may be, the mid-term prospect of benefits coming from accession overshadows the short-term pain. The trepidation among enterprises may be further aggravated by inevitable economic struggles in the wake of the Covid-19 pandemic. The governments of Ukraine, Georgia and Moldova may soon face the unenviable task of balancing between keeping the economies afloat and meeting their respective obligations under the Association Agreements. One should not be surprised if requests for re-negotiation of law approximation deadlines follow in the coming months.

[34] See further Khvorostankina 2014; Petrov 2014; Gabrichidze 2014. In this respect, the procedures and institutions share similarities with institutional set-ups for accession to the European Union. See, for instance, Łazowski and Vlašić Feketija 2014.

[35] See further Franco 2016.

10.3 European Agendas and Other Policy Tools

By limiting the present analysis only to law approximation, one would risk not seeing the wood for the trees. When it comes to implementation of the Association Agreements with Ukraine, Georgia and Moldova it is of paramount importance to see the big picture, that is, the policy context in which all three agreements developed. In broad terms, their genesis goes back to the early 2000s, when the foundations of the European Neighbourhood Policy (ENP) were laid down by the European Commission.[36] As well-known and documented in the academic literature, the initial effort focused on development of policy instruments, that is, the jointly agreed action plans, supplemented by a fairly modest financial envelope.[37] At the early stages of the ENP, the legal foundations remained untouched: the existing Association Agreements with the Mediterranean countries[38] and rather basic Partnership and Co-operation Agreements with the former Soviet Union countries.[39] The three Association Agreements discussed in the present chapter, when seen through this lens, prove to be major steps forward, even though, when it comes to their enforceability in the EU Member

[36]Communication from the Commission to the Council and the European Parliament, Wider Europe—Neighbourhood: A New Framework for Relations with our Eastern and Southern Neighbours, COM (2003) 104 final.

[37]Van Vooren 2012; Gstöhl 2016b; Whitmans and Wolf 2010.

[38]Euro-Mediterranean Agreement establishing an association between the European Communities and their Member States, of the one part, and the Kingdom of Morocco, of the other part, opened for signature 26 February 1996, OJ L 70/2 (entered into force 1 March 2000); Euro-Mediterranean Agreement establishing an Association between the European Community and its Member States, of the one part, and the Republic of Lebanon, of the other part, opened for signature 17 June 2002, OJ L 143/2 (entered into force 1 April 2006); Euro-Mediterranean Agreement establishing an Association between the European Community and its Member States, of the one part, and the People's Democratic Republic of Algeria, of the other part, opened for signature 22 April 2002, OJ L 265/2 (entered into force 1 September 2005); Euro-Mediterranean Agreement establishing an Association between the European Communities and their Member States, of the one part, and the Arab Republic of Egypt, of the other part, opened for signature 25 June 2001, OJ L 304/39 (entered into force 1 June 2004); Euro-Mediterranean Agreement establishing an Association between the European Communities and their Member States, of the one part, and the Hashemite Kingdom of Jordan, of the other part, opened for signature 24 November 1997, OJ L 129/3 (entered into force 1 May 2002); Euro-Mediterranean Interim Association Agreement on trade and cooperation between the European Community, of the one part, and the Palestine Liberation Organization (PLO) for the benefit of the Palestinian Authority of the West Bank and the Gaza Strip, of the other part, opened for signature 24 February 1997, OJ L 187/3 (entered into force 1 July 1997); Euro-Mediterranean Agreement establishing an association between the European Communities and their Member States, of the one part, and the State of Israel, of the other part, opened for signature 20 November 1995, OJ L 147/3 (entered into force 1 June 2000); Euro-Mediterranean Agreement establishing an association between the European Communities and their Member States, of the one part, and the Republic of Tunisia, of the other part, opened for signature 17 May 1995, OJ L 97/2 (entered into force 1 March 1998).

[39]Agreement on partnership and cooperation establishing a partnership between the European Communities and their Member States and the Russian Federation, opened for signature 24 June 1994, OJ L 327/3 (entered into force 1 December 1997); Partnership and Cooperation Agreement between the European Communities and their Member States and the Republic of Moldova, opened

States, their lack of direct effect is anything but an upgrade.[40] In the meantime the policy framework has also developed, with—in the case of the Eastern Partnership *avant garde*—the association agendas taking the lead in relation to Georgia and Moldova. From the formal point of view, they are adopted as recommendations of the respective Association Councils. The Association Agendas lay down the priorities for three-year periods, frequently venturing into areas of political conditionality where the EU's formal competences to legislate internally are rather limited. It all falls into export of the EU values agenda,[41] underpinned by heavy conditionality.[42]

For instance, in the case of Moldova the key priorities outlined in the Association Agenda extend to, *inter alia*, political dialogue, good governance, strengthening of domestic institutions, respect for human rights, freedom of expression, children's rights, trade unions and labour law standards as well as foreign and security policy and co-operation in the area of freedom, security and justice.[43] A similar approach has been taken in the Association Agenda for Georgia.[44] For the time being, this policy tool is not being employed in relation to Ukraine.

The implementation of Eastern Partnership objectives is further strengthened by a wide suite of initiatives undertaken by the European Commission focusing on key priority areas. They include support for businesses, investment in people, export of EU values focusing on the usual mantra of combatting corruption, judicial reforms, public administration reform. Many of them are outlined in the already

---

for signature 28 November 1994, OJ L 181/3 (entered into force 1 July 1998); Partnership and Cooperation Agreement between the European Communities and their Member States and the Republic of Georgia, opened for signature 22 April 1996, OJ L 205/3 (entered into force 1 July 1999); Partnership and Cooperation Agreement between the European Communities and their Member States and Ukraine, opened for signature 14 June 1994, OJ L 49/3 (entered into force 1 March 1998); Partnership and Cooperation Agreement between the European Communities and their Member States and the Republic of Kazakhstan, opened for signature 23 January 1995, OJ 196/3 (entered into force 1 July 1999); Partnership and Cooperation Agreement between the European Communities and their Member States, of the one part, and the Republic of Azerbaijan, of the other part, opened for signature 22 April 1996, OJ L 246/3 (entered into force 1 July 1999); Partnership and Cooperation Agreement establishing a partnership between the European Communities and their Member States, of the one part, and the Kyrgyz Republic, of the other part, opened for signature 9 February 1995, OJ L 196/48 (entered into force 1 July 1999); Partnership and Cooperation Agreement establishing a partnership between the European Communities and their Member States, of the one part, and the Republic of Uzbekistan, of the other part, opened for signature 21 June 1996, OJ L 229/3 (entered into force 1 July 1999); Partnership and Cooperation Agreement establishing a partnership between the European Communities and their Member States, of the one part, and the Republic of Tajikistan, of the other part, opened for signature 11 October 2004, OJ L 350/3 (entered into force 1 January 2010). Partnership and Cooperation Agreement between the European Communities and their Member States, of the one part, and the Republic of Armenia, opened for signature 22 April 1996, OJ L 293/3 (entered into force 1 July 1999).

[40] See further Ghazaryan 2018.

[41] See further, *inter alia*, Poli 2016; Ghazaryan 2014.

[42] See further Şemşit 2016.

[43] Recommendation No 1/2017 of the EU-Republic of Moldova Association Council of 4 August 2017 on the EU-Republic of Moldova Association Agenda [2017] OJ L 215/3.

[44] Recommendation No 1/2007 of the EU-Georgia Association Council on the EU-Georgia Association Agenda [2017] L 344/65.

mentioned recent EaP Strategic Paper published in March 2020. It is also notable that the EU has been offering financial assistance to the EaP countries,[45] including—most recently—tailor-made macro-economic financial assistance in the wake of the Covid-19 pandemic.[46] All these initiatives are a useful and complementary addition to the Association Agreements themselves and, consequentially, they expand the EU's offering to the neighbouring countries. The trouble is, however, that many of them are fairly modest endeavours suffering from the lack of a long-term strategic vision. Furthermore, the EU's legitimacy to pursue rule-of-law-based conditionality is currently under a serious threat from within. A fundamental challenge is how to marry the desiderata anchored in independence of the judiciary and the prerequisite of democratic governance with acts of political and constitutional vandalism courtesy of Kaczyński, Orban *et consortes*.[47] The mere fact that the EU has on board states breaching fundamental democratic principles, combined with its inherent weakness to effectively prosecute behaviour undermining the values laid down in Article 2 TEU, keeps on eroding its credibility.

10.4 *Quo Vadis*?

10.4.1 Introduction

As alluded to in the introduction to the present chapter, standing still is not part of the EU's DNA. This argument applies in equal measure to the domestic dimension of the European Union and to the external face of the European integration endeavour. Hence, a genuine question emerges as to the next steps of the European Neighbourhood Policy, its eastern dimension (Eastern Partnership) and the discussed Association Agreements. In this respect one can concur with Blockmans, who persuasively argues that the ENP is coming to the end of the road.[48] At the same time, for a host of reasons, the ENP may be kept on life support for quite a while. In the meantime, however, the European Union will in the future have to address calls for an upgrade of the existing legal framework laid down in the Association Agreements. The EaP *avant garde* is becoming rather vocal about the drive to deeper integration. It is enough to mention here a recent Joint Statement on the Future of Eastern Partnership, which not only calls for expansion of the substantive scope of respective Association Agreements but also openly refers to applications for EU

[45] In the current EU Financial Framework the funds are available *qua* the European Neighbourhood Instrument. See Regulation (EU) No 232/2014 of the European Parliament and of the Council of 11 March 2014 establishing a European Neighbourhood Instrument [2014] OJ L 77/27.

[46] Decision (EU) 2020/701 of the European Parliament and of the Council of 25 May 2020 on providing macro-financial assistance to enlargement and neighbourhood partners in the context of the COVID-19 pandemic [2020] OJ L 165/31.

[47] See Sadurski 2019.

[48] See Blockmans 2017.

membership, when the time comes.[49] In this vein, the Georgian Government in 2019 adopted the RoadMap2EU: a strategic document outlining future steps *en route* to EU accession.[50]

10.4.2 Upgrades to the Association Agreements

There is no denying that the painfully negotiated and concluded Association Agreements with Ukraine, Georgia and Moldova will be here to stay for quite a while. Their lifespan is likely to exceed the one experienced by the Europe Agreements concluded by the then European Communities with the countries of Central and Eastern Europe.[51] At the same time, they may not reach the stage of a long-term engagement akin to the Ankara Agreement, which for over five decades has remained

[49] Joint Statement by the Ministers of Foreign Affairs of Georgia, the Republic of Moldova and Ukraine on the Future of Eastern Partnership (5 December 2019, Bratislava), available at: https://3dcftas.eu/library/documents/joint-statement-by-the-ministers-of-foreign-affairs-of-georgia,-the-republic-of-moldova-and-ukraine-on-the-future-of-eastern-partnership.

[50] Ministry of Foreign Affairs of Georgia 2019.

[51] Europe Agreement establishing an association between the European Communities and their Member States, of the one part, and the Republic of Poland, of the other part, opened for signature 16 December 1991, OJ L 348/2 (entered into force 1 February 1994); Europe Agreement establishing an association between the European Communities and their Member States, of the one part, and the Republic of Hungary, of the other part, opened for signature 16 December 1991, OJ L 347/2 (entered into force 1 February 1994); Europe Agreement establishing an association between the European Communities and their Member States, of the one part, and the Czech Republic, of the other part, opened for signature 4 October 1993, OJ L 360/2 (entered into force 1 February 1995); Europe Agreement establishing an association between the European Communities and their Member States, of the one part, and the Slovak Republic, of the other part, opened for signature 4 October 1993, OJ L 359/2 (entered into force 1 February 1995); Europe Agreement establishing an association between the European Communities and their Member States, of the one part, and Romania, of the other part, 1 February 1993, OJ L 357/2 (entered into force 1 February 1995); Europe Agreement establishing an association between the European Communities and their Member States, of the one part, and the Republic of Bulgaria, of the other part, opened for signature 8 March 1993, OJ L 358/3 (entered into force 1 February 1995); Europe Agreement establishing an association between the European Communities and their Member States, of the one part, and the Republic of Lithuania, of the other part, opened for signature 12 June 1995, OJ L 51/3 (entered into force 1 February 1998); Europe Agreement establishing an association between the European Communities and their Member States, of the one part, and the Republic of Latvia, of the other part, opened for signature 12 June 1995, OJ L 26/3 (entered into force 1 February 1998); Europe Agreement establishing an association between the European Communities and their Member States, of the one part, and the Republic of Estonia, of the other part, opened for signature 12 June 1995, OJ L 68/3 (entered into force 1 February 1998); Europe Agreement establishing an association between the European Communities and their Member States, acting within the framework of the European Union, of the one part, and the Republic of Slovenia, of the other part, opened for signature 10 June 1996, OJ L 51/3 (entered into force 1 February 1999). See further Ott and Inglis 2002.

a foundation for association between the EU and Turkey.[52] So, the question which for now remains unanswered is whether the three Association Agreements are ends in themselves or whether, possibly, they may evolve into vehicles for EU membership.[53] In the short term, however, it is rather obvious that the EU and the associated countries ought to focus their efforts on updating the lists of *acquis* provided in the Association Agreements. This, as argued in the academic literature, is a two-edged sword. On the one hand, there is no doubt that the pieces of *acquis* listed therein may be replaced by newly adopted EU legislation by means of decisions of joint bodies established under the Association Agreements. On the other hand, it is doubtful if the lists in question may be expanded by way of the kitchen door even further to cover the areas not listed before.[54] Such a manoeuvre may in fact require a fully-fledged revision of the Association Agreements, translating into ratification by all EU Member States as well as the associated countries. Should that happen, it would be worth taking the association—in more general terms—to new levels. At least two strands of reforms could be put under consideration.

A deepening of economic integration could amount to an expansion of lists of EU *acquis* to areas not ventured into before or, at least, the obligation to approximate could go down to the level of implementing and delegated acts, which—as things stand today—are largely not included in the current parameters of a *rapprochement*. Furthermore, the politics of association in the present form dictate enhancement of institutional relations between the EU and its neighbours. It is striking that only the EU-Ukraine Association Agreement envisages regular joint high level summits. *Au contraire*, such options are not on the menu in the Association Agreements with Georgia and Moldova. Furthermore, a new paradigm for the institutional framework has recently emerged in relations with Switzerland[55] as well as the United Kingdom (as far as the Withdrawal Agreement is concerned).[56] Some elements could surely be borrowed to shape upgraded institutional frameworks with Ukraine, Georgia and Moldova.[57] This could include, for instance, enhanced access to the EU agencies and working groups prevalent in the early stages of the EU decision-making process.

---

[52] Agreement Creating an Association between the European Economic Community and Turkey, opened for signature 12 September 1963, OJ L 361/29 (entered into force 1 December 1964). See further Rogers 2000; Szigetvári 2016; Terzi 2019.

[53] As was the case with European Agreements with Central and Eastern European countries. See Inglis 2000.

[54] Van der Loo and Akhvlediani 2020, pp. 9–10.

[55] Kaddous 2019; Łazowski 2021b.

[56] Agreement on the withdrawal of the United Kingdom of Great Britain and Northern Ireland from the European Union and the European Atomic Energy Community, opened for signature 24 January 2020, OJ C 384I (entered into force 1 February 2020); See further Dougan 2020; Łazowski 2021c.

[57] On the current institutional set-up, see Van Der Loo 2019.

10.4.3 Beyond the Association Agreements

In the long term one could entertain some ideas, which have been floating around for quite a while, but so far, have failed to bear fruit. For instance, perhaps the time has come—drawing from the experience gained in the EEA[58]—to return to the concept of joint economic space between the EU and EaP countries.[59] As an alternative, it would surely be intellectually tempting to contemplate the potential accession of Ukraine, Georgia and Moldova to the European Economic Area (either as an end in itself, or a steppingstone towards EU membership). This, however, would not only require prior membership of EFTA but also a fair degree of political will in the three EEA-EFTA countries and the EU Member States.[60] Alas, such good will is—at least for now—in short supply. The question also remains how Brexit will change the dynamics within the European Union and the multispeed trajectory it has found itself in.[61] The time may be right to reconsider the option of partial membership that could be on offer for some of the neighbouring countries, which are expressing no desire to join, or fall short of meeting the accession criteria. The latter option would surely require a treaty revision that, in the current political climate, does not seem to be the preferred way forward.[62]

10.5 Conclusions

Analysis of the experience gained with the Association Agreements with Ukraine, Georgia and Moldova offers a mixed bag. On the one hand, they serve as platforms for association with the European Union and the creation of DCFTAs. Combined with a heavy rule-of-law component, based on political conditionality, they offer a broad framework for co-operation. For some, they are the epitome of the EU operating as a normative power.[63] For others, they may be proof of the EU acting as a hegemon. The most recent post-Brexit debacles show yet another phenomenon. Such models for a *rapprochement*, when looked at from Kyiv, Tbilisi and Chișinău, are tools for a decisive policy shift and a way to escape from the Soviet past. Seen from Westminster, they are vicious devices imposing shackles on third countries. In the great scheme of things, this cacophony is hardly surprising. Ukraine, Georgia and Moldova have been, for years now, forced to stand up to existential threats coming from Moscow and the

---

[58] See Frommelt 2016.

[59] This was mentioned *en passant* by the European Commission in one of its ENP Strategy Papers, however this idea failed to take off properly and skipped in the subsequent ENP papers. See Communication from the Commission to the Council and the European Parliament on Strengthening of the European Neighbourhood Policy, COM (2006) 726 final, p. 5.

[60] See Baur 2016.

[61] See De Witte et al. 2017.

[62] On the mechanics of treaty revisions see, *inter alia*, De Witte 2011.

[63] Manners 2010.

economic/social fallout from the Soviet days, while the authorities in London keep on operating in a comfort zone, indulging in an intellectual extravaganza of (long gone) imperial power. When the UK was leaving the European Union, risking an economic calamity, the EaP *avant garde* was hoping for an even closer *rapprochement*. Alas, with no explicit EU membership promise in sight, the EU is at risk of undermining the implementation of the Association Agreements as the authorities in the associated countries may feel less inclined to pursue reforms, which at times deliver benefits with considerable delay. As this chapter argues, many steps have been taken to fulfil the potential of the Association Agreements. Yet, much more effort is still required, on both sides, to make sure that the Agreements live up to their potential. In the short term, the European Union should roll up its sleeves and pursue upgrades of the Association Agreements in a more dynamic fashion, including long overdue updates of lists of *acquis* pencilled in for law approximation. At the same time, the Ukrainian, Georgian and Moldovan authorities should—in their own interest—approach the changing legal environment with a degree of caution. Self-interest should prevail, especially in the light of the economic havoc caused by the Covid-19 pandemic. In the mid- and long-term perspective, the association should be upgraded to the next levels. Which form they will take is—at this stage—unclear. However, it would be advisable for the European Union to do its homework. The most recent EaP revision lacks a strategic vision and does not live up to its expectations. At the same time, the recent recommendation of the European Parliament brings some hope.[64] With this in mind one should remember the words of ancient Demosthenes: all speech is vain and empty unless it be accompanied by action. The grand objectives behind the ENP/EaP are still to reach their potential, or risk demise.

References

Arnesen F et al. (eds) (2018) Agreement on The European Economic Area: A Commentary. CH Beck/Hart Publishing/Nomos Verlag, Oxford/Portland

Association4U (2018) Огляд прецедентного права Суду Європейського Союзу у сферах, що регулюються Угодою про асоціацію між Україною та ЄС [Review of case law of the Court of Justice of the European Union in the areas governed by the Association Agreement between Ukraine and the EU]. https://eu-ua.org/sites/default/files/imce/ohliad-pretsedentnoho-prava-sudu-yevropeiskogo-soiuzu-sferi-shcho-rehuliuiutsia-uhodoiu-pro-asotsiatsiiu.pdf. Accessed 2 July 2020

Baudenbacher C (ed) (2015) The Handbook of EEA Law. Springer

Baur G (2016) Who Can Join the European Economic Area? In: Gstöhl S, Phinnemore D (eds) The Proliferation of Privileged Partnerships between the European Union and Its Neighbours. Routledge, pp. 55–71

Blockmans S (2017) The Obsolescence of the European Neighbourhood Policy. Rowman and Littlefield International

[64] See Report on a European Parliament recommendation to the Council, the Commission and the Vice-President of the Commission/High Representative of the Union for Foreign Affairs and Security Policy on the Eastern Partnership, in the run-up to the June 2020 Summit, A9-0112/2020.

Blockmans S, Van Vooren B (2012) Revitalizing the European 'Neighbourhood Economic Community': The Case for Legally Binding Sectoral Multilateralism. EFARev 17:577–604

Brsakoska Bazerkoska J (2016) The European Union and (Frozen) Conflicts in its Neighbourhood: The SAP and the ENP Compared. In: Gstöhl S, Phinnemore D (eds) The Proliferation of Privileged Partnerships between the European Union and Its Neighbours. Routledge, pp. 235–255

Buschle D (2016) Challenges in Exporting the Internal Market: Lessons from the Energy Community. In: Gstöhl S (ed) The European Neighbourhood Policy in a Comparative Perspective: Models, Challenges, Lessons. Routledge, pp. 72–91

Buschle D, Karova R (2019) The EU's Sectoral Communities with Neighbours: the case of the Energy Community. In: Gstöhl S, Phinnemore D (eds) The Proliferation of Privileged Partnerships between the European Union and its Neighbours. Routledge, pp. 139–156

Buschle D, Talus K (eds) (2015) The Energy Community: A New Energy Governance System. Intersentia

De Witte B (2011) Treaty Revision Procedures after Lisbon. In: Biondi A, Eeckhout P, Ripley S (eds) EU Law after Lisbon. Oxford University Press, pp. 107–127

De Witte B, Ott A, Vos E (eds) (2017) Between Flexibility and Disintegration: The Trajectory of Differentiation in EU Law. Edward Elgar Publishing

Dougan M (2020) So Long, Farewell, auf Wiedersehen, Goodbye: The UK'S Withdrawal Package. CMLRev 57:631–704

Emerson M, Cenuşa D (eds) (2018) Deeping EU-Moldovan Relations. What, Why and How? https://www.ceps.eu/ceps-publications/deepening-eu-moldovan-relations-what-why-and-how/. Accessed 3 July 2020

Emerson M, Konstanyan H (2013) Putin's Grand Design to Destroy the EU's Eastern Partnership and Replace it with a Disastrous Neighbourhood Policy of His Own. https://www.ceps.eu/ceps-publications/putins-grand-design-destroy-eus-eastern-partnership-and-replace-it-disastrous/. Accessed 3 July 2020

Emerson M, Kovziridze (eds) (2018) Deepening EU-Georgian Relations. What, why and how? https://www.ceps.eu/ceps-publications/deepening-eu-georgian-relations-what-why-and-how-second-edition/. Accessed 3 July 2020

Emerson M, Movchan V (eds) (2018) Deepening EU-Ukrainian Relations. What, why and how? https://www.ceps.eu/ceps-publications/deepening-eu-ukrainian-relations-what-why-and-how-second-edition/. Accessed 3 July 2020

Emerson M, Blockmans S, Cenusa D, Kovziridze T, Movchan V (2020) Eastern Partnership Policy beyond 2020: Advances and Omissions in a Vast Agenda. https://www.ceps.eu/ceps-publications/eastern-partnership-policy-beyond-2020/. Accessed 3 July 2020

Franco M (2016) The Effectiveness of Institutional Arrangements in the European Union's Relations with its Neighbours. In: Gstöhl S (ed) The European Neighbourhood Policy in a Comparative Perspective: Models, Challenges, Lessons. Routledge, pp. 183–198

Frommelt C (2016) Differentiated Integration in the European Economic Area: What Lessons Can Be Drawn for the European Neighbourhood Policy? In: Gstöhl S (ed) The European Neighbourhood Policy in a Comparative Perspective: Models, Challenges, Lessons. Routledge, pp. 33–54

Gabrichidze G (2014) Legislative Approximation and Application of EU law in Georgia. In: Van Elsuwege P, Petrov R (eds) Legislative Approximation and Application of EU Law in the Eastern Neighbourhood of the European Union: Towards a Common Regulatory Space? Routledge pp. 179–190

Ghazaryan N (2014) The European Neighbourhood Policy and the Democratic Values of the EU: A Legal Analysis. Hart Publishing

Ghazaryan N (2018) Who Are the 'Gatekeepers'?: In Continuation of the Debate on the Direct Applicability and the Direct Effect of EU International Agreements. YEL 37:27–74

Gstöhl S (2016a) Mapping the European Union's Neighbourhood Relations: The European Economic Area as a 'Prototype' for the Integration of EU Neighbours? In: Gstöhl S (ed) The

European Neighbourhood Policy in a Comparative Perspective: Models, challenges, lessons. Routledge, pp. 15–30
Gstöhl S (ed) (2016b) The European Neighbourhood Policy in a Comparative Perspective: Models, challenges, lessons. Routledge
Inglis K (2000) The Europe Agreements Compared in the Light of Their Pre-Accession Reorientation. CMLRev 37:1173–1210
Joint Statement by the Ministers of Foreign Affairs of Georgia, the Republic of Moldova and Ukraine on the Future of Eastern Partnership (2019) https://3dcftas.eu/library/documents/joint-statement-by-the-ministers-of-foreign-affairs-of-georgia,-the-republic-of-moldova-and-ukraine-on-the-future-of-eastern-partnership. Accessed 3 July 2020
Kaddous C (2019) Switzerland and the EU: Current Issues and New Challenges under the Draft Institutional Framework Agreement. In: Gstöhl S, Phinnemore D (eds) The Proliferation of Privileged Partnerships between the European Union and its Neighbours, Routledge, pp. 68–83
Khvorostankina A (2014) Legislative Approximation and Application of EU law in Moldova. In: Van Elsuwege P, Petrov R (eds) Legislative Approximation and Application of EU Law in the Eastern Neighbourhood of the European Union: Towards a Common Regulatory Space? Routledge, pp. 159–178
Łazowski A (2020) Exporting Cherries for the Tops of Cakes: The Charter of Fundamental Rights in Domestic Courts of the EU's Neighbourhood. In: Bobek M, Prassl J (eds) Ten Years of Charter of Fundamental Rights. Hart Publishing, pp. 499–523
Łazowski A (2021a) How to Move the EU Enlargement out of the Cul-de-sac? SIEPS, forthcoming
Łazowski A (2021b) Draft EU-Swiss Institutional Agreement: Towards a New Institutional Paradigm? In: Biondi A, Sangiuolo G (eds) Judicial Protection and EU FTAs. Edward Elgar Publishing, forthcoming
Łazowski A (2021c) Withdrawal from the European Union: A Legal Appraisal. Edward Elgar Publishing forthcoming
Łazowski A, Blockmans S (2014) Between Dreams and Reality: Challenges to the Legal Rapprochement of the Western Balkans. In: Van Elsuwege P, Petrov R (eds) Legislative Approximation and Application of EU Law in the Eastern Neighbourhood of the European Union: towards a Common Regulatory Space? Routledge, pp. 108–133
Łazowski A, Vlašić Feketija M (2014) The Seventh EU Enlargement and Beyond: Pre-Accession Policy vis-à-vis the Western Balkans Revisited. CYELP 10:1–37
Manners I (2010) As You Like It: European Union Normative Power in the European Neighbourhood Policy. In: Whitman R, Wolff S (eds) The European Neighbourhood Policy in Perspective: Context, Implementation and Impact. Palgrave, pp. 29–50
Melo Araujo BA (2016) The EU Deep Trade Agenda: Law and Policy. Oxford University Press
Ministry of Foreign Affairs of Georgia (2019) European Union Integration Roadmap: RoadMap2EU. Better Integration for New Opportunities! https://mfa.gov.ge/News/%E2%80%8Bsaqartvelo-evrokavshiris-asocirebis-sabchos-me-5.aspx?CatID=5&lang=en-US. Accessed 3 July 2020
Nizhnikau R (2019) EU Induced Institutional Change in Post-Soviet Space: Promoting Reforms in Moldova and Ukraine. Routledge
Ott A, Inglis K (eds) (2002) Handbook on European Enlargement: A Commentary on the Enlargement Process. T.M.C. Asser Press, The Hague
Petrov R (2014) Legislative Approximation and Application of EU law in Ukraine. In: Van Elsuwege P, Petrov R (eds) Legislative Approximation and Application of EU Law in the Eastern Neighbourhood of the European Union: towards a Common Regulatory Space? Routledge, pp. 137–158
Petrov R, Kalinichenko P (2011) The Europeanization of Third Country Judiciaries through the Application of the EU Acquis: The Cases of Russia and Ukraine. ICLQ 60:325–353
Phinnemore D (2003) Stabilisation and Association Agreements: Europe Agreements for the Western Balkans. EFARev 8:77–103
Poli S (ed) (2016) The European Neighbourhood Policy – Values and Principles. Routledge

Refit EU (2018) Making EU law Simpler, Less Costly and Future Proof. https://ec.europa.eu/info/law/law-making-process/evaluating-and-improving-existing-laws/refit-making-eu-law-simpler-and-less-costly_en#2018-commission-proposals-potential-benefits. Accessed 2 July 2020
Rodin S, Perišin T (eds) (2015) Judicial Application of International Law in Southeast Europe. Springer
Rogers N (2000) A Practitioner's Guide to the EC-Turkey Association Agreement. Kluwer Law International
Rosas A, Levits E, Bot Y (eds) (2013) The Court of Justice and the Construction of Europe: Analyses and Perspectives on Sixty Years of Case-law - La Cour de Justice et la Construction de l'Europe: Analyses et Perspectives de Soixante Ans de Jurisprudence. T.M.C. Asser Press, The Hague
Sadurski W (2019) Poland's Constitutional Breakdown. Oxford University Press
Saurugger S, Terpan F (2016) The Court of Justice of the European Union and the Politics of Law. Palgrave
Şemşit S (2016) The EU's Enlargement and Neighbourhood Policy Strategies: The Role of Political Conditionality. In: Gstöhl S (ed) The European Neighbourhood Policy in a Comparative Perspective: Models, Challenges, Lessons. Routledge, pp. 218–234
Sindbjerg Martinsen D (2015) An Ever More Powerful Court? The Political Constraints of Legal Integration in the European Union. Oxford University Press
Szigetvári T (2016) EU-Turkey Relations: Customs Union and More… or Less? In: Gstöhl S (ed) The European Neighbourhood Policy in a Comparative Perspective: Models, Challenges, Lessons. Routledge, pp. 107–124
Terzi Ö (2019) The EU–Turkey Customs Union: Shortcomings and Prospects for Modernization. In: Gstöhl S, Phinnemore D (eds) The Proliferation of Privileged Partnerships between the European Union and its Neighbours. Routledge, pp. 121–138
Van Der Loo G (2016) The EU-Ukraine Association Agreement and Deep and Comprehensive Free Trade Area: A New Legal Instrument for EU Integration Without Membership. Brill Publishing
Van Der Loo G (2019) The Institutional Framework of the Eastern Partnership Association Agreements and the Deep and Comprehensive Free Trade Areas. In: Gstöhl S, Phinnemore D (eds) The Proliferation of Privileged Partnerships between the European Union and its Neighbours. Routledge, pp. 102–120
Van Der Loo G, Akhvlediani T (2020) Catch Me if You Can: Updating the Eastern Partnership Association Agreements and DCFTAs. https://www.ceps.eu/ceps-publications/catch-me-if-you-can/. Accessed 3 July 2020
Van Vooren (2012) EU External Relations Law and the European Neighbourhood Policy: A Paradigm for Coherence. Routledge
Vilpišauskas R (2016) European Union or Eurasian Union? A Dilemma for the Eastern Partnership Countries. In: Gstöhl S, Phinnemore D (eds) The Proliferation of Privileged Partnerships between the European Union and its Neighbours. Routledge, pp. 259–281
Wernø Holter D (2017) Legislative Homogeneity. In: Baudenbacher C (ed) The Fundamental Principles of EEA Law: EEA-ities. Springer
Wessel R, Van Der Loo G (2017) The Non-Ratification of Mixed Agreements: Legal Consequences and Solutions. CMLRev 54:735–770
Whitman R, Wolff S (eds) (2010) The European Neighbourhood Policy in Perspective: Context, Implementation and Impact. Palgrave

A. Łazowski is Professor of EU Law at the University of Westminster in London in the United Kingdom and Visiting Professor at the College of Europe (Natolin). The views and opinions expressed in this chapter belong solely to the author.

Chapter 11
Legal Status of the United Kingdom as a Third State: Strange *Déjá Vu*

M. Gatti

Contents

Abstract The UK government envisaged a clean break from the Union but, under the Withdrawal Agreement, the UK's legal position as a "third state" is ambiguous. Throughout the transition period, the UK is in many respects hardly distinguishable from an EU member state. After the transition period, the UK remains outside Union institutions, but applies core EU rules in respect of specific persons (EU citizens settled in the UK) or areas (Northern Ireland). Furthermore, UK authorities must apply these EU rules in light of EU principles and are, by and large, subject to the control of EU institutions, particularly the Court of Justice. Several aspects of the new legal status of the UK are a *déjà vu*, since the Withdrawal Agreement is relatively similar to "integration-oriented agreements", such as Association Agreements. To be sure, this similitude is imperfect, as the degree of integration of the United Kingdom varies considerably, depending on the subject matter, the persons and regions concerned, and/or the moment when the law is applied. The UK's legal position, therefore, remains complex and contradictory: as it was the least integrated member of the Union, it is now a very integrated third state.

Keywords Brexit · withdrawal · citizenship · free movement of goods · Court of Justice · EU institutions

---

M. Gatti (✉)
University of Bologna, Via Zamboni 27/29, 40126 Bologna, Italy
e-mail: m.gatti@unibo.it

W. Th. Douma et al. (eds.), *The Evolving Nature of EU External Relations Law*,
https://doi.org/10.1007/978-94-6265-423-5_11

11.1 Introduction

After its withdrawal from the Union, the legal status of the UK shifted from "member state" to "third state". But what does it really mean, to be a "third state"?[1]

The legal status of a "member state" or "third state" corresponds to the legal position of that country in the legal order of the Union, i.e. the sum of its rights and obligations in the EU legal system.[2] EU Treaties distinguish clearly member states from third states, at least from a formal perspective. Member states are subject to a set of rights and obligations under EU primary law, while third states are described by the Treaties as objects of cooperation[3] or entities the EU may interact with.[4] From a substantive viewpoint, however, the distinction is not that straightforward, since the scope of rights and obligations of member states and third states may vary.[5] For instance, Switzerland (a third state) is in the Schengen area, unlike some EU member states, such as Ireland.

Some elements, linked to the nature of the European Union, arguably characterise the position of EU member states, and set them apart from third states, at least in principle. According to the case law of the Court of Justice,[6] EU Treaties established a new legal order, characterised by the "establishment of *institutions* endowed with sovereign rights".[7] EU law is defined by "its *primacy* over the laws of the Member States and by the *direct effect* of a whole series of provisions which are *applicable to their nationals*" and to the member states themselves.[8] To ensure that those specific characteristics are preserved, "the Treaties have established a *judicial system* intended to ensure consistency and uniformity in the interpretation of EU law".[9]

The status of member states may thus be linked to at least five essential elements that arguably define their position. The member states (1) are bound by EU Treaties

---

[1] On the meaning of the expression "third state", see Bosse Platière and Rapoport 2014, pp. 17–18.

[2] On the notion of legal status, see *inter alia* Trisciuoglio 2019, p. 11.

[3] See e.g. Consolidated Version of the Treaty on the European Union, 2012, OJ C326 (TEU) articles 21(1) and 43(1).

[4] See e.g. Consolidated Version of the Treaty on the Functioning of the European Union, 2012, OJ C 326 (TFEU) articles 216 and 218.

[5] See, in this sense Abderamane 2018, p. 217.

[6] On the relationship between the status of EU member states and the principles enucleated in the case law of the Court of justice, see Potvin-Solis 2018, pp. 17–18.

[7] Court of Justice, *Van Gend en Loos*, Judgment, 5 February 1963, Case 26-62, EU:C:1963:1, p. 12, emphasis added.

[8] Court of Justice, *Wightman,* Judgment, 10 December 2018, Case C-621/18, EU:C:2018:999, paras 44–45; Court of Justice, *Achmea*, Judgment of 6 March 2018, Case C-284/16, EU:C:2018:158, para 33; Court of Justice, *Draft Agreement on the Accession of the European Union to the European Convention for the Protection of Human Rights and Fundamental Freedoms,* Opinion 2/13 of 18 December 2014, EU:C:2014:2454, paras 165–166 (emphases added).

[9] Court of Justice, *Comprehensive Economic and Trade Agreement between Canada, of the one part, and the European Union and its Member States, of the other part (CETA),* Opinion of the Court of 30 April 2019, Opinion 1/17, ECLI:EU:C:2019:341, paras 110–111; Court of Justice, *Les Verts,* Judgment, 23 April 1986, Case 294/83, EU:C:1986:166, para 23; *Van Gend en Loos*, above n. 7, p. 12 (emphasis added).

and the principles of EU law, such as sincere cooperation, uniform interpretation and application of EU law, as well as primacy and direct effect; consequently, they apply EU law to individuals, especially in respect of free movement of (2) citizens and (3) goods; and participate in (4) the EU judicial system[10] and (5) EU institutions, bodies, offices or agencies.

Although, in principle, these elements characterise the position of EU member states, they may concern, to a certain extent, some third states, too. Through the conclusion of international agreements with the EU, third states may engage in "integration without membership".[11] It is the case, for example, of the European Economic Area (EEA),[12] composed of the European Union and three members of the European Free Trade Area (EFTA), i.e. Iceland, Liechtenstein, and Norway (hereafter, EFTA states).[13] EFTA states ensure, to a large extent, free movement of persons, apply EU internal market law[14] and are subject to the jurisdiction of the EFTA Court, which interprets the EEA Agreement in light of EU principles and the case law of the Court of Justice.[15]

This chapter investigates the status of the UK as a third state by referring to the five aforementioned elements that characterise the legal position of EU member states. To elucidate the specificities of the UK's status, the analysis compares the position of the UK to the status of other third states that have a close relationship with the Union. It is submitted that, after Brexit, the UK has an unprecedentedly complex status. In some areas, the UK's position is analogous to the status of Associated countries, particularly EFTA states. Although the Withdrawal Agreement is a "disintegration-oriented" instrument, it is relatively similar to "integration-oriented agreements", such as the EEA Agreement or other Association Agreements.[16] In any event, this similitude is imperfect, as the degree of integration of the United Kingdom varies considerably: *certain* EU rules concerning *certain* topics apply in *certain* regions of the UK, to *certain* persons, and/or for a *certain* period. If one wanted to represent

---

[10]Court of Justice, *Popławski II,* Judgment, 24 June 2019, Case C-573/17, EU:C:2019:530, para 52; *Achmea*, above n. 8, para 35; Opinion 2/13 *(Accession to the ECHR)*, above n. 8, para 174; there are, of course, other elements that might possibly characterise EU member states, such as common values, see Article 2 TEU; Court of Justice, *Commission v. Poland*, Judgment, 24 June 2019, Case C-619/18, EU:C:2019:531, paras 42, 43, and 58; Opinion 2/13 *(Accession to the ECHR)*, above n. 8, paras 168 and 173. The EU purportedly shares "values" with several third countries, too, see e.g. Agreement on the European Economic Area, opened for signature 02 May 1992, OJ L 1/3–522, (entered into force 1 January 1994) (EEA Agreement), preamble (referring to "common values"); Cooperation Agreement between the European Community and the Socialist Republic of Vietnam, opened for signature 17 July 1995, OJ L329/8 (entered into force 1 June 1996) preamble (referring to "shared values").

[11]Łazowski 2008; see also Ott 2015 and Maresceau 2013.

[12]EEA Agreement, above n. 10.

[13]Cf. EEA Agreement, above n. 10, article 2(b).

[14]Baur et al. 2018, p. 64; Van Elsuwege and Chamon 2019, p. 28.

[15]See below, Sects. 11.2, 11.3, 11.4 and 11.5.

[16]Cf. Rapoport 2017, p. 104; see also Ott 2015, p. 10; Maresceau 2012, p. 319; Maresceau 2013, p. 153.

third countries on a sliding scale of "closeness" to EU membership, the UK would be contemporarily "very close" in some respects and quite "far" in others.

It is worth noting that, at the time of writing, the EU and the UK have concluded a Withdrawal Agreement (hereinafter: WA), including a Protocol on Ireland/Northern Ireland (hereinafter: NI Protocol) and a Protocol relating to the Sovereign Base Areas in Cyprus, and a Protocol on Gibraltar,[17] and have adopted a (nonbinding) Political Declaration.[18] The UK and the EU are currently negotiating a "Future Relationship" agreement, regarding cooperation on issues not covered by the Withdrawal Agreement, which might modify the status of the UK.[19] This contribution focuses on the aspects of the UK's status that are already discernible on the basis of the WA. The analysis does not intend to address all the details connected to the UK position, such as the treatment of British citizens in the EU, the treatment of goods exported from the UK to the EU, or the external relations of the UK after Brexit.

Section 11.2 investigates the application to the UK of core constitutional principles of the Union. Then, the attention turns to the application of EU law to individuals in the UK, concerning the movement of citizens (Sect. 11.3) and goods (Sect. 11.4). Section 11.5 focuses on the participation of the UK in the EU judicial system and Sect. 11.6 discusses the UK's participation in the EU's institutional structure. The conclusion suggests that certain elements of the UK's status are modelled on previous experiences, but they are combined in a novel and uniquely intricate manner (Sect. 11.7).

11.2 Application of EU Constitutional Principles to and in the UK

EU Treaties, by definition, bind EU member states but are *res inter alios acta* from the perspective of third states. Nonetheless, rules and principles of EU primary law (as well as secondary rules based on primary law) may be applicable to third states, albeit indirectly, by virtue of international agreements concluded with the Union.

This is the case, in particular, of the UK during the "transition period", which started with the UK's withdrawal and is expected to last until the end of 2020, and may be extended once up to two years (December 2022).[20] During this period,

[17] Agreement on the withdrawal of the United Kingdom of Great Britain and Northern Ireland from the European Union and the European Atomic Energy Community, opened for signature 24 January 2020, OJ C 384I (entered into force 1 February 2020) (UK WA).

[18] European Commission 2019.

[19] Council Decision (EU, Euratom) 2020/266 of 25 February 2020 authorising the opening of negotiations with the United Kingdom of Great Britain and Northern Ireland for a new partnership agreement, OJ 2020 L58/53.

"Union law" as such is "applicable to and in the United Kingdom",[21] though there are exceptions relating, for instance, to participation in EU institutions (see Sect. 11.6 below).[22]

After the transition period, the status of the UK changes considerably in terms of the application of EU law. This section discusses the application of EU constitutional principles to and in the UK, by virtue of the Withdrawal Agreement. The following sections focus on the application of EU rules in respect of free movement of persons, free movement of goods, the jurisdiction of the Court of Justice and the UK's participation in EU organs.

EU law is characterised by several constitutional principles, some of which are particularly relevant.[23] The list of core EU principles obviously includes *direct effect* and *primacy*, which are connected to *sincere cooperation*.[24] *Uniform interpretation* and application of EU law arguably constitutes another core constitutional principle of EU law[25] and ensures "its consistency, its full effect and its autonomy as well as, ultimately, the particular nature of the law established by the Treaties".[26] The uniformity of interpretation of the Treaties is the primary mission of the Court of Justice, which fosters it, in particular, through the preliminary reference procedure.[27]

EU constitutional principles generally apply to EU member states, but international agreements may lead to the application of EU constitutional principles—or the application of principles modelled on EU law—to and in third states. The EEA Agreement constitutes a useful term of comparison for the Withdrawal Agreement in this respect.[28] In the first place, both Agreements refer, explicitly or implicitly, to

---

20 UK WA, above n. 17, articles 126 and 132.

21 Ibid., article 127; see also articles 7, 128 and 129.

22 Ibid., article 129(3), which enables the UK to conclude international agreements with third countries in areas subject to the EU's exclusive competence, such as trade, provided such agreements do not apply during the transition period. See further Neframi 2019, pp. 220–221.

23 Cf. Constantinesco 2001.

24 See *Achmea,* above n. 8, para 34. See also Court of Justice, *Costa v Enel,* Judgment, 15 July 1964, Case 6/64, EU:C:1964:66: "the executive force of community law cannot vary from one state to another in deference to subsequent domestic laws, without jeopardizing the attainment of the objectives of the treaty set out in article 5(2)" (providing for the obligation of sincere cooperation). See further Casolari 2019b, pp. 50–51.

25 On the characterisation of uniform interpretation and application of EU law as a principle, see *inter alia* Court of Justice, *Océ van der Grinten,* Judgment, 25 September 2003, Case C-58/01, EU:C:2003:495, para 53; Court of Justice, *Soledad Duarte Hueros,* Opinion of Advocate General Kokott of 28 February 2013, Case C-32/12, EU:C:2013:128, para 20; Constantinesco 2001; Burchardt 2019.

26 Opinion 2/13 *(Accession to the ECHR),* above n. 8, para 174; see also Court of Justice, *Draft Agreement on the Creation of a Unified Patent Litigation System,* Opinion of 8 March 2011, Opinion 1/09, ECLI:EU:C:2011:123, paras 67 and 83.

27 See, *inter alia,* Opinion 1/17 *(CETA),* above n.9, paras 110–111; Court of Justice, *Rosneft,* Judgment, 28 March 2017, Case C-71/15, EU:C:2017:236, para 80.

28 The EEA Agreement does not extend the legal order of the Union to EFTA countries, because it pursues specific objectives in a specific context (Neframi and Lacchi 2018, p. 240) but makes applicable principles modelled on EU law, as shown below.

sincere cooperation. The EEA Agreement does not mention sincere cooperation as such but its Article 3 mirrors to a certain extent Article 4(3) TEU, by stipulating that the Contracting Parties must take appropriate measures to ensure fulfilment of the obligations arising out of the Agreement and abstain from any measure which could jeopardize the attainment of its objectives. The obligation of sincere cooperation enshrined in Article 3 of the EEA Agreement has been used by the EFTA Court as a legal foundation for the introduction, in the EEA legal order, of principles linked to sincere cooperation, such as state liability[29] and consistent interpretation.[30]

The Withdrawal Agreement may seem different from the EEA Agreement: Article 5 WA stipulates that the parties "shall, in full mutual respect and good faith, assist each other in carrying out tasks which flow from this Agreement". Being titled "Good faith" and referring to "good faith", this provision might suggest that the international principle of good faith, and not the more expansive EU law principle of sincere cooperation, should apply in this ambit.[31] However, Article 5(3) WA clarifies that "This Article is without prejudice to the application of Union law pursuant to this Agreement, in particular the *principle of sincere cooperation*."[32] Moreover, Article 5(1) and (2) WA are almost identical to Article 4(3) TEU;[33] the WA is even closer to the wording of the TEU than the EEA Agreement. This suggests that the WA, and the EU rules it refers to, should be applied in the UK consistently with the principle of sincere cooperation. Moreover, UK judges, like the EFTA Court, should arguably "import" in their legal order principles linked to sincere cooperation, such as state liability and consistent interpretation. The British judiciary should apply also the *ERTA* case law (which is based on the duty of sincere cooperation)[34] in respect of the EU's rules applied in the UK by virtue of the Withdrawal Agreement. For instance, after the end of the transition period, the UK should not assume international obligations which might affect or alter the scope of the internal market rules applicable to Northern Ireland (see below, Sect. 11.4).

Secondly, the Withdrawal Agreement and the EEA Agreement ensure application, to a certain extent, of *direct effect* and *primacy*. To preserve the dualistic approach

---

[29] EFTA Court, *Sveinbjörnsdóttir*, Advisory Opinion of 10 December 1998, E-9/97, E1997J0009 para 6; EFTA Court, *Kolbeinsson*, Judgment, 10 December 2010, E-2/10, para 85. On the relationship between state liability and sincere cooperation, see Neframi 2018, p. 355.

[30] EFTA Court, *Criminal proceedings against A,* Judgment of 3 October 2007, E-1/07, para 39; EFTA Court, *L'Oréal,* Judgment, 8 July 2008, Joined Cases E-9/07 and E-10/07, para 22. See further Hreinsson 2016, pp. 357–359; Lourenço 2019, p. 541; Neframi and Lacchi 2018, pp. 245–246. On the link between consistent interpretation and sincere cooperation, see Court of Justice, *Von Colson,* Judgment, 10 April 1984, Case 14/83, EU:C:1984:153, para 26.

[31] On the difference between good faith and sincere cooperation, see Constantinesco 1987 and Klamert 2014, pp. 42–46.

[32] Emphasis added.

[33] Differently from TEU, above n. 3, article 4(3), Article 5 WA, above n. 17, stipulates that the parties assist in each other "in good faith" and does not require them to facilitate the achievement of the Union's tasks. See further Casolari 2019a, pp. 1027–1028; Casolari 2019b, pp. 72–73.

[34] Court of Justice, *European Agreement on Road Transport*, Judgment, 31 March 1971, Case 22-70, EU:C:1971:32, paras 21–22.

of some EFTA states, EEA law was not expressly given direct effect and primacy.[35] The EFTA Court has rejected arguments for making the principles of direct effect and primacy part of the EEA legal order.[36] To partially compensate for the absence of direct effect, Article 7 of the EEA Agreement affirms that the acts referred to in decisions of the EEA Joint Committee (typically, EU secondary legislation) must "be, or be made" part of the internal legal order of the parties.[37] Furthermore, Protocol 35 to the EEA Agreement introduces a so-called "*ersatz* primacy", by stipulating that "for cases of possible conflicts between implemented EEA rules and other statutory provisions, the EFTA States undertake to introduce, if necessary, a statutory provision to the effect that EEA rules prevail in these cases." This "*ersatz* primacy", however, applies only to EEA norms implemented in national legal orders.[38]

The Withdrawal Agreement is more straightforward. According to Article 4(1) WA, "legal or natural persons shall in particular be able to *rely directly* on the provisions contained or referred to in this Agreement which meet the conditions for direct effect under Union law."[39] Moreover, the UK must ensure compliance with the duty to give EU provisions the same effect that they have in the EU legal order, "including as regards the required powers of its judicial and administrative authorities to disapply inconsistent or incompatible domestic provisions, through domestic primary legislation" (Article 4(2) WA). As in the case of the EEA's *ersatz* primacy, the UK must adopt "primary legislation" to enable domestic judicial and administrative authorities to disapply any national legislation inconsistent with the WA (and the EU rules it refers to). Unlike the EEA's *ersatz* primacy, though, the WA's primacy arguably applies, not only to EU norms implemented in the UK legal order, but to all the "provisions of Union law" made applicable by the WA.[40]

Thirdly, the Withdrawal Agreement, like the EEA Agreement, introduces extensive obligations in respect of the *uniform interpretation and application of EU law*.[41] Although the EEA Agreement creates an autonomous legal order, it aims at creating "a homogeneous European Economic Area" by ensuring "uniform interpretation and application" of EEA norms and those provisions of EU legislation which are substantially reproduced in EEA Agreement.[42] For the sake of a homogeneous application of the law, the EEA Joint Committee takes decisions incorporating (with adaptations)

[35] See Protocol 35 (On the Implementation of EEA Rules) to the EEA Agreement.

[36] EFTA Court, *Karlsson,* Judgment, 30 May 2002, E-4/01, para 28; *Criminal Proceedings against A,* above n. 30, para 40.

[37] Hreinsson 2016, pp. 384–385.

[38] See further Hreinsson 2016, pp. 384–386.

[39] Emphasis added.

[40] UK WA, above n. 17, articles 4(1) and (2). There may, in any event, be some issues with the application of the WA's primacy under UK law, see UK's European Union (Withdrawal Agreement) Act 2020, section 38; Dougan 2020, p. 21.

[41] Cf. Court of Justice, *Ruska Federacija*, Judgment, 2 April 2020, Case C-897/19 PPU, EU:C:2020:262, para 50; for a broader comparison of homogeneity clauses in integration-oriented agreements, see Ott 2015, pp. 18–23.

[42] EEA Agreement, above n. 10, Recitals 4, 6 and 15 and article 1(1); EFTA Court, *L'Oréal,* above n. 30, para 27; see further Neframi and Lacchi 2018, pp. 240–241; Hreinsson 2016, pp. 350.

new pieces of EU secondary law in annexes of the EEA Agreement, thereby making them binding on EFTA states.[43] Moreover, the provisions of the EEA agreement, when identical in substance to corresponding rules of EU law, must be interpreted "in conformity with" the relevant rulings of the Court of Justice handed down *prior* to the date of signature of the EEA Agreement.[44] By contrast, the EFTA Court must "pay due account to" the principles laid down by the rulings by the Court of Justice *after* the date of signature of the EEA Agreement.[45] "Paying due account to" presumably means less than "in conformity with". The EFTA Court is at least obliged to examine the case-law of the Court of justice and make this clear in its reasoning.[46] In practice, the EFTA Court tends to follow the case law of the Court of Justice, unless there are "compelling grounds for divergent interpretations",[47] linked to the specific context and objectives of the EEA Agreement.[48]

Like the EEA Agreement, the Withdrawal Agreement fosters uniformity in the application of EU law. To be sure, the EEA Agreement and the Withdrawal Agreement have different objectives: while the former promotes integration (a homogeneous EEA), the latter is intended to facilitate disintegration (the UK withdrawal). Nonetheless, both agreements make applicable EU rules to one or more third states, either by referring to EU sources or by restating their content.[49] Uniform interpretation and application of such rules is essential, not only for the EEA, but also for the UK. The WA promotes the "orderly withdrawal" of the UK, to "prevent disruption and to provide legal certainty" to citizens, economic operators, and judicial and administrative authorities in the Union and in the UK.[50] To attain this goal, a uniform and, therefore, predictable application of the law is arguably indispensable. The WA itself implicitly calls for uniform interpretation and application of EU rules: under Article 4(3), WA provisions "referring to Union law or to concepts or provisions thereof" must be interpreted and applied in accordance with the methods and general principles of Union law.[51]

---

[43]EEA Agreement, above n. 10, article 102; see further Sif Tynes 2018, pp. 25–26.

[44]EEA Agreement, above n. 10, articles 6 and 119; see further Court of First Instance, *Opel Austria*, Judgment, 22 January 1997, Case T-115/94, EU:T:1997:3, para 110; Court of Justice, *A*, Judgment, 19 July 2012, Case C-48/11, EU:C:2012:485, para 22; Court of Justice, *Fonnship A/S*, Judgment, 8 July 2014, Case C-83/13, EU:C:2014:2053, para 41.

[45]Agreement between the EFTA States on the Establishment of a Surveillance Authority and a Court of Justice, opened for signature 02 May 1992, OJ L 344 (entered into force 1 January 1993), article 3(2).

[46]Baudenbacher 2016, p. 181.

[47]EFTA Court, *L'Oréal,* above n. 30, paras 31, 37; see also Baur et al. 2018, pp. 76–77; Baudenbacher 2016, p. 183; Tatham 2016, p. 115–116.

[48]Cf. Neframi and Lacchi 2018, pp. 242–243.

[49]For instance, Article 5(5) NI Protocol stipulates that (*i*) "Articles 30 and 110 TFEU" apply to and in the UK in respect of Northern Ireland and (*ii*) "quantitative restrictions on exports and imports" are prohibited. See Protocol on Ireland and Northern Ireland to the UK WA (NI Protocol).

[50]UK WA, above n. 17, preamble, recitals 5 and 7.

[51]To be sure, in the case of the UK WA, this interpretation is performed by national (UK) courts, not by an international tribunal (such as the EFTA Court).

Differently from the EEA agreement, the WA does not include a general expectation of automatic adaptation to new EU legislation: references to Union law are understood as references to Union law "as applicable on the last day of the transition period" (Article 6(1) WA).[52] Nonetheless, the interpretation of the EU law provisions referred to in the WA follows the same rules set in the EEA Agreement. EU law provisions made applicable by the WA must be interpreted "in conformity" with the case law of the Court of Justice handed down *before* the end of the transition period (Article 4(4) WA). UK judicial and administrative authorities are generally required to have only "due regard" to relevant case law handed down *after* the end of the transition period (para 5).[53] Presumably, the concept of "due regard" is equivalent to "due account" under the EEA Agreement (see above). Since the concern for the "uniform interpretation and application" of EU law underlies the WA, as much as the EEA Agreement, British judges should, in principle, follow the example of the EFTA Court and respect the case law of the Court of Justice in its entirety—unless there are "compelling grounds" for divergent interpretations.

The Withdrawal Agreement fosters uniformity in the interpretation of EU law, not only by requesting British courts to take into account the case law of the Court of justice, but by extending the competence of the Court. This issue is discussed below, in Sect. 11.5. Before addressing that topic, the analysis focuses on the main rules whose uniformity of interpretation should be ensured, regarding free movement of citizens (Sect. 11.3) and goods (Sect. 11.4).

11.3 Free Movement of EU Citizens in the UK

By virtue of their sovereignty, states generally are entitled to control the entry of aliens into their territories and their residence there.[54] EU member states, having transferred part of their sovereign powers to the EU, should generally grant all EU citizens the right to move and reside freely within their territories.[55] Some third states have undertaken similar obligations via the conclusion of international agreements with the EU. The EEA Agreement, in particular, grants all EEA citizens free movement rights similar (though not identical) to those protected by EU law.[56]

---

[52] An exception concerns the coordination of social security systems; see UK WA, above n. 17, article 36; another exception is provided in NI Protocol, above n. 49, article 13(3); see further below, Sect. 11.4.

[53] The NI Protocol makes exception to the "due regard" rule, see below, Sect. 11.5.

[54] European Court of Human Rights, *Üner v. the Netherlands,* Judgment, 18 October 2006, App. 46410/99, para 54; see also Mariani 2019, p. 669.

[55] See in particular TFEU, above n. 4, article 20; Charter of Fundamental Rights of the EU, 2002, OJ C364/1, article 45.

[56] See EEA Agreement, above n. 10, articles 28–39; see also Decision of the EEA Joint Committee No 158/2007 of 7 December 2007, OJ 2008 L 124/20; EFTA Court, *Jabbi,* Judgment of the Court of 26 July 2016, E-28/15, para 71; see further Björgvinsson 2016, pp. 473–500.

Such an arrangement was unacceptable for UK authorities and, probably, public opinion. Restraining freedom of movement of persons has been a leitmotiv of the Brexit campaign, epitomised by the xenophobic rhetoric of Nigel Farage.[57]

However, the Withdrawal Agreement does not eliminate freedom of movement completely. During the transition period, EU citizens fully benefit from freedom of movement in the UK, as Union law is applicable to and in the UK during this period (see above, Sect. 11.2). After the end of the transition period, EU citizens generally do not benefit from freedom of movement in the UK, with an important exception: Union citizens who exercised their right to reside in the United Kingdom or their right as frontier workers in the UK "before the end of the transition period" (hereafter, Protected EU citizens), as well as their family members, enjoy rights that are, to large extent, similar to the freedom of movement rights guaranteed by EU primary and secondary law (notably, Directive 2004/38/EC).[58] Protected EU citizens enjoy these rights "for their lifetime" (Article 39 WA), assuming they continue to reside in the UK.[59]

In other words, the Withdrawal Agreement creates two categories of EU citizens: protected EU citizens, who moved to the UK before the end of the transition period (and who can enjoy free movement rights in the UK for the duration of their lives) and other EU citizens (who do not enjoy free movement in the UK after the transition period). Protected EU citizens may enjoy several rights after the end of the transition period, including:[60] (*i*) The right to *enter* and *exit* the UK with a valid passport "or national identity card";[61] the UK cannot impose on protected EU citizens "exit visa, entry visa or equivalent formality" (Article 14(1) and (2) WA).[62] (*ii*) The right to *reside* in the UK, under conditions similar to those imposed by EU law for the exercise of the right to residence in EU member states (Article 13 WA).[63] (*iii*) The right to *permanent residence*, under the conditions set out in EU law for permanent residence in EU member states (Article 15 WA).[64] The UK may not impose any additional limitations or conditions for obtaining, retaining or losing residence rights

[57] For instance, Farage's campaign included a poster showing "a queue of migrants, mostly men and brown-skinned", with the slogan "Breaking Point: the EU has failed us all", Evolvi 2018, p. 4; see also Pitcher 2019, pp. 2491–2492.

[58] See, in particular, UK WA, above n. 17, articles 10(1)(a), (c) and (e). On the notion of EU citizens and their family members, see Article 2 of Directive 2004/38, OJ 2004 L 158/77.

[59] Under the UK WA, the right of permanent residence is lost only through absence from the host State for a period exceeding 5 consecutive years (whereas under EU law the period is 2 years), see UK WA, above n. 17, article 15(3); see further Dougan 2020, pp. 32–33.

[60] This list of rights of EU citizens in the UK after Brexit is non-exhaustive; see, for instance, the right to equal treatment in the UK WA, above n. 17, article 23; see further Mariani 2019, p. 664; Piernas López 2019, pp. 287–289; Dougan 2020, pp. 30–31.

[61] Cf. Article 4 and 5 of Directive 2004/38/EC, cit. It is worth noting that the UK may decide no longer to accept identity cards five years after the end of the transition period, but only if they do not include a chip complying with the applicable International Civil Aviation Organisation standards, see UK WA, above n. 17, article 14(1).

[62] Cf. Article 4(2) and 5(1) of Directive 2004/38/EC, cit.

[63] UK WA, above n. 17, article 13.

[64] See, however, n. 59.

other than those provided for in the Withdrawal Agreement and "there shall be no discretion in applying the limitations and conditions provided for in the Agreement, other than in favour of the person concerned" (Article 13(4) WA).

The Withdrawal Agreement introduces two main limitations to the freedom of movement of protected EU citizens.[65] In the first place, the Withdrawal Agreement widens the scope of the public policy exception to freedom of movement. Under EU Law, an EU citizen who exercised his/her right to freedom of movement may be regarded as posing a threat to public policy only if his/her individual conduct represents a "genuine, present and sufficiently serious threat affecting one of the fundamental interests of the society of the Member State concerned".[66] Under the WA, the UK may exercise wider discretion: the conduct of protected EU citizens occurred after the end of the transition period may constitute grounds for restricting their right of entry (for frontier workers) and residence (for other EU citizens) "in accordance with national legislation".[67] UK parliament and courts may, therefore, adopt a broader understanding of "public security" than the EU legislature and judiciary, and consequently introduce greater restrictions to the right to entry, exit, and residence.[68]

Secondly, and most importantly, the Withdrawal Agreement introduces new procedural obligations for EU citizens. Union citizens do not require a permit to exercise their rights to freedom of movement in the Union but EU citizens residing in the UK may be required to apply for a new residence status which "confers the rights" to freedom of movement (Article 18(1) WA). The UK has indeed introduced the obligation to apply for a residence permit ("EU Settlement Scheme"). In principle, this procedural obligation should not constitute an unassailable obstacle. The Withdrawal Agreement expressly stipulates that EU citizens have "a right to be granted the residence status" if they comply with the conditions set in the Agreement—in particular, if they moved to the UK before the end of the transition period (Article 18(1)(a) WA).[69] Applications must be "smooth, transparent and simple" and the document evidencing the residence status must be issued free of charge (or for a charge not exceeding that imposed on UK citizens for the issuing of similar documents) (Article

[65] The list of limitations is not exhaustive. For instance, the range of family members entitled to rights by association with a protected EU citizen is reduced, see Dougan 2020, p. 33. Moreover, procedural safeguards in case of removal seem reduced, see UK WA, above n. 17, article 20(4) and Peers 2019.

[66] Court of Justice, *G.S. and V.G.*, Judgment, 12 December 2019, Joined Cases C-381/18 and C-382/18, EU:C:2019:1072, para 53; Court of Justice, *Orfanopoulos and Oliveri*, Judgments, 29 April 2004, Joined cases C-482/01 and C-493/01, EU:C:2004:262, paras 66 and 67; Court of Justice, *Coman and Others*, Judgement, 05 June 2018C-673/16, EU:C:2018:385, para 44; see also Article 27(2) of Directive 2004/38/EC, cit.

[67] UK WA, above n. 17, article 20(2).

[68] See also Piernas López 2019, p. 284.

[69] The UK might also require EU citizens to comply with the conditions for enjoying the right to residence under EU law, e.g. being workers or having sufficient resources and sickness insurance, see Article 7(1)(a) and (b) of directive 2004/38; see further Smismans 2018, p. 448; Dougan 2020, p. 31.

18(1)(e), and (g) WA).[70] The deadline for submitting the application is not too strict, as it must not be less than 6 months from the end of the transition period (Article 18(1)(b) WA).[71]

However, some commentators expressed concerns about the application of the EU Settlement Scheme in practice: for instance, EU citizens may allegedly face problems with evidence required for the Settlement Scheme application, since they may lack the means to prove their stay in the UK or may not be properly informed about the need to apply for a residence document.[72] The potential misapplication of the WA in this area is very problematic: if an EU citizen failed to obtain the residence status in the immediate aftermath of the transition period, he/she probably would be unable to secure his/her rights afterwards.[73] The "hostile environment" for migration created by the UK Home Office does not ease the concerns regarding the application of the Withdrawal Agreement.[74]

To avert the risk of misapplication of EU law during the transition period, the WA introduces two institutional solutions. On the one hand, the creation of an "authority", which may receive complaints from EU citizens in the UK and has the right to bring legal action before an UK court (Article 159 WA).[75] On the other hand, the extension of the Court of Justice's jurisdiction to give preliminary rulings concerning EU citizens' rights, which is discussed below, in Sect. 11.5.

The rules on the free movement of EU citizens in the Withdrawal Agreement suggest that, with respect to EU citizens entering the UK *after* the transitional period, the UK's position has indeed changed. But the UK's obligations vis-à-vis EU citizens exercising their movement rights *before* the end of the transitional period are to a large extent unmodified. And these rights must be interpreted and applied consistently with the principles of EU law, such as direct effect and primacy (see above, Sect. 11.2). The Withdrawal Agreement thus injects in the UK legal order parts of EU citizenship law. A similar injection occurs with respect to other EU rules applicable to individuals, concerning freedom of movement of goods.

11.4 Free Movement of Goods to and from the UK

Internal market arguably constitutes, together with citizenship law, the main body of EU norms applicable to individuals and, as such, characterises EU membership. Freedom of movement of goods and the customs union may be seen as the core of the internal market. Some third states apply EU rules (or rules modelled on EU

[70] See also, in particular, UK WA, above n. 17, articles 18(1)(f), (j), (k) and (l).

[71] Ibid., article 18(1).

[72] Smismans 2018, p. 449; Benson et al. 2019.

[73] See however UK WA, above n. 17, article 18(1).

[74] Smismans 2018, pp. 444–445, 450; Benson et al. 2019; Dougan 2020, pp. 29–30.

[75] The Joint Committee may abolish the authority eight years after the end of the transition period, see UK WA, above n. 17, article 159.

law): for instance, EFTA states apply EU internal market law, while the EU-Turkey Association Agreement ensures freedom of movement of goods and establishes a customs union.[76]

Neither the EEA nor the Turkey model were acceptable for the UK, which sought to restore its regulatory autonomy and conduct its own policy on international trade. At the same time, the UK's exit from the EU's customs union could not be complete, as it might have determined the re-establishment of border checks between the Republic of Ireland (i.e. the EU) and Northern Ireland (the UK).[77] To solve this conundrum, the May government and the Union negotiated a complex solution, known as "backstop" and contained principally in a Protocol on Ireland/Northern Ireland.[78] During the transition period, EU law would have applied in the UK. Had the UK and the EU failed to conclude a Future Relationship agreement before the end of the transition period, the entire UK would have aligned with the EU customs union; furthermore, the UK would have committed to respect EU-equivalent standards in several areas, such as labour or environmental law (the so-called "Level Playing Field").[79]

The Johnson government re-negotiated the NI Protocol. The new NI Protocol, which was approved by both Parties as part of the Withdrawal Agreement, confirms the applicability of substantive EU law provisions in the UK during the transition period.[80] After the transition period the UK ceases to be part of the EU's single market for goods and customs union.[81] The UK can also define its own regulatory standards, as the new NI Protocol no longer refers to the Level Playing Field.[82]

However, Northern Ireland is subject to special rules. It becomes "part of the customs territory of the United Kingdom" (Article 4(1) of the NI Protocol)[83] but remains closely aligned with EU law regarding the movement of goods. By virtue of the NI Protocol, most primary and secondary EU law rules on the movement of goods are applied in Northern Ireland after the end of the transition period. This is the case, for instance, of the prohibition of customs duties, discriminatory taxation, and quantitative restrictions in respect of trade between the Union and Northern Ireland (Article 5(5) NI Protocol). The NI Protocol also requires the application in Northern Ireland of the numerous EU acts regarding the customs union, including the Customs Code (Article 5(4) NI Protocol and Annex II to the Protocol). EU State aid law also

---

[76] Decision No 1/95 of the EC-Turkey Association Council of 22 December 1995 on implementing the final phase of the Customs Union, OJ 1996 L35/1.

[77] See further Harvey and Kramer 2018, pp. 68–69.

[78] See further on the "backstop" Ares et al. 2019, pp. 105–114.

[79] Ibid., pp. 108–111, 116–122.

[80] See above, n. 21.

[81] See NI Protocol, above n. 49, articles 4 and 5.

[82] The only reference to this concept is found in the Political Declaration, which is a political commitment that does not significantly affect the UK's legal position, see Political Declaration, cit., para 77.

[83] The UK, therefore, can include Northern Ireland in the territorial scope of trade agreements with other countries (provided that those agreements do not prejudice the application of the NI Protocol); see NI Protocol, above n. 49, articles 4(2)(3) and (4).

applies to the entire UK in respect of measures that affect trade between Northern Ireland and the EU (Article 10(1) NI Protocol).[84]

Whereas EU law provisions referred to in the WA are generally intended as the provisions applicable "on the last day of the transition period",[85] the references contained in the NI Protocol refer to the act "as amended or replaced" (Article 13(3) NI Protocol). Moreover, while UK judges should generally have "due regard" to the case law of the Court Justice handed down after the end of the transition period,[86] they should always rule "in conformity" with the case law of the Court relating to provisions referred to in the NI Protocol, including post-transition case law (Article 13(2) NI Protocol).

Northern Ireland seems more integrated in the Union than EFTA states, since the EFTA Court is bound only by the pre-EEA case law of the Court of Justice, at least in principle (see above, Sect. 11.2). The position of Northern Ireland comes close to that of Turkey: EU rules on freedom of movement of goods and the customs union applicable to Turkey must be interpreted "in conformity with the relevant decisions of the Court of Justice",[87] including decisions issued after the signature of the EU-Turkey Association Agreement.[88]

The NI Protocol goes even beyond any association agreement, by enabling EU "institutions, bodies, offices, and agencies" to exercise their powers regarding the implementation of the key norms applicable to Northern Ireland, notably with regard to free movement of goods[89] (Article 12(4) NI Protocol). The Court of Justice has the competence provided for in the Treaties in this respect and may receive preliminary references from British courts regarding the application of EU rules made applicable by the NI Protocol in respect of Northern Ireland (see further below, Sect. 11.5). In addition, Union organs may supervise British authorities. Union representatives have a right to be present during any activities of UK authorities relating to the implementation of provisions of Union law made applicable by the NI Protocol (e.g. the Customs Code); they also have a right to receive "all relevant information" relating to such activities. Union representatives may even request British authorities to perform control measures in individual cases (e.g. on a certain good imported in Northern Ireland) and the latter must comply with the request (Article 12(2) NI Protocol).

In other words, while Great Britain exits the EU's customs union and single market for goods both *de jure* and *de facto,* Northern Ireland remains, to a large extent, within them—even more so than other third countries. There are, at any rate, three major differences between Northern Ireland and EU member states from the perspective of free movement of goods.

[84] Ibid., Annex 5 to the NI Protocol.

[85] UK WA, above n. 17, article 6(1), see above, Sect. 11.2.

[86] Ibid., article 4(5); see above, Sect. 11.2.

[87] Ibid., article 66.

[88] See, to this effect, Ott 2015, p. 22.

[89] *Rectius,* EU organs exercise their powers in respect of article 5, articles 7–10 and article 12(2)(2) NI Protocol.

In the first place, the UK applies in Northern Ireland only certain provisions of EU primary law, as well as the pieces of secondary law listed in Annex II to the NI Protocol, as amended or replaced. If the EU adopts a new piece of law, the UK-EU Joint Committee can either add it to an Annex to the Protocol or "examine all further possibilities" to ensure the functioning of the Protocol (Article 13(4) NI). This procedure is reminiscent of the adaptation of EEA law to EU law (see above, Sect. 11.2). As the Joint Committee decides by mutual consent of the UK and the EU,[90] it might not manage to adopt a decision "within a reasonable time"; in that case, the EU can adopt "appropriate remedial measures" (Article 14(4) NI Protocol). The vagueness of these rules might foster disputes between the parties. For instance, the Protocol does not specify to what extent amending (or replacing) EU acts may contain new elements compared to the amended (or replaced) act. Should the Union include "new" provisions in an amending act, the UK may bring the issue to the arbitration panel, which would have to decide whether an EU provision "amends" a previous EU act or is indeed "new".[91]

Secondly, the NI Protocol apparently enables some restrictions to the trade in goods between Northern Ireland and the EU. Article 5(5) of the Protocol stipulates that Article 30 TFEU (prohibition of customs duties and charges having equivalent effect) and Article 110 TFEU (prohibition of discriminatory taxation) apply in respect of Northern Ireland. Then, it affirms that "quantitative restrictions on exports and imports" are prohibited but mentions neither "measures having equivalent effect" nor Article 34 TFEU (prohibiting both quantitative restrictions and measures having equivalent effect). This formulation of the NI Protocol seems the product of a deliberate choice of the parties: the Draft Protocol on Ireland prepared by the European Commission in early 2018 mentioned both quantitative restrictions and "measures having equivalent effect", but the latter were excluded from the NI Protocol.[92] The NI Protocol implicitly refers to equivalent measures only in Article 7(1), by stipulating that "the lawfulness of placing goods on the market in Northern Ireland shall be governed by the law of the United Kingdom as well as, as regards goods imported from the Union, by Articles 34 and 36 TFEU". This arguably means that only *certain* measures having equivalent effect are prohibited (those regarding the placing of goods on the market), while others, such as inspections at the frontier[93] or "buy national" campaigns,[94] seem compatible with the NI Protocol.[95]

---

[90] UK WA, above n. 17, article 166(3).

[91] As this question deals with the interpretation of EU law, it should be settled after a preliminary reference to the Court of Justice (see below, Sect. 11.5).

[92] European Commission Draft Withdrawal Agreement on the withdrawal of the United Kingdom of Great Britain and Northern Ireland from the European Union and the European Atomic Energy Community, 28 February 2018, TF50 (2018) 33, article 4(4).

[93] See e.g. Court of Justice, *Rewe-Zentralfinanz eGmbH*, Judgment, 8 July 1975, Case 4-75, EU:C:1975:98.

[94] See e.g. Court of Justice, *Commission v Ireland*, Judgment, 24 November 1982, Case 249/81, EU:C:1982:402.

[95] It cannot be excluded that the UK intended to be set free, in particular, from the (wavering) case law of the CJEU on selling arrangements, see e.g. *Keck*, Judgment, 24 November 1993, Case C-267/91,

Thirdly, Northern Ireland is in two markets at the same time—the UK market *de jure* and the EU market *de facto*—and this may create frictions between the Parties. As the EU and UK markets are likely to have different rules, in terms of custom duties and standards for products, there must be some restrictions to trade, either between the EU and Northern Ireland, or between this region and the rest of the UK. It may seem, at first sight, that trade between Northern Ireland and the rest of the UK should generally be free, with restrictions being an exception. Article 5(1) NI Protocol indeed stipulates that "no customs duties shall be payable for a good brought into Northern Ireland from another part of the United Kingdom by direct transport [...] *unless* that good is at risk of subsequently being moved into the Union".[96] However, restrictions to intra-UK trade are likely to be the rule. Article 5(2) NI Protocol affirms that any good brought into Northern Ireland from outside the EU is "at risk of subsequently being moved into the Union", unless it is established that it will not be subject to commercial processing in Northern Ireland and it fulfils additional criteria established by the Joint Committee. This suggests that custom duties are likely to apply to several goods exported from Great Britain to Northern Ireland.[97] Moreover, exports from Great Britain to Northern Ireland may be subject to custom and regulatory checks (e.g. sanitary checks on live animals). Such checks will be performed by British authorities, but EU authorities will supervise them (see above). These intricate arrangements are likely to create conflicts between EU and British authorities: for instance, the UK government claims that checks on trade between Great Britain and Northern Ireland are not necessary.[98]

The norms regulating free movement of goods may be integrated or modified by the Future Relationship agreement and subsequent decisions of the Joint Committee. The Future Relationship agreement is expected to define, in particular, the legal regime applicable to trade between the EU and Great Britain (i.e. UK minus Northern Ireland).[99] Moreover, starting four years after the end of the transition period, the Northern Ireland Assembly will be given the possibility to decide whether to continue the application of the EU rules of freedom of movement of goods contained in the NI Protocol (Article 18 NI Protocol). In any event, the NI Protocol arguably provides for a sufficiently stable legal framework, which enables some preliminary conclusions regarding the UK's legal status in terms of free movement of goods.

The UK is treated *de facto* as a member state throughout the transition period but, after that, it becomes truly a third country, capable of defining its internal regulatory standards and its external trade policy. Nonetheless, the exit from the Union brings about two shortcomings, from the UK viewpoint. On the one hand, the so-called "Irish

EU:C:1993:905; *Commission v. Italy,* Judgment, 10 February 2009, Case C-110/05, EU:C:2009:66; *Scotch Whisky Association*, Judgment, 23 December 2015, Case C-333/14, EU:C:2015:845. I thank Giacomo Di Federico for pointing this out.

[96] Emphasis added.

[97] The Joint Committee and the UK government may, to a certain extent, ease the burden for exporters, see NI Protocol, above n. 49, articles 5(6) and 10, as well as Annex 5.

[98] O'Carroll 2019.

[99] See further Neframi 2019, pp. 226–227.

sea border" between Great Britain and Northern Ireland. It is curious that, whereas the Union is bound to respect the "territorial integrity" of its member states (Article 4(2) TEU), the first withdrawal from the Union should lead to the creation of a *de facto* customs border within the withdrawing state. On the other hand, the persisting application of parts of EU law—past, present, and future—in the UK. Whereas the UK has little to no influence on the activity of EU institutions (see below, Sect. 11.6), EU organs can adopt, implement and enforce legislation applying in the UK, albeit only in respect of EU trade with Northern Ireland.[100] The persisting jurisdiction of the Court of Justice, discussed further below, is the most striking example in this sense.

11.5 Jurisdiction of the Court of Justice on Acts Applicable to and in the UK

Being part of the EU's judicial system and being subject to the jurisdiction of the Court of Justice is a key element of the membership of the Union. As repeatedly affirmed by the Court of Justice, EU Treaties have established a judicial system intended to ensure consistency and uniformity in the interpretation of EU law.[101] It is for the "national courts and tribunals *and the Court of Justice*" to ensure the full application of EU law in all member states.[102] The preliminary ruling procedure, which sets up a dialogue between the Court of Justice and the courts and tribunals of the Member States, constitutes the keystone of this judicial system.[103]

In the Brexit debate, the Court of Justice was often presented as a pro-integration court, prone to overstep its mandate, and whose jurisdiction in the UK had to be terminated. The government of Theresa May embraced this approach, by affirming that "We will bring an end to the jurisdiction of the [Court of Justice] in the UK".[104] This result was achieved through the WA, though not completely. The Court of Justice maintains its jurisdiction virtually untouched throughout the transition period. For example, the Commission can bring infringement proceedings against the UK and British judges can issue preliminary references until the end of the transition period.[105]

---

[100] Cf. UK House of Lords, EU Committee 2020, para 168.

[101] *Achmea,* above n. 8, para 35; Opinion 2/13 *(Accession to the ECHR),* above n 8, para 174; see also TEU, above n. 3, article 19.

[102] *Achmea,* above n. 8, para 36, emphasis added; Opinion 1/09 *(Patent Court),* above n. 26, paras 68–69; Court of Justice, *Associação Sindical dos Juízes Portugueses,* Judgment, 27 February 2018, Case C-64/16, EU:C:2018:117, para 33.

[103] Achmea, above n. 8, para 37; see also, *inter alia,* Opinion 2/13 *(Accession to the ECHR),* above n. 8, para 176.

[104] UK Government 2017b, paras 2.2–2.3.

[105] Moreover, the Court will maintain its jurisdiction, after the transition period, on proceedings brought by or against the United Kingdom and requests from UK tribunals made before the end of the transition period, see UK WA, above n. 17, article 86.

After the transition, the Court of Justice will play a role in several areas. In some fields, the Court's post-transition powers are limited in time. The Court has jurisdiction on infringement and state aid proceedings brought by the Commission against the UK "within 4 years" after the end of the transition period, provided that the UK has failed to fulfil one of its obligations under EU Treaties or under Part Four of the Withdrawal Agreement (relating to the transition) before the end of the transition period (Article 87 WA).

Moreover, the Court of Justice has time-bound jurisdiction on preliminary references regarding free movement of citizens. Any court or tribunal in the UK may, in a case which "commenced at first instance within 8 years from the end of the transition period", request the Court of Justice to give a preliminary ruling concerning the interpretation of Part Two of the Withdrawal Agreement, which concerns citizens' rights (Article 158 WA).[106] The judgments of the Court of Justice have the same effects as preliminary rulings under Article 267 TFEU. The Court's time-bound jurisdiction in this field probably is aimed at ensuring the correct application of EU citizenship law in respect of the issuance of residence documents. As noted above (Sect. 11.3), the EU citizens that do not obtain residence documents after the transition period risk losing their free movement rights in the UK forever. The Court may provide UK judges with guidance about crucial questions such as the definition of "EU citizen" or "residence in the host state",[107] or the prohibition for UK authorities to exercise "discretion in applying the limitations" to residence rights.[108] This solution is satisfactory in principle, but there is the risk that British judges might fail to formulate preliminary questions, especially because they (including last instance judges) "may", but are not required to, do so.

In other areas, the powers of the Court of Justice have indefinite duration. This is the case of the Protocol relating to the Sovereign Base Areas in Cyprus[109] and the infringement proceedings and preliminary references relating to certain UK financial obligations to the Union (e.g. the contribution to Union programmes committed under the Multiannual Financial Framework 2014–2020).[110]

The jurisdiction of the Court has indefinite duration also in respect of the implementation of the NI Protocol. As noted above (Sect. 11.4), the NI Protocol enables EU "institutions, bodies, offices, and agencies" to exercise their powers concerning the application of EU rules (mostly, on free movement of goods and the customs union) in relation to the UK and persons resident or established in the UK. The Court of Justice, in particular, has "the jurisdiction provided for in the Treaties in this respect. The second and third paragraphs of Article 267 TFEU shall apply to and in the United Kingdom in this respect" (Article 12(4) NI Protocol). Like the acts

[106] Ibid., article 158(2), which provides for a partial exception to this rule in case of residence applications made during the transition period.

[107] Ibid., articles 108(1)(a) and (f).

[108] Ibid., article 13(4).

[109] See Protocol No 3 on the Sovereign Base Areas of the United Kingdom of Great Britain and Northern Ireland in Cyprus of 23 September 2003, OJ L236, article 12(1).

[110] UK WA, above n. 17, article 160.

of other "institutions, bodies, offices, and agencies", the judgments of the Court of Justice produce with regard to and in the United Kingdom the same legal effects as those which they produce within the Union and its Member States (Article 12(5) NI Protocol). By affirming that the Court of Justice has "the jurisdiction provided for in the Treaties" in respect of the application of certain EU rules, the NI Protocol arguably suggests that all judicial procedures may be applicable in this area. For instance, the Commission may bring infringement proceedings against the UK. Preliminary references, at any rate, are likely to be more common. By referring to the "second and third paragraphs of Article 267 TFEU", the NI Protocol makes applicable the general preliminary reference procedure to freedom of movement of goods and customs union in Northern Ireland. Therefore, a UK judge "may" request the Court of Justice to give a ruling (second subparagraph of Article 267 TFEU) and judges of last instance "shall bring the matter before the Court" (third subparagraph).

Finally, the Court's competence has indefinite duration in respect of *sui generis* preliminary references regarding the settlement of disputes between the Contracting Parties. The UK and EU soon agreed that the WA requires some form of dispute settlement, which may be problematic under EU law.[111] Given the numerous references to EU law in the Withdrawal Agreement, it is likely that a dispute may raise a question of interpretation of a concept of Union law. Under the case law of the Court of Justice, dispute settlement procedures cannot bind the Union to a particular interpretation of EU rules;[112] probably, international tribunals and arbitrators cannot even "interpret" rules of EU law.[113] Some association agreements bypass this problem, by stipulating that arbitration panels established under those agreements "shall not give an interpretation of the *acquis communautaire*".[114] The Association Agreements with Ukraine, Moldova and Georgia go a step further, by affirming that, if a dispute raises a question of interpretation of one of the several provisions of EU law made applicable by the agreements, the arbitration panel shall not decide the question, but "request the Court of Justice of the European Union to give a ruling on the question".[115] The ruling is binding on the panel.[116] The Withdrawal Agreement followed the example set by these Association Agreements. In case of a dispute regarding the

[111]To be sure, the starting positions of the Contracting parties diverged considerably on a number of key points, see Odermatt 2018, p. 300.

[112]Cf. Court of Justice, *Draft Agreement between the European Community and non-Member States on the establishment of a European Common Aviation Area (ECAA)*, Opinion of 18 April 2002, Opinion 1/00, ECLI:EU:C:2002:231, para 13; Opinion 2/13 *(Accession to the ECHR)*, above n. 8, para 184.

[113]Opinion 1/17 *(CETA)*, above n. 9, para 120; *Achmea*, above n. 8, para 39.

[114]E.g. Stabilisation and Association Agreement between the European Communities and their Member States, of the one part, and Bosnia and Herzegovina, of the other part, opened for signature 16 June 2008, OJ L164/2 (entered into force 1 June 2015), Protocol 7, article 13.

[115]E.g. Association Agreement between the European Union and its Member States, of the one part, and Ukraine, of the other part, opened for signature 21 March 2014, OJ L 161/3–2137 (entered into force 1 September 2017) (EU-Ukraine AA), article 322; see further Van Elsuwege and Chamon 2019, p. 46. The EEA Agreement contains a comparable, but not identical, mechanism, see EEA Agreement, above n. 10, article 111(3); see further Baur et al. 2018, pp. 168–169.

[116]See further Van der Loo 2016, pp. 296–300.

interpretation and application of the provisions of the WA and its Protocols, the UK and the EU may enter in consultation and, eventually, each of the parties may demand the establishment of an arbitration panel, whose ruling is binding (Article 170 and 175 WA).[117] If a dispute raises a question of interpretation of EU law, the panel must request the Court of Justice to give a ruling to the question, which is binding on the panel (Article 174 WA).[118]

The *sui generis* preliminary ruling procedure in the dispute settlement mechanism, the Court's preliminary jurisdiction regarding citizens' rights (for a limited time) and free movement of goods (concerning a limited area), combined with the British court's duty to take into account the case law of the Court of justice (see above, in Sect. 11.2), should contribute to foster a consistent application of EU law in and to the UK. The effectiveness of most of these mechanisms, however, depends on the cooperation of British courts, which should conduct a dialogue with the Court of Justice as if they were courts of a member state—despite being the courts of a third state. At a time when even the Constitutional Court of a member state disregards a judgment of the Court of Justice, labelling it as "simply not comprehensible",[119] the cooperation of the courts of a third countries can hardly be taken for granted.

11.6 UK Participation in EU Institutions, Bodies, Offices, or Agencies

EU member states participate, not only in the judicial system of the Union, but also in its institutional machinery. The "establishment of institutions endowed with sovereign rights, the exercise of which affects Member States and also their citizens" has always been a defining feature of the European Union.[120] The member states participate directly in these institutions (e.g. the Council) or contribute to their nomination or election (e.g. the Commission).[121] The right to participate in EU institutions, bodies, offices or agencies (hereafter, collectively, EU organs) may be seen as complementary to the obligation to apply Union law, discussed in the previous sections. Under the WA, however, the UK's participation in the work of EU organs is not symmetrical to its obligations to apply EU law.

---

[117] See also UK WA, above n. 17, article 182. One may note that, since the arbitrators cannot be "members, officials or other servants of the Union institutions", the members of the Court of Justice cannot be part of the panel (article 171(2)).

[118] Cf. Court of Justice, *Draft Agreement relating to the creation of the European Economic Area*, Opinion of 14 December 1991, Opinion 1/91, ECLI:EU:C:1991:490, para 61.

[119] German Constitutional Court, Judgment of the Second Senate of 5 May 2020, 2 BvR 859/15, para 118.

[120] *Van Gend en Loos*, above n. 7; see also *Costa* v *Enel,* above n. 24. More generally, participation in the institutional structure of international organisations is one of the constant elements of the status of member states, see Pustorino 2012, p. 176.

[121] See further Dony 2018, pp. 299–313.

Third states are generally excluded from the activity of EU organs.[122] The Union is, in this respect, different from most other international organisations, that grant some form of observer status to non-member states.[123] The exclusion of third states from EU organs is arguably a corollary of the EU's autonomy, which requires that "the essential character of the powers of the [Union] and its institutions as conceived in the Treaty remain unaltered".[124] The autonomy of EU law indeed presupposes "the capacity of the Union to operate autonomously within its unique constitutional framework".[125]

Nonetheless, certain third states have some relationships with EU organs. EFTA states, in particular, have a right to be consulted by the Commission regarding the proposal of new legislation in a EEA-related field, but their views are not binding; similarly, the experts of EFTA states participate in comitology committees, but they do not have the right to vote.[126] More generally, third states may participate in some EU agencies but do not have voting rights.[127]

Third states may also set up joint organs under international agreements together with EU institutions but this should not result in an alteration of the "essential character" of the powers of EU organs, which should remain clearly separate "from an institutional point of view".[128] Several agreements create international bodies where the Union is represented separately from third States. For instance, the EEA Joint Committee (composed of representatives of the Union and EFTA states) facilitates exchange of information, adopts decisions (especially in respect of the incorporation of EU acts in the EEA agreement) and may settle disputes between the Union and EFTA states.[129]

In institutional terms, the status of the UK does not differ significantly from the position of other third states. The Withdrawal agreement sets up a Joint UK-EU Committee that supervises the implementation of the agreement and is similar to the EEA Joint Committee.[130]

---

[122] One may note that non-EU EEA member states are consulted during the EU decision-making process relating to acts relevant for the EEA, but their opinion is not binding on the Union, Lourenço 2019, p. 535.

[123] Schermers and Blokker 2011, para 173ff.

[124] Opinion 1/00 *(ECAA)*, above n. 112, para 12; see also Opinion 1/91 *(EEA)*, above n. 118, paras 61–65; Court of Justice, *Draft agreement between the Community, on the one hand, and the countries of the European Free Trade Association, on the other, relating to the creation of the European Economic Area,* Opinion of 10 April 1992, Opinion 1/92, ECLI:EU:C:1992:189 paras 32 and 41. See also Guillard 2014, p. 458.

[125] Opinion 1/17 *(CETA)*, above n. 9, para 150.

[126] EEA Agreement, above n. 10, articles 99(1) and 100. See further Baur et al. 2018, pp. 119–124; Lourenco 2019, p. 535.

[127] Tovo 2016, pp. 72–83; Chamon 2019, pp. 1517 and 1522; Bekkedal 2019.

[128] Opinion 1/00 *(ECAA)*, above n. 112, paras 6–22.

[129] Baur et al. 2018, pp. 94–95; see also, e.g., the Association Council established by the EU-Ukraine AA, above n. 115, articles 460–463.

[130] UK WA, above n. 17, articles 164–166. See, to that effect, EU Law Analysis 2019, para 127. See also the Specialised Committee overseeing the implementation of the Protocol on Northern Ireland, Protocol on NI, above n. 49, article 14.

Furthermore, the WA prevents the UK from participating in EU organs since the day of its withdrawal from the Union, including the transition period. In its guidelines on the Brexit negotiations (December 2017), the European Council stated that "the United Kingdom, as a third country, will no longer participate in or nominate or elect members of the EU institutions".[131] The UK government had similar priorities, since it sought to extricate itself from the EU machinery even *before* the transition: the UK did not take up the rotating presidency of the Council in 2017 and refused to propose a British member of the European Commission in 2019.[132] The WA reflects the intention to separate the UK from the EU as soon as withdrawal takes place, by stipulating, e.g., that the UK loses the ability to introduce legislative proposals and its parliament may not be considered as a parliament of a member state for the purpose of subsidiarity control during the transition period.[133]

The WA introduces only minor limitations to the UK's exclusion from EU organs during the transition period. Although the British Parliament does not have the right to exercise any subsidiarity control under Protocol 1, it has the right to receive the legislative proposals introduced by the Commission.[134] Moreover, British representatives *may* be invited by EU institutions to take part in comitology meetings and international bodies where the EU is represented.[135] The UK's involvement in EU organs during the transition period is even weaker than that of non-EU EEA member states, which at least have a *right* to be consulted at the stages of initiative and implementation, concerning EEA-related areas (see above).

The almost complete exclusion of the UK from EU organs during the transition period, albeit consistent with the established approach of the EU vis-à-vis third states, is remarkable, as the position of the UK during this period is unusually similar to that of a member state (see above, in Sect. 11.2). In other words, the UK's integration in the EU's institutional structure seems to be at its lowest during the transition period (when the UK is subject to almost all the obligations applicable to EU member states) but, paradoxically, might possibly grow *after* the transition period (when EU obligations for the UK are likely to be fewer).

In fact, the WA does not regulate the UK's involvement in EU organs after the transition period; this issue is touched upon in the Political Declaration and will presumably be addressed by the Future Relationship agreement or other UK-EU agreements. The Political Declaration expresses the intention of the parties to establish, after the transition, a dialogue or cooperation on various subjects, such as emerging technologies, nuclear safety,[136] healthcare, and police.[137] The expectation of cooperation seems particularly high in respect of foreign policy, security and defence. Among others, the Declaration mentions, the adoption of "agreed statements, demarches and

[131] European Council (Article 50) Meeting, 15 December 2017, Guidelines, EUCO XT 20011/17.

[132] See EC Europa 2019.

[133] UK WA, above n. 17, articles 128(2) and (3); see also articles 128 (4) and 129(7).

[134] Ibid., article 128(2).

[135] Ibid., article 128(2)(b) and 129(2); see also article 129(5).

[136] Political Declaration, paras 40 and 66.

[137] Ibid., paras 23, 40, and 66. See also paras 45, 49, 63, 65, 83, 86, 88.

shared positions", "exchange of information on listings" for sanctions, and "early consultation" in the area of defence to facilitate the UK's participation in CSDP missions.[138] It cannot be excluded that, in the long run, the UK's integration in the EU's institutions might be strongest in the area—CFSP—where European integration is weakest.

11.7 Conclusion

The UK government apparently envisaged a clean break from the Union: "Leaving the European Union will mean that our laws will be made in Westminster, Edinburgh, Cardiff and Belfast. And those laws will be interpreted by judges not in Luxembourg but in courts across this country".[139] After the conclusion of the Withdrawal Agreement the legal position of the UK seems more complicated.

Throughout the transition period, the UK is many respects indistinguishable from a member state—though it does not participate in EU institutions and organs. After the transition period, the UK remains outside the EU institutional framework but must apply core EU rules and principles in respect of specific persons or areas. Northern Ireland, in particular, remains *de facto* in the EU's customs union. And some EU citizens—who settled in the UK before the end of the transition period—can exercise their free movement rights in the UK.

These rules are likely to be applied to and in the UK for a long time: for the duration of protected EU citizens' lives and even indefinitely, in the case of free movement of goods in Northern Ireland. Not only is the UK bound by EU rules but must apply and interpret them in light of EU principles, including those defining the Union and distinguishing it from other international organisations, such as direct effect and primacy. The UK also remains, in several respects, subject to the control of EU institutions, particularly the Court of Justice. In a way, EU citizens and goods entering the UK may bring with them into the British system parts of the EU's legal order, including rules, principles, and judicial procedures.

Therefore, the status of the UK under the Withdrawal Agreement is ambiguous. Several aspects of the UK's position are a *déjà vu*, as they echo agreements between the Union and other third countries. For instance, the EEA Agreement inspires the WA rules on the relationship with the case law of the Court of Justice, while the *sui generis* preliminary references in the context of dispute settlement are probably modelled on recent Association Agreements (see Sects. 11.2 and 11.6). It is perhaps ironic that the Withdrawal Agreement, a "disintegration-oriented" instrument, should be similar to "integration-oriented agreements" such as Association Agreements.[140]

The similitudes with past experiences are accompanied by elements of novelty, which complicate the framework: under the WA, *certain* EU rules concerning *certain*

---

[138] Ibid., para 93.

[139] UK Government 2017a.

[140] See above, n. 16.

topics apply in *certain* regions of the UK, to *certain* persons, and/or for a *certain* period. These apparently strange arrangements of the WA constitute a compromise between the UK's government intention to showcase a "clean break" from the Union and the practical necessity to protect the interests of citizens and economic actors, as well as the stability of Northern Ireland. Combining established solutions in original ways prevented a "hard" Brexit but gave the UK a uniquely multifaceted status as a "third country". The Future Relationship Agreement might possibly simplify the legal framework, but such a simplification cannot be taken for granted.

By withdrawing from the Union, the UK may have changed its status, but its legal position remains complex: as it was the least integrated member of the Union,[141] it is now a very integrated third state.

Acknowledgements I thank the editors who assisted me with my contribution, Marco Borraccetti, Federico Casolari, Giacomo Di Federico, Giulia Evolvi, Eleftheria Neframi, Pietro Manzini, and Carlo Tovo for their comments. All errors remain mine.

References

Abderamane K (2018) L'Ancrage de l'Engagement des États Membres dans l'Ordre Constitutionnel de l'Union : Les principes de Loyauté et de Solidarité [The Principles of Loyalty and Solidarity]. In: Potvin-Solis L (ed) Le statut d'état membre de l'Union européenne. Bruylant, Brussels, pp 205–256

Ares E et al (2019) The UK's EU Withdrawal Agreement. UK House of Commons https://commonslibrary.parliament.uk/research-briefings/cbp-8453/ Accessed 15 March 2020

Baudenbacher C (2016) The Relationship Between the EFTA Court and the Court of Justice of the European Union. In: Baudenbacher (ed) The Handbook of EEA Law. Springer, Heidelberg, pp 179–194

Baur G et al (2018) European Free Trade Association (EFTA) and the European Economic Area (EEA). Kluwer, Alphen aan den Rijn

Bekkedal T (2019) Third State Participation in EU Agencies: Exploring the EEA Precedent. CMLRev 56:381–416

Benson M et al (2019) Brexit's Effect on Citizens, Human Rights & Immigration. City Law School (CLS) Research Paper No. 2019/03, https://openaccess.city.ac.uk/id/eprint/22848/ Accessed 15 March 2020

Björgvinsson KB (2016) Free Movement of Persons. In: Baudenbacher C (ed) The Handbook of EEA Law. Springer, Heidelberg, pp 473–500

Bosse-Platière I, Rapoport C (2014) L'État Tiers Appréhendé par le Droit de l'Union Européenne [The Third State under EU Law]. In: Bosse-Platière I, Rapoport C (eds) L'État Tiers en Droit de l'Union Européenne [The Third State in EU Law]. Bruylant, Brussels, pp 9–40

Burchardt D (2019) The relationship between the Law of the European Union and the Law of its Member States - a Norm - Based Conceptual Framework. European Constitutional Law Review 15: 73–103

Casolari F (2019a) Il Recesso dall'Unione Europea: per una Lettura dell'art. 50 TUE tra Diritto Sovranazionale e Diritto Internazionale [Withdrawal from the European Union: A Reading of Art. 50 TEU between Supranational Law and International Law]. Rivista di Diritto Internazionale 102:1006–1039

[141] Poinsignon 2018, pp. 580–583.

Casolari F (2019b) EU Loyalty and the Protection of Member States' National Interests-A Mapping of the Law. In: Varju M (ed) Between Compliance and Particularism-Member State Interests and European Union Law. Springer, Heidelberg, pp 49–78
Chamon M (2019) A Constitutional Twilight Zone: EU Decentralized Agencies' External Relations. CMLRev 56:1509–1548
Constantinesco V (1987) L'article 5 CEE, de la Bonne Foi à la Loyauté Communautaire [Art. 5 EEC, from good Faith to Community Loyalty]. In: Capotorti F et al (eds) Du Droit International au Droit de l'Intégration: Liber Amicorum Pescatore. Nomos, Baden-Baden, pp 97–114
Constantinesco V (2001) The ECJ as Law-maker: Praeter aut Contra Legem? In O'Keeffe D, Bavasso A (eds) Judicial Review in European Law: Essays in Honour of Lord Slynn. Kluwer, Alphen aan den Rijn, pp 73–79
Dony M (2018) Statut d'État Membre et Participation à la Fonction Normative Européenne [Member State status and participation in the European Law-Making Function]. In: Potvin-Solis L (ed) Le statut d'État Membre de l'Union Européenne. Bruylant, Brussels, pp 281–314
Dougan M (2020) So Long, Farewell, Auf Wiedersehen, Goodbye: The UK's Withdrawal Package. Social Sciences Research Network, https://papers.ssrn.com/sol3/papers.cfm?abstract_id=3553407 Accessed 15 March 2020
EC Europa (2019) European Commission Launches Infringement Proceedings Against the UK Following its Failure to Name a Candidate for EU Commissioner. https://ec.europa.eu/commission/presscorner/detail/en/ip_19_6286
EU Law Analysis (2019) http://eulawanalysis.blogspot.com/2019/10/analysis-5-of-revised-brexit-withdrawal.html Accessed 3 July 2020
European Commission (2019) Revised Political Declaration setting out the Framework for the Future Relationship between the EU and the UK. https://ec.europa.eu/commission/publications/revised-political-declaration_en Accessed 15 March 2020
Evolvi G (2018) Hate in a Tweet: Exploring Internet-Based Islamophobic Discourses. Religions 9
Guillard C (2014) L'ex-Etat Membre de l'Union Européenne: un État tiers comme les autres ? [The Former Member State of the EU: A Third State like the Others?]. In Bosse-Platière I and Rapoport C (eds) L'État tiers en droit de l'Union européenne [The Third State in EU Law]. Bruylant, Brussels, pp 443–466
Harvey C, Kramer A (2018) Brexit and Ireland/Northern Ireland. In: Biondi A et al (eds) Brexit: the Legal Implications. Kluwer, Alphen aan den Rijn, pp 59–74
Hreinsson P (2016) General Principles. In: Baudenbacher C (ed) The Handbook of EEA Law. Springer, Heidelberg, pp 339–390
Klamert M (2014) The Principle of Loyalty in EU Law. Oxford University Press, Oxford
Łazowski A (2008) Enhanced multilateralism and enhanced bilateralism: Integration without Membership in the European Union. CMLRev 45:1433–1458
Lourenço L (2019) European Economic Area (EEA) and European Free Trade Association (EFTA). In: Wessel RA, Odermatt J (eds) Research Handbook on the European Union and International Organizations. Edward Elgar, Cheltenham
Maresceau M (2012) Turkey: A Candidate State Destined to Join the Union. In: Nic Shuibhne N, Gormley LW (eds) From Single Market to Economic Union, Essays in Memory of John A. Usher. Oxford University Press, Oxford
Maresceau M (2013) Les Accords d'Intégration dans les Relations de Proximité de l'Union Européenne [Integration agreements in the proximity relations of the European Union]. In: Blumann C (ed) Les Frontieres de l'Union Européenne [The Frontiers of the European Union]. Bruylant, Brussels
Mariani MP (2019) La Protection des Citoyens et des Opérateurs Économiques à la Suite de la Sortie du Royaume Uni de l'Union Européenne : Régimes Transitoires et Droits Acquis [Protection of Citizens and Economic Operators after the Withdrawal of the United Kingdom from the European Union]. Révue Générale de Droit International Public 123:653–681

Neframi E (2018) La Force Intégrative du Statut de l'État Membre dans la Fonction Juridictionnelle [Integrative Impact of Member State Status on the Judicial Function]. In: Potvin-Solis L (ed) Le Statut d'État Membre de l'Union Européenne. Bruylant, Brussels, pp 333–357

Neframi E (2019) L'Action Extérieure de l'Union Européenne à la Lumière du Brexit [The External Action of the European Union in the light of Brexit]. European Review of Public Law 31:209–239

Neframi E, Lacchi C (2018) Une Approche Particulière du Dialogue des Juges au sein de l'Espace Économique Européen [A specific Approach of the Judicial Dialogue in the European Economic Area]. In: Monjal P-Y et al (eds) La Concurrence des Juges en Europe. Clément Juglar, Nancy, pp 237–251

O'Carroll L (2019) UK faces 'catastrophe' if Tories continue with 'no checks in Irish Sea' claim. The Guardian https://www.theguardian.com/uk-news/2020/mar/04/uk-faces-catastrophe-if-tories-continue-with-no-checks-in-irish-sea-claim-northern-ireland-johnson Accessed 15 March 2020

Odermatt J (2018) How to Resolve Disputes Arising from Brexit: Comparing International Models. International Organizations Law Review 15:295–320

Ott A (2015) The EU-Turkey Association and Other EU Parallel Legal Orders in the European Legal Space. Legal Issues of Economic Integration 42:5–30

Peers S (2019) Analysis 4 of the revised Brexit Withdrawal Agreement: Citizens' Rights. EU Law Analysis, http://eulawanalysis.blogspot.com/2019/10/analysis-4-of-revised-brexit-withdrawal.html Accessed 15 March 2020

Piernas López JJ (2019) Derechos de los Ciudadanos de la Unión Europea y del Reino Unido después del Brexit [Rights of Citizens of the European Union and the United Kingdom after Brexit]. Anuario Español de Derecho Internacional 35:261–295

Pitcher B (2019) Racism and Brexit: Notes Towards an Antiracist Populism. Ethnic and Racial Studies 2490

Poinsignon D (2018) Le Retrait de l'Union Européenne et le statut d'Etat Membre : le cas du Brexit. In: Potvin-Solis L (ed) Le statut d'état membre de l'Union européenne. Bruylant, Brussels, pp 579–614

Potvin-Solis L (2018) Propos introductifs. Le Statut d'État Membre et le Cadre Constitutionnel de l'Union Européenne [Introductory remarks. The status of Member State and the Institutional Framework of the European Union]. In: Potvin-Solis L (ed) Le Statut d'État Membre de l'Union Européenne. Bruylant, Brussels, pp 15–50

Pustorino P (2012) Lo Status di Membro delle Organizzazioni Internazionali [The status of Member State of International Organisations]. In: Del Vecchio A (ed) Diritto delle Organizzazioni Internazionali. Edizioni Scientifiche Italiane, Naples, pp 140–204

Rapoport C (2017) La Redéfinition des Relations entre l'Union Européenne et le Royaume-Uni : les Modèles de Coopération Envisageables [The Redefinition of the Relations between the European Union and the United Kingdom: The Possible Cooperation Models]. In: Bahurel C et al (eds) Le Brexit - Enjeux Régionaux, Nationaux et Internationaux [Brexit: Regional, National and International Issues]. Bruylant, Brussels, pp. 97–119

Schermers HG, Blokker MR (2011) International Institutional Law. Brill, Leiden

Sif Tynes D (2018) The Future Is Not What It Used to Be: Some Reflections on the UK and the EEA. In: Biondi A et al (eds) Brexit: The Legal Implications. Kluwer, Alphen aan den Rijn

Smismans S (2018) EU Citizens' Rights post Brexit: why direct effect beyond the EU is not enough. European Constitutional Law Review 14:443–474

Tovo C (2016) Le Agenzie Decentrate dell'Unione Europea [Decentralised Agencies of the European Union]. Editoriale scientifica, Naples

UK Government (2017) The Government's Negotiating Objectives for Exiting the EU: PM speech. https://www.gov.uk/government/speeches/the-governments-negotiating-objectives-for-exiting-the-eu-pm-speech Accessed 15 March 2020

UK Government (2017) The United Kingdom's Exit from and New Partnership with the European Union.https://assets.publishing.service.gov.uk/government/uploads/system/uploads/att

achment_data/file/589191/The_United_Kingdoms_exit_from_and_partnership_with_the_EU_Web.pdf Accessed 15 March 2020
UK House of Lords, EU Committee (2020) Brexit: The Revised Withdrawal Agreement and Political Declaration. https://publications.parliament.uk/pa/ld5801/ldselect/ldeucom/4/402.htm Accessed 15 March 2020
Tatham A (2016) Where Culture, Language and Politics Meet: Is there any Place for National Identity in the EEA Legal System? UNIO - EU Law Journal 2:108–122
Trisciuoglio A (2019) Historical Overview of the Status Topic. In: Bartolini A et al (eds) Dictionary of Statuses within EU Law: The Individual Statuses as Pillar of European Union Integration. Springer, Heidelberg, pp 9–16
Van der Loo G (2016) The EU-Ukraine Association Agreement and Deep and Comprehensive Free Trade Area. Brill, Leiden
Van Elsuwege P, Chamon M (2019) The Meaning of 'Association' under EU Law: A Study on the Law and Practice of EU Association Agreements. European Parliament, Brussels

Chapter 12
Brexit and the 'Great British Trade-Off': The Future of the EU's and the UK's External Treaty Relations

J. Larik

Contents

Abstract The United Kingdom has left the European Union. While both sides continue to shape their future relationship, Brexit also reveals a distinctly global dimension. The UK government is negotiating "continuity agreements" with countries around the world to replace agreements concluded by the EU, while also aiming to strike new agreements where the EU has failed to do so thus far. At the same time, the EU as a global treaty-maker is not standing still either. This setting provides a fertile ground for a comparative analysis of the performance of both the UK and EU as international treaty negotiators, especially in the area of trade. This chapter argues that such a comparison serves as an unprecedented opportunity for testing some of the core assumptions of both Eurosceptics and proponents of European integration. The assumptions can be grouped under two opposing narratives designated here as "Global Britain" and "Market Power Europe", respectively. While the former suggests that the UK will be better off "unshackled" from the EU by becoming a more agile and effective international actor, the latter argues that the benefits of being able to rely on the collective economic power of the EU outweigh the costs of heterogeneity of interests and more burdensome decision-making. Comparing the ability of both the EU and UK to conclude trade agreements with partners around the world, and comparing the respective terms accorded to them, will enable researchers to provide insights into the costs and benefits of "non-Europe" on the international stage. However, in order to produce meaningful findings, numerical, normative, relative and cumulative methodological challenges will have to be overcome. Therefore,

J. Larik (✉)
Leiden University, The Hague, The Netherlands
e-mail: j.e.larik@luc.leidenuniv.nl

W. Th. Douma et al. (eds.), *The Evolving Nature of EU External Relations Law*,
https://doi.org/10.1007/978-94-6265-423-5_12

a new interdisciplinary approach is required that combines rigorous legal analysis with empirical-legal, qualitative, and economic methods to answer a fundamental question: was striking out on its own in the world "worth it" for the first country that left the EU?

Keywords Brexit · EU External Relations · International Agreements · International Trade · United Kingdom

12.1 Introduction: From *Verdrittstaatlichung* to Global Competition

On the night of 31 January 2020 to 1 February 2020, the world witnessed the first case of the *Verdrittstaatlichung* of a country,[1] i.e., the transformation of a European Union (EU) Member State into a "third country". That night, Brexit "got done", to use the campaign slogan of Boris Johnson and his Conservative Party.[2] It was accomplished in the sense that the United Kingdom (UK) ceased to be a Member State of the EU. As confirmed before by the *Wightman* judgment of the Court of Justice of the EU (CJEU), before this moment, the UK could have stopped the withdrawal process and remained a Member State with all the rights and obligations it already had.[3] However, this did not happen and thus the UK's very special status, replete with rebates, opt-outs, opt-ins,[4] is now consigned to history. Henceforth, the UK is an outsider from the point of view of the EU.[5]

Nevertheless, the aftermath of Brexit continues. First, the UK and EU went through a "transition period" as envisaged by the Withdrawal Agreement to give form to their future relations.[6] Moreover, Brexit also entails a rupture and need for a recalibration of the UK's treaty relations with numerous countries around the world, due to the fact that many treaties concluded by the EU will no longer be applicable to it.[7] As a consequence, the UK has been engaged in signing so-called "continuity agreements" in the area of trade to fill the gap.[8] At the same time, the idea that the UK,

---

[1]The author proudly claims authorship of this German compound neologism.

[2]See Perrigo B (2019) 'Get Brexit Done.' The 3 Words That Helped Boris Johnson Win Britain's 2019 Election. https://time.com/5749478/get-brexit-done-slogan-uk-election/. Accessed 1 June 2020.

[3]Court of Justice, *Wightman and Others v Secretary of State for Exiting the European Union*, Judgment of the (full) Court, 10 December 2018, Case C-621/18, ECLI:EU:C:2018:999, para 74.

[4]See Keedus et al. 2018; Gowland 2016, pp. 219–30; and George 1998, pp. 39–41.

[5]See Chap. 11 and this chapter; see also Larik 2020a, pp. 9–12.

[6]Agreement on the withdrawal of the United Kingdom of Great Britain and Northern Ireland from the European Union and the European Atomic Energy Community, opened for signature 24 January 2020, OJ C 384I (entered into force 1 February 2020) (UK WA), articles 126 and 184.

[7]McClean P (2017) After Brexit: The UK Will Need to Renegotiate at Least 759 Treaties, Financial Times. https://www.ft.com/content/f1435a8e-372b-11e7-bce4-9023f8c0fd2e. Accessed 01 June 2020.

[8]Larik 2020b.

under the "Global Britain" banner, will strike lucrative trade and other agreements around the world, unencumbered by the sluggish EU, was a prominent theme during the campaign to leave the EU, during which "Vote Leave initially focused on the economic and sovereignty arguments, not least the ability of a non-EU UK to negotiate its own trade deals", before migration assumed a prominent role in the discourse as well.[9] Also subsequently, this idea was reiterated by leading Brexiteers. According to Prime Minister Johnson, Brexit is an opportunity "to recover [the UK's] natural and historic role as an enterprising, outward-looking and truly global Britain."[10] The EU, on its part, is not standing still either as an international treaty-maker in the area of trade in view of an evolving international environment.[11]

The need to deliver on "Global Britain" puts the British government—and those favouring leaving the EU more generally—under pressure. If the UK suffers instead of thrives post-Brexit, this may be seen as proof that the country would have been "better off" remaining in the EU. However, the EU—and those favouring regional integration more generally—are equally under pressure. The fundamental question they face is: What if the UK prospers after its departure from the EU? More specifically, what if "Global Britain" actually manages to outperform the EU in global trade negotiations? In that sense, Brexit has created the background conditions for a large-scale comparative experiment that could allow scholars to test some core assumptions of both proponents of European integration and Eurosceptics alike.

While it is still too early for any firm conclusions on this matter, the 10th anniversary of the Centre for the Law of EU External Relations (CLEER), which this volume commemorates, is an apt opportunity to look forward into the next ten years for the EU as a global actor. This chapter, therefore, expounds the grand competition onto which the EU and UK are now embarking, including its international legal dimension as well as its opposing underlying narratives and economic and political stakes. Moreover, it outlines an assessment framework and highlights some of the main methodological challenges that research in this area will face. These challenges, while considerable, can be tackled by combining rigorous legal research with empirical-legal, qualitative, and economic analysis.

12.2 The Great British Trade-Off: "Global Britain" Versus "Market Power Europe"

What is called here the "Great British Trade-Off" (not to be confused with the "Great British Bake Off", a TV show where the stakes are considerably lower) is the idea that the UK will gain agility and flexibility outside of the EU in its international

---

[9] Oliver 2018, p. 67.

[10] Prime Minister's Office 2019. The UK will also negotiate treaties in other areas. However, due to the prominence of trade deals in the political and public discourse as well as due to the transactional nature of most trade agreements, the present chapter will focus on this area.

[11] Weiß 2020, p. 29; Larik 2020a, pp. 13–14.

treaty negotiations, in particular trade negotiations, while at the same time losing the ability to rely on the EU's combined economic weight, in particular its combined market power. In this sense, the concept harks back to the enquiry of economists Alberto Alesina and Enrico Spolaore on the "optimal size" of countries, which they frame as a trade-off between the benefits of combined capacities and the costs of heterogeneity.[12]

In a similar vein, Brexit can be understood here as a large-scale experiment for determining the "cost of non-Europe". This concept was popularized in the 1988 Cecchini Report.[13] Back then, it was used in an introspective and prospective way. It sought to determine how much better the Member States would be off economically if they completed the Single Market.

With regard to Brexit, by contrast, the "cost of non-Europe" takes on a meaning that is both outward-looking and comparative. All "continuity" agreements which the UK will agree on with other countries can be compared to pre-existing agreements concluded by the EU. This, in turn, will lead to insights into the added value of being inside or outside the EU in global trade and other negotiations.

Whether Brexit will make the UK "better off" as an international treaty negotiator (see Sect. 12.4 *infra* on the methodological issues related to this) is a fundamental question for both the Brexiteers and proponents of European integration alike. In essence, it will serve to confirm or challenge their respective assumptions about leaving the EU—and the added value of regional integration more broadly. In the following paragraphs, these main assumptions, encapsulated in the two opposing narratives called "Global Britain" and "Market Power Europe", are presented.[14]

12.2.1 "Global Britain"

The vision of a "Global Britain" that would be freed from the constraints of EU membership and hence would be able to strike trade deals around the world was a prominent theme both during the campaign and afterwards. This narrative's premise is that by acceding to the EU, figuratively speaking, the UK "shackled [itself] to a corpse".[15] This image captures well the key elements of this narrative, which posits that the UK would be better off outside the EU, which has been holding it back.

Adherents of "Global Britain" lament the EU's slow economic growth compared to the rest of the world. To quote Boris Johnson during the campaign to leave: "The

---

[12] Alesina and Spolaore 2005.

[13] Cecchini et al. 1988.

[14] The following two sub-sections draw on Larik 2020b.

[15] As quoted in Mason R (2012) Britain "shackled to corpse" of EU, says Douglas Carswell, The Telegraph, 22 October 2012. https://www.telegraph.co.uk/news/politics/9636417/Britain-shackled-to-corpse-of-EU-says-Douglas-Carswell.html. Accessed 1 June 2020.

only continent with weaker economic growth than Europe is Antarctica."[16] They criticise, moreover, the Union's alleged sluggishness as a treaty negotiator, which failed to take British interests to heart. For instance, Conservative politician David Davis stated that "trade agreements negotiated by the EU take a very long time to conclude", that British "interests are not well represented in trade negotiations" and, hence, "that these trade deals are not tailored to [the UK's] requirements".[17] This was echoed by fellow Conservative party member Rishi Sunak, who stressed in the lead-up to the referendum that "the agility of independent, mid-sized nations has proven more effective at tapping into the global economy than the sluggish, horse trading between 28 different EU nations, each protecting their own special interests".[18]

Hence, according to the proponents of Brexit, the UK would be better off once it left the EU. The country would prosper, including and especially in its relations with the wider world. On the day the revised Withdrawal Agreement was announced, this outlook was summarized in rather emphatic terms by senior Conservative Jacob Rees-Mogg:

> We will be able to implement our own free trade deals. We will be able to set our own regulations. We will be in charge of our own laws. … it will be a golden age for the United Kingdom when we are free of the heavy yoke of the European Union, which has bowed us down for generations and made us less competitive, less efficient and higher-cost.[19]

This idea is reinforced by arguments that the UK would be more agile in its trade negotiations, not having to wait for EU-internal compromises to be hammered out and no longer having to take into account interests from other Member States and their industries, which are not shared by the UK. Thus, the UK could tailor trade agreements better to its own preferences. In addition, it could avail itself of its "soft power" and historical ties, in particular the Commonwealth and the "special relationship" with the U.S. As the UK government noted in its Trade Policy White Paper of 2017,

> The Commonwealth is home to a third of the world's population, many of its fastest growing economies, and half of the globe's top 20 emerging cities. This vast network of growing markets, with which the UK has long-established relationships, presents a significant opportunity for UK business and enhances the UK's ability to promote free trade in a multilateral rules-based system.[20]

In a certain sense, "Brexiteers" could be understood as constructivists of sorts from the point of view of international relations theory due to their emphasis on identity

---

[16] Johnson (2016) The only continent with weaker economic growth than Europe is Antarctica, Telegraph. https://www.telegraph.co.uk/news/2016/05/29/the-only-continent-with-weaker-economic-growth-than-europe-is-an/. Accessed 1 June 2020.

[17] Davis 2016.

[18] Sunak R (2016) One Glance at the EU's Dismal Trade Policy Simply Destroys the Economic Argument for Remain. https://www.telegraph.co.uk/news/2016/06/01/one-glance-at-the-eus-dismal-trade-policy-simply-destroys-the-ec/. Accessed 1 June 2020.

[19] UK House of Commons 2019.

[20] UK Department for International Trade 2017.

and "the power of ideational variables"[21] as opposed to material factors in the form of economic weight. This vision of "Global Britain", which is as scathing about the EU as it is optimistic about the UK as an international actor, can be contrasted with that of the EU as collective global actor benefitting all of its members.

12.2.2 "Market Power Europe"

A diametrically opposing narrative is espoused by what can be called "Market Power Europe".[22] As explained by Chad Damro, "as a major economic power with a large single market, the EU is capable of externalizing various internal policies, in particular its regulatory standards".[23] It can wield this power "specifically through the relative size of its market."[24] Aggregate market power is seen as the key to success in negotiations with external partners.

The EU's market power is particularly felt by smaller economies in the EU's neighbourhood, which can be seen to make significant commitments in order to gain access to the internal market. The prime examples here are the countries of the European Economic Area (EEA), which follow important parts of EU standards and regulations, subject themselves to a supranational architecture (the EFTA Surveillance Authority and EFTA Court), and even contribute to the EU budget, without have a vote in EU decision-making processes.[25]

Consequently, a country leaving the EU collective would entail being confronted with harsher conditions in trade negotiations because of a loss of relative market size and thus leverage. In 2017, the UK accounted for 15.2% of the EU's total GDP.[26] This makes the UK still one of the world's largest economies. However, the UK will have a smaller market to use for bargaining purposes compared to the U.S. and China, as well as the EU (of twenty-seven) and Japan. Its relative weight compared to other economies will also have decreased.

The principle rationale for collective action is the EU's ability to obtain more concessions in trade negotiations, which is due to a favourable economic power differential with the external trading partner. In other words, relative economic size matters. The European Commission stressed the importance of combined strength through the internal market in its 2015 *Trade for All* strategy:

> The EU is the world's largest exporter and importer of goods and services taken together, the largest foreign direct investor and the most important destination for foreign direct investment (FDI). This scale makes the EU the largest trading partner of about 80 countries and the second most important partner for another 40. The EU should use this strength to

[21] Andreatta 2011, p. 36.

[22] Damro 2012.

[23] Ibid., p. 686.

[24] Ibid., p. 686.

[25] See Baur et al. 2018.

[26] Eurostat 2018.

> benefit both its own citizens and those in other parts of the world, particularly those in the world's poorest countries.[27]

Thus, according to the "Market Power Europe" narrative, the UK should experience the downside of negotiating on its own. As Ramses Wessel puts it,

> the UK will have to start from scratch, although it may in some cases aim at what could largely be a copy of the agreements that were concluded by the EU. This, of course, assumes that the other contracting parties would agree to such a solution. In fact, this should not be taken as a given. One thing is to negotiate a trade agreement with the biggest trade block in the world, quite another to negotiate it with a medium-size country on the fringes of Europe.[28]

In his own emphatic style, the European Parliament's Brexit coordinator Guy Verhofstadt warned that the Brexiteers will "drag their country down a path strewn with uprooted trade ties and substantial new barriers to commerce."[29] Lambasting the idea of "Global Britain", he noted how the EU had managed to wield its combined market power to its own advantage:

> The real global trading power, of course, is the EU, which has recently concluded trade deals with Japan, South Korea and Canada. As an EU member state, the UK automatically benefits from the 40 trade agreements the bloc has in place with more than 70 countries.[30]

In fact, as observed by Anu Bradford, businesses and governments outside the EU may adopt EU standards and regulations even in the absence of trade agreements imposing a legal duty to do so due to the "size and attractiveness of its market".[31] This is what she has termed the "Brussels Effect", meaning "the EU's unilateral ability to regulate the global marketplace."[32] For the EU, she argues, the ability to set global rules, including through trade agreements, serves also "to prove to its critics that it remains relevant as a global economic power."[33]

Proponents of the "Market Power Europe" narrative can thus be understood as positivists of sorts, in the meaning of the term in international relations theory, due to their emphasis on economic power,[34] which is then also the EU's foremost foreign policy tool to pursue its interests and values.[35]

Until Brexit, these narratives remained largely unproven assumptions, or in any event assumptions that are very difficult to verify due to the lack of a direct

---

[27] European Commission 2015.

[28] Wessel 2018, p. 116.

[29] Verhofstadt G (2019) Boris Johnson's Talk of 'Global Britain' is about to Look even more Ridiculous. https://www.theguardian.com/commentisfree/2019/jun/27/boris-johnson-global-britain-eu-trade-deal. Accessed 1 June 2020.

[30] Ibid.

[31] Bradford 2020, p. 2.

[32] Ibid.

[33] Ibid., p. 24.

[34] Stressing economic power over military power also causes some international relations scholars to classify such a perspective as "liberal", Andreatta 2011, p. 27.

[35] Larik 2011, pp. 23–30.

comparator. With the UK having left the EU and having embarked on a worldwide effort of negotiating its own international agreements under the banner of "Global Britain", this will allow for a more direct comparison between the performance of the EU and the UK on the international stage. However, due to the transition period of the Withdrawal Agreement, the UK is slowly phased into its new position.

12.3 "The Great British Trade-Off" as an International Legal Issue

That Brexit is not only an intra-European affair but has wide-ranging consequences for international treaty relations has by now been well documented by a number of scholars.[36] This concerns, on the one hand, treaties that no longer apply to the UK. On the other, this is about the UK's increased freedom from the constraints of EU law in negotiating and concluding new international agreements.

Regarding treaties that would no longer apply to the UK, the *Financial Times* reported in 2017 that this would be the case for approximately 750 international agreements concluded by the EU with 168 different third countries, once it is no longer a Member State.[37] As noted by the *BBC*, these include 40 trade agreements with more than 70 countries.[38]

A legal debate ensued regarding the different categories of these agreements, of which three can be distinguished. First, there are agreements concluded by the EU alone (i.e., without the Member States) with one or several third parties. Since the UK was never a party to these in its own right, these are generally considered to no longer apply to the former Member State.[39] Second, there are "multilateral mixed agreements", i.e. agreements that include as parties the EU, (some of) its Member States, and several third countries. Prominent examples for this type of setting are the main WTO Agreements and the UN Convention on the Law of the Sea. Here, the UK was already a party, and will remain one, with the main difference being that it is no longer constrained by EU law, in particular the need to respect the EU's exclusive powers and the duty of sincere cooperation as laid down in Article 4(3) TEU.[40] Third, there are "bilateral mixed agreements", i.e. treaties that have as parties the EU and its Member States on one side, and one third party on the other.

---

[36]See Łazowski and Wessel 2016; Odermatt 2017; Wessel 2018; Silvereke 2018; Larik 2018; and Larik 2020b.

[37]See https://www.ft.com/content/f1435a8e-372b-11e7-bce4-9023f8c0fd2e. Accessed 1 June 2020. For some critical remarks on how to count such international agreements, see Larik 2018, pp. 19–24.

[38]Edington T (2020) Brexit: What Trade Deals has the UK done so far? https://www.bbc.com/news/uk-47213842. Accessed 1 June 2020.

[39]Silvereke 2018, p. 339; and Odermatt 2017, p. 1056.

[40]See Chamon and Govaere 2020. There may also be other issues to sort out. In the WTO context, for instance, tariff rate quotas needed to be split up between the UK and the EU.

"Bilateral mixed agreements" are arguably the trickiest category when it comes to determining the UK's post-Brexit status. While the UK was a party to these agreement in its own right and was exercising some powers of its own in their conclusion and implementation, a number of scholars pointed out the bilateral setup of these agreements.[41] In a nutshell, bilateral mixed agreements did not foresee the situation of an EU Member State becoming a third country. Their provisions on territorial application and institutional mechanisms, for instance, are written to apply to the EU and its Member States as a collective entity and the respective third country. They are not designed for accommodating an additional third country.[42] The British government's practice seems to confirm the view that these agreements would no longer apply to the UK, as the UK has signed continuity agreement with certain countries with which the EU has mixed bilateral agreements.[43]

According to the Withdrawal Agreement between the EU and UK, the "Union will notify the other parties to these [external] agreements that during the transition period the United Kingdom is to be treated as a Member State for the purposes of these agreements."[44] This means that the EU's external agreements should continue to apply to the UK during the transition period, to the extent that the respective third countries go along with this request. At the same time, the Withdrawal Agreement allows the UK to "negotiate, sign and ratify international agreements entered into in its own capacity in the areas of exclusive competence of the Union, provided those agreements do not enter into force or apply during the transition period, unless so authorised by the Union."[45] In doing so, the UK is to respect "the principle of sincere cooperation" according to which "the United Kingdom shall refrain, during the transition period, from any action or initiative which is likely to be prejudicial to the Union's interests".[46]

These provisions in the Withdrawal Agreements apply to both continuity agreements that the UK may wish to negotiate as well as agreements that are not aimed at replacing treaties concluded by the EU. Through these provisions, the Withdrawal Agreement itself provides a legal framework for a gradual easing into the "Great

---

[41] Wessel 2018, p. 120; Odermatt 2017, pp. 1059–60; and Sacerdoti 2017, p. 82.

[42] See, e.g., Comprehensive Economic and Trade Agreement (CETA) between Canada, of the one part, and the European Union and its Member States, of the other part, opened for signature 30 October 2016, OJ L 11/23 (entered into force (provisionally) 21 September 2017), article 1.3 on the geographical scope of application and article 26.1(1) on the composition of the Joint Committee.

[43] See, e.g., Free trade Agreement between the European Union and its Member States, of the one part, and the Republic of Korea, of the other part, opened for signature 06 October 2010, OJ L127/6 (entered into force 13 December 2015); and Free Trade Agreement between the United Kingdom of Great Britain and Northern Ireland and the Republic of Korea (with Exchange of Notes), opened for signature 22 August 2019 (CP 167). See further Larik 2020b, pp. 448–49.

[44] UK WA, above n. 6, article 129(1), n. 1.

[45] Ibid., article 129(4).

[46] Ibid., article 129(3).

British Trade-Off'. While the UK remains largely bound by EU law during the transition period,[47] while having lost its without voting rights,[48] it can start negotiations with third countries, as long as its continuity and new agreements do not enter into force before the end of the transition.

12.4 An Assessment Framework and Its Methodological Challenges

By the time the UK had left the EU, it had already signed a number of continuity trade agreements with countries around the world.[49] However, the time for direct comparisons of the performance of the EU and UK viewed through the terms of international agreements with the rest of the world is not quite ripe yet due to the abovementioned transition as well as the fact that additional agreements are likely to take time be negotiated, especially if they will not be based on the template of a pre-existing agreement concluded by the EU. Nevertheless, it is already possible—and indeed timely—to theorize about an assessment framework for verifying the claims of both proponents of what has been termed here "Global Britain" and "Market Power Europe".

To provide evidence-based answers to questioning these narratives, a framework is required for assessing the UK's post-Brexit performance as opposed to the EU's in international treaty negotiations. On the one hand, where the UK manages to extract more favourable terms from an external trade partner, that would have to be considered a success for "Global Britain". Despite reduced market size, it managed to outperform the EU in such cases. This may vindicate the premises of "Global Britain", such as greater flexibility or bringing its soft power to bear. The latter factor in particular would have certain theoretical implications as well since it may be seen as evidence that shared identities and ideas can outweigh sheer material, economic power in international relations.

In addition, it is argued here that even instances where the UK manages to extract the same terms as before, for instance by "incorporating" a pre-existing agreement concluded by the EU virtually in its entirety, should be considered a success. That is so because also here, despite its reduced market power, the UK managed to obtain the same result, demonstrating that there was no added value of being part of the EU, at least in this particular context.

On the other hand, where the UK fails to obtain the same or better terms than the EU managed to do, this can be considered a sign of the global costs of no longer being part of the bloc. This would vindicate the premises of "Market Power Europe" and could be seen as evidence of the added value of being part of the EU. On a more theoretical level, such a result may also be seen as evidence of material, economic

[47] Ibid., article 127.

[48] Ibid., article 7(1).

[49] Larik 2020b, p. 452.

power prevailing over ideational factors—at any rate those touted by the proponents of "Global Britain".

However, establishing and applying such an assessment framework, as any ambitious project, comes with a range of methodological challenges. These include the following four:

- Numerical, i.e., the ability to analyse considerable amounts of legal materials;
- Normative, i.e., a definition of "better" and "worse terms";
- Relative; i.e., factoring in economic power differentials;
- Cumulative, i.e., offsetting the sum of "Global Britain" wins against Brexit losses.

Firstly, the numerical challenge lies in the fact that Brexit has caused a rupture of hundreds of treaty relations. Nevertheless, the analysis of larger numbers of international agreements is made possible through advances in empirical-legal studies, where larger samples of treaties have been compared.[50] A focus on trade agreement narrows down the number, with an estimated 40 trade agreements in need of replacement.[51] Using this smaller sample and/or making use of empirical-legal tools, would make textual comparisons of individual treaties more feasible.

This is especially the case for continuity agreements, some of which follow the so-called "short-form" format. In those cases, the EU agreement is "incorporated into and made part of"[52] the new agreement, while deviations are spelled out. Here, the negotiators do the comparative work for future researchers as differences with the agreement concluded by the EU are made explicit. Also for "long-form" agreements, where the entire content is copied and modified in certain regards, a simple side-by-side comparison can reveal the differences. As regards new agreements, these may be compared to similar agreements concluded by the EU with that same third country, to the extent that they exist. If there is none, such as a comprehensive trade agreement with the United States or China, for instance, conclusions will have to be drawn from the UK managing to do so.

Secondly, once textual differences are revealed, tackling the normative challenge means drawing conclusions from the comparisons of the terms of agreements concluded by the EU and UK with the same external partners. In essence, this means determining whose terms are "better" or "worse". In some instances, this will be easy. For example, where the UK would receive less market access from a trading partner compared to the EU in the form of (higher) tariffs. Concerning tariff rate quotas, the assessment needs to take into account also the UK's market size and previous export levels to the third country. The issue of non-tariff barriers such as regulatory restrictions will be more difficult to evaluate.

The normative analysis of comparing EU and UK trade agreements would therefore benefit from supplementing the comparison of the legal texts with qualitative

[50] See, e.g., Alschner and Skougarevskiy 2016; and Verdier and Versteeg 2015.

[51] See https://www.bbc.com/news/uk-47213842. Accessed 1 June 2020.

[52] See, e.g., Agreement Establishing an Association Between the United Kingdom of Great Britain and Northern Ireland and the Republic of Chile, opened for signature 30 January 2019, CP 35, article 3(1).

research methods. These would include taking into account sources from the different countries giving insights into these countries' respective interests in trade negotiations and how these were achieved, or where concessions were made, to the UK or EU. Semi-structured interviews with government, industry, and civil society representatives could be particularly useful to gain targeted data for evaluating the respective terms in the trade agreements accorded to the EU and UK.

Thirdly, such a comparative analysis of terms obtained in trade agreements will have to factor in relative economic power differentials. The UK represented about one sixth of the EU's gross domestic product (GDP) before its departure. On its own, it represents a much smaller market. At the same time, it still is the world's fifth largest economy in terms of nominal GDP according to the World Bank.[53] Therefore, it will doubtlessly continue to be a significant trading power and a larger market than most other countries. For a comparative analysis with the EU in trade negotiations, these different economic power differentials need to be taken into account.

For instance, for small economies, including least developed countries, the economic power differential will still be very favourable to the UK despite no longer being able to rely on the EU's combined market leverage. For example, Zambia's and El Salvador's GDP (in nominal terms) is less than 1% of both the UK's and the EU's.[54] By contrast, at the other end of the spectrum, the UK will be the smaller market compared to economic heavyweights such as Japan. According the "Market Power Europe" narrative, it is here that the UK would experience particular difficulties in achieving terms comparable to the EU. Both additional economic analysis and country-specific qualitative research will be needed to take these relative economic power differentials and bilateral trading profiles fully into account.

Fourthly, once texts are compared and differences are explained, the results need to be contextualized with the future relationship between the EU and UK. At any rate, this will become relevant in case the analysis reveals the UK achieving more favourable terms than the EU in its trade agreements with global partners. On their own, these could be interpreted as validating the "Global Britain" narrative. However, one may object that any such wins would have to be offset against any losses in market access the UK would experience in its relationship with the EU post-transition. This would be the case according to economic forecasts, especially in scenarios where the EU and UK would only have a CETA-style trade agreement or fall back onto WTO rules.[55] As of 2020, the EU is still the UK's main trading partner, accounting for about half the latter's trade.[56] Therefore, the cumulative effect of better terms obtained by the UK compared to the EU would need to be brought in a relation to losses suffered in relation to trade with the EU.

---

[53] World Bank (2020) GDP (current US$)—All Countries and Economies. https://data.worldbank.org/indicator/NY.GDP.MKTP.CD?most_recent_value_desc = true&year_high_desc = true. Accessed 1 June 2020.

[54] Ibid.

[55] See Ries et al. 2017, pp. 47–73.

[56] https://www.bbc.com/news/uk-47213842. Accessed 1 June 2020.

Additional economic analysis would be required to meaningfully combine these different effects. Even where the UK manages to extract better terms from certain non-EU trading partners, the theory of "gravity" in international trade will need to be accounted for, i.e. that countries tend to trade more with larger and closer markets.[57] The EU fulfils both criteria and could show in this way that the UK will find it difficult to escape from its economic orbit. In any event, trade patterns may also take longer times to adjust. Hence, longitudinal analyses across many years would be necessary to keep checking how trade relations evolve.

In sum, a meaningful comparative analysis of the EU and UK's post-Brexit—or rather post-transition—performance as international treaty negotiators in the area of trade has considerable potential in terms of providing evidence for verifying the opposing narrative of "Global Britain" and "Market Power Europe". However, this evidence is not easily established. While rigorous legal analysis will remain essential, this needs to be supplemented with legal-empirical, qualitative and economic research methods.

12.5 Conclusion: Was Leaving "Worth It"?

This chapter has sought to highlight the international dimension of Brexit and its wider importance for the EU as an international (legal) actor. Beyond the intra-European dimension of fashioning a future relationship between the EU and UK, Brexit has a distinctly global dimension. And beyond the more immediate need for the UK to ensure "continuity" of a range of treaty relations with the rest of the world due to its departure from the EU, larger questions of the respective futures of both the EU and UK on the global stage are looming on the horizon.

While it is too early to draw any conclusions yet at a time when the transition period has just ended, now is an opportune moment to reflect on the aftermath of Brexit as an unprecedented opportunity to check some of the core assumptions of the main opposing narratives of the costs and benefits of European integration in an international context. These have been designated here, respectively, as "Global Britain" and "Market Power Europe". Rather than blindly or implicitly subscribing to either narrative, it is incumbent upon scholars to be critical of either and to seek ways to test them on the basis of objectifiable evidence.

Such evidence, it has been argued here, is forthcoming in the form of scores of new international agreements the UK seeks to conclude with partners around the world, largely to replace existing EU agreements but also to forge new legal ties where the EU has not managed to do so yet. Making sense of this evidence requires an interdisciplinary research agenda in order to meet the numerical, normative, relative, and cumulative methodological challenges that such an endeavour poses.

Rigorous legal analyses will remain crucial to provide an accurate understanding of these new materials. Given their volume, legal-empirical methods will be useful to

[57] Lowe 2018.

process them and to condense findings. Qualitative research methods will be essential for explaining differences in terms accorded to the UK and EU, respectively, in the analysed agreements. This will be particularly important for determining whose terms are more favourable. Last but certainly not least, economic analyses will be indispensable to balance relative economic power differentials and for offsetting any gains made by the UK with the rest of the world against loss of access to the EU's internal market.

None of this is easy, and none of this will be done quickly. However, further refining and applying this methodology seems a worthwhile endeavour, for the prize that beckons is considerable: The answer to the question "Was striking out on its own in the world worth it for the first country that left the EU?"

References

Alesina A, Spolaore E (2005) The Size of Nations. MIT Press, Cambridge

Alschner W, Skougarevskiy D (2016) Mapping the Universe of International Investment Agreements. JIEL 19:561–588

Andreatta F (2011) The European Union's International Relations: A Theoretical View. In: Hill C, Smith M (eds) International Relations and the European Union, 2nd edn. Oxford University Press, Oxford, pp 21–43

Baur G, Sánchez Rydelski M, Zatschler C (2018) European Free Trade Association (EFTA) and the European Economic Area (EEA), 2nd edn. Wolters Kluwer, Alphen aan den Rijn

Bradford A (2020) The Brussels Effect: How the European Union Rules the World. Oxford University Press, Oxford

Cecchini P et al. (1988) The European Challenge—1992: The Benefits of a Single Market. Wildwood House, Aldershot

Chamon M, Govaere I (eds) (2020) EU External Relations Post-Lisbon: The Law and Practice of Facultative Mixity. Brill, Leiden/Boston

Damro C (2012) Market Power Europe. Journal of European Public Policy 19:682–699

Davis D (2016) Britain would be better off out of the EU – And here's why https://www.conservativehome.com/platform/2016/02/david-davis-britain-would-be-better-off-out-of-the-eu-and-heres-why.html Accessed 1 June 2020

European Commission (2015) Trade for all: Towards a more Responsible Trade and Investment Policy https://trade.ec.europa.eu/doclib/docs/2015/october/tradoc_153846.pdf Accessed 3 July 2020

Eurostat (2018) Which Member States have the largest share of EU's GDP? https://ec.europa.eu/eurostat/web/products-eurostat-news/-/DDN-20180511-1?inheritRedirect=true Accessed 1 June 2020

George S (1998) An Awkward Partner: Britain in the European Community, 3rd edn. Oxford University Press, Oxford

Gowland D (2016) Britain and the European Union. Routledge, Abingdon

Keedus L et al. (2018) The British Rebate and the Single European Act: Political Ramifications of an Economic Reform. In: Ramiro Troitiño D, Kerikmäe T, Chochia A (eds) Brexit: History, Reasoning and Perspectives. Springer, Berlin, pp 141–152

Larik J (2011) Much More Than Trade: The Common Commercial Policy in a Global Context. In: Evans M, Koutrakos P (eds) Beyond the Established Legal Orders: Policy Interconnections Between the EU and the Rest of the World. Hart Publishing, Oxford, pp 13–45

Larik J (2018) The New Transatlantic Trigonometry: "Brexit" and Europe's Treaty Relations with the United States. University of Pennsylvania Journal of International Law 40:1–81
Larik J (2020a) EU External Relations law and Brexit: 'When Pluto was a Planet'. Europe and the World: A Law Review 4:1–18
Larik J (2020b) Brexit, the Withdrawal Agreement, and Global Treaty (Re-)Negotiations. AJIL 114:443–462
Łazowski A, Wessel RA (2016) The External Dimension of Withdrawal from the European Union. Revue des Affaires Européennes 4:623–638
Lowe S (2018) Last Word: Global Britain? The Trade Debate. Political Insight 9:40
Odermatt J (2017) Brexit and International law: Disentangling Legal Orders. Emory International Law Review, 31:1051–1073
Oliver T (2018) Understanding Brexit: A Concise Introduction. Policy Press, Bristol
Prime Minister's Office (2019) Press Release: Boris Johnson's First Speech as Prime Minister. https://www.gov.uk/government/speeches/boris-johnsons-first-speech-as-prime-minister-24-july-2019 Accessed 1 June 2020
Ries CP et al. (2017) After Brexit: Alternate form of Brexit and their Implications for the United Kingdom, the European Union and the United States. Rand Corporation, Santa Monica
Sacerdoti G (2017) The Prospects: The UK Trade Regime with the EU and the World: Options and Constraints Post-Brexit. In: Fabbrini F (ed) The Law & Politics of Brexit. Oxford University Press, Oxford, pp 71–91
Silvereke S (2018) Withdrawal from the EU and Bilateral Free Trade Agreements: Being Divorced is Worse? IOLR 15:321–340
UK House of Commons (2019) Hansard, Business of the House, 66:490. https://hansard.parliament.uk/Commons/2019-10-17/debates/C7D5E220-3549-4DF1-AF9E-07079573464C/BusinessOfTheHouse(Saturday19October) Accessed 1 June 2020
Verdier P-H, Versteeg M (2015) International Law in National Legal Systems: An Empirical Investigation. AJIL 109:514–533
Weiß W (2020) EU Multilateral Trade Policy in a Changing, Multipolar World: The Way Forward. In: Weiß W, Furculita C (eds) Global Politics and EU Trade Policy: Facing the Challenges to a Multilateral Approach. European Yearbook of International Economic Law Special Issue:17–39
Wessel RA (2018) Consequences of Brexit for International Agreements Concluded by the EU and its Member States. CMLRev 55:101–131

Part IV
The EU and Migration Policies

Chapter 13
Two Years After the Adoption of the Global Compact for Migration: Some Thoughts on the Role Played by the EU

P. Melin

Contents

Abstract In December 2018, all the media attention was on the adoption of the Global Compact for Migration at the Marrakesh intergovernmental conference. Developed as an international answer to the migration crisis, the Global Compact for Migration became a political symbol for many States, including some EU Member States, in holding an anti-migration discourse. By contrast, the EU has played a great role in shaping the Global Compact for Migration since the beginning of the negotiations in 2017. The gradual lack of support of some EU Member States created a situation where the unity of EU representation on the international scene has been injured. Two years after its adoption, this contribution aims to offer some thoughts on the EU's role in the process of negotiation and adoption of the Global Compact for Migration. It aims to discuss the (lack of) an EU legal framework for negotiations of international soft law instruments by looking at the case-law of the Court of Justice, notably *Council v. Commission* (C-660/13).

P. Melin (✉)
Maastricht University, Maastricht, The Netherlands

W. Th. Douma et al. (eds.), *The Evolving Nature of EU External Relations Law*,
https://doi.org/10.1007/978-94-6265-423-5_13

Keywords Global Compact for Migration · United Nations · International Soft Law · EU External Relations · Unity of Representation · Principle of Sincere Cooperation

13.1 Introduction[1]

In the aftermath of what was often referred to as the 'refugee crisis', the EU and its Member States have shaped their discourse on migration as a management strategy ranging from addressing the root causes of migration in developing countries to responding to the issue of human trafficking. This management strategy is heavily dependent on the collaboration with third countries and international organizations such as the UN. In that context, the EU and its Member States have adopted "The European Consensus on Development"[2] where they agreed to support the elaboration of the UN Global Compact for Safe, Orderly and Regular Migration (hereinafter 'the Global Compact for Migration') in 2017. Together with the Global Compact for Refugees, the Global Compact for Migration was meant to provide an international answer to the global phenomenon that is migration. Negotiated under the UN auspices, the Global Compact for Migration was adopted at an intergovernmental conference held in Morocco on 10 and 11 December 2018 and further endorsed as an UN General Assembly Resolution on 19 December 2018.

The final stages of the negotiating process of the Global Compact for Migration attracted a lot of attention in the media due to a number of countries distancing themselves from the very idea of the Global Compact. Two years after its adoption, the Global Compact is in its implementation phase. And two years after its adoption, barely anyone still speaks about the Global Compact for Migration. Is it because the migration crisis seems far away or is it due to the fact that we have passed the political moment of its adoption? In any case, the Global Compact for Migration was off to a good start on 19 September 2016 when the UN General Assembly adopted the New York Declaration. Through that declaration, 193 Heads of State and Government recognized the need for developing an international cooperation on migration.[3] In April 2017, the negotiations of the Global Compact for Migration started in a good spirit of international cooperation that soon faded. In December 2017, the USA announced that it would no longer participate in the negotiation of the Global Compact for Migration. Soon after that, Hungary, followed by several EU Member States, started to voice discomfort with the Global Compact for Migration. This led to the withdrawal of Hungary from the negotiating process in July 2018 after the adoption of the Final Draft of the Global Compact. However, it was not until the withdrawal announcement made by Austria that doubts about the Global

[1] Some elements of this contribution were presented at the CLEER Annual Conference in December 2018, summarized in a blog post on EU Law Analysis (Melin 2018) and first published in the European Journal of Migration Law (Melin 2019).

[2] European Parliament, Council, European Commission 2017.

[3] UNGA 2016b.

Compact spread in many EU Member States creating uncertainties as to whom in the EU would be supporting the adoption of the Global Compact in the end.

In contrast with the discomfort of some Member States, the EU was a strong supporter of the Global Compact. Since the beginning of the negotiations, the EU had been active in delivering EU statements by the Union delegation at the UN. The contradictory stances adopted by some Member States and by the EU created a situation where it was unclear who would support the Global Compact in the Marrakesh Conference. Ultimately, the unity of representation of the EU was impaired. The purpose of this contribution is to reflect on the negotiation of the Global Compact for Migration from an EU external relations point of view and to draw some conclusions which could be applicable for future negotiations of similar instruments. This contribution starts with a section devoted to the nature of the Global Compact for Migration as well as its context and where it stands now. Defining the legal nature of the Global Compact for Migration is important for the discussion on the role played by the EU in its negotiation. The second section of this contribution analyses the elaboration and the negotiation of the Global Compact for Migration from an EU external relations perspective. The EU participated in the drafting process of the Global Compact for Migration since April 2017 through Union delegation's statements. At the time, there was no Council Decision authorizing the European Commission to start the negotiation of the Global Compact on behalf of the EU and its Member States. It was only in April 2018 that the European Commission adopted two proposals of Council Decisions authorizing the Commission to conclude the Global Compact on behalf of the Union.[4] The second section hence questions the lack of a clear negotiating mandate for the Commission and the timing of the Commission's proposals. Through the use of the law of the Court, such as *Council v. Commission* on the Swiss MoU (C-660/13), this contribution ultimately scrutinizes the EU involvement and the attitude of the Member States in the drafting process of the Global Compact for Migration by considering their duty of sincere cooperation and the unity of Union representation.

13.2 The Global Compact for Migration and Its Legal Nature

13.2.1 The Negotiation, Adoption and Implementation of the Global Compact for Migration

The first step towards the adoption of the Global Compact for Migration was taken on 19 September 2016 in the New York Declaration whereby the need for developing an international cooperation on migration was stressed by the UN General Assembly. Whereas Annex I concerned the framework for the negotiation and adoption of the

[4]European Commission 2018.

Global Compact for Refugees, Annex II of the New York Declaration set out the bases for negotiation of the Global Compact for Migration.

The drafting process of the Global Compacts started in April 2017. Throughout the negotiations, three drafts have been made publicly available: the Zero Draft on 5 February 2018,[5] the Zero Draft Plus on 5 March 2018[6] and the Final Draft on 11 July 2018.[7] The modalities regarding the negotiation of the Global Compact for Migration were set out by a UN General Assembly Resolution.[8] One of the major points of the New York Declaration was to recognize formally the IOM as the global leading agency and to ensure its close cooperation with the UN.[9] As a result, it was agreed that the Secretariat of the UN and the IOM would jointly organize the negotiations. The Secretariat of the UN offered the capacity and the support, while the IOM provided the technical and policy expertise.[10]

At the end of the negotiation process, the Final Draft was endorsed at an intergovernmental conference held in Morocco from 10 to 11 December 2018. It was then adopted as a UN General Assembly Resolution on 19 December 2018.[11] Currently, the Global Compact for Migration is under implementation. The UN Network on Migration has been created in order to take care of the implementation. It held its first annual meeting on 11 December 2019, exactly one year after the endorsement of the Global Compact in Marrakesh. The Network is composed of 38 UN members,[12] including the IOM who serves as the Coordinator and Secretariat of the Network. The main objectives of the Network are to propose ideas for shaping the implementation of the Global Compact as well as to support and coordinate the actions of the Member States. Hence, the Network has published a workplan[13] and is working on the identification of "*priority-or-pilot-countries who can help lead the way*".[14] At the moment, the main concrete achievement of the Network is the establishment of a Start-up Fund.[15] Established in May 2019 and formally launched in July 2019, the Start-up Fund aims at funding joint initiatives of Member States of the UN who would like to cooperate in the context of the Global Compact.

---

[5]UNGA 2018b.

[6]UNGA 2018c.

[7]UNGA 2018d.

[8]UNGA 2017b.

[9]UNGA 2016a, p. 49.

[10]UNGA 2016b, Annex 2, p. 12.

[11]UNGA 2018d.

[12]For a complete list of the members, see UN Network on Migration 2018, Annex II.

[13]United Nations Network on Migration 2020.

[14]Coordinator of the United Nations Network on Migration (2019) Update on the UN Network on Migration by the Coordinator. http://migrationnetwork.un.org/update-un-network-migration-coordinator. Accessed 25 February 2020.

[15]Start-up Fund for Safe, Orderly and Regular Migration. http://mptf.undp.org/factsheet/fund/MIG00. Accessed 25 February 2020.

13.2.2 The Positions of the EU Member States and the EU

Since the EU is not a member of the UN, some modalities needed to be taken by the UN in order to make the EU participation possible. With the idea to render the negotiation process as inclusive as possible,[16] the UN General Assembly Resolution on Modalities for the Intergovernmental Negotiations of the Compacts called for participation of all its State Members, all members of specialized agencies that have an observer status with the General Assembly, intergovernmental organizations and other entities having received a standing invitation.[17] Consequently, the EU, as a regional group, was granted standing status in order to participate in the negotiations and the conclusion of the Global Compacts.[18]

From the EU side, the European Commission took the lead in the negotiation and draft process of the Global Compact for Migration as representative of the Union and its Member States. This is not surprising as, according to Article 17(1) TEU, the European Commission shall have the task of external representation of the Union for all matters except CFSP matters.[19] Furthermore, the representative agents of the Union at the UN are the Union delegations according to Article 221(1) TFEU. Hence, the EU participated in the negotiation of the Global Compact through the delivery of Union delegation statements.

According to the European Commission, the Union delegation statements delivered in the context of the negotiation of the Global Compact were "*EU coordinated statements*" constituting an "*unified EU approach*".[20] In several occasions during the negotiations of the Global Compact, the Union delegation indeed had given EU statements containing a unified position of the EU and its Member States.[21] However, the unified EU approach did not last. In March 2018, Hungary held a different stance in the process of negotiations of the Global Compact for Migration and made contradictory statements to the ones presented by the Union delegation.[22] The disagreements between that Member State and the European Commission were not a secret. In her speech to the European Parliament on 13 March 2018, the High Representative regretted that one of the Member States had presented a position that was not in line with the position of the 27 other Member States.[23] The efforts of the High Representative as head of the European External Action Service in ensuring consistency

[16]For a more detailed discussion on the negotiating process of the Global Compacts, elements of participation and consultation, see Guild and Grant 2017b.

[17]UNGA 2017b.

[18]UNGA 2017a; UNGA 2018f.

[19]For CFSP matters, the tasks of external representation are split between the High Representative and the President of the European Council. See Consolidated Version of the Treaty on the European Union, 2012, OJ C326 (TEU), Articles 15(6) and 27(2). For a more detailed overview of the Union's role at the UN, see Wouters and Chané 2016, pp. 299–323.

[20]European Commission 2018, p.1.

[21]EEAS 2017a; EEAS 2017b; EEAS 2017c.

[22]Hungarian delegation at the UN 2018.

[23]High Representative of the EU 2018.

in the Union's external action[24] were vain as Hungary announced in July 2018 that it will not sign the Global Compacts for Migration and for Refugees.[25] The withdrawal of Hungary in July 2018 was not really a surprise considering its stance during the negotiation of the Global Compact. In fact, since May 2018, the Union delegation was giving statements "*on behalf of 27 Member States*" thereby formally excluding the position of Hungary.[26]

The withdrawal of Austria was, on the other hand, surprising considering the fact that Austria supported the Global Compact and a unified EU approach when holding the Presidency of the Council. Despite its role as leader, Austria announced at the end of October 2018 that it would not endorse the Global Compact for Migration.[27]

The withdrawal of Austria caused uncertainties regarding the adoption of the Global Compact for many Member States such as Belgium, Germany, or Italy. In fact, at the beginning of November 2018, it was easier to identify for which Member States the Global Compact did not form a problem than the opposite. By mid-November 2018, Bulgaria, Poland, and the Czech Republic had followed the Hungarian and Austrian withdrawals.[28] The Latvian parliament rejected the Global Compact in December 2018.[29]

The adoption of the Global Compact triggered political crises for several governments of EU Member States. Slovakia announced that it would not support the Global Compact while its Foreign Minister, Miroslav Lajcak, was a strong supporter of the Global Compact and was the president of the UN General Assembly when it adopted the Final Draft of the Global Compact in July 2018. The Global Compact ultimately caused the fall of the federal government in Belgium in December 2018 after the refusal by one of the political party to support the Global Compact.[30] Finally, Italy held an inconsistent stance in the process of the negotiations and adoption of the Global Compact. In September 2018, the Prime Minister, Giuseppe Conte made a speech at the UN affirming his support for the Global Compact.[31] However, two

[24]TEU, above n. 18, Article 18(4) TEU and 21(3); Council Decision 2010/427/EU establishing the Organisation and functioning of the European External Action Service, OJ L 201/30, Article 3(1).

[25]The New York Times (2018) Hungary Pulls Out of UN Global Migration Agreement. https://www.nytimes.com/2018/07/18/world/europe/hungary-migration-united-nations.html. Accessed 25 February 2020.

[26]EEAS 2018b.

[27]EU observer (2018) Austria will not sign UN migration pact. https://euobserver.com/tickers/143261. Accessed 25 February 2020.

[28]Politico (2018) Czech Republic latest EU country to reject UN migration treaty. https://www.politico.eu/article/czech-republic-migration-refugees-latest-eu-country-to-reject-united-nations-treaty/. Accessed 25 February 2020.

[29]France 24 (2018) Latvia rejects UN migration pact. https://www.france24.com/en/20181206-latvia-rejects-un-migration-pact. Accessed 25 February 2020.

[30]Politico (2018) Belgium's identity crisis isn't about migration. https://www.politico.eu/article/belgium-government-charles-michel-identity-crisis-isnt-about-migration/. Accessed 25 February 2020.

[31]UNGA 2018a.

months later, the Interior Minister, Matteo Salvini, announced that the government would not support it and would leave the issue up to the national parliament.[32]

In the end, the Global Compact for Migration was adopted by the UN General Assembly with 152 votes in favour on 19 December 2018. Fourteen EU Member States (Belgium, Croatia, Cyprus, Estonia, Finland, France, Germany, Greece, Ireland, Luxembourg, Portugal, Slovenia, Spain, and Sweden) approved the Global Compact without any additional note. Five EU Member States (Denmark, Lithuania, Malta, the Netherlands, and the United Kingdom) approved the Global Compact attaching an explanatory note stressing their national sovereignty in migration matters. Five EU Member States (Austria, Bulgaria, Italy, Latvia, and Romania) abstained from voting.[33] One EU Member State, Slovakia, was not at the UN General Assembly on that day and therefore could not vote. The probable reason for that absence was the important role played by the Foreign Minister, Miroslav Lajcak, who was the president of the UN General Assembly when it adopted the Final Draft of the Global Compact in July 2018. Despite his support, the Slovakian Parliament decided that its government should not support the final vote of the Global Compact. In light of that national political context, the lack of attendance of the Slovak delegation at the UN General Assembly on the day of the adoption of the Global Compact can be understood. Finally, three EU Member States (the Czech Republic, Hungary, and Poland) opposed to the Global Compact.[34]

13.2.3 The Nature and Content of the Global Compact for Migration

One of the most controversial elements during the negotiation of the Global Compact for Migration was its legal nature. The main concerns for many States were that the Global Compact would create legal obligations, thereby impeding their state sovereignty over migration issues.

From a legal perspective, it must be said that the form of an instrument is not relevant for the finding of its legal nature. This view is shared by the International Court of Justice[35] and by the Court of Justice of the European Union.[36] Furthermore,

---

[32] ANSA (2018) Italy not signing Global Compact- Salvini. http://www.ansa.it/english/news/politics/2018/11/28/italy-not-signing-global-compact-salvini_fde75c34-ea73-4358-bd17-df80c94e5c2d.html. Accessed 25 February 2020.

[33] In total, twelve countries abstained from the vote.

[34] In total, five countries opposed the Global Compact. The other two countries, apart from the three EU Member States, were the USA and Israel.

[35] ICJ, *Greece v Turkey (Agean Sea Continental Shelf Case)*, Judgment, 19 December 1978, Rep. 1978/3; ICJ, *Case concerning Maritime Delimitation and Territorial Questions Qatar and Bahrain*, Judgment, 01 July 1994 Rep. 1994/112. For a more detailed discussion on this matter, see den Heijer and Spijkerboer 2016.

[36] Court of Justice, *Parliament* v *Council and Commission*, Judgment, 30 June 1993, Joined cases C-181/91 and C-248/91, ECLI:EU:C:1993:271. See also the *NF* case on the EU-Turkey "deal"

it must be added that, under EU law, the legal nature of the instrument will depend on whether it intends to produce legal effects.[37] In order to establish whether the Global Compact for Migration intends to produce legal effects, one needs to look at the content of the Global Compact and the intention of its authors expressed therein.

Firstly, the intention of the authors to have a non-legally binding instrument is expressed throughout the drafting process. From the Zero Draft until the Final Draft, the formulation has not changed: "*this Global Compact presents* ***a non-legally binding****, cooperative framework that builds on the commitments agreed upon by Member States in the New York Declaration for Refugees and Migrants.*" (emphasis added).[38]

Secondly, in terms of the actual content of the Global Compact for Migration, Annex II of the New York Declaration mentioned that it will comprise "a range of principles, commitments and understandings among Member States regarding international migration in all its dimensions". Some elements already identified by Annex II of the New York Declaration[39] became 23 objectives agreed in the Final Draft of the Global Compact for Migration published in July 2018. At the time of the negotiations of the Global Compact for Migration, Guild and Grant have considered that it is likely that the Global Compact would contain three types of engagement with different legal content: (1) principles that can be used to interpret legislation; (2) actionable commitments; (3) understandings.[40] According to Guild and Grant, only the second type, the actionable commitments, could be legally binding depending on how international commitments are considered under national constitutional law.[41]

However, now that the Final Draft has been published and adopted, it seems that all the objectives set out in the Global Compact for Migration are meant to be achieved through non-legally binding commitments. The Final Draft stresses that the Global Compact for Migration is a "*non-legally binding, cooperative framework that builds on the commitments agreed upon by Member States in the New York Declaration for Refugees and Migrants*".[42] Within that cooperative framework, 23 objectives are identified. For each objective, commitments in the form of a plan for actions are established. The commitments are worded in a rather vague way. Despite using the words "*we commit*", the plan for actions is worded in "*will*" rather than "*shall*". The plan for actions in fact envisages future actions to be taken in

---

although the Court there refused to look at the EU-Turkey Statement due to the fact that the statement was not adopted by the European Council but by Member States gathered at the European Council; General Court, *NF v. European Council*, Order of the Court, 28 February 2017, Case T-192/16, ECLI:EU:T:2017:128. For a discussion on the legal nature of the EU-Turkey Statement, see Carrera et al. 2017; Ott 2017; den Heijer and Spijkerboer 2016.

[37]Pursuant to Article 263 TFEU, the Court only reviews the legality of acts intended to produce legal effects. See Consolidated Version of the Treaty on the Functioning of the European Union, 2012, OJ C 326 (TFEU), Article 263.

[38]UNGA 2018b, above n. 5, p. 5; UNGA 2018c, above n. 6, p. 6; UNGA 2018d, above n. 7, p. 7.

[39]UNGA 2016b, Annex 2, p. 8.

[40]Guild and Grant 2017b, p. 12.

[41]Guild and Grant 2017b, p. 12.

[42]UNGA 2018d, above n. 7, p. 7.

the form of bilateral or multilateral agreements. As an example, on the objective of enhancing availability and flexibility of pathways for regular migration, States commit that they will draw actions on the facilitation of regional and cross-regional labour mobility through international and bilateral cooperation arrangements, such as free movement regimes, visa liberalization or multiple-country visas and labour cooperation frameworks.[43]

In addition, there are two final sections of the Final Draft of the Global Compact for Migration which are worth mentioning for the purpose of defining the legal nature of the Global Compact. These are the section on implementation and the section on the follow-up and review of the Global Compact for Migration. Those sections essentially provide for a system of monitoring of the implementation process via an International Migration Review Forum which should take place every four years, starting in 2022. The result of the review process will be an agreed Progress Declaration. It seems that the tool is therefore political peer-pressure to ensure implementation of the Global Compact.

Due to its wording stressing the non-legally binding character of the Global Compact, it is unlikely that the Global Compact intends to produce legal effects. Nonetheless, its relevance should not be underestimated.[44] On one hand, the Global Compact reaffirms some human rights obligations such as the principle of non-discrimination[45] or the principle of the best interests of the child.[46] The preamble of the Global Compact for Migration recalls that the Compact is founded on the Universal Declaration of Human Rights and core international human rights treaties.[47][48] In the implementation of the Global Compact for Migration, States will have to pay due regard to the international human rights treaties cited therein. As such, the Global Compact for Migration does not create new legal obligations but reinforces already existing ones.

On the other hand, the Global Compact is politically binding. It is a strong signal sent by the States who have approved it that there is a willingness to cooperate globally on the issue of migration. It could form the basis for the adoption of future

[43] Ibid., p. 21.

[44] This is the view of many authors, see Gammeltoft-Hanse et al. 2017; Guild and Grant 2017a; Allinson et al. 2019.

[45] UNGA 2018g, p. 15(f).

[46] UNGA 2018e, p. 15(h).

[47] International Convention on the Elimination of All Forms of Racial Discrimination, opened for signature 21 December 1965, UNTS 660 195 (entered into force 4 January 1969); Convention on the Elimination of All Forms of Discrimination against Women, Convention against Torture and Other Cruel, Inhuman or Degrading Treatment or Punishment, opened for signature 10 December 1984, UNTS 1249 13 (entered into force 26 June 1987); Convention on the Rights of the Child, International Convention on the Protection of the Rights of All Migrant Workers and Members of Their Families, opened for signature 18 December 1990, UNTS 2220 3 (entered into force 1 July 2003); International Convention for the Protection of All Persons from Enforced Disappearance, opened for signature 20 December 2006, UNTS 2716 3 (entered into force 23 December 2010); and Convention on the Rights of Persons with Disabilities, opened for signature 13 December 2006, UNTS 2515 3 (entered into force 3 May 2008).

[48] UNGA 2018e, p. 2.

bilateral and multilateral agreements on specific issues, such as visa liberalization, related to migration. However, States would still need to agree on whether they adopt future bilateral and multilateral agreements. If States decide to adopt such agreements in order to give flesh to the political commitments agreed upon in the Global Compact for Migration, it could become a tool to interpret the bilateral and multilateral agreements.

13.3 The Negotiation of the Global Compact for Migration Viewed from an EU External Relations Perspective

As discussed, the Global Compact for Migration is not a legally binding instrument. In case C-233/02 *France v. Commission*, the Court held that the conclusion of non-binding international instruments does not fall within the scope of Article 300 EC (now Article 218 TFEU).[49] As a result, the procedure of Article 218 TFEU did not apply to the Global Compact for Migration.

Since the Global Compact is to be considered as an international soft law instrument, there is no procedure for the negotiation and adoption of such an instrument under EU law. That being said, the fact that the procedure of Article 218 TFEU does not apply to international soft law instruments does not mean that the EU has *carte blanche* in negotiating and adopting such instruments.

13.3.1 The Lack of Negotiating Mandate and the Power of Representation

In *France v. Commission*, the Court warned that the fact that an instrument is non-binding does not entail that the Commission is responsible for its conclusion.[50] In light of the principles of conferral and institutional balance, the Court seemed to indicate that the conclusion of the instrument should reflect on the procedure of the specific policy the instrument is targeting.[51]

In practice, the negotiation and conclusion of international soft law instruments follow the same procedure as the conclusion of international agreements whereby

[49]Court of Justice, *France v. Commission*, Judgment, 23 March 2004, Case C-233/02 ECLI:EU:C:2004:173.

[50]Ibid., para 40.

[51]Ibid., "Nevertheless, this judgment cannot be construed as upholding the Commission's argument that the fact that a measure such as the Guidelines is not binding is sufficient to confer on that institution the competence to adopt it. Determining the conditions under which such a measure may be adopted requires that the division of powers and the institutional balance established by the Treaty in the field of the common commercial policy be duly taken into account, since in this case the measure seeks to reduce the risk of conflict related to the existence of technical barriers to trade in goods."

the Commission negotiates and signs the negotiated text, but the Council remains responsible for the actual conclusion of the agreement.[52]

In addition, it must be said that, pursuant to the case C-660/13 *Council v. Commission* on the Swiss Memorandum of Understanding (MoU), the Commission would need a Council Decision authorizing it to sign the negotiated text of a soft law instrument before it can approve it on behalf of the Union.[53] Case C-660/13 concerned the conclusion of an addendum to the MoU between the EU and the Swiss Confederation on an adaptation of the financial contribution by the Swiss Confederation in exchange for free access to the enlarged Internal Market. The interesting fact in this case was that there were Council Conclusions adopted in 2012 authorizing the start of the negotiation between the Swiss Confederation and the EU. In those Council Conclusions, the content of the negotiation as well as the designation of the European Commission as the negotiator could be found.[54] Hence, there was a negotiating mandate for the European Commission given by the Council. The European Commission then considered that because the negotiated text was similar in content to the negotiated mandate, it could sign the negotiated text on the basis of its power of representation, pursuant to Article 17(1) TEU.[55] However, the Court disagreed with the European Commission by finding that neither Article 17(1) TEU nor the negotiating mandate were sufficient and that the European Commission should have had a Council Decision before signing the text on behalf of the Union.[56]

In the context of the negotiation of the Global Compact for Migration, there was no Council Decision authorizing the European Commission to start the negotiation and setting out the content of those negotiations. The European Commission relied on two documents in order to justify its negotiating mandate: the European Council Conclusions on Migration from October 2016 and the European Consensus on Development from 2017.[57] In the European Council Conclusions on Migration, it is simply mentioned that the European Council welcomes the New York Declaration. In the European Consensus on Development from 2017, it is stated that the EU and its Member States will actively support the elaboration of the UN Global Compacts on Migration and Refugees. While the two documents could be considered as an indication that there was a willingness from the European Council to have a common position in the negotiations of the Global Compacts for Migration and Refugees, there is nothing in the documents either identifying the European Commission as the negotiator on behalf of the Union and its Member States nor indicating what the content of that common position would be. Furthermore, compared to the situation in case C-660/13, both the European Consensus on Development and the European Council

[52] Van Vooren and Wessel 2014, p. 53.

[53] Court of Justice, *Council v. Commission*, Judgment, 28 July 2016, Case C-660/13 ECLI:EU:C:2016:616.

[54] Ibid., para 8.

[55] Ibid., para 35.

[56] Ibid., paras 36–43.

[57] European Commission 2018, p.1.

Conclusions on Migration are documents coming from the European Council and not the Council.

That being said, the lack of Council Decision authorizing the European Commission to start the negotiation of the Global Compact on behalf of the Union and its Member States does not necessarily mean that the European Commission failed to respect the principle of conferral (Article 5(2) TEU) and the principle of institutional balance (Article 13(2) TEU). After case C-660/13, uncertainty remains whether a Council Decision authorizing the European Commission to start the negotiation on behalf of the Union and its Member States is needed. After all, case C-660/13 was not about whether a Council Decision authorizing the European Commission to start negotiation on behalf of the Union and its Member States was necessary for the start of the negotiation of a non-legally binding instrument. This case is solely about the need of a Council Decision authorizing the Commission to sign the negotiated text. The uncertainty is there because, in that specific case, there was a Council Decision authorizing the European Commission to start the negotiations. Ultimately, requiring a Council Decision would in fact render the procedure for the negotiation and conclusion of international agreements under Article 218 TFEU applicable to international soft law instruments. Hence, it would probably go too far as to affirm that the European Commission did not respect the principle of conferral and the principle of institutional balance in the context of the negotiations of the Global Compact for Migration.

Nonetheless, the lack of a Council Decision setting out a clear mandate for the European Commission did not stay without consequences. Without an official document attesting the negotiating mandate of the European Commission, it let the door open for the Member States to express contradictory statements to the ones made by the Union delegations.

13.3.2 The Lack of Respect for the Principle of Sincere Cooperation and the Unity of Union Representation

Despite the lack of a clear (official) negotiating mandate for the European Commission, the principle of sincere cooperation and the unity of Union representation should have prevented the Member States from making statements that were in contradiction with the ones presented by the Union delegation at the UN.

According to Article 4(3) TEU, Member States need to respect the principle of sincere cooperation in all policy areas including external actions of the Union. In *Commission v. Spain*, the Court held that the principle of sincere cooperation is 'of general application' in EU external actions, irrespective of the nature of the EU competences.[58] Furthermore, for CFSP matters, Article 24(3) TEU reinforces that the Member States are "*to refrain from any action which is contrary to the interests*

[58]Court of Justice, *Commission v. Sweden*, Case C-246/07, Judgment, 20 April 2010, ECLI:EU:C:2010:203.

of the Union or likely to impair its effectiveness as a cohesive force in international relations". The duty of sincere cooperation in external actions is further restated in Article 34(1) TEU which asks from the Member States to coordinate their actions in international organizations and at international conferences and to uphold the Union's positions in such forums.[59]

According to settled case law, the duty of sincere cooperation in fact flows from the requirement of unity in the international representation of the Union.[60] In order to ensure uniformity in Union external actions, the EU institutions and the Member States must coordinate internally their positions. The Union's position usually consists of general strategies concerning the Union's priorities agreed in the Council in Brussels and the details left to the Union delegations who act on the ground.[61] For files to be discussed at the UN, the common position of the Union is established at the Council's United Nations Working Party (CONUN) meetings who can be extended to other interested Council's working groups such as the High-Level Working Group on Asylum and Migration (HLWG). At UN level, where the Union does not have a member status, it is important that the EU institutions and the Member States reach an agreement on the Union's position. Furthermore, an agreement on the Union's position is important in light of the *PFOS* case.

From the *PFOS* case, it seems that the principle of sincere cooperation whereby the Member States should support the position expressed by the EU or, at least, abstain from contradicting it starts from the moment there is an established common position.[62] In this case, Sweden had submitted a proposal to list the chemical substance PFOS in Annex A of the Stockholm Convention on Persistent Organic Pollutants while a Commission proposal for a Council Decision authorizing the Commission to submit on behalf of the Union and its Member States a list of chemicals to be added in the Annexes of the Convention did not comprise PFOS within the list. Firstly, the Court recalled that the submission by the Commission of a Council proposal for the authorization to start the negotiation of a multilateral agreement represents the point of departure for a concerted action even though the proposal has not been adopted by the Council.[63] The Court added that the establishment of a common position through a Council Decision was not a prerequisite for its existence as long as "*the content of*

[59]For a historical account on the development of the principle of sincere cooperation in external relations, see Van Vooren and Wessel 2014, pp. 192–205.

[60]Court of Justice, *International Agreement on Natural Rubber*, Opinion of the Court, 4 October 1979, Opinion 1/78, ECLI:EU:C:1979:224, paras 34–36; Court of Justice, *ILO Convention 170*, Opinion 2/91, 19 March 1993, ECLI:EU:C:1993:106, para 36; Court of Justice, *Competence of the Community to conclude international agreements concerning services and the protection of intellectual property*, Opinion of the Court, 15 November 1994, Opinion 1/94, ECLI:EU:C:1994:384, para 108; Court of Justice, *Council v. Commission*, Judgment, 19 March 1996, Case C-25/94, ECLI:EU:C:1996:114, para 48; Court of Justice, *Commission v. Sweden*, Judgment, 20 April 2010, Case C-246/07, ECLI:EU:C:2010:203, para 73.

[61]Wouters and Chané 2016, pp. 312–313.

[62]*Commission v. Sweden*, above n. 59, para 89.

[63]Ibid., para 74.

that position can be established to the requisite legal standards".[64] In the *PFOS* case, the Court found that the fact that Council's conclusions and minutes of the meeting of the Council's Working Party on International Environmental Issues were sufficient evidences of an established common position which the Member States should support or, at least, abstain from contradicting.[65] As a result, the Court does not seem to follow a formalistic approach but instead focuses on whether the content of the common position can be established to the requisite legal standards. This threshold of being "*established to the requisite legal standards*" has been criticized in the literature as being rather vague.[66] In the *PFOS* case, in reference to the "*requisite legal standards*", the Court referred to another case: *Council v. Commission.*[67] In that case, the Council and the Commission had concluded an arrangement setting up a coordination procedure between the Commission and the Member States to decide on the exercise of responsibilities or on statements in the context of the UN Food and Agriculture Organization ('FAO').[68] In *Council v. Commission*, the requisite legal standards were set out in section 2.3 of the arrangement between the Commission and the Council and required a common position to be achieved through consensus.[69] What can be deduced from that case law is that, while the need for a Council Decision is not required, there is a need to have an internal discussion, according to the requisite legal standards, on a common position to be expressed at an international forum.

In the context of the drafting process of the Global Compact for Migration, one may consider the "General Arrangements for EU Statements in multilateral organisations"[70] as being the relevant requisite legal standards. Point 2 of the General Arrangements indicates that "[G]iven the sensitivity of representation and potential expectations of third parties, it is essential that, in conformity with current practice, the preparation of statements relating to the sensitive area of competences of the EU and its Member States should remain **internal and consensual**." (emphasis added). Considering the fact that internal coordination for setting a common position takes place behind closed doors, it is very difficult to ascertain that an internal coordination on the Global Compact for Migration actually took place thereby holding the Member States accountable for it. According to Mauro Gatti, the statements delivered by the Union delegation at the UN show that there was a common position up until March 2018.[71] After March 2018, the statements represented the position of the EU and 27 Member States, thereby excluding Hungary. While this might be true,

---

[64] Ibid., para 77.

[65] Ibid., para 89.

[66] Van Vooren and Wessel 2014, p. 203.

[67] *Council v. Commission*, above n. 59.

[68] *Commission v. Sweden*, above n. 59, para 77 referring to *Council v. Commission*, above n. 59, para 49.

[69] *Council v. Commission*, above n. 59, para 49.

[70] Council of the European Union 2011.

[71] Gatti 2018.

the lack of transparency about the establishment of a common position is a pity as it left an opportunity for the Member States to hold contradictory statements.

The lack of evidence is even more problematic considering that it is unclear who the Union delegation's statements represented. The General Arrangements have been adopted by the Council in 2011 following disagreements on the delivery of statements given on behalf of the Union in multilateral organizations, in particular in the UN and the OSCE.[72] According to the General Arrangements, there are three types of statements representing different actors.[73] The first type of statements are statements made "*on behalf of the European Union*" for matters, including CFSP, related to exclusive actions or responsibilities of the EU. When the statement is entitled "*on behalf of the EU and its Member States*", it represents common position of the EU and its Member States in the spirit of the principle of unity of representation. And finally, when the statement is prefaced with "*on behalf of the Member States*", it is understood that the EU represents the Member States collectively in a matter relating to the exercise of the national competences.[74] If one looks on the Union delegation's website, one of those statements given in the context of the negotiation of the Global Compact is labelled "*on behalf of the EU*".[75] This seems to indicate that it is a statement representing the EU position in a matter exclusively related to EU competence.[76] However, within the text of that statement, there are several references to positions "*of the EU and its Member States*". In accordance with the General Arrangements, that wording would mean that the statements given by the Union delegation in fact represented a common position of the EU and its Member States.

While there might have been internal coordination and an agreed common position, the lack of evidence of it is in fact problematic when Member States start expressing opinions contradicting the Union position. It is problematic as it becomes hard for the European Commission to ensure that the Member States respect the common position agreed in Brussels. As a result, judicial enforcement through infringement proceedings under Article 258 and 260 TFEU would not have worked in this case.

13.3.3 The European Commission's Proposal for Two Council Decisions Authorizing It to Approve the Global Compact

In the *PFOS* case, the Court recalled that the point of departure for a concerted action is the submission by the Commission of a Council proposal for the authorization to

[72]Kuijper et al. 2015, p. 202.

[73]Council of the European Union 2011.

[74]Ibid., p. 4.

[75]EEAS 2018a.

[76]Council of the European Union 2011.

start the negotiation of a multilateral agreement.[77] Hence, one way to prove the common position and to enforce the positions agreed is through Council Decisions authorizing the European Commission to negotiate and conclude the Global Compact on behalf of the Union. As a result, the European Commission proposed two Council Decisions authorizing it to approve the Global Compact on behalf of the Union[78] on 21 March 2018 while the negotiated text of the Global Compact was only finalized in July 2018. The timing of the proposals certainly shows the uneasiness of the Commission regarding the proof of an agreed position for the negotiation of the Global Compacts. It seems that the European Commission wanted to secure its mandate not only with regard to the approval of the Global Compact on Migration but also for the negotiations of the text. Besides their timing, the European Commission's proposals also raise questions concerning their legal bases and the reasons given in order to justify the need of two separate Council Decisions.

Whereas the first Council Decision was based on Article 16 TEU in combination with Article 209 TFEU, the second Council Decision was based on Article 16 TEU together with Article 79 TFEU. Despite the fact that the Global Compact on Migration is one single instrument, the European Commission proposed two Council Decisions. The choice for adopting two separate Council Decisions appeared to have been purely political to escape the struggles of Article 79 TFEU on immigration policy. Indeed, in accordance with Protocol No 21 and No 22, Denmark does not participate in immigration policies and Ireland and the United Kingdom do not participate unless they opt-in. The timeline sought for adoption of the Council's Decisions would not have allowed the UK to make the necessary internal arrangements to take an opt-in decision.[79] In any case, the decision to propose two separate Council Decisions cannot be justified just because migration policies will trigger the application of Protocol No. 21 and No. 22. The Court has repeatedly held that the choice of legal bases must rest on objective factors amenable to judicial review, which include the aim and content of the measure.[80]

As explained above, the aim of the Global Compact for Migration is to set out commitments to improving cooperation on international migration.[81] In terms of content, if one traces back to the New York Declaration, it must be noted that the first specific commitments agreed by States were commitments related to return and readmission.[82] The name of the Global Compact itself refers to "migration". However, the overall content of the Global Compact for Migration is to be guided by the 2030 Agenda for Sustainable Development and the Addis Ababa Action Agenda

---

[77] *Commission v. Sweden*, above n. 59, para 74.

[78] European Commission 2018.

[79] UK Minister of State for Immigration 2018.

[80] Court of Justice, *Commission v. Council*, Judgment, 11 June 1991, Case C-300/89 ECLI:EU:C:1991:244, para 10; Court of Justice, *Commission v. Council,* Judgment, 29 April 2004, Case C-338/01, ECLI:EU:C:2004:253, para 54.

[81] UNGA 2018c, above n. 7, p. 8.

[82] UNGA 2016b, paras 41–42.

of the Third International Conference on Financing for Development.[83] Hence, in the New York Declaration and its Annex II as well as in the Final Draft, the link between migration and development is clearly emphasized. As a result, it seems that the aims and content of the measure are equally about migration and development.[84] Article 209 TFEU has been considered by the Court as encompassing a wide range of policies that can fall within the heading of "development".[85] Hence, Article 209 TFEU can cover other type of policies, such as migration policy, without the need to add a legal basis to cover those other policies.[86] However, a measure would need additional legal bases if the obligations and implementation of other policies are "*so extensive that they may be considered to constitute objectives distinct from those of development cooperation that are neither secondary nor indirect in relation to the latter objectives*".[87] It is therefore a case where the measure has a twofold purpose which are inseparably linked without one being secondary and indirect in relation to the other.[88] As such the selection of Article 209 TFEU and 79 TFEU as legal bases seem to be appropriate in the context of the Global Compact for Migration, contrarily to the choice of separating the Council Decisions.

13.4 Conclusion

The road leading to the adoption of the Global Compact for Migration was a difficult one. Given the sensitivity of its subject, the lack of support for the Global Compact for Migration became a symbol for many populist governments. At the beginning of the negotiation of the Global Compact, the EU had however managed to present a unified approach. That unity of EU representation did not last. The first difficulties appeared when Hungary started to adopt contradictory statements to the ones presented by the EU delegation. Then, new difficulties arose when several Member States such as Hungary, Austria, Poland, the Czech Republic and Bulgaria announced their withdrawals from the negotiation process. The contradictory stances adopted by several Member States not only impaired the unity of EU representation but also disregarded the duty of sincere cooperation in external actions.

Nonetheless, it was difficult for the European Commission to enforce judicially or politically the position (allegedly) agreed in Brussels with the Member States. The

[83] UNGA 2016b, Annex II, p. 2.

[84] The mixing of migration and development policies is often criticized by the literature. The purpose of this paper is not to enter this debate. For more details on that debate, see Andrade 2013, pp. 263–281.

[85] Court of Justice, *Portugal v. Council,* Judgment, 3 December 1996, Case C-268/94 ECLI:EU:C:1996:461, paras 37–38; Court of Justice, *Commission v. Council*, Judgment, 11 June 2014, Case C- 377/12, ECLI:EU:C:2014:1903, paras 36–38.

[86] *Portugal v. Council,* above n. 84, para 39; *Commission v. Council*, above n. 84, para 39.

[87] *Commission v. Council*, above n. 84, paras 48 and 59.

[88] Court of Justice, *Parliament v. Council*, Judgment, 19 July 2012, Case C-130/10 ECLI:EU:C:2012:472, paras 42–45.

cracks in unity of EU representation are in fact the consequences of a lack of clear negotiating mandate for the European Commission and the Union delegation. Indeed, without a Council Decision authorizing the European Commission to negotiate the Global Compact for Migration on behalf of the Union, it is difficult to prove the common position of the Union. The uneasiness of the European Commission faced by rebellious Member States can be felt through the timing of its proposals for Council Decisions authorizing it to sign the Global Compact for Migration on behalf of the Union. The European Commission adopted those proposals in March 2018 whereas the Final Draft of the Global Compact for Migration was only agreed in July 2018. In the end, those proposals were not adopted by the Council and were eventually withdrawn by the Commission.

Overall, the negotiations of the Global Compact for Migration are informative for future negotiations of international soft law instruments. It shows that the lack of a clear legal framework with a procedure for the negotiation of international soft law instrument is detrimental in cases where political support from the Member States is lacking. Indeed, the procedure of Article 218 TFEU for the negotiation and adoption of international agreements does not apply to international soft law instruments. Instead, there are uncertainties with regard to the standards framing the negotiation and adoption of international soft law instruments. The only legal boundaries are coming from the case-law of the Court in C-660/13 on the Swiss MoU. In that case, the Court has held that the Commission would need a Council Decision authorizing it to sign a negotiated soft law instrument. As for the period prior to the signature, the negotiations should respect the principles of unity of representation and sincere cooperation. However, given the lack of proof and transparency regarding common positions agreed in Brussels, there is little room for putting rebellious Member States back on track. With a clear legal framework for the negotiation and adoption of international soft law instrument outlining the rights and obligations of all actors involved, many of the political difficulties that arose in the Global Compact for Migration could have been avoided. Instead, the Global Compact will be remembered for the EU's inability to preserve its unity of representation on the international scene.

References

Allinson K, Guild E, Basaran T (2019) GCM Commentary: The Legal Status of the UN's Global Compact for Safe, Orderly and Regular Migration in International and UK Law. https://rli.blogs.sas.ac.uk/2019/01/31/gcm-commentary-the-legal-status/ Accessed 25 February 2020

Andrade P G (2013) The Legal Feasibility of the EU's External Action on Legal Migration: the Internal and External Intertwined. European Journal of Migration and Law 15:263–281

Carrera S, Den Hertog L, Stefan M (2017) It wasn't me! The Luxembourg Court Orders on the EU-Turkey Refugee Deal. https://www.ceps.eu/system/files/EU-Turkey%20Deal.pdf Accessed 25 February 2020

Council of the European Union (2011) General Arrangements on EU Statements in Multilateral Organisations http://data.consilium.europa.eu/doc/document/ST-15901-2011-INIT/en/pdf. Accessed 25 February 2020

Den Heijer M, Spijkerboer T (2016) Is the EU-Turkey refugee and migration deal a treaty? http://eulawanalysis.blogspot.com/2016/04/is-eu-turkey-refugee-and-migration-deal.html Accessed 25 February 2020

EEAS (2017a) EU statement on Global Compact for Migration https://refugeesmigrants.un.org/sites/default/files/ts1_p1234_eu.pdf. Accessed 25 February 2020

EEAS (2017b) EU statement on Global Compact for Migration https://refugeesmigrants.un.org/sites/default/files/ts3_p1234_eu.pdf. Accessed 25 February 2020

EEAS (2017c) EU statement on Global Compact for Migration https://refugeesmigrants.un.org/sites/default/files/eu_ts5.pdfs/eu_ts5.pdf. Accessed 25 February 2020

EEAS (2018a) EU statement on Global Compact on Refugees Geneva 8-10 May 2018 https://eeas.europa.eu/delegations/un-new-york/44617/global-compact-refugees-fourth-formal-consultations-draft-2-eu-statement_en. Accessed 25 February 2020

EEAS (2018b) EU statement on Global Compact for Migration 15 May 2018 https://refugeesmigrants.un.org/sites/default/files/eu_proposal_on_international_cooperation.pdf. Accessed 25 February 2020

European Commission (2018) Proposal for a COUNCIL DECISION authorising the Commission to approve, on behalf of the Union, the Global Compact for Safe, Orderly and Regular Migration in the area of immigration policy https://ec.europa.eu/transparency/regdoc/rep/1/2018/EN/COM-2018-168-F1-EN-MAIN-PART-1.PDF. Accessed 25 February 2020

European Parliament, Council, European Commission (2017) Joint statement: The New European Consensus on Development, p. 40. https://eur-lex.europa.eu/legal-content/EN/TXT/PDF/?uri=CELEX:42017Y0630(01)&from=EN. Accessed 25 February 2020

Gammeltoft-Hanse T, Guild E, Moreno-Lax V, Panizzon M, Roele I (2017) What is a Compact? Migrants' Rights and State Responsibilities Regarding the Design of the UN Global Compact for Safe, Orderly and Regular Migration, Raoul Wallenberg Institute Paper. https://rwi.lu.se/app/uploads/2017/10/RWI_What-is-a-compact-test_101017-senaste-1.pdf Accessed 25 February 2020

Gatti M (2018) EU States' Exit from the Global Compact on Migration: A Breach of Loyalty. http://eumigrationlawblog.eu/eu-states-exit-from-the-global-compact-on-migration-a-breach-of-loyalty/ Accessed 25 February 2020

Guild E, Grant S (2017a) Migration Governance in the UN: What is the Global Compact and What does it mean? https://repository.ubn.ru.nl/bitstream/handle/2066/182071/182071.pdf?sequence=1 Accessed 25 February 2020

Guild E, Grant S (2017b) What role for the EU in the UN negotiations on a Global Compact on Migration? https://www.ceps.eu/system/files/COMPACTS%20RRpt%20No%202017-05.pdf Accessed 25 February 2020

High Representative of the EU (2018) Speech at the European Plenary session on the situation in Syria https://eeas.europa.eu/delegations/russia/41270/speech-high-representativevice-president-federica-mogherini-european-parliament-plenary_en Accessed 25 February 2020

Hungarian delegation at the UN (2018) Security First: Proposals by Hungary to the UN's Global Compact on Migration

Kuijper P J, Wouters J, Hoffmeister F, De Baere G, Ramopoulos T (2015) The Law of EU External Relations. Cases, Materials, and Commentary on the EU as an International Legal Actor. Oxford University Press, Oxford

Melin P (2018) The Global Compact for Migration: Cracks in Unity of EU Representation. http://eulawanalysis.blogspot.com/2018/12/the-global-compact-for-migration-cracks.html Accessed 25 February 2020

Melin P (2019) The Global Compact for Migration: Lessons for the Unity of EU Representation, European Journal of Migration and Law 21:194–214

Ott A (2017) EU-Turkey Cooperation in Migration Matters: A Game Changer in a Multi-Layered Relationship? https://www.asser.nl/media/4085/cleer17-4_web.pdf Accessed 25 February 2020

UK Minister of State for Immigration (2018) Letter to the Chair of the European Scrutiny Committee of the House of Commons, pp. 1–2. http://europeanmemoranda.cabinetoffice.gov.uk/files/2018/

06/Letter_from_Immigration_Minister_on_7400_18_and_7391_18.pdf. Accessed 25 February 2020
UNGA (2016a) Agreement concerning the Relationship between the United Nations and the International Organization for Migration, A/RES/70/296
UNGA (2016b) New York Declaration for Refugees and Migrants, A/RES/71/1
UNGA (2017a) Modalities for the Intergovernmental Conference to Adopt the Global Compact for Safe, Orderly and Regular Migration, A/RES/72/244
UNGA (2017b) Modalities for the Intergovernmental Negotiations of the Global Compact for Safe, Orderly and Regular Migration, A/RES/71/280
UNGA (2018a) Speech by Giuseppe Conte, President of the Council of Ministers of Italy https://gadebate.un.org/en/73/italy Accessed 25 February 2020
UNGA (2018b) Zero Draft of the Global Compact for Safe, Orderly and Regular Migration https://refugeesmigrants.un.org/sites/default/files/180205_gcm_zero_draft_final.pdf Accessed 25 February 2020
UNGA (2018c) Zero Draft Plus of the Global Compact for Safe, Orderly and Regular Migration http://unipd centrodirittiumani.it/public/docs/20180503_globalcompactformigration_zerodraftplus.pdf. Accessed 25 February 2020
UNGA (2018d) Final Draft of the Global Compact for Safe, Orderly and Regular Migration https://refugeesmigrants.un.org/sites/default/files/180711_final_draft_0.pdf. Accessed 25 February 2020
UNGA (2018e) Global Compact for Safe, Orderly and Regular Migration, A/RES/73/195
UNGA (2018f) Modalities for the Intergovernmental Conference to Adopt the Global Compact for Safe, Orderly and Regular Migration, A/RES/72/308
UNGA (2018g) Outcome of the Intergovernmental Conference to Adopt the Global Compact for Safe, Orderly and Regular Migration https://undocs.org/pdf?symbol=en/a/conf.231/3 Accessed 5 July 2020
UN Network on Migration (2018) Terms of Reference http://migrationnetwork.un.org/sites/default/files/docs/UN_Network_on_Migration_TOR.PDF. Accessed 25 February 2020
UN Network on Migration (2020) Workplan https://migrationnetwork.un.org/about/united-nations-network-migration-workplan. Accessed 25 February 2020
Van Vooren B, Wessel R A (2014) EU External Relations Law. Text, Cases and Materials. Cambridge University Press, Cambridge
Wouters J, Chané A-L (2016) Brussels Meets Westphalia: the European Union and the United Nations. In: Eeckhout P, Lopez-Escudero M (eds) The European Union's External Action in Times of Crisis. Hart Publishing, Oxford, pp 299–323

Chapter 14
The Externalisation of EU Migration Policies: The Implications Arising from the Transfer of Responsibilities to Third Countries

J. Santos Vara and L. Pascual Matellán

Contents

Abstract The EU and its Member States have resorted very often to the externalisation of migration policies with the aim of preventing the access of irregular migrants and persons in need of international protection to the territory of the Member States. The transfer of responsibilities to third countries in the management of migration does not exonerate the EU and its Member States from the infringements of human rights that might take place on the territory of third countries. The aim of this chapter is to analyse the implications arising from the transfer of responsibilities to third countries in the management of migration and, in particular, the cooperation developed with Libya in recent years.

Keywords externalization of migration · Libya · Regional Disembarkation Platforms · international responsibility · non-refoulement · extraterritorial jurisdiction

---

J. Santos Vara (✉)
University of Salamanca, Salamanca, Spain
e-mail: savajuan@usal.es

L. Pascual Matellán
University of Salamanca, Salamanca, Spain
e-mail: nicte@usal.es

W. Th. Douma et al. (eds.), *The Evolving Nature of EU External Relations Law*,
https://doi.org/10.1007/978-94-6265-423-5_14

14.1 Introduction

The EU and its Member States have resorted very often to the externalisation of migration policies with the aim of preventing the access of irregular migrants and persons in need of international protection to the territory of the Member States. It has been pointed out that externalisation often amounts to a policy of deterrence preventing third countries' nationals from entering into direct contact with EU or Member States' authorities.[1] Externalization of migration controls is also presented in terms of security and/or humanitarian concerns.[2] Externalisation is sometimes considered by the EU institutions as an instrument used in order to avoid migrants taking very dangerous journeys to reach the country of their destination. Extraterritorial immigration control has been increasingly used by States aiming to prevent flows of migrants and asylum seekers towards their territory.[3] The failure to develop a common migration policy has led the EU to intensify the externalization process.[4] In this chapter, the term externalization refers to the shifting of responsibilities to third countries of origin and transit of migrants, as well as to the activities carried out by the EU and the Member States on the territory of third countries aiming to externalize the management of migration.

In a first stage, extraterritorial immigration controls have led to the intensification of visa regimes, the imposition of passenger identification duties to carriers before travel with non-compliance leading to significant sanctions and the intensification of immigration controls and surveillance before entering the territory of the Member States, including on the high seas.[5] More recently, the EU has tried to reinforce the cooperation with third countries in the management of migration, including Turkey, Libya and the Sahel countries in order to externalize migration controls.[6]

The externalization of migration controls to third countries is not totally new in the EU. Some Member States have resorted in the past to similar policies, including among others Spain.[7] The recent initiatives adopted by the EU aiming to externalize the management of migration have led to the enlistment of third countries to reinforce EU border controls with the support of the EU and its member States. The EU has provided several third countries with financial assistance, equipment, training and it has even deployed liaison officers on the ground. The externalization of EU migration policies may also lead the EU and its Member States to exercise directly effective control over migrants and persons in need of international protection on the territory of third countries on the basis of the agreements concluded with them.

[1]See Lavanex 2010, p. 329; Rijpma 2017, p. 1; Santos Vara 2020, p. 17; Santos Vara and Pascual Matellán 2020, p. 163.

[2]Frelick et al. 2016, p. 193.

[3]See Guiraudon 2003, p. 191. Mitsilegas 2019, p. 290.

[4]See González Vega 2019, p. 76.

[5]See Mitsilegas 2019, p. 294; Santos Vara 2020, p. 49.

[6]See Santos Vara 2019, p. 21.

[7]Mangas Martín 2012, p. 646.

Externalisation in the management of migration is leading to priority being given to preventing migrants from reaching the territory of the Member States over the protection of human rights.[8] As a result of the transfer of responsibilities to third countries, migrants and persons in need of international protection are often obliged to stay in the territory of third countries with a questionable human rights record. The aim of this chapter is to analyse the implications arising from the transfer of responsibilities to third countries in the management of migration and, in particular, the cooperation developed with Libya in recent years. This contribution will also devote special attention to the proposal to establish Regional Disembarkation Platforms (RDPs) on the territory of third countries. The externalisation in the management of migration raises very complex issues as regards the attribution of responsibility for breaches of human rights that might take place on the territory of third countries.

14.2 The Transfer of Responsibility in the Management of Migration to Third Countries: The Case of Libya

The EU is providing humanitarian assistance to Libya to respond to migration challenges and is supporting the Libyan authorities with the aim of reinforcing border controls and tackling the systematic problems that the detained migrants face in Libya. The financial support has been mainly channelled through the International Migration Organization (IMO) and the High Commissioner for Refugees (UNHCR), including the voluntary return of migrants to their countries of origin.[9] However, the main initiatives have been adopted within the framework of the Common Security and Defence Policy (CSDP) through the operations EU Border Assistance Mission in Libya (EUBAM Libya)[10] and EUNAVFOR MED (Operation Sophia).[11] The aim of the EUBAM Libya is to support the Libyan authorities to develop their capacity for enhancing the security of Libya's borders in the short term and "to develop a broader IBM strategy in the longer term".[12] The original objective of the Operation Sophia was to contribute to the disruption of the business model of human smuggling and trafficking networks in the Southern Central Mediterranean.[13] One year later the purpose of the operation was widened by providing training to the Libyan Coast

[8] Parliamentary Assembly Council of Europe 2018; see Atak and Crépeau 2014, p. 591.

[9] The EU's extensive cooperation programmes in Libya (of in total €467 million) are continuing despite the security situation, and new programmes have been adopted in the last months of 2019 by the EU Trust Fund for Africa. See European Commission, Progress report on the Implementation of the European Agenda on Migration, COM (2019) 481 final, 16 October 2019.

[10] Council Decision 2013/233/CFSP of 22 May 2013 on the European Union Integrated Border Management Assistance Mission in Libya (EUBAM Libya), OJ L 138, 24 May 2013, p. 15.

[11] Council Decision 2015/778 of 18 May 2015 on a European Union military operation in the Southern Central Mediterranean (EUNAVFOR MED), OJ L 122, 19 May 2015, p. 31.

[12] Council Decision 2013/233/CFSP, above n. 10, Article 2.

[13] Council Decision 2015/778 of 18 May 2015, above n. 10.

Guard and Navy and contributing to the implementation of arms trafficking within its agreed area of operation in accordance with the Security Council's resolutions.[14]

The use of a military operation to perform extraterritorial controls of migration flows has been questioned from the beginning.[15] The implementation of the Operation Sophia in cooperation with Libya, a country with a questionable human rights record, raises very serious difficulties.[16] It has been even held that as a result of the Operation Sophia migrants are forced to use smaller boats to cross the Mediterranean Sea and more dangerous routes.[17] The mandate of the Operation Sophia has been periodically extended. The deployment of the Operation's naval assets was suspended in March 2019, as Italy opposed the disembarkation of migrants rescued at sea until a solution for the resettlement of the people disembarked was agreed at EU level.[18]

The EU has also supported the cooperation on migration and border control developed by Italy with Libya. In the Malta Declaration of 3 February 2017, it is stated that "capacity building is key for the authorities to acquire control over the land and sea borders and to combat transit and smuggling activities".[19] In the Final Declaration of the Paris Summit held on 28 August 2017, the Heads of State and Government of France, Germany, Spain, Chad, Niger and Libya and the High Representative for the CFSP praised Italy for the initiatives undertaken to improve the management of migration and control of borders by the Libyan authorities.[20] In June 2018, the European Council held that the EU should further develop the approach adopted in the last years in order to definitively break the business model of the smugglers, thus preventing tragic loss of lives in the Mediterranean Sea.[21]

On 2 February 2017, Italy and Libya signed a Memorandum of Understanding on development cooperation, illegal immigration, human trafficking, fuel smuggling and reinforcement of border security (hereafter 'Memorandum').[22] Libya assumed the commitment to control the departures of irregular migrants to Europe. Italy accepted supporting and financing development programs in the regions affected

---

[14]Council Decision 2016/993 of 20 June 2016 amending Decision (CFSP) 2015/778 on a European Union military operation in the Southern Central Mediterranean (EUNAVFOR MED operation SOPHIA), OJ L 162, 21 June 2016, p. 18. See also UNSC 2011; UNSC 2016.

[15]See Mitsilegas 2019, p. 301.

[16]See Estrada-Canamares 2015, p. 181; Moreno-Lax and Papastavridis 2016.

[17]European Union Committee, 2nd Report of Session 2017–19, HL Paper 5, 12 July 2017.

[18]Council of Ministers, EUNAVFOR MED Operation Sophia: Mandate extended until 30 September 2019, 29 March 2019.

[19]EU Council 2017.

[20]Joint Statement "Addressing the Challenge of Migration and Asylum", Paris, 28 August 2017.

[21]European Council Conclusions, 28 June 2018.

[22]Memorandum of Understanding on Cooperation in the fields of Development, the Fight against Illegal Immigration, Human Trafficking and Fuel Smuggling and on reinforcing the Security of Borders between the State of Libya and the Italian Republic (MoU) 2 February 2017. Italy has concluded similar arrangements in the past with Libya that led to a very intense cooperation on migration between both countries. However, the cooperation was suspended as a result of the *Hirsi Jamaa* case. Italy was condemned by the European Court of Human Rights for infringing the principle of non-refoulement (ECtHR, *Hirsi Jamaa and Others v. Italy*, Judgment (Grand Chamber), 23 February 2012, App. No. 27765/09.

by the illegal immigration phenomenon and "to provide technical and technologic support to the Libyan institutions in charge of the fight against illegal immigration, and that are represented by the border guard and the coast guard (…)".[23] These generic obligations have given rise to more specific commitments and, among others, we could mention the following: completion of the system of border control in Southern Libya; adaptation and financing of the reception centres of migrants already active and the delivery of medicines and medical equipment for the treatment of migrants detained; training of the Libyan personnel within the above mentioned reception centres to face the clandestine immigration phenomenon and human trafficking; supporting the international organizations that are present and operate in Libya in the migration sector; and starting development programs through adequate job creation initiatives within the Libyan regions affected by illegal immigration phenomena.[24]

The Memorandum is aimed at curbing migration flows from Libya, developing the country and reinforcing migration control by Libya. The document constantly refers to clandestine or illegal migrants, lacking a substantial reference to the international protection of human rights.[25] From the beginning, it has been pointed out that the implementation of the Memorandum may lead to pushing back migrants to the Libyan southern border and transferring the persons intercepted by Libyan coastguard upon departure to Europe to local reception centres pending repatriation or voluntary return to their countries of origin.[26] These objections have not led the Italian and European authorities to stop the process of externalization. On the contrary, the shifting of responsibilities to the Libyan coastguard has continued in the last years. First, Italy has provided support to the Libyan coastguard with the aim of exercising effective control over its territorial sea and beyond.[27] Second, the EU and its Member States have progressively disengaged from search and rescue (SAR) operations on the high seas in the Central Mediterranean Sea. In practice, the Memorandum has led to a transfer of responsibility over SAR activities to the Libyan authorities in exchange for providing the capacity-building and training of the Libyan coastguard.[28] At the same time, a restrictive code of conduct for NGOs engaged in SAR operations, adopted by the Italian authorities, is part of the policy of deterring migrants from travelling to Europe.[29] Third, there is some justified scepticism as regards the final destination of the financial resources awarded to Libya in the absence of an effective central

[23]MoU, above n.22, Article 1.

[24]Ibid., Article 3.

[25]Palm 2017, p. 3. There is only one reference to human obligations in Article 5. It says that "le Parti si impegnano ad interpretare e applicare il presente Memorandum nel rispetto degli obblighi internazionali e degli accordi sui diritti umani di cui i due Paesi siano parte".

[26]Palm 2017, p. 3; Skordas 2018, p. 1.

[27]Italy has supported the establishment of a rescue coordination centre in Libya and has donated vessels to the Libyan coast guards, see Camera dei Deputati [Italian Chamber of Deputies] 2018.

[28]See Riegert 2019.

[29]Ministero dell'Interno 2017. See Sánchez Legido 2018, p. 1; Santos Vara 2020, p. 54.

authority. It has rightly stated that the development projects could not be realistically implemented without involving the militias.[30]

The Libyan authorities do not have the capacity or real means or even intention to provide migrants with assistance and protection, as well as proper access to asylum procedures. The grave violations of human rights repeatedly committed against migrants in Libya have been reported by the main NGOs and international organizations working on the ground.[31] The new role attributed to the Libyan Coast Guard has led to increased push-backs operations and distressing circumstances for both the people rescued at sea and the NGO rescue teams. As it has been held by the Parliamentary Assembly of the Council of Europe, the grave violations of human rights repeatedly reported against migrants in Libya shows clearly that people rescued cannot be returned and disembarked there in compliance with international human rights law, refugee law and maritime law.[32] According to the last report of the UN Support Mission in Libya, published in August 2019:

> Migrants and refugees continued to be vulnerable to: loss of liberty and arbitrary detention in official and unofficial places of detention; torture, including sexual violence; abduction for ransom; extortion; forced labour; and unlawful killings. Migrants continued to be detained in overcrowded, inhuman and degrading conditions, with insufficient food, water and medical care and very poor sanitation. Perpetrators of violations included State officials, members of armed groups, smugglers, traffickers and members of criminal gangs. The number of detainees rose as a result of an increase in interceptions at sea and the closure of sea routes to migrants, preventing their departure. On 25 July, up to 150 migrants reportedly died at sea after their vessel capsized.[33]

The transfer of responsibilities on migration to Libya entails serious human rights risks. It substantially increases the risk of migrants being submitted to arbitrary detention, inhuman treatment and infringing the principle of *non-refoulement*. The implications of externalising migration controls to Libya are not merely theoretic. Libya has not ratified the UN Convention relating to the Status of Refugees nor has it developed a legal framework to protect the rights of migrants or persons in need of international protection. However, the Memorandum signed in 2017 does not include any provision with the aim to improve the migrants' situation in Libya, but foresees explicitly the repatriation and voluntary return of migrants to their countries of origin.[34] Many NGOs have pointed out the risks involved in the externalisation of

[30] Walsh and Horowitz (2018) Italy, Going It Alone, Stalls the Flow of Migrants. But at What Cost? https://www.nytimes.com/2017/09/17/world/europe/italy-libya-migrant-crisis.html Accessed 4 July 2020; Skordas 2018.

[31] UNSC 2018; UN Support Mission in Libya 2018; Amnesty International 2019; Human Rights Watch 2019.

[32] Parliamentary Assembly Council of Europe 2018, above n. 8.

[33] UN Support Mission in Libya 2019.

[34] Palm 2017, p. 3; Santos Vara 2020, p. 56.

migration management.[35] It is understandable that the Italian judges and courts have already questioned the legality of the Memorandum signed with Libya.[36]

The Parliamentary Assembly of the Council of Europe has pointed out that the externalisation of the management of migration by the EU may negatively affect the following rights: the right of asylum, the right to an effective remedy, freedom of movement (including the right to leave a country), human dignity and non-discrimination, as well as the obligation of *non-refoulement.*[37] The cooperation with the Libyan authorities leads inevitably to "a high record of refoulement or chain-refoulement put in practice by Libyan authorities".[38] The prohibition to transfer or return a person to a country where there is a risk that the person might suffer torture or inhumane treatment is firmly anchored in international law.

The externalisation of the management of migration and border controls to the South of the Mediterranean shore is not going to provide a satisfactory solution to the current problems. The difficulties to depart from Libya in recent times has led migrants to use more dangerous routes or try to reach Europe through the West Mediterranean Sea, mainly towards Spain. It is not acceptable to outsource the management of migration to Libya. Apart from the fact that the human rights obligations arising from the main international instruments are not respected, the formation of a Government of national unity and the unification of key institutions has not been possible.

14.3 The Regional Disembarkation Platforms: A New Version of the Hotspots?

The proposal to establish RDPs in neighbouring countries for migrants rescued at sea is the latest development in the process of externalisation of migration. It would amount to establishing a kind of hotspot on the territory of third countries.[39] This initiative was presented within the framework of the European Council meeting that took place on 28 and 29 June 2018. The European Council called also for the establishment of "controlled centres" in the EU with the aim of processing the persons rescued at sea and disembarked in the territory of the Member States. Both centres are theoretically aimed at developing a shared approach for the processing of migrants and persons in need of international protection and breaking at the same time the business model of smugglers. In the past, similar proposals have been presented by the

---

[35] Amnesty International 2014: "the demands being placed on third countries to prevent irregular departures to Europe put refugees, asylum-seekers and migrants in those countries at risk of prolonged and arbitrary detention, *refoulement*, and ill-treatment".

[36] See Tribunale di Trapani, Sentenza a Seguito di Giudizio Abbreviato, 23 May 2019.

[37] Parliamentary Assembly Council of Europe 2018, above n. 8.

[38] Palm 2017, p. 3.

[39] See Neville and Rigon 2016, p. 26; Santos Vara 2018, p. 159; Santos Vara 2020, p. 64; Tsourdi 2016, p. 997.

EU institutions. In 2003, the Commission proposed to further explore the viability of the proposal to set up an EU Regional Task Force with the aim of identifying outside the EU the persons in need of international protection and increasing the number of arrivals, namely by setting up resettlement scheme.[40] The United Kingdom proposed also to set up "Regional Protection Zones" and "Transit Processing Centres" in regions of origin aiming at providing accessible protection and returning persons in need of international protection from the EU.[41] These proposals presented serious concerns as regards their compatibility with the ECHR and the UN Convention relating to the Status of Refugees.[42]

The European Council in its conclusions of 28–29 June invited the Council and the Commission to swiftly explore the concept of RDPs in close cooperation with relevant third countries, as well as the United Nations High Commissioner for Refugees (UNHCR) and the International Organization for Migration (IOM). The RDPs would "operate distinguishing individual situations, in full respect of international law and without creating a pull factor".[43] The idea lying behind the concept of RDPs is that the persons who are saved in SAR operations are quickly disembarked in line with international law, in a place of safety that upholds their rights including the principle of *non-refoulement*. A distinction will be made in the RDPs between persons entitled to receive international protection and irregular migrants.

The Commission presented a Non-Paper on 24 July 2018 with the aim of developing the concepts of RDPs and 'controlled centres' in the territory of EU Member States.[44] The Commission clarified that disembarkation in a third country is only possible if SAR operations are carried out in the territorial sea of that country by its coast guard or by other third country vessels. However, if SAR operations take place in international waters and involve an EU State's flag vessel, disembarkation can only take place in a third country, 'provided that the principle of *non-refoulement* is respected'.[45] The EU is willing to provide financial and operational support with the aim of establishing regional disembarkation arrangements in close cooperation with partner third countries, UNHCR and IOM. Apparently, there are many advantages in establishing RDPs in the territory of third countries. If sufficient protection is offered to asylum seekers in the country of first arrival or in third countries, migrants would not be forced to risk their lives in the journey and be subject to human smuggling. Another major advantage for the EU would be that migrants that are not entitled to international protection nor can be returned to their countries will stay in the territory of neighbouring countries that host the RDPs.

---

[40]European Commission, Towards more accessible, equitable and managed asylum systems, COM (2003) 315 final, 3 June 2003.

[41]UK Government, New International approaches to asylum processing and protection, Paper discussed at an informal meeting of EU Justice and Home Affairs (JHA) ministers, 28 March 2003.

[42]See Noll 2003, p. 303.

[43]European Commission 2018b.

[44]Ibid.

[45]European Commission 2018a.

The establishment of disembarkation centres in third countries for migrants rescued at sea raises very complex political and legal issues. It is not clear where the RDPs will be established and under what norms they would be operating for the identification and status determination of the migrants. Until now, no third country has volunteered to establish RDPs on its own territory. The IOM and UNHCR have expressed its willingness to support the States where the RDPs are established, but it seems that they would not accept running the RDPs.[46] There are two alternatives. They could be directly run by the EU with the agreement of the third country concerned or by third countries themselves with the support of the EU, IOM and UNHCR. The first solution does not seem feasible. As current law stands, the only means of getting refugee status from outside the EU is through resettlement. The Commission has admitted that 'to allow individuals to «apply» for asylum outside the EU would require the extraterritorial application of EU law which is currently neither possible nor desirable'.[47] This solution requires a major institutional transformation involving several experts from EASO and the Member States. Also, a system for distributing asylum seekers among Member States should be established. In addition to devoting substantial financial resources to operate the RDPs by the EU, the major difficulty is that the setting up of such extraterritorial centres should go hand and hand with the establishment of an EU courts system to process appeals against negative decisions and the Court of Justice would become the appellate body in the field of asylum. The Court of Justice is not well equipped to deal with mass litigation in this area. For these reasons, it has been held that 'this is an unlikely route as it would require far-reaching institutional engineering'.[48] In addition to requiring a major institutional transformation, substantial resources would need to be allocated to the new EU-asylum courts and bodies.

The only feasible solution is that the RDPs would be operated by third countries themselves with the support of the EU, IOM and UNHCR. Third countries would be responsible for the identification, reception and status determination of migrants in their territories. The third country concerned should effectively implement SAR obligations arising from international law and be considered a safe third country in order to respect the obligations arising from the ECHR. It may happen that the RDP would end up resembling ordinary 'safe third country' mechanisms already in place.[49] It has also been held that 'the concept would hold little added value in relation to current 'pull-back' and 'safe third country' practices, unless one could somehow make RDPs safe regardless of the conditions prevailing in their host State.[50] It might happen that the RDPs lead to developing arrangements similar to the Memorandum between Italy and Libya which support third countries in order to enable them to assume their SAR responsibilities.

[46] UNHCR and IOM 2018.

[47] European Commission 2018a. See also Council of the European Union 2018, above n. 45.

[48] Maiani 2018, p. 3.

[49] Ibid.

[50] Ibid.

The proposal has not been welcomed by African countries. Even though the President of the Commission said in 2019 that the initiative to establish RDP in third countries was no longer on the agenda of the institution, the African Union rejected later the EU's proposal over the new platforms.[51] It does not seem feasible to set up centres to process asylum applications on the territory of African countries. Apart from the political and legal difficulties posed by the initiative, the eventual creation of this kind of centres could attract a huge number of migrants and asylum seekers to the territory of neighbouring countries that wish to obtain the protection offered by the EU.[52]

The ambiguous and controversial proposal might end up being redirected towards the more concrete system of resettlement. In 2016, the Commission proposed a Resettlement Framework which seeks to contribute to managing inflows of third-country nationals or stateless persons applying for international protection by providing legal pathways to international protection in partnership and cooperation with third countries.[53] When identifying the regions or third countries from which resettlement shall take place, the institutions have to take into account a number of factors, among others the third countries' effective cooperation with the EU in the area of migration and asylum.[54] The introduction of a link between resettlement and cooperation in the area of migration and asylum has been criticized by several NGOs.[55] The European Parliament has also raised serious concerns as regards the proposal which gives priority to the management of migration over humanitarian considerations. The Parliament argued that "determining geographical priorities based on third countries cooperation in the area of migration and leveraging resettlement to reach foreign policy objectives would therefore de facto jeopardize a humanitarian, needs-based and international protection approach".[56] It is not surprising that the negotiations to establish a resettlement framework have not advanced in recent years.[57] It is not coherent to use the resettlement framework to further develop the process of externalising the management of migration and asylum. It seems that the Member States

[51] Reuters (2018) Juncker says North Africa Migrant 'Camps' not on EU agenda". https://www.reuters.com/article/us-europe-migrants-africa/juncker-says-north-africa-migrant-camps-not-on-eu-agenda-idUSKCN1N01TU. Accessed 4 July 2020; Boffey (2019) "African Union Seeks to kill EU Plan to Process Migrants in Africa". https://www.theguardian.com/world/2019/feb/24/african-union-seeks-to-kill-eu-plan-to-process-migrants-in-africa. Accessed 4 July 2020.

[52] Savino 2017, p. 86.

[53] Proposal for a Regulation establishing a Union Resettlement Framework and amending Regulation (EU) No 516/2014 of the European Parliament and the Council, COM (2016) 468 final, 13 July 2016.

[54] Ibid., Article 4.

[55] ECRE 2016.

[56] Report on the proposal for a regulation of the European Parliament and of the Council establishing a Union Resettlement Framework and amending Regulation (EU) No 516/2014 of the European Parliament and the Council (COM (2016) 0468–C8–0325/2016–2016/0225(COD)) 19 October17.

[57] Carrera and Cortinovis 2019, p. 9.

are reluctant to complement the establishment of RDPs with a resettlement framework. If the EU does not offer real possibilities of resettlement, third countries are not going to accept the establishment of these kind of centres in their territories.

In conclusion, despite the declared commitment to respect fundamental rights, and in particular the principle of *non-refoulement*, the establishment of the RDPs raises very complex issues as regards fundamental human rights standards laid down in the EU Charter of Fundamental Rights and the ECHR. The proposal to establish a sort of 'hotspots' in neighbouring countries does not ensure that the migrants' rights are always respected, including the principle of *non-refoulement*. There is also a risk that the RDPs serve to curb migration, at the expense of infringing the common values and principles that identify the external action of the EU.

14.4 The Externalization of Migration Policies: The Responsibility of the EU for Human Rights Violations

The transfer of responsibility to third countries in the management of migration raises the question of the attribution of responsibility for breaches of human rights that might take place in the territory of third countries.[58] The concept of jurisdiction is not framed today exclusively in territorial terms. The European Court of Human Rights (ECtHR) held that the responsibility of a Contracting Party could arise when as a consequence of military action it exercises effective control of an area outside its national territory.[59] It is also admitted that a State exercises jurisdiction over individuals held on its military bases, detention centres, or other closed facilities controlled[60] or on board crafts or vessels which are registered in that State.[61] The jurisdiction of a State can be also established when their agents exercise authority or direct control over an individual in the absence of a spatial element of control.[62] This expansive notion of extraterritorial jurisdiction imposes relevant legal constraints on migration policies.[63]

There is no doubt that when a State is exercising public authority on the territory of a third country or effective control over migrants the situation does not raise any doubt from a legal perspective. In the case of *Hirsi Jamaa and Others v. Italy,* the ECtHR dealt with an application made by eleven Somali nationals and thirteen

---

[58] Santos Vara 2020, p. 71.

[59] ECtHR, *Loizidou v. Turkey,* Judgment, 1995, App. No. 15318/89, para 62.

[60] ECtHR, *Al-Saadoon and Mufdhi v. the United Kingdom*, Judgment, 2009, App. No. 61498/08, paras 135, 140 and 155.

[61] See ECtHR *Bankovic v. Belgium*, Judgment, 2001, App. No. 52207/99, para 73; *Hirsi Jamaa v. Italy*, above n. 22, para 81.

[62] ECtHR *Al-Skeini v. United Kingdom*, Judgment, 2011, App. No. 55721/21, paras 135–142. See also *Banković v Belgium,* above n. 61, paras 59–73. See Gammeltoft-Hansen and Hathaway 2015, p. 235.

[63] Savino 2017, p. 86.

Eritrean nationals, who were intercepted by Italian ships on the high seas and forced to return to Libya.[64] The Court sustained that "whenever the State through its agents operating outside its territory exercises control and authority over an individual, and thus jurisdiction, the State is under an obligation under Article 1 to secure to that individual the rights and freedoms".[65] The ECtHR held that there has been a violation of Article 3 of the ECHR on account of the fact that the applicants were exposed to the risk of being subjected to ill-treatment in Libya.

As it has been exposed before, the Italian authorities have progressively transferred the responsibility as regards SAR operations to Libya. Unlike in the *Hirsi* case, the interception of migrants at sea is carried out directly by the Libyan authorities. The fact that such actions are carried out in the Libyan territorial waters does not absolve Italy from its obligations under the ECHR.[66] The Italian authorities have always argued that they have never returned to Libya migrants rescued at sea by Italian vessels in recent years.[67]

However, a more complex situation arises when third countries have prevented migration flows and incurred in human rights breaches as a result of the migration cooperation established with the EU and its Member States. It may be argued that in these situations the cooperation and support of the EU and its Member States to third countries amount to 'assistance' according to the law of international responsibility of States and international organizations.[68] According to Article 16 of the Project of Articles on Responsibility of States for International Wrongful Acts the State that aids or assists another States in the commission of an international wrongful act does so "with knowledge of the circumstances of the internationally wrongful act". It is not easy to demonstrate that the cooperation established with a third country to prevent migration is developed with the intention of facilitating the violation of migrants' rights. Even in the case of Libya there are clear difficulties in demonstrating that the assistance provided by the EU and Italy was given in order to facilitate the commission of a wrongful act.[69] However, it has been pointed out that "limiting responsibility only to third countries would create the very gaps in the rule of law that ECtHR attempted to address in *Hirsi*".[70] It is not easy to demonstrate that the assistance given by the Italian authorities was aimed at helping the Libyan authorities in the commission of an international wrongful act.

As regards the proposal to establish RDCs in neighbouring countries, if the centres were run directly by the EU with the agreement of the countries where the centres are located, there is no doubt that the criteria laid down in Article 16 of the Articles on

---

[64] *Hirsi Jamaa and Others v. Italy*, above n. 22.

[65] Ibid., para 74.

[66] See Commissioner of Human Rights—Council of Europe, Letter to the Minister of the Interior of Italy, CommHR/INM/sf 0345-2017, 28 September 2017.

[67] Rappresentanza Permanente D'Italia presso il Consiglio d'Europa [Permant Representation of Italy to the Council of Europe] 2017.

[68] Santos Vara 2020, p. 73.

[69] Skordas 2018, p. 2.

[70] Mitsilegas 2019, p. 302.

Responsibility of States for international wrongful acts would be fulfilled. However, if they are operated by third countries themselves with the support of the EU, it would not be easy to demonstrate that the assistance was provided with the purpose of facilitating the commission of a wrongful act, unless there is a clear link between the establishment of centres or detention camps contrary to international law and human rights obligations and the assistance provided by the EU.[71]

The ECHR has recently been called to examine the responsibility of Italy for outsourcing migration management to Libya within the framework of the Memorandum signed between both countries. A group of NGOs filed an application against Italy in May 2018 on behalf of a group of survivors that suffered a fatal incident when they were travelling in a boat carrying migrants found itself in distress off the coast of Libya.[72] This case would be an excellent opportunity to clarify the responsibility of the EU and its Member States when they transfer the management of migration and border controls to third countries. The interception was carried out by a Libyan vessel that was previously donated by Italy and the crew had been trained within the framework of the Operation Sophia. The Italian authorities coordinated the operation, but they did not exercise effective control over the migrants rescued at sea. It could be held that the relevant authorities, when receiving distress calls originating from any SAR region, should not transfer, either formally or de facto, responsibility for rescue operations to other authorities when they know or should have known that this action would lead to the exposure of people in distress at sea to serious violations of their rights protected under the ECHR.[73] This case would allow the ECtHR to clarify the responsibility of the EU and its Member States when they transfer SAR operations to third countries, in particular certain types of assistance provided to the Libyan Coast Guard, despite the fact that Libya is not a safe country.

14.5 Conclusions

The EU has constantly argued that the reinforcement of its external borders should not prevent access to the territory of the EU Member States of persons in need of international protection. However, the externalization of EU migration policies is leading to the transfer of the management of migration policies to third countries of origin and transit of migrants without providing legal pathways or opportunities for resettlement for persons in need of international protection.[74] The cooperation developed with third countries may lead in practice to prevent migrants from reaching the territory of the EU Member States and result in migrants being stranded in countries where their human rights are clearly at risk. The emphasis put by the EU on the cooperation with third countries such as Libya and Turkey may result in a

[71] *Hirsi Jamaa v. Italy*, above n. 22, para 74; and *Al-Skeini and Others*, above n. 62, paras 136–137.
[72] Human Rights at Sea 2018.
[73] See CoE Commissioner for Human Rights 2019.
[74] Santos Vara and Pascual Matellán 2020, p. 170.

model that prioritizes the prevention of migration flows over the protection of human rights. As a result of the externalization process, migrants will face more obstacles to invoke their rights conferred by the EU legal order. The transfer of responsibilities to Libya is particularly worrying. Apart from the fact that the Libyan authorities do not have the capacity or even intention of providing the migrants with assistance and protection, the grave violations of human rights committed in Libya against migrants have been reported by the main international organizations and NGOs working on the ground.

The transfer of responsibilities to Libya in the management of migration increases substantially the risk of migrants being submitted to arbitrary detention and inhuman treatment. Despite the EU's declared commitment to respect fundamental rights and, in particular, the principle of *non-refoulement*, the externalization of migration controls to third countries leads to the emergence of a specific model of action by which the EU seeks to externalize the management of migration, asylum and borders control without paying sufficient attention to the protection of human rights.

The transfer of responsibilities to third countries in the management of migration does not exonerate the EU and its Member States from the infringements of human rights that might take place on the territory of third countries. The ECtHR has accepted that a contracting party can exercise its jurisdiction extraterritorially in a broad range of circumstances. If the violations of human rights occurred as a result of the cooperation established with the EU and its Member States, they could be considered responsible on the basis of the criteria laid down in the Project of Articles on the Responsibility of States for Wrongful Acts. However, it is not easy to demonstrate the existence of a direct link between the violation of human rights and the cooperation developed with a third country in the management of migration. According to the case law of the ECtHR, the responsibility of the EU and its Member States could arise when their agents or organs exercise effective control over a territory or jurisdiction over individuals held in closed facilities or on board vessels. The jurisdiction of a State can also be established when it exercises authority or direct control in the absence of the spatial element of control. Finally, when a State provides financial support, training and vessels to the authorities of a third country or gives support towards the establishment of centres for the reception of migrants, it could lead to the violation of the ECHR as a result of the assistance given to the third country concerned.

Acknowledgements This contribution has been written within the framework of the research project on 'The externalisation and informalisation of the EU migration, asylum and border management policies: new legal challenges' (EUMABEXT), funded by the Spanish Government (RTI2018-099097-B-I00).

References

Amnesty International (2014) Letter to Foreign Affairs Council - Human Rights of Migrants and Refugees at the Core of EU relations with Neighbouring Countries

Amnesty International (2019) Europe's Shameful Failure to End the Torture and Abuse of Refugees and Migrants in Libya https://www.amnesty.org/en/latest/news/2019/03/europes-shameful-failure-to-end-the-torture-and-abuse-of-refugees-and-migrants-in-libya/ Accessed 4 July 2020

Atak I, Crépeau F (2014) Managing Migrations at the External Borders of the European Union: Meeting the Human Rights Challenges. Journal Européen des Droits de l'Homme 5:591–622

Camera dei Deputati [Italian Chamber of Deputies] (2018) Decreto Legge no 84/2018, Cessione di Unità Navali alla Libia https://temi.camera.it/leg18/temi/cessione_di_unit__navali_alla_libia.html Accessed 29 December 2019

Carrera S, Cortinovis R (2019) The EU's Role in Implementing the UN Global Compact on Refugees Contained Mobility vs. International Protection https://www.ceps.eu/ceps-publications/eus-role-implementing-un-global-compact-refugees/ Accessed 4 July 2020

CoE Commissioner for Human Rights (2019) Third party intervention by the Council of Europe Commissioner for Human Rights under Article 36, paragraph 3, of the European Convention on Human Rights in Application No. 21660/18 S.S. and others v. Italy https://rm.coe.int/third-party-intervention-before-the-european-court-of-human-rights-app/168098dd4d Accessed 4 July 2020

Council of the European Union (2018) Working Paper on Regional Disembarkation Arrangements https://www.statewatch.org/media/documents/news/2018/oct/eu-council-wk-paper-disembarkation.pdf Accessed 4 July 2020

ECRE (2016) Joint Comments Paper by: Caritas Europa, Churches' Commission for Migrants in Europe (CCME), European Council for Refugees and Exiles (ECRE), International Catholic Migration Commission (ICMC Europe), International Rescue Committee (IRC), Red Cross EU office https://www.ecre.org/wp-content/uploads/2016/11/NGO-joint-comments-resettlement-141116.pdf Accessed 4 July 2020

Estrada-Canamares M (2015) Operation Sophia Before and After UN Security Council Resolution no 2240. European Papers 1:185–191

EU Council (2017) Malta Declaration by the Members of the European Council on the External Aspects of Migration: addressing the Central Mediterranean https://www.consilium.europa.eu/en/press/press-releases/2017/02/03/malta-declaration/ Accessed 4 July 2020

European Commission (2018a) Non-Paper on Regional Disembarkation Arrangements https://ec.europa.eu/home-affairs/sites/homeaffairs/files/what-we-do/policies/european-agenda-migration/20180724_non-paper-regional-disembarkation-arrangements_en.pdf Accessed 4 July 2020

European Commission (2018b) Migration: Follow-up to the European Council Conclusions of 28 June 2018 https://ec.europa.eu/commission/publications/migration-follow-european-council-conclusions-28-june-2018_en Accessed 4 July 2020

Frelick B, Kysel M, Podkul J (2016) The Impact of Externalization of Migration Controls on the Rights of Asylum Seekers and Other Migrants. Journal on Migration and Human Security 4:190–220

Gammeltoft-Hansen T, Hathaway J C (2015) Non-Refoulement in a World of Cooperative Deterrence. Columbia Journal of Transnational Law 53:235–283

González Vega J A (2019) Non-refoulement at risk? Asylum's Disconnection Mechanisms in Recent EU practice. In: Santos Vara J, Carrera S, Strik T (eds) Constitutionalising the External Dimensions of EU Migration Policies in Times of Crisis. Legality, Rule of Law and Fundamental Rights Reconsidered. Edward Elgar Publishing, Cheltenham

Guiraudon V (2003) Before the EU Border: Remote Control of the Huddle Masses. In: Groenendijk K, Guild E, Minderhoud P (eds) In Search of Europe's Borders. Kluwer Law International, The Hague, pp 191–214

Human Rights at Sea (2018) Human Rights at Sea, 'Legal action against Italy over its Coordination of Libyan Coast Guard pull-backs resulting in Migrant Deaths and Abuse' https://www.humanr

ightsatsea.org/2018/05/08/legal-action-before-the-ecthr-against-italy-over-its-coordination-of-libyan-coast-guard-pull-backs-resulting-in-migrant-deaths-and-abuse/ Accessed 4 July 2020

Human Rights Watch (2019) No Escape from Hell EU Policies Contribute to Abuse of Migrants in Libya https://www.hrw.org/report/2019/01/21/no-escape-hell/eu-policies-contribute-abuse-migrants-libya Accessed 4 July 2020

Maiani F (2018) "Regional Disembarkation Platforms" and "Controlled Centres": Lifting the Drawbridge, Reaching out Across The Mediterranean, or Going Nowhere? EU Immigration and Asylum Law and Policy

Mangas Martín A (2012) Convenios Bilaterales de España Sobre Inmigración con Estados Africanos [Spain's Bilateral Agreements on Immigration with African States]. In: Esplugues C, Palao G, Paredés M (eds) Nuevas fronteras del Derecho de la UE: liber amicorum José Luis Iglesias Buhiges [New frontiers of EU law: liber amicorum José Luis Iglesias Buhiges]. Tirant lo Blanch, Valencia, pp 643–660

Ministero dell'Interno (2017) Codice di Condotta per le ONG Impegnate nelle Operazioni di Salvataggio dei Migranti in Mare [Code of Conduct for NGOs involved in Rescue Operations of Migrants at Sea] http://www.interno.gov.it/sites/default/files/codice_condotta_ong.pdf Accessed 4 July 2020

Mitsilegas V (2019) Extraterritorial Immigration Control, Preventive Justice and the Rule of Law in Turbulent Times: Lessons from the Anti-Smuggling Crusade. In: Santos Vara J, Carrera S, Strik T (eds) Constitutionalising the External Dimensions of EU Migration Policies in Times of Crisis. Legality, Rule of Law and Fundamental Rights Reconsidered. Edward Elgar Publishing, Cheltenham, pp 290–307

Moreno-Lax V, Papastavridis E (2016) (eds) Boat Refugees' and Migrants at Sea: A Comprehensive Approach: Integrating Maritime Security with Human Rights. Brill

Neville D, Rigon A (2016) On the Frontline: The Hotspot Approach to Managing Migration https://www.europarl.europa.eu/thinktank/en/document.html?reference=IPOL_STU(2016)556942 Accessed 4 July 2020

Noll G (2003) Visions of the Exceptional: Legal and Theoretical Issues raised by Transit Processing Centres and Protection Zones. European Journal of Migration and Law, 5:303–341

Palm A (2017) The Italy-Libya Memorandum of Understanding: The Baseline of a Policy Approach aimed at Closing all Doors to Europe? EU Immigration and Asylum Law and Policy

Parliamentary Assembly Council of Europe (2018) Human Rights Impact of the "External Dimension" of European Union Asylum and Migration Policy: out of Sight, out of Rights? http://assembly.coe.int/nw/xml/XRef/Xref-DocDetails-en.asp?FileId=24808 Accessed 4 July 2020

Pijnenburg A (2018) From Italian Pushbacks to Libyan Pullbacks: Is Hirsi 2.0 in the Making in Strasbourg? European Journal of Migration and Law 20: 396–426

Rappresentanza Permanente D'Italia presso il Consiglio d'Europa [Permant Representation of Italy to the Council of Europe] (2017) Letter of the Italian Minister of Interior Marco Minniti in reply to European Commissioner of Human Rights from the Council of Europe https://rm.coe.int/reply-of-the-minister-of-interior-to-the-commissioner-s-letter-regardi/168075dd2d Accessed 15 January 2020

Riegert B (2019) Libya takes over from Italy on Rescuing Shipwrecked Migrants. Deutsche Welle, 5.7.2018, available https://p.dw.com/p/30ue2 Accessed 19 December 2019

Rijpma J (2017) External Migration and Asylum Management: Accountability for Executive Action Outside EU-territory. European Papers 2:571–596

Sánchez Legido A (2018) ¿Héroes o villanos? ¿Las ONGs de rescaste y las políticas europeas de lucha contra la inmigración irregular (A propósito del caso Open Arms) [Heroes or Villains? Rescue NGOs and European Policies to Combat Illegal Immigration (On the Open Arms case)]. Revista General de Derecho Europeo 46: 1–52

Santos Vara J (2018) La transformación de Frontex en la Agencia Europea de la Guardia de Frontera y Costas: ¿Hacia una centralización en la gestión de las fronteras? [The Transformation of Frontex into the European Border and Coast Guard Agency: Towards Centralisation in Border Management?]. Revista de Derecho Comunitario Europeo 59:159–161

Santos Vara J (2019) Soft International Agreements on Migration Cooperation with Third Countries: A Challenge to Democratic and Judicial Controls in the EU. In: Santos Vara J, Carrera S, Strik T (eds) Constitutionalising the External Dimensions of EU Migration Policies in Times of Crisis. Legality, Rule of Law and Fundamental Rights Reconsidered. Edward Elgar Publishing, Cheltenham, pp 21–38

Santos Vara J (2020) La dimensión exterior de las políticas de inmigración de la Unión Europea [The External Dimension of the European Union's Immigration Policies]. Tirant lo Blanch, Valencia

Santos Vara J, Pascual Matellán L (2020) The Global Compact on Migration: Convergence or Divergence with EU Policies? In: Fahey E (ed) Framing Convergence with the Global Order: The EU and the World. Hart Publishing, pp 163–176

Savino M (2017) Refashioning Resettlement: from Border Externalization to Legal Pathways for Asylum. In: Carrera S et al. (eds) EU External Migration Policies in an Era of Global Mobilities: Intersecting Policy Universes. Brill Nijhoff, Leiden

Skordas A (2018) A 'Blind Spot' in the Migration Debate? International Responsibility of the EU and its Member States for Cooperating with the Libyan Coastguard and Militias. EU Immigration and Asylum Law and Policy

Tsourdi T (2016) Bottom-up Salvation? From Practical Cooperation Towards Joint Implementation Through the European Asylum Support Office. European Papers 1:997–1031

UN Support Mission in Libya (2018) Desperate and Dangerous: Report on the Human Rights Situation of Migrants and Refugees in Libya https://www.ohchr.org/Documents/Countries/LY/LibyaMigrationReport.pdf Accessed 4 July 2020

UN Support Mission in Libya (2019) Report of the Secretary-General, S/2019/682

UNHCR, IOM (2018) Proposal for a Regional Cooperative Arrangement Ensuring Predictable Disembarkation and Subsequent Processing of Persons Rescued-at-Sea https://www.unhcr.org/partners/eu/5b35e60f4/proposal-regional-cooperative-arrangement-ensuring-predictable-disembarkation.html Accessed 4 July 2020

UNSC (2011) Resolution 1970, UN Doc. No. S/RES/1970

UNSC (2016) Resolution 2292, UN Doc. No. S/RES/2292

UNSC (2018) Report of the Secretary-General on the United Nations Support Mission in Libya, UN Doc. No. S/2018/140

J. Santos Vara is Professor of Public International Law and European Law, Jean Monnet Chair in EU External Action, Coordinator of the European Joint Master's in Strategic Border Management at the University of Salamanca, Spain.

L. Pascual Matellán is Researcher in Criminal Law at the University of Salamanca, Spain.

Chapter 15
The EU's Policy Towards Combatting Trafficking in Human Beings in Its Relations with the Eastern Neighbourhood: A Human Rights-Based Approach?

N. Ghazaryan

Contents

Abstract The fight against trafficking in human beings has been on the European Union's (EU) internal and external agenda since the 1990s. Having acquired competence to regulate this matter, the EU has gradually developed a legal framework to combat this crime incorporating a human rights-based approach with an emphasis on victim protection. Cooperation with third countries, particularly those on its doorstep including the countries of the Eastern Partnership, has been essential to fight trafficking in human beings to the EU's territory. The chapter traces the security and human rights nexus embedded in these efforts in the myriad of EU instruments established with the Eastern neighbours in bilateral and regional relations. It concludes that while firmly placed within the domain of the external aspects of the area of freedom, security and justice, the EU has transposed the human rights-based approach most prominently through the reforms associated with visa liberalisation.

Keywords trafficking in human beings · European Neighbourhood Policy · Eastern Partnership · human rights · security

N. Ghazaryan (✉)
University of Nottingham, University Park, Nottingham NG7 2RD, UK
e-mail: narine.ghazaryan@nottingham.ac.uk

W. Th. Douma et al. (eds.), *The Evolving Nature of EU External Relations Law*,
https://doi.org/10.1007/978-94-6265-423-5_15

15.1 Introduction

Trafficking in human beings, as defined in the UN Palermo Protocol,[1] is a mobile phenomenon, attracting criminals around the world due the lucrative proceeds it generates.[2] It is regularly assessed as a key threat to the European Union (EU) by Europol,[3] and the 2015 European Agenda on Security reflected upon the seriousness of this crime alongside the EU's efforts to deal with it.[4] The fight against trafficking in human beings requires consolidated efforts within the EU given that a significant proportion of human trafficking takes place in an intra-EU context.[5] Trafficking of human beings *to the* EU from abroad is a 'phenomenon repeatedly illustrating connections between the EU and third countries',[6] including those in the Eastern neighbourhood comprising Ukraine, Moldova, Belarus, Georgia, Armenia and Azerbaijan. Before the EU established closer relations with its Eastern neighbours through the European Neighbourhood Policy (ENP), Moldova and Ukraine were identified as significant sources of human trafficking to the EU, mostly for sexual exploitation.[7] As suggested by empirical research, geographical proximity raises the likelihood of recruitment and exploitation as part of human trafficking.[8] Currently, according to the US Department of State, only Georgia meets the minimum standards for the elimination of trafficking, with Belarus making the least significant efforts to tackle trafficking.[9] Despite significant reforms in border control undertaken in Ukraine,

---

[1] The definition in Article 3(a) includes 'the recruitment, transportation, transfer, harbouring or receipt of persons, by means of thle threat or use of force or other forms of coerçion, of abduction, of fraud, of deception, of the abuse of power or of a position of vulnerability or of the giving or receiving of payments or benefits to achieve the consent of a person having control over another person, for the purpose of exploitation'. See UNGA 2000.

[2] According to Europol, trafficking in human beings generates over 29 billion Euro annually; Europol 2015.

[3] See EU Serious and Organised Crime Threat Assessment (SOCTA) reports. https://www.europol.europa.eu/socta-report. Accessed 7 February 2020.

[4] European Commission, *Communication on the European Agenda on Security*, COM (2015) 185 final, p. 16.

[5] Up to 70% of registered victims were EU citizens; European Commission, Report on the progress made in the fight against trafficking in human beings (2016) as required under Article 20 of Directive 2011/36/EU; See Directive 2011/36/EU of the European Parliament and of the Council of 5 April 2011 on preventing and combating trafficking in human beings and protecting its victims and replacing Council Framework Decision 2002/629/JHA, OJ 2011 L101/1, p. 4; Europol 2016, p. 3; Eurostat, 2015, p. 13.

[6] Council Action-Oriented Paper on strengthening the EU external dimension on action against trafficking in human beings, 11450/5/09, 19 November 2009, p. 3.

[7] EC 2012, p. 2; Europol 2016, pp. 4 and 24; European Commission, Ukraine ENP Country Report Staff Working Paper, COM (2004) 373 final, 12 May 2004, p. 14; IOM 2008d, p. 36; European Commission, Moldova ENP Country Report, Staff Working Paper, COM (2004) 373 final, p. 12.

[8] Hernandez and Rudolph 2015, p. 134.

[9] According to the 2019 report, Georgia is a Tier 1 country, Ukraine, Moldova and Armenia are classed as Tier 2, Azerbaijan is on Tier 2 Watch List, and Belarus is a Tier 3 country; see US Department of State 2019.

Georgia and Moldova leading to a visa-free travel regime with the EU, trafficking in human beings to the EU persists nonetheless.[10]

Human trafficking is a complex phenomenon where the issues of security and human rights intertwine. On the one hand, it is a form of highly organised cross-border crime which the EU has gradually acquired competence to deal with. On the other hand, human trafficking—as a modern or a 'new form of slavery'[11]—is a serious breach of human rights under international and EU law. The Charter of Fundamental Rights of the EU in its Article 5(3) prohibits trafficking in human beings under the heading of the prohibition of slavery and forced labour.[12] The current EU framework on combatting human trafficking set in Directive 2011/36 also embraces the so-called human rights approach to this issue representing a major step forward.[13] The so-called human rights or victims-based approach shifts the traditional emphasis from crime fighting towards the protection of and assistance to the victims of trafficking, including the safeguarding of their human rights. The Directive at the same time is 'part of a global action against trafficking in human beings, which includes action involving third countries'.[14] The EU's orientation towards global action started much earlier though.

Trafficking in human beings featured in early policy documents on ENP as one of the issues requiring 'particular attention'.[15] The subsequent ENP policy documents, as well as bilateral documents, continuously included the fight against human trafficking on the cooperation agenda. The issue was also taken forward to the new era of association, first featuring in the 2009 Association Agenda with Ukraine, and later finding its way into the Association Agreements concluded between the EU and Ukraine, Georgia and Moldova respectively.[16] The Comprehensive and Enhanced Cooperation Agreement (hereinafter CEPA) concluded with Armenia in 2017 also

[10]See most recently Dutch News (2019) Dutch police intercept bus with 65 Moldovans heading to claim asylum. https://www.dutchnews.nl/news/2019/11/dutch-police-intercept-bus-with-65-moldovans-heading-to-claim-asylum/. Accessed 7 February 2020.

[11]Scarpa 2008.

[12]Charter of Fundament Rights of the European Union, OJ 2012 C 326/02.

[13]Directive 2011/36/EU, above n. 5.

[14]Ibid., preamble, recital 2.

[15]European Commission, Communication on Wider Europe-Neighbourhood: A New Framework for Relations with our Eastern and Southern Neighbours, COM (2003) 104 final, 11 March 2003, p. 11.

[16]Association Agreement between the European Union and the European Atomic Energy Community and their Member States, of the one part, and Georgia, of the other part, opened for signature 27 June 2014, OJ L261/4 (entered into force 1 July 2016), (EU-Georgia AA); Association Agreement between the European Union and the European Atomic Energy Community and their Member States, of the one part, and the Republic of Moldova, of the other part, opened for signature 27 June 2014, OJ L260/4 (entered into force 1 July 2016) (EU-Moldova AA); Association Agreement between the European Union and the European Atomic Energy Community and its Member States, of the one part, and Ukraine, of the other part, opened for signature 21 March 2014, OJ L 161/3–2137 (entered into force 1 September 2017) (EU-Ukraine AA).

includes the combatting of human trafficking as a matter of bilateral cooperation in the area of Justice, Freedom and Security (JFS).[17]

The subject of trafficking in human beings features also within the multilateral cooperation in the Eastern neighbourhood. Already the 2004 ENP Strategy Paper included trafficking as one of the aspects of regional cooperation on the EU eastern borders in the area of Justice and Home Affairs. After the initiation of the Eastern Partnership (EaP), this matter came under the aegis of the thematic platform on democracy, good governance and stability. In 2010, the Integrated Border Management Flagship Initiative was established with the reduction of human trafficking being one of its key objectives.[18]

Within this context, the chapter addresses the interplay between the security and human rights aspects of the EU's policy towards combatting human trafficking in its Eastern neighbourhood. In particular, it aims to analyse whether the issue is dealt with as one belonging solely to the security domain, namely the Area of Freedom, Security and Justice (AFSJ) with accommodation for human rights considerations, or whether it also transcends into the EU's external framework on human rights promotion. Within this quest, the chapter questions the extent to which the EU's internal reorientation towards a human rights-based approach has been incorporated into the EU's relations with its Eastern neighbours. The chapter, first, briefly addresses the EU's internal framework and competence in this area. It then considers the EU's policy towards its Eastern neighbours. For this purpose, the chapter will take stock of the wide range of policy-specific and framework instruments. The chapter will consider both the bilateral and multilateral tracks of cooperation. The findings will be summarised in brief conclusions.

15.2 Trafficking in Human Beings in the EU Legal Order and Its External Aspects

The EU's competence in relation to trafficking in human beings is currently found among the TFEU provisions on the AFSJ.[19] The issue has gradually crystallised in the EU legal framework making a shift to a human rights-based approach eventually. The Maastricht Treaty establishing cooperation in this pillar included no specific

[17] Comprehensive and enhanced Partnership Agreement between the European Union and the European Atomic Energy Community and their Member States, of the one part, and the Republic of Armenia, of the other part, opened for signature 20 November 2017, OJ L23/4 (entered into force (provisionally) 20 November 2017).

[18] See further https://www.euneighbours.eu/en/east/stay-informed/projects/eastern-partnership-integrated-border-management-flagship-initiative. Accessed 7 February 2020.

[19] The Area of Freedom Security and Justice is defined in Article 3(2) TEU as an area 'without internal frontiers, in which the free movement of persons is ensured in conjunction with appropriate measures with respect to external border controls, asylum, immigration and the prevention and combatting of crime'; Consolidated Version of the Treaty on the Functioning of the European Union, 2012, OJ C 326 (TFEU), Title V.

provisions on human trafficking but provided for police cooperation for the purposes of preventing and combatting terrorism, unlawful drug trafficking and other serious forms of international crime.[20]

Post-Maastricht, early efforts to deal with human trafficking included the Commission's Communication on trafficking in women for the purpose of sexual exploitation.[21] While the early programmes to combat human trafficking, namely the 1996 STOP Program and the Daphne programmes were lauded for their human rights dimension, the 1997 Joint Action to Combat Trafficking in Human Beings and the sexual exploitation of children was short of content on victim protection and assistance.[22] The emphasis on the criminal law aspects of the human trafficking were seen as inevitable given that the first reference to the matter would be found in the Amsterdam Treaty under the title on police and judicial cooperation in criminal matters.[23] Due to these amendments in Amsterdam Treaty, the EU gradually developed a legal framework of certain uniformity concerning human trafficking.[24]

Chronologically, the first relevant measure was the Council Framework Decision 2001/220/JHA of 15 March 2001 on the standing of victims in criminal proceedings.[25] As a general instrument, it applied to victims of trafficking participating in criminal proceedings excluding victims who were not participants in the proceedings and offering no protection beyond the proceedings.[26] The second measure was specific to combatting human trafficking, the Council Framework Decision 2002/629/JHA on Combating Trafficking in Human Beings.[27] Focused on criminal proceedings with an emphasis on combatting the crime of human trafficking, the latter included only two substantive provisions concerning children as a vulnerable victim group and was seen as a major step back in relation to victims' rights.[28] The Framework Decision failed to embrace the human-rights approach inter alia by not accepting the proposals of the UN High Commissioners for Human Rights and for Refugees.[29]

---

[20]Treaty on European Union OJ 1992 C 191/61, Article K1.

[21]COM (96) 567 final, 20 November 1996. This was followed by a subsequent Communication, European Commission, For Further Actions in the Fight Against Trafficking in Women, COM (98) 726 final, 9 December 1998.

[22]Grundell 2015, pp. 4–5; Obokata 2006a, pp. 95–96.

[23]Treaty of Amsterdam amending the Treaty on European Union, the Treaties establishing the European Communities and certain related acts, 1997, OJ C 340/16 (Amsterdam Treaty), Article 1(11); Berman and Friesendorf 2008, p. 195; Scarpa 2008, p. 175.

[24]Ibid. (Amsterdam Treaty), revised Article 34 TEU; Obokata 2006a, pp. 390–393; Obokata 2006b, p. 97.

[25]Council Framework Decision 2001/220/JHA of 15 March 2001 on the standing of victims in criminal proceedings, OJ L82.

[26]Chaudary 2011, pp. 97–98; Obokata 2006a, pp. 100–101.

[27]Council Framework Decision 2002/629/JHA on Combating Trafficking in Human Beings, OJ L203/1.

[28]Gallagher 2010, pp. 98–99.

[29]Scarpa 2008, pp. 181–183.

The next measure, the Council Directive 2004/81/EC regulated residence granting to the victims of human trafficking provided they cooperated with authorities,[30] without creating a right to a residence permit necessarily.[31] Despite offering certain support to the victims of trafficking, the Directive's core, alongside the 2002 Framework Decision, belonged to the domain of illegal migration and crime, whereby victim protection was secondary to the crime-fighting aspects of trafficking.[32] Crucially, it was restricted to third country national victims willing to cooperate with the authorities among other shortcomings.[33] Although AFSJ-related programmatic documents adopted in this decade were primarily concerned with human trafficking in the context of illegal migration and crime,[34] by the middle of the decade, the human rights and victim-based approach found its way in the trafficking-related discourse of EU institutions set in soft law documents.[35]

With the Lisbon Treaty, trafficking in human beings has 'assumed an autonomous role within EU migration policies'.[36] Article 79 establishes the EU's competence to conduct common immigration policy inter alia aimed at 'the prevention of, and enhanced measures to combat, illegal immigration and trafficking in human beings' through the ordinary legislative procedure. Article 83 TFEU further grants the EU the competence to legislate in the area of criminal law by establishing 'minimum rules concerning the definition of criminal offences and sanctions in the areas of particularly serious crime with a cross-border dimension', including such crimes as trafficking in human beings and sexual exploitation of women and children. This competence was used to adopt Directive 2011/36 replacing the Council Framework Decision 2002/629/JHA, becoming the first area of criminal law to be regulated at EU level in the post-Lisbon era.[37] The Lisbon Treaty also granted binding legal force to the Charter of Fundamental Rights, whose relevant provisions inevitably had to influence the approach to be taken in any new legislation.

The Directive follows the best international practice, namely the 2000 United Nations Protocol to Prevent, Suppress and Punish Trafficking in Persons, Especially Women and Children and the 2005 Council of Europe (CoE) Convention on Action

[30]Council Directive 2004/81/EC of 29 April 2004 on the residence permit issued to third-country nationals who are victims of trafficking in human beings or who have been the subject of an action to facilitate illegal immigration, who cooperate with the competent authorities, OJ L261.

[31]Stoyanova 2017, pp. 136–138.

[32]Chaudary 2011, pp. 96–97; Grundell 2015, p. 6; Berman and Friesendorf 2008, p. 196; Villacampa Estiarte 2012, p. 293; Krieg 2009, p. 788; Obokata 2006b, p. 94.

[33]For detailed criticism, see Scarpa 2008, pp. 185–194; Gallagher 2010, pp. 100–103.

[34]These include the 2004 Council Hague Program and the 2009 Stockholm Program; Grundell 2015, p. 5.

[35]Council (2005/C 311/01) EU plan on best practices, standards and procedures for combating and preventing trafficking in human being, 1, 3; European Commission, Communication on Fighting Trafficking in Human Beings—An Integrated Approach and Proposals for an Action Plan, COM (2005) 514 final, 18 October 2005; European Commission, Recommendations on Identification and Referral to Services of Victims of Trafficking in Human Beings, 18 October 2007.

[36]Bressan 2012, p. 140.

[37]Bressan 2012, p. 140.

against Trafficking in Human Beings,[38] by incorporating the so-called 'three Ps'—the principles of prevention, prosecution and protection. It has expanded the definition of trafficking to include methods of exploitation not foreseen in the 2002 Framework Decision,[39] in line with the ILO and UN definition of trafficking that was incorporated in the CoE Convention above.[40] In addition to this, the human rights orientation of the Directive transpires through the references made to the EU Charter of Fundamental Rights in the preamble.[41] Most importantly, it incorporates the human rights or victims-based approach noted above as it emphasises the protection of and assistance to the victims of trafficking inter alia ruling out the prosecution or application of penalties to the victims.[42] The Directive goes further than any previous EU instrument in offering support and assistance to the victims stretching beyond the context of criminal proceedings, and with particular attention to children as a vulnerable group.

Despite making a pronounced shift to a human rights-based approach in the fight against human trafficking, the Directive has not escaped criticism. It has been suggested that its focal point continues to reside with a 'repressive law enforcement approach centred on prosecution' and 'transportation rather than exploitation'.[43] Others have pointed out the potential gaps in the protection of trafficking victims who are third country nationals.[44] Despite these shortcomings, the Directive is widely perceived to be a step forward in orientating the EU's legal framework towards human rights protection.

As noted earlier, Directive 2011/36 constitutes part of a global action on fighting human trafficking involving cooperation with third countries.[45] The fight against human trafficking on the EU's international agenda evolved alongside the external dimension of the AFSJ since the late 1990s, when the European Council urged action and called for a legislative reform.[46] The necessity of external cooperation inter alia through supporting third countries was picked up in subsequent Commission policy documents.[47] The preference for multilateralism in EU external relations

[38]Recital 9, Directive 2011/36, above n. 5; UNGA 2005; Council of Europe Convention on Action against Trafficking in Human Beings, opened for signature 16 May 2005, CETS n. 197 (entered into force 1 February 2008).

[39]It currently includes also begging, exploitation for criminal activities, removal of organs.

[40]Convention Concerning Forced or Compulsory Labour, opened for signature 28 June 1930, n. 29 (entered into force 1 May 1932); Convention concerning the Abolition of Forced Labour, opened for signature 25 June 1957, n. 105 (entered into force 17 January 1959); Campana and Varese 2015; Gromek-Brok 2011, p. 229.

[41]Directive 2011/36, above n. 5, preamble, recital 1, 8 and 33.

[42]Ibid., Article 8.

[43]Grundell 2015, p. 8; Villacampa Estiarte 2012, p. 306.

[44]Gromek-Brok 2011, p. 233.

[45]Directive 2011/36, preamble, recital 2.

[46]Tampere European Council, 15–16 October 1999, para 23; Conclusions, Santa Maria da Feira European Council, 19 and 20 June, para 52.

[47]European Commission, Communication on the Integration of Migration Issues in the EU Relations with Third Countries; the 2004 Hague Programme set the multiannual framework for the next five

set in Article 21(2) TEU chimes with the necessity for cooperation with third countries, regional and international organisations which was repeatedly stressed in the Stockholm programme, the multi-annual framework setting priorities and objectives of cooperation in Justice and Home Affairs for 2010–2014.[48]

The discourse on a human rights-based approach and victim protection was incorporated in the Conclusions of the European Council already since the end of the 1990s calling for cooperation with third countries.[49] The external dimension of the fight against human trafficking was developed in the 'milestone'[50] 2002 Brussels Declaration including third countries.[51] Among others it led to the establishment by the Commission of an expert group with international participation,[52] which in its report emphasised the necessity of incorporating a human rights-based approach.[53] Subsequently adopted soft law documents indicated that the human rights-based approach was to become an element of political dialogue and cooperation with third parties.[54] At the time of drafting the 2005 CoE Convention, however, the role of the EU was criticised by the CoE Parliamentary Assembly for '[hampering] any genuine negotiation' in order to compel the CoE 'to lower its standards to the lowest common denominator of [EU] law', when proposing amendments for victim protection.[55] The rhetoric on the human rights-based approach to combatting trafficking in EU external relations was maintained nonetheless. In 2009, the Council adopted an Action-Oriented Paper on strengthening the EU external dimension on action against trafficking in human beings by pursuing it as 'an area of cooperation in its own right',[56] stressing the necessity of pursuing a holistic and human rights-based approach when combatting human trafficking, including by adopting a gender- and children-specific prism.[57] Recently in 2017, for instance, the Commission identified the next steps in external policy regarding human trafficking with a particular

---

years; European Commission, 2005 Strategy for the External Dimension of Justice and Home Affairs, COM (2005) 491 final, 12 October 2005.

[48]The EU in particular intends to enhance its cooperation with countries where trafficking originates see The Stockholm Programme—An open and secure Europe serving and protecting the citizens' General Affairs Council/European Council, 2010, OJ C115/1.

[49]Tampere European Council, above n. 46, para 23.

[50]Scarpa 2008, p. 194.

[51]See Brussels Declaration on Preventing and Combating Trafficking in Human Beings, Council General Secretariat, 14981/02, 29 November 2002.

[52]European Commission, Decision (EC) 2003/209/EC of 25 March 2003 on setting up a consultative Experts Group on Trafficking in Human Beings.

[53]Report of the European Experts Group on Trafficking in Human Beings (EC, 2004) 226, Annex 2 (Final Report of the Experts Group).

[54]For instance, Council (2005/C 311/01) above n. 35, calls on Member States and the Commission to 'strengthen political dialogue with third countries bilaterally and multilaterally on the human rights dimensions of anti-trafficking policies and continue to raise the issue in relevant regional and multi-lateral fora', s 3, para (iv); COM (2005) 514 final, above n. 35, p. 3.

[55]As cited in Scarpa 2008, pp. 145–146.

[56]Council of the European Union 2009b, pp. 14–15.

[57]Ibid.

emphasis on women as a vulnerable group.[58] It should be noted that human rights underpins JHA external action more generally,[59] and migration and mobility particularly.[60] The human rights dimension of the fight against human trafficking also transpires through the wider internal and external policy framework of the EU,[61] including on development cooperation.[62] At the same time, human trafficking can hardly be detached from wider security concerns in external policy, evidenced also through the inclusion of the matter in the EU's vision on security and stabilisation in the 2016 Global Strategy,[63] as well as 2015 European Agenda on Security.[64]

It is this interplay between the human rights dimension and security in the fight against human trafficking that is explored below in relation to the EU's Eastern neighbours.

15.3 The EU's Policy on Human Trafficking in Relations with Its Eastern Neighbours

Among the EaP countries, Ukraine and Moldova are significant countries as sources of human trafficking to the EU, as noted earlier. Other Eastern neighbours are also sources or transit countries for trafficking of human beings to such destinations as

---

58 European Commission, Communication on Reporting on the follow-up to the EU Strategy towards the Eradication of Trafficking in Human Beings and Identifying further Concrete Actions, COM (2017) 728 final, 4 December 2012, pp. 6–7.

59 EU Annual Report on Human Rights and Democracy in the World in 2014, Council, 10152/15, 22 June 2015.

60 European Commission, Communication on the Global Approach to Migration and Mobility, COM (2011) 743 final, 18 November 2011, p. 7.

61 European Commission, Communication on 2005 Strategy for the External Dimension of Justice and Home Affairs, COM (2005) 491 final, 12 October 2005, p. 6; Communication on a European Agenda on Migration, COM (2015) 240 final, 13 May 2015; Communication on the European Agenda on Security, COM (2015) 185 final, 28 April 2015; Communication on the EU Action Plan against Migrant Smuggling (2015–2020), COM(2015) 285 final, 27 May 2015; Council, The Action Plan on Human Rights and Democracy 2015–2019;European Commission/High Representative, Joint Staff Working Document on Gender Equality and Women's Empowerment: Transforming the Lives of Girls and Women through EU External Relations 2016–2020, SWD (2015) 182 final, 21 September 2015, pp. 6, 27; European Commission, The EU's Strategic Engagement for Gender Equality 2016–2019, 14 March 2016, p. 15; European Commission, Communication towards an EU Strategy on the Rights of the Child, COM (2006) 367 Final, 4 July 2006; EU Guidelines for the Promotion and Protection of the Rights of the Child (2017), pp. 32–34; European Commission, Communication on a Special Place for Children in the EU's External Action, COM (2008) 55 final, 5 February 2008.

62 The New European Consensus on Development, 9459/17, 19 May 2017, para 40, 71.

63 A Global Strategy for the European Union's Foreign and Security Policy, June 2016, pp. 35, 38.

64 European Commission, Communication on the European Agenda on Security, COM (2015) 185 final, 28 April 2015 pp. 4, 18.

Turkey, UAE, Russia, Ukraine or Central Asia, as well as to European countries.[65] Even prior to the initiation of the ENP, the matter of human trafficking in relations with non-EU countries, members of the CoE, was picked up as one of importance by the EU.[66] The ENP's sweeping nature was inevitably to incorporate the fight against organised crime, including human trafficking within the prospective frameworks of cooperation with the relevant countries.

By that time, the Eastern neighbours had already undertaken certain measures in this area, including the signature of the Palermo Protocol mentioned above, awaiting ratification.[67] While some of the neighbours lacked a legal framework criminalising trafficking and protecting victims,[68] others were already making significant steps in that direction,[69] with the involvement of such international organisations, as the International Organisation for Migration (IMO), ILO, UNDP, OSCE.[70] The discussion below reveals the interplay between security and human rights considerations in the manner in which the issue was framed and incentivised by the EU through the ENP instruments.

15.3.1 Tracing the EU's Approach Through the ENP and EaP Policy Documents

The story behind the ENP has been told and retold, its promises and failures scrupulously analysed across various disciplines.[71] The EU's expansion to the East in 2004 challenged it with a task of addressing a myriad of issues stemming from the emergence of new borders. The ENP's aim of 'avoiding new dividing lines at the borders' was to be implemented by actually reinforcing and strengthening the newly created borders in the East.[72] Achieving security and stability were paramount to the new policy,[73] and would be expected to include measures to fight against transnational organised crime. The 'management of the new external border and

---

[65] IOM 2008b, p. 24; IOM 2008a, pp. 13, 32–33; IOM 2008c, pp .13, 35; Armenia ENP Country Report 2004, Commission Staff Working Document, COM (2005) 72 final, p. 2.5.

[66] 2002 Brussels Declaration, above n. 51, p. 4.

[67] See for instance for early efforts IOM 2008a, pp. 37–39; IOM 2008c, pp. 40, 42–44.

[68] European Commission, Azerbaijan ENP Country Report 2004, Staff Working Document SEC (2005) 286/3, 2 March 2005, p. 2.5.

[69] For instance, Moldova had already criminalised trafficking in human beings alongside other state measures to combat trafficking; European Commission, Moldova ENP Country Report 2004, Staff Working Document SEC (2004) 567, 12 May 2004, p. 12.

[70] See for instance, IOM 2008a, p. 47; IOM 2008c, pp. 45, 47–48.

[71] To name a few: Cremona and Hillion 2006; Cremona 2008; Ghazaryan 2014; Ghazaryan 2013; Van Vooren 2011; Van Elsuwege and Petrov 2011; Smith 2005; Zaiotti 2007; Lannon 2012; Dannreuther 2006; Aliboni 2005; Schumacher et al. 2018.

[72] European Commission, Communication on the European Neighbourhood Policy Strategy Paper, COM (2004) 373 final, 21 May 2004, p. 16.

[73] Cremona and Hillion 2006, pp. 22–23; Ghazaryan 2014, pp. 24–28.

trans-boundary flows' was one of the major concerns of the new geographical and political reality.[74] Migration, border management and most importantly shared security concerns, including human trafficking, were in need of bilateral and multilateral cooperation.[75] The ENP was to build upon the experience of 'Söderköping Process' including Belarus, Moldova and Ukraine and eight EU Member States establishing cross-border cooperation process on asylum and migration in the wake of the anticipated enlargement.[76] Thus, the initial policy planning documents placed human trafficking within the domain of migration control and the fight against organised crime. The 2003 European Security Strategy Paper, viewed as closely linked to the ENP,[77] also identified organised crime, such as trafficking in women and illegal migrants as one of the key threats facing Europe.[78]

Human trafficking featured in successive ENP revisions similarly placed in the domain of security and the fight against organised crime with no link to human rights protection. For instance, the 2011 Communication in response to the Arab Spring uprisings incentivised the neighbours with visa-liberalisation prospects linked to cooperation on migration, mobility and security.[79] The 2015 ENP revision similarly includes the issue within the strengthened security dimension of the policy.[80]

A regional dimension of the policy was expected to incorporate an element on human trafficking as the EU prefers to tackle issues related to AFJS through regional cooperation.[81] The 2008 EaP Communication envisaged reinforced cooperation on 'mobility and security' by offering 'pacts' to the partner countries, within which the EU would provide support in 'adopting and effectively implementing national strategies in line with EU standards to fight vigorously against organised crime, trafficking [etc.]'.[82] At the Prague EaP summit in 2009, in particular, the parties decided to strengthen cooperation and coordination in the prevention of and the fight against trafficking in human beings.[83]

In 2011, the Eastern Partnership Panel on Migration and Asylum was created as the successor of the Söderköping Process under the EaP Platform on democracy, good governance and stability.[84] Funded by the EU and implemented in cooperation

---

[74]Commission of The European Communities 2003, p. 6.

[75]Ibid., pp. 6, 11, 14; ENP Strategy Paper, p. 16.

[76]ENP Strategy Paper, p. 21.

[77]Ghazaryan 2014, p. 26; Hillion 2008, p. 314.

[78]Council of the European Union 2009a, p. 4.

[79]European Commission, Joint Communication on a New Response to a Changing Neighbourhood, COM (2011) 303 final, 25 May 2011, pp. 12–13.

[80]European Commission, Joint Communication on Review of the European Neighbourhood Policy, JOIN (2015) 50 final, 18 November 2015, pp. 12–13.

[81]European Commission, Strategy for the External Dimension of Justice and Home Affairs, COM (2005) 491 final, 12 October 2005, p. 5.

[82]European Commission, Communication on Eastern Partnership, COM (2008) 823 final, 3 December 2008, pp. 6, 8.

[83]Joint Declaration of the Eastern Partnership Summit, Warsaw, 14983/11, Press 341, 29–30 September 2011, para. 7.

[84]See further http://eapmigrationpanel.org/en/about-panel. Accessed 7 February 2020.

with such international organisations as the UNHCR and IOM, the panel was aimed at promoting cooperation and dialogue towards the harmonisation of policies and practices based on the principles of the EU Global Approach to Migration. In 2017, however, a decision was made to reconfigure the panel into a Panel on Migration, Mobility and Integrated Border Management under the EaP Platform 4 on 'Mobility and people-to-people contacts'. An overview of the Panel's programme since its inception reveals four expert and panel meetings relevant for human trafficking addressing also the issue of victim protection.[85] The Panel, thus, provides a socialisation platform where the EaP partners and EU Member States share experiences and achievements.

In addition to the regional dimension, the prevention of and the fight against human trafficking has been incorporated in the bilateral instruments involving an element of conditionality as part of the methodology of the ENP.[86]

15.3.2 A Human Rights-Based Approach: The Bilateral Context

In the bilateral context, the matter of human trafficking has been incorporated both in framework documents and in policy-specific instruments. In some cases, the ENP instruments had to build upon pre-existing initiatives. In particular, the EU and Ukraine had already developed advanced cooperation based on JHA Action Plan established in 2001 and revised periodically subsequently.[87] It was an all-encompassing JHA instrument setting a scoreboard against which Ukraine's progress had to be monitored, already incorporating elements of a human rights approach in the fight against human trafficking.[88] The document preserved its significance under the ENP for Ukraine, while for the other Eastern neighbours the ENP Action Plans (APs) were novel in inviting attention to the matter of human trafficking in a bilateral context.

[85] Expert Meeting on Preventing Facilitation of Irregular Migration, 17–18 October 2017; Panel Meeting on Irregular Migration and Trafficking in Human Beings; 14–15 April 2016; Panel Meeting on Smuggling of Human Beings; 10–11 June 2014; Expert Workshop on Victims of Trafficking in Human Beings, 21–22 May 2013.

[86] Kelley 2006; Cremona and Hillion 2006; Ghazaryan 2014; Kochenov 2008.

[87] Balzacq 2008, p. 20.

[88] For instance, it provided for the ratification and implementation of the international instruments on human rights protection when combatting organised crime, as well as providing assistance inter alia to reintegrate victims of human trafficking.

15.3.3 ENP Action Plans and Their Monitoring

The ENP APs were the first comprehensive bilateral ENP instruments, established with all Eastern partners except Belarus. Soft law in nature, they set priorities for bilateral cooperation, including in the area of JHA. In the case of Ukraine, the ENP AP instead made a reference to the JHA Action.[89] The latter, in its 2007 revised version, placed human trafficking under the heading of security, although not devoid of a human rights component.[90] In particular, it provided for promotion of a child sensitive approach in line with international law.

The ENP APs with Moldova, Georgia, Armenia and Azerbaijan varied in their approach to this issue. In case of Moldova, the stepping up of the fight against organised crime, including human trafficking was a general priority action. It stood out from the rest of the APs as it provided for priority actions on human trafficking, including legislative reform in line with international human rights standards, under the priorities on human rights and fundamental freedoms.[91] Similar, but more extensive actions were also provided under the priority heading of 'Cooperation in JHA' with a strong orientation towards human rights protection.[92] In contrast, the ENP APs with Azerbaijan, Georgia and Armenia had no such inclination. The Armenian AP did not prioritise cooperation in the area of JFS, instead including it among 'general actions'—which were flagged as a matter for further attention, but not priority for action—with little human rights content.[93] In the case of Azerbaijan and Georgia, trafficking-related actions were spread under the priority area of JFS, as well as the 'general actions' in the same area with little human rights content.[94]

The Eastern APs, thus, differed significantly in the manner in which they addressed the matter of human trafficking, with some barely making any connection with human rights protection. Such connection, however, was more consistently present within the Commission's evaluation of progress in the implementation of AP priorities. While the issue of human trafficking is addressed most commonly as part of the progress on justice, freedom of security, occasionally the progress on this matter has been assessed under human rights and fundamental freedoms.[95] Most importantly, the Commission paid equal attention to victim protection measures, at times making calls for continuous reform in relation to the protection of victims, even demanding a

[89]EU-Ukraine ENP Action Plan, s 2.1(15).

[90]Revised EU-Ukraine JHA Action Plan, s III.3.

[91]EU-Moldova ENP Action Plan, s 2.1(5).

[92]Ibid., s 2.5.

[93]Ibid., s 4.5.3; on the status of the 'general actions', see further Ghazaryan 2014, p. 132.

[94]Priority Area 9; EU-Azerbaijan ENP Action Plan, s 4.3.3; Priority Area 4; EU-Georgia ENP Action Plan, s 4.3.3. In the EU-Georgia Action Plan, developing mechanisms of protection, assistance and rehabilitation for victims is included as part of the general objectives.

[95]For instance, the Azerbaijan 2010 Progress Report (SEC (2010) 519) called for further effort as part of human rights assessment; Armenia 2012 Progress Report (SWD (2012) 110 final), p. 7; Moldova 2008 Progress Report (SEC (2008) 399), p. 4.

gender and human rights perspective on occasion.[96] The ratification of relevant international instruments, particularly the CoE-relevant Convention was also a continuous feature in the assessment of the progress made. Ultimately, all EaP countries have ratified the Convention.[97]

While the APs and the accompanying progress evaluation brought human trafficking to the attention of the partners as a JFS matter mostly, it was not necessarily devoid of a human rights component. The approach taken in sector specific instruments is considered next.

15.3.4 Visa Liberalisation and Mobility Partnerships

The Commission's 2006 Communication on strengthening the ENP set out that visa liberalisation would be necessarily linked to commitment to broader reforms in the area of JHA, including cooperation in combating trafficking and smuggling in human beings.[98] The cooperation in this area became a priority for the EaP, visa liberalisation being one of the most prominent offers to the Eastern neighbours,[99] serving as a 'powerful incentive for far-reaching reforms' across the relevant sector and human rights area.[100] The Stockholm Programme also reiterated the EU's determination to link its visa policy to 'a broader vision that takes account of relevant internal and external policy concerns'.[101] According to the Commission's 2011 Communication on Global Approach to Migration and Mobility, the fight against trafficking in human beings should be systematically included within newly concluded agreements and various frameworks of dialogue on migration and mobility.[102] This was reflective of the emerging practice in the EaP region in the so-called mobility partnerships. These non-binding instruments were the 'prime bilateral framework to address relevant migration and mobility issues of mutual concern'.[103] With the exception of Ukraine, mobility partnerships have been the primary framework used to manage migration flows between the EU and the EaP countries.[104] These instruments served

---

[96] See, for instance, Ukraine 2011 Progress Report (SEC (2011) 646), p. 15; Ukraine 2012 Progress Report (SWD (2012) 124 final), p. 4.

[97] See https://www.coe.int/en/web/conventions/full-list/-/conventions/treaty/197/signatures?desktop=false. Accessed 7 February 2020.

[98] COM (2006) 726 final, 4 December 2006, p. 6.

[99] Joint Declaration of the Prague Eastern Partnership Summit, Prague, 7 May 2009, 8435/09, Presse 78; Warsaw 2011 Eastern Partnership Summit Declaration; Joint Declaration of the Eastern Partnership Summit, Vilnius, 28–29 November 2013, 17130/13, Presse 516.

[100] Hernandez and Sagrera 2014, p. ii.

[101] Stockholm Programme, above n. 48 s 5.2.

[102] COM (2011) 743 final, above n. 60, p. 16.

[103] Council of the European Union 2012, para 42.

[104] See further https://ec.europa.eu/home-affairs/what-we-do/policies/international-affairs/eastern-partnership/mobility-partnerships-visa-facilitation-and-readmission-agreements_en. Accessed 7 February 2020.

as an umbrella framework for reforms that were required for visa facilitation and readmission arrangements.[105] As noted above, Ukraine had embarked on reform-oriented cooperation in this area earlier than other Eastern neighbours, and signed a visa facilitation and readmission agreements in 2007 without the need for a mobility partnership. With the rest of the EaP, partners mobility partnerships were signed within the period of 2008–2016.

The mobility partnerships adopt respect for human rights as the basis for pursuing wider policy objectives. The measures for bilateral cooperation evolve mostly around secure border management and the strengthening of national institutional capacities with the main emphasis on the prevention of trafficking and law enforcement. Human rights concerns come across in an ad hoc and non-systematic manner. In the Moldovan case, the country must ensure the effective implementation of the Palermo Convention and its relevant protocols. In the Azeri mobility partnership, a call is made to promote 'best practices in the field of combatting trafficking in human beings'. The mobility partnership with Belarus includes support to protect and assist victims of trafficking.[106] Most significantly, human trafficking is coupled with irregular migration with an emphasis on its prevention and readmission of individuals. This is understandable given that the partners also had visa facilitation and readmissions agreements in place or intended to sign them in the future.[107] Mobility partnerships should not therefore be seen as significant in advancing a human rights agenda in the fight against human trafficking in the Eastern partners.

The visa-liberalisation dialogue, including the implementation of VLAPs, goes further in the scope and depth of required reforms. The incentive of visa liberalisation has equipped the EU with leverage to promote a certain model in the fight against human trafficking in Ukraine, Georgia and Moldova. The visa-liberalisation process had two phases, involving legislative reforms in the first phase, and benchmarked implementation in the second.[108] Following continuous monitoring by the Commission, the process culminated in establishing a visa-free travel with all three countries as noted above. Most importantly, the visa-liberalisation action plans incorporated a human rights conditionality within its four blocks. Block 4 linked external relations and fundamental rights in all three action plans by focusing mainly on freedom of movement, issuing of identity documents, citizenship and anti-discrimination,[109] thus omitting any trafficking related human right reforms per se. The human rights dimension of the fight against trafficking instead constituted a part of Block 3 on public order and security.[110] In all three cases, the first phase required the adoption or consolidation of a legal framework on trafficking in human beings and relevant benchmarked strategies, while the second phase required the efficient implementation

---

[105] Hernandez and Sagrera 2014, pp. 3–4.

[106] Belarus Mobility Partnership, para 12.

[107] The last country to do so was Belarus, which signed the respective agreements in January 2020.

[108] Malmström 2011.

[109] EU-Ukraine Visa Liberalisation Action Plan, s 2.4.

[110] EU-Ukraine 2010 Visa Liberalisation Action Plan, s 2.3.

of the latter, including through the effective protection of victims of trafficking.[111] The Georgian VLAP elaborated further on the effective protection of victims to include 'provision of adequate infrastructures and funds ensuring decent reception and protection of the rights and dignity of trafficking victims and supporting their social and professional reintegration'.[112]

When setting the relevant actions for the first legislative and policy framework phase, the VLAPs required the adoption or consolidation of the relevant legislation according to EU and international standards. This suggests that even though there was no clear obligation to adopt the EU *acquis* in this area, the standards set in EU law, including the human rights-based approach of the Directive, should have been taken into account. The monitoring of the progress under the VLAPs demonstrates by far the most substantive and detailed assessment of the achievements during both phases, inter alia by indicating outstanding issues, including regarding the improvement of the support to the victims of human trafficking.[113] In the Georgian case, the assessment of the progress in the first phase placed less emphasis on these issues perhaps due to the country's 'well advanced' status.[114] In subsequent reports assessing the implementation of the relevant legislation the Commission, however, offered substantive scrutiny and demanded further action on the human rights dimension.[115] After successive rounds of assessment, the relevant benchmark was deemed to be achieved securing the visa liberalisation for all three countries.

The securing of visa-free travel, however, does not signal the end of scrutiny by the Commission which can resort to the visa suspension mechanism, to which extent it publishes reports. To this date, human trafficking has not been of particular concern for the Commission.[116] This, however, does not mean that there are no issues

[111] EU-Ukraine; EU-Moldova, EU-Georgia Visa Liberalisation Action Plans, s 2.3.1.

[112] Georgia Visa Liberalisation Action Plan, S 2.3.1.

[113] Third Report on the Implementation by Ukraine of the Action Plan on Visa Liberalisation, COM (2013) 809 final, 15 November 2013, pp. 11–12; Fifth Progress Report on the Implementation by Ukraine of the Action Plan on Visa Liberalisation, COM (2015) 200 final, 2 March 2017 pp. 5–6; Sixth Progress Report on the Implementation by Ukraine of the Action Plan on Visa Liberalisation, COM (2015) 905 final, 18 December 2015, p. 6; First Progress Report of the Implementation by the Republic of Moldova of the Action Plan on Visa Liberalisation, SEC (2011) 1075 final, 16 September 2011, p. 7; Second Progress Report on the Implementation by the Republic of Moldova of the Action Plan on Visa Liberalisation, SWD (2012) 12 final, 27 September 2012, p. 12; Report on the Implementation by the Republic of Moldova of the Action Plan on Visa Liberalisation, COM (2012) 348 final, 22 June 2012, p. 12; Fourth Report on the Implementation by the Republic of Moldova of the Action Plan on Visa Liberalisation, COM (2013) 459 final, 21 June 2013, pp. 18–19; Fifth Report on the Implementation by the Republic of Moldova of the Action Plan on Visa Liberalisation, COM (2013) 807 final, 15 November 2013, pp. 17–18.

[114] First Progress Report on the Implementation by Georgia of the Action Plan on Visa Liberalisation, COM (2013) 808 final, 15 November 2013, p. 12.

[115] Third Progress Report on Georgia's Implementation of the Action Plan on Visa Liberalisation, COM (2015) 199 final, 8 May 2015, pp. 5–6; Fourth Progress Report on Georgia's Implementation of the Action Plan on Visa Liberalisation COM (2015) 684 final, 18 December 2015, p. 6.

[116] European Commission, First Report under the Visa Suspension Mechanism, COM (2017) 815 final, 20 December 2017; European Commission, Second Report under the Visa Suspension Mechanism, COM (2018) 856 final, 19 December 2018.

in either country as far as the fight against human trafficking, including its human rights dimension is concerned.[117] Instead, the Commission is concerned with other matters such as the rising level of irregular migration, corruption and other organised crime that might threaten the visa-free travel. Besides, other dialogue venues or instruments can be used to address outstanding or emerging issues. For Armenia, Azerbaijan and Belarus, which are not involved in the visa-liberalisation dialogue, such frameworks, including human rights dialogues, could be particularly important.

15.3.5 Human Rights Dialogues

Human rights dialogues are not specific to the ENP. Instead, they are EU foreign policy tools,[118] constituting a part of wider political dialogue within which the EU institutions can raise the matter of human trafficking.[119] The usefulness of the human rights dialogues was stressed by the Court of Auditors in terms of placing a stronger emphasis on human trafficking in another region.[120] Human rights dialogues have been established with all EaP countries with the exception of Azerbaijan. An examination of the statements following the successive rounds of dialogues with the EaP countries reveals that human trafficking is rarely referenced during the dialogue appearing only on two occasions across the region.[121] In case of Azerbaijan, the matter of human trafficking is part of the dialogue taking place through the Subcommittee on Justice, Freedom, Security and Human Rights established under the Partnership and Cooperation Agreement, which occasionally makes a reference to human trafficking.[122] Even these occasional references can be interpreted as evidence of the EU's approach of embracing this issue within its human rights agenda. Besides, the agenda of these meetings appears to be dominated by more pressing matters of political reforms and first-generation human rights.

---

[117] See, for instance, US Department of State 2018.

[118] EU Guidelines on human rights dialogues with non-EU countries, 16526/08, 22 December 2008.

[119] Reliefweb 2019, p. 79; EEAS 2010, p. 51.

[120] European Court of Auditors 2017.

[121] As a matter of exception, the 2010 Moldova human dialogue and the Georgia 2016 human rights dialogue make such a reference.

[122] https://eeas.europa.eu/headquarters/headquarters-homepage/34108/eu-azerbaijan-subcommittee-justice-freedom-security-and-human-rights-and-democracy-meets_en. Accessed 7 February 2020.

15.3.6 *New Generation Agreements and Related Framework Instruments*

With the EaP came a reinforced promise of new contractual framework between the parties. By then negotiations had already commenced with Ukraine in 2007. An association agreement was chosen as a template used also for the subsequent negotiations with Moldova, Georgia and Armenia. While the Association Agreements eventually materialised with Ukraine, Moldova and Georgia despite the political turbulence in the neighbourhood, Armenia retracted from the prospect of Association Agreement in lieu of joining the Eurasian Economic Union under pressure from Russia.[123] In 2017, the CEPA was signed instead. Negotiations on a new agreement are also under way with Azerbaijan.[124]

The 2009 Council Action-Oriented Paper specifically noted the need for promoting EU goals in the fight against human trafficking through the ENP and the relevant contractual framework.[125] It was therefore anticipated that the Association Agreements and the CEPA would contain trafficking-related provisions. Before turning to their relevant provisions, it should be noted that according to the EU's 2012–2016 strategy towards the eradication of trafficking in human beings, 'as a severe violation of human rights mentioned in the Charter of Fundamental Rights, trafficking in human beings will continue to be covered under the Human Rights Clauses in the EU's agreements with third countries … providing the basis for cooperation on and promotion of human rights'.[126] While the EU Charter of Fundamental Rights as such is not referenced in the human rights clauses with the Eastern neighbours, the partner countries should abide by other international instruments, which in the case of Ukraine and Armenia is an open-ended list.[127] The human rights clauses, most importantly, set a positive framework of engagement across all areas of cooperation between the EU and the relevant partners, including in the domain of AFSJ.[128]

In the Ukrainian case, the path towards the Association Agreement was paved through successive Association Agendas. The fight against human trafficking invariably featured as part of the cooperation on JFS without any emphasis on a human rights approach, with the exception of child trafficking being included within the domain of human rights and fundamental freedoms.[129] It should be noted that the first Association Agenda was adopted in 2009 shortly preceding the VLAP which was the main instrument incorporating conditionality in AFSJ. The new agreement,

---

[123] Ghazaryan and Delcour 2018; Alieva et al. 2017.

[124] https://www.consilium.europa.eu/en/press/press-releases/2016/11/14/azerbaijan/. Accessed 5 July 2020.

[125] European Commission 2009, p. 14.

[126] EC 2012, p. 11.

[127] EU-Ukraine AA, above n. 16, Article 2; CEPA, Article 2.

[128] Fierro 2001; Ghazaryan 2015.

[129] 20009 EU-Ukraine Association Agenda, S 2.1(f), s 3; 2011–2012 EU-Ukraine Association Agenda, s 3; 2013 EU-Ukraine Association Agenda s 2.1(f), s 3.

however, is important in setting the legal framework beyond the visa liberalisation, which is the case also for Georgia and Moldova. For Armenia, the CEPA is the first bilateral instrument providing for comprehensive cooperation in the AFSJ.

The new agreements share in common a strong commitment to the respect for human rights which shall 'guide' the cooperation in the AFSJ.[130] In all agreements, trafficking in human beings features both under the cooperation on migration, asylum and border management, and a separate article on the fight against organised crime. As part of the provisions on the fight against organised crime, the main emphasis is on combatting and preventing various transnational crimes, including human trafficking. As part of the provisions on cooperation on migration, asylum and border management, smuggling of and trafficking in human beings is one of the issues on which the parties 'reaffirm the importance of joint management'.[131] The EU-Ukraine Association Agreement notes that the cooperation will take place in accordance 'with the relevant Union and national legislation in force', implying that Ukraine would undertake relevant actions in accordance with EU law.[132] This should be juxtaposed to the relevant provisions in the Association Agreements with Georgia and Moldova respectively, as well as the CEPA with Armenia, where the cooperation will be based and will be implemented 'in accordance with [the parties'] relevant legislation in force'.[133]

The overview of the actions constituting cooperation in the relevant areas demonstrate that the agreements are comparable in terms of their emphasis on prevention and law enforcement. The action most relevant to the fight against human trafficking calls for 'establishing together an effective and preventive policy against illegal migration, smuggling of migrants and trafficking in human beings', which includes combatting networks of smugglers and traffickers and the protection of the victims of such trafficking.[134] It thus incorporates a general reference to human rights approach, which appears to be subsumed in the 'effective and preventative policy' against human trafficking. It can be suggested that in the case of the Association Agreements with Ukraine, Moldova and Georgia, given the reforms the countries have already undertaken, there is no need to elaborate upon this issue in a framework agreement. The position is the same in CEPA, even though Armenia has not undergone an EU-driven reform in this area in the absence of a visa-liberalisation dialogue. This can be explained by the possibility of substantiating the required reforms in further instruments.

The subsequent Association Agendas supporting the implementation of the agreements in Ukraine, Moldova and Georgia by setting specific actions, demonstrate the

---

[130] EU-Ukraine AA, above n. 16, Article 14; CEPA, Article 12(3); EU-Moldova AA, above n. 16, Article 12(3); EU-Georgia AA, above n. 16, Article 13(3).

[131] EU-Ukraine AA, above n. 16, Article 16(1); EU-Moldova AA, above n. 16, Article 14(1); EU-Georgia AA, above n. 16, Article 15(1); CEPA, Article 14(1).

[132] EU-Ukraine AA, above n. 16, Article 16(2).

[133] CEPA, Article 14(2); EU-Moldova AA, above n. 16, Article 14(2); EU-Georgia AA, above n. 16, Article 15(2).

[134] EU-Moldova AA, above n. 16, Article 14(2)(d); EU-Ukraine AA, above n. 16, Article 16(2)(b); EU-Georgia AA, above n. 16(2)d; CEPA, Article 14(2)(d).

incorporation of a human rights-based approach. Measures relevant for human trafficking are included either under the heading of ensuring respect for human rights and fundamental freedoms,[135] or the relevant priority actions regarding police cooperation and organised crime—at times with evident human rights orientation with actions on effective victim protection, including through strengthening procedural rights[136] or both. The relevant priorities can shift from the heading of respect of human rights to cooperation on freedom, security and justice.[137] Most commonly the actions require the efficient implementation of the national action plans on the fight against human trafficking without stressing a specific human rights dimension. It should be noted that the Partnership Priorities established with Armenia (the equivalent of the Association Agenda) contain no provisions concerning the fight against human trafficking. This might be motivated by the lesser importance of human trafficking in the Armenian case as the country is not a major source of trafficking to the EU, even though Armenian victims are trafficked elsewhere.

15.4 Conclusion

The fight against the trafficking in human beings has become a composite part of the EU's external agenda on AFSJ and its external human rights policy in the Eastern neighbourhood. The EU's gradually evolved internal legal framework incorporating a human rights-based approach has been undoubtedly diffused into the bilateral and multilateral instruments with a varying intensity depending on a number of factors.

The ENP with its emphasis on security and stability elevated the issue of trafficking in human beings in relations between the parties as part of an intensified cooperation in the AFSJ. The ENP policy documents demanded action in this area, which also found its way into the EaP framework via the establishment of the relevant panel. The relocation of the panel from the EaP's Platform 1 to Platform 4 demonstrates that the matter of human trafficking is an inherent part of the cooperation on AFSJ. Framing the issue as belonging only to the domain of human rights and fundamental freedoms would fragment it as it cannot be uncoupled from the fight against human trafficking as a transnational crime. The most suitable approach is to incorporate a human rights dimension in the fight against human trafficking as part of AFSJ cooperation, as well as demonstrating awareness of the human rights aspects of the fight against human trafficking in the cooperation on human rights and fundamental freedoms. This dual

[135] 2015 EU-Ukraine Association Agenda, S 2.1.(f); 2014 EU-Moldova Association Agenda, s 2.1(iii).

[136] 2015 EU-Ukraine Association Agenda, s 3.5(iii); EU-Georgia 2014, 2017–2020 Association Agenda.

[137] For instance, in the 2017 EU-Moldova Association Agenda, the implementation of the national action plan on preventing and combatting human trafficking was moved to the area of cooperation on freedom, security and justice, whereas in the 2014 Association Agenda it was placed under the respect of human rights and fundamental freedoms.

approach does transpire in the Eastern dimension of the ENP mostly through placing the matter under the umbrella of AFSJ with a human rights dimension to it.

The ENP APs (in the Ukrainian case vicariously through the JHA AP) demonstrate that human trafficking has been more of a concern for the EU in Ukraine and Moldova receiving more substantive attention, including to its human rights dimension. The Armenian, Georgian and Azeri ENP APs instead reveal a lesser emphasis on this issue with a much weaker human rights dimension. The Commission's Progress Reports, nonetheless, bring to the fore the expectation of incorporating a human rights approach in tackling this phenomenon in all countries concerned.

The examination of migration and mobility specific instruments reveal further nuances. Instruments, such as mobility partnerships are primarily concerned with prevention of illegal migration and readmission of individuals. The VLAPs are more helpful in tracing the security and human rights linkages. These documents reveal a pronounced human rights dimension to the fight against human trafficking linked to the visa-liberalisation incentive but only as part of the block on public order and security. In the end, the countries which are not involved in a visa-liberalisation dialogue do not face the same pressure to develop the human rights dimension of the fight against human trafficking.

As far as the new generation of agreements in the East are concerned, they demonstrate a stronger awareness of human rights in the area of AFSJ. In relation to trafficking in human beings, a general reference to victim protection is made as part of the cooperation on effective and preventative policies on human trafficking among other crimes. Although the wording can be criticised for subsuming victim protection under preventative policies, it is a welcome development that the security-related obligations in the agreements are intertwined with human rights protection.

Ultimately, while the human rights approach became part of the EU's policies on fighting the trafficking in human beings in its Eastern neighbourhood, it materialised most prominently within the visa-liberalisation dialogues with Ukraine, Georgia and Moldova.

References

Aliboni R (2005) The Geopolitical Implications of the European Neighbourhood Policy. EFAR 10:1

Alieva L, Delcour L, Kostanyan H (2017) EU Relations with Armenia and Azerbaijan, European Parliament. AFET

Balzacq T (2008) The External Dimension of EU Justice and Home Affairs: Tools, Processes, Outcomes, CEPS Working Document No. 303

Berman J, Friesendorf C (2008) EU Foreign Policy and the Fight Against Human Trafficking: Coercive Governance as Crime Control. EFAR 13:189–209

Bressan S (2012) Criminal Law against Human Trafficking within the EU: A Comparison of an Approximated Legislation. EJCCL&CJ 20:137–163

Campana P, Varese F (2015) Exploitation in Human Trafficking and Smuggling. EJCPR 22:89–105

Chaudary S (2011) Trafficking in Europe: An Analysis of the Effectiveness of European Law. Michigan Journal of International Law 33:77–99

Commission of The European Communities (2003) Wider Europe Communication. http://eeas.europa.eu/archives/docs/enp/pdf/pdf/com03_104_en.pdf Accessed 5 July 2020
Council of the European Union (2009a) European Security Strategy - A secure Europe in a better world https://www.consilium.europa.eu/media/30823/qc7809568enc.pdf Accessed 5 July 2020
Council of the European Union (2009b) Towards Global EU Action against Trafficking in Human Beings http://register.consilium.europa.eu/doc/srv?l=EN&f=ST%2011450%202009%20REV%205 Accessed 5 July 2020
Council of the European Union (2012) Conclusions on the Global Approach to Migration and Mobility http://register.consilium.europa.eu/doc/srv?l=EN&f=ST%209417%202012%20INIT Accessed 7 February 2020
Cremona M (2008) The European Neighbourhood Policy: More than a Partnership. In: Cremona M (ed) Developments in EU External Relations Law. OUP, Oxford, pp 244–299
Cremona M, Hillion C (2006) L'Union fait la force? Potential and Limitations of the ENP as an Integrated EU Foreign and Security Policy. In: Copsey N, Mayhew A (eds) European Neighbourhood Policy: The Case of Europe. Sussex European Institute, SEI Seminar Papers Series Number 1, pp 20–44
Dannreuther R (2006) Developing the Alternative to Enlargement: The European Neighbourhood Policy. EFAR 11:183
EC (2012) EU Strategy towards the Eradication of Trafficking in Human Beings 2012–2016 https://ec.europa.eu/anti-trafficking/eu-policy/eu-strategy-towards-eradication-trafficking-human-beings-2012-2016_en Accessed 5 July 2020
EEAS (2010) EU Annual Report on Human Rights and Democracy in the World in 2010 https://eeas.europa.eu/topics/human-rights-democracy/8437/eu-annual-reports-human-rights-and-democratisation_en Accessed 7 February 2020
European Commission (2009) Action-Oriented Paper on strengthening the EU external dimension on action against trafficking in human beings; Towards Global EU Action against Trafficking in Human Beings. https://ec.europa.eu/anti-trafficking/eu-policy/action-oriented-paper-strengthening-eu-external-dimension-against-trafficking-human-beings_en Accessed 5 July 2020
European Court of Auditors (2017) EU Support to Fight Human Trafficking in South/South-East Asia. https://www.eca.europa.eu/en/Pages/DocItem.aspx?did=41523 Accessed 5 July 2020
Europol (2015) The THB Financial Business Model, Assessing the Current State of Knowledge https://www.google.com/search?q=Europol%2C+%E2%80%98The+THB+Financial+Business+Model%2C+Assessing+the+Current+State+of+Knowledge&rlz=1C1JZAP_enNL839NL839&oq=Europol%2C+%E2%80%98The+THB+Financial+Business+Model%2C+Assessing+the+Current+State+of+Knowledge&aqs=chrome.69i57.192j0j1&sourceid=chrome&ie=UTF-8Accessed 5 July 2020
Europol (2016) Trafficking in Human Beings in the EU.https://www.europol.europa.eu/publications-documents/trafficking-in-human-beings-in-eu Accessed 5 July 2020
Eurostat (2015) Trafficking in Human Beings https://ec.europa.eu/anti-trafficking/publications/trafficking-human-beings-eurostat-2015-edition_en Accessed 5 July 2020
Fierro E (2001) Legal Basis and Scope of the Human Rights Clauses in EC Bilateral Agreements: Any Room for Positive Interpretation? ELJ 7:41–68
Gallagher AT (2010) The International Law of Human Trafficking. Cambridge University Press, Cambridge
Ghazaryan N (2013) The Law and Political Objectives of the European Neighbourhood Policy in the East: A Difficult Marriage or Singing in Unison. CYELS 15:619–641
Ghazaryan N (2014) The European Neighbourhood Policy and the Democratic Values of the EU A Legal Analysis. Hart Publishing, Oxford
Ghazaryan N (2015) A New Generation of Human Rights Clauses? The Case of Association Agreements in the Eastern Neighbourhood. ELR 40:391–410
Ghazaryan N, Delcour L (2018) From EU Integration Process to the Eurasian Economic Union: The Case of Armenia. In: Petrov R, Van Elsuwege P (eds) Post-Soviet Constitutions and Challenges of Regional Integration: Adapting to European and Eurasian Integration Projects. Routledge, Oxon

Gromek-Brok K (2011) EU Directive on Preventing and Combating Trafficking in Human Beings and Protecting Victims: Will It Be Effective? Nova et Vetera 20:227–237
Grundell LR (2015) EU Anti-Trafficking Policies: from Migration and Crime Control to Prevention and Protection. EUI Migration Policy Centre 2015/09
Hernandez D, Rudolph A (2015) Modern Day Slavery: What Drives Human Trafficking in Europe? EJPE 38:118–139
Hernandez R, Sagrera R (2014) The Impact of Visa Liberalisation in Eastern Partnership Countries, Russia and Turkey on Trans-Border Mobility. CEPS Papers in Liberty and Security No. 63
Hillion C (2008) The EU's Neighbourhood Policy towards Eastern Europe. In: Dashwood A, Maresceasu M (eds) Law and Practice of EU External Relations. CUP, Cambridge, pp 309–333
IOM (2008a) Migration in Armenia: A Country Profile. https://publications.iom.int/books/migration-armenia-country-profile-2008#:~:text=%E2%80%9CMigration%20in%20Armenia%3A%20A%20Country,funded%20from%20IOM's%201035%20Facility.&text=However%2C%20migrants'%20remittances%20constitute%20the%20largest%20source%20of%20foreign%20exchange. Accessed 5 July 2020
IOM (2008b) Migration in Azerbaijan: A Country Profile https://publications.iom.int/books/migration-republic-azerbaijan-country-profile-2008 Accessed 5 July 2020
IOM (2008c) Migration in Georgia: A Country Profile. https://publications.iom.int/books/migration-georgia-country-profile-2008 Accessed 5 July 2020
IOM (2008d) Migration in Ukraine: A Country Profile https://publications.iom.int/fr/system/files/pdf/ukraine_profile2008.pdf Accessed 5 July 2020
Kelley J (2006) New Wine in Old Wineskins: Policy Learning and Adaptation in the New European Neighbourhood Policy. JCMS 44:29–55
Kochenov D (2008) The ENP Conditionality: Pre-Accession Mistakes Repeated. In: Delcour L, Tulmets E (eds) Pioneer Europe? Testing EU Foreign Policy in the Neighbourhood. Nomos, Baden-Baden, pp 105–120
Krieg SH (2009) Trafficking in Human Beings: The EU Approach between Border Control. Law Enforcement and Human Rights. ELJ 15:775–790
Lannon E (ed) (2012) The European Neighbourhood Policy's Challenges. College of Europe Studies, Peter Lang, Brussels
Malmström C (2011) The Way Forward for EU Home Affairs Cooperation with Eastern Partners. Chişinău
Obokata T (2006a) EU Action against Trafficking of Human Beings: Past, Present and Future. In: Guild E, Minderhoud P (eds) Immigration and Criminal Law in the European Union. Martinus Nijhoff, Leiden, pp 387–406
Obokata T (2006b) Trafficking of Human Beings from a Human Rights Perspective: Towards a Holistic Approach. Martinus Nijhoff, Leiden
Reliefweb (2019) Human Rights and Democracy in the World: Report on EU Action July 2008 to December 2009 https://reliefweb.int/report/world/human-rights-and-democracy-world-report-eu-action-july-2008-december-2009 Accessed 5 July 2020
Scarpa S (2008) Trafficking in Human Beings: Modern Slavery. Oxford University Press, Oxford
Schumacher T, Marchetti A, Demmelhuber T (eds) (2018) The Routledge Handbook on the European Neihbourhood Policy. Routledge Oxon
Smith KE (2005) The Outsiders: The European Neighbourhood Policy. International Affairs 81:757–773
Stoyanova V (2017) Human Trafficking and Slavery Reconsidered: Conceptual Limits and State's Positive Obligations in European Law. Cambridge University Press, Cambridge
UNGA (2000) Protocol to Prevent, Suppress and Punish Trafficking in Persons Especially Women and Children, supplementing the United Nations Convention against Transnational Organized Crime, A/RES/55/25
UNGA (2005) Protocol to Prevent, Suppress and Punish Trafficking in Persons Especially Women and Children, supplementing the United Nations Convention against Transnational Organized Crime, A/RES/55/25

US Department of State (2018) Trafficking in Persons 2018 Report: Country Narratives. https://www.state.gov/wp-content/uploads/2019/01/282798.pdf Accessed 7 February 2020
US Department of State (2019) Trafficking in Persons Report https://www.state.gov/wp-content/uploads/2019/06/2019-Trafficking-in-Persons-Report.pdf Accessed 7 February 2020
Van Elsuwege P, Petrov R (2011) Article 8 TEU: Towards a New Generation of Agreements with the Neighbouring Countries of the European Union? ELR 36:688–703
Van Vooren B (2011) EU External Relations Law and the European Neighbourhood Policy: A Paradigm for Coherence. Routledge, London
Villacampa Estiarte C (2012) The European Directive on Preventing and Combating Trafficking in Human Beings and the Victim-Centric Treatment of This Criminal Phenomenon. ECLR 2:291–317
Zaiotti R (2007) Of Friends and Fences: Europe's Neighbourhood Policy and the 'Gated Community Syndrome'. European Integration 29:143–162

Dr N. Ghazaryan is Associate Professor in Law at the School of Law of the University of Nottingham, Nottingham, UK.

Chapter 16
EU Cooperation with Third Countries on Migration and Asylum: The Case of Libya Revisited

A. dos Santos Soares and S. Beck-Mannagetta

Contents

Abstract The so-called "migration crisis" that Europe has been facing since 2015 has led the European Union (UE) to reconsider its partnership with countries of origin and transit, especially Libya, as crucial in the fight against migration. In the meantime, extremely worrying accounts of horrors and serious human rights violations (including slave auctions) perpetrated against migrants and asylum-seekers detained in Libya by members of the Libyan security forces, armed groups and criminal gangs emerge from that country. From this observation and using an effort of analysis and critical reflection based on review of the relevant literature, this chapter attempts to answer the following two key questions: (i) To what extent can it be assumed that the EU indirectly exposes migrants and asylum seekers to unimaginable horrors by directly funding their detention system in Libya? (ii) Is EU cooperation with Libya undertaken in accordance with the values and principles enshrined in Articles 2 and 21 of the Treaty on European Union (TEU), on which the EU is founded? In this

A. dos Santos Soares (✉)
Universidad Pontificia Comillas, Madrid, Spain
e-mail: adossantos@comillas.edu

S. Beck-Mannagetta
Munich, Germany
e-mail: sophia_beck-mannagetta@yahoo.de

W. Th. Douma et al. (eds.), *The Evolving Nature of EU External Relations Law*,
https://doi.org/10.1007/978-94-6265-423-5_16

sense, the axial goal of this chapter is to analyse the adequacy or lack of adequacy to international and European law of ongoing EU cooperation with Libya in the area of migration and asylum. It therefore concludes by arguing that, to become a true "civil power" and contribute to good global governance of human mobility, the EU must align its migration control policies with its founding principles and values under European and international law.

Keywords human mobility · human rights · third countries · partnership · externalization · migration policies · compliance · international responsibility · trafficked and smuggled migrants · development aid · conditionality

16.1 Introduction

Over the past five years, the "migration crisis" that broke out in Europe in 2015, became the most important key force shaping the European Union (hereinafter EU or Union) policy agenda, and its mismanagement made it a powerful test to the EU project, undermining some of its fundamental pillars, especially the Schengen Agreement on free movement.[1]

In order to cope with it, the EU adopted in May 2015 its *European Migration Agenda*, which sets the EU's migration policy, comprising six key aspects. Under the first one (Collaborate with countries of origin and transit), a number of migration dialogues have been launched and held and frameworks for cooperation with relevant third countries have been established. In 2015, European leaders agreed on the *Valletta Action Plan* to respond to the influx of migrants into the EU, mainly from African countries. In 2016, the European Council approved the establishment of a new *Migration Partnership Framework* to deepen cooperation with priority countries of origin. In the same year, the *EU-Turkey Declaration* was adopted to address the flow of asylum seekers and migrants through Turkey to the EU.

Determined to close the Central Mediterranean route and halt the flow of African migrants, EU leaders agreed to increase cooperation with Libya. Thanks to this cooperation migrant arrivals on the Central Mediterranean route have fallen by almost 70% in the third quarter of 2017 compared to the same period in 2016,[2] and by 87% by end of 2018.[3]

Meanwhile, extremely worrying accounts of horrors and serious human rights violations (including slave auctions) perpetrated against migrants and asylum-seekers

---

[1]Convention implementing the Schengen Agreement of 14 June 1985 between the Governments of the States of the Benelux Economic Union, the Federal Republic of Germany and the French Republic on the gradual abolition of checks at their common borders, opened for signature 14 June 1985, OJ L239 (entered into force 26 March 1995), pp. 19–62.

[2]European Council (2017) News on migration, digital Europe, security and defence. https://www.consilium.europa.eu/es/meetings/european-council/2017/10/19-20/. Accessed 1 December 2019.

[3]Frontex 2019, p. 16.

detained in Libya by members of the Libyan security forces, armed groups and criminal gangs emerge from that country.

With all that in mind and using an effort of analysis and reflection supported by a review of the relevant literature, this chapter assesses the effectiveness, security and humanitarian character of EU cooperation ('compacts') on migration and asylum with third countries, in particular, Libya, from a human rights and refugee law perspective.

Structured into five sections, this chapter starts by examining the real dimension of the so-called "migratory crisis" (Sect. 16.2). It then reviews the EU's response to this "crisis" (Sect. 16.3), paying particular attention to the legal, political and operational tools used in cooperation with third countries on migration and asylum issues, which are deeply marked by conditionality (Sect. 16.4). Finally, it analyses the extent to which interest in the fight against irregular migration prevails in the EU's "pact" with Libya over the defence and promotion of dignity and human rights (Sect. 16.5). All of this is followed by a few brief conclusions in the form of a critical appraisal.

16.2 The "Unprecedented Migratory Crisis", Its Real Dimension and Political Relevance

In 2015, over one million third-country citizens arrived in the EU.[4] The vast majority of them (more than 80%) were applicants for international protection[5] who, fleeing from barbarism in Syria (50%), Afghanistan (21%), Iraq (9%), Eritrea (4%) or Pakistan (3%) among other places,[6] reached the European territory using several migratory routes,[7] among which those of the eastern and central Mediterranean

[4]European Parliament (2017) EU migrant crisis: facts and figures. https://www.europarl.europa.eu/news/en/headlines/society/20170629STO78630/asylum-and-migration-in-the-eu-facts-and-figures. Accessed 21 October 2018; European Commission (2017) The EU and the migration crisis. https://op.europa.eu/webpub/com/factsheets/migration-crisis/en/. Accessed 21 October 2018.

[5]Kingsley P (2015) 10 truths about Europe's migrant crisis. https://www.theguardian.com/uk-news/2015/aug/10/10-truths-about-europes-refugee-crisis. Accessed 2 December 2019; in his own words, Gil Arias, Deputy Director of the European Agency for the Management of Operational Cooperation at the External Borders (Frontex), said: "We call them immigrants for the sake of simplicity, but perhaps the term refugees should be used. The situation today is that more than 80% of immigrants arriving in Europe are potential beneficiaries of international protection. See Sanmartín O R (2015) Frontex: 'El 80% de los inmigrantes que llegan a Europa son potenciales refugiados' [80% of immigrants arriving in Europe are potential refugees]. https://www.elmundo.es/internacional/2015/04/30/554221e5e2704e9f668b4571.html. Accessed 2 December 2019.

[6]UNHCR 2015.

[7]According to the European Border and Coast Guard Agency, the Frontex successor, in 2015 international airports were one of the major entry routes for immigrants into the EU, since most of those residing irregularly in the EU had initially come into possession of valid travel documents and an expired visa. By land and sea, the main migratory routes to the EU were: West Africa; the Western Mediterranean; the Central Mediterranean; Apulia and Calabria; Albania to Greece; the

stand also out for their extreme dangerousness. In fact, a total of 3,782 people were reported dead or missing during that same year, in an attempt to reach European shores using those routes. In 2016 that figure rose to 5,143 and reached 3,139 in 2017.[8] The Mediterranean Sea has arguably become a mass grave for thousands of people fleeing conflict and persecution, including hunger and misery.

Eurostat[9] reveals that 1,255,600 first time asylum seekers applied for international protection in the EU member states, in 2015, a number more than double that of the previous year. The highest number of them were registered in Germany (with 441,800 or 35% of all first time applicants in the EU Member States), followed by Hungary (174,400, or 14%), Sweden (156,100, or 12%), Austria (85,500, or 7%), Italy (83,200, or 7%) and France (70,600, or 6%). Compared with the previous year, the number of first time asylum applicants in 2015 increased the most in Finland (+822%), ahead of Hungary (+323%), Austria (+233%), Belgium (+178%), Spain (+167%) and Germany (+155%). Compared with the population of each member state, the highest number of registered first time applicants in 2015 was recorded in Hungary (17,699 first time applicants per million inhabitants), ahead of Sweden (16,016), Austria (9,970), Finland (5,876) and Germany (5,441). In contrast, the lowest numbers were observed in Croatia (34 applicants per million inhabitants), Slovakia (50), Romania (62), Portugal (80) and Lithuania (93).

All the foregoing gave rise to the so-called "unprecedented migratory crisis", which has pushed migration to the very top of the EU's political agenda over the last three years. This is in spite of the numerical insignificance of the aforementioned migrants' arrivals, representing just 0.3% of the total population of the Union (508 million) and 0.027% of the total population of Europe (740 million).

Such numerical insignificance is even more evident from a comparative perspective with the neighbouring countries of those in conflict, particularly Turkey, Pakistan, Lebanon, Iran, Ethiopia, Jordan, Kenia, Uganda, D.R. Congo and Chad. Some of them were facing (or are still facing) a breakdown of their social infrastructure due to the high number of refugees hosted.

Lebanon is the most obvious example housing 1.2 million Syrian refugees within a total population of roughly 4.5 million (refugees representing 17% of the country's total population). This country that is more than 100 times smaller than the EU has already taken in more than 50 times as many refugees as the EU will even consider resettling in the future. Jordan is another obvious example of a country in "refugee crisis", having hosted over 635,000 Syrian refugees, in 2015, representing 8% of its total population.

It should be noted that by the end of 2015, forced displacement induced by armed conflict and socio-political crisis reached 65.3 million people. The overwhelming

---

Western Balkans; and the Eastern Mediterranean, in addition to the Eastern border route. See in this regard https://frontex.europa.eu/along-eu-borders/migratory-map/ (link no longer active).

[8]See International Organization for Migration (IOM) 2017 Missing Migrants: tracking deaths along migratory routes. https://missingmigrants.iom.int/. Accessed 5 December 2019. An updated review to 2018 of the main migratory routes towards the EU can be found, *inter alia*, in Atanassov and Radjenovic 2018, pp. 20–22.

[9]Eurostat 2016.

majority of them, 40.8 million, were internally displaced, refugees numbered 21.3 million, and 3.2 million were asylum-seekers. European countries (including the EU member states) hosted only 6% of that forcibly displaced people global figure.[10] This is despite the fact that the flows of forcibly displaced persons have been seriously aggravated by actions undertaken by the United States of America and some EU member states to provoke regime change in the North African and Middle Eastern countries.

As indicated above, the arrivals of migrants and applicants for international protection in the EU have been reduced by a high percentage since the end of 2015. In the meantime, the majority of the world's refugees (85% of the world's 25.4 million refugees in 2017) continue to be hosted by countries in developing regions. In fact, according to the evidence compiled by UNHCR,[11] at the end of 2017, with 3.5 million refugees Turkey remained the country that hosted the largest number of refugees worldwide. It was followed by Pakistan and Uganda, both with 1.4 million. With a figure just under 1 million (998,900), Lebanon was the fourth largest country of asylum in the world. With 979,400 refugees, the Islamic Republic of Iran ranked fifth among the world's major refugee host countries. The sixth refugee host country was Germany, with 970,400 refugees. Bangladesh was the seventh country, hosting 932,200 refugees. With 906,600 refugees, Sudan was the eighth host country. The ninth and tenth places were occupied by Ethiopia and Jordan, hosting 889,400 and 691,000 refugees, respectively.

Furthermore, the measurement of the dimension of the "migration crisis" in the EU cannot overlook the fact that, in addition to the already appalling number of people displaced by wars, forced displacements also occur both in the context of climate change and in that of large-scale development projects.

In that sense, it should be noted that, confirming the bleak predictions of the Intergovernmental Panel on Climate Change (IPCC) in assessment reports published since 1990, climate change threatens to become the most powerful force inducing forced displacement, given its enormous capacity to operate as a factor exacerbating wars and other aspects of socio-economic vulnerability. In fact, the Internal Displacement Monitoring Centre (IDMC), which has embarked on the enormous task of statistically quantifying environmental displacements, estimates that, since 2008, environmental disasters, many of which are linked to climate change, have displaced an average of 26.4 million people per year,[12] which is three times more than the number of victims resulting from armed conflict.[13]

In close synergy with the wars and environmental disasters taking place in the context of climate change, are the so-called large-scale development projects, which currently constitute the third main driver of forced displacement worldwide, with an annual average of 15 million victims.[14] This is an inherent reality of the unstoppable

[10] UNHCR 2015, above n. 6.

[11] UNHCR 2018, pp. 15–18.

[12] IDMC 2015, p. 11.

[13] IDMC 2017, p. 4.

[14] Terminski 2013, p. 13.

and exponential increase in inequalities at all levels, local, national and global.[15] In this context, involuntary mobility is nothing more than the high price that millions of people are forced to pay for a perverse and deeply iniquitous development model, which cancels out rights, concentrates economic resources in the hands of a few, exacerbates the extreme poverty of the vast majority and, moreover, operates as a sophisticated weapon of socio-economic exclusion and "ethnic cleansing in disguise".[16]

To be coherent in both its objective and subjective dimensions, the measurement of the real scale and political relevance of the "migratory crisis" in the EU must also take into account the dimension of contemporary human mobility. In this sense, it is estimated that of the approximately one billion migrants worldwide, the total number of international migrants is 272 million people, equivalent to 3.5% of today's world population of over 7.6 billion. The vast majority of migrants (740 million) move within their respective countries or, at most, within their regional scope, thus establishing networks between the developing areas themselves and strengthening so-called South-South mobility, which tends to be as or more numerous than South-North mobility.[17]

All of the above suggests a certain political exploitation of the "refugee emergency" that erupted in 2015, turning it, in narrative terms, into an "unprecedented migration crisis" and, as such, overestimated and placed at the forefront of the EU's political agenda. With that said, the following section will briefly analyse the response of the EU and its member states to such fearsome "migration crisis". This involves critically reviewing specific measures different in nature taken by the EU to deal with the "crisis".

16.3 The EU's Response to the "Migration Crisis": A Brief Overview

The issue of migration reached an emergency level in the EU when, alongside the aforementioned unprecedented increase in the number of migrant arrivals, on 18 April 2015 an overloaded migrant ship from Libya sank in the Mediterranean Sea, leaving more than 700 dead and missing. On the following days, such alarming tragedy and dizzying increase in the number of deaths in the Mediterranean of migrants and people in need of international protection led the European Commission (the Commission) to present to the Council of the EU (the Council), in a joint special meeting of the Ministers of Foreign Affairs and Internal Administration, on 20 April 2015, an action plan with measures for immediate response to the "crisis". These

[15]For more on this thorny subject, see, among others, Alvaredo et al 2017.

[16]Rajagopal B (2001) The Violence of Development. https://www.washingtonpost.com/archive/opinions/2001/08/09/the-violence-of-development/1b169574-3992-44ec-bff9-a1e42857f192/. Accessed 21 November 2019.

[17]See International Organization for Migration—IOM 2019; Bakewell 2009, p. 18.

measures included a commitment to examine options for creating an "emergency relocation" mechanism.[18]

The European Council, in turn, meeting in extraordinary session on 23 April 2015,[19] after noting "the tragic situation in the Mediterranean", established as an "immediate priority" "to prevent more people from dying at sea". To this end, the joint Frontex surveillance and rescue operations at the Mediterranean external borders should be strengthened, reinforcing EU Operations Triton and Poseidon by at least tripling the financial resources for this purpose in 2015 and 2016; traffickers should be combated in accordance with international law; illegal migration flows should be prevented, and solidarity and responsibility at internal level should be strengthened. Moreover, the European Council urged the Commission to present a European Agenda for Migration, "in order to develop a more systemic and geographically comprehensive approach to migration".[20]

On 13 May 2015, the Commission presented the European Agenda on Migration[21] in the form of a communication to the European Parliament, the Council, the Economic and Social Committee and the Committee of the Regions. In it, the Commission made public its intention to activate the emergency intervention mechanism provided for in Article 78(3) TFEU[22] in order to better distribute asylum seekers within the Union. To this end, the Commission announced a compulsory relocation programme for Member States (intended for those persons in manifest need of international protection who were already within the EU) and, in parallel, an EU-wide resettlement scheme for 20,000 people should be undertaken. At the same time, according to the Agenda, all those who were in an irregular situation on European soil without being in need of international protection should return to their countries of origin. On the other hand, in order to assist "frontline Member States" at the external borders of the Union, the Commission launched the "Hotspot areas" concept, under which, coordinated by the Commission, European Asylum Support Office (EASO), Frontex and Europol should work on the ground in such "frontline Member States" in order to identify, record and fingerprint migrants as quickly as possible and to coordinate return.[23]

Explicitly stating its position on the common asylum policy, the Agenda notes as one of the weaknesses of this policy "the lack of mutual trust between Member States, in particular due to the persistent fragmentation of the asylum system". It then advocates strengthening the provisions on the concept of a safe country of origin, as

---

[18]European Commission 2015b.

[19]For further details, see European Council (2015) Special meeting of the European Council, 23 April 2015—statement. https://www.consilium.europa.eu/en/meetings/european-council/2015/04/23/. Accessed 9 December 2019.

[20]Ibid.

[21]European Commission 2015a.

[22]Which reads as follows: "In the event of one or more Member States being confronted by an emergency situation characterised by a sudden inflow of nationals of third countries, the Council, on a proposal from the Commission, may adopt provisional measures for the benefit of the Member State(s) concerned. It shall act after consulting the European Parliament."

[23]European Commission 2015a, above n. 21.

set out in the Procedures Directive, which is intended to support the rapid processing of asylum applications from asylum seekers from countries considered to be safe.

The Agenda also makes a strong commitment to cooperation with third countries as an indispensable aspect of its model for responding to the migration crisis. It refers to Turkey as a good example of where there is much to be gained from stepping up cooperation.

It should also be noted that on 3 September 2015, one day after the shocking image of the corpse of the Syrian child Alan Kurdi drowned in the sea and found on a beach in Bodrum (Turkey), in a joint initiative German Chancellor Angela Merkel and French President François Hollande addressed to the European Council, the Commission and the Presidency of the Council a letter containing an action plan urging the full and immediate implementation of the initiatives and decisions taken at EU level.[24] Thus, in line with what had previously been advanced by the European Agenda on Migration, the Franco-German axis recalled and put on the table the following six concrete measures: (i) the creation of "Hotspot areas" at certain points on the external borders of Italy and Greece to proceed, as soon as possible, to the identification, recording and collection of fingerprints of new arrivals and to eliminate their protection needs (ii) the need to observe and apply properly the Common European Asylum System (CEAS) with regard to procedures and standards for the reception of refugees; (iii) the equitable, solidarity-based and responsible sharing among the Member States of persons manifestly in need of international protection, with the Commission presenting a complementary proposal for a permanent and compulsory mechanism for the relocation of such persons; (iv) effectively expel irregular immigrants by promoting their readmission to third countries of origin and transit; (v) establish a common list of safe countries of origin, to ensure coherent action at EU level and a uniform basis for decisions by national asylum authorities; in this respect, EU candidate countries, in particular those of the Western Balkans should be considered as safe countries of origin; (vi) further expand efforts to dismantle criminal networks of trafficking in human beings.

All this is at the origin of what are considered to be the three main measures adopted at EU level in its "fair, robust and realistic" response to the migration crisis: the creation of "Hotspot areas", the adoption of interim measures in the field of international protection in favour of Italy and Greece, and the "EU-Turkey Declaration" of 18 March 2016.[25] While the first two have an essentially internal dimension, the third is clearly external to the Union. However, as Nuno Piçarra puts it,[26] all of them are united by their largely circumstantial character and their proven diminutive effectiveness. In addition, they have all been accompanied by unilateral measures taken by the Member States of transit and destination of migrants. Such measures range

---

[24] Stroobants J and Revault d'Allonnes D (2015) La lettre commune de François Hollande et d'Angela Merkel pour accueillir les réfugiés en Europe. https://www.lemonde.fr/europe/article/2015/09/05/la-lettre-commune-de-francois-hollande-et-d-angela-merkel-pour-accueillir-les-refugies-en-europe_4745852_3214.html. Accessed 24 May 2020.

[25] For a critical review of these measures, see, among others, Piçarra 2016, pp. 30–38.

[26] Piçarra 2016, p. 30.

from the reintroduction of controls at internal borders to the construction of walls at external borders, through announcements of rejection or quantitative restrictions to the reception of applicants for international protection.

At present, it seems clear that more than an "unprecedented migration and refugee crisis", what is really at stake is a crisis of the EU itself and its migration and asylum policy, which has proven unable to adequately consider the plight of people in need for international protection, nor the concerns of the Member States most affected by migrant flows. In other words, it should be stated, in general terms, that the EU's policy responses to the "migration crisis", both internally and externally through cooperation with third countries, "have by and large lacked a *multi-policy sector* approach". Instead, priority has been given to security concerns and military interests; attention to border controls, return of migrants and the fight against smuggling has generally prevailed over the guarantee and full compliance with fundamental human rights standards and principles, this being one of the Achilles' heels of the current European Migration Agenda, according to some analysts.[27]

It should be highlighted though that while, on the one hand, the EU Member States continue to be very divided over the common internal migration and asylum policy, a division clearly evidenced by the persistent disagreements over the reform of the CEAS as the legal expression of that policy, on the other hand they appear united around the goal of strengthening the EU's external migration policy through cooperation with third countries of origin and transit of migrants.

16.4 Cooperation with Third Countries on Migration and Asylum: Toolbox and Conditionality

The inclusion of migration in the EU's external action is not recent. In fact, it has been a key component of such action since the early 1990s, when the EU started the construction of a complex architecture of migration external governance. The so-called "migration crisis" revealed its weaknesses neglected from the outset. And it led the EU to refocus this policy area towards "tailor-made", "global" and "mutually beneficial" migration partnerships. The idea was, according to Federica Mogherini, former High Representative of the European Union for Foreign Affairs and Security Policy/Vice-President of the European Commission,[28] to move from an old approach to a mutually beneficial partnership, a two-way partnership in which each party has its own responsibilities, and both seek the best possible way to manage the complex migration phenomenon together.

---

[27] Carrera et al. 2015, p. 2.

[28] Delegation of the European Union to Mali (2016) Remarks by the HRVP Federica Mogherini at the press conference on the progress under the Migration Partnership Framework. https://eeas.europa.eu/delegations/mali/12352/remarks-by-the-hrvp-federica-mogherini-at-the-press-conference-on-the-progress-under-the-migration-partnership-framework_it. Accessed 3 November 2019.

However, an analysis of this announced shift from the "old approach" to the "new one" reveals that these weaknesses were not overcome. On the contrary, to a large extent they were aggravated by being adapted to a crisis response model, characterized by "an immense prioritisation of migration, an increase and flexibilization of funding, and a renewed focus on transactional bilateral migration "deals"", which lays strong emphasis on "conditionality" and almost completely exclude the interests and human rights of migrants.[29]

16.4.1 Legal, Political and Operational Instruments

It follows from the above that as of today the overarching objectives of the EU's external migration policy, practically, remain unchanged since they started being formulated, in 2005, and, in 2011, were grouped in four pillars under the Global Approach to Migration and Mobility (GAMM),[30] "designed to address all relevant aspects of migration in a balanced and comprehensive way, in partnership with non-EU countries".[31] Such pillars are as follows: (i) fostering legal migration and well-managed mobility; (ii) preventing irregular migration and eradicating human trafficking; (iii) maximising the positive impact of migration on development; and (iv) promoting international protection.

Formulated like this, on paper the goals of the EU's external migration policy seem to pursue comprehensiveness and balance between the interests of the EU, those of third countries and those of the migrants themselves. In practice, however, the accentuated primary focus on the fight against irregular migration has always prevailed over other aspects of this policy and has systematically unbalanced cooperation relations with third countries, whose specific interests and perspectives have not received enough attention. That's not to mention the practical exclusion from such cooperation of the interests and rights of migrants themselves, especially those in need of international protection.

All that seems to have become even more sharpened in the wake of the European Migration Agenda and, most notably, the Migration Partnership Framework,[32] which, in a sort of *aggiornamento* of the EU's external migration policy, rewrites and establishes its short and long-term objectives as follows: (i) save lives in the Mediterranean sea; (ii) increase the rate of returns to countries of origin and transit; (iii) enable migrants and refugees to stay close to home and to avoid taking dangerous journeys; (iv) address the root causes of irregular migration and forced displacement; and (v) foster sustainable development.

In order to implement these objectives, the EU has been progressively adopting and using a number of legal, political and operational instruments. Visa facilitation

[29] Koenig 2017, pp. 4–6.

[30] European Commission 2011.

[31] Ibid., p. 3.

[32] European Commission 2016.

and readmission agreements as well as migration clauses in global agreements are the main legal instruments. Among the political ones are the regional and bilateral dialogues, action plans, the common agendas for migration and mobility (CAMMs) as well as the mobility partnerships. In turn, operational instruments consist mainly of regional protection programmes (RPPs) and regional development and protection programmes (RDPPs), Frontex working arrangements, and EASO cooperation with third countries.[33]

16.4.2 Conditionality

After all, the Migration Partnership Framework (MPF) is nothing other than the consolidation of the tailor-made migratory compacts model, marked by a strong emphasis on conditionality and assumed as the key component of the overall relationships between the EU and third countries of origin or transit.[34] In this regard, comprehensive incentive packages are being developed and proposed to the relevant third countries of origin and transit in order to ensure effective return and readmission of migrants. In other words, the EU embraces cooperation on readmission and return as a key test of the partnership on migration and asylum. Based on this premise, third partner countries may receive positive incentives (“more for more”) or sanctions (“less for less”) depending on the degree of their willingness and effective commitment to this European assignment. As an example, the Austrian Chancellor Kurz threatened to cancel development aid for countries which do not cooperate with deportations of their citizens, e.g. by issuing their documents.[35]

The foregoing arguably points to a sort of instrumentalization of development aid and the externalisation of migration and asylum management by the EU in its fight against irregular and unwanted migration. In this sense, two of the earlier mentioned instruments are particularly relevant both for their increasingly widespread use and their controversial nature. They are, on the one hand, the Trust Funds and, on the other, the tailor-made migration compacts.

As noted above, one of the features of the EU’s response to the “migration crisis” is an increase and flexibilization of collective funding. In this sense, the centrality of migration among the EU’s external priorities is reflected in three new instruments created by the Union since 2015 and used to “flexibly pool funds from the member states as well as various EU budget envelopes including humanitarian and development aid, the European Neighbourhood Policy Instrument and the Instrument for Pre-Accession”: (i) the Facility for Refugees in Turkey (2016–17), made up of

[33]For a detailed analysis of such instruments, see García Andrade and Martín 2015, pp. 22–50.

[34]European Commission 2016, above n. 32, p. 6.

[35]Süddeutsche Zeitung (2016) Wien droht Herkunftsländern von Flüchtlingen mit Sanktionen [Vienna threatens refugees’ countries of origin with sanctions]. https://www.sueddeutsche.de/politik/abschiebungen-wien-droht-herkunftslaendern-von-fluechtlingen-mit-sanktionen-1.3313876. Accessed 1 December 2019.

€1 billion from the EU budget + €2 billion from the member states; (ii) the EU Regional Trust Fund in Response to the Syrian Crisis (2015–19), with an amount of €500 million from the EU budget + €500 million from the member states or other donors; and (iii) the EU Emergency Trust Fund for stability and addressing the root causes of irregular migration and displaced persons in Africa (2015–20), which is comprised by €1.8 billion from the EU budget + €1.8 billion from the member states.[36]

As of today, the EU Emergency Trust Fund for Africa (EUTF) stands out as the main instrument for EU's political engagement with African partners in the field of migration and asylum. Launched in November 2015 at the Valetta Summit and presented as an innovative and flexible mechanism and as a key instrument to implement the Valetta Action Plan,[37] this fund makes predominant use (90%) of Official Development Assistance (ODA), mostly from the European Development Fund (EDF), which demonstrates a clear and striking instrumentalization of aid, rather than respect for the development effectiveness key principles that should guide the implementation of international development cooperation programmes.[38] Not surprisingly, many critical voices consider that in order to stop migration movements, even before the EU's external borders, the implementation of the EUTF is largely neglecting both the local contexts and regional dynamics of the partner countries as well as the migrant's rights.[39]

Closely associated with the EUTF instrumentalization of development aid in favour of the fight against irregular migration are the "tailor-made agreements" (migration compacts), a partnership framework introducing positive and negative conditionalities regarding cooperation with third countries in the field of migration and strengthening the externalisation of EU migration and asylum policies. It is by no means a recent instrument. However, in the aftermath of the November 2015 Valletta Summit, its use has been increased and even institutionalised, encouraged by the European Council in order to ensure effective returns and readmission.

[36]Koenig 2017, p. 5.

[37]European Council, Valletta summit on migration, 11–12 November 2015—action plan and political declaration. http://www.consilium.europa.eu/en/press/pressreleases/2015/11/12-valletta-final-docs/. Accessed 23 December 2019. Adopted by leaders from the EU and Africa, the Valletta action plan sets out five priority domains of cooperation: (1) addressing the root causes of irregular migration and developing the benefits of migration; (2) promoting regular migration and mobility; (3) reinforcing protection and asylum policies; (4) fighting against human trafficking and migrant smuggling; and (5) strengthening cooperation to facilitate return and reintegration of irregular migrants.

[38]CINI and CONCORD 2018, p. 6.

[39]Koch et al. 2018.

It is well known that in early 2016, the EU offered Jordan[40] and Lebanon[41] bilateral migration compacts, which were adopted as an annex to the corresponding Association Council Decisions. However, it can be indicated that the beginning of the current "migration compacts" approach was marked by the New Partnership Approach, adopted by the EU on 6 June 2016, based on similar incentives compared to the EU-Turkey Statement of 18 March 2016.[42] According to such a New Partnership Approach,[43] a mix of negative and positive incentives should be integrated notably into the EU's development and trade policies to reward those countries willing to cooperate effectively with the EU on migration management and ensure there are consequences for those who do not cooperate. As noted above, the European Council considers the cooperation on readmissions and returns as the key test of the Partnership.[44]

From the very beginning Mali, Nigeria, Niger, Senegal and Ethiopia were identified as priority partners. However, the reach of this new approach was soon extended to a broad range of countries including Libya. The growing relevance of this country as an EU priority partner in terms of migration compacts is more than evident. So much so that in January and February 2017, the Joint Communication on the Central Mediterranean Route[45] and the Malta Declaration[46] called for additional operational measures focusing on the development of border management capacity in the countries concerned, in particular Libya.

---

[40] EU-Jordan Association Council (2016) Council Decision No 1/2016 of 19 December 2016 agreeing on EU-Jordan Partnership Priorities [2016/2388]. https://eur-lex.europa.eu/legal-content/EN/TXT/PDF/?uri=CELEX:22016D2388&from=EN. Accessed 24 May 2020.

[41] EU-Lebanon Association Council (2016) Council Decision No 1/2016 of 11 November 2016 agreeing on EU-Lebanon Partnership Priorities [2016/2368]. https://eur-lex.europa.eu/legal-content/EN/TXT/PDF/?uri=CELEX:22016D2368&from=SV. Accessed 24 May 2020.

[42] European Council (2016) EU-Turkey statement, 18 March 2016. https://www.consilium.europa.eu/en/press/press-releases/2016/03/18/eu-turkey-statement/. Accessed 22 November 2019. Controversial and heavily criticized by human rights organisations, the deal was simultaneously hailed as a success by the European Commission and several EU member states. It meant that, with the aim of lowering the death tolls in the Mediterranean Sea, Turkey would strengthen its border patrols and coast guards, ensuring that asylum seekers and migrants would not be able to leave Turkey for Europe. In return Turkey would receive €6 billion in aid from the EU.

[43] European Council (2016) Conclusions. https://www.consilium.europa.eu/media/21645/28-euco-conclusions.pdf. Accessed 26 December 2019. http://www.consilium.europa.eu/en/press/press-releases/2016/06/28-euco-conclusions/. Accessed 24 May 2020.

[44] Ibid.

[45] European Commission 2017a.

[46] European Council and Council of the EU (2017) Malta Declaration by the members of the European Council on the external aspects of migration: addressing the Central Mediterranean route. https://www.consilium.europa.eu/en/press/press-releases/2017/02/03/malta-declaration/. Accessed 14 December 2019.

16.5 Migration Compact with Libya: Human Rights and EU Values at Stake?

16.5.1 EU's Obligations on Migration and Development Cooperation: Legal References at a Glance

As recognised by the European Council itself,[47] thanks to the tight collaboration of the EU and its Member States, in particular Italy, with Libya and its Coast Guard by providing them training, equipment and funding, migrants arrivals on the Central Mediterranean route have fallen by almost 70% in the third quarter of 2017 compared to the same period in 2016. Meanwhile, extremely worrying accounts of horrors and serious human rights violations (including slave auctions)[48] perpetrated against migrants and asylum-seekers detained in Libya by members of the Libyan security forces, armed groups and criminal gangs emerge from that country. Stemming from this harsh observation, it makes sense to ask to what extent can it be assumed that the EU unintentionally contributes to expose migrants and asylum seekers to unimaginable horrors by directly financing the detention system in Libya? Can this situation lead to international responsibility of the EU or/and its Member States? To what degree is the EU's cooperation with Libya in the field of migration conducted in accordance with the law and the founding values of the EU itself?

Characterised, from the outset, by the humanitarian community as a "humanitarian emergency", the "migration crisis" that erupted in 2015 should be addressed on the basis of respect for the values on which the Union is founded: human dignity, freedom, democracy, equality, the rule of law and human rights, including the rights of persons belonging to minorities, as well as social pluralism, non-discrimination, tolerance, justice, solidarity and equality between women and men. These are, in short, universal and indivisible values and the common principles on which the EU is founded, solemnly proclaimed in Article 2 TEU[49] and in the Preamble to the Charter of Fundamental Rights of the EU (hereinafter "the Charter").[50]

In addition, Article 18 of the Charter guarantees the right to asylum in compliance with the 1951 Convention relating to the Status of Refugees[51] and its 1967 Protocol.[52] Moreover, Article 19 of the Charter states categorically that "collective expulsions

---

[47]European Council and Council of the EU (2017) European Council, 19–20 October 2017. http://www.consilium.europa.eu/es/meetings/european-council/2017/10/19-20/. Accessed 14 December 2019.

[48]CNN (2017) United Nations (UN) chief: Libya slave auctions may be crimes against humanity. http://edition.cnn.com/2017/11/20/africa/un-secretary-general-libya-slave-auctions/index.html. Accessed 17 December 2019.

[49]Consolidated Version of the Treaty on the European Union, 2012, OJ C326.

[50]Charter of Fundamental Rights of the EU, 2002, OJ C364/1.

[51]Convention Relating to the Status of Refugees, opened for signature 28 July 1951, UNTS 189:37 (entered into force 22 April 1954).

[52]Protocol to the Convention Relating to the Status of Refugees, opened for signature 31 January 1967, UNTS 606:267 (entered into force 4 October 1967).

are prohibited" and that "no one shall be transferred, expelled or extradited to a State where there is a grave risk of being subjected to the death penalty, torture or other inhuman or degrading treatment or punishment".

In accordance with Article 21 of the TEU, the EU shall base its external relations, including those related to migration, on the principles of democracy, human rights and solidarity. In turn, Article 80 of the Treaty on the Functioning of the European Union (TFEU)[53] establishes the basic principle of solidarity and fair sharing of responsibilities, which should govern the implementation of EU policies on asylum, border controls and immigration. The same principle is expressed in Article 4(3) TEU in terms of "sincere cooperation". According to Phillippe De Bruycker and Evangelia Tsourdi, this "sincere cooperation" is referring to loyalty and solidarity and includes "a positive obligation (taking measures to ensure fulfilment of obligations), and a negative obligation (abstaining from measures that could jeopardize this fulfilment)".[54] At the same time, Article 78 TFEU is particularly relevant for the understanding of EU policies and rules on asylum, border controls and immigration, in the framework of the still emerging Common European Asylum System (CEAS).[55] It serves as the legal basis of the "Dublin System",[56] which determines which European Member State is responsible for the examination of an Asylum application in the EU. The Dublin System has been heavily criticised for the asymmetric burdens it puts on certain Member States due to their geographical location and questions the credible implementation of the principles of "fair sharing of responsibilities", "solidarity" and "sincere cooperation". Even though not all of these principles are defined in detail, it is noteworthy that the precise wording of "fair sharing of responsibilities" does not require Member States to first fulfil their responsibilities according the Dublin Regulations in order to "deserve" solidarity and support, but actually emphasizes the solidarity through the description of the "fair sharing" of responsibilities.[57]

Finally, Article 208(1) TFEU on development cooperation assists with the systematic interpretation of "sincere cooperation" by stating that the "Union development cooperation policy shall have as its primary objective the reduction and, in the long term, the eradication of poverty. The Union shall take account of the objectives of development cooperation in the policies that it implements which are likely to affect developing countries".

So far, the orientations and premises are flawless. But what about their fulfilment on the ground, particularly in the case of Libya?

---

[53]Consolidated Version of the Treaty on the Functioning of the European Union, 2012, OJ C 326 (TFEU).

[54]De Bruycker and Tsourdi 2016.

[55]For a more in-depth description and analysis of the legislative acts that make up the Common European Asylum System to date, see Piçarra 2016, above n. 25.

[56]Regulation (EU) No 604/2013 of 26 June 2013 establishing the criteria and mechanisms for determining the Member State responsible for examining an application for international protection lodged in one of the Member States by a third-country national or a stateless person (Dublin Regulation III), OJ L 180/31, 29 June 2013.

[57]De Bruycker and Tsourdi 2016.

16.5.2 *Is the Fight Against Irregular Migration Prevailing Over Human Rights?*

In 2011, in the heat of the so-called "Arab Spring", perceiving as imminent the possibility of a massacre in Benghazi at the hands of the troops of the Gaddafi regime, the United Nations (UN), through Resolution 1973 of its Security Council,[58] authorized an international military intervention in Libya with the aim of protecting the civilian population. With a military operation led by North Atlantic Treaty Organization (NATO), whose mandate did not contemplate the objective of overthrowing the regime, that intervention in Libya was the first experience of implementing the principle of the Responsibility to Protect in its aspect of foreign military intervention. But it also meant the collapse of the Libyan state and the rise of a number of different political and military forces fighting for power. Indeed, the country has since then been confronted with overlapping crises of security and governance. This includes rival governments and armed militias competing for territorial control and power, as well as terrorists, smugglers and traffickers who use the ensuing vacuum to establish themselves in the country.

Such a widespread instability in the country in a state of civil war since 2014 has facilitated the transit of irregular migrants, making Libya one of the largest sources and gateways of departures for migrants attempting to reach Europe through the Mediterranean. In fact, European Commission data[59] indicate that in 2016, Libya was the main gateway, accounting for approximately 90% of the departures of some 181,400 immigrants arriving in Europe via the Central Mediterranean route. This not counting the shocking figure of 5,143 people who, in the course of the same year, lost their lives in the attempt to do so.[60] As of August 2018, the country hosted an estimated population of 669,176 migrants. To this figure must be added 193,581 internally displaced persons (IDPs) and 382,222 returnees.[61]

All this led to Libya increasingly becoming a key partner of the EU in the field of migration. The adoption in January and February 2017 of the earlier mentioned Joint Communication on the Central Mediterranean Route and the Malta Declaration marked a particular deepening of the EU's collaboration with the UN-backed Libyan Government of National Accord (GNA) led by Fayez Al-Sarraj, a collaboration translated into many millions of euros for Libya under the EUTF framework.

It is well known that, along with Malta, Italy has been the first and most important destination for migrants leaving Libya. That said, it is striking to note with the Danish Refugee Council that

> The numbers of people who arrived in Italy by sea dropped from 181,400 in 2016 to 119,400 in 2017 and then to 18,500 in the first half of 2018. A key factor of this trend has been the increased 'efficiency' of the Libyan Coast Guard to apprehend people at sea. While the

---

[58] UNSC 2011.

[59] European Commission 2016, above n. 32.

[60] IOM 2016.

[61] IOM 2017.

> actual number of people apprehended at sea did not increase significantly – 14,332 in 2016, 15,3558 in 2017 and 13,898 as of October 2018 - the proportion of people apprehended by the Libyan Coast Guard relative to the total number of people who attempted to cross the sea has skyrocketed from 7% in 2016 to 38% in 2018. Similarly, while the actual number of people who died while attempting to reach Europe by sea decreased from 5,143 in 2016 to 3,139 in 2017 and to 1,719 as of September 2018, the actual death rate along the Libya-Italy axis – the number of deaths relative to the number of people who attempted to cross the sea – rose from 1.9% in 2015 to 2.1% in 2017 and 3.2% so far in 2018.[62]

Meanwhile, there is an incessant dribble of news reporting on the horrific conditions of detention of migrants and asylum-seekers in Libya, exposed to trafficking, abductions, torture, rape and other sexual violence, forced labour, migrants, slavery, exploitation, severe physical violence, hunger and other atrocities. As Nicole Koenig sums up, "UN-backed Libyan government is hardly able to establish full territorial control over its own capital. Furthermore, there is ample evidence that the Libyan authorities violate migrants' human rights. There have been reports of the Libyan coastguard shooting at migrants. If migrants are intercepted in Libya's territorial waters they are unlawfully detained".[63] She adds that a report leaked by German diplomats went so far as to equate conditions in Libyan detention centres with those in "concentration camps". IOM and UNHCR have very limited access to these centres, where, according to witnesses, daily executions take place "to accommodate new arrivals". Therefore, "the EU's focus on the prevention of deaths in the Mediterranean is thus likely to shift these deaths to places where they are not seen", Koenig argues.

The situation of migrants' human rights violations in Libya is so serious that in November 2017 the United Nations High Commissioner for Human Rights, Zeid Ra'ad Al Hussein, stated that "the suffering of migrants in Libya outrage to conscience of humanity".[64] So it is not surprising that one of the twelve migrants rescued in the Mediterranean end November 2018 by the Spanish-flagged fishing boat *Nuestra Madre de Loreto* categorically stated while Spain was negotiating their return to Libya: "I am not afraid of dying, I am afraid of Libya".[65]

In this regard, it is necessary to mention the ongoing investigations of the ICC examining the responsibility of the EU, its member states officials and agents for acts and omissions of crimes against humanity due to the cooperation with Libya. To be

---

[62] Danish Refugee Council (DRC) 2018, p. 3.

[63] Koenig 2017, p. 16.

[64] UN (2017) "Suffering of migrants in Libya outrage to conscience of humanity" says the UN human rights chief. https://www.ohchr.org/EN/NewsEvents/Pages/DisplayNews.aspx?NewsID=22393. Accessed 24 May 2020.

[65] Martín M, Burgos R and D'Agostino L (2018) Spain ignores pleas to not send rescued migrants back to Libya. https://english.elpais.com/elpais/2018/11/28/inenglish/1543393941_790926.html. Accessed 28 November 2019. "I entered Libya when I was 12. The Libyans only want money; they put us in jail so we will pay them. They put me in prison for one year and I was not able to shower even once. When I was on the boat and I saw the Libyan Coast Guard coming near I jumped in the water, because I am not afraid of dying, I am afraid of Libya", said a young Sudanese man among the rescued migrants by the fishing boat *Nuestra Madre de Loreto*.

precise, the accusations concern criminal liability for EU policies which, allegedly, result in "(i) the deaths by drowning of thousands of migrants, (ii) the refoulement of tens of thousands of migrants attempting to flee Libya, and (iii) complicity in the subsequent crimes of deportation, murder, imprisonment, enslavement, torture, rape, persecution and other inhuman acts, taking place in Libyan detention camps and torture houses".[66]

Moreover, the European Court of Human Rights (ECtHR) found in Hirsi Jamaa and Others v. Italy that the collective expulsion of asylum seekers, who were intercepted near Malta by the Italian Revenue Police and Coastguard and then directly handed over the Libyan Authorities without identification or possibility to apply for asylum, constituted a violation of various human rights, including Article 3 of the Convention for the Protection of Human Rights and Fundamental Freedoms regarding the real risk of ill-treatment in the third country (Libya) due to reports of torture and ill-treatment and the real risk of arbitrary repatriation from there, Article 14 of the same Convention, the right to effective remedy, and Article 4 of Protocol No. 4 to the Convention for the Protection of Human Rights and Fundamental Freedoms, the prohibition of collective expulsions of aliens. Even though the judgment dates back to 2012,[67] the reports of torture, ill-treatment and even more severe human rights violations have not stopped but increased, therefore it can be highly doubted if the EU's collaboration with Libya is consistent with its own principles and the jurisprudence of the ECtHR.

In addition, the UN Committee on the Rights of the Child decided in the case of D.D. vs. Spain that the common practice in Ceuta and Melilla of directly returning migrants at the border "without access to any procedure to safeguard their fundamental rights",[68] including unaccompanied minors, constituted a violation of various core principles of the Convention of the Rights of the Child, namely Article 20, to provide special protection and assistance, Article 37, the exposure to the risk of violence, inhuman or degrading treatment due to the return to Morocco and Article 3, the duty to primarily take into consideration the best interests of the child.

All of the above makes the EU's cooperation with Libya a matter of extreme controversy. The humanitarian community as a whole continues to denounce it, accusing the EU of paying little attention to the country's real needs, supporting a fragile government with poor governance, endangering migrants' human rights, feeding into the detention and smuggling industry and encouraging forced return.[69]

These accusations, however, have not yet prevented the EU from continuing to regard its partnership with Libya on migration as strategic and a priority. To this end, it has adopted a series of political and operational measures and instruments of a

---

[66]European Council on Refugees and Exiles (ECRE) (2019) ICC Submission Seeks to Hold the EU Accountable for Creation of "World's Deadliest Migration Route". https://www.ecre.org/icc-submission-seeks-to-hold-the-eu-accountable-for-creation-of-worlds-deadliest-migration-route/. Accessed 17 November 2019.

[67]ECtHR, *Hirsi Jamaa and Others v. Italy,* Judgment (Grand Chamber), 23 February 2012, App. No. 27765/09.

[68]Wriedt 2019.

[69]CINI and CONCORD 2018, pp. 19–20.

diplomatic, economic and security nature, which the European Commission itself identifies and details in its Fifth Progress Report on the Partnership Framework with third countries under the European Agenda on Migration,[70] which came to light in September 2017.

EU-Libya partnership started with high-level political dialogue with the internationally recognized (interim) Government of National Accord (GNA) led by Ali Fayez Al-Sarraj, whose role as a key partner is manifest, for example, in his participation in the initiatives held by the Contact Group for the Mediterranean.

In association with the high-level political dialogue are the diplomatic efforts which the EU claims to be pursuing, underpinned by EU financial support from the Instrument contributing to Stability and Peace, aimed at stabilising Libya and facilitating conflict mediation between leaders in the Libya-Niger border region and in eastern Libya.

The EU Trust Fund for Africa represents the most important funding instrument for the overall projects aimed at increasing the capacity of Libyan authorities in migration management. This includes activities to strengthen the operational capacities of the Libyan Coast Guards and their control operations, to conduct technical assessments for a fully-fledged National Coordination Centre and a Maritime Rescue Coordination Centre in Tripoli, and to strengthen the operational capacity of the Libyan border guards along the southern borders. It also includes financial support to United Nations agencies—UNHCR and IOM—for the protection and return of migrants from Libya to their countries of origin.

Another of the relevant instruments comprised in the EU-Libya partnership is the SEAHORSE Mediterranean Project, "which aims at enhancing the situational awareness and reaction capacity of North African countries on the irregular migration flows and illicit trafficking in particular those taking place in their coastal regions and territorial waters, was pursued". In addition, EUNAVFOR Med Operation Sophia is aimed at anti-smuggling operations as well as the complementary training and capacity building of the Libyan Coast Guard. In turn, the EU Border Assistance Mission in Libya (EUBAM) is intended to work with the authorities on border management reform for Libya and with the United Nations Support Mission in Libya and the United Nations Development Programme on supporting the civilian aspects of the Libyan security plans, among other tasks.

Along with the complex socio-political and migratory context in Libya examined above, the handling of all these instruments of partnership between the EU and Libya in the field of migration highlights the EU's growing interest in security measures that prevail over the humanitarian and human rights focus.

[70]European Commission 2017b, pp. 10–14.

16.6 Conclusion

The axial objective of this chapter was to analyse the adequacy or lack of adequacy to international and European legislation of the current EU cooperation with Libya in the field of migration and asylum. Our purpose was to attempt to answer the following two key questions: To what extent can it be assumed that the EU indirectly exposes migrants and asylum seekers to unimaginable horrors by directly funding its detention system in Libya? Is EU cooperation with Libya carried out in accordance with the values and principles enshrined in Articles 2 and 21 of the TEU, on which the EU is based?

The United Nations, humanitarian and human rights organizations insist on pointing out that, since 2011, Libya has become a death trap in the middle of the Mediterranean. Far from being a "safe port", Libya is a hell for migrants and asylum seekers, with thousands of them exposed to abuse and torture, sex trafficking and the sale of slaves. In this context, EU cooperation with that country has been described as "inhumane", since it leads to the condemnation of thousands of migrants and potential refugees to arbitrary and indefinite detention and exposes them to torture, rape, forced labour, exploitation and extortion.

Certainly, the current EU cooperation with Libya in the field of migration and asylum is an extremely complex, controversial and politically sensitive issue, to which this writing does not go beyond a mere approach from the perspective of international human rights and refugee law. However, this approximation leads to the conclusion that, at its current extremes, such cooperation is only possible as long as the EU and its Member State carefully avoid triggering the application of the EU Charter of Fundamental Rights and the principles and values on which the EU itself is based, as enshrined in the Treaty on EU and the TFEU. Such contradiction or lack of coherence largely delegitimizes the EU, its claim to be a "Great Civilian Power" and its leading role in the protection of human rights. The EU is probably playing much of its prestige on this cooperation with Libya. For the time being, it appears that, driven by a certain political pragmatism which, in the fight against irregular immigration, leads it to clearly put its interests before its principles and values, the EU has become a necessary collaborator and financer of the perpetrators of the serious human rights violations committed against migrants and asylum seekers in Libya. This circumstance arguably weakens the EU's capacity as a global player with a high impact factor by promoting norms and values in global governance. The EU's collaboration and funding of these severe human rights violations in Libya may even lead to its being held internationally responsible for the atrocious crimes taking place in that country.

References

Alvaredo F, Chancel L, Piketty T, Saez E, Zucman G (eds) (2017) World Inequality Report 2018. https://wir2018.wid.world/files/download/wir2018-full-report-english.pdf Accessed 1 December 2019

Atanassov N, Radjenovic A (2018) EU Asylum, Borders and External Cooperation on Migration. Recent Developments. European Parliamentary Research Service (EPRS) N°. PE 625.194

Bakewell O (2009) South-South Migration and Human Development: Reflections on African Experiences. https://www.migrationinstitute.org/publications/wp-15-09 Accessed 2 December 2019

Carrera S, Blockmans S, Gross D, Guild E (2015) The EU's Response to the Refugee Crisis Taking Stock and Setting Policy Priorities. CEPS Essay No. 20

CINI and CONCORD (2018) Partnership or Conditionality? Monitoring the Migration Compacts and EU Trust Fund for Africa. https://concordeurope.org/wp-content/uploads/2018/01/CONCORD_EUTrustFundReport_2018_online.pdf Accessed 4 July 2020

Danish Refugee Council (DRC) (2018) EU-Libya migration cooperation: Shipwrecked values of humanity. https://drc.ngo/media/4912148/drc-policy-brief_eu-libya-migration-cooperation_final29102018.pdf Accessed 20 December 2019

De Bruycker P, Tsourdi E (2016) The Bratislava Declaration on Migration: European irresponsibility instead of solidarity. http://eumigrationlawblog.eu/the-bratislava-declaration-on-migration/ Accessed 24 May 2020

European Commission (2011) Communication from the Commission to the European Parliament, the Council, the European Economic and Social Committee and the Committee of the Regions. The Global Approach to Migration and Mobility. https://eur-lex.europa.eu/legal-content/EN/TXT/HTML/?uri=CELEX:52011DC0743&from=GA Accessed 4 July 2020

European Commission (2015) Communication from the Commission to the European Parliament, the Council, the European Economic and Social Committee and the Committee of the Regions. A European Agenda on Migration https://ec.europa.eu/home-affairs/sites/homeaffairs/files/what-we-do/policies/european-agenda-migration/background-information/docs/communication_on_the_european_agenda_on_migration_en.pdf Accessed 4 July 2020

European Commission (2015) Joint Foreign and Home Affairs Council: Ten point action plan on migration. https://ec.europa.eu/commission/presscorner/detail/en/IP_15_4813 Accessed 24 May 2020

European Commission (2016) Communication from the Commission to the European Parliament, the European Council, the Council and the European Investment Bank on establishing a new Partnership Framework with third countries under the European Agenda on Migration. https://ec.europa.eu/home-affairs/sites/homeaffairs/files/what-we-do/policies/european-agenda-migration/proposal-implementation-package/docs/20160607/communication_external_aspects_eam_towards_new_migration_ompact_en.pdf Accessed 24 May 2020

European Commission (2017a) Joint Communication to the European Parliament, the European Council and the Council: Migration on the Central Mediterranean Route – Managing flows, saving lives. https://eur-lex.europa.eu/resource.html?uri=cellar:6e6590bb-e2fa-11e6-ad7c-01aa75ed71a1.0001.02/DOC_1&format=PDF Accessed 4 July 2020

European Commission (2017b) Fifth Progress Report on the Partnership Framework with third countries under the European Agenda on Migration. https://eeas.europa.eu/sites/eeas/files/20170906_fifth_progress_report_on_the_partnership_framework_with_third_countries_under_the_eam_en_0.pdf Accessed 31 December 2019

Eurostat (2016) Asylum in the EU Member States - Record number of over 1.2 million first time asylum seekers registered in 2015 - Syrians, Afghans and Iraqis: top citizenships. https://ec.europa.eu/eurostat/documents/2995521/7203832/3-04032016-AP-EN.pdf/790eba01-381c-4163-bcd2-a54959b99ed6 Accessed 23 November 2019

Frontex (2019) Risk Analysis for 2019. https://frontex.europa.eu/assets/Publications/Risk_Analysis/Risk_Analysis/Risk_Analysis_for_2019.pdf Accessed 4 December 2019

García Andrade P, Martín I (2015) EU cooperation with third countries in the field of migration. http://www.europarl.europa.eu/RegData/etudes/STUD/2015/536469/IPOL_STU%282015%29536469_EN.pdf Accessed 1 December 2019
IDMC (2015) Global estimates 2015: People displaced by disasters. https://www.internal-displacement.org/sites/default/files/inline-files/20150713-global-estimates-2015-en-v1.pdf Accessed 4 July 2020
IDMC (2017) Global Report on Internal Displacement. https://www.internal-displacement.org/global-report/grid2017/ Accessed 4 July 2020
International Organization for Migration – IOM (2019) World Migration Report 2020. https://publications.iom.int/books/world-migration-report-2020 Accessed 24 May 2020
IOM (2016) Missing Migrants: tracking deaths along migratory routes. https://missingmigrants.iom.int/ Accessed 29 December 2019
IOM (2017) Libya's Migrant Report. http://www.globaldtm.info/libya/ Accessed 27 December 2019
Kingsley P (2015) 10 truths about Europe's migrant crisis. https://www.theguardian.com/uk-news/2015/aug/10/10-truths-about-europe's-refugee-crisis Accessed 2 December 2019
Koch A, Weber A, Werenfels I (eds) (2018) Profiteers of Migration? Authoritarian States in Africa and European Migration Management. SWP Research Paper 4
Koenig N (2017) The EU's External Migration Policy: towards win-win-win partnerships https://hertieschool-f4e6.kxcdn.com/fileadmin/user_upload/20170406_ExternalMigrationPolicy-NKoenig.pdf Accessed 1 December 2019
Martín M et al. (2018) Spain ignores pleas to not send rescued migrants back to Libya. https://english.elpais.com/elpais/2018/11/28/inenglish/1543393941_790926.html Accessed 28 November 2019
Piçarra N (2016) The European Union and the 'unprecedented migratory and refugee crisis': brief chronicle of a rupture of the Common European Asylum System. e-Pública: Revista Eletrónica de Direito Público 3(2):1–40
Rajagopal B (2001) The Violence of Development. https://www.washingtonpost.com/archive/opinions/2001/08/09/the-violence-of-development/1b169574-3992-44ec-bff9-a1e42857f192/ Accessed 21 November 2019
Sanmartín O R (2015) Frontex: 'El 80% de los inmigrantes que llegan a Europa son potenciales refugiados' [80% of immigrants arriving in Europe are potential refugees]. https://www.elmundo.es/internacional/2015/04/30/554221e5e2704e9f668b4571.html Accessed 2 December 2019
Süddeutsche Zeitung (2016) Wien droht Herkunftsländern von Flüchtlingen mit Sanktionen [Vienna threatens refugees' countries of origin with sanctions]. https://www.sueddeutsche.de/politik/abschiebungen-wien-droht-herkunftslaendern-von-fluechtlingen-mit-sanktionen-1.3313876 Accessed 1 December 2019
Terminski B (2013) Development-induced displacement and resettlement: social problem and human rights issue. https://ssrn.com/abstract=2026410 Accessed 1 December 2019
UNHCR (2015) Global Trends 2015: Forced Displacement in 2015. https://www.unhcr.org/statistics/unhcrstats/576408cd7/unhcr-global-trends-2015.html Accessed 24 May 2020
UNHCR (2018) Global Trends: displacement in 2017. https://www.unhcr.org/globaltrends2018/ Accessed 24 May 2020
UNSC (2011) Resolution 1973, UN Doc. No. S/RES/1973
Wriedt V (2019) Push-backs Rejected: D.D. v. Spain and the rights of minors at EU borders. http://eumigrationlawblog.eu/push-backs-rejected-d-d-v-spain-and-the-rights-of-minors-at-eu-borders/ Accessed 29 November 2019